saur

Catalogues of the
International Youth Library

Kataloge der
Internationalen Jugendbibliothek

2

Children's Prize Books

An international listing of
193 children's literature prizes

Preisgekrönte Kinderbücher

Ein internationales Verzeichnis von
193 Kinderbuchpreisen

Ouvrages pour Enfants

dotés d'un Prix littéraire
Un répertoire international comprenant
193 prix

Edited by / Herausgegeben von / Edité par
Jess R. Moransee

With an introduction by / Mit einer Einführung von
Avec un avant-propos par
Walter Scherf

K·G·Saur München·New York·London·Paris 1983

CIP — Kurztitelaufnahme der Deutschen Bibliothek

Children's prize books : an internat. listing of 193 children's literature prizes = Preisgekrönte Kinderbücher / ed. by Jess R. Moransee. With an introd. by Walter Scherf. — 2., rev. and enl. ed. — München ; New York ; London ; Paris : Saur, 1983. — ca. XXII, 580 S.
(Catalogues of the International Youth Library ; 2)
ISBN 3-598-03250-1

NE: Moransee, Jess R. [Hrsg.]; Internationale Jugendbibliothek ⟨München⟩: Kataloge der Internationalen Jugendbibliothek

2nd revised and enlarged Edition
2. überarbeitete und erweiterte Auflage
2me Edition, révisée et augmentée

Printed in the Federal Republic of Germany

Phototypesetting by Ähren-Verlag, München
Printed by grafik + druck GmbH & Co., München
Bound by Großbuchbinderei Gebhardt, Ansbach

ISBN 3-598-03250-1

Contents / Inhalt

Brazil/Brasilien

Bulgaria/Bulgarien

Canada/Kanada

Colombia/Kolumbien

Cuba/Kuba

Czechoslovakia/Tschechoslowakei

Norway/Norwegen

Peru/Peru

Poland/Polen

Portugal/Portugal

Rumania/Rumänien

South Africa/Südafrika

Soviet Union/Sowjetunion

International Prizes/Internationale Preise

Index / Register

List of Illustrations

Introduction
Book-awards, and some insight to be gained from them

Awards reflect the views of an era. The lists of prize-winning titles give evidence of our period's ideas on education more forcefully and authentically than it could be found anywhere else. Members of juries always make their choices first as exponents of society, no matter how different their individual dispositions may be. The majority decisions of a jury will always prevail against the differing preferences of individual jury members and the brave fights they might have put up for them. Those decisions reveal the general attitudes of an era, beyond individually held beliefs; they reflect the common hope to find the right book, first and always, the book that will help point the way for future generations.

This is perfectly legitimate. Since time immemorial, the old have told the young fables and stories which deal with "right behaviour", ("adjustment" may possibly be the more modern term). The question is: will this be done superficially, in an arbitrary, over-simplified way; will this be burdened with emotionalism. "Advice for the young" ("Lebenshilfen") of that sort is often nothing but an author's means to turn those who are ignorant and incapable of judgment into mere partisans of his personal convictions, (however valid they may be). The question is, moreover, whether tendentious literature, — obvious or subtle in procedure — is used for the surreptitious insertion of a morale for adult life which is quite different from the one it preaches, or whether juries will have the courage to cast aside all other but strictly artistic and psychological considerations. It is obvious, that the artistic ideas and the psychological discoveries of our time will find their expression in the book-awards. And the majority decisions of juries are the result of a series of complex deliberations which culminate in a particular conclusion. It is interesting to examine, how strongly literature and art of a certain period will stand up against cliché, convention and the fashion of the day. After all, there are now, and there always have been times, and social groups, which will not participate in the intellectual activities and discussions of the day. The rewards of such an attitude are dubious, at best.

It makes little sense to look on the compilations of prize-winning books simply as reference lists for translations and adaptations. The programmatic competitions and special awards alone should be viewed with a wary eye. One jury may find, with some reason, that our young people should be brought closer to the world of technical progress, while another wants to do something about the deplorable quality of reading matter for young girls; a third may have detected gaps in the historical catalogue, and a fourth has come to the conclusion that a childhood without tales of poetic imagination is a poor childhood indeed. And lo and behold: amongst the texts and pictures thus elicited we find — just as we do anywhere else — some outstanding and original things between the run-of-the-mill and the plain miserable. Was it worth, then, to pamper production with such special awards? Why not. Without enticement and challenge, there would be no handicraft and no art. To quote Brecht: "One has to tear the wisdom from the wise ..."

The true value of a comprehensive compilation of book-awards can be found first in the numerous suggestions it offers for creative translating, and second in the opportunity it presents for research. But there is a third aspect. We are living in a time, which as no other before, tends to transcend national boundaries. We really take notice of the things which are produced in other nations and under different sociological and national conditions. We purposely offer our children books which were written under conditions different from ours, show other sets of values, other modes of behaviour. Books of that sort bring, in artistic and convincing ways, knowledge of other cultural developments and traditions into our playpens. As a result, a great number of jury-members in all parts of the world are consciously seeking out comparison with the artistic and psychological values of other literatures, their pedagogical tendencies and production trends. And, what is the most important aspect: activities of jurors are being noticed and observed. The jurors know this and strive for ever higher standards, both in the books and in themselves. The most outstanding example is the art of illustration. Over the last decade, a fundamental change has taken place in this field. This change has spread to every country, and this largely because of award-giving practices.

It is an essential task of the IYL to foster international comparison in the field of children's literature. Publishers form East and West offer their books for documentation. We offer our thanks to publishers, individual contributors, to many public and private institutions for their help and not simply with reference-lists. We also aspire to create a dependable compilation of special reference material as a practical tool for research and the business of publishing. Book-awards, in our opinion, hold a key position.

Walter Scherf

Einführung: Auszeichnungen und einige Lehren daraus

Preise spiegeln die Auffassungen ihrer Zeit. Wer in den Titelreihen eines Preises zu lesen versteht, findet die pädagogischen Ideen einer Epoche in einer Verdichtung und Authentizität, wie sie an keiner anderen Stelle geboten werden. Die Juroren, so verschieden ihre Individualität sein mag, wählen als Exponenten einer Gesellschaft aus. Vielleicht hatten sie persönlich ganz andere Favoriten, vielleicht haben sie sogar für ihre persönlichen Favoriten gekämpft — aber in den Mehrheitsentscheidungen einer Jury treten die überindividuellen Ideen einer Epoche zutage, die gemeinsame Hoffnung, man finde die rechten Bücher, um der nachfolgenden Generation einen Weg zu weisen.

Das ist durchaus legitim. So alt die Menschheit ist, haben die Älteren den Jüngeren stets Fabeln und Beispielgeschichten erzählt, aus denen "rechtes Verhalten" hervorgeht (moderner nennt man das möglicherweise adjustment). Die Frage ist nur, ob es kurzschlüssig und simpel geschieht, ob vordergründig oder gar gefühlsüberfrachtet sogenannte "Lebenshilfen" ausgesucht werden, ob die Beeinflussung der Jugend sich heimlich eine andere Moral für das Erwachsenenleben sichert, ob man durch offene oder verkappte Tendenz unwissende, nie zu einer persönlichen Entscheidung gelangte Schildknappen für die eigene (vielleicht zu Recht bestehende) Überzeugung rekrutieren möchte, oder ob man den Mut besitzt, sich auf die künstlerische und psychologische Auswahl zu beschränken. Denn auch die künstlerischen Ideen und die psychologischen Erkenntnisse einer Epoche spiegeln sich in den Preisen. Und die Mehrheitsentscheidungen einer Jury gehen hervor aus einer sehr komplexen Reihe, über die das Integral des Beschlusses gezogen wird. Mit welchem Gewicht Literatur und Kunst einer Zeit neben Klischee, Konvention und Mode einer Zeit sich behaupten — das ist eine Frage, der nachzugehen sich besonders lohnt. Schließlich gab es und gibt es Zeiten und Gesellschaftsgruppen, die sich mit zweifelhaftem Erfolg von der geistigen Auseinandersetzung isolieren.

Wer Preisbuchlisten unkritisch als Vorschlagslisten für Übersetzungen und Neubearbeitungen läse, käme nicht weit. Allein die programmatischen Ausschreibungen und Sonderpreise sollten uns vorsichtig zu Werke gehen lassen. Da scheint es der einen Jury, sicherlich mit gewissem Recht, als müsse die Jugend besser in die Welt der Technik eingeführt werden, während die andere etwas gegen die notorischen Mißstände des Mädchenbuches tun möchte, eine dritte Jury hat Lücken im historischen Katalog entdeckt, und eine vierte kommt zur Einsicht, daß eine Kinderstube ohne Poesie beklagenswert arm ist. Und o Wunder: Unter den hervorgelockten Texten und Bildern gibt es (im selben Verhältnis wie sonst überall in der Welt) Originelles und Unübertreffliches neben dem programmatisch Mitlaufenden und dem Miserablen. Hat es sich also gelohnt, mit derartigen Sonderpreisen die Produktion zu beeinflussen? Warum nicht. Ohne Auftrag und Herausforderung gäbe es weder Kunst noch Handwerk. Wie Brecht sagte: Man muß dem Weisen seine Weisheit erst entreißen ...

Zweifellos liegt der eigentliche Wert eines umfassenden Preisverzeichnisses sowohl in den geradezu unerschöpflichen Anregungen zu übersetzen, als auch in den Studienmöglichkeiten. Aber es gibt noch eine dritte Bedeutung. Wir leben in einer Zeit, die wie keine andere zuvor die nationalen Beschränkungen überschreitet (noch). Wir nehmen wirklich zur Kenntnis, was bei anderen Nationen und aus anderen nationalen und soziologischen Bedingungen entsteht. Ja, wir bieten unseren Kindern bewußt Bücher an, die aus anderen Bedingungen stammen, andere Verhaltensweisen zeigen und in künstlerisch überzeugender Verdichtung andere Kulturen und Traditionen in unsere Kinderstuben bringen. Das wirkt sich unter anderem so aus, daß ein großer Teil der Juroren in den unterschiedlichsten Ländern den Vergleich sucht, die künstlerischen und psychologischen Werte in anderen Literaturen mißt und die pädagogischen Tendenzen und Produktionsakzente zu erfassen trachtet. Und, das aber ist das wichtigste, die Juroren fühlen sich beachtet und beobachtet, und mithin schrauben sie die Anforderungen hinaus, die sie sowohl an die Bücher als auch an sich selbst stellen. Das eklatanteste Beispiel ist die Illustrationskunst. Hier ist im letzten Jahrzehnt ein grundlegender Wandel vonstatten gegangen. Er hat, nicht zuletzt über die Preise, schöpferischen Einfluß in jedem Lande genommen.

Für die IJB ist es eine wesentliche Aufgabe, den internationalen Vergleich auf dem Gebiete der Kinderliteratur zu ermöglichen. Die Verleger aus Ost und West stellen ihre Bücher zur Dokumentation zur Verfügung — aber unsere Dankbarkeit für das Vertrauen und die tatkräftige Hilfe, die wir von dieser Seite und von seiten so vieler öffentlicher und privater Institutionen, Organisationen und einzelner Persönlichkeiten erfahren, sei nicht nur mit der bibliothekarischen Erschließung abgetan. Wir bemühen uns, praktisches Handwerkszeug für Forschung und Verlagsarbeit bereitzustellen, zuverlässiges Nachschlagematerial auf speziell interessierenden Gebieten. Die Preise, so meinen wir, besitzen eine Schlüsselfunktion.

Walter Scherf

Editor's Preface

The International Youth Library takes pride in the publication of the 2nd and enlarged edition of Children's Prize Books. This catalogue of children's literature prizes contains 187 awards from 38 countries, including 6 international awards. Of course, the count given above most certainly does not exhaust the number of prizes existent in the world, but this work had to be held to its present size because of time and manpower limitations. And, it must also be noted that new awards are continually being created. Another point which must be noted is that several of the prizes listed in this book have not been completed up to the present date. The reason for this is that either the information was not forthcoming, or arrived after the printer's deadline and could not be included. Therefore, what is lacking in this edition will have to be included in a future edition, which in its turn will probably be incomplete for basically the same reasons.

Apart from being used as a source of documentation, this catalogue may also be utilized in other ways. Librarians can use it as a reference tool and as a guide for purchasing foreign titles. Publishers and editors may use it to select new titles for translation. Teachers of children's literature, as well as teachers of foreign languages, can utilize it to find new material to enhance their lectures and to select supplementary reading material for their students. Children's literature experts should find in this catalogue a means of keeping abreast of what is and has been published in other countries.

In order to increase the universality of this catalogue, the text above each prize list has been rendered in both English and German. As for each book mentioned, the title appears first in the original language, followed by an English and German translation of that title placed in parenthesis. The author, illustrator, publisher and place and date of publication are also given. Example:

> Staes, Guido: Kinderen van de vrede. (Children of peace; Kinder des Friedens.) Ill.: Gerbrand Jespers.
> Averbode: Altiora 1972.

In the case of a translation receiving a prize, the form is as follows:

Andersen, Hans Christian: Skazki. (Fairy tales; Märchen; Dan.orig.title: Eventyr og historier.) Ill.: A. Kokorin. Moskva: Moskovskij raboćij 1976.

I wish to thank the publishers who have given us their books, all of our correspondents from many different countries, public and private institutions and the staff members of the IYL for their generous cooperation in helping to obtain the information which has resulted in the publication of this work. Warm thanks are also due to the publisher Klaus G. Saur for making the printing of this catalogue possible. I wish to offer very special thanks to my esteemed colleague, Erika von Engelbrechten, head of the IYL reference section, for the translation of numerous titles and part of the text into German and for proofreading the entire German text of the manuscript. Without her untiring assistance, the task of making this book would have been extremely difficult. I also wish to express my sincere gratitude to Walter Scherf, director of the International Youth Library, for writing the introduction to this edition and also for his valuable suggestions and advice.

Jess R. Moransee,
Editor

Vorwort des Herausgebers

Die Internationale Jugendbibliothek legt hiermit die 2. und erweiterte Auflage des Kataloges "Preisgekrönte Kinderbücher" vor. Der Katalog mit den Auszeichnungen zur Kinderliteratur enthält 187 Preise aus 38 Ländern und 6 internationale Preise. Wahrscheinlich sind nicht alle in der Welt existierenden Preise berücksichtigt worden, jedoch muß das Buch seinen jetzigen Umfang beibehalten und es werden ja laufend neue Preise ins Leben gerufen. Außerdem muß hier festgehalten werden, daß die im Buch enthaltenen Preise nicht bis zum heutigen Tag vervollständigt werden konnten. Der Grund für die Unvollständigkeit ist, daß die Informationen noch nicht erschienen waren oder erst nach dem Abgabetermin des Druckers eintrafen und somit nicht mehr aufgenommen werden konnten. Deshalb werden alle Angaben, die in dieser Ausgabe fehlen, in die nächste Auflage übernommen werden, diese wiederum wird dann aus den gleichen Gründen nicht komplett sein.

Abgesehen davon, daß der Katalog als Dokumentation benutzt wird, kann er auch auf andere Weise verwendet werden. Bibliothekare können ihn als Auskunftsmittel benutzen und als Führer für fremdsprachige Titel. Verleger und Herausgeber werden neue Titel zur Übersetzung auswählen. Lehrer für Kinderliteratur, Dozenten, ebenso wie Lehrer für Fremdsprachen finden neues Material, um ihre Vorlesungen zu bereichern und ergänzende Lektüre für ihre Studenten bereitzuhalten. Experten der Kinderliteratur finden hier die Titel, die in anderen Ländern veröffentlicht wurden.

Um die Vielseitigkeit des Kataloges zu erhöhen, wurde der Text jeder Preisliste sowohl ins Englische als auch ins Deutsche übersetzt. Wie bei jedem Buch angegeben, erscheint zuerst der Originaltitel, dann die Übersetzung ins Englische und Deutsche in Klammern. Autor, Illustrator, Verleger, Ort des Verlages und Jahr der Veröffentlichung werden auch angegeben. Hier ein Beispiel:

> Staes, Guido: Kinderen van de vrede. (Children of peace; Kinder des Friedens.) Ill.: Gerbrand Jespers.
> Averbode: Altiora 1972.

Wenn eine Übersetzung einen Preis bekommen hat, dann ist die Form der Darstellung wie folgt:

Andersen, Hans Christian: Skazki. (Fairy tales; Märchen; Dan. orig. title: Eventyr og historier.)
Ill.: A. Kokorin.
Moskva: Moskovskij rabocij 1976.

Ich möchte an dieser Stelle den Verlegern danken, die uns ihre Bücher zur Verfügung stellen; unseren Korrespondenten in aller Welt; öffentlichen und privaten Instituten; und den Mitarbeitern der IJB für ihre ausdauernde Mitarbeit, um die nötigen Informationen zu erhalten. Ich möchte auch dem Verleger Klaus G. Saur danken, der den Druck des Kataloges möglich gemacht hat. Meiner geschätzten Kollegin Erika v. Engelbrechten, Leiterin der Zentralen Referenz in der IJB, möchte ich besonders danken für die Übersetzung zahlreicher Titel, Teile des Textes in Deutsch und der Korrektur des gesamten deutschen Textes des Manuskriptes. Ohne ihre unermüdliche Hilfe wäre das Zustandekommen des Buches äußerst schwierig geworden. Nicht zuletzt möchte ich meine aufrichtige Dankbarkeit Walter Scherf, dem Direktor der Internationalen Jugendbibliothek bezeigen, für seine wertvollen Vorschläge und Ratschläge und für seine Einleitung zu diesem Buch.

Jess R. Moransee
Editor

Prizes /
Verzeichnis der Preise

Argentina / Argentinien

Premio Argentina de Escritores (S.A.D.E.)

The "ribbon of honour" of the Society of Argentinian Writers is given annually to the best children's book. The prize was established in 1972 through the initiative of the presidents of CAPLI (Committee of Assessment and Promotion of Children's and Youth Literature) and IBBY (International Board on Books for Young People), Marta Salotti and Maria Hortensia Locari, and other well know children's and youth book authors.

Ill. 1 Leopoldo Durañona in I. Bornemann: El espejo distraido

The competing authors of the prize must be members of S.A.D.E. and are obliged to submit four copies of each title that is to be judged in the competition. Each year, three different persons are selected to serve on the jury that chooses the prize-winning book.

Das Ehrenband des argentinischen Schriftstellerverbandes, das jährlich an das beste Kinderbuch verliehen wird, wurde 1972 auf den Vorschlag der Präsidenten von CAPLI (Kommitee zur Beurteilung und Verbreitung von Kinder- und Jugendbuch), Marta Salotti und Maria Hortensia Locari gemeinsam mit anderen bekannten Autoren der Kinder- und Jugendliteratur gegründet. Die Autoren, die an dem Wettbewerb teilnehmen wollen, müssen Mitglied des S.A.D.E. sein und je 4 Exemplare ihres Buches zur Verfügung stellen. Von den Mitgliedern des S.A.D.E. werden jedes Jahr drei Schriftsteller als Jury für den besagten Wettbewerb gewählt.

1973 *Bornemann, Elsa Isabel:* **El espejo distraido.** (The absent-minded mirror; Der vergeßliche Spiegel.) Ill.: Antonio Vilar.
Buenos Aires: Ed. Edicón 1971.

1974 Poletti, Syria: **Reportajes supersónicos.** (Supersonic reports; Überschallgeschwindigkeits-Nachrichten.) Ill.: Antonio Vilar.
Buenos Aires: Ed. Sigmar 1972.

1975 Granata, Maria: **El ángel que perdió un ala.** (The angel who lost a wing; Der Engel, der einen Flügel verlor.) Ill.: Adriana Frattantoni.
Buenos Aires: Ed. Acme 1974.

1976 Giménez Pastor, Martha: **La pancita del gato.** (The cat's little tummy; Das Bäuchlein der Katze.) Ill.: Kitty Lorefice de Passalia.
Buenos Aires: Ed. Plus Ultra 1975.

1977 Finkel, Berta: **Castillito de papel.** (The paper castle; Die Burg aus Papier.) Ill.: Kitty Lorefice de Passalia.
Buenos Aires: Ed. Plus Ultra 1976.

1978 Cupit, Aarón: **La isla del cielo.** (The island of the sky; Die Insel am Himmel.)
Buenos Aires: Ed. Orión 1977.
(Ex aequo)

Vega, Adriana: **La chinchilla maravilla.** (The marvelous chinchilla; Der wunderbare Chinchilla.) Ill.: Chacha.
Buenos Aires: Ed. Plus Ultra 1977.
(Ex aequo)

Premio Nacional de Literatura Infantil

This prize was created by the Cultural Section of the National Ministry of Education in 1978 to promote Argentinian children's literature. Works of poetry, theatre pieces and stories written between 1974 and 1978 were eligible for the prize competition.

Das Sekretariat des Kulturinstitutes, dem Ministerium für Erziehung angeschlossen vergab 1978 zum ersten Mal einen Preis um Jugendbuchautoren anzuregen. Drei verschiedene Gattungen (Erzählung, Poesie und Theater) argentinischer Kinderliteratur wurden im Zeitraum zwischen 1974—1978 zum ersten Mal vorgestellt.

1978 *1st prize/1. Preis*
The prize was not given; Der Preis wurde nicht vergeben.

2nd prize/2. Preis
The prize was not given; Der Preis wurde nicht vergeben.

3rd prize/3. Preis
Requeni, Antonio: **El pirata Malapata.** *(Malapata,* the pirate; *Malapata,* der Pirat.)
Buenos Aires: Plus Ultra 1976.

Premios del Poema Infantil Ilustrado S.A.D.E.

This annual prize for illustrated poems was founded in 1978 by the Society of Argentinian Writers (S.A.D.E.). The award is given to children's works which are prime examples of the important relationship between illustrations and text.

Der Preis, der jährlich für illustrierte Gedichte verliehen wird, wurde 1978 von der Argentinischen Autorenvereinigung (S.A.D.E.) gestiftet. Der Preis wird für Kinderbücher vergeben, die beispielhaft die enge Beziehung zwischen Illustration und Text verdeutlichen.

1978 *1st prize/1. Preis*
Corbacho, Oscar: **El tren.** (The train; Der Zug.) Ill.: José Rainer. (Unpublished; Unveröffentlicht.)

2nd prize/2. Preis
Devetach, Laura: **Coplas de la humedad.** (Couplets of dew; Lieder der Feuchtigkeit.) Ill.: Raúl Fortín.
Buenos Aires: Biliken 1979.

3rd prize/3. Preis
Viola, Miguel Angel: **El colectivo fantástico.** (The fantastic autobus; Der phantastische Autobus.) Ill.: Estanislao Gonczaresky.
(Unpublished; Unveröffentlicht.)

Australia / Australien

The Book of the Year Award

From 1946 to 1964, the Children's Book Council of New South Wales annually conferred a prize in the form of a medal upon the best children's and picture books. In 1964, all of the Australian State Councils combined to form the Children's Book Council of Australia which, since, has made the annual award presentations. The prize is only given when prize-worthy books have been published. The jury is composed of the members of the Children's Book Council and of school and youth librarians in the public service.

Von 1946–1964 vergab der Kinderbuchrat von Neu-Südwales (Children's Book Council of New South Wales) jährlich einen Preis in Form einer Medaille für die besten Kinder- und Bilderbücher. 1964 schlossen sich alle australischen "State Councils" zum Children's Book Council of Australia zusammen; seitdem beteiligen sie sich alle an der Preisverleihung. Der Preis wird nur vergeben, wenn wirklich preiswürdige Bücher vorliegen. Die Jury setzt sich aus Mitgliedern des Children's Book Council zusammen sowie aus Schul- und Kinderbibliothekaren im öffentlichen Dienst.

Ill. 2 Peter Pavey in: One dragon's dream

1946 Rees, Leslie Clarke: **Karrawingi, the emu.** *Karrawingi,* das Emu.) Ill.: Walter Cunningham.
Sydney: Sands 1946.

1947 The prize was not given; Der Preis wurde nicht vergeben.

1948 Hurley, Frank: **Shackleton's argonauts.** A saga of the Antarctic ice-packs. *(Shackletons* Argonauten. Eine Legende von den Antarktis-Eisbergen.) Photos: Frank Hurley.
Sydney: Angus & Robertson 1948.

1949 The prize was not given; Der Preis wurde nicht vergeben.

1950 Villiers, Alan John: **Whalers of the midnight sun.** A story of modern whaling in the Antarctic. (Walfänger der Mitternachtssonne. Eine Geschichte des modernen Walfangs in der Antarktis.) Ill.: Charles Pont.
Sydney: Angus & Robertson 1950.

1951 Williams, Ruth C.: **Verity of Sydney Town.** *(Verity* aus Sydney.) Ill.: Rhys Williams.
Sydney: Angus & Robertson 1950.

1952 Pownall, Eve (i.e. Marjorie Evelyn Pownall): **The Australia book.** (Das Buch über Australien). Ill.: Margaret Senior.
Sydney: Sands (Angus & Robertson) 1952.

1953 Martin, James Henry/Martin, William Donald: **Aircraft of today and tomorrow.** (Flugzeuge heute und morgen). Photos.
Sydney: Angus & Robertson 1953.
Phipson, Joan: **Good luck to the rider.** (Viel Glück dem Reiter.) Ill.: Margaret Horder.
Sydney: Angus & Robertson 1953.

1954 Parker, K. Langloh (i.e. Catherine Somerville Parker): **Australian legendary tales.** Australische legendenhafte Erzählungen.) Ill.: Elizabeth Durack.
Sydney: Angus & Robertson 1953.

1955 Tindale, Norman B./Lindsay, H.A.: **First walkabout.** (Erster Spaziergang.) Ill.: Madeleine Boyce.
Melbourne: Longmans 1956.

1956 *Picture book/Bilderbuch*
Barnard, Peggy: **Wish and the magic nut.** (Der Wunsch und die Zaubernuß.) Ill.: Sheila Hawkins.
Sydney: Angus & Robertson 1956.
Children's book/Kinderbuch
Wrightson, Patricia: **The crooked snake.** (Die krumme Schlange.) Ill.: Margaret Horder.
Sydney, London, Melbourne: Angus & Robertson 1955.

1957 *Picture book/Bilderbuch*
The prize was not given; Der Preis wurde nicht vergeben.
Children's book/Kinderbuch
Moodie, Heddle Enid: **The boomerang book of legendary tales.** (Das Bumerang-Buch mit legendenhaften Erzählungen.) Ill.: Nancy Parker.
Melbourne, London: Longmans, Green 1957.

1958 *Picture book/Bilderbuch*
Poignant, Axel: **Piccaninny walkabout.** A story of two aboriginal children. (Kinderspaziergang. Eine Geschichte von zwei kleinen Ureinwohnern.) Photos: Axel Poignant.
Sydney, Melbourne, London, Wellington: Angus & Robertson 1957.
Children's book/Kinderbuch
Chauncy, Nan: **Tiger in the bush.** (Tiger im Busch.) Ill.: Margaret Horder.
Melbourne, London: Oxford University Press 1957.

1959 *Picture book/Bilderbuch*
The prize was not given; Der Preis wurde nicht vergeben.
Childrens book/Kinderbuch
Chauncy, Nan: **Devil's hill.** (Der Teufelsberg.) Ill.: Geraldine Spence.
Melbourne, London: Oxford University Press 1958.
Gunn, John: **Sea menace.** (Gefahren der See.) Ill.: Brian Keogh.
London: Constable 1958.

1960 *Picture book/Bilderbuch*
The prize was not given; Der Preis wurde nicht vergeben.
Children's book/Kinderbuch
Tennant, Kylie: **All the proud tribesmen.** (Alle stolzen Stammesangehörigen.) Ill.: Clem Seale.
Melbourne, London: Macmillan 1959.

1961 *Picture book/Bilderbuch*
The prize was not given; Der Preis wurde nicht vergeben.
Children's book/Kinderbuch
Chauncy, Nan: **Tangara.** Let us set off again. (Tangara. Lasst uns wieder aufbrechen.) Ill.: Brian Wildsmith.
Melbourne, London: Oxford University Press 1960.

1962 *Picture book/Bilderbuch*
The prize was not given; Der Preis wurde nicht vergeben.

Children's book/Kinderbuch
Evers, Leonard Herbert: **The Racketty Street gang.** (Die Bande von der *Racketty-Strasse.)*
London: Parrish 1961.

1963 *Picture book/Bilderbuch*
The prize was not awarded; Der Preis wurde nicht vergeben.
Children's book/Kinderbuch
Phipson, Joan: **The family conspiracy.** (Die Familien-Verschwörung.) Ill.: Margaret Horder.
Sydney: Angus & Robertson 1962.

1964 *Picture book/Bilderbuch*
The prize was not given; Der Preis wurde nicht vergeben.
Children's book/Kinderbuch
Spence, Eleanor: **The green laurel.** (Der grüne Lorbeer.)
Melbourne, London: Oxford University Press 1963.

1965 *Picture book/Bilderbuch*
MacIntyre, Elisabeth: **Hugh's zoo.** *(Hughs* Zoo.) Ill.: Elisabeth MacIntyre.
London: Constable 1964.
Children's book/Kinderbuch
Brinsmead, Hesba Fay Hungerford: **Pastures of the blue crane.** (Die Weiden des blauen Kranichs.) Ill.: Annette Macarthur-Onslow.
Melbourne: Oxford University Press 1964.

1966 *Picture book/Bilderbuch*
The prize was not given; Der Preis wurde nicht vergeben.
Children's book/Kinderbuch
Southall, Ivan: **Ash road.** (Eschenweg.) Ill.: Clem Seale.
Sydney, London, Melbourne: Angus & Robertson 1965.

1967 *Picture book/Bilderbuch*
The prize was not given; Der Preis wurde nicht vergeben.
Children's book/Kinderbuch
Clarke, Mavis Thorpe: **The min-min.** (Das "*Min-Min*" = ein Geist.) Ill.: Genevieve Melrose.
Melbourne: Lansdowne Press 1966.

1968 *Picture book/Bilderbuch*
The prize was not given; Der Preis wurde nicht vergeben.
Children's book/Kinderbuch
Southall, Ivan: **To the wild sky.** (Am wilden Himmel.) Ill.: Jennifer Tuckwell.
Sydney, London, Melbourne: Angus & Robertson 1967.

1969 *Picture book/Bilderbuch*
Southall, Ivan: **Sly old wardrobe.** (Schlauer alter Kleiderschrank.) Ill.: Ted Greenwood.
Melbourne: Cheshire 1968.

Children's book/Kinderbuch
Balderson, Margaret: **When jays fly to Bárbmo.** (Wenn die Häher nach *Bárbmo* fliegen.) Ill.: Victor G. Ambrus (i.e. Gyösö László Ambrus).
London: Oxford University Press 1968.

1970 *Picture book/Bilderbuch*
The prize was not given; Der Preis wurde nicht vergeben.

Children's book/Kinderbuch
Macarthur-Onslow, Annette: **Uhu.** *(Uhu.) Ill.: Annette Macarthur-Onslow.*
Sydney: Ure Smith 1969.

1971 Picture book/Bilderbuch
Paterson, Andrew Barton: **Waltzing Matilda.** (Die Walzer tanzende *Mathilda.*) Ill.: Desmond Digby.
Sydney: Collins 1970.

Children's book/Kinderbuch
Southall, Ivan: **Bread and honey.** (Brot und Honig.)
Sydney: Angus & Robertson 1970.

1972 *Picture book/Bilderbuch*
The prize was not given; Der Preis wurde nicht vergeben.

Children's book/Kinderbuch
Brinsmead, Hesba Fay Hungerford: **Longtime passing.** (Eine lange Zeit vergeht.)
Sydney: Angus & Robertson 1971.

1973 *Picture book/Bilderbuch*
The prize was not given; Der Preis wurde nicht vergeben.

Children's book/Kinderbuch
Shelley, Noreen: **The family at the lookout.** (Die Familie am Ausblick.) Ill.: Robert Micklewright.
London: Oxford University Press 1973.

1974 *Picture book/Bilderbuch*
Wagner, Jenny: **The bunyip of Berkeley's Creek.** Das Bunyip vom *Berkeley*-Bach.) Ill.: Ron Brooks.
Melbourne: Longman Young 1973.

Children's book/Kinderbuch
Wrightson, Patricia: **The nargun and the stars.** (Der Nargun und die Sterne.)
Richmond: Hutchinson 1973.

1975 *Picture book/Bilderbuch*
Paterson, Andrew Barton: **The man from Ironbark.** (Der Mann aus *Ironbark.*) Ill.: Quentin Hole.
Sydney: Collins 1974.

Children's book/Kinderbuch
The prize was not given; Der Preis wurde nicht vergeben.

1976 *Picture book/Bilderbuch*
Roughsey, Dick: **The rainbow serpent.** Die regenbogenfarbene Schlange.) Ill.: Dick Roughsey.
Sydney: Collins 1975.

Children's book/Kinderbuch
Southall, Ivan: **Fly west.** (Flug nach Westen.)
Sydney: Angus & Robertson 1975.

1977 *Picture book/Bilderbuch*
The prize was not given; Der Preis wurde nicht vergeben.

Children's book/Kinderbuch
Spence, Eleanor: **The October child.** (Das Oktoberkind.)
London: Oxford University Press 1976.

1978 *Picture book/Bilderbuch*
Wagner, Jenny: **John Brown, Rose and the midnight cat.** (*John Brown, Rose* und die Mitternachtskatze.) Ill.: Ron Brooks.
Harmondworth: Kestrel 1977.

Children's book/Kinderbuch
Wrightson, Patricia: **The ice is coming.** (Das Eis kommt.)
Richmond: Hutchinson 1977.

1979 *Picture book/Bilderbuch*
Trezise, Percy: **The Quikins.** (Die *Quinkins* = Geister.) Ill. Dick Roughsey.
Sydney: Collins 1978.

Children's book/Kinderbuch
Manley, Ruth: **The Plum-Rain Scroll.** Die Pflaumenregenschriftrolle.)
Lane Cove: Hodder & Stoughton 1978.

1980 *Picture book/Bilderbuch*
Pavey, Peter: **One dragon's dream.** Der Traum eines Drachen.) Ill.: Peter Pavey.
West Melbourne: Nelson 1979.
Children's book/Kinderbuch
Harding, Lee: **Displaced person.** (Eine verschleppte Person.)
Yarra, Vic.: Hyland House 1979.

1981 *Picture book/Bilderbuch*
The prize was not given; Der Preis wurde nicht vergeben.
Children's book/Kinderbuch
Park, Ruth: *Playing Beatie Bow.* (*Beatie-Bow*-Spielen.)
Melbourne: Nelson 1980.

Visual Arts Award

This award was first offered in 1974 by the Visual Arts Board of the Australian Book Council to an artist on the merit of the visual content of his book. In 1977, however, the Visual Arts Board decided to henceforth give the prize-money to the Children's Book Council of Australia for the picture book category of their Book of the Year Award.

Dieser Preis wurde 1974 zum erstenmal vom "Visual Arts Board" des "Australian Book Council" vergeben. Und zwar an einen Künstler, der vortrefflich den sichtbaren Inhalt eines Buches darstellen kann. 1977 jedoch beschloß "Visual Arts Board", von nun an den Preisbetrag dem "Children's Book Council", von Australien für die Bilderbuchsektion des Preis-Buches des Jahres zu übergeben.

1974 Niland, Deborah/Niland, Kilmeny in:
Paterson, Andrew Barton: **Mulga Bill's bicycle.** (*Mulga Bills* Fahrrad.)
Sydney: Collins 1973.

1975 Haldane, Roger in:
Thiele, Colin Milton: **Magpie Island.** (Elster-Insel.)
Adelaide: Rigby 1974.

1976 Greenwood, Ted in:
Greenwood, Ted: **Terry's brrrmmm GT.** (*Terrys* brummender GT = Kraftfahrzeug.)
Sydney: Angus & Robertson 1975.

Austria / Österreich

Österreichischer Staatspreis für Kinder- und Jugendliteratur

Since 1955, the Secretary of Education and Art presents annually state awards in the form of a cash prize to living Austrian authors to promote good literature for children and young adults. Beginning in 1966, translations were also made eligible for the award. The books under consideration for the award must have been published in Austria within the last three years prior to the time of selection, and they must have appeared on the list of recommended books compiled by the Austrian Commission on Young People's Literature of the Federal Secretariat of Education.

Ill. 3 Angelika Kaufmann in M. Lobe: Der Apfelbaum

In 1958 the Austrian State Award was divided into two categories: children's books and youth books. Since that time further divisions have come about and today there exist the following categories: small children's book (up to 8 years); children's book I (8 to 11 years); children's book II (11 to 14 years); youth book; non-fiction; illustration; translation. In addition to the prize winning books, an honour list of other noteworthy books has been published since 1956 (these titles are not listed below).
The Austrian Ministry of Education and Art, in order to insure the promotion of good children's literature, purchases numerous copies of the prize-winning titles for distribution to institutions dealing with children and young people.

Der Bundesminister für Unterricht und Kunst verleiht seit 1955 "zur Förderung wertvoller Kinder- und Jugendliteratur ... für die besten Werke der laufenden österreichischen Verlagsproduktion" jährlich Staatspreise in Form einer Geldprämie an lebende Schriftsteller. Seit 1966 werden auch Übersetzungen berücksichtigt. Das preisgekrönte Werk muß während der vergangenen drei Jahre in einem österreichischen Verlag erschienen und von der Österreichischen Jugendschriftenkommission beim Bundesministerium für Unterricht und Kunst in die Jugendbuch-Empfehlungsliste aufgenommen worden sein. Seit 1958 findet eine Trennung zwischen Kinder- und Jugendbuchpreis statt, weitere Differenzierungen folgten später. Heute umfaßt der Preis drei Österreichische Kinderbuchpreise: Kleinkinderalter bis zum 8. Lebensjahr; Kinderbuchpreise I (8.—11. Lebensjahr); Förderungspreis für das Kind- und jugendgemäße Sachbuch; Förderungspreise für die Illustration von Kinder- und Jugendbüchern; Förderungspreis für die Übersetzung von Kinder- und Jugendbüchern. Seit 1956 wird neben den preisgekrönten Büchern eine "Ehrenliste" veröffentlicht, die besonders empfehlenswerte Bücher nennt. Zur Förderung und Werbung für wertvolle Jugendliteratur werden vom Bundesministerium für Unterricht und Kunst Exemplare der prämiierten Bücher im Gesamtwert von 100.000.— Schilling angekauft und kostenlos gemeinnützigen Einrichtungen für Kinder und Jugendliche zur Verfügung gestellt.
Literatur: Preisgekrönte Kinder- und Jugendbücher. 1954—1961. Hrsg.: Institut für Wissenschaft und Kunst. (Wien): Verlag für Jugend und Volk (1961). 85 S. mit Ill.

1955 Stappen, Gerhard/Huber, Otto: **Servus, Pinguin!** (Hello penguin!) Photos.
Wien: Österreichischer Bundesverlag 1955.

Stemmer, Irene: **Prinz Seifenblase und andere märchenhafte Geschichten.** (Prince *Soap Bubble* and other fairy tales.) Ill.: Hans Cornaro.
Wien: Verlag Jungbrunnen 1954.

1956 Bruckner, Karl: **Der Weltmeister.** Roman. (The champion. Novel.) Ill.: Adalbert Pilch.
Wien: Verlag für Jugend und Volk 1956.

Koenig, Lilli: **Gringolo.** Eine Siebenschläfergeschichte. (*Gringolo.* A dormouse story.) Ill.: Lilli Koenig.
Wien: Verlag für Jugend und Volk 1956.

Lechner, Auguste: **Das Licht auf Montsalvat.** Die Abenteuer Parzifals. (The light from Montsalvat. The adventure of *Parsifal.*) Ill.: Hans Vonmetz.
Innsbruck, Wien, München: Tyrolia-Verlag 1956.

1957 Tauschinski, Oskar Jan: **Wer ist diese Frau?** (Who ist this woman?)
Wien: Verlag Jungbrunnen 1957.

1958 *Children's book/Kinderbuch*
Lobe, Mira: **Titi im Urwald.** (*Titi* in the jungle.) Ill.: Susanne Weigel.
Wien: Verlag Jungbrunnen 1957.

Youth book/Jugendbuch
Braumann, Franz: **Ritt nach Barantola.** Die Abenteuer des Tibetreisenden Johannes Grueber. (Ride to Barantola. The travel adventures of *Johannes Grueber* in Tibet.) Ill.: Rudolf Angerer.
Wien: Herder 1958.

1959 *Children's book/Kinderbuch*
Busta, Christine: **Die Sternenmühle.** Gedichte für Kinder und ihre Freunde. (The star mill. Poems for children and their friends.) Ill.: Johannes Grüger.
Salzburg, Wien, Freilassing: O. Müller 1959.

Youth book/Jugenbuch
Ellert, Gerhart (i.e. Gertrud Schmirger): **Auf endlosen Straßen.** Abenteuer der Menschheit. (On endless streets. Adventure of mankind.) Ill.: Hilde Seidl.
Wien, München: Österreichischer Bundesverlag 1959.

1960 *Small children's book/Kleinkinderbuch*
Eigl, Kurt: **Alle brauchen Moro.** (Everybody needs *Moro.*) Ill.: Wilfried Zeller-Zellenberg.
Wien: Forum Verlag; Verlag für Jugend und Volk 1960.

Children's book/Kinderbuch
Leiter, Helmut: **Martin gegen Martin.** Ein heiterer Kinderroman. (*Martin* versus *Martin.* A happy children's novel.) Ill.: Wilfried Zeller-Zellenberg.
Wien, München: Österreichischer Bundesverlag 1960.

Youth book/Jugendbuch
The prize was not given; Der Preis wurde nicht vergeben.
Illustration
Zeller-Zellenberg, Wilfried in: Eigl, Kurt: **Alle brauchen Moro.** (Everybody needs *Moro.*)
Wien: Forum Verlag; Verlag für Jugend und Volk 1960.

1961 *Children's book/Kinderbuch*
Recheis, Käthe: **Kleiner Adler und Silberstern.** (*Little Eagle* and *Silver Star.*) Ill.: Atelier Schmid.
Wien: Herder 1961.

Youth book/Jugendbuch
Bruckner, Karl: **Sadako will leben! (Sadako** wants to live!)
Wien: Verlag für Jugend und Volk 1961.

Lang, Othmar Franz: **Vielleicht in fünf, sechs Jahren . . .** (Perhaps in five, six years . .) Ill.: Ingrid Zeitler.
Wien, München: Österreichischer Bundesverlag 1961.

Illustration
Wallenta, Emanuela in:
Bamberger, Richard: **Mein erstes großes Märchenbuch.** (My first big fairy tale book.)
Wien: Verlag für Jugend und Volk 1960.

1962 *Small children's book/Kleinkinderbuch*
Ferra-Mikura, Vera: **Der alte und der junge und der kleine Stanislaus.** (The old and the young and the little *Stanislaus.*) Ill.: Romulus Candea.
Wien: Verlag Jungbrunnen 1962.

Children's book/Kinderbuch
Steiner, Alexis (i.e. Alois Franz Rottensteiner): **Die stille, heilige Nacht.** (The quiet, holy night.) Ill.: Adalbert Pilch.
Wien, München: Österreichischer Bundesverlag 1962.

Youth book/Jugendbuch
Schreiber, Georg: **Schwert ohne Krone.** Ein Roman um Konradin, den letzten Hohenstaufen, und Friedrich von Österreich. (Sword without a crown. A novel about *Konradin,* the last *Hohenstaufen,* and *Friedrich* of Austria.) Ill.: Gottfried Pils.
Graz, Wien, Köln: Styria Verlag 1962.

Tauschinski, Oskar Jan: **Die Liebenden sind stärker.** Ein Suttner Roman. (Lovers are stronger. A *Suttner* novel.)
Wien, München: Österreichischer Bundesverlag 1962.

Illustration
Pils, Gottfried in:
Schreiber, Georg: **Schwert ohne Krone.** Ein Roman von *Konradin,* den letzten Hohenstaufen, und *Friedrich* von Österreich. (Sword without a crown. A novel about *Konradin,* the last *Hohenstaufen,* and *Friedrich* of Austria.)
Graz, Wien, Köln: Styria Verlag 1962.

1963 *Small children's book/Kleinkinderbuch*
Ferra-Mikura, Vera: **Unsere drei Stanisläuse.** (Our three *Stanislauses.*) Ill.: Romulus Candea.
Wien: Verlag Jungbrunnen 1963.

Children's book/Kinderbuch
Recheis, Käthe: **Der kleine Biber und seine Freunde.** The little beaver and his friends.) Ill.: Herbert Lentz.
Wien: Herder 1963.

Youth book/Jugendbuch
Habeck, Fritz: **Der einäugige Reiter.** (The one-eyed rider.) Ill.: Gottfried Pils.
Wien, München: Verlag für Jugend und Volk 1963.

Illustration
Jaruska, Wilhelm in:
Steiner, Alexis (i.e. Alois Franz Rottensteiner): **Alle meine Pferde.** All my horses.)
Wien: Verlag für Jugend und Volk 1963.

1964 *Small children's book/Kleinkinderbuch*
Ferra-Mikura, Vera: **Lustig singt die Regentonne.** (Gayly sings the rain barrel.) Ill.: Romulus Candea.
Wien: Verlag Jungbrunnen 1964.

Children's book/Kinderbuch
Stebich, Max: **Aus Moor und Heide.** Sagen und Märchen. (From moor and heather. Legends and fairy tales.) Ill.: Hildegard Hostnig.
Wien: Breitschopf 1964.

Urban, Gustav: **Die Stimme des Jogi.** (The voice of the yogi.)
Wien, München: Verlag für Jugend und Volk 1964.

Youth book/Jugendbuch
Recheis, Käthe: **Das Schattennetz.** Erzählung. (The shadow net. A story.)
Wien, Freiburg, Basel: Herder 1964.

Illustration
Hostnig, Hildegard in:
Stebich, Max: **Aus Moor und Heide.** Sagen und Märchen. (From moor and heather. Legends and fairy tales.)
Wien: Breitschopf 1964.

1965 *Small children's book/Kleinkinderbuch*
Schaller, Ilse: **Himpel, Hampel, Humpel und der Vogel Hui.** (*Himpel, Hampel, Humpel* and *Hui* the bird.) Ill.: Emanuela Delignon.
Wien: Österreichischer Bundesverlag 1965.

Children's book/Kinderbuch
Lobe, Mira: **Die Omama im Apfelbaum.** (The grandmother in the apple tree.) Ill.: Susi Weigel.
Wien: Verlag Jungbrunnen 1965.

Youth book/Jugendbuch
Bruckner, Winfried: **Die Pfoten des Feuers.** (The paws of the fire.)
Wien: Verlag Jungbrunnen 1965.

Mayer-Skumanz, Lene: **Ein Engel für Monika.** (An angel for *Monika.*)
Wien, München: Österreichischer Bundesverlag 1965.

1966 *Small children's book/Kleinkinderbuch*
Hofbauer, Friedl: **Die Wippschaukel.** (The see-saw.) Ill.: Frizzi Weidner.
Wien, München: Verlag für Jugend und Volk 1966.

Children's book/Kinderbuch
Tichy, Herbert: **Der weiße Sahib.** (The white sahib.)
Wien, München: Österreichischer Bundesverlag 1966.

Youth book/Jugendbuch
Rutgers van der Loeff-Basenau, An: **Mensch oder Wolf?** (Man or Wolf?)
Wien: Verlag für Jugend und Volk 1966.

1967 *Picture book/Bilderbuch*
Berger, Eleonore: **Geschichten vom Hanselmann.** (Stories about *Hanselmann.*) Ill.: Emanuela Wallenta.
Wien: Verlag für Jugend und Volk; München: Hirundo Verlag 1967.

Children's book I/Kinderbuch I
Čtvrtek, Václav: **Die Geschichte vom Kreidemännlein.** (The story about the little chalk men.) Ill.: Olga Čechova.
Wien: Braumüller 1967.

Wilkeshuis, Cornelis: **Die goldene Schatztruhe.** (The golden treasure chest.) Ill.: Jenny Dalenoord.
Wien, Heidelberg: Ueberreuter 1966.

Children's book II/Kinderbuch II
Habeck, Fritz: **Aufstand der Salzknechte.** (The revolt of the peasant salt-miners.) Ill.: Haimo Lauth.
Wien, München: Verlag für Jugend und Volk 1967.

Recheis, Käthe: **Red Boy.** *(Red Boy.)* Ill.: Herwig Schubert.
Wien, Freiburg, Basel: Herder 1967.

Youth book/Jugendbuch
Rekimies, Erkki: **Jagt den Wolf.** (Hunt the wolf.) Ill.: Kurt Röschl.
Wien: Österreichischer Bundesverlag 1967.

Ruck-Pauquèt, Gina: **Joschko.** *(Joschko.)* Ill.: Sigrid Heuck.
Wien: Breitschopf 1967.

1968 *Picture book/Bilderbuch*
Galler, Helga: **Der kleine Nerino.** (Little *Nerino.*) Ill.: Helga Galler.
Bad Goisern: Neugebauer Press 1968.

Children's book/Kinderbuch
Bolt, Robert: **Der kleine dicke Ritter.** (The little fat knight.) Adapted from/Bearb. von Carl Schanze. Ill.: Horst Lemke.
Wien: Obelisk Verlag 1968.

Schmidt, Annie (i.e. Anna Maria Geertruida Schmidt): **Wiplala.** (*Wiplala.*) Ill.: Jenny Dalenoord.
Wien: Verlag Jungbrunnen 1967.

1969 *Picture book/Bilderbuch*
The prize was not given; Der Preis wurde nicht vergeben.

Children's book/Kinderbuch
Hofbauer, Friedl: **Der Brummkreisel.** (The humming top.) Ill.: Frizzi Weidner.
Wien: Verlag für Jugend und Volk 1969.

Chapman, Jean: **Die Wunschkatze.** (The wish cat.) Ill.: Eva Hülsmann.
Wien: Obelisk Verlag 1969.

1970 *Picture book/Bilderbuch*
The prize was not given; Der Preis wurde nicht vergeben.

Children's book/Kinderbuch
Meissel, Wilhelm: **Die Spur führt in die Höhle.** (The trail leads into the cave.)
Wien: Verlag für Jugend und Volk 1969.

Tauschinski, Oskar Jan: **Der Jüngling im Baumstamm.** (The youth in the tree trunk.) Ill.: Frizzi Weidner.
Wien: Verlag für Jugend und Volk 1969.

Youth book/Jugendbuch
The prize was not given; Der Preis wurde nicht vergeben.

1971 *Picture book/Bilderbuch*
The prize was not given; Der Preis wurde nicht vergeben.

Children's book I/Kinderbuch I
Ferra-Mikura, Vera: **Valentin pfeift auf dem Grashalm.** (*Valentin* whistles with a blade of grass.) Ill.: Romulus Candea.
Wien: Verlag Jungbrunnen 1970.

Recheis, Käthe: **Martin und die Regengeister.** (*Martin* and the rain spirits.) Ill.: Monika Laimgruber.
Wien: Herder 1971.

Children's book II/Kinderbuch II
Lee, Mildred: **Die Rollschuhbahn.** (The roller-skating rink.)
Wien: Verlag Jungbrunnen 1971.

Wippersberg, W.J.M.: **Schlafen auf dem Wind.** (Sleeping on the wind.) Ill.: Sieglinde Meder.
Wien: Obelisk Verlag 1971.

Youth book/Jugendbuch
Domagalik, Janusz: **Ich habe mich entschieden.** (I have decided; Pol.orig.title: Koniec wakacji.)
Wien: Verlag für Jugend und Volk 1971.

Illustration
Weigel, Susi in:
Lobe, Mira: **Das Städtchen Drumherum.** (The little town *"Drumherum"* = Round about.)
Wien: Verlag Jungbrunnen 1970.

Translation/Übersetzung
Tauschinski, Oskar Jan in:
Domagalik, Janusz: **Ich habe mich entschieden.** (I have decided; Pol.orig.title: Koniec wakacji.)
Wien: Verlag für Jugend und Volk 1971.

1972 *Picture book/Bilderbuch*
Lobe, Mira: **Das kleine Ich bin ich.** (The little I am I.) Ill.: Susi Weigel.
Wien: Verlag Jungbrunnen 1972.

Children's book I/Kinderbuch I
Frischmuth, Barbara: **Ida — und ob.** (*Ida* — of course.)
Wien: Verlag Jugend und Volk 1972.

Children's book II/Kinderbuch II
Fussenegger, Gertrud: **Bibel-Geschichten.** (Bible stories.) Ill.: Janusz Grabianski.
Wien: Ueberreuter 1972.

Recheis, Käthe: **Fallensteller am Bibersee.** (Trappers at *Beaver Lake.)* Ill.: Herwig Schubert.
Wien: Herder 1972.

Youth book/Jugendbuch
Wölfel, Ursula: **Die grauen und die grünen Felder.** The grey and the green fields.)
Wien: Fährmann Verlag 1971.

Illustration
The prize was not given; Der Preis wurde nicht vergeben.

Translation/Übersetzung
Ebner, Jeannie in: Harris, Rosemary: **Eine Katz für Noahs Arche.** (A cat for *Noah's* ark; Amer.orig.title: The moon in the cloud.) Ill.: Walter Schmoegner.
Wien: Verlag für Jugend und Volk 1972.

1973 *Picture book/Bilderbuch*
Peter, Brigitte: **Lollobien.** *(Lollobien.)* Ill.: Angelika Kaufmann.
Wien: Verlag Jungbrunnen 1973.

Children's book I/Kinderbuch I
Ferra-Mikura, Vera: **Sigismund hat einen Zaun.** (*Sigismund* has a fence.) Ill.: Elisabeth Mikura.
Wien: Verlag Jungbrunnen 1973.

Children's book II/Kinderbuch II
Terlouw, Jan: **Kampf um Katoren.** (Battle at Katoren.) Ill.: Herbert Holzing.
Innsbruck: Obelisk Verlag 1973.

Youth book/Jugendbuch
Weiss, Walter: **Der Tod der Tupilaks.** (The death of the *Tupilaks.*)
Wien: Verlag für Jugend und Volk 1973.

Non-fiction/Sachbuch
Chinery, Michael: **Tier Gemeinschaften.** (Animal communities.) Ill.
Wien: Österreichischer Bundesverlag 1973.

Illustration
Kaufmann, Angelika in:
Peter, Brigitte: **Lollobien.** *(Lollobien.)*
Wien: Verlag Jungbrunnen 1973.

Kaufmann, Angelika in:
Lachs, Minna: **Was raschelt da im Bauernhof.** (What's rustling there in the farm yard.)
Wien: Verlag für Jugend und Volk 1973.

1974 The Österreichische Staatspreis was not given; Der Österreichische Staatspreis wurde nicht vergeben.

1975 *Picture book/Bilderbuch*
Recheis, Käthe: **Kleiner Bruder Watomi.** (Little brother *Watomi.*) Ill.: Monika Laimgruber.
Wien: Herder 1974.

Children's book I/Kinderbuch I
Tauschinski, Oskar Jan: **Der Spiegel im Brunnen.** (The mirror in the well.) Ill.: Helga Lauth.
Wien: Verlag Jungbrunnen 1974.

Children's book II/Kinderbuch II
Nöstlinger, Christine: **Achtung, Vranek sieht ganz harmlos aus.** (Careful. *Vranek* seems to be totally harmless.) Ill.: Christine Nöstlinger.
Wien: Verlag für Jugend und Volk 1974.

Youth book/Jugendbuch
Bayer, Ingeborg: **Die vier Freiheiten der Hanna B.** (The four freedoms of *Hanna B.*
Wien: Fährmann Verlag 1974.

Non-fiction/Sachbuch
Das Sprachbastelbuch. (The wordcraft book.) Ill.: Gerri Zotter.
Wien: Verlag für Jugend und Volk 1975.

Illustration
Ohta, Daihachi in:
Kanzawa, Toshiko: **Regentaro.** (Raintaro.)
Mödling: Verlag St. Gabriel 1974.

Translation/Übersetzung
Rukschcio, Gertrud in:
Kanzawa, Toshiko: **Regentaro.** *(Raintaro.)* Ill.: Daihachi Ohta.
Mödling: Verlag St. Gabriel 1974.

1976 *Picture book/Bilderbuch*
Harranth, Wolf: **Michael hat einen Seemann.** (*Michael* has a seaman.) Ill.: Josef Paleček.
Wien: Verlag Jungbrunnen 1975.

Children's book I/Kinderbuch I
Eckert, Allan W.: **Es geschah in der Prärie.** (It happened on the prairie; Amer.orig.title: Incident at *Hawk's Hill.*) Ill.: John Schoenherr.
Mödling: Verlag St. Gabriel 1975.

Children's book II/Kinderbuch II
O'Brien, Robert: **Frau Frisby und die Ratten von Nimh;** Amer.orig.title: Mrs. *Frisby* and the rats of *Nimh.*) Ill.: Zena Bernstein.
Wien: Verlag Jungbrunnen 1975.

Youth book/Jugendbuch
Recheis, Käthe: **London — 13. Juli.** (*London* — July 13th.)
Wien: Herder 1975.

Non-fiction/Sachbuch
Peter, Brigitte: **Im Dschungel der Gargar.** (In the jungle of *Gargar.*) Ill.
Wien: Verlag für Jugend und Volk 1975.

Illustration
Paleček, Josef in:
Harranth, Wolf: **Michael hat einen Seeman.** (*Michael* has a seaman.)
Wien: Verlag Jungbrunnen 1975.

Translation/Übersetzung
Junker, Stella in:
O'Brien, Robert: **Frau Frisby und die Ratten von Nimh;** Amer.orig.title: Mrs. *Frisby* and the rats from *Nimh.*) Ill.: Zena Bernstein.
Wien: Verlag Jungbrunnen 1975.

1977 Picture book/Bilderbuch
Lobe, Mira: **Der ist ganz anders als ihr glaubt.** (He ist totally different from what you think.) Ill.: Susi Weigel.
Wien: Verlag Jungbrunnen 1976.

Children's book I/Kinderbuch I
Rodari, Gianni: **Der Zaubertrommler.** (The magic drummer; Ital.orig.title: Tante storie per giocare.) Ill.: Gianni Pegoraro.
Wien: Verlag für Jugend und Volk 1976.

Sachs, Marilyn: **Das Bärenhaus und ich.** (The bear-house and I.) Ill.: Edith Schindler.
Innsbruck: Obelisk Verlag 1976.

Children's book II/Kinderbuch II
Valencak, Hannelore: **Regenzauber.** (Rain magic.)
Wien: Ueberreuter 1976.

Welsh, Renate: **Empfänger unbekannt — zurück!** (Address unknown — return to sender.)
Wien, München: Verlag Jungbrunnen 1976.

Youth book/Jugendbuch
The prize was not given; Der Preis wurde nicht vergeben.

Non-fiction/Sachbuch
The prize was not given; Der Preis wurde nicht vergeben.

Illustration
Haldane, Roger in:
Thiele, Colin: **Die Insel des Flötenvogels.** (Austral.orig.title: Magpie Island.)
Mödling: Verlag St. Gabriel 1976.

Translation/Übersetzung
Weixelbaumer, Ingrid in:
Elwood, Roger: **Jenseits von morgen.** (Amer.orig.title: The other side of tomorrow.)
Wien: Ueberreuter 1976.

1978 *Picture book/Bilderbuch*
Jansson, Tove: **Wer soll den Lillan trösten?** (Who will comfort *Lillan?* Swed.orig.title: Vem ska trösta knyttet?)
Mödling: Verlag St. Gabriel 1977.

Children's book I/Kinderbuch I
Welsh, Renate: **. . .und Terpsi geht zum Zirkus.** (. . . and *Terpsi* joins the circus.) Ill.: Wilfried Zeller-Zellenberg.
Wien: Verlag für Jugend und Volk 1977.

Children's book II/Kinderbuch II
Breen, Else: **Warte nicht auf einen Engel** (Don't wait for an angel; Nor.orig.title: I stripete genser.)
Wien, München: Verlag Jungbrunnen 1977.

Manzi, Alberto: **Amigo, ich singe im Herzen.** (Friend, I sing in my heart; Ital.orig.title: La luna nelle baracche.) Ill.: Roberto Innocent.
Wien: Verlag für Jugend und Volk 1978.

Youth book/Jugendbuch
Holman, Felice: **Vorhölle.** (Amer.orig.title: Slake's limbo.)
Innsbruck: Obelisk Verlag 1977.

Non-fiction/Sachbuch
The prize was not given; Der Preis wurde nicht vergeben.

Illustration
Oppermann-Dimow, Christine in:
Lobe, Mira: **Ein Vogel wollte Hochzeit machen.** (A bird wishes to get married.)
Innsbruck: Tyrolia Verlag 1977.

Translation/Übersetzung
Herrnstadt-Steinmetz, Gundl in:
Manzi, Alberto: **Amigo, ich singe im Herzen.** (Friend, I sing in my heart; Ital.orig.title: La luna nelle baracche.) Ill.: Roberto Innocent.
Wien: Verlag für Jugend und Volk 1978.

1979 *Picture book/Bilderbuch*
The prize was not given; Der Preis wurde nicht vergeben.

Children's book I/Kinderbuch I
Nöstlinger, Christine: **Rosa Riedl, Schutzgespenst.** (*Rosa Riedl*, guardian ghost.) Ill.: Christine Nöstlinger.
Wien, München: Jugend und Volk 1979.

Thiele, Colin: **Die Ttupak.** (The *Sknuks.*) Ill.: Mary Milton.
Mödling: St. Gabriel 1978.

Children's book II/Kinderbuch II
Recheis, Käthe: **Der weite Weg des Nataiyu.** (*Nataiyu's* long journey.)
Wien: Herder 1978.

Youth book/Jugendbuch
The prize was not given; Der Preis wurde nicht vergeben.

Non-fiction/Sachbuch
The prize was not given; Der Preis wurde nicht vergeben.

Illustration
Wiberg, Harald in:
Peterson, Hans: **Der große Schneesturm.** (The big snowstorm.)
Mödling: Verlag St. Gabriel 1978.

Translation/Übersetzung
Baumann, Hans in:
Tiergeschichten aus Rußland. (Animal stories from Russia.)
Heidelberg: Ueberreuter 1979.

1980 *Picture book/Bilderbuch*
Recheis, Käthe: **Wo die Wölfe glücklich sind.** (Where the wolves are happy.) Ill.: Alicia Sancha.
Wien: Herder 1979.

Children's book I/Kinderbuch I
Sklenitzka, Franz Sales: **Drachen haben nichts zu lachen.** (Dragons have nothing to laugh about.) Ill.: Franz Sales Sklenitzka.
Wien: Jugend und Volk 1979.

Children's book II/Kinderbuch II
Bachér, Ingrid: **Morgen werde ich fliegen.** (Tomorrow I will fly.)
Innsbruck: Obelisk 1979.

Fährmann, Willi: **Der lange Weg des Lukas B.** (The long path of *Lukas B.*)
Wien: Österreichischer Bundesverlag 1980.

Youth book/Jugendbuch
Domagalik, Janusz: **Grüne Kastanien.** (Green chestnuts; Pol.orig. title: Zielone kasztany.)
Wien: Jugend und Volk 1979.

Non-fiction/Sachbuch
Domenego, Hans: **Wer—wie—was.** (Who—how—what.)
Wien: Jugend und Volk 1980.

Illustration
Lucht, Irmgard in:
Lucht, Irmgard: **Die Baum-Uhr.** (The tree clock.)
Wien: Kremayr und Scheriau 1979.

Translation/Übersetzung
Tauschinski, Oskar Jan in:
Domagalik, Janusz: **Grüne Kastanien.** (Green chestnuts; Pol.orig.title: Zielone kasztany.)
Wien: Jugend und Volk 1979.

Kinder- und Jugendbuchpreis der Stadt Wien

This prize from the city of Vienna was first presented in 1954. Ten specialists nominated by the Office for Culture, Education and School Administration make up the jury. The prize is based upon the returns of the "Kulturgroschen" (culture tax). Only living Austrian authors whose books have been published by Viennese publishers are elgible for the award. The honoured author receives a certificate and a cash-award. Outstanding illustrations are also selected. The separation of the children's book award from the youth book award was affected in 1960. Since 1968, books for the youngest readers (picture books) are considered for the award as well. The city of Vienna has special funds available for the annual purchase of the distinguished books.

Der Kinder- und Jugendbuchpreis der Stadt Wien besteht seit 1954. Die Jury setzt sich aus 10 Fachleuten zusammen, die vom Amt für Kultur, Volksbildung und Schulverwaltung ernannt werden. Der Preis, aus dem Gewinn des "Kulturgroschens" gestiftet, kann nur an lebende österreichische Autoren für Bücher vergeben werden, die in Wiener Verlagen erschienen sind. Er ist mit der Verleihung eines Diploms und eines Geldbetrages verbunden. Außerdem werden herausragende Illustrationen prämiiert. Die Trennung zwischen Kinder- und Jugendbuchpreis wurde 1960 eingeführt, seit 1968 wird auch ein Bilderbuchpreis vergeben. Für den Ankauf der preisgekrönten Bücher stellt die Stadt Wien jährlich eine bestimmte Summe zur Verfügung.

1954 Bruckner, Karl: **Giovanna und der Sumpf.** (*Giovanna* and the marsh.) Ill.: Hedwig Zum Tobel.
Wien: Verlag Jungbrunnen 1953.

1955 Lang, Othmar Franz: **Die Männer von Kaprun.** (The men from *Kaprun.*). Photos: Franz Hubmann.
Wien: Österreichischer Bundesverlag 1955.

Schreiber, Georg: **Der Weg des Bruders.** Ein Roman aus dem alten Rom. (The way of the brothers. A novel of ancient Rome. Ill.: Karl Langer.
Wien: Verlag Jungbrunnen 1954.

1956 Ferra-Mikura, Vera: **Der Teppich der schönen Träume und andere Märchen.** (The carpet of beautiful dreams and other fairy tales.) Ill.: Ernst Schrom and Magda Widhalm.
Wien: Kremayr & Scheriau 1955.

Koenig, Lilli: **Gringolo. Eine Siebenschläfergeschichte.** (*Gringolo.* A dormouse story.) Ill.: Lilli Koenig.
Wien: Verlag für Jugend und Volk 1956.

Illustration
Jaruska, Wilhelm in:
Steiner, Alexis (i.e. Alois Franz Rottensteiner): **Kriki, das tapfere Entlein.** (*Kriki,* the courageous little duck.)
Wien: Verlag für Jugend und Volk 1956.

1957 Bruckner, Karl: **Der goldene Pharao.** Gräber, Abenteuer, Forscher. (The golden pharaoh. Graves, adventures and researchers.) Ill.: Hans Thomas.
Wien: Verlag für Jugend und Volk 1957.

Illustration
Candea, Romulus in:
Ferra-Mikura, Vera: **Zaubermeister Opequeh.** (Master magician *Opequeh.*)
Wien: Verlag Jungbrunnen 1956.

1958 Bruckner, Karl: **Lale die Türkin.** (*Lale* the Turkish girl.) Ill.: Emanuela Wallenta.
Wien: Verlag für Jugend und Volk 1958.

Feiks-Waldhäusl, Emmy: **Das Pestbüblein.** Erzählung. (The plague boy. A story.)
Wien: Herder 1958.

Pohl, Helga: **Der Elefant von Amsterdam.** (The elephant from *Amsterdam.*) Photos.
München, Wien: Andermann 1957.

Illustration
Weidner, Fritzi in:
Leiter, Hilde/Leiter, Helmut: **Das kleine Wetterhaus.** Geschichten für alle Kinder. (The little weather house. Stories for all children.)
Wien: Verlag für Jugend und Volk 1958.

1959 Busta, Christine: **Die Sternenmühle.** Gedichte für Kinder und ihre Freunde. (The star mill. Poems for children and their friends.) Ill.: Johannes Grüger.
Salzburg, Wien, Freilassing: O. Müller 1959.

Illustration
Candea, Romulus in:
Ferra-Mikura, Vera: **Willi Einhorn auf fremden Straßen.** (*Willi Unicorn* on strange streets.)
Wien: Verlag Jungbrunnen 1958.

1960 *Children's book/Kinderbuch*
Leiter, Helmut: **Martin gegen Martin.** (*Martin* versus *Martin.*) Ill.: Wilfried Zeller-Zellenberg.
Wien, München: Österreichischer Bundesverlag 1960.

Youth book/Jugendbuch
Habeck, Fritz: **Der Kampf um die Barbacane.** (The battle around the *Barbacane.*). Ill.: Lajos Horvath.
Wien: Verlag für Jugend und Volk 1960.

Illustration
Zeller-Zellenberg, Wilfried in:
Eigl, Kurt: **Alle brauchen Moro.** (Everybody needs *Moro.*)
Wien: Forum Verlag; Verlag für Jugend und Volk 1960.

1961 *Children's book/Kinderbuch*
Lobe, Mira: **Hannes und sein Bumpan.** (*Hannes* and his pal.) Ill.: Susi Weigel.
Wien: Verlag für Jugend und Volk 1961.

Youth book/Jugendbuch
Bruckner, Karl: **Sadako will leben!** (*Sadako* wants to live!)
Wien: Verlag für Jugend und Volk 1961.

Habeck, Fritz: **Die Stadt der grauen Gesichter.** (The city of grey faces.) Ill.: Kurt Röschl.
Wien: Verlag für Jugend und Volk 1961.

Illustration
Weigel, Susi in:
Lobe, Mira: **Hannes und sein Bumpan.** (*Hannes* and his pal.)
Wien: Verlag für Jugend und Volk 1961.

1962 *Children's book/Kinderbuch*
Ferra-Mikura, Vera: **Der alte und der junge und der kleine Stanislaus.** (The old, the young and the little *Stanislaus.*). Ill.: Romulus Candea.
Wien: Verlag Jungbrunnen 1962.

Youth book/Jugendbuch
Tauschinski, Oskar Jan: **Die Liebenden sind stärker.** Ein Suttner Roman. (The loving are stronger. A Suttner novel.)
Wien, München: Österreichischer Bundesverlag 1962.

Tichy, Herbert: **Unterwegs.** (Under way.) Photos.
Wien, München: Verlag für Jugend und Volk 1962.

Illustration
Candea, Romulus in:
Ferra-Mikura, Vera: **Der alte und der junge und der kleine Stanislaus.** (The old and the young and the little *Stanislaus.*).
Wien: Verlag Jungbrunnen 1962.

1963 *Children's book/Kinderbuch*
Ferra-Mikura, Vera: **Unsere drei Stanisläuse.** (Our three Stanislauses.) Ill.: Romulus Candea.
Wien: Verlag Jungbrunnen 1963.

Youth book/Jugendbuch
Habeck, Fritz: **Der einäugige Reiter.** (The one-eyed rider.) Ill.: Gottfried Pils.
Wien, München: Verlag für Jugend und Volk 1963.

Illustration
Candea, Romulus in:
Ferra-Mikura, Vera: **Unsere drei Stanisläuse.** (Our three *Stanislauses.*)
Wien: Verlag Jungbrunnen 1963.

Jaruska, Wilhelm in:
Steiner, Alexis (i.e. Alois Franz Rottensteiner): **Alle meine Pferde.** (All my horses.)
Wien: Verlag für Jugend und Volk 1963.

1964 *Children's book/Kinderbuch*
Ferra-Mikura, Vera: **Lustig singt die Regentonne.** (Merrily sings the rain barrel.) Ill.: Romulus Candea.
Wien: Verlag Jungbrunnen 1964.

Youth book/Jugendbuch
Recheis, Käthe: **Das Schattennetz.** Erzählung. (The shadow net. A story.)
Wien, Freiburg, Basel: Herder 1964.

Illustration
Candea, Romulus in:
Ferra-Mikura, Vera: **Lustig singt die Regentonne.** (Merrily sings the rain barrel.)
Wien: Verlag Jungbrunnen 1964.

1965 *Children's book/Kinderbuch*
Lobe, Mira: **Die Omama im Apfelbaum.** (Grandmama in the apple tree.) Ill.: Susi Weigel.
Wien: Verlag Jungbrunnen 1965.

Haushofer, Marlen: **Brav sein ist schwer.** (It's difficult to be good.) Ill.: Ilon Wikland.
Wien, München: Verlag für Jugend und Volk 1965.

Youth book/Jugendbuch
Lobe, Mira: **Meister Thomas in St. Wolfgang.** (Master *Thomas* in *St. Wolfgang.*) Photos.
Wien, München: Verlag für Jugend und Volk 1965.

Illustration
Demmer, Helga in:
Demmer, Elly: **Was kribbelt und krabbelt und leuchtet und blüht.** (What creeps and crawls and shines and blossoms.)
Wien, München: Österreichischer Bundesverlag 1965.

1966 *Children's book/Kinderbuch*
Hofbauer, Friedl: **Die Wippschaukel** (The see-saw.) Ill.: Fritzi Weidner.
Wien, München: Verlag für Jugend und Volk 1966.

Youth book/Jugendbuch
Benesch, Kurt: **Die Frau mit den hundert Schicksalen.** Das Leben der Marie von Ebner-Eschenbach. (The woman with a hundred fates. The life of *Marie von Ebner-Eschenbach.*)
Wien, München: Österreichischer Bundesverlag 1966.

Illustration
Zeller-Zellenberg, Wilfried in:
Recheis, Käthe: **66 plus 1 im Bäckerhaus.** (66 plus 1 in the baker's house.)
Wien: Herder 1966.

1967 *Children's book/Kinderbuch*
Berger, Eleonore: **Geschichten vom Hanselmann.** (Stories about *Hanselmann.*). Ill.: Emanuela Wallenta.
Wien: Verlag für Jugend und Volk; München: Hirundo Verlag 1967.

Haushofer, Marlen: **Müssen Tiere draussenbleiben?** (Must animals stay out of doors?) Ill.: Gertraud Eben.
Wien, München: Verlag für Jugend und Volk 1967.

Youth book/Jugendbuch
Habeck, Fritz: **Aufstand der Salzknechte.** (Revolt of the salt miners.) Ill.: Haimo Lauth.
Wien, München: Verlag für Jugend und Volk 1967.

Illustration
Wallenta, Emanuela in:
Berger, Eleonore: **Geschichten vom Hanselmann.** (Stories about *Hanselmann.*)
Wien: Verlag für Jugend und Volk; München: Hirundo Verlag 1967.

1968 *Picture book/Bilderbuch*
Lobe, Mira: **Das blaue Känguruh.** (The blue kangaroo.) Ill.: Susi Weigel.
Wien, München: Verlag Jungbrunnen 1968.

Children's book/Kinderbuch
Pritz, Rudolf: **Die Rabenbergbande.** (The *Raven Hill* gang.) Ill.: Maria Sorger.
Wien, München: Verlag für Jugend und Volk 1968.

Recheis, Käthe: **Nikel, der Fuchs.** (*Nikel* the fox.) Photos: Engelbert Handlbauer.
Wien, Freiburg i. Br., Basel: Herder 1968.

Youth book/Jugendbuch
Tichy, Herbert: **Keine Zeit für Götter.** (No time for gods.)
Wien, München: Österreichischer Bundesverlag 1967.

1969 *Picture book/Bilderbuch*
Hofbauer, Friedl: **Der Brummkreisel.** (The humming top.) Ill.: Fritzi Weidner.
Wien: Verlag für Jugend und Volk 1969.

Children's book/Kinderbuch
Ferra-Mikura, Vera: **Lieber Freund Tulli.** (Dear friend *Tulli.*) Ill.: Elisabeth Mikura.
Wien: Verlag Jungbrunnen 1969.

Tauschinski, Oskar Jan: **Der Jüngling im Baumstamm.** (The youth in the tree trunk.) Ill.: Fritzi Weidner.
Wien: Verlag für Jugend und Volk 1969.

Youth book/Jugendbuch
Bruckner, Winfried: **Der traurige Sherrif.** (The sad sherrif.) Ill.: Franz Stadlmann.
Wien: Verlag für Jugend und Volk 1969.

Meissel, Wilhelm: **Die Spur führt in die Höhle.** (The trail leads into the cave.)
Wien: Verlag für Jugend und Volk 1969.

Illustration
Stadlmann, Winfried: **Der traurige Sherrif.** (The sad sherrif.)
Wien: Verlag für Jugend und Volk 1969.

1970 *Picture book/Bilderbuch*
Ferra-Mikura, Vera: **Herr Plusterflaum erlebt etwas.** (The adventures of Mr. *Plusterflaum.*). Ill.: Romulus Candea.
Wien: Verlag Jungbrunnen 1970.

Children's book/Kinderbuch
Haushofer, Marlen: **Schlimmsein ist auch kein Vergnügen.** (Being naughty is not funny.) Ill.: Ilon Wikland.
Wien: Verlag für Jugend und Volk 1970.

Lobe, Mira: **Das Städtchen Drumherum.** (The little town *"Drumherum"* = Round About.) Ill.: Susi Weigel.
Wien: Verlag Jungbrunnen 1970.

Youth book/Jugendbuch
Habeck, Fritz: **Taten und Abenteuer des Dr. Faustus.** (Deeds and adventures of Dr. *Faustus.*). Ill.: Helga Lauth.
Wien: Verlag für Jugend und Volk 1970.

Illustration
Weigel, Susi in:
Lobe, Mira: **Das Städtchen Drumherum.** (The little town *"Drumherum"* = Round About.)
Wien: Verlag Jungbrunnen 1970.

1971 *Picture book/Bilderbuch*
Demmer, Elly: **Ob's stürmt oder schneit.** (Whether it storms or snows.) Ill.: Helga Demmer.
Wien: Österreichischer Bundesverlag 1971.

Children's book/Kinderbuch
Recheis, Käthe: **Martin und die Regengeister.** (*Martin* and the rain spirits.) Ill.: Monika Laimgruber.
Wien: Herder 1971.

Youth book/Jugendbuch
Tichy, Herbert: **Honig vom Binungabaum.** (Honey from the binunga tree.) Photos: Herbert Tichy.
Wien: Ueberreuter 1971.

Weiss, Walter: **Die Piste ins Tibesti.** (The road to *Tibesti.*)
Wien: Verlag für Jugend und Volk 1971.

Illustration
Kaufmann, Angelika in:
Mayröcker, Friederike: **Sinclair Sofokles, der Baby-Saurier.** (*Sinclair Sofokles,* the baby saurian.)
Wien: Verlag für Jugend und Volk 1971.

1972 *Picture book/Bilderbuch*
Lobe, Mira: **Das kleine Ich bin ich.** (The little I am I.) Ill.: Susi Weigel.
Wien: Verlag Jungbrunnen 1972.

Children's book/Kinderbuch
Wippersberg, W.J.M.: **Schlafen auf dem Wind.** (Sleeping on the wind.) Ill.: Sieglinde Meder.
Wien: Obelisk Verlag 1971.

Youth book/Jugendbuch
Recheis, Käthe: **Fallensteller am Bibersee.** (Trappers at *Beaver Lake.*) Ill.: Herwig Schubert.
Wien: Herder 1972.

Illustration
Paleček, Josef in:
Harranth, Wolf: "Das ist eine wunderschöne Wiese", sagt Herr Timtim. ("That is a wonderful meadow", says Mr. *Timtim.*)
Wien: Verlag Jungbrunnen 1972.

1973 *Picture book/Bilderbuch*
Peter, Brigitte: **Lollobien.** *(Lollobien.)* Ill.: Angelika Kaufmann.
Wien: Verlag Jungbrunnen 1973.

Children's book/Kinderbuch
Ferra-Mikura, Vera: **Sigismund hat einen Zaun.** (*Sigismund* has a fence.) Ill.: Elisabeth Mikura.
Wien: Verlag Jungbrunnen 1973.

Youth book/Jugendbuch
Recheis, Käthe: **Professor, Du siehst Gespenster.** (Professor, you see ghosts.)
Wien: Herder 1973.

Habeck, Fritz: **Schwarzer Hund im goldenen Feld.** (Black dog in golden fields.)
Wien: Verlag für Jugend und Volk 1973.

Illustration
Kaufmann, Angelika in:
Peter, Brigitte: **Lollobien.** *(Lollobien).*
Wien: Verlag Jungbrunnen 1973.

1974 The prize was not given; Der Preis wurde nicht vergeben.

1975 *Picture book/Bilderbuch*
Lobe, Mira: **Komm, sagte die Katze.** (Come, said the cat.) Ill.: Angelika Kaufmann.
Wien: Verlag für Jugend und Volk 1975.

Recheis, Käthe: **Kleiner Brunder Watomi.** (Little brother *Watomi.*) Ill.: Monika Laimgruber.
Wien: Herder 1974.

Children's book/Kinderbuch
Tauschinski, Jan Oskar: **Der Spiegel im Brunnen.** (The mirror in the well.) Ill.: Helga Lauth.
Wien: Verlag Jungbrunnen 1974.

Youth book/Jugendbuch
Hofbauer, Friedel: **Die Kirschkernkette.** (The cherry pit chain.)
Wien: Ueberreuter 1974.

Valencak, Hannelore: **Ich bin Barbara.** (I am *Barbara.*).
Wien: Ueberreuter 1974.

Illustration
Kaufmann, Angelika in:
Lobe, Mira: **Komm, sagte die Katze.**
(Come, said the cat.)
Wien: Verlag für Jugend und Volk 1975.

1976 *Picture book/Bilderbuch*
Ferra-Mikura, Vera: **Meine Kuh trägt himmelblaue Socken.** (My cow wears sky-blue socks.) Ill.: Romulus Candea.
Wien: Verlag Jungbrunnen 1975.

Harranth, Wolf: **Michael hat einen Seemann.** (*Michael* has a sailor.) Ill.: Josef Palaček.
Wien: Verlag Jungbrunnen 1975.

Children's book/Kinderbuch
Peter, Brigitte: **Im Dschungel der Gargar.** (In the jungle of *Gargar.*). Ill.
Wien: Verlag für Jugend und Volk 1976.

Wippersberg, W.J.M.: **Augenzeugen.** (Eye witnesses.)
Innsbruck: Obelisk Verlag 1976.

Youth book/Jugendbuch
Recheis, Käthe: **London — 13. Juli.** (*London* — July 13th.)
Wien: Herder 1975.

Illustration
Delignon, Emanuela in:
Welsch, Renate: **Thomas und Billy.** (Thomas and *Billy.*)
Wien: Verlag für Jugend und Volk 1975.

1977 *Picture book/Bilderbuch*
Lobe, Mira: **Es ist ganz anders als ihr glaubt.** (It is completely otherwise from what you think.) Ill.: Susi Weigel.
Wien: Verlag Jungbrunnen 1976.

Children's book/Kinderbuch
Domengo, Hans/Leiter, Hilde: **Im Fliederbusch das Krokodil singt wundervolle Weisen.** (In the elder bush, the crocodile sings wonderful melodies.) Ill.: Christina Oppermann-Dimow.
Wien: Verlag für Jugend und Volk 1977.

Valencak, Hannelore: **Regenzauber.** (Rain magic.)
Wien: Ueberreuter 1976.

Youth book/Jugendbuch
Welsh, Renate: **Empfänger unbekannt — zurück.** (Person unknown — return to sender.)
Wien: Verlag Jungbrunnen 1976.

Illustration
Reinl, Edda in:
Lechner, Auguste: **Die schönsten Fabeln von La Fontaine.** (The most beautiful fables of *La Fontaine.*)
Innsbruck: Tyrolia 1976.

Resch, Barbara in:
Harranth, Wolf: **Der Vogel singt, der König springt.** (The bird sings, the king jumps.)
Wien: Verlag Jungbrunnen 1976.

1978 *Picture book/Bilderbuch*
Lobe, Mira: **Dann rufen alle Hoppelpopp.** (Then we all call *Hoppelpopp.*) Ill.: Angelika Kaufmann.
Wien: Verlag für Jugend und Volk 1977.

Children's book/Kinderbuch
Welsh, Renate: **. . . und Terpsi geht zum Zirkus . . .** (. . . and *Terpsi* joins the circus.) Ill.: Wilfried Zeller-Zellenberg.
Wien: Verlag für Jugend und Volk 1977.

Youth book/Jugendbuch
Peter, Brigitte: **Der schlafende Bumerang.** (The sleeping boomerang.) Photos: Hanns Peter and Brigitte Peter.
Wien: Verlag für Jugend und Volk 1978.

Illustration
Treiber, Sepp in:
Mayer-Skumanz, Lene: **. . . weil sie mich nicht lassen.** (. . . because they don't let me.)
Wien: Herder 1977.

1979 *Picture book/Bilderbuch*
Harranth, Wolf: **Claudia mit einer Mütze voll Zeit.** (*Claudia* with a cap full of time.) Ill.: Josef Paleček.
Wien: Verlag Jungbrunnen 1978.

Children's book/Kinderbuch
Recheis, Käthe: **Der weite Weg des Nataiyu.** (*Nataiyu's* long journey.)
Wien: Herder 1978.

Youth book/Jugendbuch
Damals war ich vierzehn. (I was fourteen at that time.)
Wien: Verlag für Jugend und Volk 1978.

Illustration
Paleček, Josef in:
Harranth, Wolf: **Claudia mit einer Mütze voll Zeit.** (*Claudia* with a cap full of time.)
Wien: Verlag Jungbrunnen 1978.

1980 *Picture book/Bilderbuch*
Lobe, Mira: **Der Apfelbaum.** (The apple tree.) Ill.: Angelika Kaufmann.
Wien: Verlag für Jugend und Volk 1980.

Children's book/Kinderbuch
Nöstlinger, Christine: **Dschi Dsche-i Dschunior.** *(Dschi Dsche-i Dschunior.)* Ill.: Franz Sales Sklenitzka.
Wien: Verlag für Jugend und Volk 1980.

Youth book/Jugendbuch
Welsh, Renate: **Johanna.** *(Johanna.)*
Wien: Verlag für Jugend und Volk 1979.

Illustration
Sklenitzka, Franz Sales in:
Sklenitzka, Franz Sales: **Drachen haben nichts zu lachen.** (Dragons have nothing to laugh about.)
Wien: Verlag für Jugend und Volk 1979.

Sklenitzka, Franz Sales in:
Nöstlinger, Christine: **Dschi Dsche-i Dschunior.** *(Dschi Dsche-i Dschunior.)*
Wien: Verlag für Jugend und Volk 1980.

Belgium / Belgien

Prijs van de provincie Antwerpen (formerly, Provinciale premie ter bevordering van de Vlaamse letterkunde)

The provincial administration of Antwerp offers this prize annually for the promotion of Dutch literature in Belgium and it is only given to authors of Belgian nationality who write in the Dutch language. A further condition is that the authors must be Antwerp-born and currently living there, also. The prizes, which were first presented in 1926 (our list begins from the year 1928), are given to literary works which have appearred in the last three years prior to the award presentation. Lists of outstanding titles are complied, forming the basis of the selections. An author who has already received the State Award or the Award for Flemish Literature is not eligible for the prize. The deadline for entries is the first of April. The award winners are announced in the autumn.

Die Provinzialverwaltung Antwerpen verleiht jährlich Preise zur Förderung der niederländischen Literatur in Belgien. Sie werden nur an niederländisch schreibende Autoren verliehen, die in Antwerpen geboren oder wohnhaft sind. Die Preise, die 1926 zum ersten Mal verliehen wurden (unsere Liste beginnt 1928), werden an Werke vergeben, die innerhalb der drei vorhergehenden Jahre erschienen sind. Listen mit hervorragenden Titeln werden gesammelt, die die Grundlage der Auswahl bilden. Ein Autor, der bereits einen Staatspreis oder den Preis der Flämischen Literatur erhalten hat, wird nicht mehr berücksichtigt. Der letzte Einsendetermin für Manuskripte oder für die Vorschläge ist 1. April jeden Jahres. Der Preis wird im Herbst bekanntgegeben.

Ill. 4 Gerbrand Jespers in I. Willems: Zazapina in de zoo

1928 Velde, Anton van de: **Lotje.** Pretting speel-verhaaltje in 3 deelen. (*Lotje.* Pretty game story in three parts; *Lotje.* Hübsche Spielgeschichten in 3 Teilen.) Ill.: A. Ost.
Antwerpen: Leeslust; Eindhoven; Lecturis 1928.

Ill. 5 René Hausman in: Bestiaire insolite

1929 Longerstaey, Antoon: **Lobbe en Sefa.** (*Lobe* and *Sefa.*) Ill.: Elza van Hagendoren (i.e. Else Magdalena Oosterwijk van Hagendoren).
Antwerpen: De Sikkel; Utrecht: De Gemeenschap 1928.

1930 Peeters, Jan: **Het vertelsel van Goedeziel, Grimbert en Volbloed.** (Stories about *Goedeziel, Grimbert* and *Volbloed*; Die Geschichten von *Goedeziel, Grimbert* und *Volbloed.*)
Gent: Van Rysselberghe en Rombaut 1928.

1932 Lannoy, Maria de: **Bezem-Krelis.** (*Cornelius,* the broom; Der Besen-*Kornelius.*)
Brussel: De wilde roos 1931.

1934 Velde, Anton van de: **Knagelijn, 'n leuke historie uit de muizenwereld.** (*Knagelijn.* A nice story about the mouse world; *Knagelijn.* Eine nette Geschichte aus der Welt der Mäuse.) Ill.: M.R. Coenegrachts.
Antwerpen: Vlaamsche Boekcentrale 1934.

1935 Boon, Jozef: **Zwarte Piet.** Een Sint-Niklaas-sprookje. (*Black Peter.* A St. *Nicholas* story; Der schwarze *Peter.* Eine St.-*Nikolaus*-Geschichte.)
Antwerpen: Leeslust 1934.

1937 Kiroul, Paul (i.e. Edward Peeters): **Collected works;** Gesamtschaffen.

1938 Walschap, Gerard: **De vierde koning.** Een vertelsel voor mijn kinderen. (The fourth king. A story for my children; Der 4. König. Eine Erzählung für meine Kinder.) Ill.: Edgar Tijtgat.
Rotterdam: Nijgh & Van Ditmar 1935.

1941 Peeters, Jan: **Holderdebolder.** Een nieuwe reeks kinderverzen. (*"Holderdebolder"* = Helter-skelter. A new collection of children's rhymes; Holtertiepolter. Eine neue Sammlung von Kinderreimen.)
Antwerpen: De Sikkel 1940.

Peeters, Jan: **Kleuterrijmpjes.** (Verse for small children; Verse für kleine Kinder.) Ill.: Elsa van Hagendoren (i.e. Else Magdalena Oosterwijk van Hagendoren).
Antwerpen: De Sikkel 1939.

1945 Boni, Armand: **De jonge Edision.** Een geromanceerd jeugdbeeld. (The young *Edison.* A youth portrait; Der junge *Edison.* Ein Jugendbild.) Ill.: Martha van Coppenolle.
Antwerpen: Vlaamsche Boekcentrale 1943.

1947 Albe (i.e. Renaat Antoon Joostens): **Ossenwagens op de kim.** (Oxcart on the horizon; Ochsenwagen am Horizont.) Ill.: E. Hermans.
Brussel: De Pijl 1946.

1948 Maeldere, G. van den (i.e. G. Müller): **Toch zijn eigen weg.** De roeping van Carl Linnaeus den groten natuurhistoricus. (Pursuing his own way. The profession of *Carl Linnaeus*, the great natural historian; Sein eigener Weg. Die Berufung des *Carl Linnaeus*, dem großen Naturhistoriker.) Ill.: Nelly Degouy.
Antwerpen: Vlaamsche Boekcentrale 1947.

1950 Marcke, Leen van (i.e. Madeleine Suzanne Eugenie Peters-van Marcke): **Schipperskind.** (The cabin Boy; Das Schifferkind.) Ill.: Alice Vrebos.
Brussel: Van Belle 1949.

1951 Blommaert, Alois: **Vier woudloupers en een dubbele knoop.** (Four woodmen and a double knot; Vier Waldläufer und ein doppelter Knoten.) Ill.: Anny Lebbe.
Lier: Van In 1948.

Lamend, A. Margareta: **Het hartje uit Fantasia.** Een sprookje uit onze tijd. (The heart of fantasy. A fairy tale of our times; Das Herz aus Fantasie. Ein Märchen aus unserer Zeit.) Ill.: Godelieve Schatteman.
Leuven: Davidsfonds 1950.

1952 Peeters, Maurits: **Papperlapap.** Voor kinderen van 7—10 jaar. (*"Papperlapap"* = nonsense. For children from 7 to 10 years; *Papperlapap.* Für Kinder von 7 bis 10 Jahren.) Ill.: Maurits Peeters.
Tongerlo: St. Norbertus-Boekhandel; Rotterdam: De Forel 1950.

1953 *Youth book/Jugendbuch*
Lindekruis, T. (i.e. Antoon Aarts): **Lied van mijn land!** (Songs from my land; Das Lied von meinem Land.) Ill.: Martha van Coppenolle.
Antwerpen: Vlaamsche Boekcentrale 1952.

Best first-work/Bestes Erstlingswerk
Melis, Godelieve: **Sprookjes en verhalten voor groot en klein.** (Fairy tales and stories for large and small; Märchen und Erzählungen für Groß und Klein.) Ill.: Ludo Laagland.
Borgerhout-Antwerpen: Het Fonteintje 1951.

1954 *Best manuscript/Bestes Manuskript*
Christiaens, Jan: **Kili het konijn.** (*Kili*, the king; *Kili*, der König.) Ill.: Elly van Beek.
's-Gravenhage: Van Goor 1958.

1955 *Children's book/Kinderbuch*
Hagendoren, Elsa van (i.e. Else Magdalena Oosterwijk-van Hagendoren): **De beek.** (The creek; Der Bach.) Ill.: Elsa van Hagendoren.
Antwerpen: De Dikkel 1953.

Hagendoren, Elsa van (i.e. Elsa Magdalena Oosterwijk-van Hagendoren): **De weide.** (The pasture; Die Weide.) Ill.: Elsa van Hagendoren. Antwerpen: De Sikkel; Amsterdam: L.J. Veen 1953.

Youth book/Jugendbuch

Rosseels, Maria: **Spieghelken.** Dagboek van een jong meisje. (*Spieghelken.* Diary of a young girl; *Spieghelken.* Das Tagebuch eines jungen Mädchens.)
Tielt: Lannoo 1952.

1956 *Children's book/Kinderbuch*

Suls, Erik: **Het boek van Lew de Boerekat.** (The book about *Lew,* the farm cat; Das Buch von *Lew,* der Bauernkatze.) Ill.: Geert van Wanrooy.
Schoten: Imago 1955.

Youth book/Jugendbuch

Berkhof, Aster (i.e. Louis van den Bergh): **Paavo, de Lap.** (*Paavo,* the Laplander; *Paavo,* der Lappe.)
Amsterdam: Wereldbibliothek 1955.

1957 *Children's book/Kinderbuch*

Leeman, Cor Ria (i.e. Corneel Alfons van Kuyck): **Jan Klassen.** (Jan Klassen.) vol. 1. Ill.: Betty Verdcourt.
Antwerpen: 't Groeit 1956.

Youth book/Jugendbuch

Vleeschouwer-Verbraeken, Maria Elisa Justina de: **Een uil vloog over!** (An owl flew over; Eine Eule flog darüber.)
Antwerpen: Sheed & Ward 1955.

1958 *Children's book/Kinderbuch*

Nerum, Albert van: **Reintje, Roodbaartje en Geelstaartje.** (*Reintje, Roodbaartje* and *Geelstaartje.*) Ill.: Ivo Queeckers.
Antwerpen: De Branding; Amsterdam: de Boer 1957.

Nerum, Albert van: **Reintje trekt de wereld in.** (*Reintje* travels around the world; *Reintje* fährt um die Welt.) Ill.: Ivo Queeckers.
Antwerpen: De Branding; Amsterdam: de Boer 1957.

Nerum, Albert van: **Reintje en de stropers.** (*Reintje* and the poachers; *Reintje* und die Wilderer.) Ill.: Ivo Queeckers.
Antwerpen: De Branding; Amsterdam: de Boer 1957.

Nerum, Albert van: **Reintje en Rankje.** (*Reintje* and *Rankje.*) Ill.: Ivo Queeckers.
Antwerpen: De Branding; Amsterdam: de Boer 1957.

Youth book/Jugendbuch

Terklaveren, P.E.: **De papierraper van Tientsin.** (The paper collec-

tor from *Tientsin;* Die Papiersammler von *Tientsin.*) Ill.: Désiré Acket.
Antwerpen: De Sikkel 1955.

1959 *Children's book/Kinderbuch*
Knop, André de/Pirreault, Jozef: **Indiaantje.** (The Indian child; Das Indianerkind) Ill.: P. van den Broeck.
Antwerpen: Ontwikkeling 1958.

Youth book/Jugendbuch
Marcke, Leen van (i.e. Madeleine Suzanne Eugenie Peeters-van Marcke): **De zon breekt door.** (The sun shines through; Die Sonne bricht durch.) Ill.: Rein van Looy.
Antwerpen: De Branding 1957.

1960 *Children's book/Kinderbuch*
Roelants, Leo (i.e. Leo van Tichelen): **George Stephenson.** Het leven van een werker. (*George Stephenson.* The life of a worker; *George Stephenson.* Das Leben eines Arbeiters.) Ill.: Jan Waterschoot.
Antwerpen: De Sikkel 1957.

Youth book/Jugendbuch
Trio, Dita: **Guusje op Kleuterhof.** (*Guusje* from *Kleuterhof; Guusje* vom *Kleuterhof.*)
Antwerpen: Zuid-Nederlandse Uitg.; Amsterdam: Standaardboekhandel 1958.

1961 *Children's book/Kinderbuch*
Wachter, Jos de: **Koning Jan.** (King *Jan;* König *Jan.*) Ill.: Nelly Degouy.
Antwerpen: De Sikkel 1959.

Youth book/Jugendbuch
Luytens, Jozef Maria Karel: **Stormen waaien uit het noorden.** (Storm blows from the north; Stürme wehen aus dem Norden.)
Brasschaat: Hidawa 1959.

1962 *Children's book/Kinderbuch*
Marcke, Leen van (i.e. Madeleine Suzanne Eugenie Peeters-van Marcke): **O, die Pino.** (Oh, this *Pino;* O, dieser *Pino.*) Ill.: Rein van Looy.
Hilversum: de Boer 1961.

Youth book/Jugendbuch
Weyts, Staf: **Gebed om verzoening.** (Prayer for reconciliation; Gebet zur Versöhnung.)
Leuven: Davidsfonds 1961.

1963 *Children's book/Kinderbuch*
Buyle, Ivo: **Jodokus.** *(Jodokus.)* Ill.: Hermann Denkens.
Antwerpen: Diogenes 1962.

Youth book/Jugendbuch
Zeldenthuis, Kapitein (i.e. Renaat Antoon Joostens): **Het vergeten paradijs.** (The forgotten paradise; Das vergessene Paradies.)
Hasselt: Heideland 1961.

1964 *Children's book/Kinderbuch*
Staes, Guido: **De blikken buis.** (The metal pipe; Das Blechrohr.) Ill.: Van Avermaet.
Hasselt: Heideland 1961.

Youth book/Jugendbuch
Suls, Erik: **Het eiland op de Schelde.** (Island on the *Schelde;* Die Insel in der *Schelde.*) Ill.: Maria van den Eynde.
Antwerpen, Amsterdam: Standaard-boekhandel 1963.

1965 *Children's book/Kinderbuch*
Timmermans, Lia: **Janneke en Mieke en de slimme rode kraai.** (*Janneke* and *Mieke* and the naughty red crow; *Janneke* und *Mieke* und die schlimme rote Krähe.) Ill.: Tonet Meyer.
Antwerpen: Standaard-boekhandel 1963.

Youth book/Jugendbuch
Nerum, Albert van: **Gevederde slang.** (The feathered snake; Gefiederte Schlange.) Ill.: Hilde Maes.
Antwerpen, Amsterdam: Standaard-boekhandel 1963.

1966 *Children's book/Kinderbuch*
Vanderloo, Jos: **De wonderlijke avonturen van Hokus en Pokus.** (The wonderful adventures of *Hokus* and *Pokus;* Die wunderlichen Abenteuer von *Hokus* und *Pokus.*) Ill.: Gérard Bouwman.
Utrecht: Het Spectrum 1963.

Youth book/Jugendbuch
Leeman, Cor Ria (i.e. Corneel Alfons van Kuyck): **De gouden dolk.** (The golden dagger; Der goldene Dolch.)
Lier: Van In 1966.

1967 *Children's book/Kinderbuch*
Cleemput, Gerda van: **Het meisje dat de zon niet zag.** (The girl who did not see the sun; Das Mädchen, das die Sonne nicht sah.)
Averbode: Altiora 1966.

Youth book/Jugendbuch
Marcke, Leen van (i.e. Madeleine Suzanne Eugenie Peeters-van Marcke): **Hatsjepsoet.** *Hatsjepsoet.)*
Brussel: Van Belle 1966.

1968 *Children's book/Kinderbuch*
Durnez, Gaston: **Sire.** *(Sire.)* Ill.: Gommaar Timmermans.
Lier: Van In 1968.

Youth book/Jugendbuch
Hemeldonck, Emiel van: **Spookschip.** (The ghost ship; Das Spukschiff.) Ill.: Mon van Dijck.
Averbode: Altiora 1967.

1969 *Children's book/Kinderbuch*
Auwera, Ferdnand: **Karel Kruisdegen en de inktvissen.** (*Karel Kruisdegen* and the squid; *Karel Kruisdegen* und die Tintenfische.)
Kapellen: De Sikkel 1966.

Youth book/Jugendbuch
Camp, Gaston van: **Twee jongens voor een wolvinnetje.** (Two boys and a wolf; Zwei Jungen und eine Wölfin.)
Antwerpen: Standaard-boekhandel 1968.

1970 *Children's book/Kinderbuch*
Vermeulen, Lo: **Groot Groot Wombie-boek.** (The big *Wombie* book; Das große *Wombie*-Buch.) Ill.: Henri Branton.
Antwerpen: Standaard-boekhandel 1968.

Youth book/Jugendbuch
Albe (i.e. Renaat Antoon Joostens): **De jonge Odysseus.** (The young *Odysseus;* Der junge *Odysseus.*)
Hasselt: Heideland 1967.

1971 *Children's book/Kinderbuch*
Buyle, Ilvos: **De jacht met de handkarren.** (The hunt with the hand-cart; Die Jagd mit dem Handkarren.) Ill.: Pierre Wagemans.
Antwerpen: De Sikkel 1970.

Youth book/Jugendbuch
Hagendoren, Elsa van (i.e. Else Magdalena Oosterwijk-van Hagendoren): **Kraterland.** *(Kraterland.)*
Hasselt: Heideland-Orbis 1970.

1972 *Children's book/Kinderbuch*
Broek, Walter van der: **Mietje Porcelein en Lili-spring-in-'t-veld.** (*Mietje Procelain* and *Lili-spring-in-the-field; Mietje Porzellan* und *Lili-Spring-ins-Feld.*) Ill.: Bob Vanderveen.
Antwerpen: Brito 1970.

Youth book/Jugendbuch
Blauwers, Frank: **Wovoka van het zilverland.** (*Wovoka* from silverland; *Wovoka* von Silberland.)
Hasselt: Heideland-Orbis 1971.

1973 *Children's book/Kinderbuch*
Depeuter, Frans: **De kleine oorlog van koddige Koen.** (The little war of humorous *Conrad;* Der kleine Krieg vom lustigen *Konrad.*) Ill.: Bob Vanderveen.
Antwerpen: Brito 1970.

Youth book/Jugendbuch
Staes, Guido: **De kinderen van de vrede.** (The children of peace; Die Kinder des Friedens.)
Averbode: Altiora 1972.

1974 *Children's book/Kinderbuch*
Cottonje, Mireille: **Het grote onrecht.** (The great wrong; Das große Unrecht.) Ill.: Step van Stipout.
Antwerpen: Standaard-boekhandel 1973.

Youth book/Jugendbuch
Timmermans, Gommaar: **De kip, de keizer en de tsaar.** (The hen, the emperor and the czar; Die Henne, der Kaiser und der Zar.)
Haarlem: Schuyt 1973.

1975 *Children's book/Kinderbuch*
Staes, Guido: **Het zeepbellen meisje.** (The soap-bubble girl; Das Seifenblasen-Mädchen.) Ill.: Ghis.
Tielt: Lannoo 1973.

Youth book/Jugendbuch
Verleyen, Karel: **Dag stad, ik ben Sanja.** (Good day city, I am *Sanja;* Guten Tag Stadt, ich bin *Sanja.*)
Antwerpen: Opdebeek 1974.

1976 *Children's book/Kinderbuch*
Willems, Liva: **Zazapina in de zoo.** (*Zazapina* at the zoo; *Zazapina* im Zoo.) Ill.: Gerbrand Jespers.
Tielt: Lannoo 1975.

Youth book/Jugendbuch
Luyten, Christiane: **Het eiland in de nevel.** (The island in the mist; Die Insel im Nebel.)
Brugge: Die Keure 1974.

1977 *Children's book/Kinderbuch*
Durnez, Gaston: **Faantje in het circus.** (*Faantje* in the circus; *Faantje* im Zirkus.) Ill.: Cis Verhamme.
Tielt: Lannoo 1975.

Youth book/Jugendbuch
Laenen, Gie: **Leven overleven.** (Life and survival; Leben und überleben.) Ill.: Cis Verhamme.
Tielt: Lannoo 1975.

1978 *Children's book/Kinderbuch*
Auwera, Fernand: **De Gnokkel.** (The *Gnokkel;* Die *Gnokkel.*) Ill.: Stef Van Stiphout.
Lier: Van In 1976.

Youth book/Jugendbuch
Camp, Gaston van: **Ik ben Harry van de achterbuurt.** (I am *Harry* from the slums; Ich bin *Harry* aus dem Armenviertel.) Ill.
Tielt: Lannoo 1976.

Prijs van de Bond van Grote en Jonge Gezinnen

For many years, "De Bond" (The League), the weekly paper of the "Bond voor Grote en Jonge Gezinnen" (The League of Large and Small Families) has been publishing information concerning children's and youth literature. As a logical consequence of this useful service on the part of De Bond, a literature prize was created in cooperation with Lannoo publishers. All authors who write in the Dutch language may participate in the competition.

Viele Jahre brachte "der Bund", die wöchentliche Zeitschrift von "Bund für große und kleine Familien" ("Bond voor Grote en Jonge Gezinnen") Informationen über Kinder- und Jugendliteratur heraus. Als logische Folgerung dieses nützlichen Dienstes von "De Bond", wurde in Zusammenarbeit mit Lannoo Verlegern ein Literaturpreis geschaffen. Die Teilnahme ist allen Autoren gestattet, die in holländischer Sprache schreiben.

1974 Leanen, Gie: **Leven oberleven.** (Living, over-living; Leben, überleben.) Ill.: Cis Verhamme.
Tielt: Lannoo 1975.

1978 Colijn, Marianne: **Merel Veronica Wereldkind.** (*Merel Veronica,* world child; *Merel Veronica,* Weltkind.) Ill.: Marion Faber.
Tielt: Lannoo 1978.

Prijs beste Jeugdboek van Knokke-Heist

This prize for the best juvenile book was organized by the Knokke-Heist Section of the National Christian Middle Classes Union (Nationaal Christelijk Middenstandsverbond) in cooperation with the Cultural Union "Davidsfonds" under the auspices of the Municipality of Knokke-Heist and the local Cultural Advice Council of the town. Only authors who write in the Dutch language may participate.

Dieser Preis für das beste Jugendbuch wurde von der Abteilung Knokke-Heist des National Christlichen Mittelstandsvereinigung (Nationaal Christelijk Mid-

denstandsverbond) in Zusammenarbeit mit der Kulturvereinigung "Davidsfonds" vergeben, unter der Leitung der Stadtgemeinde von Knokke-Heist und der Öffentlichen Kulturratversammlung der Stadt. Nur Autoren, die in niederländischer Sprache schreiben, ist die Teilnahme gestattet.

1969 Struelens, René: **Vlucht langs de Anapoer.** (Flight along the *Anapoer;* Flucht entlang der *Anapoer.*) Ill.: Stef van Stiphout.
Antwerpen: Standaard 1971.
(ex aequo)

Swartenbroekx, René: **Ali, de guerillero.** (*Ali,* the guerrilla; *Ali,* der Freischärler.) Ill.: W. Haest, Stef van Stiphout.
Antwerpen: Standaard 1971.
(ex aequo)

1972 Cottenje, Mireille: **Het grote onrecht.** (The great injustice; Das große Unrecht.) Ill.: Stef van Stiphout.
Antwerpen: Standaard 1973.

1975 The prize was not given; Der Preis wurde nicht vergeben.

1977 Daele, Henri van: **De radijsjeskoning.** (The radish king; Der Radieschenkönig.) Ill.: Nestje Delanghe.
Leuven: Davidsfonds 1978.

Provinciale Prijs van Oost-Vlaanderen

In 1956 the Provincial Council of East Flanders established this prize for children's and youth books. Only authors who have been living for at least five years in East Flanders may participate. The first award presentation was made in 1957.

1956 stiftete der Provinzrat von Ost-Flandern diesen Preis für Kinder- und Jugendliteratur. Nur Autoren, die seit 5 Jahren in Ost-Flandern leben, dürfen teilnehmen. Der Preis wurde 1957 zum ersten Mal vergeben.

1957 *Children's book/Kinderbuch*
Gucht, Gaston M. van der: **De madonna van de knechtjes.** (The madonna of the peasants; Die Madonna der Knechte.) Ill.: D. van den Broeck.
Leuven: Davidsfonds 1959.

Youth book/Jugendbuch
The prize was not given; Der Preis wurde nicht vergeben.

1959 *Children's book/Kinderbuch*
Remoortere, Julien van: **Vlug, het wilde paard.** (*Vlug,* the wild horse; *Vlug,* das Wildpferd.) Ill.: C. Vété.
Brugge: De Brouwer, Desclee 1959.

Youth book/Jugendbuch
The prize was not given; Der Preis wurde nicht vergeben.

1961 *Children's book/Kinderbuch*
Dier, Omer de: **Het sapje Sim.** (*Sim*, the little monkey; Das Äffchen, *Sim*.) Ill.: A. Herckenrath.
Averbode: Altiora 1962.

Youth book/Jugendbuch
The prize was not given; Der Preis wurde nicht vergeben.

1962 *Children's book/Kinderbuch*
The prize was not given; Der Preis wurde nicht vergeben.

Youth book/Jugendbuch
Remoortere, Julien van: **Het eiland Kimokimono.** (The island, *Kimokimono;* Die Insel *Kimokimono.*) Ill.
Leuven: Davidsfonds 1965.

Remoortere, Julien van: **Ger en de wilde paarden.** (*Ger* and the wild horses; *Ger* und die wilden Pferde.) Ill.: J. Kuiper.
Antwerpen: De Nederlandsche Boekhandel 1962.

1964 *Children's book/Kinderbuch*
The prize was not given; Der Preis wurde nicht vergeben.

Youth book/Jugendbuch
Dalschaert, Angèle: **De zwanen van Groendale.** (The swans from *Green Valley;* Die Schwäne von *Grüntal.*) Ill.: Jos van den Abeele.
Borgerhout: Het Fonteintje 1964.

1966 *Children's book/Kinderbuch*
Librecht, Julien: **Dagboek uit Vietnam.** (Notebook from Vietnam; Tagebuch aus Vietnam.) Ill.: M. Verschueren.
Antwerpen: Opdebeek 1971.

Youth book/Jugendbuch
The prize was not given; Der Preis wurde nicht vergeben.

1969 *Children's book/Kinderbuch*
The prize was not given; Der Preis wurde nicht vergeben.

Youth book/Jugendbuch
Librecht, Julien: **Zwarte Handen.** (Black hands; Schwarze Hände.) (Unpublished/Unveröffentlicht.)

Lie (i.e. Lieve Weynants-Schatteman): **Het meisje Sandrien.** (The maiden, *Sandrien;* Das Mädchen *Sandrien.*) Ill.: Stef van Stiphout.
Lier: Van In 1970.

1971 *Children's book/Kinderbuch*
The prize was not given; Der Preis wurde nicht vergeben.

Youth book/Jugendbuch
Willemijns, R.: **Kanaal 64.** (Canal 64; Kanal 64.) Ill.
Averbode: Altiora 1971.

1972 *Children's book/Kinderbuch*
Lie (i.e. Lieve Weynants-Schatteman: **Jonas en Toetela.** (*Jonas* and *Toetela.*) Ill.: Lie.
Tielt: Lannoo 1969.

Lie (i.e. Lieve Weynants-Schatteman: **De wondere tocht van Jonas en Toetela;** The wonderful light of *Jonas* and *Toetela;* Das wundersame Licht von *Jonas* und *Toetela.*) Ill.: Lie.
Tielt: Lannoo 1972.

1974 *Children's book/Kinderbuch*
The prize was not given; Der Preis wurde nicht vergeben.
Youth book/Jugendbuch
Daele, Henri van: **De andere Bonaparte.** (The other *Bonaparte;* Der andere *Bonaparte.*) Ill.: Marcel Steurbaut.
Borgerhout: Het Fonteintje 1973.

Daele, Henri van: **Het jaar van de boze kabouter.** (The year of the wicked elves; Das Jahr des bösen Kobolds.) Ill.: Marcel Steurbaut.
Brugge: Roya 1975.

1978 *Children's book/Kinderbuch*
The prize was not given; Der Preis wurde nicht vergeben.
Youth book/Jugendbuch
Guirlande, Christina: **Het lied van de Condor.** (The song of the condor; Das Lied vom Condor.)
Averbode: Altiora 1979.

Martens, Claudine: **De rode Sokkenboom.** (The red sock tree; Der rote Sockenbaum.)
Averbode: Altiora 1978.

Bekroning Vereniging te Bevordering van het Vlaamse Boekwezen

The Association for the Promotion of the Flemish book Industry (Vereniging ter Bevordering van het Vlaamse Boekwezen) organized this prize in 1962. Participation is limited to Flemish authors who write in the Dutch language.

Die Vereinigung zur Förderung des flämischen Buchwesens (Vereniging ter Bevordering van het Vlaamse Boekwezen) vergab 1962 den Preis zum ersten Mal. Teilnahme ist nur flämischen Autoren gestattet, die in holländischer Sprache schreiben.

1962 Auwera, Fernand: **Okidoki's reis naar de sterren.** (*Okidoki's* journey to the stars; *Okidokis* Reise zu den Sternen.) Ill.
Antwerpen: Opdebeek 1961.

Remoorte, Julien van: **Ger van de Bongostam.** (*Ger* of the Bongo tribe; *Ger* vom Stamm der Bongos.) Ill.: Jan Kuiper.
Antwerpen: De Nederlandsche Boekhandel 1961.

Kerckhoven, Ronny van: **Benny en Lineke.** (*Benny* and *Lineke; Benny* und *Lineke.*) Ill.: Fred Garrels.
Antwerpen: De Sikkel 1962.

1963 Buyle, Ivo: **Judokus.** *(Judokus.)* Ill.: Herman Denkens.
Antwerpen: Diogenes 1962.

Vleeschouwer, Maria de: **Marieke over de stroom.** (Little *Marie* on the stream; *Mariechen* am Strom.) Ill.: Maria Baete.
Antwerpen: Standaard 1962.

Dierckx, Rik: **Stalen haaien.** (Steel sharks; Stählerne Haifische.) Ill.: Jozef Broeckx.
Antwerpen: Standaard 1962.

Zeldenthuis (i.e. Albe R. Joostens): **Het vergeten paradijs.** (The forgotten paradise; Das vergessene Paradies.) Ill.
Hasselt: Heideland 1962.

Suls, Erik: **Mit nummer O op de Schelde.** (With number O on the river, Schelde; Mit Nummer O auf der Schelde.) Ill.: Maria van den Eynde.
Antwerpen: Standaard 1962.

1964 Verheyen, Henk: **Gil.** *(Gil.)* Ill.: Reint T. de Jonge.
Antwerpen: De Branding 1963.

Carlier, Libera: **Het geheim van de Altamare.** (The mystery of *Altamare;* Das Geheimnis von *Altamare.*)
Antwerpen: Standaard 1963.

Nerum, Albert van: **Gevederde slang.** (Feathered snake; Gefiederte Schlange.) Ill.: Hilde Maes.
Antwerpen: Standaard 1963.

Marcke, Leen van: **Zeven, zeven, zeven.** (Seven, seven, seven; Sieben, sieben, sieben.) Ill.: Fred Garrels.
Antwerpen: De Branding 1963.

Gypen, Lieven/Vermeiren, Leopold: **Vlaanderen, mijn land.** (Flanders, my land; Flandern, mein Land.) Photos.
Antwerpen: Standard 1963.

1965 Gysen, Marnix: **Van een kat die te veel pretentie had.** (The cat who wanted too much; Von einer Katze die zuviel wollte.) Ill.: M. Segers. Antwerpen: Diogenes 1964.

Struelens, René: **Duel met fortuna.** (Duel with fortune; Duell mit dem Glück.) Ill.: Pil.
Bruxelles: Van Belle 1964.

Gronon, Rose: **Gouden regen.** (Golden rain; Goldener Regen.) Ill. Leuven: Wolters 1964.

Lie (i.e. Lieve Weynants-Schatteman): **Prins Oeki-Loeki.** Prince *Oeki Loeki;* Prinz *Oeki-Loeki.*) Ill.: Lie.
Tielt: Lannoo 1964.

1966 Remoortere, Julien van: **Met een wolkje op reis.** (On a journey with a cloud; Mit einer Wolke auf Reisen.) Ill.: Belleke Dolhain.
Den Haag: Van Goor 1965.

Toen, Alice: **Ventje glas, ventje hout, ventje ijzer.** (The little fellow of glass, the little fellow of wood, the little fellow of iron; Das Kerlchen aus Glas, das Kerlchen aus Holz, das Kerlchen aus Eisen.) Ill.: André Deroo.
Antwerpen: De Sikkel 1965.

Leeman, Cor Ria (i.e. Corneel Alfons van Kuyck): **Chris en Lex, de schoenpoetsers van Athene.** (*Chris* and *Lex,* the shoe polishers of Athens; *Chris* und *Lex,* die Schuhputzer aus Athen.) Ill.: Stef van Stiphout.
Lier: Van In 1965.

Timmermans, Lia: **Janneke en Mieke en het geheimzinnige blauwe duifje.** (*Janneke* and *Mieke* and the mysterious blue pigeon; *Janneke* und *Mieke* und die geheimnisvolle blaue Taube.) Ill.: Tonet Meyer-Timmermans.
Antwerpen: Standaard 1965.

Rompaey, Pierre van: **Vonk en Fanny.** (*Vonk* and *Fanny; Vonk* und *Fanny.*) Ill.
Antwerpen: Ontwikkeling 1965.

1967 The prize was not given; Der Preis wurde nicht vergeben.

1968 The prize was not given; Der Preis wurde nicht vergeben.

1969 Vermeulen, Lo: **Het groot Wombieboek.** (The great *Wombie-Book;* Das große *Wombiebuch.*) Ill.: Henri Branton.
Antwerpen: Standaard 1968.

Cleemput, Gerda van: **Maruja van de zonnekust.** (*Maruja* from the sunny coast; *Maruja* von der Sonnenküste.) Ill.: Mon van Dijck.
Averbode: Altiora 1968.

Vanhalewijn, Mariette: **Simon en de wondervlinder.** (*Simon* and the wonderful butterfly; *Simon* und der Wunderschmetterling.) Ill.: Jaklien Moerman.
Tielt: Lannoo 1968.

Marijn, Jessy: **Het begon met een muts.** (It began with a mouse; Es begann mit einer Maus.) Ill.: M. van den Eynden.
Antwerpen: Standaard 1967.

Albe (i.e. Renaat Antoon Joosten): **De jonge Odysseus.** (The young *Odysseus;* Der junge *Odysseus.*) Ill.: Paul Voet.
Hasselt: Heideland 1967.

1970 Lie (i.e. Lieve Weynants-Schatteman): **Het meisje Sandrien.** (The girl, *Sandrien;* Das Mädchen *Sandrien.*) Ill.: Lie.
Lier: Van In 1970.

Camp, Gaston van: **Het bonte boeketboek.** (The coloured book bouquet for youth; Das bunte Strauss-Buch für die Jugend.) Ill.: Lode Mols.
Borgerhout: Het Fonteintje 1969.

Staes, Guido: **De laatsten van het regiment.** (The last of the regiments; Die Letzten des Regiments.) Ill.: Herman Denkens.
Borgerhout: Het Fonteintje 1969.

Struelens, René: **Erik Brand en de indiaanse amulet.** (*Erik Brand* and the Indian amulet; *Erik Brand* und das indianische Amulett.) Ill.: Stef van Stiphout.
Antwerpen: Standaard 1969.

1971 Soetaert, Miriam: **Sprookjes en legenden uit Vietnam.** (Tales and legends from Vietman; Märchen und Legenden aus Vietnam.) Ill.: Ruud Nelissen.
Schelle: De Goudvink 1970.

1972 Vanhalewijn, Mariette: **Simon in het vergeten straatje.** (*Simon* in the forgotten street; *Simon* in der vergessenen Straße.) Ill.: Jaklien Moerman.
Tielt: Lanno 1971.

Willems, Lieve: **Samen een verkeersboek maken.** (Let's make a traffic book together; Wir machen zusammen ein Buch über den Verkehr.) Ill.: Herman Denkens.
Tielt: Lannoo 1971.

Vandeloo, Jos: **Nieuwe avonturen van Hokus en Pokus.** (New adventures of *Hokus* and *Pokus;* Neue Abenteuer von *Hokus* und *Pokus.*) Ill.: Leo Fabri.
Antwerpen: Standaard 1970.

Hemeldonck, Emiel van: **Avonturen van een scheepsjongen.** (Adventures of a cabin boy; Die Abenteuer eines Schiffsjungen.) Ill.: Lode Mols.
Averbode: Altiora 1970.

Swartenborekx, René: **Ali, de guerillero.** (*Ali,* the guerrilla; *Ali,* der Freischärler.) Ill.: W. Haest, Stef van Stiphout.
Leuven: Davidsfonds; Antwerpen: Standaard 1971.

1973 Staes, Guido: **De kinderen van de vrede.** (The children of peace; Die Kinder des Friedens.) Ill.: Gerbrand Jespers.
Averbode: Altiora 1972.

Timmermans, Gommaar: **De stotterende koekoek.** (The stuttering cuckoo; Der stotternde Kuckuck.) Ill.: Gommaar Timmermans.
Brugge: Angelet & Branton 1972.

Lefeber, A./Rossenau, H.: **Ben en zijn vrienden.** (*Ben* and his friends; *Ben* und seine Freunde.) Ill.: Cel Overberghe.
Antwerpen: De Sikkel 1972.

1974 Bovee, Juul: **Femios in het spoor van Odysseus.** (*Femios* on the trail of *Odysseus; Femios* auf der Spur des *Odysseus.*) Ill.: Stef van Stiphout.
Antwerpen: Standaard 1973.

Vanhalewijn, Mariette/Moerman, Jaklien: **Floris en Floriaan.** (*Floris* and *Florian; Floris* und *Florian.*) Ill.: Jaklien Moerman.
Tielt: Lannoo 1973.

Verleyen, Cyriel: **De boodschap van de onzichtbare.** (The ambassador of the invisible; Die Botschaft des Unsichtbaren.) Ill.
Lier: Van In 1973.

Guirlande, Christina: **Vaarwel Tonka.** (Farewell, *Tonka;* Lebewohl, *Tonka.*) Ill.: Christina Guirlande.
Westerlo: Saeftinge 1973.

Marijn, Jessy: **Raki en Sebastiaan.** (*Raki* and *Sebastian;* Raki und *Sebastian.*) Ill.: Annelies Vossen.
Tielt: Lannoo 1973.

1975 Leeman, Cor Ria (i.e. Corneel Alfons van Kuyck): **Het meisje Asmin.** (The girl, *Asmin;* Das Mädchen *Asmin.*) Ill.: Lode Mols.
Leuven: Davidsfonds 1974.

Verleyen, Karel: **Dag stad, ik ben Sanja.** (Good day town, I am *Sanja;* Guten Tag Stadt, ich bin *Sanja.*) Ill.
Antwerpen: Opdebeek 1974.

Berkhof, Aster (i.e. Louis van den Bergh): Goliath. (*Goliath.*) Ill.: Chris Fontijn.
Antwerpen: Standaard 1975.

Lie (i.e. Lieve Weynants. Schatteman): **Jonas en sofie . . . en Toetela natuurlijk.** (*Jonas* and *Sofie* . . . and *Toetela,* naturally; *Jonas* und *Sofie* . . . und *Toetela* natürlich.) Ill.: Lie.
Tielt: Lannoo 1974.

Swartenbroekx, René: **Reis tussen twee dromen.** (Journey between two dreams; Die Reise zwischen zwei Träumen.) Ill.: Stef van Stiphout.
Antwerpen: Standaard 1974.

1976 Struelens, René: **Alarm in Woudam.** (Alarm in *Woudam.*) Ill.: A.G.M. Mertens.
Averbode: Altiora 1975.

Durnez, Gaston: **Faantje in het circus.** (*Faantje* in the circus; *Faantje* im Zirkus.) Ill.: Cis Verhamme.
Tielt: Lannoo 1975.

Willems, Liva: **Zazapina in de zoo.** (*Zazapina* at the zoo; *Zazapina* im Zoo.) Ill.: Gerbrand Jespers.
Tielt: Lannoo 1975.

Auwera, Fernand: **De Gnokkel.** (The *Gnokkel;* Der *Gnokkel.*) Ill.: Stef van Stiphout.
Lier: Van In 1976.

Daele, Henri van: **Het jaar van de boze kabouter.** (The year of the wicked elves; Das Jahr des bösen Kobolds.) Ill.: Marcel Steurbaut.
Brugge: Roya 1975.

1977 Marijn, Jessy: **De weg liep over de bergen.** (The way goes over the mountains; Der Weg führt über die Berge.) Ill.: Annelies Vossen.
Tielt: Lannoo 1976.

Laenen, Gie: **Paultje, ze gaan weer vechten.** (*Paul,* they continue to fight; *Paul,* sie kämpfen weiter.) Ill.
Tielt: Lannoo 1977.

Swartenbroekx, René: **Abdoe en de bende van de bruinhemden.** (*Abdoe* and the ribbons of the brown shirts; *Abdoe* und die Bänder der braunen Hemden.) Ill.
Tielt: Lannoo 1976.

Vanhalewijn, Mariette: **Een schaap met witte voetjes.** (A sheep with white feet; Ein Schaf mit weißen Füßen.) Ill.: Jaklien Moerman.
Antwerpen: Standaard 1976.

1978 Cleemput, Gerda van: **Het huis in de jongel.** (The house in the jungle; Das Haus im Dschungel.) Ill.
Averbode: Altiora 1977.

Guirlande, Christina: **Avontuur op de Rietkraag.** (Adventure in the swamp; Abenteuer auf dem Schilfgürtel.) Ill.: A.G.M. Mertens.
Averbode: Altiora 1977.

Camp, Gaston van/Sollie, André: **Geweld eindigt waar liefde begint.** (Force ends where love begins; Gewalt endet wo Liebe beginnt.) Ill.: André Sollie.
Tielt: Lannoo; Leuven: Davidsfonds 1977.

Heylen, Maria: **De blauwe galabia.** (The blue galabia; Die blaue Galabia.) Ill.: Maria Heylen.
Antwerpen: Standaard 1977.

Prijs voor Letterkunde van de Vlaamse Provincies

Apart from the prizes for literature which are offered by the State of Belgium and the different provinces and academies, the provinces of Antwerp, Limburg and East and West Flanders have jointly offered together since 1930 awards to Belgian authors writing in the Dutch language. This prize is presented every four years.

Neben den Literaturpreisen, die vom belgischen Staat, von einzelnen Provinzen und Akademien verliehen werden, vergeben seit 1930 die Provinzen Antwerpen, Limburg, Ostflandern und Westflandern gemeinsam Preise an niederländisch schreibende Autoren belgischer Staatsangehörigkeit. Diese Preise werden alle vier Jahre vergeben.

1933 Velde, Anton van de: **Woe's wondere wandel.** 'n plezierig boek voor de jonkheid. (*Woe's* wonderful change; *Woes* wunderbarer Wandel.) Ill.: Christiane van de Plas.
Antwerpen: Leeslust 1933.

1936 Lannoy, Maria de: **Rozemarie in kabouterland.** (*Rosemary* in elf land; *Rosemarie* im Koboldland.) Ill.: Jan Waterschoot.
Antwerpen: De Oogst 1934.

Lannoy, Maria de: **Hoe Rozemarie haar ouders vond.** (How *Rosemary* found her parents; Wie *Rosemarie* ihre Eltern fand.) Ill.: Jan Waterschoot.
Antwerpen: De Oogst 1935.

Lannoy, Maria de: **Rozemarie en haar parels.** (*Rosemary* and her pearls; *Rosemarie* und ihre Perlen.) Ill.: Jan Waterschoot.
Antwerpen: De Oogst 1935.

Marcke, Leen van: **Kabouter Tip-Top.** (*Tip-Top* the elf; Kobold *Tip-Top.*) Ill.: Leo Sebregts.
Antwerpen: De wilde roos 1934.

1939 Lavki, Lod (i.e. Ludovic van Winkel): **Siee-krath.** Een avontuurverhaal uit den oertijd. (*Siee-krath.* An adventure story of prehistoric times; *Siee-Krath.* Eine abenteuerliche Geschichte aus der Urzeit.)
Antwerpen: Leeslust 1937.

1943 Buckinx-Luykx, Antoinette: **Het wonderbare sprookje.** (The wonderful fairy tale; Das wunderbare Märchen.) Ill.: Martha van Coppenolle.
Antwerpen: Vlaamshe Boekcentrale 1941.

Buckinx-Luykx, Antoinette: **Het waren twee cononcskinderen.** (Once there was two children of a king; Es waren einmal zwei Königskinder.) Ill.: C. van Steen.
Tongerloo: St. Norbertus-drukkerij 1942.

Opdebeeck, Leo: **Bij de vlieghaven.** (At the airport; Am Flughafen.) Ill.: Theo Opdebeeck.
Turnhout: Proost 1944.

Opdebeeck, Leo: **Bonte Tienling.** *(Bonte Tienling.)* Ill.: Theo Opdebeeck.
Antwerpen: Opdebeeck 1941.

1949 *Children's book/Kinderbuch*
Waegemans, Yvonne: **De kleine ree.** (The little deer; Das kleine Reh.) Ill.: Renaat Demoen.
Averbode: Geode Pers, Altiora 1944.

Waegemans, Yvonne: **De sprookjesplant.** (The fairy tale plant; Die Märchenpflanze.) Ill.: Renaat Demoen.
Averbode: Goede Pers, Altiora 1944.

Youth book/Jugendbuch
Laer, Jos van: **Tboec van den Cnape Ewyn.** (*Tboec* from *Cnape Ewyn; Tboec* von der *Cnape Ewyn.*)
Gent: Die Grael 1947.

1954 *Children's book/Kinderbuch*
Melis, Godelieve: **Vertel me voort.** Sprookjes en verhalen voor groot en klein. (Tell me more. Fairy tales and stories for big and small; Erzähl mir weiter. Märchen und Geschichten für Groß und Klein.) Ill.: Aimé van Avermaet.
Borgerhout-Antwerpen: Het Fonteinje 1951.

Youth book/Jugendbuch
Inghelram, Daan: **Om u treur ik, Jonathan.** (I pity you, *Jonathan;* Um dich trauere ich, *Jonathan.*)
Brugge: Desclée de Brouwer 1953.

1959 *Children's book/Kinderbuch*
Leeman, Cor Ria (i.e. Corneel Alfons van Kuyck): **Jan Klaassen.** vols. 1.2. *(Jan Klassen.)* Ill.: Betty Verdcourt.
Antwerpen: 't Groeit 1958.

Vermeulen, Lo: **Penge de pygmee.** (*Penge*, the pygmy; *Penge*, der Pygmäe.) Ill.: Elsa van Hagendoren.
Antwerpen: De Sikkel 1955.

Youth book/Jugendbuch
Vleeschouwer-Verbraeken, Maria de: **Een uil vloog over!** (An owl flew over! Eine Eule flog vorbei!)
Antwerpen: Sheed & Ward 1955.

1963 *Children's book/Kinderbuch*
Peeters, Jan: **Kattepootjes.** (Cat paws; Katzenpfötchen.) Ill.: Fred Garrels.
Antwerpen: De Sikkel 1960.

Youth book/Jugendbuch
Remoortere, Julien van: **Ger en de wilde paarden.** (*Ger* and the wilde horses; *Ger* und die wilden Pferde.) Ill.: Jan Kuiper.
's-Gravenhage: Van Goor 1962.

1967 *Children's book/Kinderbuch*
Dalschaert, Angèle: **Piekhaar.** *(Piekhaar.)* Ill.: Jos van den Abeele.
Borgerhout: Het Fonteintje 1963.

Youth book/Jugendbuch
Marcke, Leen van (i.e. Madeleine Suzanne Eugenie Peeters van Marcke): **Hatjepsoet.** *(Hatjepsoet.)*
Brussel: Van Belle 1966.

1975 *Children's book/Kinderbuch*
Lie (i.e. Lieve Weynants-Schatteman): **Jonas en Toetela.** (*Jonas* and *Toetela.*) Ill.: Lie.
Tielt: Lannoo 1971.

Youth book/Jugendbuch
Bovée, Juul: **Femios in het spoor van Odysseus.** (*Femios* on the trail of *Odysseus; Femios* auf der Spur von *Odysseus.*) Ill.: Stef van Stiphout.
Antwerpen: Standaard 1973.

Provinciale Prijs van West-Vlaanderen

Since 1925, the province of West Flanders has awarded a prize for literature in general, but in 1972 the provincial government decided to create a specific prize for children's and youth books. Participation is limited to authors who were either born or have lived in West Flanders for several years.

Seit 1925 vergibt die Provinz West-Flandern einen Preis für Literatur; 1972 beschloß die Landesregierung einen speziellen Preis für Kinder- und Jugendliteratur zu schaffen. Nur Autoren, die entweder in West-Flandern geboren oder mehrere Jahre dort gelebt haben, ist die Teilnahme gestattet.

1959 Dalle, Felix: **Klabbatse.** *(Klabbatse.)* Ill.: Marcel Notebaert. Antwerpen: Standaard 1962.

1963 The prize was not given; Der Preis wurde nicht vergeben.

1967 Maele, Pros van de: **Het paradijs aan de hertenrivier.** (The paradise on the deer river; Das Paradies am Hirschfluß.) Ill. Leuven: Davidsfonds 1969.

1971 Claeys, André: **Onder het teken van de regenboog.** (Under the sign of the rainbow; Unter dem Zeichen des Regenbogens.) Leuven: De Clauwaert 1972.

1975 Vanhalewijn, Mariette: **Met de maan als schuitje.** (With the moon as a gondola; Mit dem Mond als Gondel.) Ill.: Jaklien Moerman. Tielt: Lannoo 1972.

Cottenjé, Mireille: **Het grote onrecht.** (The great injustice; Das große Unrecht.) Ill.: Stef van Stiphout. Antwerpen: Standaard 1973.

Driejaarlijkse Staatsprijs voor Jeugdliteratur van Vlaanderen

This prize is awarded every three years by the Ministry for Dutch Culture.

Dieser Preis wird alle drei Jahre vom Ministerium für Niederländische Kultur vergeben.

1971 Struelens, René: **Vlucht langs de Anapoer.** (Flight along the *Anapoer;* Flucht entlang der *Anapoer.*) Ill.: Stef van Stiphout. Antwerpen: Standaard 1971.

1974 Staes, Guido: **Kinderen van de vrede.** (Children of peace; Kinder des Friedens.) Ill.: Gerbrand Jespers. Averbode: Altiora 1972.

1977 The prize was not given; Der Preis wurde nicht vergeben.

Prix Jeunesse du Ministère de la Communauté Française

This prize was founded in 1972 by the Belgian Ministry of French Culture. The prize is awarded to an already published children's book or a manuscript written in the French language by a Belgian author. One year the prize is given to a children's book and the following year to a youth book.

1972 hat das belgische Ministerium der französischen Kultur den Preis für Manuskripte oder bereits veröffentlichte Kinderbücher gestiftet, die von belgischen Autoren in französisch geschrieben wurden. Der Preis widmet sich der erzählenden Literatur: ein Jahr für Kinder, das zweite Jahr für Jugendliche.

1972 Bastia, France: **Une autruche dans le ciel.** (A bouquet in the sky; Ein Strauss am Himmel.) Ill.: Yolande Baurin.
Gembloux: Duculot 1971.

1973 Hausman, René: **Le bestiare insolite.** (Unusual animal stories; Ungewöhnliche Tiererzählungen.)
Bruxelles: Dupuis 1972.

1974 Victor, Gine: **Patte à ressort.**)Paw with feather; Pfote mit Feder.) (Manuscript; Manuskript.)

1975 Bastia, France: **L'herbe naive.** (The naive grass; Das naive Gras.)
Gembloux: Duculot 1975.

1976 Vinck, Antoine de: **Jérôme et Agasson.** (*Jerome* and *Agasson.*) Ill.: Françoise Souply-Clabots.
Gembloux: Duculot 1976.

1977 Lacq, Gil: **Les bannis de l'île aus huîtres.** (The exiles on the island of the oysters; Die Verbannten der Austerninsel.)
Paris: Ed. G.P. 1977.

1978 Rocourt, Jean: **Mais le plus surprenant fut le numéro du magicien Dijwou Djinepou.** (But the most surprising thing was the number of *Dijwou Djinepou* the magician; Aber das Überraschendste war die Nummer vom Zauberer *Dijwou Djinepou.*)
(Manuscript; Manuskript.)

1979 Piscaglia, Christian: **S.O.S. Radiations.** (S.O.S. Radiation; S.O.S. Strahlung.) Ill.: Christopher Smith.
Paris: Hachette 1979.

1980 Sacré, Marie-José: **Le tribut des malotrus.** (The tribute of the boors; Der Tribut der Flegel.) Ill.: Marie-José Sacré.
Paris, Gembloux: Duculot 1980.

BRAZIL / BRASILIEN

Prêmio João de Barro

This prize, named after a bird which is the emblem of the city of Belo Horizonte, was founded by the prefecture of the city in 1973. A children's jury and an adult jury each make their own selections. The first award presentation took place in 1974.

Dieser Preis, der nach dem Wappenvogel der Stadt Belo Horizonte benannt ist, wurde 1973 von der Präfektur dieser Stadt gestiftet. Die erste Verleihung erfolgte 1974. Unabhängig voneinander entscheiden eine Kinder- und eine Erwachsenenjury über die Preisträger.

1974 *Adult's jury/Erwachsenenjury*
Monteiro, Graziela Lidia: **O diário de Abner.** (*Abner's* diary; *Abners* Tagebuch.)
Belo Horizonte: Impresa Oficial 1974.
Children's jury/Kinderjury
Noronha, Maria Tereza Guimares: **Xande, o grande.** (*Xande,* the great; *Xande,* der Grosse.)
Belo Horizonte: Impresa Oficial 1974.

1975 *Adult's jury/Erwachsenenjury*
Botelho, Mariza Andrade Maia: **O Caraoco.** (The *Caraoco;* Der *Caraoco.*) Ill.: Ricardo.
Belo Horizonte: Comunicação; Prefeitura Municipal de Belo Horizonte 1976.

Ill. 6 Gian Calvi in L Nunes: Os colegas

Children's jury/Kinderjury
Monteiro, Graziela Lidia: **O circo viramundo e o palhaco Estouro.** (The traveling circus and *Estouro* the clown; Der Wanderzirkus und der Clown *Estouro.*)
Ill.: Ricardo.
Belo Horizonte: Comunicação; Prefeitura Municipal de Belo Horizonte 1976.

1976 *Adult's jury/Erwachsenenjury*
Catarino, Ana Maria Bohrer: **A gatinha impressora.** (The cat bookprinter; Die Katze als Buchdrucker.) Ill.: Virgilio.
Belo Horizonte: Comunicação; Sec. Municipal de Cultura 1976.

Children's jury/Kinderjury
Sabino, Eliane: **Bitolinha.** *(Bitolinha.)*
Ill.: Virgilio.
Belo Horizonte: Comunicação; Sec. Municipal de Cultura 1976.

1977 *Adult's jury/Erwachsenenjury*
Machado, Ana Maria: **História meio ao contrário.** (Half upsidedown stories; Halb verkehrte Geschichten.) Ill.: Virgilio.
Belo Horizonte: Comunicação; Sec. Municipal de Cultura 1978.

Children's jury/Kinderjury
Ottini, Margarida: **Aventuras no fundo do mar.** (Adventures on the bottem of the sea; Abenteuer auf dem Meeresgrund.) Ill.: Joyce Brandão.
Belo Horizonte: Comunicação; Sec. Municipal de Cultura 1978.

1978 *Adult's jury/Erwachsenenjury*
Amorin, Antonio César Drummond: **Xixi na cama.** (I wet the bed; Ich pisse ins Bett.) Ill. Helder Augusto Neves Waldolato.
Belo Horizonte: Comunicação; Prefeitura Municipal de Belo Horizonte 1979.

Children's jury/Kinderjury
Cury, Felipe Machado: **Venturas e desventuras de Zé Teixeira.** (Adventures and misadventures of *Zé Teixeira;* Abenteuer und Mißgeschicke von *Zé Teixeira.)* Ill.: Melado.
Belo Horizonte: Comunicação; Prefeitura Municipal de Belo Horizonte 1979.

1979 The prize was not given; Der Preis wurde nicht vergeben.

1980 *Adult's jury/Erwachsenenjury*
Rocha, Ruth: **Davi ataca outra vez.** (*Davi* attacks again; *Davi* greift wieder an).
(Unpublished; Unveröffentlicht.)

Children's jury/Kinderjury
Nicolelis, Giselda Laporta: **Laura, meu amor.** (*Laura,* my love; *Laura,* meine Liebe.)
(Unpublished; Unveröffentlicht.)

Prêmio INL

The Instituto Nacional do Livro (INL) established this prize in 1968. It was originally named Prêmio Viriato Corréa, but is now called Prêmio INL and is awarded biennally. The first presentation was made in 1969.

Das Instituto Nacional do Livro (INL) begründete diesen Preis, der ursprünglich Prêmio Viriato Corréa heißt, 1968. Er wird alle zwei Jahre verliehen, die erste Verleihung erfolgte 1969.

1969 Mazzetti, Maria: **Entrou por uma porta.** (Coming in by one door; Zu einer Tür herein.) Ill.: Evilimar M. Oliveira.
Rio de Janeiro: Cadernos Didáticos; Brasilia: INL 1970.

1971 Nunes, Lygia Bojunga: **Os colegas.** (The comrades; Die Kameraden.) Ill.: Gian Calvi.
Rio de Janeiro: Sabiá; Brasilia: INL 1972.

1972 Ayala, Walmir: **A toca da coruja.** (The owl's hole; Die Höhle der Eule.) Ill.: Gian Calvi.
São Paulo: Lisa; Brasilia: INL 1973.

1974 Martins, Martha Maria Rezende: **Papitoco procura um amigo.** (*Papitoco* looks for a friend; *Papitoco* sucht einen Freund.) Ill.: Gerson Lopes de Andrade.
São Paulo: Editora do Brasil; Brasilia: INL 1975.

1976 Pannunzio, Martha de Azevedo: **Veludinho.** (Little velvet; Kleiner Samt.) Ill. Eliardo Franca.
Rio de Janeiro: José Olympio; Brasilia: INL 1978.

1978 Alvarez, Reynaldo Valinho: **As aventuras de Princés, o principe sem medo.** (Adventures of *Princés,* the fearless prince; *Princés* Abenteuer, der furchtlose Prinz.) Ill.: Wilma Dantas.
Rio de Janeiro: Salamandra; Brasilia: INL 1980.

1980 Ganem, Eliane: **Matade de quase nada.** (Half of almost nothing; Die Hälfte von fast nichts.)
(Unpublished; Unveröffentlicht.)

Prêmio Jabuti

This prize, sponsored by the Camera Brasileira do Livro in São Paulo, was begun in 1958. It is given annually to the best children's book and the youth best book published during the preceding year. The award presentation takes place during Book Week in October of each year.

Dieser Preis, der 1958 von der Camera Brasileira do Livro angeregt wurde, wird jährlich für das beste Kinderbuch der Vorjahresproduktion vergeben. Die Preisverleihung erfolgt während der jährlichen Buchwoche im Oktober.

1958 *Children's book/Kinderbuch*
Fleury, Renato Sêneca: **Proezas na roca.** (Heroic exploits on the estate; Heldentaten auf dem Landgut.) Ill.: Zaé Júnior.
São Paulo: Melhoramentos 1958.
Youth book/Jugendbuch
Leal, Isa Silveira: **Glorinha.** (Little *Gloria;* Kleine *Gloria.)* Ill.: Paolo Vasta.
São Paulo: Brasiliense 1958.

1959 *Children's book/Kinderbuch*
The prize was not given; Der Preis wurde nicht vergeben.
Youth book/Jugendbuch
Giacomo, Arnaldo Magalhães de: **Villa-Lobos,** alma sonora do Brasil. *(Villa-Lobos,* musical soul of Brazil; *Villa-Lobos,* Brasiliens klingende Seele.)
São Paulo: Melhoramentos 1959.

1960 *Children's book/Kinderbuch*
The prize was not given; Der Preis wurde nicht vergeben.
Youth book/Jugendbuch
Barros Junior, Francisco de: **Tres escoteiros em férias no rio Paraguai.** (Three boy scouts vacation on the *Paraguay* river; Drei Pfadfinder in Ferien am *Paragui*-Fluß.)
São Paulo: Melhoramentos 1960.

1961 *Children's book/Kinderbuch*
Ribeiro, Jannart Moutinho: **O circo.** (The circus; Der Zirkus.)
São Paulo: Melhoramentos 1961.
Youth book/Jugendbuch
Leal, Isa Silveira: **Unico amor de Ana Maria.** *(Ana Maria's* only love; *Ana Marias* einzige Liebe.)Ill. Manuel Victor Filho.
São Paulo: Ed. das Américas 1961.

1962 *Children's book/Kinderbuch*
Sand, Elos: **Aventuras de Eduardo.** *(Edward's* adventures; *Eduardos* Abenteuer.)
São Paulo: Martins 1962.
Youth book/Jugendbuch
The prize was not given; Der Preis wurde nicht vergeben.

1963 *Children's book/Kinderbuch*
Dupré, Maria José: **Aventuras do cachorrinho Samba na Rússia.** (The adventures of *Samba* the dog in Russia; Die Abenteuer des Hundes *Samba* in Russland.) Ill.: Francisco Xavier de Paiva Andrade.
São Paulo: Saraiva 1963.
Youth book/Jugendbuch
The prize was not given; Der Preis wurde nicht vergeben.

1964 *Children's book/Kinderbuch*
Mycielski, Wanda: **Zuzuquinho, um elefante de pano.** *(Zuzuquinho* a cloth elephant; *Zuzuquinho,* ein Elefant aus Stoff.) Ill.: Wanda Mycielski, Cristina Mycielski.
São Paulo: Melhoramentos 1964.
Youth book/Jugendbuch
The prize was not given; Der Preis wurde nicht vergeben.

1965 *Children's book/Kinderbuch*
Goulart, Mauricio: **Joana.** (*Joanna; Johanna.)*
Ill. Noèmia Graciliano, Clovis Graciliano.
São Paulo: Martins 1965.
Youth book/Jugendbuch
The prize was not given; Der Preis wurde nicht vergeben.

1966 *Children's book/Kinderbuch*
The prize was not given; Der Preis wurde nicht vergeben.
Youth book/Jugendbuch
The prize was not given; Der Preis wurde nicht vergeben.

1967 *Children's books/Kinderbuch*
Andrade, Thales Castanho de: **Encanto e verdade.** (Enchantment and truth; Verzauberung und Wahrheit.) Ill. Francisco Richter.
São Paulo: Melhoramentos 1967.
Youth book/Jugenbuch
Almeida, Lúcia Machado de: **Xisto no espaco.** (Xisto in space; *Xisto* im Weltraum.)
São Paulo: Ed. Brasiliense 1967.

1968 *Children's book/Kinderbuch*
Ribeiro, Jannert Moutinho: **Aventuras de Dito Carreiro.** (*Dito Carreiro's* adventures; Die Abenteuer von *Dito Carreiro.)*
São Paulo: Melhoramentos 1968.
Youth book/Jugendbuch
Leal, Isa Silveira: **O menino de Palmerés.** (The boy from *Palmares;* Der Junge aus Palmares.) Ill.: Tom Lucas.
São Paulo: Brasiliense 1968.

1969 *Children's book/Kinderbuch*
Queiroz, Rachel de: **O menino mágico.** (The little magician; Der kleine Zauberkünstler.)
Rio de Janeiro: Ed. J. Olympio 1969.
Youth book/Jugendbuch
The prize was not given; Der Preis wurde nicht vergeben.

1970 *Children's book/Kinderbuch*
Almeida, Fernanda de: **Soprinho.** (A light breath; Ein kurzer Hauch.) Ill.: Liana Paolo Rabioglio.
São Paulo: Melhoramentos 1970.
Youth book/Jugendbuch
The prize was not given; Der Preis wurde nicht vergeben.

1971 *Children's book/Kinderbuch*
The prize was not given; Der Preis wurde nicht vergeben.
Youth book/Jugendbuch
Prado, Lucilia de Almeida: **Um rua como aquela.** (A road like that; Eine Strasse wie diese.)
São Paulo: Martins 1971.

1972 *Children's book/Kinderbuch*
Cesar, Camila Cerqueira: **Estoria de Tonzeca, o calhambeque de Nhoton.** (The story about *Tonzeca, Nhoton's* old auto; Die Geschichte von *Tonzeca,* dem alten Auto von *Nhoton.)*
Ill.: Camila Cerqueira Cesar.
São Paulo: Melhoramentos 1972.
Youth book/Jugendbuch
The prize was not given; Der Preis wurde nicht vergeben.

1973 *Children's book/Kinderbuch*
Nunes, Lygia Bojunga: **Os colegas.** (The comrades; Die Kameraden.)
Ill.: Gian Calvi.
Rio de Janeiro: Sabiá 1972.
Youth book/Jugendbuch
The prize was not given; Der Preis wurde nicht vergeben.

1974 *Children's book/Kinderbuch*
Giacomo, Maria Thereza Cunha de: **Lendas brasileiras.** (Brazilian legends; Brasilianische Sagen.)
São Paulo: Melhoramentos 1974.
Youth book/Jugendbuch
The prize was not given; Der Preis wurde nicht vergeben.

1975 *Children's book/Kinderbuch*
The prize was not given; Der Preis wurde nicht vergeben.
Youth book/Jugendbuch
Lima, Edy: **A vaca probida.** (The forbidden cow; Die verbotene Kuh.) Ill.: Jayme Cortez.
São Paulo: Melhoramentos 1974.

1976 *Children's book/Kinderbuch*
Fontes, Ofélia: **Cem noites tapuias.** (Hundred nights with the *Tapuias; Hundert Nächte bei den Tapuias.)*
Ill.: Jandira Lorenz.
São Paulo: Atica 1976.
Youth book/Jugendbuch
The prize was not given; Der Preis wurde nicht vergeben.

1977 *Children's book/Kinderbuch*
Gonçalves, Lourdes: **Calunga.** (*Calunga.*)
Rio de Janeiro: Orientação Cultural 1977.
Youth book/Jugendbuch
Piroli, Wander: **Os rios morrem de sede.** (The rivers die of thirst; Die Flüsse sterben vor Durst.) Ill.: James Scliar.
Belo Horizonte: Comunicacão 1976.

1978 *Children's book/Kinderbuch*
Machado, Ana Maria: **História meio ao contrário.** (Half upside-down stories; Halb verkehrte Geschichten.) Ill.: Virgilio Velosa.
Belo Horizonte: Comunicação; Sec. Municipal de Cultura 1978.
Youth book/Jugendbuch
The prize was not given; Der Preis wurde nicht vergeben.

1979 *Children's book/Kinderbuch*
Editora Atica S.A.: **Coleção para crianças.** (Collection for children; Sammlung für Kinder.)
São Paulo: Atica 1978.
Youth book/Jugendbuch
Santos, Joel Rufino dos: **Uma estranha aventura em Talalai.** A strange adventure in Talalai; Ein sonderbares Abenteuer in *Talalai.)*
Ill.: Massao Hotoshi.
São Paulo: Pioneira 1978.

1980 *Children's book/Kinderbuch*
Vigna, Elvira: **Lã de umbigo.** (Wool from the navel; Wolle vom Nabel.) Ill.: Elvira Vigna.
Rio de Janeiro: Edições Antares; Brasilia: INL 1979.

Youth book/Jugendbuch
Bruno, Haroldo: **O misterioso rapto de flor de sereno.** (The mysterious rapture of the flower of stillness; Der mysteriöse Raub der Blume Ruhe.)
Rio de Janeiro: Salamandra 1979.

Prêmio Monteiro Lobato

This biennial prize was established in 1965 by the Academia Brasileira de Letras (Brazilian Academy of Letters) and is awarded to original manuscripts or published works for children. The prize was named after the noted Brazilian author, journalist and critic, José Bento Monteiro Lobato (1882-1948).
Dieser Preis wird seit 1965 alle zwei Jahre von der Academia Brasileira de Letras (Die brasilianische Akademie der Schönen Literatur) für ein Kinderbuch oder ein noch unveröffentlichtes Manuskript vergeben. Er wurde nach dem bekannten brasilianischen Autor, Journalist und Kritiker José Bento Monteiro Lobato (1882-1948) benannt.

1965 Antonio, Leo: **As diabruras da Comradro Raposa.** (The tricks of Master *Fox;* Die Streiche von Meister Fuchs.) (Unpublished; Unveröffentlicht.)

1967 The prize was not given; Der Preis wurde nicht vergeben.

1969 Jardim, Luis: **Proezas do Menino Jesus.** (The deeds of child *Jesus;* Die Heldentaten des *Jesus*kindes.) Ill.: Luis Jardim.
Rio de Janeiro: Olympio 1970.

1971 Barros Malferrari, Lilia de: **Camilinha no país das cores.** *(Camilinha* in the land of colours; *Camilinha* im Land der Farben.) Ill.: Liana Paolo Rabioglio.
São Paulo: Melhoramentos 1970.

Mott, Odette de Barros: **Justino, o retirante.** (*Justino,* the refugee; *Justino,* der Flüchtling.)
São Paulo: Ed. Brasiliense 1970.

1973 Pernambuco, Lucia Margarida: **Minidiário de Lucinha.** (The minidiary of *Lucinha; Lucinhas* Minitagebuch.)
(Unpublished; Unveröffentlicht.)

1975 The prize was not given; Der Preis wurde nicht vergeben.

1977 Guimarães, Vicente: **O mundo mágico de Vovó Felício.** (Grandpa *Felicio's* magic world; Großvater *Felicios* Zauberwelt.) Ill.: Jarbas Juarez e Weiss.
Belo Horizonte: Comunicação 1976.

1979 Leonardos, Stella: **Macaquezas do macaco Malaquias.** (The tricks of *Malaquias* the monkey; Die Tricks des Affen *Malaquias.)* Ill.: Eliardo França.
Rio de Janeiro: Brasil América 1977.

Prêmio Christiane Malburg

This prize was sponsored by the newspaper "O Estado de Minas"in memory of a child, Christiana Malburg. It was financed by Christiana's father. The prize was established at the end of 1967 and was awarded to either published or unpublished texts for children. After the 1969 presentation, the prize was discontinued.

Dieser Preis wurde von der Zeitung "O Estado de Minas" zur Erinnerung an ein Kind namens Christiana Malburg gestiftet, dessen Vater auch die Preisfinanzierung übernahm. 1967 wurde er erstmals für veröffentlichte und unveröffentlichte Texte für Kinder ausgeschrieben. 1969 wurde er zum letzten Mal vergeben.

1968 *1st prize/1. Preis*
Souza e Melo, Maria de Lourdes Guanabarino: **O O do outro lado da lua.** (The O from the other side of the moon; Das O von der anderen Seite des Mondes.)
(Unpublished; Unveröffentlicht.)

2nd prize/2. Preis
Suzuki, Eico: **Dick, aventuras de um cão dinamarques.** (*Dick,* adventures of a Danish dog; *Dick,* Abenteuer eines dänischen Hundes.) Ill.: Eico Suzuki.
Saõ Paulo: Editora do escritor 1972.

1969 *1st prize/1. Preis*
Sales, Herberto: **O sobradinho dos pardais.** (The sparrow's villa; Die Villa der Spatzen.) Ill.: Gioconda Uliana Campos.
São Paulo: Melhoramentos 1973.

2nd prize/2. Preis
Soares, Terezinha: **Luno e Lunika no país do futuro.** (*Luno* and *Lunika* in the land of the future; *Luno* und *Lunika* im Land der Zukunft.) Ill.: Miriam Monteiro.
Belo Horizonte: Imprensa Oficial 1968.

Laurea "O melhor para a criança"

This prize was established in 1974 by the Fundaçõ Nacional do Livro Infantil e Juvenil (Brazilian Section of IBBY) and is awarded annually to the best children's book. While making the selection of the prize winning book, the jury takes into account the text, illustration and lay-out. The award presentation takes place on International Children's Book Day, April 2nd of each year.

Dieser Preis wurde 1974 von der Fundação Nacional do Livro Infantil e Juvenil (Brasilianische Sektion von IBBY) gestiftet und wird jährlich dem besten Kinderbuch verliehen. Bei der Preisvergabe berücksichtigt die Jury sowohl den Text als auch die Illustrationen und die grafische Gestaltung des Buches. Die Verleihung erfolgt jeweils am Internationalen Kinderbuchtag, dem 2. April.

1974 França, Eliardo: **O rei de quase tudo.** (The king of almost everything; Der König von fast allem.) Ill.: Eliardo Francą.
Rio de Janeiro: Orientação Cultural 1974.

1975 Nunes, Lygia Bojunga: **Angélica.** (*Angelica.*) Ill.: Vilma Pasqualini.
Rio de Janeiro: Agir 1975.

1976 Nunes, Lygia Bojunga: **A bolsa amarela.** (The yellow bag; Die gelbe Tasche.) Ill.: Marie Louise Nery.
Rio de Janeiro: Agir 1976.

1977 Queiroz, Bartolomeu Campos: **Pedro, o menino que tinha o coração cheio de domingo.** (*Peter,* the boy who had a heart full of Sundays; *Peter,* der Junge, der ein Herz voll von Sonntagen hatte.) Ill.: Sara Avila de Oliveira.
Belo Horizonte: Vega 1977.

1978 França, Mary: **Coleção Gato e Rato.** (Collection, *Cat* and *Rat*; Sammlung, *Katze* und *Ratte.*) Ill.: Eliardo França.
São Paulo: Ática 1978.

1979 Machado, Ana Maria: **Raul da ferrugem azul.** (*Raul* from the blue rust; *Raul* vom blauen Rost.) Ill.: Patricia Gwinner.
Rio de Janeiro: Salamandra 1979.

1980 Santos, Joel Rufino dos: **O curumim que virou gigante.** (The child who became a giant; Das Kind, das ein Riese wurde.) Ill.: Lucia Lacourt.
São Paulo: Atica 1980.

Laurea "O melhor para o jovem"

in addition to "O melhor para a criançāo Nacional do Livro Infantil e Juvenil created in 1978 "O melhor para o jovem" (The best for youth). The creation of this prize was motivated by the growing need for good books for young people.

Zusätzlich zu dem Preis "O melhor para a criança" stiftete die Fundação Nacional do Livro Infantil e Juvenil 1978 den Preis "O melhor para o jovem" (Das Beste für die Jugend) Die Einrichtung dieses Preises wurde durch den wachsenden Bedarf an guten Büchern für Jugendliche angeregt.

1978 Nunes, Lygia Bojunga; **A casa dasa da madrinha.** (The godmother's house; Das Haus der Patin.) Ill.: Regina Yolanda.
Rio de Janeiro: Agir 1978.

1979 Colasanti, Marina: **Uma idéia toda azul.** (An all blue idea; Eine ganz blaue Idee.) Ill.: Marina Colasanti.
Rio de Janeiro: Nórdica 1979.

1980 Nunes, Lygia Bojunga: **O sofá estampado.** (The patterned sofa; Das gemusterte Sofa.) Ill.: Elvira Vigna.
Rio de Janeiro: Civilização Brasileira 1980.

Prêmio Jannart Moutinho Ribeiro

This prize was established in 1977 by the Cámara Brasileira do Livro to honour Jannart Moutinho Ribeiro, the author of numerous children's books, who died in that year. The purpose of this prize is to encourage new writers of books for children and adolescents.

Dieser Preis wurde von der Cámara Brasileira do Livro zu Ehren des brasilianischen Kinderbuchautors Jannart Moutinho Ribeiro in dessen Todesjahr, 1977, gestiftet. Der Zweck dieses Preises ist es, neue Autoren von Kinder- und Jugendbüchern zu ermutigen.

1977 Gonçalves, Lourdes: **Calunga.** (*Calunga.*)
Rio de Janeiro: Orientação Cultural 1977.

1977 The prize was not given; Der Preis wurde nicht vergeben.

1979 Pannunzio, Martha Azevedo: **Veludinho.** (Little velvet; Kleiner Samt.) Ill.: Eliardo França.
Rio de Janeiro: José Olympio; Brasilia: INL 1978.

1980 Quintella, Ary: **Cão vivo, leão morto; era apenas um indio.** (Dog alive, lion dead; it was only an Indian; Hund lebt, Löwe tot; es war nur ein Indianer.)
Belo Horizonte: Communicação 1980.

Bulgaria / Bulgarien

Nagrada Boris Angelušev

This award was founded by the Bulgarian Artist's Union and is given every two years to illustrators for their complete works. The prize was named after Boris Dimitrov Angelušev (1902–), an important Bulgarian painter and graphic artist.

Ill. 7 Rumen Skorčev in M. Markovski: Pjasŭčko

Dieser Preis wurde vom Bulgarischen Künstlerverband gestiftet und wird alle zwei Jahre an einen Illustrator für dessen Gesamtwerk verliehen. Der Preis ist nach dem bulgarischen Graphiker und Maler Boris Dimitrov Angelušev (1902–) benannt.

1976 *1st prize/1. Preis*
Ljuben Zidarov
2nd prize/2. Preis
Christo Nejkov
3rd prize/3. Preis
Neva Tuzsuzova

1978 *1st prize/1. Preis*
Nikolaj Stojanov
2nd prize/2. Preis
Olga Jončeva
3rd prize/3. Preis
Žeko Aleksiev
Bogdan Mavrodinov

1980 *1st prize/1. Preis*
Aleksandur Poplilov
2nd prize/2. Preis
Mana Parpulova
3rd prize/3. Preis
Kančo Kančev

Nagrada za iljustracii

This prize is awarded annually to the best illustrated children's book.

Mit diesem Preis wird jährlich das bestillustrierte Kinderbuch ausgezeichnet.

1968 Zidarov, Ljuben in:
Andersen, Hans Christian: **Andersenovi prikazki.** (*Andersen's* fairy tales; *Andersens* Märchen.)
Sofija: Narodna mladež 1968.

1969 Dimanov, Ljuben in:
Isaev, Mladen: **Visoki, sini planini.** (High blue mountains: Hohe blaue Berge.)
Sofija: Narodna mladež 1969.

1970 Denkov, Aleksandur in:
Paspaleeva, Vesa: **Roj zvezdici.** (A swarm of stars; Sternchenschwarm.)
Sofija: Bůlgarski pisatel 1970.

1971 Denkov, Aleksandŭr in:
Karalijčev, Angel: **Bulgarski narodni prikazki.** (Bulgarian folk tales; Bulgarische Volksmärchen.)
Sofija: Narodna mladež 1971.

1972 Skorčev, Rumen in:
Markovski, Mile: **Gŭba pod čadŭr.** (Mushroom under an umbrella; Ein Pilz unter dem Regenschirm.)
Sofija: Bŭlgarski pisatel 1972.

1973 Kožucharov, Ivan in:
Kern, Ludovik Ježi: **Ferdinand velikolepni.** (*Ferdinand,* the glorious; *Ferdinand* der Prächtige.)
Sofija: Narodna mladež 1973.

1974 Skorčev, Rumen in:
Otkŭde izvira Dunava, latvijska prikazka. (The source of the *Danube.* A Latvian tale; Die *Donau*quelle. Lettisches Märchen.)
Sofija: Narodna mladež 1974.

1975 Zidarov, Ljuben in:
Rajnov, Nikolaj: **Prikazki ot cjal svjat.** (Tales from all over the world; Märchen aus der ganzen Welt.)
Sofija: Narodna kultura 1974.

Zidarov, Ljuben in:
Rusafov, Georgi: **Vaklin i negovijat veren kon.** (*Vaklin* and his faithful horse; *Vaklin* und sein treues Pferd.)
Sofija: Narodna mladež 1969.

1976 Dimov, Ivan in:
Šopov, Anton: **Alena sleda.** (The scarlet trail; Die rote Spur.)
Sofija: Narodna mladež 1976.

1977 Zidarov, Ljuben in:
Stevenson, Robert Louis: **Ostrovŭt na sŭkrovištata.** (Eng.orig.title: Treasure Island; Die Schatzinsel.)
Sofija: Narodna mladež 1977.

1978 Dimov, Ivan in:
Stowe, Harriet Beecher: **Čičo Tomovata koliba.** (Amer.orig.title: Uncle *Tom's* cabin; Onkel *Toms* Hütte.)
Sofija: Narodna mladež 1978.

1979 Dimov, Ivan in:
Sienkiewicz, Henryk: **Janko muzikantŭt.** (*Janko* the musician; *Janko,* der Musikant; Pol.orig.title: *Janko* muzykant.)
Sofija: Otečestvo 1979.

1980 Dimov, Ivan in:
Stevenson, Robert Louis: **Novi chiljada i edna nǒst.** (New Arabian nights; Neue arabische Nächte.)
Sofija: Otečestvo 1979.

Nagrada na komitet za knigoizdavane i na komitet za izkustvo i kultura

This prize was founded by the Committee for Book Publishing and the Committee for Arts and Letters. It is awarded every two years to illustrators for their complete works.

Dieser Preis wurde vom Komitee für Verlagswesen und vom Komitee für Kunst und Literatur gestiftet. Er wird alle zwei Jahre an einen Illustrator für dessen Gesamtwerk verliehen.

1976 *1st prize/1. Preis*
Nikolaj Stojanov
Stojmen Stojmenov
Simeon Venov
2nd prize/2. Preis
Tekla Aleksieva
Stefan Markov
3rd prize/3. Preis
Ivan Kenarov
Vladimir Konovalov
Vladimir Korenev

1978 *1st prize/1. Preis*
Stojmen Stojlov
2nd prize/2. Preis
Damjan Damjanov
Mana Parpulova
Šǔtneva
Ani Tuzsuzova
3rd prize/3. Preis
Tonja Goranova
Anri Kulev
Ralica Nikolova

1980 *1st prize/1. Preis*
Ivan K'osev
Todor Panajotov
Borislav Stoev

2nd prize/2. Preis
Ivan Dimov
Stojmen Stojlov
Ani Tuzsuzova

3rd prize/3. Preis
Tonja Goranova
Ralica Nikolova

Nagrada na sedmica na izkustvo i literatura na deca

This prize is awarded annually to the best children's and youth books during Children's Arts and Letters Week.

Dieser Preis wird jährlich während der Literatur- und Kunstwoche für Kinder an die besten Kinder- und Jugendbücher vergeben.

1957 Mileva, Leda: **Sividreško i Bŭrzobežko.** (*Grey Coat* and *Long Ear; Graupelz* und *Langohr.*) Ill.: Vadim Lazarkevič.
Sofija: Bŭlgarski pisatel 1956.

Stančev, Lŭčezar: **Pionerska trŭba.** (The pioneer's trumpet; Die Pioniertrompete.) Ill.: Vladimir Korenev.
Sofija: Bŭlgarski pisatel 1956.

1958 Bosev, Asen: **Prikazi, gatanki, veseli istorii.** (Fairy tales, riddles, funny stories; Märchen, Rätsel, lustige Geschichten.) Ill.: Nikolaj Stojanov.
Sofija: Narodna mladež 1957.

Zidarov, Nikolaj: **Sŭrce pod červenata vrŭzka.** (The heart under the pioneer's red neckerchief; Ein Herz unter dem roten Pioniertuch.) Ill.: Ljubomir Zidarov.
Sofija: Narodna kultura 1957.

1959 Kalčev, Kamen: **Smelijat kapitan.** (The brave captain; Der tapfere Kapitän.) Ill.: Christo Nejkov.
Sofija: Narodna mladež 1958.

Pavlov, Anastas: **Brigadata na majstor Čuk.** (The crew of Master *Hammer:* Die Brigade von Meister *Hammer.*)
Ill.: Aleksandŭr mladež 1958.

1960 Angelov, Cvetan: **Naši poznajnici.** (Our acquaintances; Unsere Bekannten.) Ill.: Borislav Stoev.
Sofija: Bŭlgarski pisatel 1959.

Bosev, Asen: **Čudo nečuvano.** (Unheard of wonder; Unerhörtes Wunder.) Ill.: Georgi Anastasov.
Sofija: Bŭlgarski pisatel 1959.

1961 Angelov, Cvetan: **Pionerska petiletka.** (The pioneer's five-year plan; Fünfjahresplan der Pioniere.) Ill.: Mana Parpulova.
Sofija: Bŭlgarski pisatel 1960.

Davidkov, Ivan: **U doma.** (At home; Zu Hause.) Ill.
Sofija: Bŭlgarski pisatel 1960.

1962 Gabe, Dora: **Pet'ovoto sŭrce.** (*Pete's* heart; Das Herz von *Peter.*) Ill.: Kuna Haglund.
Sofija: Bŭlgarski pisatel 1961.

Lamar: **Edinak.** (The loner; Der Einzelgänger.) Ill.: Georgi Zlatanov.
Sofija: Narodna mladež 1961.

1963 Radevski, Christo: **Kitna rodina.** (My beautiful country; Schöne Heimat.) Ill.: Georgi Zlatanov.
Sofija: Bŭlgarski pisatel 1962.

Georgiev, Koljo: **Naj-chubavoto na toja svjat.** (The best thing in the world; Das Schönste auf dieser Welt.) Ill.: Ivan Kožucharov.
Sofija: Narodna mladež 1962.

1964 Angelov, Cvetan: **Pŭtečki na radosta.** (Paths of happiness; Pfade der Freude.) Ill.: Borislav Stoev.
Sofija: Bŭlgarski pisatel 1963.

Srebrov, Zdravko: **Malka povest za ptičeto, semkata i mladata kruša.** (A story about the bird, the seed and the young pear tree; Eine Erzählung von dem Vöglein, dem Samenkern und der jungen Birne.) Ill.: Borislav Stoev.
Sofija: Narodna mladež 1963.

1965 Isaev, Mladen: **Krila.** (Wings; Flügel.) Ill.: Aleksandŭr Denkov.
Sofija: Narodna mladež 1964.

Mišev, Georgi: **Chlapeto.** (The rascal; Der Bengel.) Ill.: Ivan Gongalov.
Sofija: Bŭlgarski pisatel 1964.

1966 Bosev, Asen: **Ej če interesno.** (That is interesting; Ist das aber interessant.) Ill.: Ivan Jorčev.
Sofija: Narodna mladež 1965.

Karalijčev, Angel: **Toplata rŭkavička.** (A warm glove; Ein warmer Handschuh.) Ill.: Nikola Mirčev.
Sofija: Bŭlgarski chudožnik 1965.

1967 Golev, Vladimir: **Dŭch na Zvŭnika.** (The smell of Canterbury-bells; Der Duft von Glockenblumen.) Ill.: Ljuben Zidarov.
Sofija: Bŭlgarski pisatel 1966.

Stojanov, Anastas: **Zvezda zapali seloto.** (A star illuminates the village; Ein Stern beleuchtet das Dorf.) Ill.: Ivan Kirkov.
Sofija: Narodna mladež 1966.

1968 Stančev, Lŭčezar: **Bički sestrički.** (My paints, my friends; Geschwister Farbstifte.) Ill.: Rumen Skorčev.
Sofija: Bŭlgarski pisatel 1967.

Tadžer, Salis: **Žakito.** *(Žakito.)* Ill.: Simeon Venov.
Sofija: Narodna mladež 1967.

1969 Zidarov, Nikolaj: **Pesenta me vodi za rŭka.** (Hand in hand with my song; Das Lied führt mich an der Hand.) Ill.: Genčo Denčev.
Sofija: Bŭlgarski pisatel 1968.

Ignatov, Rangel: **Neulovimijat Šiško.** (The elusive *Sisko;* Der ungreifbare *Sisko.*) Ill.: Juli Mincev.
Sofija: Az sŭm bŭlgarče 1968.

1970 Bosev, Asen: **Za rodinata rasta.** (I grow for my country; Ich wachse für das Vaterland.) Ill.: Ivan Kirkov.
Sofija: Az sŭm bŭlgarče 1969.

Strumski, Georgi: **Nasko Zaštoro.** *(Nasko Why; Nasko Warum.)* Ill.: Ivan Kirkov.
Sofija: Narodna mladež 1969.

1971 Gabe, Dora: **Majka Paraškeva.** (Mother *Paraškeva;* Mutter *Paraškeva.*) Ill.: Ivan K'osev.
Sofija: Narodna mladež 1970.

Stefanov, Dimitŭr: **Slŭnčevi zajčeta.** (The sun rabbits; Die Sonnenhäschen.) Ill.: Rumen Skorčev.
Sofija: Bŭlgarski pisatel 1970.

1972 Gulev, Dimitŭr: **Tajnata komanda.** (The secret crew; Das geheime Kommando.) Ill.: Ljudmil Čechlarov.
Sofija: Bŭlgarski pisatel 1971.

Davidkov, Ivan: **Pŭtekite na zornicata.** (The paths of the morning star; Die Pfade des Morgensterns.) Ill.: Ivan K'osev.
Sofija: Bŭlgarski pisatel 1971.

1973 Germanov, Andrej: **Ogledalce.** (Tiny mirror; Spiegelchen.) Ill.: Ivan Dimov.
Sofija: Bŭlgarski pisatel 1972.

Apostolov, Kiril: **Otivat si korabite.** (The ships are leaving; Die Schiffe legen ab.) Ill.: Rumen Rakšiev.
Sofija: Bŭlgarski pisatel 1972.

1974 Markovski, Mile: **Pjasŭčko.** (Sandman; Sandmännchen.) Ill.: Rumen Skorčev.
Sofija: Bŭlgarski pisatel 1973.

Stefanov, Dimitŭr: **Zvezda s fenerče.** (The star with a lantern; Der Stern mit einer Laterne.) Ill.: Rumen Skorčev.
Sofija: Bŭlgarski pisatel 1973.

1975 *Poetry/Poesie*

Radevski, Christo: **Odumki.** (Gossipy tales; Klatschgeschichten.) Ill.: Boris Dimovski.
Sofija: Bŭlgarski pisatel 1974.

Kirov, Radoj: **Momče i slŭmčev lŭč.** (The boy and the sunbeam; Der Junge und der Sonnenstrahl.) Ill.: Boris Dimovski.
Sofija: Bŭlgarski pisatel 1975.

Fiction/Prosa

Dragonov, Nedelčo: **Srebŭrnata tromba.** (The silver trumpet; Die silberne Trompete.) Ill.: Ljuben Dimanov.
Sofija: Narodna mladež 1975.

Krumov, Boris: **Po sledite na mečkite.** (On the trail of the bears; Auf den Spuren der Bären.)
Sofija: Bŭlgarski pisatel 1975.

Literary criticism/Literaturkritik

Jankov, Nikolaj: **Detska literatura.** Istorija i kritika. (Children's literature. History and criticism; Kinderliteratur. Geschichte und Kritik.)
Sofija: Bŭlgarski pisatel 1975.

1976 *Poetry/Poesie*

Bosev, Asen: **Skok-podskok.** (Hoppity-hop; Hoppla-Hopp.) Ill.: Georgi Anastasov.
Sofija: Bŭlgarski pisatel 1975.

Kechlibareva, Nadja: **Paunovi porti.** (Peacock gates; Pfauentore.)
Sofija: Narodna mladež 1975.

Avgarski, Georgi: **Svirka-razdumka.** (The babbling flute; Die plappernde Flöte.) Ill.: Miglena Konstantinova.
Sofija: Bŭlgarski pisatel 1976.

Special prize for a first book/Ein Sonderpreis für das erste Buch eines Autors

Nikolov, Velizar: **Svirki ot kajsija.** (Apricot flutes; Aprikosenflöten.) Ill.: Simeon Spiridonov.
Sofija: Narodna mladež 1976.

Fiction/Prosa

Strandžev, Kosta: **Najchrabrata zvezda.** (The bravest star; Der tapferste Stern.) Ill.: Ivan Kožucharov.
Sofija: Bŭlgarski pisatel 1976.

Chinkova, Vasilka: **Kŭde svŭrčva nebeto.** (Where the sky ends; Wo der Himmel endet.) Ill.: Petŭr Čuklev.
Sodija: Narodna mladež 1976.

Bozakov, Dimitŭr: **Gnevno ljato.** (A wrathful summer; Ein zorniger Sommer.)
Sofija: Dŭržavno voenno izdatelstvo 1976.

Peevski, Ljubomir: **V stranata na černata Snežinka.** (In the country of the black snowflakes; Im Land der schwarzen Schneeflocken.)
Sofija: Narodna mladež 1976.

Literary criticism/Literaturkritik

Dimitrov-Rudar, Petŭr: **Za detskata literatura.** (On children's literature; Über Kinderliteratur.)
Sofija: Bŭlgarski pisatel 1976.

1977 *Poetry/Poesie*

Muratov, Aleksandŭr: **Prozorče budno.** (Wakeful window; Wachsames Fensterchen.) Ill.: Ljuben Zidarov.
Sofija: Bŭlgarski pisatel 1976.

Stanišev, Krŭst'o: **Vrana s prana perušina.** (The crow with washed feathers; Die Krähe mit dem gewaschenen Gefieder.) Ill.: Ivan Dimov.
Sofija: Bŭlgarski pisatel 1977.

Kolev, Petko: **Bodlivko.** (The prickly one; Das Stacheltier.) Ill.: Milko Dikov.
Sofija: Narodna mladeź 1977.

Fiction/Prosa

Stojanov, Anastas: **Sto prikazki.** (One hundred tales; Hundert Geschichten.) Ill.: Boris Dimovski.
Sofija: Bŭlgarski pisatel 1977.

Bobev, Petŭr: **Dragota — morski chajdutin.** (*Dragota* — pirate; *Dragota* — der Seeräuber.) Ill.: Anna Bobeva.
Sofija: Dŭržavno voenno izdatelstvo 1976.

Janev, Simeon: **Den i nošt, nošt i den.** (Day and night, night and day; Tag und Nacht, Nacht und Tag.) Ill.: Peter Rashkov.
Sofija: Bŭlgarski pisatel 1976.

1978 *Poetry/Poesie*

Nikolov, Ivan: **Razni raboti.** (Various things; Verschiedene Sachen.) Ill.: Christo Žabljanov.
Sofija: Bŭlgarski pisatel 1978.

Jordanov, Nedjalko: **Krasimir i Vladimir.** (*Krasimir* and *Vladimir.*). Ill.: Christo Žabljanov.
Sofija: Narodna mladež 1978.

Kančev, Nikolaj: **Ochljuvata kŭšta.** (The snail house; Das Schneckenhaus.)
Sofija: Narodna mladež 1978.

Fiction/Prosa
Denev, Mladen: **Kŭsni izpiti.** (Late exams; Späte Prüfungen.) Ill.: Petŭr Petrov.
Sofija: Bŭlgarski pisatel 1978.

Gulev, Dimitŭr: **Zdravej i zbogom, Don Kichot.** (Hello and goodbye, Don *Quixote;* Sei gegrüsst und Leb wohl, Don *Quichotte.*)
Sofija: Bŭlgarski pisatel 1978.

1979 *Poetry/Poesie*
Jotev, Dobri: **Za vas deča nevinni, ot pet do sto i pet godini.** (To you innocent children between the ages of five and a hundred and five; Für Euch ihr unschuldigen Kinder, von fünf bis einhundertundfünf.)
Sofija: Narodna mladež 1979.

Daskalova, Liana: **Vrabčova družina.** (The sparrow's band; Die Spatzengesellschaft.)
Sofija: Bŭlgarski pisatel 1979.

Jordanova, Petja: **Mamina svetulka.** (Mummy's firefly; Mamis Leuchtkäfer.) Ill.: Christo Žabljanov.
Sofija: Narodna mladež 1979.

Fiction/Prosa
Božilov, Kiril: **Počti po mŭžki.** (Almost like a man; Fast männlich.) Ill.: Roza Chalačeva.
Sofija: Otečestvo 1979.

Damjanov, Damjan: **Chvŭrčiloto se zavrŭšta.** (The kite comes back; Der Drachen kommt zurück.)
Sofija: Bŭlgarski pisatel 1978.

Kolev, Konstantin: **Spomeni na edno seljanče.** (Memories of a country boy; Erinnerungen eines Jungen vom Land.) Ill.: Dobri Jankov.
Sofija: Bŭlgarski pisatel 1979.

1980 *Poetry/Poesie*
Angelov, Cvetan: **Kŭšturka za veselie s tri komminčeta.** (The little fun house with three chimneys; Das fröhliche Häuschen mit drei Kaminen.)
Sofija: Bŭlgarski pisatel 1980.

Stojčev, Dimitŭr: **Chitruški.** (The sly ones; Schlaumeier.)
Sofija: Narodna mladež 1980.

Nazarov, Kiril: **Chorovod.** (The round-dance leader; Der Reigentänzer.)
Sofija: Narodna mladež 1980.

Asenov, Petko: **Goricvet.** (Forest flower; Waldblume.)
Sofija: Narodna mladež 1980.

Petrov, Janaki: **Čičo Čičopej.** (Uncle *Sing-Uncle;* Onkel *Singonkel.*)
Sofija: Bŭlgarski pisatel 1980.

Fiction/Prosa

Mutafčieva, Vera: **Predrečeno ot Pagane.** (Predicted by *Pagane:* Von *Pagane* vorhergesagt.)
Sofija: Otečestvo 1980.

Markovski, Georgi: **Selski kalendar.** (A village calendar; Ein Dorfkalender.)
Sofija: Otečestvo 1980.

Bachvarova, Svoboda: **Priključenijata na Filio i Makenzen.** (The adventures of *Filio* and *Makenzen:* Die Abenteuer von *Filio* und *Makenzen.*)
Sofija: Narodna mladež 1980.

Marinovski, Vasil: **Ruffo, červenokosijat.** (*Ruffo,* the redhead: *Ruffo,* der Rothaarige.)
Sofija: Otečestvo 1980.

Literary criticism/Literaturkritik

Hadžikosev, Simeon: **Zavrŭštane v detstvoto.** (A return to childhood; Rückkehr in die Kindheit.)
Sofija: Otečestvo 1980.

Nagrada na Petko Račev Slavejkov

This prize was named after Petko Račev Slavejlov, the first important Bulgarian writer for children. The prize is awarded annually.

Dieser Preis wurde nach Petko Raćev Slavejkov benannt, dem ersten bedeutenden Schriftsteller für Kinder. Der Preis wird jährlich verliehen.

1972 Bosev, Asen: **Nie, vie, te.** (We, you, they; Wir, ihr, sie.) Ill.: Ivan Kirkov.
Sofija: Bŭlgarski pisatel 1971.

1973 Strumski, Georgi: **Bjalo, zeleno, červeno.** (White, green, red; Weiss, grün, rot.) Ill.: Kiril Gjulemetov.
Sofija: Bŭlgarski pisatel 1972.

1974 Angelov, Cvetan: **Vaza s Margaritki.** (A vase of daisies; Eine Vase mit Margariten.) Ill.: Georgi Trifonov.
Sofija: Bŭlgarski pisatel 1973.

1975 Lŭkatnik Michail: **Alenata čajka.** (The purple seagull; Die purpurrote Möwe.) Ill.: Christo Zabljanov.
Sofija: Bŭlgarski pisatel 1974.

1976 Koralov, Emil: **Bengalski ogŭn.** (Bengal light; Bengalisches Feuer.) Ill.: Georgi Caušev.
Sofija: Narodna mladež 1975.

1977 Zidarov, Nikolaj: **Sini vakancii moi.** (My blue holidays; Meine himmelblauen Ferien.) Ill.: Ilija Saruiliev.
Sofija: Bŭlgarski pisatel 1976.

1978 Kalina, Malina: **Kŭm mesečko.** (To the tiny moon; Zum kleinen Mond.) Ill.: Nadežda Jončeva.
Sofija: Bŭlgarski pisatel 1977.

1979 Jankov, Nikolaj: **Ljubimata kniga.** Razkazi za i okolo "Pod igoto". (The favorite book. Stories about the novel "Under the yoke"; Das Lieblingsbuch. Geschichten über den Roman "Unter dem Joch".)
Sofija: Otečestvo 1978.

1980 Gabe, Dora for: **Complete works for children.** Gesamtschaffen für Kinder.

Nagrada Sŭjuz na bŭlgarskite pisateli

This prize is awarded by the Bulgarian Writer's Union to the author of the best children's or youth book.

Dieser Preis wird von dem bulgarischen Schriftstellerverband für das beste Kinder- oder Jugendbuch verliehen.

1957 Bosev, Asen: **Čudni vremena.** (Wonderful times; Wundervolle Zeiten.) Ill.: Slav Slavov.
Sofija: Narodna kultura 1966.

1964 Kalčev, Kamen: **Pri izvora na života.** (At the source of life; An der Lebensquelle.) Ill.: Ivan K'osev.
Sofija: Narodna kultura 1963.

1965 Karalijčev, Angel: **Naj-skŭpijat podarŭk.** (The most precious gift; Das teuerste Geschenk.) Ill.: Stojan Iliev.
Varna: Dŭržavno izd. 1964.

1968 Zidarov, Nikolaj: **Legendi ot brŭšljan.** (Ivy legends; Efeulegenden.) Ill.: Genčo Denčev.
Sofija: Az sŭm Bŭlgarce 1967.

1969 Angelov, Cvetan: **Cvetuška.** (Tiny flower; Blümelein.) Ill.: Nikolaj Stojanov.
Sofija: Bŭlgarski pisateli 1968.

1970 Daskalov, Stojan Cekov: **Urok za Bŭlgarija.** (A lesson about Bulgaria; Unterrichtsstunde über Bulgarien.) Ill.: Georgi Trifonov.
Sofija: Bŭlgarski pisatel 1969.

1975 Markovski, Mile: **Pjasŭčko.** (Sandman; Sandmännchen.) Ill.: Rumen Skorčev.
Sofija: Bŭlgarski pisatel 1974.

1977 Evtimov, Evtim: **Učilište na vŭrcha.** (The school on the hill; Die Schule auf dem Hügel.) Ill.: Christo Zabljanov.
Sofija: Bŭlgarski pisatel 1976.

1978 *1st prize/1. Preis*
Mileva, Leda: **Černoto flamingo.** (The black flamingo; Der schwarze Flamingo.) Ill.: Assen Stareishinski.
Sofija: Bŭlgarski pisatel 1978.

2nd prize/2. Preis
Petrov, Valeri: **Bjala Prikazka.** (A white tale; Eine weisse Erzählung.) Ill.: Danail Raikov.
Sofija: Otečestvo 1978.

1979 Končev, Dončo: **Slučki v dvora, kraj gorata, iz vŭzducha i pod vodata.** (Events in the garden, near the forest, in the air and under the water; Ereignisse im Hof, im Wald, in der Luft und unter Wasser.)
Sofija: Otečestvo 1979.

1980 Zidarov, Nikolaj: **Chiljada i trista proleti.** (One thousand and three hundred springs; Tausenddreihundert Frühlinge.) Ill.: Stefan Markov.
Sofija: Narodna mladež 1980.

The People's Education Ministry Prize

This prize was established in 1955 for the best children's book by the Bulgarian Ministry of Education. The award is presented during the Week of Children's Arts and Letters. Each year, the Ministry appoints a commission made up of delegates from the Ministry of Education, the Writer's Association, the House of Children's Arts and Letters and the Youth Organisation, DKMS.

1955 wurde ein Preis des bulgarischen Volksbildungsministeriums für das beste Kinderbuch gestiftet, der während der im Frühling durchgeführten Literatur- und Kunstwoche für Kinder und Jugendliche verteilt wird. Das Bildungsministerium ernennt jährlich eine Kommission, die sich aus Vertretern des Ministeriums, des Schriftstellerverbandes, des Hauses für Literatur und Kunst für Kinder und Jugendliche und der Jugendorganisation (DKMS) zusammensetzt.

1956 Zidarov, Nikolaj: **Pionersko sŭrce.** (A pioneer's heart; Pionierherz.) Ill.: Stojan Anastasov.
Sofija: Narodna kultura 1955.

1957 Kjuljavkov, Krum: **Chljab i ošte nešto.** (Bread and something else; Brot und noch etwas.)
Sofija: Narodna mladež 1956.

1958 The prize was not given; Der Preis wurde nicht vergeben.

1959 Belev, Gjončo: **Patilata na edno momče.** (The sufferings of a boy; Die Leiden eines Jungen.)
Sofija: Narodna mladež 1958.

1960 Bosev, Asen: **Čude nečuvano.** (An unheard of wonder; Unerhörtes Wunder.) Ill.: Georgi Atanasov.
Sofija: Bŭlgarski pisatel 1959.

Karalijčev, Angel: **Topla rŭkavička.** (A warm glove; Ein warmer Handschuh.) Ill.: Nikola Mirčev.
Sofija: Bŭlgarski pisatel 1959.

1961 The prize was not given; Der Preis wurde nicht vergeben.

1962 Davidkov, Ivan: **Sŭzvedieto na svetulkite.** The constellation of fireflies; Das Sternbild der Leuchtkäferchen.) Ill.: Ivan Kjosev.
Sofija: Narodna mladež 1961.

1963 Radevski, Christo: **Kitna rodina.** (My beautiful country; Schöne Heimat.) Ill.: Georgi Zlatanov.
Sofija: Bŭlgarski pisatel 1962.

1964/1966 The prize was not given; Der Preis wurde nicht vergeben.

1967 Stojanov, Anastas: **Zvezda zapali seloto.** (A star lighted the village; Ein Stern erleuchtete das Dorf.)
Sofija: Narodna mladež 1966.

1968 Davidkov, Ivan: **Dalečni brodove.** (Ships far away; Ferne Schiffe.)
Sofija: Narodna mladež 1967.

Canada/Kanada

Book of the Year Award

The Book of the Year Award, a bronze medal, is presented annually by the children's librarians' section of the Canadian Library Association for the best children's book written in English by a Canadian author. Until 1973, an award was also given for a children's book written in the French language. Since 1966, the prize-winning titles have been announced one year after the date of publication during Canadian Children's Book Week.

Der "Book of the Year Award", eine Bronzemedaille, wird jährlich von den Kinderbibliothekaren der kanadischen Bibliotheksvereinigung an das beste Kinderbuch eines englischsprachigen Kanadiers verliehen. Bis 1973 wurde ein Preis auch für ein französischsprachiges Kinderbuch vergeben.

Ill. 8 Elizabeth Cleaver in W. Toye: The Loon's necklace

Seit 1966 wird der Preis ein Jahr nach Veröffentlichung des Buches während der kanadischen Kinderbuchwoche verliehen.

1947 Haig-Brown, Roderick Langmere: **Starbuck valley winter.** (Winter im Starbucktal.) Ill.: Charles DeFeo.
Toronto: Collins 1946.

1948 Dunham, Bertha Mabel: **Kristli's trees.** (*Kristlis* Bäume.) Ill.: Selwyn Dewdney.
Toronto: McClelland & Stewart 1948.

1949 The prize was not given; Der Preis wurde nicht vergeben.

1950 Lambert, Richard Stanton: **Franklin of the Arctic.** A life of adventure. (*Franklin* aus der Arktis. Ein Leben voller Abenteuer.) Maps: Julius Griffith.
Toronto: McClelland & Stewart 1949.

1951 The prize was not given; Der Preis wurde nicht vergeben.

1952 Clark, Catherine Anthony: **The sun horse.** (Das Sonnenpferd.) Ill.: Clare Bice.
Toronto: Macmillan 1951.

1953 The prize was not given; Der Preis wurde nicht vergeben.

1954 Gervais, Emile: **Le vénérable François de Montmorency-Laval.** (The venerable François de *MontmorencyLaval;* Der ehrwürdige *François de Montmorency-Laval.) Ill.: Maurice Petitdidier. Montréal: Comité des Fondateurs de l'Eglise Canadienne 1953.*

1955 The prize was not given; Der Preis wurde nicht vergeben.

1956 Riley, Louise: **Train for Tiger Lily.** (Ein Zug für *Tiger Lily.)* Ill.: Christine Price.
Toronto: Macmillan 1954.

1957 Macmillan, Cyrus: **Glooskap's country and other Indian tales.** (*Glooskaps* Land und andere indianische Erzählungen.) Ill.: John A. Hall.
Toronto: Oxford University Press 1956.

1958 Clément, Béatrice: **Le chevalier du roi.** Vie de Saint Ignace de Loyola. (The king's knight. The life of Saint *Ignatius Loyola;* Der Diener des Königs. Das Leben des Hl. *Ignatius von Loyola.)* Ill.: Thérèse Robichon.
Montréal: Ed. de l'Atelier 1956.

Mowat, Farley: **Lost in the barrens.** (Verloren in den Tundren.) Ill.: Charles Geer.
Boston, Toronto: Little, Brown 1956.

1959 Flamme, Hélène: **Un drôle de petit cheval.** (A funny little horse; Ein lustiges kleines Pferd.) Ill.: Viat.
Montréal: Leméac 1957.

Hayes, John Francis: **The dangerous cove.** A story of the early days in Newfoundland. (Die gefährliche Bucht. Eine Geschichte aus den Gründertagen von Neufundland.) Ill.: Fred Finley.
Montréal, Toronto, Vancouver: Copp Clark 1957.

1960 Daveluy, Paule: **L'été enchanté. Roman.** (The enchanted summer. Romance; Der wunderbare Sommer. Roman.)
Montréal: Ed. de l'Atelier 1958.

Barbeau, Charles Marius: **The golden phoenix and other French-Canadian fairy tales.** (Der goldene Phönix und andere französisch-kanadische Märchen.)
Adapt.: Michael Hornyansky. Ill.: Arthur Price.
Toronto: Oxford University Press 1958.

1961 Gauvreau, Marcelle: **Plantes vagabondes.** (Wandering plants; Wandernde Pflanzen.) Ill.: Hélène Gagné-Dufresne, Marcel Cailloux.
Montréal: Centre de Psychologie et de Pédagogie 1959.

Toye, William: **The St. Lawrence.** (Der St. *Lawrence.) Ill.: Leo Rampen.*
Toronto: Oxford University Press 1959.

1962 Aubry, Claude: **Les îles du roi Maha Maha II. Conte fantaisiste canadien.** (The islands of King *Maha Maha II.* A fantistic Canadian story; Die Inseln des Königs *Maha Maha II.* Fantastische Erzählung aus Kanada.) Ill.: Edouard Perret.
Québec: Ed. du Pélican 1960.

1963 Daveluy, Paule: **Drôle d'automne.** (Droll autumn; Komischer Herbst.)
Québec: Ed. du Pélican 1961.

Burnford, Sheila: **The incredible journey.** (Die unglaubliche Reise.) Ill.: Carl Burger.
Boston, Toronto: Little, Brown 1961.

1964 Chabot, Cécile: **Férie.** (Holiday; Feiertag.)
Montréal: Beauchemin 1963.

Haig-Brown, Roderick Langemere Haig: **The whale people;** (Das Walvolk.) Ill.: Mary Weiler.
Don Mills: Longmans 1962.

1965 Aubry, Claude: **Le loup de Noël.** (The Christmas wolf; Der Weihnachtswolf.) Ill.: Edouard Perret.
Montréal: Centre de Psychologie et de Pédagogie 1962.

Reid, Dorothy M.: **Tales of Nanabozho.** (Erzählungen von *Nanabozho.)* Ill.: Donald Grant.
Toronto: Oxford University Press 1963.

1966 Corriveau, Monique: **Le wapiti.** (The wapiti; Der Wapiti.)
Québec: Ed. Jeunesse 1964.

Maillet, Andrée: **Le chêne des tempêtes.** (The storm oak; Die Gewitter-Eiche.)
Montréal: Ed. Fides 1965.

Houston, James A.: **Tiktaliktak. An Eskimo legend.** (*Tiktaliktak.* Eine Eskimosage.) Ill.: James A. Houston.
Don Mills: Longmans 1965.

McNeill, James: **The double knights. More tales from around the world.** (Die doppelten Ritter. Mehr Geschichten aus aller Welt.) Ill.: Theo Dimson.
Toronto: Oxford University Press 1964.

1967 Harris, Christie: **Ravens cry.** (Der Schrei des Raben.) Ill.: Bill Reid.
Toronto: McClelland & Stewart 1966.

1968 Mélançon, Claude: **Légendes indiennes du Canada.** (Indian legends of Canada; Indianersagen aus Kanada.) Ill.
Montréal: Ed. du Jour 1967.

Houston, James A.: **The white archer.** (Der weisse Bogenschütze.) Ill.: James A. Houston.
Don Mills: Longmans 1967.

1969 Hill, Kay: **And tomorrow the stars.** The story of *John Cabot.* (Und morgen die Sterne. Die Geschichte von *John Cabot.)* Ill.: Laszlo Kubinyi.
New York: Dodd, Mead 1969.

1970 Gendron, Lionel: **La merveilleuse histoire de la naissance.** (The wonderful story of birth; Die wunderbare Geschichte der Geburt.) Ill.: Jack Tremblay.
Montréal: Ed. de l'Homme 1969.

Fowke, Edith Margaret: **Sally go round the sun. 300 songs, rhymes and games of Canadian children.** (Sally umkreist die Sonne. 300 Lieder, Reime und Spiele kanadischer Kinder.)
Ill.: Carlos Marchiori.
Toronto: McClelland & Stewart 1969.

1971 Major, Henriette: **La surprise de Dame Chenille.** (The surprise of Lady *Caterpillar;* Die Überraschung der Raupendame.) Ill.: Claude Lafortune. Photos: Jean-Louis Frund.
Montréal: Centre de Psychologie et de Pédagogie 1970.

Toye, William: **Cartier discovers the St. Lawrence.** *(Cartier* entdeckt den St. *Lawrence*-Strom.) Ill.: Lászlo Gal.
Toronto: Oxford University Press 1970.

1972 Blades, Ann: **Mary of Mile 18.** (*Mary* von Kilometer 18.) Ill.: Ann Blades.
Montréal: Tundra Books 1971.

1973 Bussières, Simone: **Le petit sapin qui a poussé sur une étoile.** (The little fir tree which grew on a star; Die kleine Fichte, die auf einem Stern wuchs.) Ill.: Cécile Chabot.
Notre-Dame-des-Laurentides: Presses Laurentiennes 1972.

Nichols, Ruth: **The marrow of the world.** (Der Kern der Welt.) Ill.: Trina Schart Hyman.
Toronto: Macmillan 1972.

1974 Cleaver, Elizabeth: **The miraculous hind. A Hungarian legend.** (Die wunderbare Hirschkuh. Eine ungarische Sage.) Ill.: Elizabeth Cleaver.
Toronto: Holt, Rinehart and Winston 1973.

1975 Lee, Dennis: **Alligator pie.** (Alligator-Kuchen.) Ill.: Frank Newfeld.
Toronto: Macmillan 1974.

1976 Richler, Mordecai: **Jacob Two-Two meets the Hooded Fang.** (*Jacob Two-Two* trifft den *Hooded Fang.) Ill.: Fritz Wegner.*
Toronto: McClelland & Stewart 1975.

1977 Harris, Christie: **The mouse woman and the vanished princesses.** (Die Maus und die verschwundenen Prinzessinnen.) Ill.: Douglas Tait.
Toronto: McClelland & Stewart 1976.

1978 Lee, Dennis: **Garbage delight.** (Müllvergnügen) Ill.: Franz Newfeld.
Toronto: Macmillan 1977.

1979 Major, Kevin: **Hold fast.** (Halte fest.)
Toronto, Vancouver: Clarke, Irwin 1978.

1980 Huston, James: **River runners.** (Flußschiffer.)
Toronto: McClelland and Stewart 1979.

1981 Kushner, Donn: **The violin maker's gift.** (Das Geschenk des Geigenbauers.)
Toronto: Macmillan 1980.

Canada Council Award for Children's Literature/Prix Littérature de Jeunesse du Conseil des Arts du Canada

This award, which was established in 1975, consists of two annual prizes of 5 000 dollars each and is given in recognition of outstanding contributions to Canadian literature for children in both the English and French languages. The prize is awarded by the Canada Council.

Im Jahre 1975 stiftete das Canada Council zwei Preise jährlich in Höhe von je 5 000 Dollar für je ein englischsprachiges und ein französischsprachiges Kinder- oder Jugendbuch.

1976 *English/Englisch*
Freeman, Bill: **Shantymen of Cache Lake.** (Holzfäller aus *Cache-Lake.)*
Toronto: James Lorimer 1975.

French/Französisch
Aylwin, Louise: **Raminagradu; histoires extraordinaires pour enfants extraordinaires.** (*Raminagradu:* extraordinary stories for extraordinary children; *Raminagradu:* Ausserordentliche Erzählungen für ausserordentliche Kinder.) Ill.: Louise Aylwin.
Montréal: Editions du Jour 1975.

1977 *English/Englisch*
Paperny, Myra: **The wooden people.** (Die hölzernen Menschen.) Ill.: Ken Stampnick.
Toronto: Little, Brown 1976.

French/Französisch
Renaud, Bernadette: **Emilie, la baignoire à pattes.** (*Emilie,* the bathtub with feet; *Emilie,* die Badewanne mit Füssen.) Ill.: France Bédard.
Saint-Lambert: Les Editions Héritage 1976

1978 *English/Englisch*
Little, Jean: **Listen for the singing.** (Hör auf den Gesang.)
Toronto: Clarke Irwin 1977.

French/Französisch
Houle, Denise: **Lune de neige.** (Snow moon; Schneemond.) Ill.: Frédéric Castel.
Montréal: La Société de Belles-Lettres Guy Maheux 1977.

Illustration
Lafortune, Claude in:
Major, Henriette: **L'évangile en papier.** (The gospel out of paper; Das Evangelium aus Papier.)
Montréal, Paris: Fides-Centurion 1977.

1979 *English/Englisch*
Major, Kevin: **Hold fast.** (Halte fest.)
Toronto, Vancouver: Clarke, Irwin 1978.

Waterton, Betty: **A salmon for Simon.** (Ein Lachs für *Simon.)* Ill.: Ann Blades.
Vancouver: Douglas & McIntyre 1978.

French/Französisch
Anfousse, Ginette: **La chicane.** (Chicanery; Schikane.) Ill.: Ginette Anfousse.
Montréal: La Courte Échelle 1978.

Anfousse, Ginette: **La varicelle.** (Chicken pox; Die Windpocken.) Ill.: Ginette Anfousse.
Montréal: La Courte Échelle 1978.

1980 *English/Englisch*
Smucker, Barbara: **Days of terror.** (Schreckenstage.)
Toronto, Vancouver: Clarke, Irwin 1979.

Illustration
Gal, Laszlo in:
Lunn, Janet: **The twelve dancing princesses; A fairy tale retold.** (Die 12 tanzenden Prinzessinen: Ein Märchen wiedererzählt.)
Agincourt, Ontario: Methuen 1979.

French/Französisch
Roy, Gabrielle: **Courte-queue.** (Bob-tail; Kurzschwanz.) Ill.: François Olivier.
Montréal: Stanké 1979.

Illustration
Paré, Roger in:
Plante, Raymond: **Une fenêtre dans ma tête.** (A window in my head; Ein Fenster in meinem Kopf.)
Montréal: La Courte Échelle 1979.

1981 *English/Englisch*
Harris, Christie: **The trouble with princesses.** (Die Probleme mit Prinzessinnen.) Ill.: Douglas Tait.
Toronto: McClelland & Stewart 1980.

Illustration
Cleaver, Elizabeth in:
Cleaver, Elizabeth: **Petrouchka.** *(Petrouchka.)*
Don Mills, Ont.: Oxford University Press 1980.

French/Französisch
Gauthier, Bernard: Hébert Luée. *(Hébert Luée.)* Ill.: Marie-Louise Gay.
Montréal: La Courte Échelle 1980.

Illustration
Tanobe, Miyuki in:
Vigneault, Jean: **Les gens de mon pays.** (The people of my country; Die Leute aus meiner Heimat.)
Montréal: La Courte Échelle 1980.

Prix Marie-Claire Daveluy

This prize was founded in 1970 by the Association Canadienne des Bibliothécaires de Langue Française (Canadian Association of French speaking librarians) and was named in honour of Marie-Claire Daveluy, an important authoress of historical novels. The authors competing for this prize must be between 15 and 21 years of age and must also be French-speaking. Novels, fairy tales, theatre pieces and poetry collections can be submitted.

1970 wurde der Preis von der Association Canadienne des Bibliothécaires de Langue Française (Kanadische Vereinigung der französischsprechenden Bibliothekare) gestiftet und wurde zu Ehren von Marie-Claire Daveluy, einer wichtigen Autorin historischer Romane, benannt. Der Autor soll französischsprachig und zwischen 15 und 21 Jahre alt sein. Es kann sich um einen Roman, ein Märchen, ein Theaterstück oder eine Gedichtsammlung handeln.

1970 Chavarie, Robert: **Opium en fraude.** (Smuggled opium; Geschmuggeltes Opium.) Ill.: Robert Chavarie.
Sherbrooke: Paulines 1971.

1971 Sabella, Monique: **L'inconnue des Laurentides.** (The unknown of of the *Laurentides;* Die Unbekannte von der *Laurentides.) Ill.: Gabriel de Beney.*
Sherbrooke: Paulines 1972.

1972 Desrosiers, Christian: **Lavabosse, ou légendes du pays perdu.** *(Lavabosse,* or legends of lost lands; *Lavabosse,* oder Sagen des verlorenen Landes.)
(Unpublished; Unveröffentlicht.)

1973 Charland, Jean-Pierre: **Le naufrage.** (The shipwreck; Der Schiffbruch.)
Montréal: Editions du Jour 1975.

1974 Aylwin, Louise: **Raminagradu: histoires extraordinaires pour enfants extraordinaires.** (*Raminagradu:* extraordinary stories for extraordinary children; *Raminagradu:* ausserordentliche Erzählungen für ausserordentliche Kinder.) Ill.: Louise Aylwin.
Montréal: Editions du Jour 1975.

1975 Côté, Laurier: **L'éveil d'un somnambule.** (The awakening of a sleepwalker; Das Aufwachen eines Nachtwandlers.)
(Unpublished; Unveröffentlicht.)

1976 The prize was not given; Der Preis wurde nicht vergeben.

1977 The prize was not given; Der Preis wurde nicht vergeben.

1978 Sergi, Christina: **Arabesque.** (Arabesque; Arabeske.)
(Unpublished; Unveröffentlicht.)
(1st prize/1. Preis)

Bérubé, Isabelle: **Le lion des mers.** (The lion of the seas; Der Löwe der Meere.)
(Unpublished; Unveröffentlicht.)
(2nd prize/2. Preis)

1979 Chassay, Jean-François: **Dont act.** (Decreed; Ausgefertigt.)
(Unpublished; Unveröffentlicht.)

1980 Bérard, Diane: **Au-delà des rêves.** (Beyond dreams; Jenseits der Träume.)
(Unpublished; Unveröffentlicht.)
(1st prize/1. Preis)

Lafrance, Roger: **Photo périlleuse.** (Dangerous photo; Gefährliche Aufnahme.)
(Unpublished; Unveröffentlicht.)
(2nd prize/2. Preis.)

Amelia Frances Howard-Gibbon Award

This award, in the form of a bronze medal, has been given annually since 1971 by the Canadian Association of Children's Librarians for the best illustrated book published during the calendar year. The illustrator must be a Canadian resident. The award honours and commemorates the illustrator of "An illustrated Comic Alphabet", considered to be the first Canadian picture book, published in 1859.

Dieser Preis (in Form einer Bronze-Medaille) wird seit 1971 jährlich von der Kanadischen Vereinigung der Kinderbibliothekare verliehen und zwar für das beste im Laufe des Jahres erschienene illustrierte Buch. Der Illustrator muss aus Kanada stammen oder dort leben. Der Preis ehrt das Andenken der ersten kanadischen Kinderbuch-Illustratorin, die im Jahre 1859 das "Illustrated Comic Alphabet" schuf.

1971 Cleaver, Elizabeth in:
Downie, Mary Alice/Robertson, Barbara: **The wind has wings. Poems from Canada.** (Der Wind hat Flügel. Gedichte aus Kanada.)
Toronto: Oxford University Press 1968.

1972 Takashima, Shizuye in:
Takashima, Shizuye: **A child in prison camp.** (Ein Kind im Gefangenenlager.)
Montréal: Tundra Books 1971.

1973 Roussan, Jacques de in:
Roussan, Jacques de: **Au-delà du soleil.** (Beyond the sun; Hinter der Sonne.)
Montréal: Tundra Books 1972.

1974 Kurelek, William in:
Kurelek,William: **A prairie boy's winter.** (Der Winter eines Jungen in der Prärie.)
Montréal: Tundra Books 1973.

1975 Italiano, Carlo in:
Italiano, Carlo: **The sleighs of my childhood.** Les traineaux de mon enfance. (Die Schlitten meiner Kindheit.)
Montréal: Tundra Books 1975.

1976 Kurelek, William in:
Kurelek, William: **The prairie boy's summer.** (Der Sommer eines Jungen in der Prärie.)
Montréal: Tundra Books 1975.

1977 Hall, Pam in:
Pittman, Al: **Down by Jim Long's stage.** (Bei *Jim Longs* Kutschenstation.)
Portugal Cove, Newfoundland: Breakwater 1976.

1978 Cleaver, Elizabeth in:
Toye, William: **The loon's necklace.** (Die Kette des Eistauchers.)
Toronto: Oxford University Press 1977.

1979 Blades, Ann in:
Waterton, Betty: **A salmon for Simon.** (Ein Lachs für *Simon.*)
Vancouver: Douglas & McIntyre 1978.

1980 Gal, Laszlo in:
Lunn, Janet: **The twelve dancing princesses:** A fairy tale retold. (Die 12 tanzenden Prinzessinnen: Ein Märchen wiedererzählt.)
Agincourt: Methuen 1979.

1981 Tait, Douglas in:
Harris, Christie: **The trouble with princesses.** (Die Probleme mit Prinzessinnen.)
Toronto: McClelland & Stewart 1980.

Prix Lettérature de Jeunesse

This prize was established in 1964 by the Ministry of Culture in Québec.

1964 wurde der Preis vom Kulturministerium in Québec gegründet.

1964 Corriveau, Monique: **Le wapiti.** (The wapiti; Der Wapiti.) Ill.: Melinda Wilson.
Québec: Ed. Jeunesse 1964.

1965 Maillet, Andrée: **Le chêne des tempêtes.** (The storm oak; Die Gewitter-Eiche.)
Montréal: Ed. Fides 1965.

1966 Corriveau, Monique: **Le maître de Messire.** (The master from *Messire;* Der Meister von *Messire.*). Ill.: Guy Paradis.
Québec: Ed. Jeunesse 1965.

Durand, Lucile: **Togo, apprenti-remorquer.** (*Togo,* the tow-away truck apprentice; *Togo,* der Schlepper-Neuling.) Ill.: Jean Letarte.
Montréal: Centre de Psychologie et de Pédagogie 1965.

1968 Benoit, Jacques: **Jos Carbone.** *(Jos Carbone.)*
Montréal: Ed. du Jour 1967.

Pinsonneault, Jean-Paul: **Terre d'aube.** (Land of sunrise; Land des Morgenrots.)
Montréal: Ed. Fides 1967.

1970 Lacerte, Rolande: **Le soleil des profondeurs.** (The sun of the depths: Die Sonne der Tiefe.) Ill.: Marcel Martin.
Montréal: Ed. Jeunesse 1968.

Gagnon, Cécile: **Martine aux oiseaux.** (*Martine* with the birds; *Martine* mit den Vögeln.) Ill.: Cécile Gagnon.
Québec: Pelican 1968.

Vicky Metcalf Award

This annual award of 1000 dollars is donated by Mrs. Vicky Metcalf, who has a vital interest in the promotion of Canadian children's literature. The award is administered by the Canadian Author's Association. The purpose of the prize is to stimulate writing for children and it is awarded to an author for the body of his of her work which is of interest to young people.

Vicky Metcalf, die sich für kanadische Jugendliteratur interessiert, stiftete diesen Preis (1000 Dollar). Er wird von der kanadischen Autoren-Vereinigung verliehen und soll dazu anregen, Kinder- und Jugendbücher zu schreiben. Ein Autor bekommt ihn jeweils für sein Gesamtwerk.

1963 Kerr Wood
1964 John Francis Hayes
1965 Roderick Haig-Brown
1966 Fred Swayze
1967 John Patrick Gillese
1968 Lorrie McLaughlin
1969 Audrey McKim
1970 Farley McGill Mowat
1971 Kathleen Louise Hill
1972 William Toye
1973 Christie Harris
1974 Jean Little
1975 Lyn Harrington
1976 Suzanne Martell
1977 James Archibald Houston
1978 Lyn Cook
1979 Cliff Faulknor
1980 John Craig
1981 Monica Hughes

Ruth Schwartz Foundation Award

This award of 2000 dollars was established in 1975 in memory of the Toronto bookseller, Ruth Schwartz. The prize is given annually by the Canadian Bookseller's Association for the best children's book written in English and published in Canada.

Zum Gedenken an die Buchhändlerin Ruth Schwartz aus Toronto wurde dieser Preis (in Höhe von 2000 Dollar) im Jahre 1975 gestiftet. Er wird jährlich vom Kanadischen Buchhändlerverband verliehen und zeichnet das beste englischsprachige Buch aus, das in Kanada erschienen ist.

1976 Richler, Mordecai: **Jacob Two-Two meets the Hooded Fang.** (*Jacob Two-Two* trifft den *Hooded Fang.*) Ill.: Fritz Wegner.
Toronto: McClelland & Stewart 1975.

1977 Allen, Robert Thomas: **The violin.** (Die Geige.)
Scarborough: McGraw-Hill 1976.

1978 Lee, Dennis: **Garbage delight.** (Müllvergnügen.) Ill.: Frank Newfeld.
Toronto: Macmillan 1977.

1979 Major, Kevin: **Hold fast.** (Halte fest.)
Toronto: Clarke, Irwin 1978.

1980 Smucker, Barbara Claassen: **Days of terror.** (Tage des Terrors.)
Toronto: Clarke, Irwin 1979.

Colombia / Kolumbien

Concurso ENKA de Literatura Infantil

This prize was founded in 1976 by the firm "ENKA of Colombia S.A." to promote the development of children's literature in Colombia. The organization and coordination of the prize was carried out by the Ministry of Education and the Colombian Institute of Culture. The first presentation of the award took place in 1977.

Dieser Preis wurde 1976 von der kolumbianischen Firma ENKA GmbH gestiftet um die Entwicklung der kolumbianischen Kinderliteratur zu fördern. Die Organisation und die Durchführung der Preisvergabe liegt beim Erziehungsministerium und beim kolumbianischen Kulturinstitut. Der Preis wurde 1977 zum ersten Mal vergeben.

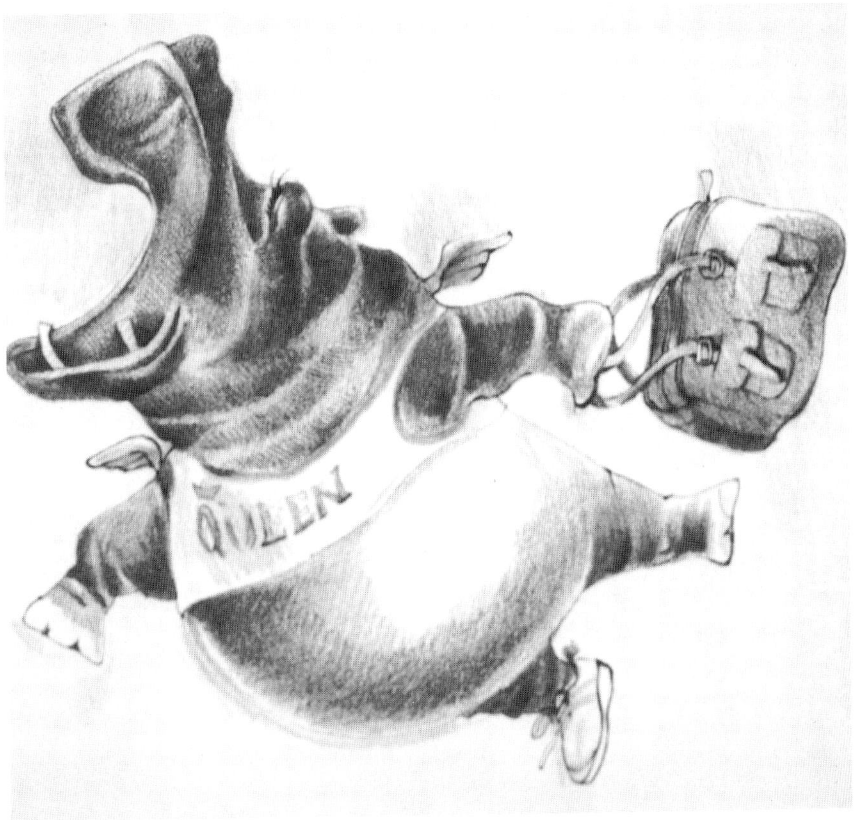

Ill. 9 Victoria Paz in R. Vélez: Hip hipopótamo vagabundo

1977 Niño, Jairo Anibal: **Zoro.** *(Zoro.)* Ill.: Enrique Grau.
Medellín: Colina 1977.

1979 Román, Celso: **Los amigos del hombre.** (The friends of man; Die Freunde der Menschheit.) Ill.: Celso Román.
Medellín: Colina 1979.

Cuba / Kuba

Premio Ismaelillo

This prize was founded in 1973 by "La Unión de Escritores y Artistas de Cuba" (Union of Cuban Writers and Artists) in honour of Cuba's national hero, José Martí. The name of the prize was taken from a children's book written by Martí, "Ismaelillo". A jury of three members makes the selections and a cash-prize of 1000 dollars is awarded to each prize-winning author. The award can be given for works of poetry, novels, stories, plays, essays and biographies written by Cuban authors for children and young people.

Ill. 10 Luis G. Fresquet in I. Altarriba: Como te iba diciendo

Der Preis wurde 1973 von der "Unión de Escritores y Artistas de Cuba" (Schriftsteller- und Künstlerverband Kubas) zu Ehren von José Martí, dem kubanischen Nationalhelden, gestiftet. Der Name des Preises stammt von dem gleichnamigen Kinderbuch Matrís: "Ismaelillo". Eine dreiköpfige Jury trifft die Auswahl. Jeder preisgekrönte Autor erhält einen Geldpreis von 1000 Dollar. Der Preis wird verliehen für Gedichte, Romane, Erzählungen, Dramen, Essays und Biografien, die von kubanischen Autoren verfaßt sind.

1973 *Prose/Prosa*
Miranda, Anisia: **Los cuentos del compay Grillo.** (The stories of godfather, *Grillo;* Die Geschichten des Gevatters *Grillo.*) Ill.: Manuel Bu.
La Habana: UNEAC 1975.

Poetry/Poesie
Balmaseda, Alfredo: **Cantando y adivinando.** (Singing and riddling; Singen und raten.) Ill.: Dario Mora.
La Habana: UNEAC 1975.

1974 *Poetry/Poesie*
Calzadilla Núñez, Julia: **Los poemas cantarines.** (Lyrical poems; Singende Verse.) Ill.: Manuel Bu.
La Habana: UNEAC 1975.

1975 *Poetry/Poesie*
Rodríguez, Giordano: **Para Camilo.** (For *Camilo;* Für *Camilo.*) Ill.: Manuel Bu.
La Habana: UNEAC 1981.

Theatre/Theater
Rodríguez Bouben, Ramón: **Había una vez un jardín.** (There was once a garden; Es war einmal ein Garten.) Ill.: Félix Beltrán.
La Habana: UNEAC 1981.

1976 *Prose/Prosa*
Rodríguez, Antonio Orlando: **Siffig y el Vramontoro.** (*Siffig* and the *Vramontoro; Siffig* und das *Vramontoro.*)
La Habana: UNEAC 1978.

Poetry/Poesie
González Fernández, Orlando: **Lula.** *(Lula.)*
La Habana: UNEAC 1978.

1977 *Poetry/Poesie*
Tormes, Concha: **Nanas para el príncipe Igor.** (Lullabies for prince *Igor:* Wiegenlieder für Prinz *Igor.*) Ill.: Eduardo Abela Alonso.
La Habana: UNEAC 1980.

1978 *Prose/Prosa*
Vilasís, Mayra: **Los días de Serafín Quintero.** (The days of *Serafin Quintero;* Die Tage des *Serafin Quintero.*)
La Habana: UNEAC 1981.

Poetry/Poesie
Martí Fuentes, Adolfo: **Por el ancho camino.** (The wide road; Den breiten Weg entlang.)
La Habana: UNEAC 1981.

Premio de Literatura para Niños y Jóvenes "13 de Marzo"

This annual prize for children's and youth literature was founded in 1975 by the University of Havana. It was established to commemorate the uprising on March 13, 1957 against the regime of Fulgencio Baptista, led by the university student; José Antonio Echeverría.

Der Preis, der seit 1975 verliehen wird, wurde von der Universität Havanna gestiftet. Er erinnert an den Aufstand vom 13. März 1957 gegen das Regime Fulgencio Baptista. Der Aufstand wurde von dem Studenten José Antonio Echeverría angeführt.

1975 Vian, Enid: **Cuentos de sol y luna.** (Stories of sun and moon; Geschichten von Sonne und Mond.) Ill.: Luís G. Fresquet (i.e. Chamaco).
La Habana: Universidad de la Habana 1977.

1976 Gonzalez Lopez, Waldo: **Poemas y canciones.** (Poems and songs; Gedichte und Lieder.) Ill.: Luís G. Fresquet (i.e. Chamaco.)
La Habana: Universidad de La Habana 1977.

1977 Vian Altarriba, Ivette: **Como te iba diciendo ..** (As you were saying . . .; Wie gesagt . . .) Ill.: Luís G. Fresquet (i.e. Chamaco).
La Habana: Universidad de la Habana 1977.

1978 Gutierrez, José A.: **Por entre los sueños.** Canto. (Between dreams. Verse; Zwischen den Träumen. Verse.)
(Unpublished; Unveröffentlicht.

1979 Yanez, Alberto Jorge: **Cuentos de Penélope.** (Stories about *Penelope;* Geschichten von *Penelope.*)
(Unpublished; Unveröffentlicht.)

1980 The prize was not given; Der Preis wurde nicht vergeben.

1981 Gallegos, Emilia: **Para un niño travieso.** (For a naughty child; Für ein unartiges Kind.)
(Unpublished; Unveröffentlicht.)

Czechoslovakia / Tschechoslowakei

Cena Zväzu slovenských spisovateľov

This prize offered by the Slovakian Writer's Union is awarded annually to the best children's book published during the previous year.

Der Preis des Slovakischen Schriftstellerverbandes für Kinder- und Jugendliteratur wird für ein bedeutendes Werk aus der Kinder- und Jugendbuchproduktion des vergangenen Jahres verliehen.

1970 Jarunková, Klára: **Brat mlčanlivého vlka.** (The brother of the taciturn wolf; Der Bruder des schweigenden Wolfes.) Ill.: Ivan Schurman.
Bratislava: Mladé letá 1967.

Válek, Miroslav: **Do Trantarie.** (To *Tramtaria;* Nach *Tramtarien.*) Ill.: Miroslav Cipár.
Bratislava: Mladé letá 1969.

1971 Moric, Rudo: **Collected works in the area of children's literature;** Für sein Gesamtschaffen auf dem Gebiet der Kinderliteratur.

1972 Gašparová, Eleonóra: **Collected works in the area of children's literature;** Für ihr Gesamtschaffen auf dem Gebiet der Kinderliteratur.

1973 Bendová, Krista: **Osmijankove rozpravký.** (*Osmijanko's* stories; *Osmijankos* Geschichten.) Ill.: Božena Plochánová-Hajdučíková.
Bratislava: Mladé letá 1971.

1974 Beňo, Jan: **Škola sa začína v máji.** (School begins in May; Die Schule beginnt im Mai.) Ill.: Peter Ondreicka.
Bratislava: Mladé letá 1974.

1975 Feldek, Lubomír: **Modrá kniha rozprávok.** (The blue fairy tale book; Das blaue Märchenbuch.) Ill.: Albín Brunovský.
Bratislava: Mladé letá 1974.

1976 Rúfus, Milan: **Kniha rozprávok.** (Fairy tale book; Märchenbuch.) Ill.: Viera Krajčová.
Bratislava: Mladé letá 1975.

1977 Handzová, Viera: **Davno sa tmy nebojím.** (For a long time now, I am no longer afraid of the dark; Ich fürchte mich schon lange nicht mehr vor der Finsternis.) Ill.: Vladimír Chovan.
Bratislava: Mladé letá 1977.

1978 Ďuričková, Mária: **Dunajská král'ovná.** (The Danube queen; Die Donaukönigin.) Ill.: Miroslav Cipár.
Bratislava: Mladé letá 1976.

Ill. 11 Karel Svolinský in: Červená labuť

Ill. 12 Marián Minarovič in J. Navrátil: Lampáš malého plavčika

Ďuričková, Mária: **Prešporsky zvon.** (The *Pressburg* bell; Die *Pressburger* Glocke.) Ill.: Miroslav Cipár.
Bratislava: Mladé letá 1978.

1979 Jančová, Mária: **Žofkine rozprávky.** (*Sophie's* fairy tale; *Sophies* Märchen.) Ill.: Igor Rumanský.
Bratislava: Mladé letá 1979.

1980 Moric, Rudo: **Podivuhodné príbehy Adama Brezuľu.** (The wonderful adventures of *Adam Brezula;* Die wunderbaren Abenteuer des *Adam Brezula.*) Ill.: Igor Rumanský.
Bratislava: Mladé letá 1980.

Prémie Ceského Literarního Fondu

This prize founded by the Czech Literature Foundation is awarded annually to the most exemplary children's books and theoretical and critical works dealing with children's literature. The prize was first given in 1977.

Der "Preis des Čechischen Literaturfonds" wird von diesem jährlich für die bedeutendsten Werke aus dem Bereich der Kinderliteratur und aus der Literaturwissenschaft und -kritik der Kinderliteratur verliehen. Der Preis wurde erstmals im Jahre 1977 verliehen.

1977 Bezděková, Zdeňka: **Děvčatko Zdena a moudrý pes.** (The girl, *Zdena,* and the wise dog; Das Mädchen *Zdena* und der kluge Hund.)
Praha: Albatros 1977.

Kovářík, Vladimír: **Literární toulky po Čechach.** (Literary travel through Bohemia; Literarische Wanderungen durch Böhmen.)
Praha: Albatros 1977.

Šusta, Stanislav: **Na rozcestí dějin.** (At the crossroads of history; Am Scheideweg der Geschichte.) Ill.: Antonie Pvondrová.
Praha: Albatros 1977.

Scholarly work and criticism/Literaturwissenschaft und -kritik
Holešovský, František: **Ilustrace pro děti.** (Illustrations for children; Illustrationen für Kinder.)
Praha: Albatros 1977.

1978 Černík, Michal: **Kdy má pampeliška svátek.** (When the dandelion had its name day; Wenn der Löwenzahn Namenstag hat.) Ill.: Olga Franzová.
Praha: Albatros 1978.

Hercíková, Iva: **Andrsenka.** (Little *Andersen; Andersenchen.*) Ill.: František Klenský.
Praha: Albatros 1978.

Klevis, Vladimír: **Setkaní s Michaelou.** (The encounter with *Michaela;* Die Begegnung mit *Michaela.*) Ill.: Josef Duchoň.
Praha: Albatros 1978.

Šmahelová, Helena: **Kdy přijde Dora.** (When *Dora* comes; Wenn *Dora* kommt.) Ill.: Dagmar Berková.
Praha: Albatros 1977.

Žáček, Jiři: **Aprílová škola.** (The April school; Die Aprilschule.) Ill.: Adolf Born.
Praha: Albatros 1978.

Scholarly work and criticism/Literaturwissenschaft und -kritik
Strnadel, Josef: **Rodná řeč poezie.** (Mother tongue poetry; Muttersprache Poesie.)
Praha: Albatros 1978.

1979 Křenek, Petr: **Devět Martinových dnů.** (*Martin's* nine days; Neun Tage *Martins.*) Ill.: Zdeněk Filip.
Praha: Albatros 1979.

Cena Nakladatelství Albatros

After the regulations of the Marie Majerová Prize were changed (now given exclusively to the collected works of authors and illustrators), there still remained the need for a prize which could be given to outstanding books published each year. The prize of the SNDK Publishing House was established for this purpose. The prize consists of a cash award. In 1969 the name, SNDK, was chenged to Albatros Publishers.

Nachdem die Statuten des Marie-Majerová-Preises geändert und der Preis nunmehr für das Gesamtschaffen eines Autors oder Illustrators verliehen wird, blieb doch die Notwendigkeit bestehen, beste Bücher unter den Neuerscheinungen hervorzuheben. Für diesen Zweck wurde der Preis des Verlages SNDK gestiftet. Er wird verliehen in Form eines Geldbetrages. Der Verlag SNDK wurde umbenannt und heißt seit 1969 Albatros Verlag.

1966 Kocourek, Vítězslav: **Vesmír, země, člověk — a my děti.** (The cosmos, the earth, mankind and we children; Der Kosmos, die Erde, der Mensch und wir Kinder.) Ill.: Jiří Rathouský and Dora Novákova.
Praha: SNDK 1966.

Macourek, Miloš: **Mravenéčník v početnici.** (The anteater in the copybook; Der Ameisenbär im Rechenheft.) Ill.: Miroslav Štěpánek.
Paraha: SNDK 1966.

Mrázková, Daisy: **Neplač, neplač, muchomůrko.** (Don't cry, little toadstool; Weine nicht, kleiner Fliegenpilz.) Ill.: Daisy Mrázková.
Praha: SNDK 1965.

Illustration
Kolíbal, Stanislav in:
Reis, Vladimir: **Kristálové sestry.** (The crystal sisters; Die kristallenen Schwestern.)
Praha: SNDK 1965.

Mrázková, Daisy in:
Mrázková, Daisy: **Neplač, neplač, muchomůrko.** (Don't cry little toadstool; Weine nicht, kleiner Fliegenpilz.)
Praha: SNDK 1965.

Nováková, Dora in:
Kocourek, Vítězslav: **Vermír, země, člověk – a my děti.** (The cosmos, the earth, mankind and we children; Der Kosmos, die Erde, der Mensch und wir Kinder.)
Praha: SNDK 1966.
Rathouský, Jiři in:
Kocourek, Vítězslav: **Vesmír, země, člověk – a my děti.** (The cosmos, the earth, mankind and we children; Der Kosmos, die Erde, der Mensch und wir Kinder.)
Praha: SNDK 1966.

Layout/Ausstattung
Sekal, Zbyněk for:
Albatros book series; Buchreihe Albatros.

1967 Aškenazy, Ludvík: **Malá vánoční povídka.** (Little Christmas fairy tales; Das kleine Weihnachtsmärchen.) Ill.: Hana Štěpánová.
Praha: SNDK 1966.

Bodláková, Jitka: **Erich Kästner.** *(Erich Kästner.)*
Praha: SNDK 1966.

Hazlík, Josef: **Sněhová hvězdička.** (Snow flakes; Schneeflöckchen.)
Ill.: Květa Pacovská.
Praha: SNDK 1966.

Seifert, Jaroslav: **Halleyova kometa.** *(Halley's Comet; Halleys Komet.)*
Ill.: Jiří Trnka.
Praha: SNDK 1966.

Illustration
Bednářová, Eva in:
Franková, Hermína: **Blázni a Pythagoras.** (The fools and *Pythagoras;* Die Narren und *Pythagoras.*)
Praha: SNDK 1966.

Bednářová, Eva in:
Bezděková, Zdeňka: **Říkali mi Leni.** They called me *Leni;* Man nannte mich *Leni.*)
Praha: SNDK 1967.

Bednářová, Eva in:
Pujmanová, Marie: **Předtucha.** (The foreboding; Die Vorahnung.)
Praha: SNDK 1967.

Pacovská, Květa in:
Hanzlík, Josef: **Sněhová hvězdička.** (Snow flakes; Schneeflöckchen.)
Praha: SNDK 1966.

Editor/Herausgeber
Brousek, Antonín in:
Postavit vejce po Kolumbovi. (To stand the egg on end as *Columbus* did; Das Ei des *Kolumbus.*)
Praha: SNDK 1967.

Hirsal, Josef in:
Postavit vejce po Kolumbovi. (To stand the egg on end as *Columbus* did; Das Ei des *Kolumbus.*)
Praha: SNDK 1967.

1968 Brukner, Josef: **Z Ladovy zahrádky.** (From *Lada's* garden; aus *Ladas Garten.)* Ill.: Josef Lada.
Praha: SNDK 1968.

Florian, Miroslav: **Jake oči má vítr.** (What kind of eyes has the wind; Was für Augen hat der Wind.) Ill.: Josef Palaček.
Praha: SNDK 1968.

Heřman, Zdeněk: **Bohumil Říha.** *(Bohumil Říha.)*
Praha: SNDK 1968.

Kupka, Jiři S: **Prázdniny s Dominkou.** (Vacation with *Dominica;* Ferien mit *Dominika.*) Ill.: Jan Brychta.
Praha: SNDK 1968.

Lukešová, Milena: **Bačkůrky z mechu.** (Moss slippers; Pantöffelchen aus Moos.) Ill.: Mirko Hanák.
Praha: SNDK 1968.

Šolc, Václav/Hořejš, Petr: **Najstarši Američané.** (The oldest Americans; Die ältesten Amerikaner.) Ill.: Jaromir Vrastil
Praha: SNDK 1968.

Vladislav, Jan: **Král sedmi závojů.** (King of the seven veils; König der sieben Schleier.) Ill.: Zdenek Seydl.
Praha: SNDK 1968.

Illustration
Kudláček, Jan in:
Claudius, Eduard: **Když se ryby pásly na nebil.** (When the fish grazed in the sky; Als die Fische am Himmel weideten; Germ.orig.title: Als die Fische die Sterne schluckten.)
Praha: SNDK 1967.

Vimr, Luděk in:
Zucconi, Guiglem: **Klaun Skaramakaj.** (Clown, *Skaramakai;* Ital.orig.title: *Scaramacai* e la donna Baronessa.)
Praha: SNDK 1968.

Graphic design/Grafische Gestaltung
Grygar, Milan for:
Brukner, Josef: **Z Ladovy zahrádky.** (From *Lada's* garden; Aus *Ladas* Garten.) Ill.: Josef Lada.
Praha: SNDK 1968.

Grygar, Milan for:
Daudet, Alfons: **Tartarin z Tarascon;** (*Tartarin* from Tarascon; *Tartarin* von Tarascon; Fr.orig.title: *Tartarin* de Tarascon.) Ill.: Vladimir Tesar.
Praha: SNDK 1968.

Pavalová, Olga for:
Kratký, Radovan: **Báje, žerta, pohádky a dobrodružné zkazy o putováni na Mesic.** (Myths, wittitcisms, fairy tales and adventure stories about traveling to the moon; Mythen, Witze, Märchen und abenteuerliche Geschichten über Reisen zum Mond.) Ill.
Praha: SNDK 1967.

1969 Kleibl, Josef: **Cesta za Adamem.** (On the trail of *Adam;* Auf *Adams* Spuren.) Ill.: Zdeněk Burian/Jindřich Hegr.
Praha: Albatros 1969.

Kovařík, Vladimír: **Staropražske romance.** (Romance of old Prague; Alt-Prager Romanzen.) Photos.
Praha: Albatros 1969.

Strnadel, Josef: **Zamrzlá studánka.** (The frozen spring; Der zugefrorene Brunnen.) Ill.: Antonín Strnadel.
Praha: Albatros 1969.

Trefulka, Jan: **Tajemstvi tajemníka Růdamóra.** (Secrets of the secretary, Rudamor; Geheimnisse des Sekretärs *Rudamor.*) Ill.: Jan Zbanek.
Praha: Albatros 1969.

Illustration
Procházka, František in:
Mezera, Alois: **Nase stromy a kere.** (Our trees and shrubs; Unsere Bäume und Sträucher.)
Praha: Albatros 1969.

Strnadel, Antonín in:
Strnadel, Josef:
Zamrzlá studánka. (The frozen spring; Der zugefrorene Brunnen.)
Praha: Albatros 1969.

Graphic design/Grafische Gestaltung
Grygar, Milan for:
Hejna, Olga: **Povidali, že mu hráli.** (Don't pull my leg; Mach mir doch nichts vor.) Ill.: Jan Brychta, Stanislav Kolíbal, et al.
Praha: Albatros 1969.

1970 Hanzák, Jan: **Světem zviřat.** Sv. 1—5. (Through the animal world. Vol. 1—5; Durch die Welt der Tiere. Bd. 1—5.) Ill.: Antonín Pospíšil.
Praha: Albatros 1970.

Translation/Übersetzung
Kornelová, Marie for:
Adaptation and translation/Bearbeitung und Übersetzung of Grimm, Jakob/Grimm, Wilhelm: Pohádky bratři Grimů. (Fairy tales of the brothers *Grimm;* Märchen der Brüder *Grimm;* Germ.orig.title: Kinder- und Hausmärchen.) Ill.: Jiři Trnka.
Praha: Albatros 1969.

Illustration
Hanák, Mirko in:
Williamson, Henry: **Vodni poutník Tarka.** (*Tarka,* the otter; *Tarka,* die Otter; Eng.orig.title: *Tarka,* the otter.)
Praha: Albatros 1970.

Pospísil, Antonín in:
Hanzák, Jan: **Světem zviřat.** Sv. 1—5. (Through the animal world. Vo. 1—5; Durch die Tierwelt. Bd. 1—5.)
Praha: Albatros 1970.

Seydl, Zdenek in:
Dvořáčková, Vlasta: **Uletělo čapi pero.** (The stork feather flew away; Die Storchenfeder flog fort.)
Praha: Albatros 1970.

1971 Čtvrtek, Václav: **Kočičiny kocourka Damiána.** (Music of *Damian* the cat; Katzenmusik des Katers *Damian.*) Ill.: Gabriela Dubská.
Praha: Albatros 1971.

Petiška, Eduard: **Čtení o hradech.** (Stories about castles; Erzählungen über Burgen.) Ill.: Zdeněk Mézl.
Praha: Albatros 1971.

Říha, Václav: **Po stopách života.** (On the trail of life; Auf den Spuren des Lebens.) Ill.: Vaclav Bláha/Zdenek/Dušan Říha.
Praha Albatros 1971.

Translation/Übersetzung
Gel, František for:
Doyle, Sir Arthur Conan: **Ztracený svět.** (The lost world; Die verlorene Welt; Eng.orig.title: The lost world.)
Ill.: Pavel Brom.
Praha: Albatros 1971.

Illustration
Čechová, Olga for:
Children's book illustrations, 1971; Illustrationen in Kinderbüchern 1971.

Zmatlíková, Helena in:
Hain-Týnecký, Josef: **Vrabec tulák. Kmotr ježek.** (Sparrow, the tramp. Brother hedgehog; Spatz, der Landstreicher. Gevatter Igel.)
Praha: Albatros 1971.

Graphic design/Grafische Gestaltung
Kopřiva, Milan for:
Petiška, Eduard: **Čtení o hradech.** (Stories about castles; Erzählungen über Burgen.) Ill.: Zdeněk Mézl.
Praha: Albatros 1971.

Kopřiva, Milan for:
Landau, Lev D./Rumer, Jurij B.: **Co to je relativity.** (The theory of relativity; Was ist Relativitätstheorie; Russ.orig.title: Čto takoje teorija otnositelnosti.) Ill.: Jaroslav Malák.
Praha: Albatros 1971.

Kopřiva, Milan for:
Sigsgaars, Jens: **Míta sám na světe.** (*Mitya* alone in the world; *Mitja* allein auf der Welt; Dan.orig.title: *Palle* alene i verden.) Ill.: Adolf Born.
Praha: Albatros 1971.

Honourable mention illustration prize/Illustrations-Ehrenpreise
Sigmundová, Jana in:
Hanzlík, Josef: **Princ v zeleném království.** (The prince in the green kingdom; Der Prinz im grünen Königreich.)
Praha: Albatros 1971.

Honourable mention/Ehrenvolle Erwähnung
Čarek, Jan for:
Selections from his poetic work, "Čarokruh"; Auswahl aus seinem poetischen Werk *"Čarokruh"*.
Praha: Albatros 1971.

1972 Branislav, František: **Básně dětem.** (Poetry for children; Gedichte für Kinder.) Ill.: Karel Beneš.
Praha: Albatros 1971.

Adla, Zdeněk: **100 kapek.** (100 drops; 100 Tropfen.) Ill.: Zdeněk Adla.
Praha: Albatros 1971.

Chaloupka, Otokar: **Horizonty čtenářství.** (Reader-horizon; Leserhorizonte.)
Praha: Albatros 1971.

Syrovátka, Oldřich: **Pohádky z duhové zahrádky.** (Fairy tales from the rainbow garden; Märchen aus dem Regenbogengarten.) Ill.: Helena Zmatlíková.
Praha: Albatros 1972.

Illustration
Born, Adolf in:
Kadecková, Helena: **Oli, tvůj kamarád z Islandu.** (*Oli,* your friend from Iceland: *Oli,* dein Kamerad aus Island.)
Praha: Albatros 1972.

Born, Adolf in:
Kopřuvy, Milan: **Míťa sám na světě.** (*Mitja,* alone in the world; *Mitja* allein auf der Welt; Dan.orig.title: *Palle* alene i verden.)
Praha: Albatros 1971.

Born, Adolf in:
Syrovátka, Oldrich: **Zatoulané písmenko.** (The lost letter; Der verlorengegangene Buchstabe.)
Praha: Albatros 1972.

Honourable mention/Ehrenvolle Erwähnung
Nezkusil, Vladimír: **Spor o specifičnost dětské literatury.** (Controversy over the specific nature of children's literature; Streit über die Besonderheit der Kinderliteratur.)
Praha: Albatros 1971.

Graphic design/Grafische Gestaltung
Hegar, Milan for:
Feld, Friedrich (i.e. Friedrich Rosenfeld): **Mistr z Mohuče.** (The master from Mainz; Germ.orig.title: Der Meister von Mainz.) Ill.
Praha: Albatros 1972.

1973 Bořkocová, Hana: **My tři cvoci.** (The crazy three; Wir drei Spinner.) Ill.: Kamil Lhoták.
Praha: Albatros 1973.

Translation/Übersetzung
Hulák, Jaroslav for:
Standjukovič, Konstantin: **Muž přez palubu.** (A man overboard; Ein Mann über Bord.) Ill.: Dagmar Sedlácková.
Praha: Albatros 1973.

Vritšova, Jiřina for:
Asbjörnsen, Peter Christen/Moe, Jörgen: **Princezny z Modrého vrchu.**) (Princesses from *Blue Hill;* Prinzessinnen vom *Blauem Hügel;* Nor.orig.title: Norske folke eventyr.) Ill.: Václav Kabát.
Praha: Albatros 1973.

Illustration
Hísek, Dvětoslav in:
Deyl, Miloš: **Naše květiny.** (Our flowers; Unsere Blumen.)
Praha: Albatros 1973.

Kabát, Václav in:
Asbjörnsen, Peter Christen/Moe, Jörgen: **Princezny z Modrého vrchu.**)Princesses from *Blue Hill;* Prinzessinnen vom *Blauen Hügel.*)
Praha: Albatros 1973.

Graphic design/Grafische Gestaltung
Grygar, Milan for:
series/Reihe: "Zlatoroh". (Goldhorn.)

1974 Adlová, Věra/Adla, Zdeněk: **Vyprávěmie o veliké zemi.** (Stories from a big land; Erzählungen von einem großen Land.) Ill.: Zdenek Mlćoch.
Praha: Albatros 1974.

Hofmann, Ota: **Červená kůlna.** (The red shelters; Der rote Schuppen.) Photos: Jan Kudela.
Praha: Albatros 1974.

Říha, Bohumil: **Jak jel Vítek do Prahy.** (How little *Vitek* went to Prague; Wie der kleine *Vitek* nach Prag fuhr). Ill.: Adolf Born.
Praha: Albatros 1973.

Řiha, Bohumil: **Vítek je zase doma.** (*Vitek* is home again; *Vitek* ist wieder zu Hause.) Ill.: Adolf Born.
Praha: Albatros 1974.

Translation/Übersetzung
Pražaková, Hana for:
O lesním carovi. Ukrajinsó pohádky. (The lord of the woods.

Ukrainian fairy tales; Der Herrscher des Waldes. Ukrainische Märchen.) Ill.: Jiří Šindler.
Praha: Albatros 1974.

New edition/Neuauflage
Huplach, Vladimír for:
New adaptation/Nacherzählung; **Návrat Operného hada.** (The return of the feathered snake; Die Rückkehr der gefiederten Schlange.) Ill.: Miroslav Troup.
Praha: Albatros 1974.

Illustration
Born, Adolf in:
Říha, Bohumil: **Jak jel Vítek do Prahy.** (How little *Vitek* went to Prague; Wie der kleine *Vitek* nach Prag fuhr.)
Praha: Albatros 1973.

Born, Adolf in:
Říha, Bohumil: **Vítek je zase doma.** (*Vitek* is home again; Der kleine *Vitek* ist wieder zu Hause.)
Praha: Albatros 1974.

Vraštil, Jaromir in:
Salgari, Emilio: **Město malomocného krále.** (The town of the powerless King; Die Stadt des machtlosen Königs.)
Praha: Albatros 1974.

Zábranský, Adolf in:
Zábranský, Adolf: **Česke a moravské pohďky.** (Czech and Moravian fairy tales; Tschechische und mährische Märchen.)
Praha: Albatros 1974.

1975 Bernadinová, Eva: **Kluci, holky a stodůlky.** (Boys, girls and *Stodulky;* Jungen, Mädchen und *Stodulky.*) Ill.: Alena Ladová.
Praha: Albatros 1975.

Ryska, Jan: **Martin v ráji.** (*Martin* in paradise; *Martin* im Paradies.) Ill.: Helena Rokytová.
Praha: Albatros 1975.

Illustration
Müller, Karel in:
Hinderks-Kutscher, Rotraut: **Malý Wolfgang Amadeus.** (Little *Wolfgang Amadeus:* Der kleine *Wolfgang Amadeus;* Germ.orig.title: Donnerblitzbub *Wolfgang Amadeus.*)
Praha: Albatros 1975.

1976 *New edition/Neuauflage*
Michl, Karel: **Babiččino údoli.** (Grandmother's valley; Grossmuttertal.) Photos: Zdeněk Manec.
Praha: Albatros 1976.

Illustration
Paleček, Josef in:
Nepil, František: **Makový mužiček.** (The poppyman; Das Mohnmännchen.)
Praha: Albatros 1976.

1977 Doskočilová, Hana: **Eliška a táta Král.** (*Eliška* and *Daddy King;* Eliška und *Papa König.*) Ill.: Jaroslav Malák.
Praha: Albatros 1977.

Šusta, Stanislav: **Na rozcesti dějin.** (At the crossroads of history; Am Scheideweg der Geschichte.) Ill.: Antonie Povondrová.
Praha: Albatros 1977.

Urbánková, Jarmila: **Mladá vichřice.** (The young whirlwind; Der junge Sturmwind.) Ill.: Denisa Wagnerová.
Praha: Albatros 1977.

Illustration
Kalousek, Jiří in:
Říha, Bohumil: **Dětská enciklopedie.** (Children's encyclopedia; Kinderlexikon.)
Praha: Albatros 1977.

Mézl, Zdeněk in:
Zlatá kniha historických prběhů. (The golden book of historical events; Das goldene Buch der historischen Ereignisse.)
Praha: Albatros 1977.

Translation/Übersetzung
Fromková, Jarmila in:
Fadeev, Aleksandr Aleksandrovič: **Příběhy našeho mládí.** (Novel of our youth; Roman unserer Jugend.)
Praha: Albatros 1977.

1978 Kovářík, Vladimír: **Literárni toulky Moravou.** (Literary tours through Moravia; Literarische Wanderungen durch Mähren.) Photos: Pavel Štecha. Maps: Jiří Tesař.
Praha: Albatros 1978.

Bernardinová, Eva: **Kluci, holky a Stodůlky.** (Boys, girls and one hundred valleys; Jungen, Mädchen und hundert Täler.) Ill.: Alena Ladová.
Praha: Albatros 1978.

Illustration
Jágr, Miloslav in:
Sirovátka, Oldřich: **Plny pytel pohádek.** (A sack full of fairy tales; Ein Sack voll Märchen.)
Praha: Albatros 1978.

Honourable mention/Ehrenverleihung
Lukešová, Milena: Zimní knížka pro Lucinku. (A winter book for *Lucinka;* Ein Winterbuch für *Lucinka.*) Ill.: Jana Sigmundová.
Praha: Albatros 1978.

Safír, Marcel: **Hmyz je docela jiný.** (An insect is completely different; Ein Insekt ist ganz anders.) Photos: Marcel Safír.
Praha: Albatros 1977.

Cibula, Václav: **Cid a jeho věrní.** (The *Cid* and his loyal follwers; Der *Cid* und seine Getreuen.) Ill.: Karel Teissing.
Praha: Albatros 1978.

1979 Petiška, Eduard: **Čtení o zámcích a městech.** (Reading selections about castles and towns; Lesestücke über Schlösser und Städte.) Ill.: Zdeněk Mézl.
Praha: Albatros 1979.

Šmahelová, Helena: **Dora na cestách.** (*Dora,* traveling; *Dora* auf Reisen.) Ill.: Josef Novák.
Praha: Albatros 1978.

Illustration
Novák, Josef in:
North, Sterling: **Dareba.** (Amer.orig.title: Rascal; *Rascal,* der Waschbär.)
Praha: Albatros 1978.

Honourable mention/Ehrenverleihung
Vančurová, Eva: **Bystrozraký Filip.** (Sharp-sighted *Philipp;* Der scharfsichtige *Philipp.*) Ill.: Miloš Noll.
Praha: Albatros 1976.

Černý, Jan in:
Vivierová, C. (i.e. Colette Vivier): Malé divadlo. (The little theater; Das kleine Theater; Fr.orig.title: Le petit théâtre.)
Praha: Albatros 1979.

Černý, Jan in:
LeRoy, Eugène: **Trhan Kuba.** (*Jacquon* the rebel; *Jacquon* der Rebell.)
Praha: Albatros 1979.

1980 Klevis, Vladimír: **Jakub a Ingrid.** (*Jacob* and *Ingrid; Jacob* und *Ingrid.*) Ill.: Pavel Sivko.
Praha: Albatros 1980.

Lukešová, Milena: **Jak je bosé noze v rose.** (Barefoot through the dew; Barfuss durch den Tau.) Ill.: Jitka Walterová.
Praha: Albatros 1981.

Illustration
Svolinský, Karel in:
Červená labuť. Jedenáct pohádek. (The red swan. Eleven fairy tales; Der rote Schwan. Elf Märchen.)
Praha: Albatros 1980.

Honourable mention/Ehrenverleihung
Holeček, Jaroslav/Vacková, Marie: **Osamelá vlčice.** (The lonesome she-wolf; Die einsame Wölfin.) Photos: Jaroslav Holeček.
Praha: Albatros 1980.

Illustration
Mikulka, Alois in:
Čukovskij, Kornej: **Hádanky a povídačky děda Kořena.** (Grandfather *Root's* stories and riddles; Rätsel und Erzählungen von Großvater Wurzel; Russ.orig.title: Čudo-derevo i drugie skazki.)
Praha: Albatros 1980.

Mikulka, Alois in:
Feldek, Ľubomír: **Rýmy a šprýmy.** (Verses and jokes; Verse und Possen.)
Praha: Albatros 1980.

Mrázková, Daisy in:
Mrázková, Daisy: **Co by se stalo, kdyby . . .** (What would happen if . . . Was würde geschehen, wenn . . .)
Praha: Albatros 1980.

Cena Ľudovíta Fullu

This prize, formerly a part of the Fraňo Kráľ Prize, was created in 1977 and is named after Ludovit Fulla (1902—), the famous Slovakian illustrator. It is awarded annually to an outstanding illustrator.

Dieser Illustrationspreis, der früher Teil des Fraňo Kráľ Preises war, wurde 1977 ins Leben gerufen und nach dem berühmten slowakischen Illustrator Ludovit Fulla (1902—) benannt. Er wird jährlich an einen herausragenden Illustrator vergeben.

1977 Ladislav Nesselman
1978 Vladimír Machaj
1979 Miroslav Cipár
1980 Mária Želibská
1981 Ľuba Končeková-Veselá

Cena Fraňa Kráľa

The Slovak Minister for Cultural Affairs and Information presents the Fraňo Kráľ Prize annually following the recommendation of the Circle of Friends of the Children's Book. It is awarded for outstanding achievement in the field of juvenile literature. In special cases the award is given in memoriam. Since 1977, the prize for illustration has been given separately from the literature prize and is now called the Cena Ľudovíta Fullu. In addition to a cash award the recipient receives a bronze plaque. The prize is named after the founder of the Slovak socialist realist juvenile literature, Fraňo Kráľ (1903—1954).

Vom slovakischen Kultur- und Informationsminister wird auf Vorschlag des Kreises der Kinderbuchfreunde alljährlich der Fraňo-Kráľ-Preis für ein Gesamtwerk oder aussergewöhnliche Verdienste auf dem Gebiet der Kinder- und Jugendliteratur verliehen (ausnahmsweise auch in memoriam.) Seit 1977 wird die Auszeichnung für Illustration — unter dem Namen Cena Ľudovíta Fullu — vom literarischen Preis getrennt vergeben. Der Preisträger wird mit einer Bronzeplakette ausgezeichnet und erhält darüber hinaus eine Geldprämie. Benannt wurde der Preis nach dem Begründer der slovakischen sozialistisch-realistischen Kinderliteratur, dem Schriftsteller Fraňo Kráľ (1903—1954).

1965 *Literature/Literatur*
Jozef Horák
Ľudo Ondrejov (in memoriam)
Mária Rázusová-Martákova (in memoriam)
Illustration
Ľudovít Fulla

1966 *Literature/Literatur*
Ľudo Zúbek
Illustration
Vincent Hložník

1967 *Literature/Literatur*
Rudo Moric
Illustration
Jaroslav Vodrážka

1968 *Literature/Literatur*
Mária Ďuríčková
Illustrator
Štefan Cpin

1969 *Literature/Literatur*
Krista Bendová
Illustration
Albín Brunovský

1970 *Literature/Literatur*
Mária Jančová
Dominik Štubňa-Źámostský (in memoriam)
Illustration
Ľubomír Kellenberger

1971 *Literature/Literatur*
Elena Čepčeková
Illustration
Alojz Klimo

1972 *Literature/Literatur*
Ľubomír Feldek
Illustration
Róbert Dúbravec

1973/ *Literature/Literatur*
1974 Miroslav Válek
Illustration
Jozef Baláž

1975 *Literature/Literatur*
Klára Jarunková
Illustration
Viera Bombová

1976 *Literature/Literatur*
Ján Bedenek
Ferdinand Hložník

1977 Vojtech Zamarovský

1978 Eleonóra Gašparová
Ján Poliak (in memoriam)

1979 Hans Zelinová

1980 Ján Navrátil

1981 Stanislav Šmatlák

Cena Marie Majerové

The Circle of the Friends of the Children's Book, Prague (Kruh přatel dětské knihy) presents the Marie Majerová Prize to authors and illustrators of the best Czech children's books. This is equivalent to the Frano Kráľ Prize which is given to Slovak authors and illustrators in Bratislava. Because of the establishment of the Albatros Prize, the regulations of the Marie Majerová Prize were changed in 1965. Upon the suggestion of the jury of the Circle of Friends of the Children's Book, the Minister of Cultural Affairs now presents the prize every other year to a living author or illustrator for their collected works. The prize is named after the children's book authoress, Marie Bartošová (1882—1967), who won internatinal fame under her pseudonym, Marie Majerová.

Der Kreis der Freunde des Kinderbuches in Prag (Kruh prátel détské knihy) erteilt Autoren und Illustratoren bester tschechischer Kinderbücher den Marie-Majerová-Preis. Er entspricht dem in Pressburg (Bratislava) erteilten Fraňo-Král-Preis für slovakische Kinderbücher, Autoren und Illustratoren. 1965 wurden wegen der Einführung des Verlagspreises von SNDK (jetzt Albatros) die Statuten geändert. Auf Antrag der Jury des Kreises der Freunde des Kinderbuches verleiht nunmehr (in einem Turnus von zwei Jahren) der Kultusminister lebenden Autoren oder Illustratoren für ihr gesamtes bisheriges Schaffen den Marie-Majerová-Preis. Der Preis wurde benannt nach der Kinder- und Jugendbuchautorin Marie Bartośová (1882—1967), die unter dem Pseudonym Marie Majerová international bekannt wurde.

1961 Čivrný, Lumír: **Čokoládová princezna a juné pohádky školní a předškolní.** (The chocolate princess and other fairy tales for school and pre-school children; Die Schokoladenprinzessin und andere Märchen für Schul- und Vorschulkinder.) Ill.: Vratislav Hlavatý.
Praha: SNDK 1961.

Gel, František: **Přemožitel neviditelný dravců.** (Conqueror of the invisible parasites; Der Überwinder der unsichtbaren Schädlinge.) Ill.
Praha: SNDK 1959.

Kriebel, Zdeněk: **Koulej se sluníčko, kutálej.** (Roll and turn, sun; Rolle Sonne, dreh dich.) Ill.: Jiří Trnky.
Praha: SNDK 1961.

Mareš, Jan: **Brácha a já.** (My brother and I; Mein Bruder und ich.) Ill.: Jan Brychta.
Praha: SNDK 1961.

Říha, Bohumil: **Dětská encyklopedie.** (Children's encyclopedia; Lexikon für Kinder.) Ill.: Vladimír Fuka.
Praha: SNDK 1959.

Šmahelová, Helena: **Karlínská číslo 5.** (No. 5 *Karlínská* Street; *Karlínská*strasse 5.) Ill.: Jarmila Fenclová.
Praha: SNDK 1961.

Illustration
Fuka, Vladimír in:
Říha, Bohumil: **Dětská encyklopedie.** (Children's encyclopedia; Lexikon für Kinder.)
Praha: SNDK 1959.

Trnky, Jiří in:
Jirásek, Alois: **Staré pověsti české.** (Old Bohemian legends; Alte böhmische Sagen.)
Praha: SNDK 1961.

1962 Sojová, Kamila: **Jeřabinky.** (Mountain-ash berries; Die Vogelbeeren.) Ill.: Otokar Jelínek.
Praha: SNDK 1962.

Tomeček, Jaromír: **Admirál na Dyji.** (Admiral on the river *Thaya;* Admiral auf dem Fluss *Thaya.*) Ill.: Mirko Hanák.
Praha: SNDK 1962.

Secondary literature/Sekundärliteratur
Stejskal, Václav: **Moderní česká literature pro děti.** (Modern Czech children's literature; Moderne tschechische Kinderliteratur.)
Praha: SNDK 1962.

Illustration
Svolinský, Karel in:
Vladislav, Jan (i.e. Ladislav Bambásek): **Příběhy třinácti bohatyru.** (Adventure of 13 heroes; Abenteuer der 13 Helden.)
Praha: SNDK 1962.

1963 Čtvrtek, Václav: **Kosí strom.** (The blackbird tree; Der Amselbaum.) Ill.: Alena Ladová.
Praha: SNDK 1963.

Dvořák, Ladislav: **Kam chodí slunce spát.** (Where the sun goes to sleep; Wohin die Sonne zum Schlafen geht.) Ill.: Ota Janaček.
Praha: SNDK 1963.

Hrubín, František: **Kolik je sluníček!** (How many suns exist? Wieviele Sonnen gibt es?) Ill.: Milada Králova.
Praha: SNDK 1963.

Zapletal, Miloš: **Kouzelné brýle.** (The magic spectacles; Die Zauberbrille.) Ill.: Jan Schmid.
Praha: SNDK 1963.

Secondary literature/Sekundärliteratur

Šmatlák, Stanislav: **Básnik a diet'a.** Reflexie o detskej poézil. (Poet and child. Reflexions over children's poetry; Dichter und Kind. Reflexionen über Kinderpoesie.)
Bratislava: Mladé letá 1963.

Illustration

Janeček, Ota in:
Vladislav, Jan (i.e. Ladislav Bambásek): **Princezna s lískovými oříšky.** Anglické. (The princess with the hazel nuts. English fairy tales; Die Prinzessin mit den Haselnüssen. Englische Märchen.)
Praha: SNDK 1963.

1964 *Poetry/Poesie*

Kainar, Josef: **Nevídáno, neslýcháno.** (Never heard, never seen; Nie gehört, nie gesehen.) Ill.: Josef Kainar.
Praha: SNDK 1964.

Kriebel, Zdeněk: **Stradivárky z neónu.** Posměšky na plot. (Neon Stradivarius. Mockery on a fence; Stradivari aus Neon. Spott auf den Zaun.) Ill.: Vladimír Fuka.
Praha SNDK 1964.

Prose/Prosa

Adlová, Věra: **Mirka to ví nejlíp.** (*Mirka* knows best; *Mirka* weiss es am besten.) Ill.: Adolf Born.
Praha: SNDK 1964.

Souček, Ludvík: **(Cesta slepých ptáků.** (The way of the blind birds; Der Weg der blinden Vögel.) Ill.: Kamil Lhoták.
Praha: SNDK 1964.

Translation/Übersetzung

Skoumal, Aloys/Skoumalová, Hana for:
Carroll, Lewis (i.e. Charles Lutwidge Dodgson): **Alenka v kraji divů a za zrcadlem.** (*Alice* in wonderland; *Alice* im Wunderland.) Ill.: Dagmar Berková.
Praha: SNDK 1961.

Skoumal, Aloys for:
Swift, Jonathan: **Gulliverovy cesty.** (*Gulliver's* travels; *Gullivers* Reisen.) Ill.: Cyril Bouda.
Praha: SNDK 1960.

Skoumal, Aloys/Skoumalová, Hana for:
Steinbeck, John: **Ryzácek.** (The red pony; Der rote Pony.) Ill.: Jitka Kolínská.
Praha: SNDK 1962.

Skoumalová, Hana for:
Milne, Alan Alexander: **Medvídek Pú.** *(Winnie-the-Pooh;* Pu der Bär.) Ill.: Jaromír Zápal.
Praha: SNDK 1964.

Illustration
Sklenář, Zdeněk in:
Petiška, Eduard: **Staré řecké báje a pověsti.** (Old Greek legends; Alte griechische Sagen.)
Praha: SNDK 1964.

1965 The prize was not given; Der Preis wurde nicht vergeben.

1966 *Literature/Literatur*
Ondřej Sekory
Illustration
Antonín Strnadel

1968 *Literature/Literatur*
František Hrubín
Illustration
Kamil Lhoták

1970 *Literature/Literatur*
Josef Věromír Pleva
Illustration
Cyril Bouda

1972 *Literature/Literatur*
Bohumil Říha
Illustration
Adolf Zábranský

1974 *Literature/Literatur*
Jaromír Tomeček
Illustration
Mirko Hanák

1976 *Literature/Literatur*
Helená Šmahelová
Illustration
Karel Svolinský

1978 *Literature/Literatur*
Eduard Petiška

Illustration
Helena Zmatlíková

1980 *Literature/Literatur*
Věra Adlová
Illustration
Dagmar Berková

Cena vydavateľstva Mladé letá

The publisher, Mladé letá, in Bratislava, annually presents a prize for the best children's and youth books. Works of the following types can receive the prize: prose, poetry, popular science literature, illustration, translation. Also, any outstanding editorial work which was published during the previous year. The prize consists of a certificate and a cash award.

Der Verlag Mladé letá in Pressburg (Bratislava) verleiht jährlich einen Preis für das beste Werk der Kinder- und Jugendliteratur. Prämiiert werden Bücher aus folgenden Gebieten: Prosa, Poesie, populärwissenschaftliche Literatur, Illustration, Übersetzung oder ein besonders gutes editorisches Werk, das im vergangenen Jahr erschienen ist. Der Preisträger erhält ein Diplom und einen Geldpreis.

1953 *Poetry/Poesie*
Rázusová-Martháková, Mária: **Pieseň o Váhu.** (The song of the scale; Das Lied von der Waage.) Ill.: František Kráľ.
Bratislava: SNDK 1953.

1954 Jančová, Mária: **Rospravky starej matere.** (Fairy tales of the old mother; Märchen der alten Mutter.) Ill.: Ľudovít Ilečko.
Bratislava: SNDK 1953.

1955 Šmatlák, Stanislav für:
Compilation of, and commentary on the poems of/Zusammenstellung und Begleittext der Poesie von: Hviezdoslav, Pavol Országh: **Výber z diela.** (Selection of poetry; Auswahl aus dem Werk.) Ill.: Martin Benka.
Bratislava: SNDK 1954.

1956 Moric, Rudo: **Z poľovníckej kapsy.** (From the hunter's bag; Aus des Jägers Tasche.) Ill.: Fedor Klimáček.
Bratislava: Mladé letá 1957.

1957 Figuli, Margita: **Mladosť.** (The youth; Die Jugend.) Ill.: Ladislav Nesselman.
Bratislava: SNDK 1956.

Zúbek, Ľudo: **Doktor Jesenius.** Doctor *Jesenius;* Doktor *Jesenius.*) Ill.: Václav Fiala.
Bratislava: SNDK 1956.

Poetry/Poesie

Bendová, Krista: **Bola raz jedna trieda.** (Once there was a class; Es war einmal eine Klasse.) Ill.: Božena Hajdučíková.
Bratislava: Mladé letá 1958.

1958 Handzová, Viera: **Madlenka.** *(Madlenka.)* Ill.: Ladislav Nesselman.
Bratislava: Mladé letá 1957.

Mňačko, Ladislav: **Marxova ulica.** (Marx Street; Marxstrasse.) Ill.: Viliam Weiskopf.
Bratislava: Mladé letá 1957.

Štefanovićová, Elena: **Rástli bez mamy.** (Grown up without mother; Ohne Mutter aufgewachsen.) Ill.: Ladislav Nesselman.
Bratislava: Mladé letá 1957.

1959 Krno, Miloš: **Vrátim sa živý.** (I came back alive; Ich kam lebend zurück.) Ill.: Július Nemčík.
Bratislava: Mladé letá 1958.

Moric, Rudo: **Pri zakliatej rieke.** (The bewitched river; Der verwunschene Fluss.) Ill.: Ľubomír Kellenberger.
Bratislava: Mladé letá 1958.

1960 Horák, Jozef: **Lendacké zvony.** (*Lendack* bells; *Lendacker* Glocken.) From the collection, Kremnický zlatý človek/Aus der Sammlung Kremnický zlatý človek. Ill.: Václar Boukal.
Bratislava: Mladé letá 1959.

Jarunková, Klára: **Hrdinský zápisník.** (The diary of a hero; Das Tagebuch eines Helden.) Ill.: Božena Hajdučíková.
Bratislava: Mladé letá 1960.

1961 Ďuríčková, Mária (i.e. Mária Masaryková): **Danka a Janka.** (*Danka* and *Janka.*) Ill.: Božena Hajdučíková.
Bratislava: Mladé letá 1961.

Illustration

Gergeľova, Viera in:
Podjavorinská, Ľudmila (i.e. Ľudmila Riznerová): **Ćin-ćin.** *(Čin-čin.)*
Bratislava: Mladé letá 1961.

Hložník, Vincent in:
Maržak, Samuil Jakovlevič: **Mačkin dom.** Rozprávková knižka i hra pre javiská. (The cat house. A fairy tale book and theatre piece; Das Katzenhaus. Märchenbuch und Bühnenstück.)
Bratislava: Mladé letá 1961.

Translation/Übersetzung
Válek, Miroslav for:
Tuwim, Julian: **Zázraky a divy.** (Wonder upon wonder; Wunder über Wunder; Pol.orig.title: Preložil Jan Pilař.) Ill.: Vladimír Fuka.
Bratislava: Mladé letá 1961.

1962 Blažková, Jaroslava: **Ohňostroj pre deduška.** (The firework for grandfather; Ein Feuerwerk für Grossvater.) Ill.: Alois Mikulka.
Bratislava: Mladé letá 1962.

Zamarovský, Vojtech: **Objavenie Troje.** (The discovery of Troy; Die Entdeckung Trojas.) Ill.: Antonín Jukl.
Bratislava: Mladé letá 1962.

Poetry/Poesie
Bendová, Krista: **Čiernobiela rozprávka.** (The black-white fairy tale; Das schwarzweisse Märchen.) Ill.: Orla Čechová.
Bratislava: Mladé letá 1962.

Illustration
Brunovský, Albín in:
Ibis a mesiac. Rozprávky z južných mori. (The ibis and the moon. Stories from the South Sea; Der Ibis und der Mond. Erzählungen von der Südsee.)
Bratislava: Mladé letá 1962.

Lebiš, Ján in:
Puškin, Aleksandr Sergejevič: **Rozprávky.** (Fairy tales; Märchen.)
Bratislava: Mladé letá 1962.

1963 Ďuríčková, Mária (i.e. Mária Masarykovà): **Jasietka.** *(Jasietka.)* Ill.: Vincent Hložník.
Bratislava: Mladé letá 1963.

Poetry/Poesie
Ferko, Milan: **Snehový strom a ine dobrodružné rosprávky.** (The snow tree and other adventure fairy tales; Der Schneebaum und andere Abenteuermärchen.) Ill.: Viera Gergel'ová.
Bratislava: Mladé letá 1963.

Theory/Theorie
Poliak, Jan/Klátik, Zlatko: **O literature pre mládež.** Učebnica pre pedagogické inštitúty. (Youth literature. Textbook for teaching institutes; Jugendliteratur. Lehrbuch für Pädagogische Institute.)
Bratislava: Slovenské pedagogické nakladatel'stvo 1963.

Illustration
Klimo, Alojz in:
Tolstoj, Lev Nikolajevič: **Rozprávky a bájky.** (Fairy tales and fables; Märchen und Fabeln.)
Bratislava: Mladé letá 1963.

1964 Tanská, Nataša: **Počkaj, ešte nehrámel,** (Stop, we are not playing yet; Halt, wir spielen noch nicht.) Ill.: Milan Vavro.
Bratislava: Mladé letá 1964.

Poetry/Poesie
Válek, Miroslav: **Velka cestovná horúčka pre malých cestovateľov.** (High travel fever for little travelers; Hohes Reisefieber für kleine Reisende.) Ill.: Miroslav Cipár.
Bratislava: Mladé letá 1964.

Theory/Theorie
Kovač, Bohuš: **Svet dieťaťa a umelecká fantázia.** (The world of children and the artistic force of imagination; Die Welt des Kindes und die künstlerische Einbildungskraft.)
Bratislava: Mladé letá 1964.

Illustration
Bombová, Viera in:
Bodenek, Ján: **Ivkova biela mat'.** (*Ivko's* white mother; *Ivkos* weisse Mutter.)
Bratislava: Mladé letá 1964.

Cpin. Štefan in:
Drevený, trón. Bulharské rosprávky. (The wooden throne. Bulgarian fairy tales; Der hölzerne Thron. Bulgarische Märchen.) Selected by/Ausgewählt von: Georgi Vlčev.
Bratislava: Mladé letá 1964.

1965 Ťažký, Ladislav: **Kŕdeľdivých Adamov.** (*Adam's* wild flock; *Adams* wilde Herde.)
Bratislava: Mladé letá 1965.

Zúbek, L'udo: **Gaudeamus igitur alebo sladký život študentský.** (Gaudeamus igitur or the sweet student life; Gaudeamus igitur oder das süsse Studentenleben.) Ill.: Jozef Cesnak.
Bratislava: Mladé letá 1965.

Illustration
Hložnik, Vincent in:
Hauff, Wilhelm: **Rozprávky z půšte i mora.** (The desert and the sea; Die Wüste und die See; Germ.orig.title: Märchen.)
Bratislava: Mladé letá 1965.

Klimo, Alojz in:
Němcová, Božena: **Kráľ času.** (The king of time; Der König der Zeit.)
Bratislava: Mladé letá 1965.

Lebiš, Jan in:
La Fontaine, Jean de: **Bájky.** (Fables; Fabeln.)
Bratislava: Mladé letá 1965.

Translation/Übersetzung

Ďuričková, Mária (i.e. Mária Masaryková) for:
Bohatier Kremienok. Ruské ľudové rozprávky. (Russian fairy tales; Russische Märchen.) Ill.: Mária Želibská.
Bratislava: Mladé letá 1965.

Krupa, Viktor for:
Obrova stupaj. Maorijské rozprávky. (Giant footsteps. Maori fairy tales; Riesen-Fusspuren. Maorie-Märchen.) Ill.: Viera Bombová.
Bratislava: Mladé letá 1965.

1966 Navrátil, Ján: **Cestovanie s orangutanom.** (The journey with an orangutan; Die Reise mit einem Orang-Utan.) Ill.: Ján Meisner.
Bratislava: Mladé letá 1966.

Zamarovský, Vojtech: **Na počiatku bol Sumer.** (In the beginning was *Sumer;* Am Anfang war *Sumer.*) Photos.
Bratislava: Mladé letá 1966.

Illustration

Hübel, František in:
Strmeňova, Jirina: **Živá voda zadarmo.** (Life-water is free; Lebenswasser ist umsonst.)
Bratislava: Mladé letá 1966.

Kraicová, Viera in:
Rázusová-Mártaková, Mária: **Sedmikráska.** (The daisy; Das Gänseblümchen.)
Bratislava: Mladé letá 1966.

Nesselman, Ladislav in:
Zelinová, Hana: **Do videnia Zuzanka.** (Goodbye, *Susanne;* Auf Wiedersehen, *Susanne.*)
Bratislava: Mladé letá 1966.

Translation/Übersetzung

Rúfus, Milan for:
Hrubin, František: **Dvakrát sedem rozprávok.** (Two times seven fairy tales; Zweimal sieben Märchen.)
Bratislava: Mladé letá 1966.

1967 Bendová, Krista: **Opice z našej police.** (Monkeys from our shelf; Affen aus unserem Regal.) Ill.: Božena Plocháňová.
Bratislava: Mladé letá 1966.

Bendová, Krista: **Osmijanko rozpráva osem Rozprávok o Zvieratkách.** (*Osmijanko* tells eight animal stories; *Osmijanko* erzählt acht Tiermärchen.) Ill.: Božena Hajdučiková.
Bratislava: Mladé letá 1967.

Feldek, Ľubomir: **Hlava, ktorú som mal vtedy.** (The head I had that time; Den Kopf, den ich zu jener Zeit hatte.) Ill.: Miroslav Cipár.
Bratislava: Mladé letá 1967.

Feldek, Ľudbomir: **O hluchej Babke a vnúčikovi Zlatúšikovi.** (About the deaf grandmother and her grandson, *Golden Ear;* Von der tauben Grossmutter und ihrem Enkel Goldöhrchen.) Ill.: Michal Studený.
Bratislava: Mladé letá 1967.

Zubek, Ľudo: **Rytieri bze meca.** (The knights without swords; Die Ritter ohne Schwert.) Ill.: Jozef Cesnak.
Bratislava: Mladé letá 1967.

Illustration
Plocháňová-Hajdučiková, Božena in:
Rodari, Gianni: **Cibul'kove dobrodružstvá.** (Onion adventures; Zwiebelabenteuer; Ital.orig.title: Le avventure di *Cipollino.*)
Bratislava: Mladé letá 1967.

Plocháňová-Hajdučiková, Božena in:
Bendová, Krista: **Opice z našej police.** (Monkeys from our shelf; Affen aus unserem Regal.)
Bratislava: Mladé letá 1966.

Tarasová, Irena in:
Miller, Arthur: **Jankina prikrývka.** (Amer.orig.title: *Jane's* blanket; *Jankins* Decke.)
Bratislava: Mladé letá 1967.

Translation/Übersetzung
Ferko, Milan for:
Radovič, Dušan: **Rozprávky pre Gordonu.** (Fairy tales for *Gordonu,* Märchen für *Gordonu.*) Ill.: Jozef Baláž.
Bratislava: Mladé letá 1967.

1968 Feldek, Ľubomir: **Zelené jelene.** (The green deer; Die grünen Hirsche.) Ill.: Ondrej Zimka.
Bratislava: Mladé letá 1968.

Stodola, Ivan: **Nas strýko Aurel.** (Our uncle *Aurel*; Unser Onkel *Aurel*.) Ill.
Bratislava: Mladé letá 1968.

Translation/Übersetzung
Hornis, Juraj for:
O'Faolain, Eileen: **Irske sagy.** (Irish sagas; Irische Sagen; Eng.orig.title: Irish sagas and folk tales.) Ill.: Rudolf Fila.
Bratislava: Mladé letá 1968.

Illustration
Cipar, Miroslav in:
Navrátil, Ján: **Kamzik a bambus.** (Chamois and bamboo; Gemse und Bambus.)
Bratislava: Mladé letá 1968.

Hübel, František in:
London, Jack: **Biely Tesák. — Volanie divočiny.** (The white wolf. — The call of the wild; Der weisse Wolf. — Ruf der Wildnis; Amer.orig.title: *White Fang.* — The call of the wild.)
Bratislava: Mladé letá 1968.

1969 Ferko, Milan: **Keby som mal pušku.** (If I had a gun; Wenn ich eine Flinte hätte.) Ill.: Josef Baláž.
Bratislava: Mladé letá 1969.

Moric, Rudo: **Sen o chlebe.** (The dream of bread; Der Traum vom Brot.) Ill.: Ivan Schurmann.
Bratislava: Mladé letá 1969.

Zamarovský, Vojtech: **Bohovia a hrdinovia antických baji.** (Gods and heroes of classical times; Götter und Helden der Antike.) Ill.
Bratislava: Mladé letá 1969.

Zúbek, Ľudo: **Rĭsa Svätoplukova.** (The kingdom of *Svatopluk*; Das Reich des *Svatopluk*.) Ill.: František Hübel.
Bratislava: Mladé letá 1969.

Illustration
Schnitzer, Teodor in:
Cooper, James Fenimore: **Posledný Mohykán.** (Amer.orig.title: Last of the Mohicans; Der letzte Mohikaner.)
Bratislava: Mladé letá 1969.

Zimka, Ondrej in:
Hranko, Martin: **Furko a Murko.** (*Furko* and *Murko*.)
Bratislava: Mladé letá 1969.

1970 Navrátil, Ján: **Len srdce prvej veľ kosti.** (Only a heart of importance; Nur ein Herz ersten Ranges.) Ill.: Juraj Deák.
Bratislava: Mladé letá 1970.

Sliacky, Ondrej: **Bibliografia literatúry pre deti a mľádež.** (Bibliography of children's and youth literature; Bibliografie der Kinder- und Jugendliteratur.)
Bratislava: Mladé letá 1970.

Sliacky, Ondrej: **Slovnik slovenských spisovateľov pre mládež.** (Dictionary of Slovak youth Literature; Lexikon der slovakischen Jugendliteratur.)
Bratislava: Mladé letá 1970.

Translation/Übersetzung
Hečke, Blahoslav for:
Boccaccio, Giovanni: **Príbehy z Dekameronu.** (Tales of the Decameron; Erzählungen aus dem Dekameron.) Ill.: Miroslav Cipár.
Bratislava: Mladé letá 1970.

Turcány, Viliam for:
Ovidius, Naso Publius: **Premeny.** (Metamorphosis; Metamorphosen.) Ill.: Viera Kraicová.
Bratislava: Mladé letá 1970.

Illustration
Beňo, Jozef in:
Ďuričková, Mária: **Janček Palček.** (*Little Johnny Thumb*; *Hänschen Däumling*.)
Bratislava: Mladé letá 1970.

Cipár, Miroslav in:
Válek, Miroslav: **Do Tramtárie.** (To *Tramtaria;* Nach *Tramtarien.*)
Bratislava: Mladé letá 1970.

Machaj, Vladimir in:
Hronský, Jozef Ciger: **Zakopany meč.** (The buried sword; Das vergrabene Schwert.)
Bratislava: Mladé letá 1970.

1971 Gašparová, Eleonóra: **Fontána pre Zuzanu.** (A fountain for *Susanne;* Der Springbrunnen für *Susanne.*) Ill.: Igor Rumanský.
Bratislava: Mladé letá 1971.

Juriček, Ján: **Ľudovit Štúr.** (*Ĺudovit Śtur.*) Photos.
Bratislava: Mladé letá 1971.

Stiavnický, Ján: **Šaty malej Dominiky.** (Little *Dominica's* dress; Die Kleider der kleinen Dominika.) Ill.: František Hübel.
Bratislava: Mladé letá 1971.

Translation/Übersetzung
Feldek, Ľubomir/Doležalová, Anna for:
Povest o krásnej Ašme. (The legend about beautiful *Asma*; Die Sage von der schönen *Asma*.) Ill.: Viera Bombová.
Bratislava: Mladé letá 1971.

Illustration
Bombová, Viera in:
Povest o krásnej Ašme. (The legend about beautiful *Asma*; Die Sage von der schönen *Asma*.)
Bratislava: Mladé letá 1971.

Hübel, František in:
Čepčeková, Elena: **Móda — nemóda.** (Fashion — non-fashion; Mode — Nichtmode.)
Bratislava: Mladé letá 1971.

Typography/Typografie
Šulc, Dušan for:
Vrchlická, Eva: **Z orieška královnej Mab.** (From the little nut of queen *Mab;* Aus dem Nüsslein der Königin *Mab.*) Ill.: Vincent Hložnik.
Bratislava: Mladé letá 1971.

Šulc, Dušan for:
Defoe, Daniel: **Robinson Crusoe.** (*Robinson Crusoe.*) Ill.: Vincent Hložnik.
Bratislava: Mladé letá 1971.

1972 Horák, Jozef: **Leteli sokoli nad Javorinou.** (The falcons fly over *Javorina;* Die Falken flogen über *Javorina.*) Ill.: Dušan Kállay.
Bratislava: Mladé letá 1972.

Pavlovič, Jozef: **Bračekovia mravčekovia.** (The little ant brothers; Brüderchen Ameischen.) Ill.: Jarmila Dicová.
Bratislava: Mladé letá 1972.

Valehrachová, Margita: **Zabudnutý vynálezca.** (The forgotten explorer; Der vergessene Erfinder. Ill.: Milan Veselý.
Bratislava: Mladé letá 1972.

Translation/Übersetzung
Komorovský, Ján for:
Alpamyš. (*Alpamyš = Usbekian national epic; Alpamysch* = Usbekisches Nationalepos.) Ill.: Ivan Vychlopen.
Bratislava: Mladé letá 1972.

Illustration
Brunovský, Albin in:
Tri princezné v Belasej skale. (Three princesses on the blue cliff; Drei Prinzessinnen im blauen Felsen.
Bratislava: Mladé letá 1972.

Gergeľova, Viera in:
Tanska, Nataša: Puf a Muf. (*Puff* and *Muff*)
Bratislava: Mladé letá 1972.

Kállay, Dušan in:
Čepčeková, Elena: **Serenáda pre Martinu.** (Serenade for *Martina;* Serenade für *Martina.*)
Bratislava: Mladé letá 1972.

1973 Ďuričková, Mária: **Biela kňažná.** (The white princess; Die weisse Fürstin.) Ill.: Miroslav Cipár.
Bratislava: Mladé letá 1973.

Jarunková, Klára: **Tulák.** (The tramp; Der Landstreicher.) Ill.: Dušan Kállay.
Bratislava: Mladé letá 1973.

Šrámková, Jana: **Biela stužka v tvojich vlasoch.** (The white ribbon in your hair; Das weisse Band in deinem Haar.) Ill.: Eugénia Lehotská.
Bratislava: Mladé letá 1973.

Sliacky, Ondrej: **Slovenská literatura pre mladež v národnom obrodeni.** (Slovakian youth literature during the national rebirth; Slovakische Jugendliteratur während der nationalen Wiedergeburt.)
Bratislava: Mladé letá 1973.

Illustration
Cipár, Miroslav in:
Ďuričková, Mária: **Biela kňažná.** (The white princess; Die weisse Fürstin.)
Bratislava: Mladé letá 1973.

Nesselman, Ladislav in:
Navrátil, Ján.: **Uzlik a Nitka.** (*Little Knot* and *Little Thread; Knötchen* und *Fädchen.*)
Bratislava: Mladé letá 1973.

1974 Feldek, Ľubomir/Brunovský, Albin/Krátky, Ľubomir: **Modrá kniha rozpravok.** (The blue fairy tale book; Das blaue Märchenbuch.) Ill.: Albin Brunovský. Typog: Ľubomir Krátky.
Bratislava: Mladé letá 1974.

(The prize was equally awarded to all three of the abovenamed persons for excellent collaboration: Alle drei wurden für die gute Zusammenarbeit ausgezeichnet.)

Gašparová, Eleonóra: **Koncert bez ruži.** (Concert without roses; Konzert ohne Rosen.) Ill.: Stanislav Dusik.
Bratislava: Mladé letá 1974.

Sliacky, Ondrej: **Otpusť te, mamička.** (Forgive me, mommy; Verzeiht, Mütterchen.) Ill.: Jako Movák/Ľudovit Ilečko.
Bratislava: Mladé letá 1974.

Zamarovský, Vojtech: **Grécky zázrak.** (The Greek miracle; Das griechische Wunder.) Photos: Vojtech Zamarovský.
Maps: Otokar Pok.
Bratislava: Mladé letá 1974.

Translation/Übersetzung

Križanová-Brindzová, Helena for:
Bohatierske byliny. (*Bohatierske byliny* = epic poetry; *Bohatierske byliny* = Helden-Epen.) Ill.: Róbert Dúbravec.
Bratislava: Mladé letá 1974.

Illustration

Dúbravec, Róbert in:
Križanová-Brindzová, Helena: **Bohatierske byliny.** (*Bohatierske byliny* = epic poetry; *Bohatierske byliny* = Helende-Epen.)
Bratislava: Mladé letá 1974.

Končekova-Veselá, Ľuba in:
Ďuričková, Mária: **Laponček Sampo.** (*Sampo,* the little Laplander; Der kleine Lappe *Sampo.*)
Bratislava: Mladé letá 1974.

Končeková-Veselá, Ľuba in:
Trilecová, Božena: **Ako si kvety šijú sukničky.** (How the flowers sew their dresses; Wie die Blumen sich Röckchen nähen.)
Bratislava: Mladé letá 1974.

Typography/Typografie

(The books of Jules Verne published by Mladé letá; Die Bücher von Jules Verne, die bei Mladé letá erschienen sind.

1975 Rúfus, Milan: **Kniha rozprávok.** (Fairy tale book; Das Märchenbuch.) Ill.: Viera Kraicová.
Bratislava: Mladé letá 1975.

Illustration
Baláž, Jozef in:
Ďuričkova, Mária: Sedemfarebný kvietok. (Flowers of seven colours; Das siebenfarbige Blümchen.)
Bratislava: Mladé letá 1975.

1976 Gašparová, Eleonóra: **Ťažko je mustangovi.** (A mustang has it hard; Ein Mustang hat es schwer.) Ill.: Nad'a Rappensbergerová.
Bratislava: Mladé letá 1976.

Illustration
Končeková-Veslá, Ľuba in: **Kalevala.** (*Kalevala.*)
Bratislava: Mladé letá 1976.

1977 Kováčik, Peter: **Jablká nášho detestva.** (The apples of our childhood; Die Äpfel unserer Kindheit.) Ill.: Karol Ondreička.
Bratislava: Mladé letá 1977.

Illustration
Dúbravec, Róbert in:
Ondrejka, Kliment: **Poviestki spod piecky.** (Stories around the oven; Geschichten am Ofen.)
Bratislava: Mladé letá 1977.

1978 Ferko, Vladimir: **Kniha o Slovensku.** (A book about Slovakia; Ein Buch über die Slovakei.) Photos: L. Bláha et al.
Bratislava: Mladé letá 1978.

Kováč, Dušan: **Tajomstvá** (Secrets; Geheimnisse.) Ill.: Ján Zelenák.
Bratislava: Mladé letá 1978.

Illustration
Rumanský, Igor in:
Hrubin, František: **Ako sa chytá radost.** (How to be happy; Wie man glücklich wird.)
Bratislava: Mladé letá 1978.

1979 Janovic, Tomáš: **Drevený tato.** (Wooden father; Holzpapi.) Ill.: Ondrej Zimka.
Bratislava: Mladé letá 1979.

Illustration
Kállay, Dušan in:
Wotte, Herbert: **Magalhaesova cesta okolo sveta.** (*Magellan's* voyage around the world; Magellans Reise um die Welt.)
Bratislava: Mladé letá 1979.

1980 Navrátil, Ján: **Lampáš malého plavčika.** (The little cabin-boy's lantern; Die Laterne des kleinen Schiffsjungen.) Ill. Marián Minarovič.
Bratislava: Mladé letá 1980.

Illustration
Klimo, Alojz in:
Rázusová-Martáková, Mária: **Jarné vtáča.** (Little spring bird; Frühlingsvögelchen.)
Bratislava: Mladé letá 1980.

Nejkrásnejši knihy roku

This prize for the "most beautiful books of the year", was established in 1957. It is awarded by the Ministry of Culture of the ČSSR (Ministerstvo kultury ČSSR), the Slovakian Center for Book Culture (Slovenské ústredie knižnej kultúry), the National Writer's Archives (Památnik národniho pisemnictvi) and the Slovakian Language and Culture Association (Matica slovenská).

Den Preis "Die schönsten Bücher des Jahres" verleiht das Kultusministerium der ČSSR (Ministerstvo kultury ČSSR), das Slovakische Zentrum für Buchkultur (Slovenské ústredie knižnej kultúry), das Denkmal des nationalen Schrifttums (Památnik národniho pisemnictvi) und der Slovakische Sprach- und Kulturverein (Matica slovenská) seit 1957 jährlich an die schönsten Publikationen des Jahres.

1957 Kocourek, Vítezslav: **Za pohádkou kolem světe.** (With fairy tales through the whole world; Mit Märchen durch die ganze Welt.) Ill.: Helena Zmatliková.
Praha: SNDK 1957.

Nezval, Vitezslav: **Zlatý věk.** (The golden age; Das goldene Zeitalter.) Ill.: Jiři Trnka.
Praha: SNDK 1957.

Stowe, Harriet Elizabeth Beecher: Chaloupka strýcka Toma. (Amer.orig.title: Uncle *Tom's* cabin; Onkel *Toms* Hütte.) Ill.: Antonin Pelc.
Praha: SNDK 1957.

1958 Andersen, Hans Christian: **Pohádky.** (Fairy tales; Märchen; Dan.orig.title: Eventyr og historier.) Ill.: Jiři Trnky.
Praha: SNDK 1957.

Čivrný, Lumir: **Pohádky o kouzelném džbánu.** (The fairy tale of the magic pitcher; Das Märchen vom Zauberkrug.)
Ill.: Jindřich Kovařik.
Praha: SNDK 1958.

Hrubin, František: **Dvakrát sedm pohádek.** (Two times seven fairy tales; Zweimal sieben Märchen.) Ill.: Jiři Trnky.
Praha: SNDK 1957.

Kocourek, Vitezslav: **Se zvižatky kolem světa.** (With animals around the world; Mit Tieren rings um die Welt.) Ill.: Helena Zmatliková.
Praha: SNDK 1958.

Lada, Josef: **Nezbedné pohádky.** (Happy fairy tales; Fröhliche Märchen.) Ill.: Josef Lada.
Praha: SNDK 1958.

Majerová, Marie: **Africké vteřiny.** (African seconds; Afrikanische Sekunden.) Ill.: Karl Slovinský.
Praha: SNDK 1958.

Perovská, Olga: **Tygřik Vaska.** (*Vaska,* the tiger; Der Tiger *Vaska;* Russ.orig.title: Rebjata i zverjata.) Ill.: Mirko Hanák.
Praha: SNDK 1958.

Pražák, František: **Ráj srdce.** (Paradise of the heart; Paradies des Herzens.) Ill.: Antonín Strnadel.
Praha: SNDK 1958.

Priležajevová, Marija: **Od břehaů Medvědice.** (From the shores; Von den Ufern; Russ.orig.title: S beregov Medvedicy.) Ill.: Václav Bláha.
Praha: SNDK 1958.

Stanovský, Vladislav: **Strom pohádek z celého světa.** (Fairy tale tree from all over the world; Märchenbaum aus aller Welt.) Ill.: Stanislav Kolíbal.
Praha: SNDK 1958.

Tuwim, Julian: **Zázraky a divy.** (Astonishment and wonder; Staunen und Wunder; Pol.orig.title: Wiersze dla dzieci.) Ill.: Vladimir Fuka.
Praha: SNDK 1958.

Twain, Mark (i.e. Samuel Langhorne Clemens): **Princ a cuhdas.** (The prince and the pauper; Prinz und Bettelknabe; Amer.orig.title: The prinze and the pauper.) Ill.: Pavel Simon.
Praha: SNDK 1958.

Vildrac, Charles: **Na vlastni pěst.** (On one's own initiative; Auf eigene Faust; Fr.orig.title: Vers le traveil.) Ill.: Antonin Pelc.
Praha: SNDK 1958.

1959 Čech, Svatopluk: **Ve stínu lípy.** (In the shadow of the lime tree; Im Schatten der Linde.) Ill.: Cyril Bouda.
Praha: SNDK 1959.

Harris, Joel Chandler: **Rozprávky strýčka Remuse.** (Uncle *Remus* fairy tales; Onkel *Remus* Märchen; Amer.orig.title: Uncle *Remus.)* *Ill.: Ota Janeček.*
Praha: Albatros SNDK 1959.

Kubín, Josef Štefan: **Princezna pohádka.** (Princess fairy tales; Prinzessin Märchen.) Ill.: Adolf Zábranský.
Praha: SNDK 1959.

Mácha, Karl Hynek: **Marinka.** (*Marinka.*) Ill.: Ludmila Jirincová.
Praha: SNDK 1959.

Stanovský, Vladislav: **O dvanácti Mikitech.** (The twelve *Nikitas*; Die Zwölf *Nikitas* Ill.: Michael Romberg.
Praha: SNDK 1959.

Vladislav, Jan/Stanovský, Vladislav: **Druhý strom pohádek z celého světa.** (The second fairy tale tree from all over the world; Der zweite Märchenbaum aus aller Welt.) Ill.: Stanislav Kolíbal.
Praha: SNDK 1959.

1960 Branislav, František: **Přijďte k nam, muzikanti.** (Come to us, musicians; Kommt zu uns, Musikanten.) Ill.: Jiŕi Trnka.
Praha: SNDK 1960.

Erben, Karel Jaromir: **Kytice z pověstí národních.** (A bouquet of folk tales; Ein Volkssagenstrauß.) Ill.: Jan Zrzavý.
Praha: SNDK 1960.

Hrubín, František: **Hrajte si s námi.** (Play with us; Spielt mit uns.) Photos: Dagmar Hochová.
Praha: SNDK 1960.

Lada, Josef: **Dětem.** (For children; Für Kinder.) Ill.: Josef Lada.
Praha: SNDK 1960.

Nechvátal, František: **Medová studánka.** (The copper spring; Der Kupferbrunnen.) Ill.: Antonín Strnadel.
Praha: SNDK 1960.

Petrbok, Jaroslav: **Rostliny.** (Plants; Pflanzen.) Ill.: Karel Svolinský.
Praha: SNDK 1960.

Vrchlichá, Eva: **Z oříšku královny mab.** (From the nut of queen *Mab;* Aus der Nuß der Königin *Mab.*) Ill.: Karl Svolinský.
Praha: SNDK 1960.

1961 The prize was not awarded; Der Preis wurde nicht vergeben.

1962 The prize was not awarded; Der Preis wurde nicht vergeben.

1963 The prize was not awarded; Der Preis wurde nicht vergeben.

1964 The prize was not awarded; Der Preis wurde nicht vergeben.

1965 Aškenázy, Ludvík: **Praštěné pohádky.** (Foolish fairy tales; Närrische Märchen.) Ill.: Bohumil Štěpán.
Praha: SNDK 1965.

Kolář, Jiři/Hiršal, Josef: **Baron Prášil.** (Baron *Prášil.*) Ill.: Cyril Bouda.
Praha: SNDK 1965.

Mahler, Zdeněk: **Jak se stát bubeníkem královské gardy.** (How to become a drummer in the royal guard; Wie wird man Trommler der Königlichen Garde.) Ill.: Vladimir Fuka.
Praha: SNDK 1965.

Sandburg, Carl: **Pohádky z bramborových řádků.** (Fairy tales from the potato rows; Märchen aus den Kartoffelreihen; (Amer.orig.title: Rootabaga stories.) Ill.: Květa Pacovská.
Praha: SNDK 1965.

Illustration (Main prize/Hauptpreis)

Strnadel, Antonín: **For complete works;** für das Gesamtschaffen.

(Honourable mention/Ehrenpreis)

Serých, Jaroslav in:
Bednář, Kamil: **Labuti jezero.** (Swan Lake; Schwanensee.)
Praha: SNDK 1965.

Strnadel, Antonín in:
Kilianová, Eva/Sirovátka, Oldřich: **Čarovne ovoce.** (Magic fruit; Zauberfrüchte.)
Praha: SNDK 1965.

1966 Reis, Vladimír: **Křištalové sestry,** (The crystal sisters; Die Kristallschwestern.) Ill.: Stanislav Kolibal.
Praha: SNDK 1966.

Illustration

Janeček, Ota in:
Fournier, Alain: **Kouzelné dobrodružstvi.** (Wonderful adventure; Wunderbares Abenteuer; Fr.orig.title: Le grande Meaulnes.)
Praha: SNDK 1966.

Tesař, Vladimír in:
Hofman, Ota: **Útěk.** (The escape; Die Flucht.)
Praha: SNDK 1966.

Šejna, František (ed) for:
Dítě a svět. (The child and the world; Das Kind und die Welt.)
Praha: SNDK 1966.

1967 Claudius, Eduard: **Když se ryby pásly na nebi.** (When the fish gazed at the sky; Als die Fische am Himmel weideten; Germ.orig.title: Als die Fische die Sterne schluckten.) Ill.: Jan Kudláček.
Praha: SNDK 1967.

Hanzlik, Josef: **Sněhovná hvězdička.** (Snow stars; Schneesternchen.) Ill.: Kvéta Pacovská.
Praha: SNDK 1966.

Petiška, Eduard: **Příběhy, na které svitilo slunce.** (Adventures on which the sun shone; Abenteuer, auf die die Sonne schien.) Ill.: Karel Teissig.
Praha: SNDK 1967.

1968 Karafiát, Jan: **Broučci.** (Little firefly; Leuchtkäferchen.) Ill.: Jiři Trnka.
Praha: SNDK 1968.

Kocourek, Vítezslav/Rathouský, Jiři: **Vesmir, Zeme, Človek — a my deti.** (The cosmos, the earth, mankind and we children; Weltall, Erde, Mensch und wir Kinder.) Ill.: Jiři Rathouský.
Praha: SNDK 1966.

Lukešový, Milena: **Bačkůrky z mechu.** (Slippers of moss; Pantöffelchen aus Moos.) Ill.: Mirko Hanák.
Praha: SNDK 1968.

1969 Strnadel, Josef: **Zamrzlá studánka.** (The frozen spring; Der zugefrorene Brunnen.) Ill.: Antonín Strnadel.
Praha: SNDK 1969.

(Honourable mention prize/Ehrenpreis)
Jirásek, Alois: **Psohlavci.** (The dog-heads; Die Hundsköpfe.) Ill.: Antonín Strnadel.
Praha: SNDK 1969.

Řiha, Václav: **Pohádky.** (Fairy tales; Märchen.) Ill.: Cyril Bouda.
Praha: SNDK 1969.

Seifert, Jaroslav: **Halleyova kometa.** (Halley's Comet; Halleys Komet.) Ill.: Jiři Trnka.
Praha: SNDK 1969.

1970 Čukovskij, Kornej: **Doktor Bolíto.** (Dr. *Bolito,* Russ.orig.title: Dokotr *Ajbolit.*) Ill.: Vratislav Hlavatý.
Praha: Albatros 1970.

(Honourable mention prize/Ehrenpreis)
Čelakovský, František Ladislav: **Ohlas písni ruských, Ohlas písni českých.** (Echo of Russian songs, echo of Czech songs; Das Echo russischer Lieder, das Echo tschechischer Lieder.)
Praha: Albatros 1970.

Dvořačkova, Vlasta: **Uletělo čapi pero.** (The stork feather flew away; Die Storchenfeder flog fort.) Ill.: Zdenek Seydl.
Praha: Albatros 1969.

Šmerhovský, Karl: **Bylo — nebylo.** (It was — it was not; Es war — es war nicht.) Ill.: Jiři Behounek.
Praha: Albatros 1969.

Vladislav, Jan: **Kapitán Tulipan a princezna z Bordeaux.** (Captain *Tulipan* and the princess from Bordeaux; Kapitän *Tulipan* und die Prinzessin aus Bordeaux.) Ill.: Eva Bednářová.
Praha: Albatros 1970.

Williamson, Henry: **Vodni poutnik Tarka.** (Eng.orig.title: *Tarka* the otter; *Tarka,* die Otter.) Ill.: Mirko Hanák.
Praha: SNDK 1970.

1971 (Honourable mention prize/Ehrenpreis)

Landau, Lev D./Rumer, Jurij B.: **Coto je teorie relativity.** (Theory of relativity; Was ist Relativitätstheorie; Russ.orig.title: Čto takoje teorija otnositelnosti.) Ill.: Jaroslav Malák.
Praha: Albatros 1971.

1972 Lesueur, Nicole: **Tajemství zlutého belankú.** (The secret of the yellow balloon; Das Geheimnis des gelben Ballons; Fr.orig.title: Le secret du ballon jaune.) Ill.: Dagmar Berková.
Praha: Albatros 1971.

1973 (Honourable mention prize/Ehrenpreis)

Řiha, Bohumil: **Nový Gulliver.** (The new Gulliver: Der neue *Gulliver.*) Ill.: Jan Kudláček.
Praha: Albatros 1973.

Deyl, Miloš: **Naše květiny.** (Our plants; Unsere Pflanzen.) Ill.: Květoslav Hísek.
Praha: Albatros 1973.

Katajev, Valentin: **Na obzoru plachta bílá.** (On the horizon, a white sail; Am Horizont ein weißes Segel; Russ.orig.title: Beleet parus odinokij.) Ill.: Kamil Lhoták.
Praha: Albatros 1973.

1974 (Main prize/Hauptpreis)

Zábranský, Adolf for:
Česke a moravské pohádky. (Czech and Moravian fairy tales; Tschechische und Mährische Märchen.) Ill.: Adolf Zábranský.
Praha: Albatros 1974.

(Honourable mention prize/Ehrenpreis)

Adlová, Věra/Adla, Zdeněk: **Vyprávěnié o velike zemi.** (Stories about a big country; Erzählungen von einem großen Land.) Ill.: Zdenek Mlčoch.
Praha: Albatros 1974.

Cirkl, Jiři: **Kytička pro štěsti.** (A little bouquet of happiness; Ein Sträusschen zum Glück.) Ill.: Dagmar Berková.
Praha: Albatros 1974.

Lukešová, Milena: **Knižka pro Lucinku.** (A book for *Lucinka;* Ein Buch für *Lucinka.*) Ill.: Jana Sigmundová.
Praha: Albatros 1973.

Macourek, Milos: **Svete div se.** (World, be astonished; Welt, wundere dich.) Ill.: Adolf Born.
Praha: Albatros 1974.

1975 *In memoriam*
Strnadel, Antonín in:
Strnadel, Josef: **Vyhnal jsem ovečky až na Javorníček.** (I drove the sheep up to *Javorníček;* Ich trieb die Schafe auf den *Javorníček.*)
Praha: Albatros 1975.

Honourable mention/Ehrenpreis
Barto, Agnija: **Svět s modýma očima.** (The world with blue eyes; Die Welt mit blauen Augen; Russ.orig.title: Vybral a přel.) Ill.: Jana Sigmundová.
Praha: Albatros 1974.

Dewetter, Karel: **Neuvěřitelná dobrodružstvi Davida Damiána.** (The incredible adventures of *David Damian;* Die unglaublichen Abenteuer des *David Damian.*) Ill.: Cyril Bouda.
Praha: Albatros 1975.

Hinderks-Kutscher, Rotraut: **Malý Wolfgang Amadeus.** (The little *Wolfgang Amadeus;* Germ. orig. title: Donnerblitzbub Wolfgang Amadeus.) Ill.: Karel Müller.
Praha: Albatros 1975.

Kándlová, Marie: **Tři stromy.** (Three trees; Drei Bäume.) Ill.: Helena Zmatlíková.
Praha: Albatros 1975.

Lukešová, Milena: **Molčička a déšť.** (The girl and the rain; Das Mädchen und der Regen.) Ill.: Jan Kudláček.
Praha: Albatros 1975.

Prokofjevá, Sofija: **Mášenčiny pohádky.** (Mary's fairy tale; *Mariechens* Märchen.) Ill.: Zdenka Krejčová.
Praha: Albatros 1975.

Syrovátka, Oldřich: **Běžel zajiček z lesa.** (The rabbit came running out of the forest; Der Hase kam aus dem Wald gelaufen.) Ill.: Jindřich Kovarík.
Praha: Albatros 1975.

Tuwim, Julian: **Zázraky a divy.** (Wonder and puzzle; Wunder und Rätsel; Pol.orig.title: Wiersze dla dzieci.) Ill.: Ludek Vimr.
Praha: Albatros 1974.

1976 Lukešová, Milena/Řiha, Bohumil: **Velká obrázková knižka pro malé děti.** (Big picture book for little children; Grosses Bilderbuch für kleine Kinder.) Ill.: Helena Rokytová.
Praha: Albatros 1976.

Tolstoj, Lev Nikolaevič: **Dětem.** (For children; Für Kinder.) Ill.: Jitka Kolínská.
Praha: Albatros 1976.

Honourable mention/Ehrenpreis
Nechvatal, František: **V mámině náručí.** (In mamma's arms; In Mamis Armen.) Ill.: Jan Kudlaček.
Praha: Albatros 1975.

1977 *In memoriam*
Müller, Karel in:
Langer, František: **Putovánní s Pustrpalkem.** (A trip with *Pustrpalk;* Wanderung mit *Pustrpalk.*)
Praha: Albatros 1977.

Müller, Karel in:
Hinderks-Kutscher, Rotraut: **Malý Wolfgang Amadeus.** (Little *Wolfgang Amadeus;* Germ.orig.title: Donnerblitzbub *Wolfgang Amadeus.*)
Praha: Albatros 1975.

Honourable mention/Ehrenpreis
Florian, Miroslav: **Jaro, napověž!** (Spring, tell me a story! Frühling, erzähl!) Ill.: Josef Paleček.
Praha: Albatros 1977.

Lukešová, Milena: **Bíla zima.** (White winter; Weisser Winter.) Ill.: Jan Kudláček.
Praha: Albatros 1977.

Petiška, Eduard: **Martínkova čitanka a dvě klubčíka pohádek.** (*Martina's* reading book and two skeins of fairy tales; *Martinas* Lesebuch und zwei Knäuel Märchen.) Ill.: Helena Zmatlíková.
Praha: Albatros 1977.

Slovo o pluku Igorevě. (*Igor's* song; *Igor*lied; Russ.orig.title: Slovo o polku *Igor*eve.) Ill.: Michael Romberg.
Praha: Albatros 1977.

Šajner, Donát: **Kde louki nejvíc voni.** (Where the meadows smell most sweetly; Wo die Wiesen am stärksten duften.) Ill.: Mirko Hanák.
Praha: Albatros 1977.

Zlatá kniha historických přiběhů. (The golden books of historical events; Das goldene Buch historischer Ereignisse.) Ill.: Zdeněk Mézl.
Praha: Albatros 1977.

Honourable mention to Albatros Publishing House for/Ehrenverleihung an den Verlag Albatros für:
Urbánková, Jarmila: **Mladá vichřice.** (The young whirlwind; Der junge Sturmwind.) Ill.: Denisa Wagnerová.
Praha: Albatros 1977.

1978 Zábranský, Adolf in:
Jelen, Josef: **Od jara do jara.** (From spring to spring; Von Frühling zu Frühling.)
Praha: Albatros 1978.

Honourable mention/Ehrenpreis
Holý, Stanislav: **Procházky pana Pipa.** (Mr. *Pip's* walks; Herrn *Pips* Spaziergänge.) Ill.: Stanislav Holý.
Praha: Albatros 1978.

Sirovátka, Oldřich: **Plný pytel pohádek.** (A sack full of fairy tales; Ein Sack voll Märchen.) Ill.: Miloslav Jágr.
Praha: Albatros 1978.

Bednařová, Eva in:
Gabe, Dora: **Dávno.** (Long ago; Vor langer Zeit.)
Praha: Albatros 1978.

Sigmundová, Jana in:
Lukešová, Milena: **Zimní knížka pro Lucinku.** (A winter book for *Lucinka;* Ein Winterbuch für *Lucinka.*)
Praha: Albatros 1978.

Jágr, Miloslav in:
Sirovátka, Oldřich: **Plný patel pohádek.** (A sack full of fairy tales; Ein Sack voll Märchen.)
Praha: Albatros 1978.

1979 Honourable mention to Albatros Publishing House for the series; Ehrenverleihung an den Verlag Albatros für die Bemühungen um das künstlerische Niveau der: Edition *Oko.*

Denmark/Dänemark

Børnebogspris

This prize for the best Danish children's and youth book was first awarded in 1954. Authors, illustrators and composers are eligible for the award. The prize-winning titles must have appeared during the previous year. Often, the Danish Writer's Association (Forfatterforening) offers an additional donation. The director of the State Library Supervision is chairman of the ministerial committee which makes the selections. The prize is presented by the Minister of Cultural Affairs. The amount of the prize is 10.000 kroner.

Der Preis für das beste dänische Kinder- und Jugendbuch (Er kann sowohl Verfassern als auch Illustratoren oder Komponisten zuerkannt werden) wurde 1954 zum ersten Mal verliehen. Der Autor des besten Kinderbuches aus dem vorhergehenden Jahr wird mit einer Prämie ausgezeichnet. Häufig stellt der Dänische Autorenverband (Forfatterforening) noch eine zusätzliche Prämie zur Verfügung. Der Direktor der Staatlichen Büchereiaufsicht ist der Vorsitzende des ministeriellen Ausschusses. Der Preis wird durch das Kultusministerium verliehen. Er besteht aus 10.000 Kronen.

Ill. 13   Ib Spang Olsen in: Lille dreng på Østerbro

1954 Johnsen, Alfred: **Den grønne flaske.** (The green bottle; Die grüne Flasche.)
København: Branner og Korch 1953.

Mathiesen, Egon: **Mis med de blå øjne.** (The blue-eyed cat; Mies mit den blauen Augen.) Ill.: Egon Mathiesen.
København: Gyldendal 1949.

1955 The prize was not given; Der Preis wurde nicht vergeben.

1956 Jeppesen, Poul: **Henrik.** (*Henry*; *Henrik*.)
København: Jespersen og Pio 1955.

1957 Lauring, Palle: **Stendolken.** (The stone dagger; Der Steindolch.) Ill.: Ib Spang Olsen.
København: Høst 1956.

1958 Ott, Estrid: **Chicos lange vandring.** (*Chico's* long walk; *Chicos* lange Wanderung.)
København: Grafisk forlag 1957.

1959 Ditlevsen, Tove: **Annelise — tretten år.** (*Annelise* — 13 years of age; Als *Annelise* dreizehn war.) Ill.: Kamma Svensson.
København: Høst 1958.

1960 Olsen, Karen Herold: **Afrika.** (Africa.)
København: Gjellerup 1959.

Plovgaard, Karen: **Sanne.** (*Sanne*.) Ill.: Jens Rosing.
København: Gad 1959.

1961 Knudsen, Poul E.: **Vaeddemålet.** (The contest; Der Wettstreit.)
København: Gyldendal 1960.

Ungermann, Arne: **Da solen blev forkølet.** (When the sun caught a cold; Als die Sonne sich erkältete.) Ill.: Arne Ungermann.
København: Spectator 1960.

1962 Birkeland, Thøger: **Når hanen galer.** (When the cock crows; Wenn der Hahn kräht.)
København: Gyldendal 1961.

1963 Bjerge Hansen, Valborg: **Helle — ikke som de andre.** (*Helle* — different from the others; *Helle* — nicht wie die anderen.)
København: Gad 1962.

Brande, Marlie: **Da skoene løb med Laura.** (When the shoes ran away with *Laura*; Als die Schuhe mit *Laura* davonliefen.) Ill.: Marlie Brande.
København: Erichsen 1962.

Spang Olsen, Ib: **Drengen i månen.** (The boy in the moon; Der Junge im Mond.) Ill.: Ib Spang Olsen.
København: Gyldendal 1962.

1964 Pedersen, Mona/Pedersen, Peter Christian: **Israel.** (Israel.) Ill.: Hans-Henrik Ley.
København: Munksgaard 1963.

Spang Olsen, Ib: Blaesten. (The wind; Der Wind.) Ill.: Ib Spang Olsen.
København: Gyldendal 1963.

Spang Olsen, Ib: **Regnen.** (The rain; Der Regen.) Ill.: Ib Spang Olsen.
København: Gyldendal 1963.

Spang Olsen, Ib: **Det lille lokomotiv.** (The little locomotive; Die kleine Lokomotive.) Ill.: Ib Spang Olsen.
København: Gad 1963.

1965 Rasmussen, Halfdan: **Børnerim.** (Children's rhymes; Kinderreime.) Ill.: Ib Spang Olsen.
København: Schøberg 1964.

1966 The prize was not given; Der Preis wurde nicht vergeben.

1967 Møller, Jan: **Borger i det gamle København.** (Citizen in old Copenhagen; Bürger im alten Kopenhagen.)
København: Gjellerup 1966.

Spang Olsen, Ib: **Mosekonens bryg.** (The moorish woman's brew; Das Gebräu der Moorfrau.) Ill.: Ib Spang Olsen.
København: Gyldendal 1966.

1968 Bødker, Cecil: **Silas og den sorte hoppe.** (*Silas* and the black mare; *Silas* und die schwarze Stute.)
København: Branner og Korch 1967.

1969 Kirkegaard, Ole Lund: **Albert.** (**Albert.**)
København: Gyldendal 1968.

1970 Haugaard, Erik Christian: **De små fisk.** (The small fish; Die kleinen Fische.)
København: Høst 1969.

1971 The prize was not given; Der Preis wurde nicht vergeben.

1972 Andersen, Benny; Snøvsen på sommerferie. (*Snøvsen* on summer holiday; *Snøvsen* hat Sommerferien.) Ill.: Signe Plesner Andersen.
København: Borgen 1970.

Knudsen, Per Holm: **Sådan får man et barn.** (How father and mother get a baby; Wie Vater und Mutter ein Kind bekommen.)
København: Borgen 1971.

1973 Kruuse, Merete: **Rode-Rikke.** (*Rode-Rikke.*)
København: Gyldendal 1972.

1974 Petersen, Palle: **50 år i jernet. Rapport fra en arbejdsplads.** (50 years in irons. Report from a work-place; 50 Jahre in Fesseln. Bericht von einem Arbeitsplatz.)
København: Borgen 1975.

1975 Krog, Inge: **Hjemmefra.** (From home; Von zu Hause.)
København: Borgen 1975.

1976 Andersen, Leif Esper: **Fremmed.** (Strange; Fremd.)
København: Gyldendal 1975.

1977 Reuter, Bjarne B.: **En dag i Hector hansen's liv.** (One day in the life of *Hector Hansen*; Ein Tag im Leben von *Hector Hansen.*) Ill.: Klaus Albrechtsen.
Kastrup: Branner og Korch 1976.

1978 Haller, Bent: **Indianeren.** (The Indian; Der Indianer.) Ill.: Palle Bregnhøi.
København: Borgen 1978.

1979 *Literature prize/Literaturpreis*
Berliner, Franz: **Haevneren. Historien om Skaevben.** (The revenger. The story of the cripple; Der Rächer. Die Geschichte des Mannes mit dem krummen Bein.) Ill.: Robert Jensen.
København: Sesam 1978.

Berliner, Franz: Ulven som jager alene. (The wolf that hunts alone; Der Wolf, der allein jagt.)
København: Sesam 1979.

Illustration
Dahlerup, Rina in:
Winding, Thomas: **Odas historie.** (*Olda's* story; Die Geschichte von *Oda.*)
København: Borgen 1978.

1980 *Literature prize/Literaturpreis*
Olsen, Lars-Henrik: **Raeven i skoven.** (The fox in the forest; Der Fuchs im Wald.) Ill.: Inger Marie and Leif Ringtved.
Klampenborg: Mallings 1980.

Illustration
Spang Olsen, Ib: Complete works; Gesamtschaffen.

Barnabókaheidourslønn Tórshavnar býráds

The prize for the best Faroese children's book was established by the town Council of Tórshavn in 1976. Authors as well as illustrators can be awarded the prize which consists of 8000 krónur. The selection committee is made up of five members: the chairman of the town cultural committee, one librarian from the municipal children's library, one teacher from the municipal schools and two other members nominated by the Town Council.

Die Vergabe des Preises für das beste färingische Kinderbuch wurde 1976 vom Stadtrat in Tórshavn beschlossen. Sowohl Autoren als auch Illustratoren können mit dem Preis ausgezeichnet werden, der aus 8000 Kronen besteht. Das Auswahlkomitee besteht aus folgenden 5 Migliedern: dem Kulturreferent der Stadt, einem Lehrer und zwei anderen Migliedern, die vom Stadtrat ernannt werden.

1976 Jacobsen, Steinbjörn Berghamar: **Hönan og hanin.** (The hen and the cock; Das Huhn und der Hahn.) Ill.: Bárđur Jacobsen.
Tórshavn: Steplid 1970.

Jacobsen, Steinbjörn Berghamar: **Hin snjóhvíti kettlingurin.** (The snow-white kitten; Das schneeweisse Kätzchen.) Ill.: Bárdur Jacobsen.
Tórshavn: Steplid 1971.

Jacobsen, Steinbjörn Berghamar: **Krákuungarnir.** (Crow children; Krähenjunge.) Ill.: Bárdur Jacobsen.
Tórshavn: Steplid 1972.

Jacobsen, Steinbjörn Berghamar: **Maeid.** (The bleating lamb; Das Bählamm.) Ill.: Bárdur Jacobsen.
Tórshavn: Steplid 1972.

Jacobsen, Steinbjörn Berghamar: **Lív og hundurin.** (*Liv* and the dog; *Liv* und der Hund.) Ill.: Bárdur Jacobsen.
Tórshavn: Emil Thomsen 1974.

Jacobsen, Steinbjörn Berghamar: **Brái steinur.** (Grey stone; Grauer Stein.) Ill.: Bárdur Jacobsen.
Tórshavn: Steplid 1975.

1977 Joensen, Sigurd: *Gráa dunna.* (The grey duck; Die graue Ente.)
Tórshavn: Steplid 1958.

Joensen, Sigurd: **Kálvamuan.** (The small calf; Das kleine Kalb.)
Tórshavn: Steplid 1959.

Joensen, Sigurd: **Lambamaeid.** (The little lamb; Das kleine Lamm.)
Tórshavn: Steplid 1960.

1978 Dahl, Marianna D.: **Burtur á heidi.** (Out in the peat bog; Im Torfmoor.)
Tórshavn: Steplid 1975.

1979 Andreasen, Andreas: **100 sangir.**
Tórshavn: Steplið 1977.

Dahl, Oli: **Við abba a floti.** (Fishing with my grandfather; Ich fische mit meinem Großvater.)
Tórshavn: Steplið 1976.

Dahl, Oli: **Við ommu til neytar.** (With my grandmother by the cows; Mit meiner Grossmutter bei den Kühen.)
Tórshavn: Steplið 1977.

Dahl, Oli: **Við gubba at kasta nót.** (Dragging the net with my father; Ich ziehe das Fischnetz mit meinem Vater ein.)
Tórshavn: Steplið 1977.

Dahl, Oli: **Við mammi i torvi.** (Cutting peat with mother; Beim Torfstechen mit meiner Mutter.)
Tórshavn: Steplið 1978.

Finland/Finnland

Tauno Karilas palkinto

The Tauno Karilas Award was established in 1969. It is awarded annually for the best youth book. The Finnish Association of Youth Book Writers act as judges for this prize.

Dieser Preis wurde 1969 zum ersten Mal verliehen. Er wird jährlich für das beste Jugendbuch vergeben. Die finnische Vereinigung der Jugendschriftsteller stellt die Jury dar.

1969 Martinheimo, Asko: **Poltaa, poltaa . . .** (It burns, it burns . . .; Es brennt, es brennt . . .)
Porvoo, Helsinki: W. Söderström 1968.

Ill. 14 Mikko Samulinen in: Tunari

1970 Haakana, Veikko: **Kivinen biisoni.** (The stone bison; Der steinerne Bison.)
Helsinki: Valistus 1969.

1971 Pakkanen, Kaija: **Sebastian tytär.** (*Sebastian's* daughter; *Sebastians* Tochter.)
Porvoo, Helsinki: W. Söderström 1970.

1972 Martinheimo, Asko: **Pääkallokiitäjä.** (Death's-head moth; Totenkopffalter.)
Porvoo, Helsinki: W. Söderström 1971.

1973 The prize was not given; Der Preis wurde nicht vergeben.

1974 Mäkelä, Hannu: **Herra Huu.** (Mr. *Huu*; Herr *Huu*.) Ill.: Hannu Mäkelä.
Helsinki: Otava 1973.

1975 Raustela, Lasse: **Piura.** (*Piura*.)
Helsinki: Tammi 1974.

1976 The prize was not given; Der Preis wurde nicht vergeben.

1977 Arjatsalo, Arvi: **Kovikset.** (Hard core; Der harte Kern.)
Helsinki: Otava 1976.

1978 Jalo, Marvi: **Ratsukesä.** (Riding holiday; Reiterferien.)
Helsinki: Tammi 1977.

1979 Nojonen, Uolevi: **Röönpöök.** (*Röönpöök*.)
Porvoo: W. Söderström 1979.

Nojonen, Uolevi: **Matkatoverit.** (Fellow travellers; Reisegefährten.)
Helsinki: Kirjayhtymä 1969.

Rudolf Koivu palkinto

The Rudolf Koivu Foundation presents annually an award to the illustrator of the best children's book of the previous year. The first presentation took place in 1949. The award is in the form of a bronze medal which was designed by Tapio Tapiovaara. It shows "The birch tree and the star", after a drawing by Koivu. The initiator of the prize was August Fr. Thitz, a friend of the artist Rudolf Koivu.

Seit 1949 verleiht die Rudolf-Koivu-Stiftung alljährlich für die beste Jugendbuchillustration des vergangenen Jahres einen Preis. Die von Tapio Tapiovaara entworfene Plakette ist in Bronze gegossen. Sie zeigt das Motiv "Die Birke und der Stern" nach einer Zeichnung von Koivu. Der Initiator des Preises war August Fr. Thitz, ein Freund von Rudolf Koivu.

1949 Mäkinen, Risto in:
Roine, Raul: **Pilvilinna.** (Castle in the air; Das Luftschloss.)
Porvoo: W. Söderström 1948.

1950 Danning, Alf in:
Pohjoismaisia kansansatuja. (Nordic fairy tales; Nordische Volksmärchen.)
Helsinki: Kuvataide 1949.

1951 Sjöstedt, Helga in:
Heino, Saara: **Pikkusiskojen satuja.** (Little sister's fairy tales; Märchen der kleinen Schwester.)
Helsinki: Valistus 1949.

1952 Tanttu, Erkki in:
Palsi, Sakari: **Minä sain kukon kiini.** (I have the rooster; Ich hab' den Hahn.)
Helsinki: Otava 1951.

1953 Tuomi, Erkki in:
Merikoski, Kaarlo/Merikoski, Ilona: **Jättiläisiä ja kääpiöitä.** (Giants and dwarves; Riesen und Zwerge.)
Helsinki: Valistus 1952.

1954 Karma, Maija in:
Nissinen, Aila: **Orriporrin talo.** (*Orriporri's* house; *Orriporris* Haus.)
Porvoo, Helsinki: W. Söderström 1953.

1955 The prize was not awarded; Der Preis wurde nicht vergeben.

1956 Tanttu, Erkki in:
Andersen, Hans Christian: **Satuja.** (Fairy tales; Märchen.)
Helsinki: Otava 1955.

1957 Lahtinen, Heljä in:
Salmelainen, Eero: **Suomen kansan satuja ja tarinoita.** (Fairy tales and sagas of the Finnish people; Märchen und Sagen des finnischen Volkes.)
Helsinki: Suomailaisen kirjallisuuden seura 1955.

Sjöstedt, Helga in:
Merikoski, Ilona/Leväluoma, Liisa: **Kansojen satuja.** (Folk tales; Volksmärchen.)
Helsinki: Valistus 1956.

1958 Jansson, Tove in:
Jansson, Tove: **Trollvinter.** (Troll winter; Trollwinter.)
Helsinki: Schildts 1957.

1959 Karma, Maija in:
Lagerlöf, Selma: **Peukaloisen retket.** (*Tom Thumb's* journey; Die Ausflüge des *Däumlings*.)
Porvoo: W. Söderström 1958.

1960 The prize was not awarded; Der Preis wurde nicht vergeben.

1961 Sjöstedt, Helga in:
Salola, Eero: **Hölmölän kylä.** (The village of simpletons; Das Dorf der Tölpel.)
Helsinki: Valistus 1960.

1962 Karma, Maija in:
Pakkanen, Kaija: **Pien-Hauska.** (Little jolly; Das Klein-Lustig.)
Porvoo, Helsinki: W. Söderström 1961.

Karma, Maija in:
Pröysen, Alf: **Pikkurillisen kepposet.** (The tricks of the little finger; Die Streiche des Fingers.)
Porvoo, Helsinki: W. Söderström 1961.

Tapiovaara, Tapio in:
Konttinen, Aili: **Lasten kultainen Kalevala IV.** (Children's golden Kalevala; Das goldene Kalevala der Kinder.)
Porvoo, Helsinki: W. Söderström 1961.

1963 Könni, Yrjö in:
Topelius, Zacharias: **Parasta Topeliusta.** (The best of *Topelius*; Das Beste von *Topelius*.)
Helsinki: Valistus 1962.

1964 Lindeberg, Alexander in:
Grimm: **Sadut.** (Fairy tales; Märchen.)
(Unpublished. Nicht veröffentlicht.)

1965 Könni, Yrjö in:
Nissinen, Aila: **Kalpeiden vuorten tarinoita.** (The story of the pale mountains; Die Geschichte von den blassen Bergen.)
Helsinki: Valistus 1964.

Karma, Maija in:
Konttinen, Aili: **Tässä tulee intiaani.** (Here comes the Indian; Hier kommt der Indianer.)
Porvoo, Helsinki: W. Söderström 1964.

1966 Lindeberg, Alexander in:
Lindeberg, Alexander: **Iloiset aapiskuvat.** (The merry ABC pictures; Die heiteren ABC-Bilder.)
Porvoo, Helsinki: W. Söderström 1965.

Mäkinen, Risto in:
Laurikainen, Mertsi-Ilmari: **Onnimanni ja Kukkaliina.** (*Onnimanni* and *Kukkaliine*; *Onnimanni* und *Kukkaliine.*)
Helsinki: Valistus 1965.

Könni, Maire in:
Salola, Eero/Kontturi, Otro: **Lukutunnin kirja VI.** (The book for reading hour VI; Das Buch der Lesestunde VI.)
Helsinki: Valistus 1965.

1967 Tanttu, Erkki in:
Satu meni saunaan. (The fairy tale went to the sauna; Das Märchen ging in die Sauna.)
Helsinki: Otava 1966.

Tanninen, Oili in:
Tanninen, Oili: **Nunnu lentää.** (*Nunnu* flies; *Nunnu* fliegt.)
Helsinki: Otava 1966.

1968 Mäkinen, Risto in:
Laitakari-Kaila, Leena-Kaisa: **Ett tu tre.** (One, two, three; Eins, zwei, drei.)
Helsinki: Valistus 1967.

1969 Karma, Maija in:
Pennanen, Lea: **Piilomaan pikku aasi.** (The little donkey of Piilomaa; Der kleine Esel von Piilomaa.)
Helsinki: Otava 1968.

Tanttu, Erkki in:
Lehtonen, Joel: **Metsän ukko.** (The old man of the woods; Der Greis des Waldes.)
Helsinki: Otava 1968.

Vanninen, Elina in:
Kunnas, Kirsi: **Aikamme aapinen.** (The ABC book of our time; Das ABC Buch unserer Zeit.)
Porvoo, Helsinki: W. Söderström 1968.

1970 The prize was not awarded; Der Preis wurde nicht vergeben.

1971 Viljamaa-Rissanen, Katriina in:
Suuri satukirja. (The great book of fairy tales; Das grosse Märchenbuch.)
Helsinki: Valitut Palat 1970.

1972 Toivola, Heka in:
Toivola, Heka: **The Hole Story — Läpinäky.** (The Hole Story — *Läpinäky.*)
Helsinki: Viherjuuri & Uusi Kivipaino Oy 1971.

1973 Nopsanen, Aarne in:
Nopsanen, Aarne: **Peruskoulun historia.** (The elementary school story; Die Geschichte der Grundschule.)

1974 Viljamaa-Rissanen, Katriina in:
Helakisa, Kaarina: **Elli-velli-karamelli.** (Nelly Kelly Pretty Jelly; Ihne-Bihne-Mandarine.)
Helsinki: Weilin & Göös 1973.

1975 Landström, Björn in:
Olipa kerran. (Once upon a time; Es war einmal.)
Helsinki: Otava 1974.

1976 Lindquist, Seppo in:
Kerrotaan satu. (Let's tell a tale; Erzählen wir ein Märchen.)
Helsinki: Otava 1975.

1977 Taina, Hannu in:
Hännikäinen, Liisa: **Doina.** (*Doina.*)
Helsinki: Otava 1976.

1978 Jansson, Tove in:
Jansson, Tove: **Den farliga resan.** (The dangerous journey; Die gefährliche Reise.)
Helsinki: Schildts 1977.

Vuori, Pekka in:
Vuori, Pekka: **Käpälämäki.** (Helter skelter; Holterdiepolter.)
Helsinki: Kirjasieppo Ky 1977.

1979 Kaila, Kaarina in:
Mikkola, Marja-Leena: **Lumijoutsen.** (The snow swan; Der Schneeschwan.)
Helsinki: Otava 1978.

Arvid Lydecken palkinto

This prize has been presented annually, since 1969, for the best picture book, children's story or fairy tale. The Finnish Association of Youth Book Writers act as judges for this competition.

Seit 1969 wird dieser Preis für das beste Bilder-, Märchen- oder Kinderbuch vergeben. Die finnische Vereinigung der Jugendschriftsteller stellt die Jury dar.

1969 Nissinen, Aila: **Terva-apila.** (The tar-clover; Der Teer-Klee.)
Helsinki: Otava 1968.

1970 Polkunen, Mirjam: **Jättiläinen, joka tahtoi muuttua karhuksi.** (The giant who wanted to change himself into a bear; Der Riese, der sich in einen Bär verwandeln möchte.) Ill.: Ulla Rantanon and Esko Tirronen.
Porvoo, Helsinki: W. Söderström 1969.

1971 Krohn, Leena: **Vihreä vallankumous.** (The green revolution; Die grüne Revolution.) Ill.: Inari Krohn.
Helsinki: Tammi 1970.

1972 Kaikusalo, Asko: **Hiiristoori.** (The mouse story; Die Mausgeschichte.) Ill.: Asko Kaikusalo and Teuvo Suominen.
Helsinki: Tammi 1971.

1973 Kunnas, Kirsi: **Puupuu ja Käpypoika.** (*Tree-tree* and *Cone-boy*; Baumbaum und der *Tannenzapfenjunge*.) Ill.: Martti Syrjä.
Porvoo, Helsinki: W. Söderström 1972.

Rintala, Paavo: **Uu ja poikanen.** (*Uu* and the little one; *Uu* und der Kleine.)
Helsinki: Otava 1972.

1974 Helakisa, Kaarina: **Elli-velli-karamelli.** (Nelly-Kelly Pretty-Jelly; Ihne-Bihne-Mandarine.) Ill.: Katriina Viljamaa-Rissanen.
Helsinki: Weilin & Göös 1973.

1975 Krohn, Leena: **Viimeinen kesävieras.** (The last summer guest; Der letzte Sommergast.) Ill.: Inari Krohn.
Helsinki: Tammi 1974.

1976 Tauriala, Anna: **Kun Leenan ällästä tuli ärrä.** (How *Leena's* L became an R; Wie *Leenas* L zu einem R wurde.) Ill.: Anna Tauriala.
Jyväskylä: Gummerus 1975.

1977 Vaijärvi, Kari/Vaijärvi, Pirre/Hietanen, Irja: **Jeppe keksii jännärin.** (*Jeppe* finds an exciting story; *Jeppe* findet eine aufregende Geschichte.)
Espoo: Weilin & Göös 1976.

1978 Mäkelä, Hannu: **Hevonen joka hukkasi silmälasinsa.** (The horse that lost his spectacles; Das Pferd, das seine Brille verlor.)
Helsinki: Otava 1977.

1979 Erkkilae, Leena: **Satakieli, Marian lintu.** (*Maria's* nightingale; *Maria's* Nachtigall.) Ill.: Ulla Vasjakallio.
Helsinki: Lasten Keskus 1979.

Topelius palkinto

This prize was established in 1947 by the publisher Werner Söderström, Porvoo and Helsinki. It is given annually by the Association of Children's Book Authors to the writer of the year's best Finnish book. The jury has four members. The prize is named after Sakari Topelius (1818 — 1898), whose stories are still read and loved.

Der vom Verlag Werner Söderström, Porvoo und Helsinki, gestiftete Preis wurde erstmals im Jahre 1947 verliehen. Er wird jährlich an einen finnischen Autor für das beste Buch des Jahres vergeben. Die Verteilung des Preises erfolgt durch den Verband der Jugendbuchautoren. Die Jury besteht aus vier Mitgliedern. Benannt wurde der Preis nach Sakari Topelius (1818—1898), der noch heute von den finnischen Kindern, und nicht nur von diesen, gelesen und geliebt wird.

1948 Konttinen, Aili: **Inkeri palasi Ruotsista.** (*Inkeri* came back from Sweden; *Inkeri* kam aus Schweden zurück.)
Porvoo, Helsinki: W. Söderström 1947.

1949 Konttinen, Aili: **Hymyile, Krisse.** (Keep smiling, *Krisse;* Lächle, *Krisse.*)
Helsinki: Tammi 1948.

Wainio, K.W.: **Perman jousi.** (The bow of *Perma;* Der Bogen von *Perma.*)
Jyväskylä: Gummerus 1948.

1950 Rautapalo, Tauno: **Rohkeita poika.** (Brave boys; Mutige Jungen.)
Helsinki: Valistus 1949.

1951 Honka, Aaro: **Sisukkaat sarvikuanot.** (The persistent rhinoceroses; Die hartnäckigen Nashörner.)
Helsinki: Valistus 1950.

Honka, Aaro: **Suurleirin seikkailijat.** (The adventure of the great camp; Die Abenteuer des grossen Lagers.)
Porvoo, Helsinki: W. Söderström 1950.

Honka, Aaro: **Teatteriteinit.** (The theater-teens; Die Theaterteens.)
Helsinki: Tammi 1950.

1952 Somersalo, Aili for:
Complete works; Gesamtschaffen.

1953 Härmä, Leena: **Tuittupää ja Rantakylän Sisu.** (*Tuittupää* and *Rantakylä's* courage; *Tuittupää* and *Rantakyläs* Mut.)
Porvoo, Helsinki: W. Söderström 1952.

1954 Kurenniemi, Marjatta: **Oli ennen Onnimanni.** (It used to be *Onnimanni;* Es war früher *Onnimanni.*)
Helsinki: Tammi 1953.

1955 Tamminen, Juuse: **Varjagien aare.** (The treasure of the *Varjags;* Der Schatz der *Waräger.*)
Porvoo, Helsinki: W. Söderström 1954.

1956 Haavio, Martti: **Kultaomena.** (The golden apple; Der goldene Apfel.) Ill.: Heljä Lahtinen.
Helsinki: W. Söderström 1955.

Haavio, Martti: **Tuhkimus.** (*Tuhkimus.*) Ill.: Heljä Lahtinen.
Porvoo, Helsinki: W. Söderström 1955.

1957 Tynni, Aale: **Heikin salaisuudet.** (*Heikki's* secrets; *Heikkis* Geheimnisse.) Ill.: Usko Laukkan.
Porvoo, Helsinki: W. Söderström 1956.

1958 Kokki, Aira: **Avattu ovi.** (The open door; Die geöffnete Tür.)
Helsinki: Otava 1957.

1959 Nissinen, Aila: **Minä olen Lammenpei.** (I am *Lammenpei;* Ich bin *Lammenpei.*) Ill.: Maija Karma.
Helsinki: W. Söderström 1958.

Nissinen, Aila: **Laulavat omenat.** (The singing apples; Die singenden Äpfel.) Ill.: Sorella Railo.
Helsinki: Valistus 1958.

1960 Karilas, Tauno for:
(Complete works; Gesamtschaffen.)

1961 Setälä, Salme: **Minä olen Marlene.** (I am *Marlene;* Ich bin *Marlene.*)
Helsinki: Valistus 1960.

1962 Otava, Merja: **Minä, Annika ÄP.** (I, *Annika* ÄP; Ich, *Annika* ÄP.)
Porvoo, Helsinki: W. Söderström 1961.

1963 Vuorinen, Esteri: **Kala-Keisarin porsas.** (The fish-emperor's pig; Das Ferkel des Fisch-Kaisers.) Ill.: Timo Martin.
Porvoo, Helsinki: W. Söderström 1962.

1964 Kojo, Pauli: **Herrankukkaro.** (The master purse; Der Meister-Beutel.)
Helsinki: Otava 1963.

1965 Helakisa, Kaarina: **Satukirja.** (Book of fairy tales; Märchenbuch.) Ill.: Kaarina Helakisa.
Porvoo, Helsinki: W. Söderström 1964.

1966 Tanninen, Oili: **Nunnu.** (*Nunnu.*) Ill.: Oili Tanninen.
Helsinki: Otava 1965.

1967 Kurenniemi, Marjatta: **Onnelin ja Annelin talo.** (The house of *Onnelli* and *Anneli*; *Onnelis* und *Annelis* Haus.) Ill.: Maija Karma.
Porvoo, Helsinki: W. Söderström 1966.

1968 Merimaa, Kaarlo for:
(Complete works; Gesamtschaffen.)

1969 Keskitalo, Margareta: **Tyttö kuunarilaiturilla.** (The girl on the bridge of the schooner; Das Mädchen auf der Schonerbrücke.)
Porvoo, Helsinki: W. Söderström 1968.

1970 Otava, Merja: **Kuuvuosi.** (The moon year; Das Mondjahr.)
Porvoo, Helsinki: W. Söderström 1969.

1971 Virtanen, Rauha S.: **Joulukussivarkaus.** (The theft of a Christmas tree; Der Diebstahl eines Weihnachtsbaumes.)
Porvoo, Helsinki: W. Söderström 1970.

1972 Keskitalo, Margareta: **Liuhuhihnaballadi.** (Assembly line ballad: Die Fliessbandballade.)
Porvoo, Helsinki: W. Söderström 1971.

1973 Nojonen, Uolevi: **Askeetti ei saa kompleseja.** (The ascetic develops no complexes; Der Asket hat keine Komplexe.)
Porvoo, Helsinki: W. Söderström 1972.

1974 Samulinen, Mikko: **Tulikavio.** (Fire hoof; Feuer Huf.)
Helsinki: Tammi 1973.

1975 Suhonen, Pekka: **Manta.** (*Manta.*)
Helsinki: Tammi 1974.

1976 Raustela, Lasse: **Noitakellot.** (Witch bells; Hexenglocken.)
Helsinki: Tammi 1975.

1977 Martinheimo, Asko: **Lassinkyynel.** (*Lassi's* tears; *Lassis* Tränen.)
Helsinki: W. Söderström 1976.

1978 Jansson, Tove: **Den farliga resan.** (The dangerous journey; Die gefährliche Reise.)
Helsingfors: Schildts 1977.

1979 Sandman Lilius, Irmelin: **Complete works;** Gesamtschaffen.

State Award

The State Award established in 1969. It is presented every year to five or six of the best books for children and young people published during the preceding year in Finland.

Der Staatspreis besteht seit 1969. Alljährlich werden fünf bis sechs hervorragende Kinder- und Jugendbücher aus der finnischen Produktion des Vorjahres ausgezeichnet.

1969 Carpelan, Bo: **Bågen.** (The bow; Der Bogen.)
Helsinki: Schildts 1968.

Kaila, Osmo: **Pakkopeli.** (The compulsive game; Das Zwangsspiel.)
Porvoo, Helsinki: W. Söderström 1968.

Keskitalo, Margareta: **Tyttö kuunarilaiturilla.** (The girl on the bridge of the schooner; Das Mädchen auf der Schonerbrücke.)
Porvoo, Helsinki: W. Söderström 1968.

Martinheimo, Asko: **Poltaa, Poltaa . . .** (It burns, it burns . . .; Es brennt, es brennt.)
Porvoo, Helsinki: W. Söderström 1968.

Nojonen, Uolevi: **Sigmund Freudin kaamea flunssa.** (*Sigmund Freud's* ghostly influenza; Die unheimliche Grippe von *Sigmund Freud.*)
Porvoo, Helsinki: W. Söderström 1968.

1970 Haakana, Veikko: **Kivinen biisoni.** (The stone bison; Der steinerne Bison.)
Helsinki: Valistus 1969.

Otava, Merja: **Kuuvuosi.** (The moon year; Das Mondjahr.)
Porvoo, Helsinki: W. Söderström 1969.

Räikönen, Erkki: **Jämä.** (*Jämä.*)
Helsinki: Weilin & Göös 1969.

Sandman-Lilius, Irmelin: **Gullkrona gränd.** (Gold Crown Lane; Goldkronengasse.)
Helsinki: Schildts 1969.

Tanninen, Oili: **Nunnu putoaa.** (*Nunnu* falls down; *Nunnu* fällt.)
Ill.: Oili Tanninen.
Helsinki: Otava 1970.

1971 Jansson, Tove: **Sent i November.** (Late in November; Spät im November.) Ill.: Tove Jansson.
Helsinki: Schildts 1970.

Krohn, Leena: **Vihreä vallankumous.** (The green revolution; Die grüne Revolution.) Ill.: Inari Krohn.
Helsinki: Tammi 1970.

Salo, Yrjö: **Mitäs me metallimiehet.** (We metal men; Wir Metallmänner.)
Helsinki: Otava 1970.

Virtanen, Rauha S.: **Joulukuusivarkaus.** (The theft of a Christmas tree; Der Diebstahl eines Weihnachtsbaumes.)
Porvoo, Helsinki: W. Söderström 1970.

Kontakti-sarja: **Kontakti series; Kontakti-Serie.)**
Helsinki: Kauppiaitten Kustannus 1970.

1972 Hietanen, Liisi: **Kananlento.** (A chicken never flies far; Ein Huhn fliegt nie sehr weit.)
Helsinki: Tammi 1971.

Kaikusalo, Asko: **Hiiristoori.** (The mouse story; Die Mausgeschichte.) Ill.: Asko Kaikusalo and Teuvo Suominen.

Keskitalo, Margareta: **Liukuhihnaballadi.** (Assembly line ballad; Die Fliessbandballade.)
Porvoo, Helsinki: W. Söderström 1971.

Kolu, Kaarina: **Konnakopla ja III B.** (The troublemakers and class III B; Die Störenfriede und die Klasse III B.)
Helsinki: Tammi 1971.

Martinheimo, Asko: **Pääkallokiitäjä.** (The death's-head moth; Der Totenkopffalter.)
Porvoo, Helsinki: W. Söderström 1971.

Samulinen, Mikko: **Hiljaisen joen aave.** (The ghost of the silent river; Das Gespenst des stillen Flusses.)
Helsinki: Tammi 1971.

1973 Bondestam, Kati: **Pikku kanin hassu päivä.** (Little rabbit's funny day; Häschens lustiger Tag.) Ill.: Camilla Mickwitz.
Helsinki: Weilin & Göös 1972.

Lappalainen, Ines: **Vastamäen Saara.** (*Sarah* from *Vastamäki*; *Sarah* von *Vastamäki*.)
Helsinki: Tammi 1972.

Lindquist, Marita: **Kottens badvända b.** (*Kotten's* turned around "b"; *Kottens* umgedrehtes b.) Ill.: Ilon Wikland.

Saarto, Tuula: **Suljetut ovet.** (The closed door; Die geschlossene Türe.)
Helsinki: Otava 1972.

Suhonen, Pekka: **Kauniiden naisten juttu.** (The story of the beautiful women; Die Geschichte der schönen Frauen.)
Helsinki: Tammi 1972.

1974 Helakisa, Kaarina: **Elli-velli-karamelli.** (Nelly Kelly Pretty Jelly; Ihne-Bihne Mandarine.) Ill.: Katriina Viljamaa-Rissanen.
Helsinki: Weilin & Göös 1973.

Lohija, Aura: **Mukana kuvassa.** (In the picture; Auf dem Bild.) Helsinki: Otava 1973.

Mäkelä, Hannu: **Herra Huu.** (Mr. *Huu;* Herr *Huu.*) Ill.: Hannu Mäkelä.
Helsinki: Otava 1973.

Suomela, Erkki K.: **Vieras kesä.** (Strange summer; Seltsamer Sommer.)
Helsinki: Gummerus 1973.

Vaijärvi, Kari/Hietanen, Irja: **Jeppe ja salaisuus.** (*Jeppe* and the secret; *Jeppe* und das Geheimnis.) Ill.: Pirre Vaijärvi.
Helsinki: Weilin & Göös 1973.

1975 Krohn, Leena: **Viimeinen kesävieras.** (The last summer guest; Der letzte Sommergast.) Ill.: Inari Krohn.
Helsinki: Tammi 1974.

Lindquist, Marita: **Kotten vågar into gå hem.** (*Kotton* dares not go home; *Kotton* hat keinen Mut nach Hause zu gehen.) Ill.: Ilon Wikland.
Helsinki: Schildts 1974.

Nojonen, Uolevi: **Tinatähti ja Anselmin aarre.** (The tin star and *Anselm's* treasure; Der Zinnstern und *Anselms* Schatz.)
Porvoo, Helsinki: W. Söderström 1974.

Raustela, Lasse: **Kuningashitti.** (On top of the list; Oben auf der Liste.)
Helsinki: Tammi 1974.

Raustela, Lasse: **Piura.** (*Piura.*)
Helsinki: Tammi 1974.

1976 Kellberg, Aarno: **Petteri pitää pintansa.** (*Peter* the staunch; *Peter* gibt nicht auf.)
Porvoo, Helsinki: W. Söderström 1975.

Kurenniemi, Marjatta: **Leenan sininen päivä.** (*Leena's* blue day; *Leenas* blauer Tag.) Ill.: Maija Karma.
Porvoo, Helsinki: W. Söderström 1975.

Mickwitz, Camilla: **Jason.** (*Jason.*) Ill.: Camilla Mickwitz.
Espoo: Weilin & Göös 1975.

1977 Kaila, Tiina: **Auringonlaskun torni.** (The tower of sundown; Der Turm des Sonnenuntergangs.)
Helsinki: Otava 1976.

Kariniemi, Annikki: **Pikku Jounin tarina.** (The story of little *Jouni;* Die Geschichte des kleinen *Jouni.*)
Hameenlinna: Karisto 1976.

Krohn, Leena: **Ihmsen vaatteissa.** (In the clothes of man; In den Kleidern des Menschen.)
Helsinki 1976.

Pakkanen, Kaija: **Huilu hilpeä.** (The cheerful flute; Die muntere Flöte.) Ill.: Pirkko Kilpelä.
Porvoo, Helsinki: W. Söderström 1976.

1978 Arjatsalo, Arvi: **Möhkämammutti.** (*Möhkä*, the mammoth; *Möhkä*, das Mammut.)
Helsinki: Otava 1977.

Kurvinen, Jorma: **Susikoira roi ja seikkailu saaristossa.** (*Roy*, the dog and the island adventure; Der Hund *Roy* und das Inselabenteuer.)
Helsinki: Otava 1977.

Mikkola, Marja-Leena: **Anni Manninen.** (*Anni Manninen.*)
Helsinki: Otava 1977.

Salo, Eeva: **Omenannahkakengät.** (The apple peel shoes; Die Apfelschalenschuhe.)
Helsinki: Sanoma 1977.

Särkilahti, Sirkaa. **Rimpatti.** (*Rimpatti.*)
Helsinki: W. Söderström 1977.

1979 Andersson, Christina: **William och Vild-Jam.** (*William* and *Wild-Jam.*) Ill.: Veronica Leo.
Helsingfors: Söderström 1978.

Helakisa, Kaarina: **Ainakin miljoona sinisträ kissaa.** (At least a million blue cats; Mindestens eine Million blaue Katzen.) Ill.: Jori Svärd.
Porvoo: W. Söderström 1978.

Samulinen, Mikko: **Tunari.** (*Tunari.*) Ill.: Mikko Samulinen.
Helsinki: Sanoma 1978.

Seppaelae, Arto: **Kättä päälle, Vasco da Gama.** (Agreed upon, *Vasco da Gama;* Abgemacht, *Vasco da Gama.*)
Porvoo: W. Söderström 1978.

Toijala, Anneli: **Filmaus seis!** (Stop showing off! Hör' auf zu protzen!)
Helsinki: Tammi 1978.

1980 Kunnas, Kirsi: **Kani Koipeliinin kuperkeikat.** (*Rabbit Longleg's* somersaults; Die Luftsprünge des *Hasen Langbein.*) Ill.: Leila Nieminen.
Porvoo: W. Söderström 1979.

Martinheimo, Asko: **Saari taivaanrannassa.** (The island on the horizon; Die Insel am Horizont.)
Porvoo: W. Söderström 1979.

Oksanen, Aulikki: **Ykä ja kuu.** (*Ykä* and the moon; *Ykä* und der Mond.) Ill.: Aulikki Oksanen.
Helsinki: Kirjayhtymä 1979.

Parkkinen, Jukka: **Korpi ja korven veikot.** (The raven and his forest brothers; Der Rabe und seine Brüder des Waldes.) Ill.: Jyrki Vuori.
Porvoo: W. Söderström 1979.

Ranivaara, Jorma: **Raamit ränniin.** (Into the blue; Ins blaue Ungewisse.)
Porvoo: W. Söderström 1979.

Soinne, Laura for: Complete works; Gesamtschaffen.

Anni Swanin Mitali

The Finnish section of the International Board on Books for Young People founded this prize, which is presented every third year for the best children's book published during the previous three years. The prize was named after the famous Finnish author, Anni Swan (1875—1958). The silver medal was designed by the sculptor, Wäinö Aaltonen.

Der von der finnischen Sektion des Internationalen Kuratoriums für das Jugendbuch gestiftete Preis wird alle drei Jahre für das beste Buch der vergangenen drei Jahre verliehen. Benannt wurde der Preis nach der berühmten finnischen Verfasserin Anni Swan (1875—1958). Die silberne Plakette wurde von dem Bildhauer Wäino Aaltonen entworfen.

1961 Otava, Merja: **Priska.** (*Priska.*)
Porvoo, Helsinki: W. Söderström 1959.

1964 Jansson, Tove: **Det osynliga barnet.** (The invisible child; Das unsichtbare Kind.) Ill.: Tove Jansson.
Helsingfors: Schildt 1962.

1967 Vuorinen, Esteri: **Köydenvetäjät.** (The rope pullers; Die Seilzieher.) Ill.: Maija Karma.
Porvoo, Helsinki: W. Söderström 1964.

Vuorinen, Esteri: **Lentojuna.** (The flying train; Der fliegende Zug.) Ill.: Maija Karma.
Porvoo, Helsinki: W. Söderström 1966.

Vuorinen, Esteri: **Martin sarviherra.** (*Marti's* horn master; *Martis* Lehrer im Hornblasen.) Ill.: Maija Karma.
Porvoo, Helsinki: W. Söderström 1965.

1970 Tanninen, Oili: **Hippu.** (Hippopotamus; Flusspferd.) Ill.: Oili Tanninen.
Helsinki: Otava 1967.

Tanninen, Oili: **Robotti Romulus.** (Robot *Romulus*; Roboter *Romulus.*) Ill.: Oili Tanninen.
Helsinki: Otava 1968.

Tanninen, Oili: **Nunnu putoaa.** (*Nunnu* falls down; *Nunnu* fällt.) Ill.: Oili Tanninen.
Helsinki: Otava 1969.

1973 Keskitalo, Margareta: **Liukuhihnaballadi.** (Assembly line ballad; Die Fliessbandballade.)
Porvoo, Helsinki: W. Söderström 1971.

1976 Mäkelä, Hannu: **Herra Huu.** (Mr. *Huu;* Herr *Huu.*) Ill.: Hannu Mäkelä.
Helsinki: Otava 1973.

1979 Krohn, Leena: **Ihmisen vaatteissa.** (In men's clothing; In Menschenkleidung.) Ill.: Leena Krohn.
Helsinki: Tammi 1976.

France/Frankreich

Prix L'Aiglon d'Or

This prize, begun in 1978, is awarded by the International Book Festival, Nice. The jury is composed of three children's book critics and three children's book sellers. The prize is given for fiction one year, and for non-

Ill. 15 Philippe Dumas in: La petite géante

fiction the next. The prize is awarded in three categories: the "Aiglon d'or" (1st prize), the "Aiglon d'argent" (2nd prize), the "Aiglon de bronze" (3rd prize).

1978 wurde der Preis beim Festival International du Livre in Nizza zum erstenmal verliehen. Die Jury besteht aus drei Kinderbuchkritikern und drei Fachbuchhändlern. Sie zeichnet jährlich drei Bücher aus mit dem "Aiglon d'or", "Aiglon d'argent" und "Aiglon de bronze" (erster, zweiter, dritter Preis). Die prämiierten Werke werden in einem Jahr aus der erzählenden Literatur, im anderen aus der Sachliteratur ausgewählt.

1978 *Fiction/Erzählende Literatur*

Garrel, Nadine: **Au pays du grand condor.** (In the land of the great condor; Im Land des großen Kondors.) Ill.: Bernad Héron.
Paris: Gallimard 1977.
(Aiglon d'or)

Dumas, Philippe: **La petite géante.** (The little giant; Die kleine Riesin.) Ill.: Philippe Dumas.
Paris: Ecole des Loisirs 1977.
(Aiglon d'argent)

Bruel, Christian/Bozellec, Anne: **Qui pleure?** (Who cries? Wer weint?)
Paris: Le souires qui mord 1977
(Aiglon de bronze)

1979 *Non-fiction/Sachbuch*

Lamblin, Simone: **Le Larousse des enfants.** (The Larousse dictionary for children; Das Larousse-Lexikon für Kinder.) Ill.: Marianne Gaunt.
Paris: Larousse 1978.
(Aiglon d'or)

Davot, Monique: **Taliko, indien de Guyane.** (*Taliko,* the Indian from Guayana; *Taliko,* der Indianer aus Guayana.) Ill.: François Davot.
Paris: Flammarion 1978.
(Aiglon d'argent)

Bergh, Catherine de/Verdet, Pierre: **A la découverte du ciel.** (On the discovery of the sky; Die Entdeckung des Himmels.) Ill.: Gérald Eveno.
Paris: Hachette 1978.
(Aiglon de bronze)

1980 *Fiction/Erzählende Literatur*
Brisou-Pellen, Evelyne: **Le mystère de la nuit des pierres.** (The mystery of the night of stones; Das Geheimnis der Nacht der Steine.) Ill.: Alain Letort.
Paris: Éd. de l'Amitié, G.T. Rageot 1980.
(Aiglon d'or)

Klotz, Claude: **Drôle de samedi soir.** (A strange Saturday evening; Ein merkwürdiger Samstag Abend.) Ill.: Gilles Bachelet.
Paris: Hachette 1979.
(Aiglon d'argent)

Dourdic, Jacques: **Le coup de pied.** (The kick; Der Fußtritt.) Ill.: François Davot.
Paris: Flammarion 1979.
(Aiglon de bronze)

Prix Jeunes Années

This prize, named after the magazine, Jeunes Années, was founded by the Fédération des Francs et Franches Camarades in 1974. The Federation has as its main concern the educational and creative use of leisure time by children and young people. They award two prizes each year for activity-oriented books: one directed towards educators, and the other towards children.

Der Preis wurde 1974 von der "Fédération des Francs et Franches Camarades" mit dem Titel der Zeitschrift dieses Verbandes gegründet. Da der Verband der erzieherischen Freizeitgestaltung für Kinder und Jugendliche dient, werden mit dem Preis jährlich zwei Beschäftigungsbücher ausgezeichnet. Eins wendet sich an die Erzieher, das andere an die Kinder selber.

1974 *Educator/Erzieher*
Gloton, Robert/Clero, Claude: **L'activité créatrice de l'enfant.** (Creative activity for children; Die schöpferische Tätigkeit des Kindes.)
Tournai: Casterman 1971.

Children/Kinder
Duflos, Solange: **Dans le pré.** (In the meadow; Auf der Wiese.) Ill.: H. Misek.
Paris: Hatier 1974.

1975 *Educator/Erzieher*
Maumené, Jean/Pineau, Gérard: **Construire des instruments, en jouer, en inventer d'autres.** (How to make musical instruments, to

play them, to invent new ones; Musikinstrumente bauen, darauf spielen, neue erfinden.)
Paris: Scarabée 1975.

Children/Kinder
Denis, Dominique: **Jouons aux clowns.** (Let's play clowns; Wir spielen Clowns.) Photos Jean-Claude DeWolf.
Paris: Hachette 1975.

1976 *Educator/Erzieher*
Gisling, Pierre: **L'imagination au galop.** (The galloping imagination; Die galoppierende Vorstellungskraft.)
Photos: Claude Huber.
Bruxelles: Plantyn 1976.

Children/Kinder
Politzer, Annie/Politzer, Michel: **Robin des Bois, mes carnets de croquis.** (The *Robin Hood* sketch book; Das Skizzenbuch von *Robin Hood.*)
Paris: Seghers & Cuenot 1975.

1977 *Educator/Erzieher*
The prize was not given; Der Preis wurde nicht vergeben.

Children/Kinder
Lepeuve, François: **Détectives et agents secrets.** (Detectives and secret agents; Detektive und Geheimagenten.) Ill.: Nicole Clareloux.
Paris: Gallimard 1976.

Cherrier, François: **Jouets scientifiques.** (Scientific toys; Technisches Spielzeug.) Ill.: François Cherrier.
Paris: Hachette 1977.

1978 The prize was not given; Der Preis wurde nicht vergeben.

1979 *Educator/Erzieher*
Charpentreau, Jacques: **La mystère en fleurs.** (The mystery of flowers; Das blühende Geheimnis.) Ill.
Paris: Éd. Ouvrières 1979.

Children/Kinder
Alégre, Jean-Paul: **Maquillages de fête.** (Festive masks; Masken mit Schminke.) Photos.
Paris: Dessain et Tolra 1978.

1980 *Educator/Erzieher*
Mayoud-Visconti, Renée: **Les aujourd'hui qui chantent.** (The todays that sing; Das singende Heute.) Ill.: Renée Mayoud-Visconti.
Paris: Le Centurion 1979.

Baget, René/Decosse, André/Feix, Monique/Flouret, Yves: **Jouons l'eau: du bouchon au bâteau.** (Playing water: from the tap to the boat; Spielen wir Wasser: vom Stöpsel zum Boot.) Ill. Photos. Paris: Scarabée 1979.

Children/Kinder

Alfaenger, Peter K.: **La musique buissonnière.** (Music is everywhere; Musik ist überall.) Ill.: Peter K. Alfaenger. Meaux: Le Chat 1979.

Prix Jeune France (formerly Prix Fantasia)

In 1972, the former Prix Fantasia, which was founded in 1956 by Magnard publishers, Paris, was renamed Prix Jeune France and is now sponsored jointly by Magnard publishers and "Foyer National des provinces Françaises". From 1968 the prize has been given every second year for a manuscript written in French for 8 to 16 year-olds. The aim of the prize is to help promote a better understanding of the world in which we live, and life in the various French regions through good books for the young. The jury is composed of writers, children's book experts and young people.

1972 wurde der 1956 gegründete Prix Fantasia zum Prix Jeune France umbenannt und gemeinsam vom Verlag Magnard und dem "Foyer National des Provences Françaises" verliehen. Der Preis wurde zunächst jährlich, von 1968 ab – alle zwei Jahre vergeben – und zwar für ein in französischer Sprache verfaßtes Manuskript, das sich an 8 bis 16jährige Leser wendet und ihnen zu einem besseren Verständnis der Welt, in der wir leben, verhilft. Auch Bücher über das Leben in den verschiedenen Provinzen Frankreichs werden einbezogen. Die Jury setzt sich aus Schriftstellern, Kinderbuch-Fachleuten und jungen Lesern zusammen.

1956 Elsie (i.e. Collin Delavaud): **Mylord et le saltimbanque.** (*Mylord* and the juggler; *Mylord* und der Gaukler.) Ill.: Collin Delavaud. Paris: Magnard 1955.

1957 Massane, Michèle: **Au vent de fortune.** (In the wind of fortune; Im Wind des Schicksals.) Ill.: Pierre Rousseau. Paris: Magnard 1956.

1958 The prize was not given; Der Preis wurde nicht vergeben.

1959 Bourliaguet, Léonce: **Les compagnons de l'arc.** (The companions of the bow; Die Bogengenossen.) Ill.: Simone Deleuil. Paris: Magnard 1958.

1960 Chaine, Lucette/Voeltzel, Anne-Marie: **Chat sauvage et sapin bleu.** (Wild cat and blue pine tree; Wilde Katze und Blautanne.)
Ill.: Simone Deleuil.
Paris: Magnard 1959.

1961 Guillot, René: **Le maître des éléphants.** (The master of the elephants; Der Meister der Elefanten.) Ill.: Maurce Raffray.
Paris: Magnard 1960.

1962 Cénac, Claude: **Quatre pattes dans l'aventure.** (Four paws in an adventure; Vier Pfoten im Abenteuer.) Ill.: Françoise Dudal.
Paris: Magnard 1961.

1963 Froelich, Jean-Claude: **Voyage au pays de la Pierre Ancienne.** (Journey to the land of the *Ancient Stone*; Reise in das Land des alten Steins.) Ill.: Xavier Saint-Justh.
Paris: Magnard 1962.

1964 Arnaud-Valence, Suzy: **La longue veille.** (The long vigil; Die lange Wache.) Ill.: Xavier Saint Justh.
Paris: Magnard 1963.

1965 The prize was not given; Der Preis wurde nicht vergeben.

1966 Antona, René: **Les champions du gas-oil.** (The oil experts; Die Ölexperten.) Ill.: Jef Colline.
Paris: Magnard 1964.

1967 Piguet, Alice: **Tonio et les traboules.** (*Tonio* and the house passages; *Tonio* und die Häuserdurchgänge.) Ill.: Xavier Saint-Justh.
Paris: Magnard 1966.

1968 Debresse, Pierre: **Le trésor de Carthage.** (The treasure of Carthage; Der Schatz von Karthago.) Ill.: Philippe Degrave.
Paris: Magnard 1967.

1970 Cervon, Jacqueline: **Joao de Tintubal.** (*Joao de Tintubal.*) Ill.: Michel Gourlier.
Paris: Magnard 1969.

1972 Fillol, Luce: **Prune.** (*Prune.*) Ill.: Patrice Harispe.
Paris: Magnard 1972.

1974 Médina, Jean-Baptiste: **Papacopain.** (Papacopain = Father-Friend; Papacopain = Vater-Freund.)
Paris: Magnard 1974.

1976 Arnaud-Valence, Suzy: **Trois graines dans un pot de grès.** (Three grains in a sandstone urn; Drei Körner in einem Sandsteintopf.)
Paris: Magnard 1976.

1978/1980 The prize was not given; Der Preis wurde nicht vergeben.

Prix Jeunesse

The Prix Jeunesse was established in 1934 by the publishing house of Bourrelier, Paris. The first presentation took place in 1935. Only unpublished manuscripts written in French and independent of political or religious influences were considered. The jury was composed of fourteen members. The selected manuscripts were published by Bourrelier. The first president of the jury was Paul Hazard, who was succeeded by Georges Duhamel and Charles Vildrac.

In 1964 the house of Bourrelier merged with Armand Colin, and the prize-winning manuscripts were thereafter published under the heading, Colin-Bourrelier. In 1968, the prize-winning manuscripts were published by Ed. de l'Amitié — G.T. Rageot, Paris. Since 1972, the prize has been discontinued.

Der Prix Jeunesse wurde im Jahre 1934 vom Verlag Bourrelier, Paris, zur Förderung französischsprachiger Autoren für ein noch nicht veröffentlichtes unpolitisches und konfessionell nicht gebundenes Jugendbuchmanuskript vergeben. Die Jury besteht aus 14 ständigen Mitgliedern. Die Preisbücher werden im Verlag Bourrelier verlegt. Erster Präsident der Jury war Paul Hazard, ihm folgten Georges Duhamel und Charles Vildrac.

Seit 1964 ist der Verlag Bourrelier mit dem Verlag Armand Colin verbunden, die Bücher erscheinen also bei Colin-Bourrelier. Die Jury des Prix Jeunesse blieb jedoch die gleiche. Nur wurden ab 1968 die prämiierten Bücher bei Ed. de. l'Amitié — G.T. Rageot, Paris, herausgegeben. Seit 1972 besteht der Preis nicht mehr.

1935 Colmont, Marie: **Rossignol des neiges.** (The nightingale of the snow; Die Schnee-Nachtigall.) Ill.: Elsie Millon.
Paris: Bourrelier 1935.

1936 The prize was not given; Der Preis wurde nicht vergeben.

1937 Nigremont, Georges: **Jeantou, le maçon creusois.** (*Jeantou,* the bricklayer from Creuse; *Jeantou,* der Maurer aus der Creuse.) Ill.: Simone Bouglé.
Paris: Bourrelier 1937.

1938 The prize was not given; Der Preis wurde nicht vergeben.

1939 Vivier, Colette: **La maison des petits bonheurs.** (The house of the little joys; Das Haus der kleinen Freuden.) Ill.: Hélène Détroyat.
Paris: Bourrelier 1940.

1940–1945 The prize was not given; Der Preis wurde nicht vergeben.

1945 Piguet, Alice: **Thérèse et le jardin.** (*Therese* and the garden; *Therese* und der Garten.) Ill.: Jacqueline Gaillard.
Paris: Bourrelier 1945.

1946 The prize was not given; Der Preis wurde nicht vergeben.

1947 Bosshard, Jean: **Le marchand de sable attendra.** (The sandman will wait; Das Sandmännchen wird warten.) Ill.: Jacques André Cante. Paris: Bourrelier 1947.

1948 Mahler, Léone: **Le secret de l'île d'or.** (The secret of the golden island; Das Geheimnis der Goldinsel.) Ill.: Jacques André Cante. Paris: Bourrelier 1948.

1949 The prize was not given; Der Preis wurde nicht vergeben.

1950 Guillot, René: **Sama, prince des éléphants.** (*Sama,* the prince of the elephants; *Sama,* der Elefantenprinz.) Ill.: Jean de la Fontinelle. Paris: Bourrelier 1950.

1951 The prize was not given; Der Preis wurde nicht vergeben.

1952 Clair, Andrée: **Moudaïna ou Deux enfants au coeur de l'Afrique.** (*Moudaina,* or Two children in the heart of Africa; *Moudaina,* oder Zwei Kinder im Herzen Afrikas.) Ill.: Jean Hartman. Paris: Bourrelier 1952.

1953 Delluc, Louis: **Le mousse de la Niña.** (The cabin boy on the *Niña;* Der Schiffsjunge auf der *Niña.*) Ill.: Raoul Auger. Paris: Bourrelier 1953.

1954 Naïm, Robert Teldy: **Sept soleils sur la neige.** (Seven suns on the snow; Sieben Sonnen auf dem Schnee.) Ill.: Pierre Leroy. Paris: Bourrelier 1954.

1955 Audrix, Claire/Fontugne, Christian: **Nic et Nick.** (*Nic* and *Nick.*) Ill.: Christian Fontugne. Paris: Bourrelier 1955.

1956 Loisy, Jeanne: **Le secret de Don Tiburcio.** (The secret of Don *Tiburcio;* Das Geheimnis von Don *Tiburcio.*) Ill.: Françoise Estachy. Paris: Bourrelier 1956.

1957 Collonges, Aimée: **L'étrange famille de la Pampa.** (The strange family from the Pampas; Die seltsame Familie von den Pampas.) Ill.: Françoise Estachy. Paris: Bourrelier 1957.

1958 Cattin, Etienne: **Rat-blanc et son chauffeur.** (*White Rat* and his chauffeur; *Weiße Ratte* und ihr Fahrer.) Françoise Estachy. Paris: Bourrelier 1958.

1959 Martin-Chauffier, Simone: **"L'Autre" chez les corsaires.** (The *"Other"* with the corsaires; Der *"Andere"* bei den Seeräubern.) Ill.: Pierre Noël. Paris: Bourrelier 1959.

1960 LeClercq, Gine Victor: **Va-comme-le-vent.** (Go like the wind; Geh wie der Wind.) Ill.: Véra Braun.
Paris: Bourrelier 1960.

1961 Gamarra, Pierre: **L'aventure du serpent à plumes.** (The adventure of the feathered serpent; Das Abenteuer der Federschlange.) Ill.: Philippe Daure.
Paris: Bourrelier 1961.

1962 Contino, Magda: **Le mystère de l'ancre coralline.** (The mystery of the coral anchor; Das Geheimnis des Korallenankers.) Ill.: Daniel Billon.
Paris: Bourrelier 1962.

1963 Alençon, May d': **Renard-Roux.** (*Red-Fox;* Rotfuchs.) Ill.: Annie-Claude Martin.
Paris: Bourrelier 1963.

1964 Verly, Jacqueline: **Sur la route des bohémiens.** (On the road of the gypsies; Auf dem Weg der Zigeuner.) Ill.: Xavier Saint-Justh.
Paris: Colin, Bourrelier 1964.

1965 Lesueur, Nicole: **Le secret du ballon jaune.** (The secret of the yellow balloon; Das Geheimnis des gelben Ballons.) Ill.: Hervé Lacoste.
Paris: Colin, Bourrelier 1965.

1966 The prize was not given; Der Preis wurde nicht vergeben.

1967 The prize was not given; Der Preis wurde nicht vergeben.

1968 Cervon, Jacqueline: **L'aiglon d'Ouarzazate.** (The eagle from *Ouarzazate;* Der Adler von *Ouarzazate.*) Ill.: Françoise Boudignon.
Paris: Ed. de. l'Amitié — G.T. Rageot 1968.

1969 The prize was not given; Der Preis wurde nicht vergeben.

1970 Baudouy, Michel-Aimé: **Alerte sur le roc blanc.** (Alert on the white rock; Alarm auf dem weißen Felsen.) Ill.: G. di Maccio.
Paris: Ed. de l'Amitié — G.T. Rageot 1970.

1971 Pelot, Pierre: **L'unique rebelle.** (The unique rebel; Die einzige Rebellin.) Ill.: G. di Maccio.
Paris: Ed. de l'Amitié — G.T. Rageot 1971.

1972 Vidal, Nicole: **La conspiration des parasols.** (The conspiracy of the umbrellas; Die Verschwörung der Sonnenschirme.) Ill.: Françoise Boudignon.
Paris: Ed. de. l'Amitié — G.T. Rageot 1972.

Prix La Joie par le Livre

This prize, as is the case with the Salon de l'Enfance award, is selected by children. It was established in 1958 by the Association La Joie par le Livre, and consists of a cash award. Originally, the prize was given to books for boys and girls in the twelve to fourteen years age level. Since 1963, however, books for readers aged nine to eleven, and illustrations are also considered. The jury is made up of seven children who are chosen by the Association. The award winning books are announced in June of each year. The last prize presentation was held in 1977; since that time, the prize has been discontinued.

Ebenso wie der Preis des Salon de l'Enfance wird auch der Prix La Joie par le Livre von Kindern vergeben. Er wurde 1958 durch die Association La Joie par le Livre (Vereinigung der Freude durch das Buch) gegründet und in Form einer Geldprämie verliehen. Ausgezeichnet werden Bücher für zwölf- bis vierzehnjährige Mädchen und Jungen, seit 1963 auch Bücher für neun- bis elfjährige, außerdem für Illustrationen. Die Jury besteht aus sieben Kindern, die von den Mitgliedern der Vereinigung ausgesucht werden. Die Preisverteilung findet stets im Juni statt. 1977 wurde der letzte Preis vergeben; seitdem existiert der Preis nicht mehr.

1959 *Boys/Jungen*
Haber, Heinz: **Notre ami l'atome.** (Our friend the atom; Unser Freund das Atom.)
Paris: Hachette 1957

Girls/Mädchen
Saint-Marcoux, Jeanne: **La guitare andalouse.** (The Andalusian guitar; Die Gitarre aus Andalusien.) Ill.: Jean Sidobre.
Paris: Éd. G.P. 1959.

1960 *Boys/Jungen*
Houot, Georges: **La découverte sous-marine.** (Underwater discovery; Unterwasser-Entdeckungen.)
Paris: Bourrelier 1958.

Girls/Mädchen
Allan, Mabel Esther: **Lise en Italie.** (*Lise* in Italy; *Lise* in Italien.) Ill.: Gilles Valdès.
Paris: Éd. G.P. 1960.

1961 *Boys/Jungen*
Massepain, André: **Le derrick aux abeilles.** (The bee's derrick; Der Bienenderrick.) Ill.: Daniel Dupuy.
Paris: Éd. G.P. 1960.

Girls/Mädchen
Miollis, Marie-Antoinette de: **Fille de pilote.** (The pilot's daughter; Die Tochter des Piloten.) Ill.: Vanni Tealdi.
Paris: Éd. G.P. 1960.

1962 *Boys/Jungen*
Pays, Jean-François: **Toukaram ou L'âge de l'amitié.** (*Toukaram* or the age of friendship; *Toukaram* oder das Alter der Freundschaft.) Ill.: Michel Gourlier.
Paris: Éd. G.P. 1960.

Girls/Mädchen
Mauffret, Yvon: **La Bell-Amarante.** (The *Belle-Amarante;* Die *Belle-Amarante.*) Ill.: Jacques Pecnard.
Paris: Éd. G.P. 1960.

1963 Déchaud-Pérouze, Monique: **Dans le vent de Camargue.** (In the wind of the Camargue; Im Wind der Camargue.) Ill.: Michel Gourlier.
Colmar, Paris: Ed. Alsatia 1962.

1964 *Boys/Jungen*
Farley, Walter: **Flamme, cheval sauvage.** (*Flame,* the wild horse; *Flamme,* das wilde Pferd.) Ill.: J.P. Ariel (i.e. Raoul Auger).
Paris: Hachette 1964

Girls/Mädchen
Clairac, Anne: **L'émeraude de la reine de Pologne.** (The emerald of the queen of Poland; Der Smaragd der Königin von Polen.) Ill.: Françoise Bertier.
Paris: Éd. G.P. 1963.

1965 *Boys and girls/Jungen und Mädchen*
Weir, Rosemary: **Autobus tout confort.** (Deluxe autobus; Bus erster Klasse.) Ill.: Pierre Le Guen.
Paris: Éd. G.P. 1964.

Boys and girls/Jungen und Mädchen
Ravous, Aline: **Tiotis ou La rose et l'épée.** (*Tiotis* or, The rose and the sword; *Tiotis* oder Die Rose und das Schwert.) Ill.: Lizzie Napoli.
Paris: Delagrave 1962.

1966 *Boys/Jungen*
Hitchcock, Alfred: **Quatre mystères.** (Four mysteries; Vier Rätsel.) Ill.: Jacques Poirer.
Paris: Hachette 1965

Girls/Mädchen
Freemann, Barbara Constance: **Le journal de Georgina.** (The diary of *Georgina;* Das Tagebuch von *Georgina.*) Ill.: Daniel Dupuy.
Paris: Éd. G.P. 1964.

1967 Aubry, Cécile: **Belle et Sébastien.** (*Belle* and *Sebastian.*) Ill.: Jean Reschofsky.
Paris: Hachette 1965

1968 *Boys/Jungen*
Antier, Jean-Jacques: **Mission dangereuse.** (Dangerous mission; Gefährliche Mission.)
Paris: Laffont 1967.

Girls/Mädchen
Cervon, Jacqueline: **Le naufragé de Rhodes.** (The ship-wrecked from Rhodes; Schiffbrüchige von Rhodos.) Ill.: Jean Reschofsky.
Paris: Éd. G.P. 1968.

1969 Reboul, Antoine: **Tu ne tueras point.** (Thou shall not kill; Du darfst nicht töten.) Ill.: François Batet.
Paris: Hachette 1968

1970 *Boys/Jungen*
Gilles, Michelle: **Le garçon qui venait de la mer.** (The boy that came from the sea; Der Junge, der vom Meer kam.) Ill.: Jean Reschofsky.
Paris: Ed. G.P. 1969.

Girls/Mädchen
La Grange, François de: **Les animaux du monde.** (The animals of the world; Die Tiere der Welt.) Ill.
Paris: Nathan 1969.

1971 Cervon, Jacqueline: **Malik, le garçon sauvage.** (*Malik,* the wild boy; *Malik,* der wilde Knabe.) Ill.: Mathieu Romain.
Paris: Magnard 1970.

1972 *Boys/Jungen*
Ebly, Philippe: **Destination Uruapan.** (Destination *Uruapan*; Bestimmungsort *Uruapan.*) Ill.: Yvon Le Gall.
Paris: Hachette 1971

Girls/Mädchen
Médina, Jean-Baptiste: **La correspondante anglaise.** (The English correspondent; Die englische Briefkorrespondentin.) Ill.: Michel Gourlier.
Paris: Magnard 1971.

1973 Ray, Hélène: **Ionel, la musique et la guerre.** (*Ionel,* the music and the war; *Ionel,* die Musik und der Krieg.) Michel Gourlier.
Paris: Magnard 1972.

1974 *Boys/Jungen*
Grimaud, Michel: **La terre des autres.** (The land of the others; Das Land der anderen.)
Paris: Ed. de l'Amitié — G.T. Rageot 1973.
Girls/Mädchen
Chevalier, Haakon Maurice: **Le dernier voyage de la Rosamond.** (The last voyage of the *Rosamond*; Die letzte Fahrt der *Rosamond.*)
Paris: Hatier 1973.

1975 Deret, Jean Claude: **Gilles aux Champs-Elysées.** (*Gilles* on the Champs-Elysées; *Gilles* auf den Champs Elyseés.) Ill.: Annie Beynel.
Paris: Hachette 1974

1976 Lesprit, Eric: **Le désert sacré.** (The sacred desert; Die heilige Wüste.) Ill.: Pierre Joubert.
Paris: Éd. Alsatia 1975.

1977 Mauffret, Yvon: **Goulven.** (*Goulven.*) Ill.: Annie-Claude Martin.
Paris: Éd. G.P. 1976.

Prix Graphique Loisirs Jeunes

The aim of the association "Loisirs-Jeunes" is to help children and young people by promoting good books, television programmes and entertaining, free-time activities. In addition to the certificates they award to approximately twenty books each year, the association established in 1972 the Prix Graphique to further the development of French children's book illustrations.

Ziel des Vereins "Loisirs-Jeunes" ist es, Kindern und Jugendlichen zu helfen, sich besser im Angebot der Bücher, Fernsehsendungen und der verschiedenen Freizeitbeschäftigungen zurechtzufinden. Außer den Diplomen, die "Loisirs-Jeunes" jährlich etwa 20 Büchern verleiht, wird seit 1972 auch der Prix Graphique zur Förderung der französischen Illustration vergeben — der sowohl die Interessen des Kindes als auch den künstlerischen Wert berücksichtigt.

1972 Couratin, Patrick in:
Couratin, Patrick: **Monsieur l'Oiseau.** (Mr. *Bird*; Herr *Vogel.*)
Paris: Harlin Quist 1971.

1973 Delaunay, Sonia in:
Damase, Jacques: **Alphabet.** Comptines retrouvées. (Alphabet. Re-

discovered counting-rhymes; Alphabet. Wiedergefundene Abzählverse.)
Paris: L'Ecole des Loisirs 1972.

1974 Claveloux, Nicole in:
Carroll, Lewis (i.e. Charles Lutwidge Dodgson): **Les aventures d'Alice au pays des merveilles.** (Eng.Orig.title: *Alice's* adventures in wonderland; Die Abenteuer von *Alice* im Wunderland.)
Paris: Grasset & Fasquelle 1974.

1975 Folon, Jean Michel in:
Folon, Jean Michel: **Lettres à Giorgio.** (Letters to *Giorgio*; Briefe an *Giorgio*.)
Paris, Genève: Alice-Chêne 1975.

1976 Dumas, Philippe in:
Dumas, Philippe: **Histoire d'Edouard.** (Story of *Edouard*; Geschichte von *Edouard*.)
Paris: Flammarion 1976.

1977 Rabier, Benjamin in:
Rabier, Benjamin: **Gédéon dans la forêt.** (*Gedeon* in the forest; *Gedeon* im Wald.)
Paris: Garnier 1977.

1978 Lemoine, Georges in:
Bosco, Henri: **L'enfant et la rivière.** (The Child and the river; Das Kind und der Fluß.)
Paris: Gallimard 1978.

1979 Ungerer, Tomi in:
Ungerer, Tomi: **Allumette.** (Amer.orig.title: Allumette.)
Paris: L'École des loisirs 1974.

Ungerer, Tomi in:
Ungerer, Tomi: **Le chapeau volant.** (Amer.orig.title: The hat; Der Hut.)
Paris: L'École des Loisirs 1971.

Ungerer, Tomi in:
Ungerer, Tomi: **Le géant de Zeralda.** (Amer.orig.title: *Zeralda's* ogre; *Zeraldas* Riese.)
Paris: L'École des loisirs 1971.

Ungerer, Tomi in:
Ungerer, Tomi: **La grosse bête de Monsieur Racine.** (Amer.orig.title: The beast of Monsieur *Racine*; Das Biest des Monsieur *Racine*.)
Paris: L'École des loisirs 1972.

Ungerer, Tomi in:
Spyri, Johanna: **Heidi devant la vie.** (*Heidi* faces life; Germ.orig.title: Heidi kann brauchen, was es gelernt hat.)
Paris: L'École des loisirs 1979.

Ungerer, Tomi in:
Ungerer, Tomi: **Les histoires farfelues de Papaski.** (Amer.orig.title: I am *Papa Snap* and these are my favorite no such stories; *Papa Schnapp* und seine noch-nie-dagewesenen Geschichten.)
Paris, Tournai: Casterman 1977.

Ungerer, Tomi in:
Ungerer, Tomi: **Jean de la lune.** (Amer.orig.title: Moon man; Der Mondmann.)
Paris: L'École des loisirs 1969.

Ungerer, Tomi in:
Ungerer, Tomi: **Les Mellops front de l'avion.** (Amer.orig.title: The *Mellops* go flying; Die *Mellops* gehen fliegen.)
Paris: L'École des loisirs 1979.

Ungerer, Tomi in:
Ungerer, Tomi: **Pas de baiser pour maman.** (Amer.orig.title: No kiss for mother; Kein Kuß für Mutter.)
Paris: L'École des loisirs 1976.

Ungerer, Tomi in:
Ungerer, Tomi: **Les trois brigands.** (Amer.orig.title: The three robbers; Die drei Räuber.)
Paris: L'École des loisirs 1979.

1980 Guéry, Catherine in:
Léon, Pierre: **Grepotame et 250 drôles d'animaux croisés.** (*Grepotame* and 250 strange, crossed animals; *Grepotame* und 250 komische Tierkreuzungen.)
Paris: Fernand Nathan 1980.

1981 Claverie, Jean in:
Nikly, Michelle: **La princesse sur une noix.** (The princess in a nut shell; Die Prinzessin in der Nußschale.)
Paris: Nord-Sud 1981.

Prix Jean Macé

This prize is named after the "French Pestalozzi", Jean Macé (1815—1894). The selections are announced at the end of each year by the "Centre laique de lecture publique". Works of fiction or non-fiction, either in manuscript or published book form, are eligible for the prize. They must be written in French for readers aged fifteen to eighteen. Outstanding entries which did not receive the award are also brought to the attention of the public; this is in keeping with the aim of the "Ligue française de l'enseignement" (founded in 1866 by Jean Macé) for the promotion of higher non-professional education. An important part of this activity is the development of interest in reading matter among young people.

Der nach dem "französischen Pestalozzi" Jean Macé (1815—1894) bekannte Preis wird am Ende jeden Jahres vom "Centre laique de lecture publique" für ein Werk der erzählenden oder der Sachliteratur verliehen. Das Buch kann in gedruckter Form oder als Manuskript vorliegen, muß aber für Jugendliche von 15—18 Jahren bestimmt und in französischer Sprache geschrieben sein. Die wertvollsten der eingereichten und nicht mit dem Preis bedachten Bücher werden ebenfalls der Öffentlichkeit vorgestellt, denn das Ziel der "Ligue française de l'enseignement" (1866 von Macé gegründet) ist auch heute noch die Förderung der Laienbildung und damit auch das Leseinteresse der Jugendlichen.

1958 Laredo, Albert/Franceschi, Joseph: **Sidi-Safi.** (*Sidi-Safi.*) Ill.: François Batet.
Paris: Hachette 1958.

1959 Counillon, Pierre: **L'extraordinaire voyage de Monsieur Ricou.** (The extraordinary voyage of Mr. *Ricou*; Die außerordentliche Reise von Herrn *Ricou.*) Ill.: Pierre Leroy.
Paris: Delagrave 1961.

1960 Cattin, Etienne: **L'express du soir.** (The evening express; Der Abendschnellzug.) Ill.: André Pec.
Paris: Bourrelier 1962.

1961 The prize was not given; Der Preis wurde nicht vergeben.

1962 Bouglione, Firmin: **Le cirque est mon royaume.** (The circus is my realm; Der Zirkus ist mein Reich.) Photos.
Paris: Presses de la Cité 1962.

1963 Antona, René: **Quatre millimètres de chance.** (Four millimetres of chance; Vier Millimeter Glück.) Ill.: Michel Jouin.
Paris: Ed. G.P. 1963.

Eydoux, Henri-Paul: **Révélations de l'archéologie.** (Revelations of archaeology; Errungenschaften der Archäologie.) Ill.
Paris: Gautier-Languereau 1963.

1964 Rousseau, Pierre: Collected works, especially; Gesamtschaffen, insbesondere: **La science du 20e siècle.** (The science of the 20th century; Die Wissenschaft im 20. Jahrhundert.) Ill.
Paris: Hachette 1964.

1965 Marion, Marc: **Le tueur de sangliers.** (The killer of wild pigs; Der Wildschweintöter.)
Paris: Presses de la Cité 1966.

1966 Belaubre, Marcelle: **Juliette.** (*Juliette.*) (Unpublished; Bisher nicht veröffentlicht.)
Rondière, Pierre: **Le Brésil.** (Brazil; Brasilien.) Photos.
Paris: Nathan 1965.

1967 Albrand, Michèle: **La clairière.** (The clearing; Die Lichtung.)
Paris: Ed. Français Réunis 1967.

1968 Clavel, Bernard: **Victoire au Mans.** (Victory at *Le Mans*; Sieg in *Le Mans.*)
Paris: Laffont 1968.

1969 Belvès, Pierre: **Le monde merveilleux de l'art raconté aux jeunes.** (Art explained for the young; Kunst für die Jugend.)
Paris: Hachette 1969.

1970 Gilles, Michelle: **Quand revient la lumière.** (When it gets light again; Wenn es wieder hell wird.) Ill.: Jean Rechofsky.
Paris: Ed. G.P. 1970.
Cazalbou, Jean: **La porte du Casteras.** (The gate of *Casteras*; Das *Cateras*-Tor.)
Paris: Ed Français Réunis 1970.

1971 Solet, Bertrand: **Il était un capitaine.** (There was a captain; Es war einmal ein Hauptmann.)
Paris: Laffont 1972.

1972 Lépidis, Clément: **Le marin de Lesbos.** (The seaman from Lesbos; Der Matrose von Lesbos.)
Paris: Ed. du Seuil 1972.

1973 Grimaud, Michel: **La terre des autres.** (The land of the others; Das Land der anderen.)
Paris: Ed. de. l'Amitié — G.T. Rageot 1973.
Paraf, Pierre: **L'homme de toutes les couleurs.** (The man of all colours; Der Mann in allen Hautfarben.)
Paris: La Farandole 1973.

1974 Bigot, Robert: **Les lumières du matin.** (The morning lights; Das Morgenlicht.)
Paris: Hachette 1975.

1975 Pérol, Huguette: **Je rentrerai tard ce soir.** (I go home late this evening; Ich gehe heute Abend spät heim.)
Paris: Ed. de. l'Amitié — G.T. Rageot 1975.

Mathieu, Lucien: **Opération survie.** (*Operation Survival; Operation Überleben.*)
Paris: La Farandole 1975.

1976 Ollivier, Jean: **Vikings, conquérants de la mer.** (Vikings, conquerors of the sea; Die Wikinger erobern die See.)
Paris: La Farandole 1975.

Touati, Lucien-Guy: **Et puis je suis parti d'Oran.** (And then I left *Oran;* Dann habe ich *Oran* verlassen.)
Paris: Ed. G.P. 1976.

1977 Pelot, Pierre: **Le renard dans la maison.** (The fox in the house; Der Fuchs im Haus.)
Paris: Ed. de. l'Amitié — G.T. Rageot 1977.

Epin, Bernard/Rongier, Max: **Profession canteur.** (Profession, singer; Beruf: Sänger.) Ill.
Paris: Lay Farandole 1977.

1978 Coué, Jean: **Un soleil glacé.** (A frozen sun; Eine gefrorene Sonne.)
Paris: Ed. de. l'Amitié — G.T. Rageot 1978.

1979 Barokas, Bernard: **La chanson de Bertram ou le marveilleux voyage de Bertram autour de la Méditerranée.** (*Bertram's* song, or the marvelous voyage of *Bertram* around the Mediterranean; *Bertrams* Lied oder *Bertrams* wunderbare Reise um das Mittelmeer.)
Paris: Grasset 1978.

Rocchi, Jean/Buissonnet, Catherine: **Informer, pourquoi? comment?** (To inform why? how? Informiere, weswegen? wie?) Ill.
Paris: La Farandole 1979.

1980 Laguionie, Jean-François: **Les puces de sable.** (The sand fleas; Die Sandflöhe.) Ill.: Jean-François Laguionie.
Paris: Léon Faure 1980.

1981 Sautereau, François: **Marelles.** (Jumping game; Hüpfspiel.) Combs-la-Ville: Éd Envol 1980.

Victor, Paul-Emile/Larivière, Jean: **Les loups.** (The wolves; Die Wölfe.) Ill.
Paris: Nathan 1980.

Prix Enfance du Monde

This prize, presented annually from 1955 until 1962, was sponsored by the Centre International de l'Enfance, Paris. It was awarded for an unpublished manuscript of juvenile literature written in the French language which promoted the spirit of international understanding. Writers from all nations were eligible to enter this competition. The jury was composed of

French citizens and members of other nations. Georges Duhamel was the first president. The last presentation took place in 1962; since that time, the prize has been discontinued.

Der Prix Enfance du Monde wurde von 1955 bis 1962 jährlich vom Centre International de l'Enfance, Paris, für ein unveröffentlichtes französischsprachiges Jugendbuchmanuskript vergeben, das dem Bemühen um internationale Verständigung diente. Zur Teilnahme am Wettbewerb waren alle Nationen berechtigt. Die Jury setzte sich aus französischen und aus Mitgliedern anderer Nationalitäten zusammen. Erster Präsident war Georges Duhamel. 1962 wurde der letzte Preis vergeben; seitdem existiert der Preis nicht mehr.

1955 Bonzon, Paul Jacques: **Les orphelins de Simitra.** (The orphans of *Simitra*; Die Waisenkinder von *Simitra.*) Ill.: Albert Chazelle.
Paris: Hachette 1955.

1956 Bourliaguet, Léonce: **Pouk et ses loups-garous.** (*Pouk* and his werewolves; *Pouk* und seine Wehrwölfe.) Ill.: Pierre Rousseau.
Paris: Magnard 1955.

1957 Baudouy, Michel-Aimé: **Le seigneur des Hautes-Buttes.** (The lord of the high hills; Der Herr der hohen Hügel.) Ill.: Claire Marchal.
Paris: Ed. de. l'Amitié — G.T. Rageot 1957.

1958 Guillot, René: **Grichka et son ours.** (*Grichka* and his bear; *Grischka* und sein Bär.) Ill.: J.P. Ariel (i.e. Raoul Auger).
Paris: Hachette 1958.

1959 Lavolle, Louise-Noëlle: **Nuno de Nazaré.** (*Nuno de Nazaré.*) Ill.: Alain d'Orange.
Paris: Fleurus, Gautier-Languereau 1959.

1960 Ollivier, Jean: **Deux oiseaux ont disparu.** (Two birds are lost; Zwei Vögel sind verschwunden.) Ill.: Pierre Le Guen.
Paris: Ed. G.P. 1960.

1961 Meynier, Yvonne: **Une petite fille attendait.** (A young girl waited; Ein kleines Mädchen wartete.) Ill.: Pierre Le Guen.
Paris: Ed. G.P. 1961.

1962 Recher, Robert: **Rüdi et la chamois.** (*Rudi* and the chamois; *Rüdi* und die Gemse.) Ill.: Maurice Raffray.
Paris: Ed. de. l'Amitié — G.T. Rageot 1962.

Grand Prix de Littérature Enfantine du Salon de l'Enfance.

This prize, established in 1953 by the Salon de l'Enfance, is given annually for an unpublished children's book manuscript written in the French language. The nationality of the author is not a determining factor in competing for the prize. The jury is made up of children aged ten to fourteen. They are outstanding pupils chosen from high schools, private institutions and communal schools. The oldest child is chosen as president of the jury. The secretariat of the Salon de l'Enfance supplies the general rules. An author, once having received the prize, is not eligible for it a second time. The manuscripts must be submitted by January 31st of each year.

Der Preis, im Jahre 1953 vom Salon de l'Enfance gestiftet, wird jährlich für ein unveröffentlichtes französischsprachiges Jugendbuchmanuskript vergeben. Der Autor kann Franzose oder Ausländer sein. Die Jury setzt sich im wesentlichen aus Kindern französischer Nationalität im Alter von 10 bis 14 Jahren zusammen, die unter den begabtesten Schülern von höheren Schulen, freien Instituten und Kommunalschulen ausgewählt werden. Das älteste Kind ist Präsident dieser Jury. Das Generalsekretariat des Salon de l'Enfance gibt allgemeine Anleitungen. Ein preisgekrönter Autor kann nicht ein zweites Mal am Preisausschreiben teilnehmen. Die Manuskripte müssen bis zum 31. Januar eingereicht werden.

1953 Recqueville, Jeanne de: **Capitan Pacha.** (Captain *Pacha*; *Kapitän Pacha.*) Ill.: Jacques Poirier.
Paris: Hachette 1954.

1954 Saint-Marcoux, Jeanne: **Princesse Cactus.** (Princess *Cactus*; Prinzessin *Kaktus.*) Ill.: Félix Lacroix.
Paris: Ed. G.P. 1954.

1955 Berna, Paul: **Le cheval sans tête.** (The horse without head; Das Pferd ohne Kopf.) Ill.: Pierre Dehay.
Paris: Ed. G.P. 1955.

1956 Diélette (i.e. Yette Jeandet and Yvonne Girault): **Laurette et la fille des pharaons.** (*Laurette* and the daughter of the pharaohs; *Laurette* und die Tochter der Pharaonen.) Ill.: Albert Chazelle.
Paris: Hachette 1956.

1957 Bouchet, José-Marie: **Coeurs sauvages d'Irlande.** (Savage hearts of Ireland; Wilde Herzen aus Irland.) Ill.: Jacques Pecnard.
Paris: Hachette 1957.

1958 Bonzon, Paul-Jacques: **L'éventail de Séville.** (The fan of Seville; Der Fächer von Sevilla.) Ill.: François Batet.
Paris: Hachette 1958.

1959 Dumesnil, Jacqueline: **Les compagnons du Cerf d'Argent.** (The society of the silver deer; Der Klub des silbernen Hirsches.) Ill.: Henri Dimpre.
Paris: Ed. G.P. 1959.

1960 Lavolle, Louise-Noëlle: **Les clés du désert.** (The keys of the desert; Die Schlüssel der Wüste.) Ill.: Jacques Daynié.
Paris: Ed. de l'Amitié — G.T. Rageot 1960.

1961 Ollivier, Jean: **L'aventure viking.** (The adventure of the vikings; Das Wikinger-Abenteuer.) Ill.: Pierre Le Guen.
Paris: Ed. G.P. 1961.

1962 Vauthier, Maurice: **Faon l'héroïque.** (The heroic fawn; Das Heldenreh.) Ill.: Pierre Joubert.
Paris: Ed. Alsatia 1962.

1963 Massepain, André: **La grotte aux ours.** (The bear cave; Die Bärenhöhle.) Ill.: Jean Sidobre.
Paris: Ed. G.P. 1963.

1964 Thiébold, Marguerite: **Le traîneau de Manuela.** (*Manuela's* sleigh; Der Schlitten von *Manuela*.) Ill.: Gaston de Sainte-Croix.
Paris: Hachette 1964.

1965 Pélerin, Yves: **Les marceassins.** (The young wild pigs; Die jungen Wildschweine.) Ill.: Paul Ordner.
Paris: Magnard 1966.

1967 Le Poëzat-Guigner, Joseph: **Le pré du roy.** (The king's meadow; Die Königswiese.) Ill.: Philippe Degrave.
Paris: Magnard 1967.

1968 Reboul, Antoine: **Tu ne tueras point.** (Thou shall not kill; Du sollst nicht töten.) Ill.: François Batet.
Paris: Hachette 1968.

1969 Celier, François: **Les chevaliers du ciel.** (The knights of heaven; Die Ritter des Himmels.) Ill.: Maurice Paulin.
Paris: Hachette 1969.

1970 Bernadet, Jeanine: **L'enfant au dahu.** (The child from nowhere; Das Kind von Nirgends.) Ill.: Jacques Pecnard.
Paris: Hachette 1971.

1971 Loiseau, Yvette: **Le mur du froid.** (The wall of cold; Die Wand der Kälte.) Ill.: Yvon Le Gall.
Paris: Hachette 1971.

Cervon, Jacqueline: **Le fouet et la cithare.** (The whip and the zither; Die Peitsche und die Zither.) Ill.: René Péron.
Paris: Ed. G.P. 1971.

Artis, Max: **Le trésor de l'île perdue.** (The treasure of the lost island; Der Schatz der verlorenen Insel.)
Paris: Bias 1971.

1972 Pierjean, Anne: **Marika.** (*Marika.*) Ill.: Monique Gorde.
Paris: Ed. G.P. 1972.

1973 Artis, Max: **Le vol du Garuda.** (The flight of *Garuda*; Der Flug des *Garuda.*) Ill.: Jean Jacques Vayssières.
Paris: Bias 1973.

1974 Laramée, Ghislaine: **Depuis toujours, c'était écrit.** (It has always been written like that; Seit eh und je war es geschrieben.) Ill.: Annie-Claude Martin.
Paris: Hachette 1974.

1975 Aurembou, Renée: **Le disparu des villes mortes.** (Disappearance in the dead cities; In den toten Städten verschwunden.) Ill.: Jean Retailleau.
Paris: Ed. G.P. 1975.

1976 Sorensen, Odette: **La prison sous les arbres.** (The prison under the trees; Das Gefängnis unter den Bäumen.) Ill.: Paul Durand.
Paris: Hachette 1976.

1977 Grenier, Christian: **Les cascadeurs du temps.** (The stuntmen of the times; Die Doubles der Zeit.) Ill.: Jean Revelin.
Paris: Magnard 1977.

1978 Gautier, Monique: **Les ronces de l'hiver.** (The thorns of winter; Die Dornen des Winters.) Ill.: Jacques Poirier.
Paris: Hachette 1978.

1979 Lacq, Gil: **Les enfants de la guerre.** (The children of war; Die Kinder des Krieges.) Ill.: Serge Colard and Didier Rudelopt.
Paris: Hachette 1979.

1980 Loiseau, Yvette: **L'Odyssée de Sandrine.** (Sandrine's odyssey; *Sandrines* Odyssee.)
(Unpublished/Unveröffentlicht)

1981 Lignerat, Jean-Louis: **Les fous du ciel.** (The madmen of the sky; Die Wahnsinnigen des Himmels.) Ill.: Chica (i.e. Marie Josèphe Tissot).
Paris: Hachette 1980.

Prix Sobrier-Arnould

This prize was founded in 1944 by the Académie Française. It is awarded annually to a book written in the French language which is expressive of high moral and educational values. This award was made possible by a legacy left by Adélaide Arnould and bears the name of both she and her husband, Jean Sobrier.

Der Preis wurde 1944 von der Académie Française gegründet und wird jährlich einem auf französisch geschriebenen Buch von herausragendem moralischen und erzieherischen Wert verliehen. Dieser Preis ist ein Vermächtnis von Adélaide Arnould und ihrem Mann Jean Sobrier. Der Preis trägt beide Namen.

1944 Surcouf, Pierre Jean: **Ainsi parlait le vent.** (So speaks the wind; So sprach der Wind.)

Dumaine, J.B.: **Bluettes et coquelicots.** (Cornflowers and poppies; Kornblümchen und Mohn.) Ill.: Henriette Gonse.
Paris: Melot 1943.

1945 Fontanes, Catherine: **Gaul des sources.** (*Gaul* of the fountain; *Gaul* von den Quellen.) Ill.: Pol Ferjac.
Paris: Toulouse: Chantal 1944.

1946 Buet, Patrice: **Les Poncet, explorateurs à 13 et à 15 ans.** (The Poncets, 13 to 15 year old explorers; Die Poncets. Forscher mit 13 und 15 Jahren.)
Paris: Ed. des Loisirs 1945.

Reicher, Gil: **L'horloger du Puy Saint-Front.** (The watchmaker from *Puy Saint-Front*; Der Uhrmacher von *Puy Saint-Front.*) Ill.: G. Libet.
Paris: Fontas 1946.

1947 D'Alesso, Marie: **Le petit Douci.** (Little *Douci*; Der kleine *Douci.*) Ill.: Jeanne Plauzeau.
Clamart: Ed de l'Olivier 1946.

Vérité, Marcell: **Soulec, le démon des brumes. Les contes de l'étang, Grand Isard.** (*Soulec,* the demon of the mist. The tales of the pond, *Great Isard*; *Soulec,* der Dämon der Nebel. Die Märchen des Sees *Großer Isard.*)
Paris: Desclée des Brouwer 1946.

1948 Richter, Charles de: **Les contes de mon oncle Frédéric.** (The tales of my uncle *Frederick*; Die Märchen meines Onkels *Friedrich.*)
Paris: Bordas 1947.

1949 Trilby, T.: **En avant. Le petit roi des foraines.** (Forward. The little king of the jugglers; Vorwärts. Der kleine König der Gaukler.) Ill.: Manon Iessel.
Paris: Flammarion 1948.

Nardy, M.T.: **Prince Charmant et Petite Reine.** (*Prince Charming* and *Little Queen*; *Charmanter Prinz* und *Kleine Königin.*) Ill.: Gal.
Paris: Ed. de la D.G.F.1947.

1950 The prize was not given; Der Preis wurde nicht vergeben.

1951 Saint Pierre, Gérard de: **Contes du temps passé.** (Tales of time past; Märchen der vergangenen Zeit.)
Lyon: La Belle Cordière 1948.

1952 Merlaud, André: **A l'assaut du ciel.** (Upwards to the sky; Aufwärts zum Himmel.) Ill.: Lucien Cavé.
Lausanne: SPES 1951.

1953 Guillemot-Magitot, G.: **J.S. Bach et ses fils.** (*J.S. Bach* and his sons; *J.S. Bach* und seine Söhne.) Ill.: Pierre Probst.
Paris: Ed. de l'Amitié 1952.

1954 Streiff, René: **Michel Ney, maréchal d'Empire.** (*Michel Ney*, marshal of the empire; *Michel Ney*, Reichsmarschall.)
Courbevoie: L'Amitié par la Plume 1953.

1955 Noël, Paul: **Fais ton chemin.** (Go your own way; Geh deinen Weg.) Ill.: Danièle Fuchs.
Saint-Chéron: Ed. Oliven 1955.

Tramond, Renée: **Contes savoyards.** (Tales from Savoy; Märchen aus Savoyen.) Ill.: Pierre Rousseau.
Paris: T. Lanore 1950.

1956 Johnny: **Missy la sauvageonne.** (*Missy*, the savage; *Missey*, die Wilde.) Ill.: Manon Iessel.
Paris: Flammarion 1955.

Capdeboscq, Jean: **Le mystère de la montagne.** (The secret of the mountain; Das Geheimnis der Berge.)
Paris: Colin 1955.

1957 Guillot, René: **Encyclopédie Larousse des enfants.** (Larousse children's encyclopedia; Larousse Kinder-Enzyklopädie.)
Paris: Larousse 1956.

1958 Regnet, François: **Madame la Peste.** (Madame *Plague;* Frau *Pest.*)
Paris: Bonne Presse 1946.

1959 The prize was not given; Der Preis wurde nicht vergeben.

1960 Billet, R.: **Trois petits contes et puis s'en vont.** (Three little tales, then away; Drei Märchen und dann gehen Sie weg.)

Richter, Charles de: **Nouveaux contes de Magali.** (New tales about *Magali*; Neue Märchen von *Magali.*)
Gap: Ophrys 1957.

1961 Vauthier, Maurice: **Écoute, petit loup.** (Listen, little wolf; Hör mal, Wölfchen.) Ill.: Michel Gourlier.
Colmar: Alsatia 1960.

1962 Guillot, René: **Mon premier atlas.** (My first atlas; Mein erster Atlas.)
Paris: Larousse 1961.

1963 Ingold, François Joseph Jean: **Dans les hautes herbes.** (In the high grass; Im hohen Gras.) Ill.: Maurice Raffray.
Paris: Magnard 1962.

Vauthier, Maurice: **Faon l'héroïque.** (The heroic fawn; Das Heldenreh.) Ill.: Pierre Joubert.
Colmar: Alsatia 1962.

1964 Piettre, André: **Lettres à la jeunesse.** (Letters to the young; Briefe an die Jugend.)
Paris: Ed. La Colombe 1963.

1965 Cervon, Jacqueline: **Ali, Jean-Luc et la gazelle.** (*Ali, Jean-Luc* and the gazelle; *Ali, Jean-Luc* und die Gazelle.) Ill.: Monique Berthoumeyrou.
Paris: Ed. G.P. 1963.

Hilpert, Hélène: **Le chevalier des Sartigues.** (The knight of the *Sartigues;* Der Ritter der *Sartigues.*) Ill.: Xavier Saint-Justh.
Paris: Ed. G.P. 1962.

Meiffret, José: **Mes rendez-vous avec la mort.** (My appointment with death; Meine Termine mit dem Tod.) Ill.
Paris: Flammarion 1965.

Lohéac-Ammoun, Blanche: **Zénobie, reine de Palmyre.** (*Zenobia,* queen of Palmyra; *Zenobia,* die Königin von Palmyr.)

1966 Richard, Colette: **Des cimes aux cavernes.** (From peaks to caverns; Von den Gipfeln zu den Höhlen.)
Mulhouse: Salvator 1965.

1967 Vauthier, Maurice: **La planète Kalgar.** (The planet, *Kalgar;* Der Planet *Kalgar.*) Ill.: Jean Reschofsky.
Paris: Hachette 1966.

1968 The prize was not given; Der Preis wurde nicht vergeben.

1969 Coué, Jean: **Kopoli, le renne guide.** (*Kopoli,* the reindeer guide; *Kopoli,* das Führer-Rentier.)
Paris: Laffont 1967.

1970 Richard, Colette: **Ma double nuit des cavernes.** (My double night in the caves; Meine zweifache Nacht in der Höhle.)
Mulhouse: Salvator 1966.

1971 Eynaud de Fay, Jacques: **Les Hourlots des Rouges-Terres.** (The *Hourlots* of the Red Lands; Die *Hourlots* der Roten Länder.) Ill.: Jean Retailleau.
Paris: Ed. G.P. 1969.

Galet, Jean-Louis: **Meurtre à Hautefaye.** (Murder in *Hautefaye;* Mord in *Hautefaye.*). Ill.: Maurice Albe.
Périgueux: Fanlac 1970.

1972 Toussaint-Samat, Maguelonne: **Récits des châteaux de la Loire.** (Tales of the Loire castles; Erzählungen über die Schlösser an der Loire.) Ill.: René Péron.
Paris: Nathan 1970.

1973 Bernard, Jean: **Le compagnonnage.** (The working years; Die Gesellenzeit.)
Paris: Presses Univeritaires de France 1972.

1974 Lefèvre, André: **La légende des trois fleurs.** (The legend of three flowers; Die Legende der drei Blumen.) Ill.: Marie-Héleǹe Bourdin.
Conty: Touret 1973.

Christiaens, J.: **Le vainqueur de la nuit ou la vie de Louis Braille.** (The vanquisher of the night, or The life of *Louis Braille*; Der Besieger der Nacht oder Das Leben von *Louis Braille.*) Ill.: Gilles Valdès.
Paris: Ed. G.P. 1973.

1975 Duflos, Solange: **Dans le pré.** (In the meadow; Auf der Wiese.) Ill.: H. Misek.
Paris: Hatier 1974.

1976 Durousseau, Serge: **Florian la rose.** (*Florian* the rose; Der *Rosenflorian.*) Ill.: Jacques Pecnard.
Paris: Ed. G.P. 1974.

Ponthier, François: **Le chien Job.** (*Job,* the dog; *Job* der Hund.) Ill.: Jean Retailleau.
Paris: Ed. G.P. 1973.

1977 The prize was not given; Der Preis wurde nicht vergeben.

1978 Baudouy, Michel-Aimé: **Allez les petits!** (Go, you little ones! Los, ihr Kleinen!) Ill.: LeGuen. Photos: Roger Daspet.
Paris: Ed. de l'Amitié — G.T. Rageot 1977.

1979 Byars, Betsy: **Le secret de l'oiseau blessé.** (Amer.orig.title: The house of wings; Das Haus der Flügel.) Ill.: Sophie Tranie.
Paris: Éd. de l'Amitié — G.T. Rageot 1978.

Duflos, Solange/Graille, Jean-Louis: **D'étangs en marais.** (The pond lives; Der Teich lebt.) Photos.
Paris: Hatier 1978.

1980 Pinguilly, Yves: **L'été des confidences et des confitures.** (A summer of confidences and jam; Der Sommer der vertraulichen Mitteilungen und der Marmaladen.) Ill.: Dominique Goupil.
Paris: Éd. de l'Amitié — G.T. Rageot 1979.

Laroche-Clerc, Gilberte: **Les loisirs de la souris verte.** (The diversions of the green mouse; Die Vergnügungen der grünen Maus.) Ill.. Nicole Théodore Le Mauff.
Paris: Bordas 1980.

Prix des Treize

This prize was established in 1966 by the "Union Nationale des Parents d'Elèves de l'Enseignement Libre", to serve the development of the child's personality. The aim is international understanding through dissemination of Christian teachings. The jury is made up of thirteen members, personalities of the church, sciences and public services. Three of the members are children. Until 1970 the prize was offered twice a year: at Christmas, for children up to 13 years, at Easter, for children 13 and older. Since then only one prize a year has been given for a book that expresses the Christian belief and Christian understanding of the world and mankind. The best books are always introduced to the public through the services of the mass media and the magazines of youth organizations.

Der Preis wurde 1966 von der "Union Nationale des Parents d'Elèves de l'Enseignement Libre" gestiftet und soll der Persönlichkeitsbildung der Kinder und Jugendlichen dienen. Ziel ist die internationale Verständigung durch Verbreitung christlichen Gedankengutes. Die Jury setzt sich aus 13 Persönlichkeiten der Kirche, der Wissenschaften und des öffentlichen Lebens zusammen. Bis 1970 wurde der Preis zweimal im Jahr vergeben: zu Weihnachten für Kinder bis zu 13 Jahren, zu Ostern für Jugendliche über 13 Jahre. Seitdem wird der Preis nur einem Buch verliehen, das sich ausgesprochen auf den christlichen Glauben beruft und den jungen Lesern ein christliches Verständnis der Welt und der Menschen vermittelt. Die besten Bücher werden regelmäßig in den Massenmedien und Zeitschriften der Jugendorganisationen vorgestellt.

1966 *Christmas/Weihnachten*
Peyramaure, Michel: **La vallée des mammouths.** (The valley of the mammoths; Das Mammut-Tal.)
Paris: Laffont 1966.

1967 *Easter/Ostern*
Tolédano, Marc: **Le franciscain de Bourges.** (The franciscan of Bourges; Der Franziskaner von Bourges.)
Paris: Flammarion 1967.

Christmas/Weihnachten
Evangile pour les enfants. (Gospel for children; Evangelium für die Kinder.) Ill.: Lizzie Napoli.
Paris: Tisné 1967.

1968 *Easter/Ostern*
Séverin, Jean: **Le soleil d'Olympie.** (The sun of Olympia; Die Sonne von Olympia.)
Paris: Laffont 1967.

Pelot, Pierre: **Dylan Stark. La couleur de Dieu.** (*Dylan Stark.* The colour of God; Die Farbe Gottes.) Ill.: Pierre Joubert.
Verviers: Gérard 1967.

Christmas/Weihnachten
Drouet, Minou: **Ouf de la forêt.** (*Ouf* of the forest; *Ouf* vom Wald.) Ill.: Jacques Pecnard.
Paris: Ed. G.P. 1968.

1969 The prize was not given; Der Preis wurde nicht vergeben.

1970 *Easter/Ostern*
Le premier livre de poésie. (The first book of poetry; Dichtung für Kinder.)
Paris: Gautier-Languereau 1970.
Christmas/Weihnachten
Lafontaine, Claude-Pascale: **Jérican et Brindisi.** (*Jerrican* and *Brindisi.*)
Paris: Tisné 1969.

1971 The prize was not given; Der Preis wurde nicht vergeben.

1972 The prize was not given; Der Preis wurde nicht vergeben.

1973 Ray, Hélène: **Ionel, la musique et la guerre.** (*Ionel,* the music and the war; *Ionel,* die Musik und der Krieg.) Ill.: Michel Gourlier.
Paris: Magnard 1972.

1974 Ames, Francis H.: **Quelque part dans l'Ouest.** (Somewhere in the west; Irgendwo im Westen; Amer.orig.title: That *Callahan* spunk!) Ill.: Jean Retailleau.
Paris: Ed. G.P. 1973.

1975 Lavolle, Louise Noëlle: **L'expédition de l'Intrépide.** (The expedition of the *Intrepid*; Die Expedition der *Intrepide.*) Ill.: Jean Retailleau.
Paris: Ed. G.P. 1974.

1976 Vidal, Nicole: **Nam de la guerre.** (*Nam* of the war; *Nam* vom Krieg.) Ill.: J.M. Serres.
Paris: Ed. de lAmitié — G.T. Rageot 1975.

1977 Fährmann, Willi: **N'oublie pas, Christina.** (Don't forget, *Christina;* Germ.orig.title: *Kristina,* vergiss nicht . . .) Ill.: Daniel Boudineau. Paris: Ed. G.P. 1976.

1978 Lacq, Gil: **Yermak le conquérant.** (*Yermak,* the conqueror; *Yermak* der Eroberer.) Ill.: Jean Retailleau. Paris: Ed. G.P. 1977.

1979 Jansson, Tove: **Le livre d'un été.** (Summer book; Sommerbuch; Swed.orig.title: Sommarboken.) Ill.: Tove Jansson. Paris: Albin Michel 1978.

1980 Carter, Forrest: **Petit arbre.** (Amer.orig.title: The education of *Little Tree*; Die Erziehung des *Little Tree* .) Paris: Stock 1979.

1981 Defromont, Jean Michel/Le mouvement "Tapori": **La boîte à musique.** (The musical box; Die Spieldose.) Ill.: Idelette Bordigoni. Pierrelaye: Éd. Science et Service 1980.

German Democratic Republic/ Deutsche Demokratische Republik

Preisausschreiben zur Förderung der sozialistischen Kinder- und Jugendliteratur

This competition, "for the creation of a new children's and youth literature", was started in 1950 by the Ministry of Education (Ministerium für Volksbildung), and is awarded annually. The Ministry of Cultural Affairs (Ministerium für Kultur) has now taken over the management of the competition. The regulations of 1961 state as follows: "Our children's and youth books shall play an important part in forming our young people into well educated and steadfast socialists; socialists, who will grow up in the spirit of socialist morale and Marxist ideology, who are willing at all times to use their strength and all their qualifications for the promotion of socialism and the preservation of peace; that they are responsible, in international solidarity, for a peaceful future of the German nation and that of all mankind."

Prizes are presented for literary and illustrative achievements. Translations are not considered. Emphasis is placed on non-fiction works about modern sciences and technical problems and achievements. Books from the previous year's production as well as manuscripts can be submitted. Originally, the competition was divided into groups according to the age levels of the readers, and to topics; this arragement was abandoned later in favour of a listing which is presented here in our text. (Because of space consideration, the lesser awards are not indicated in this listing.)

Im Jahre 1950 wurde in der DDR vom Ministerium für Volksbildung zum ersten Mal ein Preisausschreiben "zur Schaffung einer neuen Jugend- und Kinderliteratur" ausgeschrieben, das seitdem jedes Jahr wiederholt wird. Inzwischen hat das Ministerium für Kultur diese Aufgabe übernommen. In den Wettbewerbsregeln von 1961 wird das Ziel des Preisausschreibens so umrissen: "Unsere Kinder- und Jugendbücher sollen dazu beitragen, die jungen Menschen zu allseitig gebildeten und aufrechten Sozialisten zu erziehen, die im Geiste der sozialistischen Moral und der marxistischen Weltanschauung heranwachsen und jederzeit bereit sind, all ihre Kräfte und Fähigkeiten für den Aufbau des Sozialismus und die Erhaltung des Friedens einzusetzen, die sich im Sinne der internationalen Solidarität und der Völkerfreundschaft verantwortlich fühlen für die friedliche Zukunft der deutschen Nation und der ganzen Menschheit." Es werden Preise für die literarische, aber auch für die grafische Gestaltung verliehen. Übersetzungen sind ausgenommen; besonderes Gewicht wird auf Sachbücher über moderne Naturwissenschaften und die Technik gelegt; es können sowohl Bücher aus der Produktion des vergangenen Jahres eingereicht werden

Ill. 16 *Manfred Bofinger in G. Holtz-Baumert: Die drei Frauen und ich*

als auch Manuskripte. Ursprünglich wurde das Preisausschreiben in mehreren, nach Lesealter und Thematik gegliederten Gruppen veranstaltet; später erfolgte nur noch eine Gliederung nach der Höhe der vergebenen Geldprämien. (Die sehr zahlreichen kleineren Prämien konnten wir aus Platzgründen nicht mit aufführen.)

Lit.: Wegehaupt, Heinz: Ausgezeichnete Kinder- und Jugendbücher der D(eutschen D(emokratischen R(epublik. Verz. d. von 1950 bis 1965 preisgekrönten u. zu schönsten Büchern d. Jahres erklärten Kinder- und Jugendbücher. Zsgest. Berlin: Deutsche Staatsbibliothek 1966. 32 S. (Maschinenschr. vervielf.)

1950 *1st competition/1. Preisausschreiben*

Picture book/Bilderbuch

Haacken, Frans: **Das Loch in der Hose.** Ein Bilderbuch über die Entstehung des Fadens. (The hole in the trousers. A picture book about the origin of thread.) Ill.: Frans Haacken.
Berlin: Kinderbuchverlag 19561.
(3rd prize/3.Preis)

Children's book/Kinderbuch

Jürgen, Anna: **Blauvogel. Wahlsohn der Irokesen.** (*Bluebird.* Adopted son of the Iroquois.) Ill.: Kurt Zimmermann.
Berlin: Verlag Neues Leben 1950.
(1st prize/1. Preis)

Görlach-Niemetz, Hede: **Trudels Geheimnis.** (*Trudel's* secret.) Ill.: Erwin Görlach.
Weimar: Arbeitsgemeinschaft Thüringer Verleger; Knabe 1950.
(2nd prize/2. Preis)

Reinicke, E.: **Das hörst Du gern.** Sammlung von Kinderreimen. (Now you listen. Collection of children's rhymes.)
(3rd prize/3. Preis)

Youth book/Jugendbuch

Pludra, Benno: **Ein Mädchen, fünf Jungen und sechs Traktoren.** (A girl, five boys and six tractors.) *Ill.: Max Lingner.*
Berlin: Aufbau-Verlag 1951.
(2nd prize/2. Preis)

Non-fiction/Sachbuch

Brauer, Ewald: **Der Bauer und seine Umwelt.** (The farmer and his environment.)
(1st prize/1. Preis)

Raddatz, Alf: **Nur ein Stückchen Zucker?** Ein Gang durch die Zuckerfabrik. (Another piece of sugar? A tour of a sugar factory.) Berlin, Dresden: Kinderbuchverlag 1950.
(2nd prize/2. Preis)

Steiger, Willy: **Max und Molle erleben tägliche Physik.** (*Max* and *Molle's* adventures with everyday physics.)
(3rd prize/3. Preis)

1951 *2nd competition/2. Preisausschreiben*

Children's book/Kinderbuch

Pludra, Benno: **Gustel, Tapp und die Andern.** (*Gustel, Tapp* and the others.) Ill.: Ernst Jazdzewski.
Berlin: Aufbau-Verlag 1953.
(2nd prize/2. Preis)

Youth book/Jugendbuch

Hardel, Gerhard: **Wir bauen die schönsten Boote.**
(We build the finest boats.) Ill.: Ingeborg Friebel.
Berlin: Verlag Neues Leben 1951.
(1st prize/1. Preis)

Non-fiction/Sachbuch

Greulich, Rudolf: **Vom Winkelhaken zur Setzmaschine.**
Ein Gang durch die Setzerei. (From composing stick to typesetting machine. A tour of a composing room.) Ill.
Berlin: Kinderbuchverlag 1951.
(3rd prize/3. Preis)

3rd competition/3. Preisausschreiben

Picture book/Bilderbuch

Müller, Helmut: **Wer will fleissige Handwerker sehn?**
(Who wants to see diligent artisans?)
(2nd prize/2. Preis)

Children's book/Kinderbuch

Brennecke, Wolf-Dieter: **Erich und das Schulfunkstudio.**
(*Erich* in the school broadcasting studio.) Ill.: Paul Rosié.
Berlin: Kinderbuchverlag 1952.
(2nd prize/2. Preis)

Wetzel, Rose/Rudnik, Heinz: **Die Freunde und das Geigenspiel.**
(Friends playing the violin.)
(3rd prize/3. Preis)

Youth book/Jugendbuch
Welskopf-Henrich, Liselotte: **Die Söhne der Grossen Bärin.** (The sons of *Big Bear.*)
Berlin: Altberliner Verlag 1952.
(1st prize/1. Preis)

Steinmann, Hans-Jürgen: **Es geht um Hannes.** (The case about *Hannes.*)
(2nd prize/2. Preis)

Krause, Hanns: **Frischer Wind im alten Haus.** (Fresh wind in an old house.) Ill.: Horst Schönfelder.
Berlin: Altberliner Verlag 1953.
(3rd prize/3. Preis)

Non-fiction/Sachbuch
Gentz, Kurt: **Im Reiche der Fischreiher.** Heimatliche Vogelwelt erlebt und fotografiert. (In the realm of the water birds.) Photos: Kurt Gentz.
Dresden: Sachsenverlag 1952.
(2nd prize/2. Preis)

Steiger, Willy: **Fredianer und Ingenesen bleiben gesund.** (*Fredianer* and *Ingenesen* keep fit.) Ill.: Erich Gürtzig.
Berlin: Kinderbuchverlag 1953.
(3rd prize/3. Preis)

Illustration
Peschel, Hilde in:
Tornow, Klaus: **Frisch gefangen kommt der Fisch...** (Freshly caught come the fish...)
Berlin: Altberliner Verlag 1952.
(2nd prize/2. Preis)

1952 *4th competition/4. Preisausschreiben*
Picture book/Bilderbuch
Eichler, Kurt in:
Prenzel, Gisela: **Unser Dorf.** (Our village.)
Berlin: Kinderbuchverlag 1952.
(1st prize/1. Preis)

Children's book (under 7 years)/Kinderbuch (unter 7 Jahre alt)
Wiens, Paul: **Min und Go.** Ein Brief aus China. (*Min* and *Go.* A letter from China.)
Berlin: Kinderbuchverlag 1952.
(1st prize/1. Preis)

Children's book (7–14 years)/Kinderbuch (7 bis 14 Jahre alt)
Pludra, Benno: **Die Jungen aus Zelt dreizehn.** (The boys from tent 13.) Ill.: Paul Rosié.
Berlin: Kinderbuchverlag 1952.
(1st prize/1. Preis)

Zimmering, Max: **Buttje Pieter und sein Held.** (*Buttje Pieter* and his hero.)
Berlin: Dietz Verlag 1951.
(1st prize/1. Preis)

Beseler, Horst: **Die Moorbande.** (The moor band.) Ill.: Kurt Zimmermann.
Berlin: Kinderbuchverlag 1952.
(2nd prize/2. Preis)

Krack, Hans-Günter: **Jo und Hilde setzen sich durch.** (*Jo* und *Hilde* make their point.)
Berlin: Altberliner Verlag 1952.
(2nd prize/2. Preis)

Weiss, Rudolf: **Elf Jungen – ein Ball.** (Eleven boys and a ball.) Ill.: Fritz Lattke.
Weimar: Knabe 1955.
(3rd prize/3. Preis)

Non-fiction/Sachbuch
Backhaus, Günther: **Die Menschen erzwingen die Hilfe des Wassers.** (People make water work for them.)
(1st prize/1.Preis)

Wiesenack, Günther: **Kohle, Kraft, Kilowatt.** (Coal, energy, Kilowatt.) Ill.: Hans Räde.
Berlin: Kinderbuchverlag 1953.
(2nd prize/2. Preis)

Grünberg, Helma: **Ausgerechnet Tierärztin.** (A veterinarian, of all things!) Ill.: Ursula Wendorff. Photos: Heinz Krüger.
Berlin: Kinderbuchverlag 1952.
(3rd prize/3. Preis)

5th competition/5. Preisausschreiben
Picture book/Bilderbuch
Friebel, Ingeborg: **Lustig in die Badewanne.** (Into the bathtub, happily.) Ill.: Ingeborg Friebel.
Berlin: Kinderbuchverlag 1953.
(1st prize/1. Preis)

Jantschke, Gertrud: **Morgen komm' ich wieder.** (I'll come again tomorrow.)
(half 3rd prize/halber 3. Preis)

Children's book/Kinderbuch

Hardel, Lilo: **Der freche Max.** (Fresh *Max.*) Ill.: Ingeborg Friebel.
Berlin: Kinderbuchverlag 1953.
(2nd prize/2. Preis)

Documentaries and short stories/Reportagen und Kurzgeschichten

Rutte-Diehn, Rosemarie: **Die Expedition.** (The expedition.) Ill.: Heinz Ebel.
Berlin: Kinderbuchverlag 1952.
(1st prize/1. Preis)

Linke, D./Baumann, R.: **Partisanenkinder.** (Children partisans.)
(2nd prize/2. Preis)

Finster, Ernst: **Die Wälder leben.** (Living forests)
Berlin: Verlag Sport u. Technik 1955.
(3rd prize/3. Preis)

Youth book/Jugendbuch

Rudolph, Wolfgang: **Kutterbrigade "Deutschland".** (Cutter brigade "Germany".) Ill.: Gerda Altendorf.
Berlin: Verlag Neues Leben 1953.
(1st prize/1. Preis)

Wedding, Alex (i.e. Grete Weiskopf): **Das eiserne Büffelchen.** (The little iron buffalo.) Ill.: Kurt Zimmermann.
Berlin: Verlag Neues Leben 1952.
(1st prize/1. Preis)

Illustration

Jazdzewski, Ernst in:
Meinck, Willi: **Henri, der tapfere Matrose.** (*Henry,* the brave seaman.)
Berlin: Kinderbuchverlag 1952.
(1st prize/1. Preis)

Zimmermann, Kurt in:
Komarowskij, Gleb/Komarowskij, Nikolaij: **Kai-su. Die abenteuerliche Geschichte eines koreanischen Jungen.** (*Kai-su.* The adventurous story of a Korean boy.)
Berlin: Kinderbuchverlag 1952.
(2nd prize/2. Preis)

1953 *6th competition/6. Preisausschreiben*

Picture book/Bilderbuch

Meyer-Rey, Ingeborg: **Die gestohlene Nase.** (The stolen nose.) Ill.: Ingeborg Meyer-Rey.
Berlin: Kinderbuchverlag 1954.
(1st Prize/1. Preis)

Children's book/Kinderbuch

Fiedler, Heinz: **Fips schlägt Alarm.** (*Fips* sounds the alarm.) Ill.: Ingeborg Friebel.
Berlin: Kinderbuchverlag 1955.
(3rd prize/3. Preis)

Krause, Hanns: **Strupp und Trolli.** (*Strupp* and *Trolli.)*
Berlin: Kinderbuchverlag 1954
(3rd prize/3. Preis)

Documentaries and short stories/Reportagen und Kurzgeschichten

Thürk, Harry: **Träum von morgen, Julcsa...!** (Dream about tomorrow, Julcsa...!)
Berlin: Verlag Neues Leben 1953.
(1st prize/1. Preis)

Daumann, Rudolph: **Der Andenwolf.** (Wolf from the Andes.) Ill.: Heinz Rammelt.
Berlin: Verlag Kultur u. Fortschritt 1954.
(3rd prize/3. Preis)

Schmidt, Gerhard: **Das Gericht von Weinsberg,** (The court of Weinsberg.)
Berlin: Kinderbuchverlag 1954.
(3rd prize/3. Preis)

Novels and story collections/Romane und Erzählungen

Djacenko, Boris: **Das gelbe Kreuz.** (The yellow cross.)
Berlin: Verlag Neues Leben 1954.
(1st prize/1. Preis)

Meinck, Willi: **Der Herbststurm fegt durch Hamburg.** (The autumn storm rages in Hamburg.) Ill.: Kurt Zimmermann.
Berlin: Kinderbuchverlag 1954.
(2nd prize/2. Preis)

Pludra, Benno: **In Wiepershagen krähn die Hähne.** (Cocks corw in *Wiepershagen.)* Ill.: Hans Baltzer.
Berlin: Kinderbuchverlag 1953.
(2nd prize/2. Preis)

Görtz, Adolf: **Mein Bruder Hans und seine Freunde.** (My brother *Hans* and his friends.) Ill.: Ernst Jazdzewski.
Berlin: Kinderbuchverlag 1953.
(3rd prize/3. Preis)

Non-fiction/Sachbuch

Wille, Hermann Heinz: **Wunderwelt des Wassers.** (Marvellous world of water.) Ill.: Lieselotte Funke-Poser.
Berlin: Altberliner Verlag 1955.
(1st prize/1. Preis)

Quednau, Werner: **Rufa und ihre Schwestern.** *(Rufa* and her sisters.) Ill.: Alfred Will.
Berlin: Kinderbuchverlag 1953.
(2nd prize/2. Preis)

Mütze-Specht, Fanny: **Strom der Millionen Schiffchen.** (Stream of a million little ships.) Ill.: Heinz-Karl Bogdanski.
Berlin: Kinderbuchverlag 1955.
(3rd prize/3. Preis)

Adventure book/Abenteuerbuch

Legère, Werner: **Ich war in Timbuktu. (I was in Timbuktu.)**
Berlin: Altberliner Verlag 1955.
(1st prize/1. Preis)

Illustration (Photos)

Buchmann, Heinz In:
Buchmann, Heinz: **Die Schilfhütte am silbernen See.** (The reed hut at *Silver lake.)* Ill.: Helmut Kloss.
Photos: Heinz Buchmann.
Berlin: Kinderbuchverlag 1953.
(2nd prize/2. Preis)

1954 *7th competition/7. Preisausschreiben*

Children's book/Kinderbuch

Hardel, Lilo: **Max und Lottchen in der Schule.** *(Max* and *Lottchen* at school.) Ill.: Ingeborg Friebel.
Berlin: Kinderbuchverlag 1955.
(1st prize/1. Preis)

Feustel, Günther: **Mäuse, Tränen und ein Stubenzoo.** (Mice, tears and a home zoo.)
Ill.: Ingeborg Friebel.
Berlin: Kinderbuchverlag 1955.
(2nd prize/2. Preis)

Fiedler, Heinz: **Fips schlägt Alarm.** *(Fips* sounds the alarm.) Ill.: Ingeborg Friebel.
Berlin: Kinderbuchverlag 1955.
(half 3rd prize/halber 3. Preis)

Krack, Hans-Günter: **Die Geschichte vom neidischen Dorle.** (The story about envious *Dorle.*) Ill.: Fritz Lattke.
Weimar: Knabe 1955.
(half 3rd prize/halber 3. Preis)

Girl's book/Mädchenbuch

Panitz, Eberhard: **Käte.** Eine biograph. Erzählung über Käte Niederkirchner. (*Kate.* A biographical tale about *Kate Niederkirchner.*) Ill.: Eberhard Binder.
Berlin: Verlag Neues Leben 1955.
(2nd prize/2. Preis)

Quednau, Werner: **Clara Schumann.** *(Clara Schumann.)* Ill.: Ursula Volk.
Berlin: Altberliner Verlag 1955.
(2nd prize/2. Preis)

Schmied, Luise Maria: **Die magischen Strahlen.** Lebensweg einer Forscherin. (The magic rays. Life story of a female researcher.) Photos.
Berlin: Verlag Neues Leben 1955.
(3rd prize/3. Preis)

Adventure book/Abenteuerbuch

Quednau, Werner: **Die Gefangenen von Murano.** (The prisoners of Murano.) Ill.: Günter Hain.
Berlin: Altberliner Verlag 1954.

Schönrock, Hans: **Mein Freund Chinino.** (My friend *Chinino.)* Ill.: Horst Schönfelder.
Schwerin: Petermänken-Verlag 1955.
(2nd prize/2. Preis)

Hirsch, Rudolf: **Herrn Louisides bittere Mandeln.** (Mr. *Louiside's* bitter almonds.) Ill.: Eberhard Binder.
Berlin: Verlag Neues Leben 1955.
(3rd prize/3. Preis)

Novels and story collections/Romane und Erzählungen

Renn, Ludwig (i.e. Arnold Vieth von Golssenau): **Trini.** *(Trini.)* Ill.: Kurt Zimmermann.
Berlin: Kinderbuchverlag 1954.
(1st prize/1. Preis)

Strittmatter, Erwin: **Tinko.** (*Tinko.*) Ill.: Carl von Appen.
Berlin: Kinderbuchverlag 1954.
(1st prize/1. Preis)

Daumann, Rudolf: **Herzen im Sturm.** (Stormy hearts.)
Berlin: Verlag Neues Leben 1954.
(3rd prize/3. Preis)

Veken, Karl.: **Der Kellerschlüssel.** (The cellar key.) Ill.: Ingo Kirchner.
Berlin: Verlag Neues Leben 1955.
(3rd Prize/3. Preis)

Veken, Karl: **Lustige Streiche.** (Humourous tricks.)
Ill.: Werner Tübke.
Berlin: Kinderbuchverlag 1956.
(3rd prize/3. Preis)

Veken, Karl: **Vier Berliner Rangen.** (Four Berlin urchins.) Ill.: Ernst Jazdzewski.
Berlin: Kinderbuchverlag 1955
(3rd prize/3. Preis)

Biographical stories/Biographische Erzählungen

Meichner, Fritz: **Die Schatzgräber.** Eine Erzählung um Heinrich Schliemann. (The treasure hunters. A story about *Heinrich Schliemann.*)
Berlin: Verlag Neues Leben 1954.
(3rd prize/3. Preis)

Thoma, Friedrich M.: **Georg Forster.** *(Georg Forster.)*
Berlin: Verlag Neues Leben 1954
(3rd prize/3. Preis)

Non-fiction/Sachbuch

Weltall, Erde, Mensch. Ein Sammelwerk zur Entwicklungsgeschichte von Natur u. Gesellschaft. (Universe, world, man. A book about the development of nature and society.) Ed.: Gisela Buschendorf, Horst Wolffgramm, Irmgard Radant. Ill.
Berlin: Verlag Neues Leben 1954.
(1st prize/1. Preis)

Berger, Karl-Heinz: **Johann Gottlieb Fichte.** *(Johann Gottlieb Fichte.)*
Berlin: Verlag Neues Leben 1953.
(2nd prize/2. Preis)

Kauffeldt, Alfons: **Nikolaus Kopernikus.** *(Nicolas Copernicus.)*
Berlin: Verlag Neues Leben 1954.
(3rd prize/3. Preis)

Photography/Fotografie
Buchmann, Heinz in:
Buchmann, Heinz: **Piraten im Schilf.** (Pirates in the reeds.) Ill.: Helmut Kloss. Photos: Heinz Buchmann.
Berlin: Kinderbuchverlag 1956.
(3rd prize/3. Preis)

Illustration
Zimmermann, Kurt in:
Renn, Ludwig (i.e. Arnold Vieth von Golssenau): **Trini.** *(Trini.)*
Berlin: Kinderbuchverlag 1954.

Nowak-Neumann, Martin in:
Meister Krabat. Eine sorbische Sage. (Master *Krabat.* A Sorbian saga.) Adapt.: Martin Nowak-Neumann.
Berlin: Kinderbuchverlag 1954.

Klemke, Werner in:
Verne, Jules: **Die Kinder des Kapitän Grant.** (The children of Captain *Grant;* Fr.orig.title: Les enfants du capitaine *Grant.*)
Berlin: Verlag Neues Leben 1953.

Binder, Eberhard in:
Twain, Mark (i.e. Samuel Langhorne Clemens): **Tom Sawyers Abenteuer.** (Amer.orig.title: The adventures of *Tom Ssawyer.*)
Adapt.: Karl Heinz Berger.
Berlin: Verlag Neues Leben 1954.

Grossmann, Gerhard in:
Gerstäcker, Friedrich: **General Franco.** (General *Franco.*)
Berlin: Verlag Neues Leben 1954.

1955 *8th competition/8. Preisausschreiben*
Kraze, Hanna-Heide: **Des Henkers Bruder.** (The hangman's brother.) Ill.: Karl Stratil.
Berlin: Verlag Neues Leben 1956.
(1st prize/1. Preis)

Renn, Ludwig (i.e. Arnold Vieth von Golssenau): **Nobi.** *(Nobi.)* Ill.: Hans Baltzer.
Berlin: Kinderbuchverlag 1955.
(1st prize/1. Preis)

Inkusi, der Bambuti. Abenteuerliche Erzählungen aus Afrika. (*Inkusi,* the *Bambuti.* Adventurous tales from Africa.) by Bernhard Faust et al. Ill.: Eberhard Binder.
Berlin: Verlag Neues Leben 1960.
(2nd prize/2. Preis)

Ilberg, Hanna: **Clara Zetkin.** Aus dem Leben u. Wirken einer großen Sozialistin. *Clara Zetkin.* Life and work of a great socialist.)
Berlin: Verlag Neues Leben 1956.
(2nd prize/2. Preis)

Pludra, Benno: **Vor großer Fahrt.** (Before the great trip.) Ill.: Fritz Bley.
Berlin: Verlag Neues Leben 1955.
(2nd prize/2. Preis)

Quednau, Werner: **Die Schwestern der goldenen Stadt.** (Sisters of the golden city.) Ill.: Ruprecht Haller.
Berlin: Kinderbuchverlag 1955
(2nd prize/2. Preis)

Richter, Götz Rudolf: **Savvy, der Reis-Shopper.** Die Abenteuer eines Negerjungen vom Stamme der Basa-Kru. (*Savvy,* the rice shopper. Adventures of a black boy from the Basa-Kru tribe.) Ill.: Kurt Zimmermann.
Berlin: Kinderbuchverlag 1956.
(2nd prize/2. Preis)

Schröter, Hans Robert: **Der Wunderdoktor Eisenbart.** (The quack, Dr. *Eisenbart.)* Ill.: Hans Wiegandt.
Weimar: Knabe 1955.
(2nd prize/2. Preis)

Veken, Karl: **Peng und 'ne Kiste.** Eine lustige Geschichte für kleine und große Tierfreunde. (*Peng* and a box. A humourous story for lovers of animals.) Ill.: Karl Fischer.
Berlin: Verlag Neues Leben 1956.
(2nd prize/2. Preis)

Illustration

Baltzer, Hans in:
Renn, Ludwig (i.e. Arnold Vieth von Golssenau): **Nobi.** *(Nobi.)*
Berlin: Kinderbuchverlag 1955.
(1st prize/1. Preis)

Haller, Hildegard in:
Kitzing, Hans-Dieter: **Der gelbe Dickbauch.** (The yellow fat belly.)
Berlin: Holz 1955.
(1st prize/1. Preis)

Friebel, Ingeborg in:
Hardel, Lilo: **Otto und der Zauberer Faulebaul.** (*Otto* and the magician, *Faulebaul.*)
Berlin: Kinderbuchverlag 1956.
(2nd prize/2. Preis)

Meyer-Rey, Ingeborg in:
Neckel, Dorothea: **Ulrikchen, gute Nacht.** (Good night little *Ulrike.*)
Berlin: Kinderbuchverlag 1955.
(2nd prize/2. Preis)

1956 *9th competition/9. Preisausschreiben*

Meinck, Willi: **Die seltsamen Reisen des Marco Polo.** (The wondrous travels of *Marco Polo.*) Ill.: Hans Mau.
Berlin: Kinderbuchverlag 1957
(1st prize/1. Preis)

Pludra, Benno: **Haik und Paul.** (*Haik* and *Paul.*) Ill. Eberhard Binder.
Berlin: Verlag Neues Leben 1956.
(1st prize/1. Preis)

Böhm, Karl/Dörge, Rolf: **Gigant Atom.** (Giant atom.) Ill.: Eberhard Binder.
Berlin: Verlag Neues Leben 1957
(2nd prize/2. Preis)

Brézan, Jrij (i.e. Dušan Switz): **Christa.** Die Geschichte eines jungen Mädchens. (*Christa.* The story of a young girl.) Ill.: Jutta Schlichting.
Berlin: Verlag Neues Leben 1957.
(3rd prize/3. Preis)

Fischer, Rudolf: **Dem Unbekannten auf der Spur.** (On the trail of the unknown.) Ill.: Paul Rosié.
Berlin: Kinderbuchverlag 1956.
(3rd prize/3. Preis)

Friedel, Karl: **Streifzug durch Wald und Flur.** (Roving through forest and field.) Ill.: Helmut Kloss.
Berlin: Kinderbuchverlag 1955.
(3rd prize/3. Preis)

Pludra, Benno: **Sheriff Teddy.** (Sheriff *Teddy.*) Ill.: Hans Baltzer.
Berlin: Kinderbuchverlag 1956.
(3rd prize/3. Preis)

Renn, Ludwig (i.e. Arnold Vieth von Golssenau): **Herniu und der blinde Asni.** (*Herniu* and blind *Asni.*) Ill.: Kurt Zimmermann.
Berlin: Kinderbuchverlag 1956.
(3rd prize/3. Preis)

Illustration
Zimmermann, Kurt in:
Gajdar, Arkadij (i.e. Arkadij Petrovič Golikov): **Die Feuertaufe.** (The baptism of fire.)
Berlin: Kinderbuchverlag 1956.
(1st prize/1. Preis)

Baltzer, Hans in:
Pludra, Benno: **Sheriff Teddy.** (Sheriff *Teddy.*)
Berlin: Kinderbuchverlag 1956.
(2nd prize/2. Preis)

Haller, Ruprecht in:
Durian, Wolf: **Lumberjack.** Abenteuer in den Wäldern Nordamerikas. (Lumberjack. Adventures in North American forests.)
Berlin: Kinderbuchverlag 1956.
(2nd prize/2. Preis)

1957 *10th competition/10. Preisausschreiben*
Brežan, Jurij (i.e. Dušan Swith): **Der Gymnasiast.** (The high school student.)
Berlin: Verlag Neues Leben 1958.
(1st prize/1. Preis)

Görlich, Günter: **Der Schwarze Peter.** (Black *Peter.*) Ill.: Ingo Kirchner.
Berlin: Verlag Neues Leben 1958.
(2nd prize/2. Preis)

Klatt, Edith: **Neitah, ein Mädchen im hohen Norden.** (*Neitah.* A girl of the far north.)
Photos: Anna Riwkin-Brick.
Berlin: Altberliner Verlag 1956.
(2nd prize/2. Preis)

Richter, Götz Rudolf: **Schiffe, Menschen, fernes Land.** (Boats, men, far-away countries.) Ill.: Eberhard Binder.
Berlin: Verlag Kultur u. Fortschritt 1959.
(3rd prize/3. Preis)

Illustration
Gürtzig, Erich in:
Maršak, Samuil Jakovlevič (i.e. Michail Il'in): **Das Katzenhaus.** (The cat house.)
Berlin: Kinderbuchverlag 1957.
(1st prize/1. Preis)

Friebel, Ingeborg in:
Krumbach, Walter: **Der kleine Kapitän.** (The little captain.)
Berlin: Altberliner Verlag 1956.
(2nd prize/2. Preis)

Zimmermann, Kurt in:
Hugo, Victor: **Gavroche. Die Geschichte e. Pariser Jungen.** (*Gavroche.* The story of a Paris youth; Fr.orig.title: Les misérables.)
Berlin: Kinderbuchverlag 1957.
(2nd prize/2. Preis)

Haller, Ruprecht in:
Kabirov, M.N./Šachmatov, B.F.: **Die Stadt der tauben Ohren und andere uigarische Volksmärchen.** City of deaf ears and other Uigarian folk tales.)
Berlin: Holz 1957.
(3rd prize/3. Preis)

Klemke, Werner in:
Stevenson, Robert Louis: **Catriona. Die Abenteuer d. David Balfour.** (*Catriona.* The adventures of *David Balfour.*)
Berlin: Verlag Neues Leben 1957.
(3rd prize/3. Preis)

1958 *11th competition/11. Preisausschreiben*
Strittmatter, Erwin: **Pony Pedro.** (Pony *Pedro.*) Ill.: Hans Baltzer.
Berlin: Kinderbuchverlag 1959.
(1st prize/1. Preis)

Neumann, Karl: **Frank.** (*Frank.*) Ill.: Bernhard Nast.
Berlin: Kinderbuchverlag 1958.
(2nd prize/2. Preis)

Renn, Ludwig (i.e. Arnold Vieth von Golssenau): **Herniu und Armin.** (*Herniu* and *Armin.*) Ill.: Kurt Zimmermann.
Berlin: Kinderbuchverlag 1958.
(2nd prize/2. Preis)

Richter, Götz Rudolf: **Die Höhle der fliegenden Teufel.** (The cave of the flying devils.) Ill.: Kurt Zimmermann.
Berlin: Kinderbuchverlag 1958.
(2nd prize/2. Preis)

Böhm, Karl/Dörge, Rolf: **Auf dem Weg zu fernen Welten.** (Journeying to far-away worlds.) Ill.: Heinz Handschick. Techn. ill.: Heinz Handschick, Horst Boche, Joachim Arfert.
Berlin: Verlag Neues Leben 1958.
(3rd prize/3. Preis)

Harder, Irma: **Ein unbeschriebenes Blatt.** (A blank page.) Ill.: Ursula Mattheuer-Neustädt.
Berlin: Verlag Neues Leben 1958.
(3rd prize/3. Preis)

Küchenmeister, Claus/Küchenmeister, Wera: **Der Älteste war dreizehn.** (The oldest was thirteen.)
(3rd prize/3. Preis)

Werner, Ruth: **Ein ungewöhnliches Mädchen.** (An unusual girl.)
Berlin: Verlag Neues Leben 1958.
(3rd prize/3. Preis)

Illustration

Zimmermann, Kurt in:
Wiesner, Erich: **Man nannte mich Ernst.** Ein Veteran der Arbeiterjugendbewegung erzählt sein Leben. They called me *Ernst*. A veteran of the worker's youth movement recalls his life.)
Berlin: Verlag Neues Leben 1956.
(1st prize/1. Preis)

Haacken, Frans in:
Prokof'ev, Sergej Sergeevič: **Peter und der Wolf.** (*Peter* and the wolf; Russ.orig.title: *Petja* i volk.)
Berlin: Holz 1958.
(2nd prize/2. Preis)

Fischer, Karl in:
Klein, Eduard: **Der Indianer.** (The Indian.)
Berlin: Verlag Neues Leben 1958.
(3rd prize/3. Preis)

Mau, Hans in:
Mundstock, Karl: **Ali und die Bande vom Lauseplatz.** Ein Berliner Jugendroman. (*Ali* and the *Lice Square* gang. A Berlin youth novel.)
Berlin: Verlag Neues Leben 1958.
(3rd prize/3. Preis)

1959 *12th competition/12. Preisausschreiben*

Körner-Schrader, Paul: **Treibjagd im Dorf.** (Hunt in the village.) Ill.: Kurt Zimmermann.
Berlin: Kinderbuchverlag 1959.
(1st prize/1. Preis)

Wellm, Alfred: **Die Kinder von Plieversdorf.** (The children of Plieversdorf.) Ill.: Hildegard Haller.
Berlin: Kinderbuchverlag 1959.
(2nd prize/2. Preis)

Böhm, Karl/Dörge, Rolf: **Unsere Welt von morgen.** (Our world of tomorrow.) Ill.: Eberhard Binder. Techn. ill.: Heinz Handschick, Wolfgang Würfel, Rudolf Skribelka.
Berlin: Verlag Neues Leben 1959.
(3rd prize/3. Preis)

Das große Bastelbuch. (The big hobby book.) Ed.: Hans-Peter Wetzstein. Ill.: Heinz-Karl Bogdanski.
Berlin: Kinderbuchverlag 1959.
(3rd prize/3. Preis)

Illustration

Naltzer, Hans in:
Strittmatter, Erwin: **Pony Pedro.** (Pony *Pedro.*)
Berlin: Kinderbuchverlag 1959.
(2nd prize/2. Preis)

Friebel, Ingeborg in:
Fühmann, Franz: **Vom Moritz, der kein Schmutzkind mehr sein wollte.** (Tale of *Moritz,* who no longer wanted to be a dirty child.)
Berlin: Kinderbuchverlag 1959.
(2nd prize/2. Preis)

Wendorff-Weidt, Ursula in:
Gorkij, Maksim (i.e. Aleksej Maksimovič Peškov): **Vor dem Angesicht des Lebens.** Erzählungen. Eine Auswahl für die Jugend. (Facing life. Stories. A selection for the young.)
Berlin: Verlag Neues Leben 1959.
(2nd prize/2. Preis)

Binder, Eberhard in:
Belych, Grigorij Georgievič (G. Bjelych)/Panteleev, Aleksej Ivanovič (L. Pantelejew): **Schkid, die Republik der Strolche.** (*Schkid,* The tramp's republic.)
Berlin: Verlag Neues Leben 1959.
(3rd prize/3. Preis)

1960 *13th competition/13. Preisausschreiben*

Renn, Ludwig (i.e. Arnold Vieth von Golssenau): **Auf den Trümmern des Kaiserreiches.** (On the ruins of the empire.) Ill.: Paul Rosié.
Berlin: Kinderbuchverlag 1961.
(1st prize/1. Preis)

Greulich, Emil Rudolf: **Keiner wird als Held geboren.** Ein Lebensbild aus dem deutschen Widerstand. (Nobody is born a hero. A biographical sketch from the German resistance.)
Berlin: Verlag Neues Leben 1961.
(2nd prize/2. Preis)

Radetz, Walter: **Stärkere.** Ein Buch über Werner Seelenbinder. (The stronger one. A book about Werner *Seelenbinder*.)
Berlin: Sportverlag 1961.
(2nd prize/2. Preis)

Friedrich, Herbert: **Wassermärchen.** (Water fairy tales.) Ill.: Günter Blochberger.
Berlin: Kinderbuchverlag 1960.
(3rd prize/3. Preis)

Kasper, Fritz: **Die Schicksale der Gruppe G.** Nach Aufzeichnungen und Briefen. (The fates of *Group G.*, as taken from notes and letters.)
Berlin: Verlag Neues Leben 1960.

Lindemann, Werner: **Zutiefst an dich gebunden sein...** Gedichte über eine Liebe. (Bound to you deeply... Poems about love.) Ill.: Herbert Wohlert.
Berlin: Verlag Neues Leben 1961.
(3rd prize/3. Preis)

Victor, Walther: **Der beste Freund.** Friedrich Engels, sein Leben und sein Werk. (The best friend. *Friedrich Engels,* his life and work.) Ill.: Helmut Kloss.
Berlin: Kinderbuchverlag 1961.
(3rd prize/3. Preis)

1962 *14th competition/14. Preisausschreiben*

Wellm, Alfred: **Kaule.** (*Kaule.*) Ill.: Heinz Rodewald.
Berlin: Kinderbuchverlag 1962.
(1st prize/1. Preis)

Werner, Ruth: **Olga Benario.** Die Geschichte eines tapferen Lebens. (*Olga Benario.* The story of a courageous life.) Photos.
Berlin: Verlag Neues Leben 1961.
(1st prize/1. Preis)

Bekier, Erwin: **Die Insel der sieben Schiffe.** (The island of the seven ships.) Ill.
Berlin: Kinderbuchverlag 1962.
(2nd prize/2. Preis)

David, Kurt: **Der singende Pfeil.** (The singing arrow.) Ill.: Kurt Zimmermann.
Berlin: Kinderbuchverlag 1962.
(2nd prize/2. Preis)

Pludra, Benno: **Heiner und sein Hähnchen.** (*Heiner* and his little cock.) Ill.: Ingeborg Meyer-Rey.
Berlin: Kinderbuchverlag 1962.
(2nd prize/2. Preis)

Pludra, Benno: **Lütt Matten und die weiße Muschel.** (Little *Mathew* and the white shell.)
Berlin: Kinderbuchverlag 1963.
(2nd prize/2. Preis)

Reimann, Brigitte: **Ankunft im Alltag.** Erzählung.
(Arriving in a workaday world. A story.)
Berlin: Verlag Neues Leben 1961.
(2nd prize/2. Preis)

Veken, Karl: **Auf Tod und Leben.** Roman. (On life and death. A novel.)
Berlin: Verlag Neues Leben 1961.
(3rd prize/3. Preis)

Illustration

Gürtzig, Erich in:
Hähnchen Schreihals. Ein ukrainisches Volksmärchen. (Little Cock Crow. A Ukranian folk tale)
Berlin: Kinderbuchverlag 1961.
(1st prize/1. Preis)

Gürtzig, Erich in:
Anderson, Edith: **Der verlorene Schuh.** (The lost shoe.)
Berlin: Kinderbuchverlag 1962.
(2nd prize/2. Preis)

Klemke, Werner in:
Rodrian, Fred.: **Hirsch Heinrich.** Eine Bilderbuchgeschichte. (*Stag Henry.* A picture book story.)
Berlin: Kinderbuchverlag 1960.
(2nd prize/2. Preis)

Metzmacher, Gerlinde in:
Metzmacher, Gerlinde: **Kennt ihr Kuml?** (Do you know Kuml?)
(3rd prize/3. Preis)

1963 *15th competition/15. Preisausschreiben*

Picture book/Bilderbuch

Strahl, Rudi: **Sandmännchen auf der Leuchtturminsel.** (Little sandman on the lighthouse island.)
Ill.: Eberhard Binder.
Berlin: Kinderbuchverlag 1963.
(3rd prize/3. Preis)

Belletristic children's and youth books on contemporary themes/Belletristische Kinder- und Jugendbücher zu Themen unserer Gegenwart

Meinck, Willi: **Salvi Fünf oder Der Zerrissene Faden.** (*Salvi Five* or the broken thread.) Ill.: Karl Fischer.
Berlin: Kinderbuchverlag 1966.
(1st prize/1. Preis)

Schmoll, Werner: **Mit siebzehn ist man noch kein Held.** (At seventeen, one is not a hero.)
Halle/Saale: Mitteldeutscher Verlag 1962.
(2nd prize/2. Preis)

Pludra, Benno: **Die Reise nach Sundavit.** (The journey to *Sundavit.)*
Ill.: Hans Baltzer.
Berlin: Kinderbuchverlag 1965.
(3rd prize/3. Preis)

Special prize/Sonderpreis

Korn, Vilmos/Korn, Ilse: **Mohr und die Raben von London.** (*Mohr* and the ravens of London.)
Berlin: Kinderbuchverlag 1962.
(1st prize/1. Preis)

1965 *16th competition/16. Preisausschreiben*

Beseler, Horst: **Käuzchenkuhle.** (The screech owl's pit.) Ill.: Horst Bartsch.
Berlin: Verlag Neues Leben 1965.
(1st prize/1. Preis)

David, Kurt: **Der Schwarze Wolf.** (The black wolf.) Ill.: Hans Baltzer.
Berlin: Verlag Neues Leben 1966.
(2nd prize/2. Preis)

David, Kurt: **Der Spielmann vom Himmelpfortgrund.** (The minstrel from Himmelpfortgrund.) Ill.: Renate Jessel.
Berlin: Kinderbuchverlag 1964.
(2nd prize/2. Preis)

Hardel, Gerhard: **Sieben Jahre Wunderland.** (Seven years of wonderland.)
Berlin: Kinderbuchverlag 1967.
(2nd prize/2. Preis)

Hardel, Gerhard: **Marie und ihr großer Bruder.** (*Marie* and her big brother.) Ill.: Renate Jessel.
Berlin: Kinderbuchverlag 1964.
(2nd prize/2. Preis)

1967/ *17th competition/17. Preisausschreiben*
1968 Weber, Hans: **Sprung ins Riesenrad.** (Jumping into the ferris wheel.)
Berlin: Verlag Neues Leben 1968.
(1st prize/1. Preis)

Fühmann, Franz: **Shakespeare-Märchen** (*Shakespearian* fairy tales.) Ill.: Bernhard Nast.
Berlin: Kinderbuchverlag 1967.
(2nd prize/2. Preis)

Fühmann, Franz. **Das hölzerne Pferd.** (The wooden horse.) Ill.: Eberhard Binder, Elfriede Binder.
Berlin: Verlag Neues Leben 1968.
(2nd prize/2. Preis)

Kurella, Alfred: **Unterwegs zu Lenin. Erinnerungen.** (Journey to Lenin. Memories.)
Berlin: Verlag Neues Leben 1967.
(2nd prize/2. Preis)

Brězan, Jurij (i.e. Dušan Switz): **Die schwarze Mühle.** (The black mill.) Ill.: Werner Klemke.
Berlin: Verlag Neues Leben 1968.

Meinck, Willi: **Untergang der Jaguarkrieger.** (The decline of the jaguar warriors.) Ill.: Bernhard Nast.
Berlin: Kinderbuchverlag 1968.
(2nd prize/2. Preis)

1969 *18th competition/18. Preisausschreiben*

Pludra, Benno: **Tambari.** (*Tambari.*)
Berlin: Kinderbuchverlag 1969.
(1st prize/1. Preis)

Nowatny, Joachim: **Der Riese im Paradies.** (The giant in paradise.) Ill.: Kurt Zimmermann.
Berlin: Kinderbuchverlag 1969.
(2nd prize/2. Preis)

Picture Book/Bilderbuch
Stengel, Hansgeorg: **Schnurrpfeifland am Schnurrpfeifstrand.** (Funny tale land at funny tale strand.)
Ill.: Karl Schrader.
Berlin: Kinderbuchverlag 1968.

Illustration
Lahr, Gerhard in:
Hüttner, Hannes: **Bei der Feuerwehr wird der Kaffee kalt.** (At the firehouse the coffee is getting cold.)
Berlin: Kinderbuchverlag 1969.

Lahr Gerhard in:
Augustin, Barbara: **Antonella und ihr Weihnachtsmann.** (*Antonella* and her *Santa Claus.*)
Berlin: Kinderbuchverlag 1969

1971 *19th competition/19. Preisausschreiben*
David, Kurt: **Begegnung mit der Unsterblichkeit.** (Meeting with immortality.)
Berlin: Kinderbuchverlag 1970.
(1st prize/1. Preis)

Friedrich, Herbert: **Das Kristall und die Messer.** (The crystal and the knives.) Ill.: Wolfgang Würfel.
Berlin: Kinderbuchverlag 1971.
(2nd prize/2. Preis)

Friedrich, Herbert: **Die Eissee.** (The ice lake.)
Berlin: Verlag Neues Leben 1968.
(2nd prize/2. Preis)

Beseler, Horst: **Jemand kommt.** (Someone arrives.) Ill.: Thomas Schleusing.
Berlin: Kinderbuchverlag 1972.
(3rd prize/3. Preis)

Beseler, Horst: **Auf dem Flug nach Havanna.** (On the flight to Havana.) Ill.: Gertrud Zucker.
Berlin: Kinderbuchverlag 1973.
(3rd prize/3. Preis)

Picture book/Bilderbuch
Hüttner, Hannes: **Pommelpütz.** (*Pommelpütz.*) Ill.: Konrad Golz.
Berlin: Kinderbuchverlag 1971.

Illustration
Klemke, Werner in:
Rodrian, Fred: **Wir haben keinen Löwen.** (We don't have a lion.)
Berlin: Kinderbuchverlag 1969.

1974 *20th competition/20. Preisausschreiben*

Holtz-Baumert, Gerhard: **Die drei Frauen und ich.** (The three women and I.) Ill.: Manfred Bofinger.
Berlin: Kinderbuchverlag 1973.
(1st prize/1. Preis)

Holtz-Baumert, Gerhard: **Der Wunderpilz.** (The magic mushroom.)
Berlin: Kinderbuchverlag 1974.
(1st prize/1. Preis)

Karau, Gisela: **Der gute Stern des Janusz K.** (The lucky star of *Janusz K.)* Ill.: Manfred Butzmann.
Berlin: Kinderbuchverlag 1972.
(2nd prize/2. Preis)

Höricke, Lothar: **Fischzüge.** (Bringing in the catch.) Ill.: Eberhard Binder-Stassfurt.
Berlin: Verlag Neues Leben 1972.
(2nd prize/2. Preis)

Lemann, Alfred/Taubert, Hans: **Das Gastgeschenk der Transsolaren.** (The gift from the trans-solarians.) Ill.: Peter Nagengast.
Berlin: Verlag Neues Leben 1973.
(3rd prize/3. Preis)

Picture book/Bilderbuch

Hegewald, Heidrun: **Fausthandschuh.** (The mitten.) Ill.: Heidrun Hegewald.
Berlin: Altberliner Lucie Groszer 1971.

Krawitter, Herbert: **Krawatter, das Stinchen, das Minchen.** (*Krawatter,* the *Stinchen,* the *Minchen.*) Ill.: Gerhard Lahr.
Berlin: Kinderbuchverlag 1963.

Illustration

Butzmann, Manfred in:
Bernhof, Reinhard: **Die Kuckuckspfeife.** (The cuckoo flute.)
Berlin: Kinderbuchverlag 1973.

1976 *21st competition/21. Preisausschreiben*

Grand prize/Ehrenurkunde

Holtz-Baumert, Gerhard: **Trampen nach Norden.** (Hitchhiking north.) Ill.: Thomas Schleusing.
Berlin: Kinderbuchverlag 1975

Görlich, Günter: **Der blaue Helm.** (The blue helm.) Ill.: Bernhard Nosd.
Berlin: Kinderbuchverlag 1976.
(1st prize/1. Preis)

Brock, Peter: **Ich bin die Nele.** (I am *Nele.*) Ill.: Karl Schrader.
Berlin: Kinderbuchverlag 1975.
(2nd prize/2. Preis)

Hardel, Lilo: **Nadjy, mein Liebling.** (*Nadia,* my darling.) Ill.: Rolf F.A. Müller.
Berlin: Kinderbuchverlag 1975.
(3rd prize/3. Preis)

Special poetry prize/Sonderpreis für Lyrik
Streubel, Manfred: **Honig holen.** (Collecting honey.)
Halle: Mitteldeutscher Verlag 1977.

Special belletristic prize/Sonderpreis für sachbetonte Belletristik
Hardel, Gerhard: **Hellas.** Geschichten vom alten Griechenland. (*Hellas.* Stories from ancient Greece.) Ill.: Ingeborg Friebel.
Berlin: Kinderbuchverlag 1975.

Special biography prize/Sonderpreis für Biografien
Baumert, Walter: **Und wen der Teufel nicht peinigt.** Die Jugend des Dichters Georg Weerth. (And whom the devil does not tortue. The youth of the poet, *Georg Weerth.)* Ill.: Dieter Goltzsche.
Berlin: Kinderbuchverlag 1975.

New author/Neuer Autor
Bräuer, Heinrich W.: **Leuchtfeuer.** (Signal fire.) Ill.: Hille Blumfeldt.
Berlin: Neues Leben 1975.

1977 The prize was not given; Der Preis wurde nicht vergeben.

1978 The prize was not given; Der Preis wurde nicht vergeben.

1979 *22nd competition/22. Preisausschreiben*
Holtz-Baumert, Gerhard: **Sieben und dreimal sieben Geschichten.** (Seven and three-times-seven stories.) Ill.: Egbert Herfuth.
Berlin: Kinderbuchverlag 1979.
(1st prize/1. Preis)

Wellm, Alfred: **Karlchen Duckdich.** (*Karlchen Duckdich.*) Ill.: Werner Klemke.
Berlin: Kinderbuchverlag 1977.
(2nd prize/2. Preis)

Lüdemann, Hans Ulrich: **Der Plumpsack geht um.** (The knotted handkerchief goes around the circle.) Ill.: Fred Westphal.
Berlin: Kinderbuchverlag 1979.
(3rd prize/3. Preis)

Spillner, Wolf: **Der Bachstelzenorden.** (The wagtail medal.) Ill.: Thomas Schleusing.
Berlin: Kinderbuchverlag 1977.
(3rd prize/3. Preis)

Special prize for literary reportage/Sonderpreis für literarische Reportage
Christ, Richard: **Der Spinatbaum in der Wüste** (The spinach tree in the desert.)
Berlin: Kinderbuchverlag 1978.

Special prize for historical belletristic work/Sonderpreis für historische Belletristik
Schollak, Sigmar: **Das Mädchen aus Harrys Straße.** (The girl from *Harrys* Street.)
Berlin: Kinderbuchverlag 1980

Special lyric poetry prize/Sonderpreis für Lyrik
Könner, Alfred: **Der Pfau im Apfelbaum.** (The peacock in the apple tree.)
Berlin: Altberliner Verlag 1979.

Special belletristic prize/Sonderpreis für sachbetonte Belletristik
Hardel, Lilo: **Mariechens Apfelbaum erzählt aus seinem Leben.** (Little *Marie's* apple tree tells about its life.)
Berlin: Junge Welt 1979.

Special picture book prize/Sonderpreis für Bilderbuch.
Mitschin, Jutta in:
Mitschin, Jutta: **Auf dem Hügel ist was los.** (Something is happening on the hill.)
Berlin: Altberliner Verlag 1979.

Alex-Wedding-Preis

This prize is named after the Salzburg-born pioneer of the socialist children's book, Alex Wedding (Grete Weiskopf, 1905—1966; the pseudonym is a composite of Alexanderplatz and Wedding, names of East Berlin sections). Annually on June Ist, International Children's Day, the prize is presented by the German Academy of Arts for the outstanding collective output of a socialist children's book author. The Alex Wedding Prize is awarded to bellestristic children's literature, including fairy tales, stage plays, radio plays and film senarios; illustrations and overall graphic design of the book are also taken into consideration for the selections. The award consists of a diploma and a cash-prize. The recommendations for the award are examined by a jury which is made up of delegates of the department of poetics and linguistics, the director of the academy, the directors of the special departments and the delegates from the sections of Fine Arts and the Ministry of Cultural Affairs.

Benannt nach der in Salzburg geborenen Pionierin des sozialistischen Kinderbuches Alex Wedding (d.i. Grete Weiskopf, 1905—1966; ihr Pseudonym bedeutet: Alexanderplatz und Stadtteil Wedding), wird alljährlich zum Internationalen Kindertag, dem 1. Juni, von der Deutschen Akademie der Künste das herausragende Werk eines sozialistischen Kinder- oder Jugendbuchautors prämiiert. Der Alex-Wedding-Preis, besteht aus einer Urkunde und einer Geldsumme; wird für belletristische Kinder- und Jugendliteratur einschließlich Märchen, Theaterstücke, Hörspiele und Filmszenerien verliehen, wobei die Illustrationen und die künstlerische Gesamtgestaltung bei der Beurteilung mit einbezogen werden. Die Vorschläge werden von einem Ausschuß geprüft, dem Vertreter der Sektion Dichtkunst und Sprachpflege angehören, der Direktor der Akademie, der Fachgruppenleiter sowie Vertreter der Sektion Bildende Kunst und des Ministeriums für Kultur.

1968 Willy Meinck
1969 Karl Neumann
1970 Kurt David
1971 Joachim Nowotny
1972 Götz R. Richter
1973 Herbert Friedrich
1974 Edith Bergner
1975 Horst Beseler
1976 Fred Rodrian
1977 Peter Brock
1978 Gotthold Gloger
1979 Hans Weber
1980 Hildegard Schumacher/ Siegfried Schumacher
1981 Klaus Beuchler

German federal Republic/ Bundesrepublik Deutschland

Buxtehuder Bulle

Since 1971, the „Buxtehuder Bulle" has been awarded annually by the bookshop, Ziemann & Ziemann, in the town of Buxtehude for the best children's book of the year.

The prize consists of a DM 5 000 cash-award and a metal sculpture (the Buxtehuder Bulle) created by Reinhard Güthling. The jury is made up of 11 adults and 11 young people. In order not to influence the spontaneity, especially among the juvenile members of the jury, the voting and selection of the prize book is done without preliminary discussion.

Der "Buxtehuder Bulle" wurde 1971 von der Buchhandlung Ziemann & Ziemann gestiftet und wird seither jährlich für das jeweils beste Jugendbuch aus der laufenden Produktion vergeben.

Der Preis ist mit einer Geldprämie (DM 5 000) und einer Metallplastik (dem sogenannten "Buxtehuder Bulle") des Bildhauers Reinhardt Güthling verbunden. Es wird durch eine Jury von 11 Erwachsenen und 11 Jugendlichen vergeben. Die Abstimmung und Entscheidung erfolgt nach einem Punktsystem ohne

Ill. 17 Margret Rettich in: Die Reise mit der Jolle

vorherige Aussprache, um die Spontanität der Entscheidung vor allem bei den jugendlichen Juroren nicht zu beeinflussen.

1971 Neill, Alexander Sutherland: **Die grüne Wolke.** (Eng. orig. title: The last man alive.) Ill.: Friedrich K. Waechter.
Reinbek: Rowohlt 1971.

1972 Wethekam, Cili: **Tignasse.** (*Tignasse.*)
Stuttgart: Thienemann 1972.

1973 Röhrig, Tilmann: **Thoms Bericht.** (*Thom*'s report.) Mülheim a.d. Ruhr: Anrich 1973.

Nöstlinger, Christine: **Maikäfer flieg!** (Fly away, mayfly!)
Weinheim: Beltz & Gelberg 1973.

1974 Graham, Gail: **Zwischen den Feuern.** (Amer.orig.title: Cross-fire.)
Ravensburg: Maier 1974.

1975 Reiss, Johanna: **Und im Fenster der Himmel.** (And in the window, the heavens.)
Zürich, Köln: Benziger 1975.

1976 Haar, Jaap ter: **Behalt das Leben lieb.** (Keep a positive hold on life; Dutch orig.title: Het wereldje van *Beer Lighthart.*)
Recklinghausen: Bitter 1976.

1977 Pausewang, Gudrun: **Die Not der Familie Caldera.** (The poverty of the *Caldera* family.) Ill.: Hilke Peters.
Ravensburg: Maier 1977.

1978 Ossowski, Leonie: **Stern ohne Himmel.** (Star without sky.)
Weinheim: Beltz & Gelberg 1978.

1979 Ende, Michael: **Die unendliche Geschichte.** (The unending story.) Ill.: Roswitha Quadflieg.
Stuttgart: Thienemann 1979.

1980 Vincke, Hermann: **Das kurze Leben der Sophie Scholl.** (The short life of *Sophie Scholl.*)
Ravensburg: Maier 1980

Deutscher Jugendliteraturpreis

The German Youth Literature Prize (formerly, German Youth Book Prize) was established in 1956 by the Federal Ministery of the Interior; the presentation is now in the hands of the Federal Ministry of Youth, Family and Health. The responsibility for the selection and mangement is held by the "Arbeitskreis für Jugendliteratur" (the German national section of the International Board on Books for Young People). The committee is made up of delegates from every federal organization concerned with the promotion of children's and youth literature. The selection is made from outstanding titles published in German during the previous year by living, German-speaking authors. Translations of titles by living foreign authors are also eligible providing that the original language edition is not older than five years. The Arbeitskreis für Jugendliteratur appoints the independent juries, whose members can come from any professional group, providing they have knowledge and experience in the field of juvenile literature. Since 1973, two juvenile members with full voting rights have been included in the juries which judge the youth books and non-fiction books, as well as in the main jury which makes the final selections.

The German Youth Literature Prize was originally divided up into a prize for children's books and a prize for youth books. A special award was offered for a particular theme. Later a cash-prize was offered instead of the special award. In 1965 a picture book prize was added, and in 1967 a non-fiction award. An annotated selection list is published annually.

Der Deutsche Jugendliteraturpreis (früher Deutscher Jugendbuchpreis) wurde 1956 vom Bundesinnenministerium gestiftet (heute: Bundesministerium für Jugend, Familie und Gesundheit). Mit der Auswahl der Bücher und der Durchführung der Preisverleihung ist der "Arbeitskreis für Jugendliteratur" (Deutsche Sektion des Internationalen Kuratoriums für das Jugendbuch) beauftragt, in dem alle Organisationen vertreten sind, die sich auf Bundesebene um die Pflege und Förderung der Jugendliteratur bemühen. Die Auswahl wird jeweils aus der deutschsprachigen Kinder- und Jugendbuchproduktion des vorherigen Jahres getroffen. Ausgezeichnet werden können deutschsprachige Originalwerke lebender Autoren ebenso wie deutsche Übersetzungen von fremdsprachigen Werken lebender Autoren, die im Original innerhalb der letzten 5 Jahre erschienen sind.

Der Arbeitskreis für Jugendliteratur setzt die unabhängigen Jurys ein, deren Mitglieder aus den unterschiedlichsten Berufsgruppen stammen dürfen, jedoch besondere Kenntnisse und Erfahrungen auf dem Gebiet der Jugendliteratur besitzen müssen. Seit 1973 sind in den Einzeljuries "Jugendbuch" und "Sachbuch" und in der "Hauptjury", die die endgültigen Preisentscheidungen trifft, jeweils zwei Jugendliche stimmberechtigt vertreten.

Der Deutsche Jugendliteraturpreis gliederte sich zunächst in einen Kinder- und in einen Jugendbuchpreis; daneben wurde ein Sonderpreis zu einem bestimmten Thema oder Gebiet der Jugendliteratur ausgeschrieben. Später wurden statt dessen Prämien vergeben, auch kam 1965 ein Bilderbuchpreis hinzu und 1967 ein Sachbuchpreis. Darüber hinaus wird jährlich eine annotierte Auswahlliste veröffentlicht.

1956 *Children's book/Kinderbuch*
Fatio, Louise: **Der glückliche Löwe.** (Amer.orig.title: The happy lion.) Ill.: Roger Duvoisin.
Freiburg i.Br.: Herder 1955.

Youth book/Jugendbuch
Lütgen, Kurt: **Kein Winter für Wölfe.** (No winter for wolves.) Ill.: Kurt J. Blish.
Braunschweig: Westermann 1955.

Special prize: Best girl's book/Sonderpreis: Das beste Mädchenbuch
Rommel, Alberta: **Der goldene Schleier.** (The golden scarf.)
Stuttgart: Gundert 1955.

Strätling-Tölle, Helga: **...ganz einfach Doko.** (...simply *Doko.*) Ill.: Christel Hentschke.
Recklinghausen: Paulus-Verlag 1955.

1957 *Children's book/Kinderbuch*
DeJong, Meindert: **Das Rad auf der Schule.** (Amer.orig.title: The wheel on the school.) Ill.: Marianne Richter.
Köln: Schaffstein 1956.

Youth book/Jugendbuch
Kalashnikoff, Nicholas: **Fass zu, Toyon!** (Amer.orig.title: *Toyon,* a dog of the north and his people.)
Gütersloh: S. Mohn 1956.

1958 *Children's book/Kinderbuch*
Denneborg, Heinrich Maria: **Jan und das Wildpferd.** (*Jan* and the wild horse.) Ill.: Horst Lemke.
Berlin: Dressler 1957.

Youth book/Jugendbuch
Kaufmann, Herbert: **Roter Mond und Heiße Zeit.** (*Red Moon* and *Hot Time.*) Ill.: Gottfried Pils.
Graz, Köln: Styria 1957.

Special prize: Best picture book/Sonderpreis: Das beste Bilderbuch
Reidel, Marlene: **Kasimirs Weltreise.** (*Casimir's* journey around the world.) Ill.: Marlene Reidel.
München: Lentz 1957.

1959 *Children's book/Kinderbuch*
Peterson, Hans: **Matthias und das Eichhörnchen.** (*Matthias* and the squirrel.) Ill.: Ilon Wikland.
Hamburg: Oetinger 1958.

Special prize: Best non-fiction book for children under 14 years/Sonderpreis: Das beste Sachbuch für Kinder bis zu 14 Jahren.
Rutgers von der Loeff-Basenau, An: **Pioniere und ihre Enkel.** (Pioneers and their grandchildren; Dutch orig. title: *Amerika,* pioniers en hun kleinzoons.)
Hamburg: Oetinger 1958.

Schneider, Leo/Ames, Maurice, U.: **So fliegst du heute und morgen.** (Amer.orig.title: Wings in your future.) Ill.: Jeve Donovan.
Köln: Schaffstein 1958.

1960 *Children's book/Kinderbuch*
Krüss, James: **Mein Urgroßvater und ich.** (My great-grandfather and I.) Ill.: Jochen Bartsch.
Hamburg: Oetinger 1959.

Youth book/Jugendbuch
Lewis, Elizabeth Foreman: **Schanghai 41.** (Amer.orig.title: To beat a tiger — one needs a brother's help.)
Freiburg i.Br.: Herder 1959.

Special prize: The young man in his world/Sonderpreis: **Der junge Mensch in seiner Welt**
Del Castillo, Michel: **Elegie der Nacht.** (Night elegy; Fr.orig.title: *Tanguy.)*
Hamburg: Hoffmann & Campe 1959.

1961 *Children's book/Kinderbuch*
Ende, Michael: **Jim Knopf und Lukas, der Lokomotivführer,** (*Jim Knopf* and *Lukas,* the train engineer.) Ill.: Franz Josef Tripp.
Stuttgart: Thienemann 1960.

Special prize: Newly adapted children's and youth classics/Sonderpreis: Neubearbeitungen klassischer Kinder- und Jugendbücher
Alverdes, Paul for: Cooper, James Fenimore: **Der Wildtöter.** (The deerslayer.) Ill.: Heiner Rothfuchs.
München: Obpacher 1960.

1962 *children's book/Kinderbuch*
Wölfel, Ursula: **Feuerschuh und Windsandale.** (Fire shoe and wind sandal.) Ill.: Heiner Rothfuchs.
Düsseldorf: Hoch 1961.

Youth book/Jugendbuch
Asscher-Pinkhof, Clara: **Sternkinder.** (Star children; Dutch orig. title: Sterre Kinderen.)
Berlin: Dressler 1961.

Special prize: Children's and youth stories/Sonderpreis: Geschichte im Kinder- und Jugendbuch
Engelhardt, Ingeborg: **Ein Schiff nach Grönland.** (A ship to Greenland.)
Gütersloh: S. Mohn 1961.

1963 *Children's book/Kinderbuch*
Preussler, Otfried for German adaptation of: Lada, Josef: **Kater Mikesch.** (*Mikesch* the cat; Czech.orig.title: *Mikeš.*) Ill.: Josef Lada.
Aarau, Frankfurt: Sauerländer 1962.

Youth book/Jugendbuch
O'Dell, Scott: **Insel der blauen Delphine.** (Amer.orig.title: Island of the blue dolphins.)
Olten, Freiburg i.Br.: Walter 1962.

1964 *Children's book/Kinderbuch*
Allfrey, Katherine: **Delphinensommer.** (Dolphin summer.) Ill.: Ingrid Schneider.
Berlin: Dressler 1963.

Youth book/Jugendbuch
Diekmann, Miep: **Und viele Grüsse von Wancho.** (And many greetings from *Wancho*; Dutch orig.title: ...en de groeten van *Elio.*) Ill.: Jenny Dalenoord.
Braunschweig: Westermann 1963.

1965 *Picture book/Bilderbuch*
Lionni, Leo: **Swimmy.** (Amer.orig.title: *Swimmy.*) Ill.: Leo Lionni.
Köln: Middelhauve 1964.

Children's book/Kinderbuch
Jonsson, Runer: **Wickie und die starken Männer.** (*Vicky* and the strong men: Swed.orig.title: *Vicke Viking.*) Ill.: Ewert Karlsson.
Stuttgart: Herold 1964.

Youth book/Jugendbuch
Hetmann, Frederik (i.e. Hans-Christian Kirsch): **Amerika-Saga.** (America saga.) Ill.: Günther Stiller.
Freiburg i.Br.: Herder 1964.

1966 *Picture book/Bilderbuch*
Blecher, Wilfried: **Wo ist Wendelin?** (Where is *Wendelin.*) Ill.: Wilfried Blecher.
Weinheim: Beltz 1963.

Children's book/Kinderbuch
Bolliger, Max: **David.** (*David.*) Ill.: Edith Schindler.
Ravensburg: Maier 1965.

Youth book/Jugendbuch
Prager, Hans-Georg: **Florian 14: Achter Alarm.** (*Florian 14:* eighth alarm.) Ill.
Gütersloh: Bertelsmann 1965.

1967 *Picture book/Bilderbuch*
Fromm, Lilo in: Grimm, Jakob/Grimm, Wilhelm: **Der goldene Vogel.** (The golden bird.)
München: Ellermann 1966.

Children's book/Kinderbuch
Salkey, Andrew: **Achtung — Sturmwarnung Hurricane — 23.00 Uhr.** (Eng.orig.title: Hurricane.) Ill.: William Papas.
Stuttgart: Thienemann 1966.

Youth book/Jugendbuch
Berger, Peter: **Im roten Hinterhaus.** (The red house in the rear.)
Stuttgart: Schwabenverlag 1966.

Non-fiction/Sachbuch
Lütgen, Kurt: **Das Rätsel der Nordwestpassage.** (The mystery of the *Northwest Passage.*)
Braunschweig: Westermann 1966.

1968 *Picture book/Bilderbuch*
Brandt, Katrin in:
Grimm, Jakob/Grimm, Wilhelm: **Die Wichtelmänner.** (The dwarfs.)
Zürich, Freiburg i.Br.: Atlantis Verlag 1967.

Children's book/Kinderbuch
Clarke, Pauline: **Die Zwölf vom Dachboden.** (Eng.orig.title: The twelve and the genii.) Ill.: Cecil Leslie.
Berlin: Dressler 1967.

Youth book/Jugendbuch
Rodman, Maia: **Der Sohn des Toreros.** (Amer.orig.title: Shadow of the bull.) Ill.: Alvin Smith.
Stuttgart: Herold 1967

Non-fiction/Sachbuch
Heimann, Erich Herbert: **...und unter uns die Erde.** Fliegen — schneller, weiter, höher. (...and under us the earth. Flying — faster, farther, higher.) Ill.
Stuttgart: Franckh 1967.

1969 *Picture book/Bilderbuch*
Mitgutsch, Ali: **Rundherum in meiner Stadt.** (All around in my town.) Ill.: Ali Mitgutsch.
Ravensburg: Maier 1968.

Children's book/Kinderbuch
Singer, Isaac Bashevis: **Zlateh, die Geiß und andere Geschichten.** (Amer.orig.title: *Zlateh* the goat and other stories.) Ill.: Maurice Sendak.
Aarau: Sauerländer 1968.

Youth book/Jugendbuch
Procházka, Jan: **Es lebe die Republik.** (Long live the republic; Czech.orig.title: At'žije republika.)
Recklinghausen: Bitter 1968.

Honourable mention/Prämie
O'Dell, Scott: **Vor dem Richter des Königs.** (Amer.orig.title: The king's fifth.) Maps: Samuel Bryant.
Olten: Walter 1968.

1970 *Picture book/Bilderbuch*
Schröder, Wilfried: **Kunterbunter Schabernack.** (The topsy-turvy practical joke.) Ill.: Wilfried Blecher.
Recklinghausen: Bitter 1969.

Youth book/Jugendbuch
Jarunková, Klára: **Der Bruder des schweigenden Wolfes.** (The brother of the taciturn wolf; Slovak orig.title: Brat mlčanlivého Vlka.)
Hamburg: Oetinger 1969.

Non-fiction/Sachbuch
Elliot, Lawrence: **Der Mann der überlebte.** (Amer.orig.title: The man who overcame.)
Konstanz: Bahn 1969.

Honourable mention/Prämien
Bichsel, Peter: **Kindergeschichten** (Children's stories.)
Neuwied: Luchterhand 1969.

Schmaderer, Franz-Josef/Zacharias, Thomas: **Spielen, Sehen, Denken.** (Playing, seeing, thinking.) Ill.: Wanda Zacharias.
Ravensburg: Maier 1969.

1971 *Picture book/Bilderbuch*
Mari, Iela/Mair, Enzo: **Der Apfel und der Schmetterling.** (The apple and the butterfly; Ital.orig.title: La mela e la farfalla.) Ill.: Iela Mari and Enzo Mari.
München: Ellermann 1970.

Nebehay, Rene: **Mr. Beestons Tierklinik.** (Mr. *Beeston's* animal clinic.) Ill.: Walter Schmögner.
Wien, München: Jugend und Volk Verlag 1970.

Children's book/Kinderbuch
Kunze, Reiner: **Der Löwe Leopold.** (*Leopold* the lion.)
Frankfurt: S. Fischer 1970.

Youth book/Jugendbuch
Pěsek, Ludek: **Die Erde ist nah.** (The earth is near.)
Recklinghausen: Bitter 1970.

Non-fiction/Sachbuch
Gesellschaft und Staat. (Society and State.) Ed.: Hanno Drechsler, Wolfgang Hilligen and Franz Neumann.
Baden-Baden: Signal Verlag 1970.

1972 *Children's book/Kinderbuch*
Preussler, Otfried: **Krabat.** (*Krabat.*) Ill.: Herbert Holzing.
Würzburg: Arena Verlag 1971.

Youth book/Jugendbuch
Gelberg, Hans-Joachim (Ed.): **Geh und spiel mit dem Riesen.** (Go and play with the giant.) Ill.
Weinheim: Beltz & Gelberg 1971.

Non-fiction/Sachbuch
Bauer, Ernst W.: **Höhlen — Welt ohne Sonne.** (Caves — world without sun.) Ill.
Esslingen: Schreiber 1971.

1973 *Picture book/Bilderbuch*
Janikovszky, Éva: **Grosse dürfen alles.** (Grown-ups are allowed everything.) Ill.: László Réber.
Neunkirchen: Anrich 1972.

Children's book/Kinderbuch
Nöstlinger, Christine: **Wir pfeifen auf den Gurkenkönig.** (We don't give a hoot about the cucumber king.)
Ill.: Werner Maurer.
Weinheim: Beltz & Gelberg 1972.

Youth book/Jugendbuch
Wersba, Barbara: **Ein nützliches Mitglied der Gesellschaft.** (Amer.orig.title: Run softly, go fast.)
Baden-Baden: Signal Verlag 1973.

Hetman, Frederik (i.e. Hans-Christian Kirsch): **Ich habe sieben Leben.** (I have seven lives.)
Photos: Günther Stiller.
Weinheim: Beltz & Gelberg 1972.

1974 *Picture book/Bilderbuch*
Müller, Jörg: **Alle Jahre wieder saust der Presslufthammer nieder.** (Year in, year out, the pneumatic hammer crashes down.) Ill.: Jörg Müller.
Aarau: Sauerländer 1973.

Kerr, Judith: **Als Hitler das rosa Kaninchen stahl.** (Eng.orig.title: When *Hitler* stole *Pink Rabbit.*)
Ravensburg: Maier 1973.

Youth book/Jugendbuch
Ende, Michael: **Momo.** (*Momo.*) Ill.: Michael Ende.
Stuttgart: Thienemann 1973.

Non-fiction/Sachbuch
Frisch, Otto von: **Tausend Tricks der Tarnung.** (A thousand tricks of camouflage.) Ill.
Esslingen: Schreiber 1973.

1975 Waechter, Friedrich Karl: **Wir können noch viel zusammen machen.** (We can still do a lot together.)
Ill.: Friedrich Karl Waechter.
München: Parabel Verlag 1974.

Youth book/Jugendbuch
George, Jean Craighead: **Julie von den Wölfen:** (Amer.orig.title: *Julie* of the wolves.)
Aarau: Sauerländer 1974.

Non-fiction/Sachbuch
Macauley, David: **Sie bauten eine Kathedrale.** (Cathedral.) Ill.: David Macauley.
Zürich, München: Artemis Verlag 1974.

Special prize: Internatioanl Year of the Woman/Sonderpreis: Zum internationalen Jahr der Frau
Kutsch, Angelika: **Man kriegt nichts geschenkt.** (One gets nothing free.)
Stuttgart: Union Verlag 1974.

1976 *Picture book/Bilderbuch*
Borchers, Elisabeth: **Heute wünsch ich mir ein Nilpferd.** (Today I wish for an hippopotamus.) Ill.: Wilhelm Schlote.
Frankfurt: Insel Verlag 1975.

Children's book/Kinderbuch
Härtling, Peter: **Oma.** (Grandma.) Ill.: Ingrid Mizsenko.
Weinheim: Beltz & Gelberg 1975.

Youth book/Jugendbuch
Christopher, John: **Die Wächter.** (Eng.orig.title: The guardians.)
Recklinghausen: Bitter 1975.

Non-fiction/Sachbuch
Dolezol, Theodor: **Planet des Menschen.** (Planet of man) Ill.
Wien, Heidelberg: Ueberreuter 1975.

1977 *Picture book/Bilderbuch*
Heide, Florence Parry: **Schorschi schrumpft.** (Amer.orig.title: The shrinking of *Treehorn.*) Ill.: Edward Gorey.
Zürich: Diogenes Verlag 1976.

Children's book/Kinderbuch
Askenazy, Ludvik: **Wo die Füchse Blockflöte spielen.** (Where the foxes play their flutes.) Ill.: André Barbe.
Aarau, Frankfurt: Sauerländer 1976.

Youth book/Jugendbuch
Rutgers van der Loeff-Basenau, An: **Ich bin Fedde.** (I am *Fedde;* Dutch orig.title: Ik ben *Fedde.*)
Hamburg: Oetinger 1976.

Non-fiction/Sachbuch
Herbert, Wally: **Eskimos.** (Eng.orig.title: Eskimos.) Germ. adapt.: Vitalis Pantenburg. Ill.
Esslingen: Schreiber 1976.

1978 *Picture book/Bilderbuch*
Smith, Ray/Smith, Catriona: **Der große Rutsch.** (Amer.orig.title: The long slide.) Ill.: Ray Smith and Catriona Smith.
Aarau, Frankfurt: Sauerländer 1977.

Children's book/Kinderbuch
Donnelly, Elfie: **Servus Opa, sagte ich leise.** (Goodbye grandpa, I say lightly.) Ill.: Christian B. Sadil.
Hamburg: Dressler 1977.

Youth book/Jugendbuch
Reiche, Dietlof: **Der Bleisiegelfälscher.** (The lead-seal forger.)
Modautal-Neunkirchen: Anrich 1977.

Non-fiction/Sachbuch
Flanagan, Geraldine L./Morris, Sean: **Nest am Fenster.** (Eng.orig.title: Window into a nest.)
Reinbek b. Hamburg: Carlsen 1977.

Special prize for the Internatioanl Year of the Child/Sonderpreis zum Internationalen Jahr des Kindes
Wickert, Utta: **Im Jahr der Schlange.** Tizars Geschichte. (In the year of the snake. *Tizar's* story.)
Weinheim: Beltz & Gelberg 1977.

1979 *Picture book/Bilderbuch*
Janosch (i.e. Horst Eckert): **Oh, wie schön ist Panama.** (Oh, how nice Panama is.) Ill.: Janosch.
Weinheim: Beltz & Gelberg 1978.

Children's book/Kinderbuch
Tormod, Haugen: **Die Nachtvögel.** (The night birds; (Norw.orig.title: Nattfuglene.)
Zürich, Köln: Benziger 1978.

Youth book/Jugendbuch
The prize was not given; Der Preis wurde nicht vergeben.

Non-fiction/Sachbuch
Jensen, Virginia Allen/Haller, Dorcas Woodbury: **Was ist das?** (eng.orig.title: What's that?) Ill.
Aarau, Frankfurt: Sauerländer 1978.

Parks, Peter: **Das Leben unter Wasser.** (Eng.orig.title: Underwater life.) Photos: Peter Parks.
Hamburg: Tessloff 1978.

Special prize: History and politics in youth books/Sonderpreis: Geschichte und Politik im Jugendbuch
Wildermuth, Rosemarie (ed.): **Heute – und die 30 Jahre davor.** (Today – and the 30 years before.) Ill.
München: Ellermann 1978.

1980 *Picture book/Bilderbuch*
Burningham, John: **Was ist dir lieber?** (Eng.orig.title: Would you rather like...) Ill.: John Burningham.
Aarau, Frankfurt, Salzburg: Sauerländer 1979.

Children's book/Kinderbuch
Fuchs, Ursula: **Emma oder die unruhige Zeit.** (Emma or, the restless times.)
Modautal-Neunkirchen: Anrich 1979.

Youth book/Jugendbuch
Welsh, Renate: **Johanna.** (*Johanna.*)
Wien, München: Jugend und Volk 1979.

Non-fiction/Sachbuch
Fagerström, Grethe/Hansson, Gunilla: **Peter, Ida und Minimum.** (*Peter, Ida* and *Minimum.)*
Ravensburg: Otto Maier 1979.

Schmid, Heribert: **Wie Tiere sich verständigen.** (How animals communicate.) Ill.: Jürgen Wirth.
Ravensburg: Otto Maier 1979.

1981 *Picture book/Bilderbuch*
Rettich, Margret: **Die Reise mit der Jolle.** (The voyage on the Jolle.) Ill.: Margret Rettich.
Ravensburg: Otto Maier 1980.

Children's book/Kinderbuch
Spohn, Jürgen: **Drunter und Drüber.** (Topsy-turry.) Ill.: Jürgen Spohn.
München: Bertelsmann 1980.

Youth book/Jugendbuch
Fährmann, Willi: **Der lange Weg des Lukas B.** (The long path of *Lukas B.)*
Würzburg: Arena 1980.

Non-fiction/Sachbuch
Vinke, Hermann: **Das kurze Leben der Sophie Scholl.** (The short life or *Sophie Scholl.)*
Ravensburg: Otto Maier 1980.

Friedrich-Gerstäcker-Preis der Stadt Braunschweig

In 1947, the city of Braunschweig established this award in memory of Friedrich Gerstäcker, traveller and famous German writer of adventure books (1816 — 1872). Gerstäcker lived in Braunschweig during his youth and later during the last years of his life. Every second year, this prize is given to a living author, writing in the German language, whose book has been published within a three year period prior to the time of presentation of the prize. The stories which are selected must be good tales of adventure, or give knowledge of far-away places with the same sense of the dramatic and suspense which Gerstäcker desplayed in his tales. The prize-winning author is honoured by the mayor of Braunschweig, and receives a certificate and a plaque. From 1978, the amount of the cash-award was raised to DM 6 000.

Zum Andenken an den Weltreisenden und Schriftsteller Friedrich Gerstäcker (1816—1872), der seine Jugend und seine letzten Lebensjahre in Braunschweig verbrachte, hat die Stadt Braunschweig 1947 den "Friedrich-Gerstäcker-Preis" gestiftet. Der Preis wird in jedem zweiten Jahr einem lebenden Schriftsteller deutscher Sprache für ein Buch verliehen, das der Jugend in fesselnder Darstellung das Erlebnis der weiten Welt vermittelt, wie dies Friedrich Gerstäcker in seinen Büchern getan hat. Es soll in den letzten drei Jahren erschienen sein. Der Preisträger wird in einer Feierstunde in Braunschweig durch den Oberbürgermeister geehrt. Als äußeres Zeichen der Verleihung werden ihm eine Urkunde sowie eine Plakette ausgehändigt. 1978 betrug die Preissumme DM 6 000.

1952 Lütgen, Kurt: **Der große Kapitän.** (The great captain.) Ill.: Oswald Voh.
Braunschweig, Berlin, Hamburg: Westermann 1950.

1954 Mühlenweg, Fritz: **In geheimer Mission durch die Wüste Gobi.** (On secret mission through the Gobi Desert.)
Freiburg i Br.: Herder 1950.

1956 Baumann, Hans: **Die Höhlen der großen Jäger.** (The caves of the great hunters.) Ill.
Reutlingen: Ensslin & Laiblin 1953.

1958 Wustmann, Erich: **Taowaki.** *(Taowaki.)* Ill. E. Willy Widmann.
Reutlingen: Ensslin & Laiblin 1957.

1960 Kaufmann, Herbert: **Des Königs Krokodil.** (The king's crocodile.) Ill.: Gesine Bierbach.
Köln, Graz: Verlag Styria 1959.

1962 Seufert, Karl Rudolf: **Die Karawane der weißen Männer.** (The caravan of the white men.)
Freiburg i.Br., Basel, Wien: Herder 1961.

1964 Plate, Herbert: **Der — aus — dem — Dschungel — kam.** (The one who came from the jungle.)
Düsseldorf: Hoch 1963.

1966 Kohlenberg, Karl Friedrich: **Ben Ali und seine Herde.** (*Ben Ali* and his herd.) Ill.: Kurt Wendlandt.
Stuttgart: Union Verlag 1963.

1968 Welskopf-Henrich, Liselotte: **Der junge Häuptling.** (The young chief.)
Stuttgart: Union Verlag 1967.

Welskopf-Henrich, Liselotte: **Über den Missouri.** (Over the Missouri.)
Stuttgart: Union Verlag 1967.

Also taken into special consideration, Liselotte Welskopf-Henrich's collective work about the prairie Indians/Unter besonderer Berück-

sichtigung ihres Gesamtwerkes über die Prärieindianer: Die Söhne der großen Bärin. (The sons of the great bear.)
Berlin: Altberliner Verlag 1951—1963.

1970 Hagen, Christopher S.: **Geheimauftrag.** (Secret mission.) Photos.
Freiburg i.Br.: Herder 1969.

1972 Lütgen, Kurt: **Hinter den Bergen das Gold.** (The gold beyond the mountains.)
Würzburg: Arena Verlag 1971.

Lütgen, Kurt: **Kapitäne, Schiffe, Abenteurer.** (Captains, ships, adventurers.) Ill.: Walter Grieder.
Bayreuth: Loewe 1971.

Lütgen, Kurt: **Wagnis und Weite.** (Daring and wide open spaces.)
Würzburg; Arena Verlag 1969.

1974 Jeier, Thomas: **Der große Goldrausch von Alaska.** (The Alaskan gold rush.) Ill.
Freiburg i.Br.: Herder 1972.

1976 Hetman, Frederik (i.e. Hans Christian Kirsch): **Der rote Tag.** (The red day.) Photos: Werner A. Kilian.
Bayreuth: Loewe 1975.

1978 Bartos-Höppner, Barbara: **Silvermoon, weißer Hengst aus der Prärie.** (*Silvermoon.* White stallion from the Prairie.) Ill.: Ulrik Schramm.
Bayreuth: Loewe 1977.

1980 Egli, Werner J.: **Heul doch den Mond an.** (Howl at the moon.)
München: Bertelsmann 1978.

Hans-im-Glück-Preis

This newly founded prize (1978) is awarded annually by the "Verein zur Förderung der Kinder- und Jugendliteratur" (Society for the promotion of children's and youth literature). It was initiated by the author, Hans-Christian Kirsch (Frederik Hetman). It consists of a cash-award of DM 2 000, a selected piece of "Westerwälder ceramic", and, if desired, one week of undisturbed writing or editorial assistance and advice at the home of Hans-Christian Kirsch.

The jury consists of five members. The prize is given to authors whose first or second work exists in either book or manuscript form. Picture books and picture book texts are excluded.

Der Preis wird alljährlich durch den von dem Schriftsteller Hans-Christian Kirsch (Frederik Hetman) initiierten "Verein zur Förderung der Kinder- und Jugendliteratur" verliehen. Er besteht aus einer Prämie von mindestens DM 2 000, einem ausgewählten Stück Westerwälder Steingut und (wenn erwünscht) einer Woche Schreibklausur oder lektoraler Betreuung bei Hans-Christian Kirsch.

Die Jury besteht aus 5 Personen. Ausgezeichnet werden können Autoren, deren erstes oder zweites Werk der erzählenden Kinder- und Jugendliteratur im Manuskript oder gedruckt vorliegt. Ausgenommen sind Bilderbücher und Bilderbuchtexte.

1978 Donnelly, Elfie: **Servus Opa, sagte ich leise.** (Goodby grandpa, I say lightly.) Ill.: Christian B. Sadil.
Hamburg Dressler 1977.

1979 Chidolue, Dagmar: **Fieber oder Der Abschied der Gabriele Kupinski.** (Fever or, The departure of *Gabriele Kupinski.*)
Weinheim: Beltz & Gelberg 1979.

1980 Fehrmann, Helma/Weismann, Peter: **Und plötzlich willste mehr.** (And suddenly you want more.)
München: Weismann 1979.

Wilhelm-Hauff-Preis

This prize, initiated by the Berlin Bookshop, Friedrich von Kloeden, was given for the first time in 1978. It is awarded to children's and youth books "that stimulate fantasy without, at the same time, being unrealistic". The books should motivate children to adopt a courageous and positive attitude toward life and present, if possible, worthwhile examples for them to emulate. All of these elements were an important part of the literary works of the German poet, Wilhelm Hauff (1802—1827), for whom this prize is named. The award consists of a certificate of honour (a cash award is not given). Copies of the prize winning title are distributed to children's homes.

Erstmals verliehen wurde dieser von der Berliner Buchhandlung Friedrich von Kloeden gegründete Preis 1978. Es soll "Kinder- und Jugendliteratur ausgezeichnet werden, die die Fantasie angeregt, ohne unrealistisch zu sein". Sie soll Kindern "Lebensmut, Lebensbejahung und wenn möglich nachahmenswerte Vorbilder und Perspektiven " vermitteln — Grundsätze, die "auch einen wesentlichen Teil des Hauffschen Werkes" ausmachen. Der Preis ist nicht mit einer Geldprämie verbunden: der Autor erhält eine Ehrenurkunde, Exemplare seines prämiierten Buches werden an Kinderheime verteilt.

1978 Cooper, Susan: **Wintersonnenwende.** (Eng.orig.title: The dark is rising.) Ill.: Michael Keller and Günter Hugo Magnus.
München: Bertelsmann 1977.

1979 Lindgren, Astrid: **Die Brüder Löwenherz.** (The brothers, *Lionheart;* Swed.orig.title: Bröderna *Lejonhjärta.)* Ill.: Ilon Wikland.
Hamburg: Oetinger 1974.

1980 Ende, Michael: **Die unendliche Geschichte.** (The unending story.) Ill.: Roswitha Quadflieg.
Stuttgart: Thienemann 1979.

1981 Korschunow, Irina: **Ich weiß doch, daß ihr da seid.** (I know that you are here.) Ill.: Lidia Postma.
Aarau: Sauerländer 1980.

Katholischer Kinderbuchpreis

The Catholic Children's Book Prize was established in 1977 by the German Bishop's Conference and is awarded every two years by a seven-member jury. The prize consists of a cash-award of DM 10 000 and is given to authors of books or manuscripts that deal with religious experiences and which also exemplify the Christian way of life. In addition to the prize, a selection list is also published.

Der Katholische Kinderbuchpreis wurde 1977 von der Deutschen Bischofskonferenz gestiftet; er ist mit DM 10 000 dotiert und wird alle zwei Jahre von einer siebenköpfigen Jury vergeben. Ausgezeichnet werden sollen Bücher oder Manuskripte, die beispielhaft und altersgemäß religiöse Erfahrungen oder religiöses Wissen vermitteln und christliche Lebenshaltungen verdeutlichen. Gleichzeitig mit dem Preis wird eine Auswahlliste veröffentlicht.

1979 Breen, Else: **Warte nicht auf einen Engel.** (Don't wait for an angel; Nor.orig.title: I stripete genser.)
Wien: Verlag Jungbrunnen 1977.

Hock, Kurt: **Telat sucht den Regenbogen.** (*Telat* searches for the rainbow.) Ill.: Joachim Schuster.
Freiburg: Herder 1978.

1981 Mayer-Skumanz, Lene: **Geschichten vom Bruder Franz.** (Stories about Brother *Francis.)*
Mödling, Wien: Verlag St. Gabriel 1980.

Fährmann, Willi: **Der lange Weg des Lukas B.** (The long path of *Lukas B.*)
Würzburg: Arena Verlag 1980.

Kinder- und Jugendbuchpreis der Stadt Oldenburg

The "Children's and Youth Book Prize of the City of Oldenburg" is presented annually at the Oldenburg Children's Book Fair to a living, German-speaking author or illustrator publishing his or her first children's or youth book. The total prize sum of DM 10 000 can be divided up between more than one author or illustrator. The award was established and given for the first time in 1977.

Der "Kinder- und Jugendbuchpreis der Stadt Oldenburg" wird jährlich anläßlich der Oldenburger Kinderbuchmesse an lebende deutschsprachige Autoren und Illustratoren vergeben, die erstmals mit Texten oder Illustrationen auf dem Gebiet der Kinder- und Jugendliteratur an die Öffentlichkeit treten. Der Preis kann geteilt werden und ist mit einer Geldprämie von insgesamt 10 000 DM verbunden. Er wurde 1977 erstmals ausgeschrieben und verliehen.

1977 Ossowski, Leonie: **Die große Flatter.** (The great escape attempt.) Weinheim: Beltz & Gelberg 1977.

Schaaf, Hanni: **Plötzlich war es geschehen.** (Suddenly it happened.) Jugend und Volk Verlag 1977.

Reiche, Dietlof: **Der Bleisiegelfälscher.** (The lead seal forger.) Modautal-Neunkirchen: Anrich 1977.

1978 Kékule, Dagmar: **Ich bin eine Wolke.** (I am a cloud.) Reinbek: Rowohlt 1978.

1979 Friedrichson, Sabine: **Fundevogel und andere Lieblingsmärchen.** (*Fundevogel* and other beloved fairy tales.) Weinheim: Beltz & Gelberg 1979.

Pelz, Monica: **Anna im anderen Land.** (*Anna* in another country.) Wien: Verlag Jungbrunnen 1979.

1980 Pressler, Mirjam: **Bitterschokolade.** (Bitter chocolate.) Weinheim: Beltz & Gelberg 1980.

Die Silberne Feder

This prize, "The Silver Feather", was founded in 1976 by the Deutscher Ärztinnenbund (German Association of Women Doctors) and is awarded every two years to a book that in the widest sense deals with the problems of health and sickness. The prize can be given to German original titles or to translations which have been published during the last two years prior to the time of judging. Fiction, non-fiction and picture books are eligible for the prize, which is in the form of a certificate.

Together with the prize book, a list of selected titles is published. The Arbeitskreis für Jugendliteratur, München (German Section of IBBY) is authorized to deal with the organization and maintenance of the prize.

Der Jugendbuchpreis "Die Silberne Feder" wurde 1976 vom Deutschen Ärztinnenbund gestiftet und soll alle zwei Jahre für ein Buch verliehen werden, das Themen, die sich im weitesten Sinne mit Gesundheit und Krankheit befassen, beispielhaft darstellt.

Der Preis wird an deutschsprachige Originale oder Übersetzungen fremdsprachiger Werke vergeben, die in den vorangegangenen zwei Jahren erschienen sind. Er kann einem Bilderbuch, einem erzählenden Buch oder einem Sachbuch zuerkannt werden und ist nicht mit einer Geldprämie verbunden, sondern besteht aus einer Urkunde und einer silbernen Feder. Gemeinsam mit der Preisentscheidung wird eine Auswahlliste veröffentlicht. Mit der Organisation und der technischen Durchführung der Preisvergabe ist der "Arbeitskreis für Jugendliteratur" in München beauftragt.

1976 Lanners, Edi: **Meine Augen.** (My eyes.)
Photos: Noldi Lutz.
Luzern: Reich 1976.

1978 Bronnen, Barbara: **Wie mein Kind mich bekommen hat.** (How my baby got me.) Photos.
Reinbek: Rowohlt 1977.

1980 Korschunow, Irina: **Die Sache mit Christoph.** (The thing with *Christoph.*)
Zürich, Köln: Benziger 1978.

Great Britain/Großbritannien

The Library Association Carnegie Medal

First presented in 1937, this prize was established on the occasion of the 100th birthday of Andrew Carnegie (1835—1919), who left part of his fortune to promote independent library services in both Great Britain and the United States. Since the initial presentation, it has been awarded annually to an outstanding children's book receiving its first publication in the United Kingdom during the previous year. All categories of children's books are eligible for the prize. The selection is made from lists of recommendations limited to three titles only, which are complied by youth libraries in England. These lists are sent to a special committee of the British Library Association. The jury is made up of a small group of experts, appointed for their outstanding knowledge in the field of juvenile literature.

Die Carnegie-Medaille wurde zum ersten Male 1937 vergeben; seitdem wird sie jährlich als Auszeichnung für ein überdurchschnittliches Kinderbuch in englischer Sprache, das im vergangenen Jahr zuerst in Großbritannien erschienen ist, verliehen. Der Preis ist nicht an einen bestimmten Buchtyp gebunden. Das Carnegie-Preisbuch wird durch ein besonderes Komitee der britischen Bibliotheksvereinigung (British Library Association) aus den Vorschlagslisten der Ju-

Ill. 18 Janet and Allan Ahlberg in: Each peach pear plum

gendbibliothekare ganz Englands ausgewählt. Jede Liste ist auf drei Titel beschränkt. Die Jury selbst besteht aus einer kleinen Gruppe von Experten, die auf Grund ihrer Jugendbuchkenntnisse, ihrer Erfahrung und ihres anerkannt hohen kritischen Niveaus berufen werden. Der Preis wurde anläßlich des 100. Geburtstages nach Andrew Carnegie benannt (1835–1919), der einen großen Teil seines Vermögens zur Förderung des freien Bibliothekswesens in Großbritannien und den Vereinigten Staaten stiftete.

1937 Ransome, Arthur: **Pigeon post.** (Taubenpost.) Ill.: Arthur Ransome.
London: Cape 1936.

1938 Garnett, Eve: **The family from One End Street and some of their adventures.** (Die Familie aus der Einbahnstrasse und ihre Abenteuer.) Ill.: Eve Garnett.
London: Muller 1937.

1939 Streatfield, Noel: **The circus is coming.** (Der Zirkus kommt.) Ill.: Steven Spurrier.
London: Dent 1938.

1940 Doorly, Eleanor: **The radium woman.** (Die Frau der Röntgenforschung.) Ill.: Robert Gibbings.
London: Heinemann 1939.

1941 Barne, Kitty: **Visitors from London.** (Besucher aus London.) Ill.: Ruth Gervis.
London: Dent 1940.

1942 Treadgold, Mary: **We couldn't leave Dinah.** (Wir konnten *Dinah* nicht verlassen.) Ill.: Stuart Tresilian.
London: Cape 1941.

1943 BB (i.e. Denys James Watkins-Pitchford): **The little grey men.** (Die kleinen grauen Menschen.) Ill.: Denys James Watkins-Pitchford.
London: Eyre & Spottiswoode 1942.

1944 The prize was not given; Der Preis wurde nicht vergeben.

1945 Linklater, Eric: **The wind on the moon. A story for childen.** (Der Wind auf dem Mond. Eine Geschichte für Kinder.) Ill.: Nicolas Bentley.
London: Macmillan 1944.

1946 The prize was not given; Der Preis wurde nicht vergeben.

1947 Goudge, Elizabeth: **The little white horse.** (Das kleine weisse Pferd.) Ill.: Cyril Walter Hodges.
London: University of London Press 1946.

1948 De La Mare, Walter: **Collected stories for children.** (Gesammelte Geschichten für Kinder.) Ill.: Irene Hawkins.
London: Faber & Faber 1947.

1949 Armstrong, Richard: **Sea change.** (Meereswechsel.) Ill.: Michel Leszczynski.
London: Dent 1948.

1950 Allen, Agnes: **The story of your home.** (Die Geschichte von deinem Zuhause.) Ill.: Agnes Allen and Jack Allen.
London: Faber & Faber 1949.

1951 Vipont, Elfrida (i.e. Elfrida Vipont Foulds): **The lark on the wing.** (Die Lerche steigt hoch.) Ill.: Terence Reginald Freeman.
London: Oxford University Press 1950.

1952 Harnett, Cynthia: **The wool pack.** (Der Woll-Sack.) Ill.: Cynthia Harnett.
London: Methuen 1951.

1953 Norton, Mary: **The borrowers.** (Die Borgmännchen.) Ill.: Diana Stanley.
London: Dent 1952.

1954 Osmond, Edward: **A valley grows up.** (Ein Tal wächst.) Ill.: Edward Osmond.
London: Oxford University Press 1953.

1955 Welch, Ronald (i.e. Ronald Oliver Felton): **Knight crusader.** (Der Kreuzzugsritter.) Ill.: William Stobbes.
London: Oxford University Press 1954.

1956 Farjeon, Eleanor: **The little bookroom.** (Das kleine Bücherzimmer.) Ill.: Edward Ardizzone.
London: Oxford University Press 1955.

1957 Lewis, Clive Staples: **The last battle.** (Der letzte Kampf.) Ill.: Pauline Baynes.
London: Bodley Head 1956.

1958 Mayne, William: **A grass rope.** (Das Gras-Seil.) Ill.: Lynton Lamb.
London: Oxford University Press 1957.

1959 Pearce, Ann Philippa: **Tom's midnight garden.** (*Toms* Mitternachtsgarten.) Ill.: Susan Einzig.
London: Oxford University Press 1958.

1960 Sutcliff, Rosemary: **The lantern bearers.** (Die Laternenträger.) Ill.: Charles Keeping.
London: Oxford University Press 1959.

1961 Cornwall, Jan Wolfram: **The making of man.** (Die Entstehung der Menschheit.) Ill.: M. Maitland Howard.
London: Phoenix House 1960.

1962 Boston, Lucy Maria: **A stranger at Green Knowe.** (Ein Fremder auf *Green Knowe.*) Ill.: Peter Boston.
London: Faber & Faber 1961.

1963 Clarke, Pauline: **The twelve and the genii.** (Die Zwölf auf dem Dachboden.) Ill.: Cecil Leslie.
London: Faber & Faber 1962.

1964 Burton, Hester: **Time of trial.** (Zeit der Versuchung.) Ill.: Victor G. Ambrus (i.e. Gyösö László Ambrus).
London: Oxford University Press 1963.

1965 Porter, Sheena: **Nordy Bank.** (*Nordy Bank.*) Ill.: Annette Macarthur-Onslow.
London: Oxford University Press 1964.

1966 Turner, Philip: **The grange at High Force.** (Der Meierhof auf *High Force.*) Ill.: William Papas.
London: Oxford University Press 1965.

1967 The prize was not given; Der Preis wurde nicht vergeben.

1968 Garner, Alan: **The owl service.** (Das Eulen-Geschirr.)
London: Collins 1967.

1969 Harris, Rosemary: **The moon in the cloud.** (Der Mond in den Wolken.)
London: Faber & Faber 1968.

1970 Peyton, Kathleen M.: **Edge of the cloud.** (Wolkenrand.) Ill.: Victor G. Ambrus (i.e. Gyösö László Ambrus).
London: Oxford University Press 1969.

1971 Blishen, Edward/Garfield, Leon: **The god beneath the sea.** (Gott unter dem Meer.) Ill.: Charles Keeping.
London: Longman 1970.

1972 Southall, Ivan: **Josh.** (*Josh.*)
London: Angus & Robertson 1971.

1973 Adams, Richard: **Watership Down.** (*Watership down.*)
London: Rex Colings 1972.

1974 Lively, Penelope: **The ghost of Thomas Kempe.** (Das Gespenst von *Thomas Kempe.*) Ill.: Antony Maitland.
London: Heinemann 1973.

1975 Hunter, Mollie: **The stronghold.** (Der Wehrturm.)
London: Hamish Hamilton 1974.

1976 Westall, Robert: **The machine gunners.** (Die Maschinengewehre.) London: Macmillan 1975.

1977 Mark, Jan: **Thunder and lightnings.** (Donner und Blitz) Ill.: Jim Russell.
Harmondsworth: Kestrel 1976.

1978 Kemp, Gene: **The turbulent term of Tyke Tiler.** (Das turbulente Semester von *Tyke Tilers.*) Ill.: Carolyn Dinan.
London: Faber 1977.

1979 Rees, David: **The Exeter blitz.** (Der Blitz von Exeter.)
London: Hamilton 1978.

1980 Dickinson, Peter: **Tulku.** (*Tulku*)
London: Gollancz 1979.

1981 Dickinson, Peter: **City of gold.** (Die Goldstadt.) Ill.: Michael Foreman.
London: Gollancz 1980.

The Children's Book Circle Eleanor Farjeon Award.

The Children's Book Circle founded this prize in 1965. It is given to personalities who have done outstanding work in the field of children's literature. The prize is named after one of the most important British authors of children's books, the London-born Eleanor Farjeon (1881—1965). The very talented Miss Farjeon left a life's work of more than seventy titles, among them poems, plays and compositions. About half of her literary achievements were produced for children.

Der Eleanor-Farjeon-Preis wurde 1965 vom englischen Kinderbuchkreis (Children's Book Circle) gestiftet. Er kann Persönlichkeiten verliehen werden, die auf dem Gebiete des Kinderbuchs Hervorragendes leisten. Der Preis wurde nach einer der größten englischen Kinderbuchautorinnen benannt, der in London geborenen Eleanor Farjeon (1881—1965), die überaus reich begabt, ein Werk von mehr als siebzig Titeln hinterließ, auch Gedichte, Theaterstücke und Kompositionen; etwas die Hälfte ihres Werkes ist für Kinder geschrieben.

1966 Margery Fisher: **editor of "Growing Point", authoress and critic.**

1967 Jessica Jenkins: **educational officer of National Book League.**

1968 Brian W. Alderson: **lecturer, editor, author and critic.**

1969 Anne Wood: **founder of the Federation of Children's Book Groups, and editor of "Books for your Children".**

1970 Kaye Webb: **editor of Puffin Books.**

1971 Margaret Meek: **children's librarian and reviewer.**

1972 Janet Hill: **children's librarian and authoress.**

1973 Eleanaor Graham: **founder/editor of Puffin Books.**

1974 Leila Berg: **authoress and critic.**

1975 Naomi Lewis: **authoress, editor and critic.**

1976 Joyce and Court Oldmeadow: **children's bookselling services in Melbourne, Australia.**

1977 Elaine Moss: **critic, school librarian and authoress of "Children's books of the year".**

1978 Peter Kennerly: **lecturer in English, founder of school bookshop movement, editor of "School Bookshop New".**

1979 Joy Whitby: **Director of Children' Programmes, Yorkshire Television.**

1980 Dorothy Butler: **children's bookshop owner; authoress of: Cushla and her books.** (*Cushla* und ihre Bücher.)
Auckland: Hodder & Stoughton 1979.

1981 Margaret Marshall: **librarian and lecturer.**
Virginia Allen Jensen: **editor and authoress.**

The Library Association Kate Greenaway Medal

Since the Carnegie Medal is awarded to authors only, the British Library Association decided in 1955 to establish the Greenaway Medal as a special distinction for illustrators of children's books. This action on the part of the Association was prompted by the fact that illustration had begun to play an dominant role in the publication and graphic design of children's books. The medal was designed by Reginald H. Hill and was named after the famous Victorian illustrator, Kate Greenaway (1846–1901). Miss Greenaway, together with Randolph Caldecott and Walter Crane, had been one of the most influential artists in this field during the Victorian era.

Da die Carnegie-Medaille nur der Auszeichnung von Autoren dient; die Illustration aber eine zunehmend bedeutsame Rolle bei der Herausgabe guter Kinderbücher zu spielen begann, beschloß die britische Bibliotheksvereinigung (British Library Association) 1955, einen weiteren Preis für die besten Illustratoren zu vergeben: die Kate-Greenaway-Medaille. Die Medaille, zu der Reginald H. Hill den Entwurf anfertigte, ist nach der Illustratorin benannt, die sich zusammen mit Randolph Caldecott und Walter Crane auf dem Gebiete der Kinderbuchillustration außerordentlich verdient gemacht hat.

1956 The prize was not given; Der Preis wurde nicht vergeben.

1957 Ardizzone, Edward in:
Ardizzone, Edward: **Tim all alone.** (*Tim ganz allein.)*
London: Oxford University Press 1956.

1957 Drummond, Violet Hilda in:
Drummond, Violet Hilda: **Mrs. Easter and the storks.** (Frau *Easter* und die Störche.)
London: Faber & Faber 1957.

1959 The prize was not given; Der Preis wurde nicht vergeben.

1960 Stobbs, William in:
Chekhov, Anton (Anton Pavlovič Čechov): **Kashtanka.** (*Kashtanka.*)
London: Oxford University Press 1959.

Stobbs, William in:
Manning-Sanders, Ruth: **A bundle of ballads.** (Ein Bündel Balladen.)
London: Oxford University Press 1959.

1961 Rose, Gerald in:
Rose, Elizabeth: **Old Winkle and the seagulls.** (Der alte *Winkle* und die Seemöwe.)
London: Faber & Faber 1960.

1962 Maitland, Antony in:
Pearce, Ann Philippa: **Mrs. Cockle's cat.** (Die Katze von Mrs. *Cockle.*)
London: Constable 1961.

1963 Wildsmith, Brian in:
Wildsmith, Brian: **ABC.** (ABC.)
London: Oxford University Press 1962.

1964 Burningham, John in:
Burningham, John: **Borka.** (*Borka.*)
London: Cape 1963.

1965 Hodges, Cyril Walter in:
Hodges, Cyril Walter: **Shakespeare's theatre.** (*Shakespeares* Theater.)
London: Oxford University Press 1964.

1966 Ambrus, Victor G. (i.e. Gyösö László Ambrus) in:
Ambrus, Victor G.: **The three poor taylors.** (Die drei armen Schneider.)
London: Oxford University Press 1965.

Ambrus, Victor G. (i.e. Gyösö László Ambrus) in:
Ambrus, Victor G.: **The Royal Airforce.** (Die königliche Luftwaffe.)
London: Oxford University Press 1965.

1967 Briggs, Raymond in:
Briggs, Raymond: **The Mother Goose treasury.** (Der Schatz von *Mutter Gans.*)
London: Hamish Hamilton 1966.

1968 Keeping, Charles for his children's book illustrations 1967, especially/Keeping, Charles für seine Kinderbuchillustrationen 1967, insbesondere:
Keeping, Charles: **Charley, Charlotte and the golden canary.** (*Charley, Charlotte* und der goldene Kanarienvogel.)
London: Oxford University Press 1967.

1969 Baynes, Pauline in:
Uden, Grant: **Dictionary of chivalry.** (Wörterbuch des Rittertums.)
London: Longmans 1968.

1970 Oxenbury, Helen in:
Lear, Edward: **The Quangle-Wangle's hat.** (Der Hut des *Qangle-Wangle.*)
London: Heinemann 1969.

Oxenbury Helen in:
Mahy, Margaret: **The dragon of ordinary family.** (Der Drachen einer gewöhnlichen Familie.)
London: Heinemann 1969.

1971 Burningham, John in:
Burningham, John: **Mr. Gumpy's outing.** (Der Ausflug des Mr. *Gumpy.*)
London: Cape 1970.

1972 Pienkowski, Jan in:
Aiken Joan: **The Kingdom under the sea.** (Das Reich unter dem Meer.)
London: Cape 1971.

1973 Turska, Krystyna in:
Turska, Krystyna: **The woodcutter's duck.** (Die Ente des Holzfällers.)
London: Hamish Hamilton 1972.

1974 Briggs, Raymond in:
Briggs, Raymond: **Father Christmas.** (*Nikolaus.*)
London: Hamish Hamilton 1973.

1975 Hutchins, Pat in:
Hutchins, Pat: **The wind blew.** (Der Wind blies.)
London: Bodley Head 1974.

1976 Ambrus, Victor G. (i.e. Gyösö László Ambrus) in:
Ambrus, Victor G.: **Horses in battle.** (Pferde im Krieg.)
London: Oxford University Press 1975.

Ambrus, Victor G. (i.e. Gyösö László Ambrus) in:
Ambrus, Victor G.: **Mishka.** (*Mishka.*)
London: Oxford University Press 1975.

1977 Haley, Gail E. in:
Haley, Gail E.: **The post office cat.** (Die Postamtkatze.)
London: Bodley Head 1976.

1978 Hughes, Shirley in:
Hughes, Shirley: **Dogger.** (*Dogger.*)
London: Bodley Head 1977.

1979 Ahlberg, Janet in:
Ahlberg, Allan: **Each peach pear plum.** (Jeder Pfirsich, jede Birne, jede Pflaume.)
Harmondsworth: Kestrel 1979.

1980 Pienkowski, Jan in:
Pienkowski, Jan: **The haunted house.** (Das verwunschene Haus.)
London: Heinemann 1979.

1981 Blake, Quentin in:
Blake, Quentin: **Mister Magnolia.** (Herr *Magnolia.*)
London: Cape 1980.

The Guardian Award

This prize is given by the Guardian, a leading British national daily newspaper. It was founded in 1967 and is awarded annually in the sum of £ 105 to the author of an outstanding work of fiction written for children which was first published in the United Kingdom during the preceding year. The award is made on the recommendation of a panel of well known authors and reviewers of children's books.

No formal criteria are laid down, but the standards observed by the judges are literary ones. In practice the judges allow themselves to take other work by the same writer into account. Works by jury members are not considered, but winners of the award my subsequently be invited to join the panel.

Der Preis wird vom "Guardian" einer führenden überregionalen britischen Tageszeitung verliehen. 1967 zum erstenmal — wird jährlich das hervorragende Werk eines Autors mit £ 105 ausgezeichnet, (jedoch keine Sachbücher) das im vorhergehenden Jahr zum erstenmal in Großbritannien veröffentlicht worden ist. Der Preis wird auf Empfehlung von einem Ausschuß bekannter Autoren und Rezensenten von Kinderbuchern verliehen.

Formale Kriterien sind nicht festgelegt, aber die von der Jury beachteten Normen sind literarischer Natur. Die Jury nimmt auch mehrere Bücher eines Autors in die Liste auf. Werke von Jury-Mitgliedern werden nicht in Betracht gezogen, aber Preisträger können aufgefordert werden, sich nachträglich der Jury anzuschliessen.

1967 Garfield, Leon: **Devil in the fog.** (Der Teufel im Nebel.) Ill.: Antony Maitland.
London: Constable/Kestrel 1966.

1968 Garner, Alan: **The owl service.** (Das Eulen-Geschirr.)
London: Collins 1967.

1969 Aiken, Joan: **The whispering mountain.** (Der flüsternde Berg.)
London: Cape 1968.

1970 Peyton, Kathleen M.: **Flambards.** (*Flambards.*) Ill.: Victor G. Ambrus (i.e. Gyösö László Ambrus).
London: Oxford University Press 1967.

Peyton, Kathleen M.: **The edge of the cloud.** (Wolkenrand.) Ill.: Victor G. Ambrus (i.e. Gyösö László Ambrus).
London: Oxford University Press 1969.

Peyton, Kathleen M.: **Flambards in summer.** (*Flambards* im Sommer.) Ill.: Victor G. Ambrus (i.e. Gyösö László Ambrus).
London: Oxford University Press 1970.

1971 Christopher, John: **The guardians.** (Die Wächter.)
London: Hamish Hamilton 1970.

1972 Avery, Gillian: **A likely lad.** (Ein prima Kerl.) Ill.: Faith Jacques.
London: Collins 1971.

1973 Adams, Richard: **Watership Down.** (*Watership Down.*)
London: Rex Collings 1972.

1974 Willard, Barbara: **The iron lily.** (Die eiserne Lilie.)
Harmondsworth: Longman 1973.

1975 Cawley, Winifred: **Gran at Coalgate.** (Die Oma aus *Coalgate.*) Ill.: Fermin Rocker.
London: Oxford University Press 1974.

1976 Bawden, Nina: **The peppermint pig.** (Das Pfefferminz-Schwein.) Ill.: Alexy Pendle.
London: Gollancz 1975.

1977 Dickinson, Peter: **The blue hawk.** (Der blaue Falke.) Ill.: David Smee.
London: Gollancz 1976.

1978 Jones, Diana Wynne: **Charmed life.** (Das zauberhafte Leben.)
London: Macmillan 1977.

1979 Davies, Andrew: **Conrad's war.** (*Conrads* Krieg.)
London: Blackie 1978.

1980 Schlee, Ann: **The vandal.** (Der Vandale.)
London: Macmillan 1979.

1981 Carter, Peter: **The sentinels.** (Die Schildwachen.)
London: Oxford University Press 1980.

The Other Award

The Children's Rights Workshop, a voluntary agency, founded the Other Award in 1975 for non-biased children's books of literary merit. The award, given annually, consists of a commendation, only. The jury is comprised of two members from the workshop and a panel of invited specialists in the field of children's literature. The criteria used for judging are literary merit, balanced depiction of male and female roles and realistic presentation of all peoples, whatever their culture, background or occupation.

Die Arbeitsgruppe "Rechte der Kinder" ist eine unabhängige Vereinigung. "Der andere Preis" wird seit 1975 für vorurteilsfreie Kinderbücher mit literarischem Wert vergeben. Der Preis wird jährlich verliehen und besteht nur aus einer Auszeichnung. Die Jury besteht aus zwei Migliedern der Arbeitsgruppe und einigen Spezialisten der Kinderliteratur. Die Kriterien der Jury können so umschrieben werden: literarischer Wert; Sozialisation in der Kinder- und Jugendliteratur; Realismus in der Darstellung aller sozialer Schichten.

1975 Edwards, Dorothy: **Joe and Timothy together.** (*Joe* und *Timothy* zusammen.)
London: Methuen 1975.

MacGibben, Jean: **Hal.** (*Hal.*)
London: Heinemann 1975.

Price, Susan: **Twopence a tub.** (Ein paar Groschen pro Fass.)
London: Faber 1975.

1976 Ashley, Bernard: **The trouble with Donovan Croft.** (Der Kummer von *Donovan Croft.*)
London: Oxford University Press 1975.

Fitzhugh, Louise: **Nobody's family is going to change.** (Keine Familie ändert sich.)
London: Gollancz 1976.

Hughes, Shirley: **Helpers.** (Helfer.)
London: Bodley Head 1976.

1977 Dhondy, Farrukh: **East end at your feet.** (Londoner Ostende liegt dir zu Füssen.)
London: Macmillan 1976.

Kemp, Gene: **The turbulent term of Tyke Tiler.** (Das turbulente Semester von *Tyke Tilers.*) Ill.: Carol Dinan.
London: Faber 1977.

Cox, Sarah: **Building worker.** (Bauarbeiter.) Photos: Robert Golden.
Harmondsworth: Kestrel 1976.

Cox, Sarah: **Hospital worker.** (Krankenhausarbeiter.) Photos: Robert Golden.
Harmondsworth: Kestrel 1976.

Cox, Sarah: **Rail worker.** (Eisenbahnarbeiter.) Photos: Robert Golden.
Harmondsworth: Kestrel 1976.

Grice, Frederick: **(Special commendation for the complete body of his work.** All titles by Frederick Grice are published by Oxford University Press, London; Besondere Empfehlung für sein Gesamtwerk. Alle Titel bei Oxford University Press, London.)

1978 Davidson, Basil: **Discovering Africa's past.** (Die Entdeckung der Vergangenheit Afrikas.)
Harmondsworth: Longman 1977.

Naughton, Bill: **The goalkeeper's revenge.** (Die Rache des Torwarts.)
Harmondsworth: Puffin 1978.

Sutcliff, Rosemary: **Song for a dark queen.** (Lied für eine dunkle Königin.)
London: Pelham 1978.

Waterson, Mary: **Gypsy family.** (Zigeunerfamilie.) Ill. and Photos: Lance Browne.
London: A. & C. Black 1978.

1979 Cate, Dick: **Old dog, new tricks.** (Alter Hund, neue Tricks.) Ill.: Trevor Stubley.
London: Hamilton 1978.

Dhondy, Farrukh: **Come to Mecca.** (Komm *Mekka.*)
London: Collins 1978.

Mills, Roger: **A comprehensive education.** (Eine umfassende Schulausbildung.)
London: Centerprise 1979.

Wagstaff, Sue: **Two Victorian families.** (Zwei viktorianische Familien.)
London: Black 1978.

1980 Ahlberg, Allan: **Mrs. Plug the plumber.** (Frau *Plug* die Klempnerin.) Ill.: Joseph Wright.
London: Kestrel 1980.

Bull, Angela: **The machine breakers.** (Die Maschinenzerstörer.)
London: Collins 1980.

Luling, Virginia: **Aborines.** (Eingeborene.) Ill.
London: Macdonald 1979.

Rees, David: **The green bough of liberty.** (Der grüne Ast der Freiheit.)
London: Dobson 1980.

The Times Educational Supplement Information Book Awards

This award for information books was founded by the Times Educational Supplement in 1972. The sum of £ 100 is awarded to the authors of two selected books. In addition the judges reserve the right to make a further award of £ 100 to the illustrator in each case.

The judges comprise two panels: one selecting the Senior Award and the other the Junior Award. The juries are drawn from leading authors, librarians, teachers and other experts in the field of children's literature, under the chairmanship of the editor of the times Educational Supplement. To be eligible for the award, the books must have originated either in Great Britain or the British Commonwealth and published during the preceding year.

Dieser Preis für Sachbücher wird von der Times seit 1972 verliehen. Der Betrag von £ 100 wird an zwei Autoren gegeben. Außerdem behält sich die Jury vor, einen weiteren Preis von £ 100 an einen Illustratoren zu vergeben.

Die Jury besteht aus zwei Ausschüssen: einer wählt den Senioren-Preis der andere den Junioren-Preis. Die Jury setzt sich aus Autoren, Bibliothekaren, Lehrern und anderen Spezialisten auf dem Gebiet der Kinderliteratur zusammen, den Vorsitz führt der Herausgeber der pädagogischen Beilage der Times. Es kommen nur Bücher in Frage, die in Großbritannien oder im Commonwealth zum erstenmal im vergangenen Jahr erschienen sind.

1972 Magnusson, Magnus: **Introducing archaeology.** (Einführung in die Archäologie.)
London: Bodley Head 1972.

1973 *Senior award/Senioren-Preis*
Hay, David: **Human populations.** (Die menschliche Bevölkerung.)
Harmondsworth: Penguin 1973.

Junior award/Junioren-Preis
The prize was not given; Der Preis wurde nicht vergeben.

1974 *Senior award/Senioren-Preis*
Churcher, Betty: **Understanding art.** (Kunst zu verstehen.)
Edinburgh: Holmes McDougall 1974.

Junior award/Junioren-Preis
Ommanney, Dr. F.D.: **Frogs, toads and newts.** (Frösche, Kröten und Wassermolche.) Ill.: Deborah Fulford.
London: Bodley Head 1974.

1975 *Senior award/Senioren-Preis*
Flanagan, Geraldine Lux: **Window into a nest.** (Nest am Fenster.)
Photos: Sean Morris.
Harmondsworth: Kestrel 1975.

Junior award/Junioren-Preis
Whitlock, Ralph: **Spiders.** (Die Spinne.)
London: Priory Press 1975.

1976 *Senior award/Senioren-Preis*
Macdonald's encyclopedia of Africa. (*Macdonalds* Lexikon über Afrika.)
London: Macdonald Educational 1976.

Junior award/Junioren-Preis
Allen, Eleanor: **Wash and brush up.** (Waschen und Saubermachen.)
London: A. & C. Black 1976.

1977 *Senior award/Senioren-Preis*
Beazley, Mitchell: **Man and machines.** (Mensch und Maschinen.)
Oxford: Pergamon 1977.

Junior award/Junioren-Preis
Mabey, Richard: **Street flowers.** (Straßenblumen.) Ill.: Sarah Kensington.
Harmondsworth: Kestrel 1976.

1978 *Senior award/Senioren-Preis*
Gray, Dulcie: **Butterflies on my mind.** (Schmetterlinge in meinem Sinn.)
London: Angus & Robertson 1977.

Junior award/Junioren-Preis
Barber, Richard: **Tournaments.** (Turniere.)
Harmondsworth: Kestrel 1977.

1979 *Senior award/Senioren-Preis*
Cousins, Jane: **Make it happy.** (Mach es glücklich.)
London: Virage 1978.

Junior award/Junioren-Preis
Bernard, George: **The common frog.** (Der gewöhnliche Frosch.) Photos: George Bernard.
London: André Deutsch 1979.

1980 *Senior award/Senioren-Preis*
Hurd, Michael: **The Oxford junior companion to music.** (Oxfords Musiklexikon für junge Leser.)
London: Oxford University Press 1980.

Junior award/Junioren-Preis
Updegraff, Imelda/Updegraff, Robert: **Earthquakes and volcanoes.** (Erdbeben und Vulkane.)
London: Methuen 1980.

1981 *Senior award/Senioren-Preis*
Steel, Richard: **Skulls.** (Schädel.) Ill.: G. Gaskin.
London: Heinemann 1980.

Junior award/Junioren-Preis
The prize was not given; Der Preis wurde nicht vergeben.

The Tir na n-Og Award

Tir na n-Og is a Gaelic phrase, familiar to readers of Welsh literature, for the land of eternal youth. The awards were founded in 1976 with the following aims: to draw attention to children's books in Wales; to attempt to raise the overall standard of Welsh publishing for children; to encourage and promote native Welsh authors. Two prizes are awarded annually for books that appeared during the previous year — one to the author of the best children's book written in the Welsh language and the other to the author of the best English-language volume with an authentic Welsh background. The awards are valued at £ 250 each. £ 375 is given by the Welsh Arts Council and £ 125 by the Welsh Joint Education Committee (towards the Welsh prize). The selecting panel comprises representatives of the Welsh Branch of the Youth Librarians' Group, the Welsh Library Association, the Welsh Joint Education Committee and the Literature Committee of the Welsh Arts Council.

Tir na n-Og ist die gälische Bezeichnung für das Land der ewigen Jugend, Lesern walisischer Literatur vielleicht bekannt. Die Preise werden seit 1976 mit der Absicht verliehen, die Aufmerksamkeit auf das walisische Kinderbuch zu lenken, das Niveau der walisischen Kinderbuch-Veröffentlichung anzuheben und walisische Autoren zu ermutigen und zu fördern.

Zwei Preise werden jährlich an Bücher vergeben, die im Laufe des vorangegangenen Jahres erschienen sind. Ein Preis geht an den Autor des besten in walisisch verfaßten Kinderbuches, der andere an den Autor des besten englischsprachigen Buches mit authentisch walisischem Hintergrund.

Die beiden Preise in Höhe von jeweils £ 250 werden vom Rat für walisische Kunst, der £ 375 beisteuert und vom Ausschuß des Verbandes für Erziehung, das einen Beitrag von £ 125 leistet, verliehen. Die Jury setzt sich aus Vertretern der Walisischen Sektion der Jugendbibliothekare, dem Walisischen Bibliotheksverband, dem Ausschuß des Verbandes für Erziehung und dem Literatur-Ausschuß des Rates für Walisische Kunst zusammen.

1976 *Welsh language/Walisischer Sprache*
Jones, T. Llew: **Tan ar y comin.** (Fire on the heath; Feuer in der Heide.)
Llandysul, Dyfed: Gomer Press 1975.

English language/Englischer Sprache
Cooper, Susan: **The grey king.** (Der graue König.)
London: Chatto and Windus 1975.

1977 *Welsh language/Walisischer Sprache*
Lloyd, J. Selwyn: **Trysor bryniau Caspar.** (The treasure of *Caspar Hills*; Der Schatz von *Caspar Hills.*)
Llandysul, Dyfed: Gomer Press 1976.

English language/Englischer Sprache
Bond, Nancy: **A string in the harp.** (Eine Saite der Harfe.)
New York: Athenium 1976.

1978 *Welsh language/Walisischer Sprache*
Edwards, Jane: **Miriam,** (*Miriam.*)
Llandysul, Dyfed: Gomer Press 1977.

English language/Englischer Sprache
Cooper, Susan: **Silver on the tree.** (Silber auf dem Baum.)
London: Chatto and Windus 1977.

1979 *Welsh language/Walisischer Sprache*
Owen, Dyddgu: **Y flwyddyn honno** (In that year; In jenem Jahr.)
Swansea: Christopher Davies 1978.

English language/Englischer Sprache
Meyrick, Bette: **Time circles.** (Zeit-Kreise.)
London: Abelard Schuman 1978.

Greece/Griechenland

Circle of Greek Children's Books Award

This award was founded by the Circle of Greek Children's Books and is awarded to published works as well as manuscripts.

Dieser Preis wurde vom Kreis des Griechischen Kinderbuches gestiftet und wird sowohl für veröffentlichte Werke als auch für Manuskripte verliehen.

1974 Kliapha, Marual: **E eliachtida.** (The sunshine; Der Sonnenschein.) Ill.: Giannes Kalaitzes.
Athenai: Kedros 1977.

1976 Lerake, Georgia: **San aletheia kai san thauma.** (Like truth and miracle; Wie die Wahrheit und wie ein Wunder.) Ill.: Nina N. Stamatiu.
Athenai: Kedros 1976.

Ill. 19 Sofia Zarambouka in: O Phlit taxideuei

Paterake, Giolanda: **E dantellenia skuphia tes giagias.** (Grandmother's crocheted bonnet; Großmutters gehäkelte Mütze.) Ill.: Sofia Zarambouka.
Athenai: Muskakas 1976.

1977 Gumenopulu, Maria: **O Tsilibithras.** (*Tsilibithras.*) (Unpublished; Unveröffentlicht.)

Krokos, Giorges: **Chelidonopholies.** (Swallow nests; Schwalbennester.) Ill.: Demos Anagnostopulos/Rita Bergu-Charulare/Giorgos Durduphes/Petros Zampeles/Phaidon Kalogeru/Thanases Netas.
Athenai: Giorges Krokos 1977.

Krokos, Giorges: **Ta tragudia tu eliu.** (The songs of the sun; Die Lieder der Sonne.) Ill.: Giorgos Barlamos.
Athenai: Giorges Krokos 1978.

Petrobits-Andrutsopulu, Lote: **Treis phores ki' enan kairo. S'enan planete makrino.** (Thrice upon a time. On a distant planet; Es war dreimal. Auf einem entfernten Planeten.) Ill.: Anna Mendrinu-Ioannidu and Petros Zampelles.
Athenai: Ekdoseis philon 1977.

Award of the Mayor of Athens

This prize is presented by the mayor of the city of Athens and is awarded to not only published works, but to manuscripts, as well.

Dieser Preis wird vom Bürgermeister der Stadt Athen verliehen. Er wird sowohl für veröffentlichte Bücher als auch für Manuskripte vergeben.

1972 Surele, Galateia: **O Alexes kai to xylino alogo.** (*Alexis* and the wooden horse; *Alexis* und das hölzerne Pferd.) Ill.: Anna Mendrinu-Ioannidu.
Athenai: Paidikoi orizontes Apostolike Diakonia.

Tsimikale, Pipina: **E Peristera kai e alepu.** (*Peristera* and the fox; *Peristera* und der Fuchs.) Ill.
Athenai:

1973 Sphaellu, Kalliope A.: **E istoria tu Phirphire.** (The story of *Phirphires*; Die Geschichte von *Phirphires.*) Ill.
Athenai: Estia 1973.

Sphaellu, Kalliope A.: **Ta apomnemoneumata enos gatu.** (Memoirs of a tom-cat; Die Memoiren eines Katers.) Ill.
Athenai: Dorikos.

1975 Tsimikale, Pipina: **E alepu kai o lykos.** (The fox and the wolf; Der Fuchs und der Wolf.)
(Unpublished; Unveröffentlicht.)

Tsimikale, Pipina: **Sto megalo lankadi.** (The the large valley; Im großen Tal.)
(Unpublished; Unveröffentlicht.)

Women's Literary Society Award

In 1958 a small group which was later to form the core of "Gynaikeia Logotechnike Syntrophia" (Women's Literary Society) founded this prize for children's books. Meanwhile the society has grown and has become the leading body concerned with the presentation of literary awards. During the twenty years of its existence, the prize has been awarded to historical novels, fairy tales, poetry, drama and novels dealing with contemporary problems and trends. Complete bibliographical data did not arrive before this catalogue went to press; consequently, certain information may be lacking in the list below.

1958 wurde von einer kleinen Gruppe, die den Kern der "Gynaikeia Logotechnike Syntrophia" (Literarische Frauengesellschaft) bildete, zum erstenmal ein Preis für das Kinderbuch ausgeschrieben. Inzwischen ist die Literarische Frauengesellschaft zu einem beachtenswerten führenden Verein geworden, der Bücher mit mannigfachen Richtungen mit einem Preis auszeichnet. In seiner Tätigkeit von über zwanzig Jahren wurden historische Romane, Märchen, Gedichte, Theaterstücke, Romane mit aktuellen Themen und zeitgenössischer Problematik mit einem Preis gekrönt. Leider fehlt uns in dieser Richtung ausreichende Information direkt von der Quelle.

1960 Karbelle, Despo: **To Panegyri tes leuterias.** (The feast of freedom; Das Fest der Freiheit.) Ill.
Athenai: Basileiu.

Krokos, Giorges: **E megale istoria.** (The great story; Die große Geschichte.) Ill.: E. Spyridonons/ A. Tarsule/A. Alexandrake.
Athenai: Diphros 1964.

Krokos, Giorges: **Paidikoi palmoi.** (Children's heartbeats; Kindliches Herzklopfen.)
Athenai: Giorges Krokos 1961.

1961 Sakellariu, Chare: **Charumenes phones.** (Joyful voices; Fröhliche Stimmen.) Ill.
Athenai: Basileiu 1962.

1963 Sakellariu, Chare: **Sta buna kai sta lankadia tes Sacharas.** (In the mountains and valleys of Sahara; In den Bergen und in den Tälern der Sahara.) Ill.
Peiraieus: Koinonike.

1964 Nikolopulu, Angelike: **Tha perimeno te leutheria.** (I will wait for freedom; Ich warte auf die Freiheit.) Ill.
Athenai:

Sakellariu, Chare: **To therio pu merose.** (The wild animal that has been tamed; Das wilde Tier, das zahm wurde.) Ill.: K. Kornarake.
Athenai: Ekdoseis K. Loberdu "Prometheutikes"

1965 Brachnas, Giannes: **Stu pappu mu to chorio.** (In my grandfather's village; In dem Dorf meines Großvaters.) Ill.
Athenai: Giannes Brachnas.

Chatzeanagnostu, Takes: **Ite paides . . .** (Forward, Children . . .; Vorwärts Kinder . . .) Ill.: Marios Angelopulos.
Athenai: Estia.

Gynaikeia Logotechnike Syntrophia: **Paidike Protochronia.** New Year for children; Neujahr für Kinder.) Ill.: Petros Zampeles.
Athenai: Estia.

Sphaellu, Kalliope: **O boskos ki o regas.** (The shepherd and the king; Der Hirte und der König.) Ill.: Marios Angelopulos.
Athenai: Estia 1977.

1966 Barella, Angelike: **E Ellada ki' emeis.** (Greece and us; Griechenland und wir.) Ill.: Paulos Balasakes.
Athenai: Eleutherudakes 1967.

Kulures, Christos: **Tragudo ten anoixi.** (I sing the praises of spring; Ich besinge den Frühling.) Ill.
Athenai: Nea skepsis.

Sakellariu, Chare: **Treis mikroi kosmonautes.** (Three astronauts; Drei Astronauten.) Ill.: M Meliote.
Athenai: Ekdoseis K. Loberdu "Prometheutike 1967."

Solomu, Basa: **Ieros Lochos.** (Holy legion; Heilige Legion.) Ill.: Basa Solomu.
Athenai: Basa Solomu.

1967 Palaiologu, Galateia: **Me to podelato.** (With the bicycle; Mit dem Fahrrad.) Ill.: Chara Biena.
Athenai: Galateia Palaiologu 1967.

Skiadas, Nikos: **Ta deka paidia.** (The ten children; Die zehn Kinder.) Ill.: Ch. Papageorgiu.
Athenai: Nike.

Sphaellu, Kalliope: **To liontaropulo.** (The young lion; Der junge Löwe.) Ill.
Athenai: Estia.

1968 Gulime, Alke: **O chrysaphenios krinos.** (The mystery of the golden lily; Die wilde Lilie vom Parnaß.) Ill.: Sebaste Karabokyre-Georgakopulu.
Athenai: Eletheurudakes 1978.

Kalapanida, K.: **Kubenta me t' asteria.** (Speaking with the stars; Gespräche mit den Sternen.) Ill.
Athenai:

Kubala, Gumenopulu: **Perna, perna e Melissa.** (Gone, gone the bee; Vorbei, vorbei ist die Biene.) Ill.
Sthenai: Gumenopulu Kubala.

Stathatu, Phranse: **Etan kapote mia neraida.** (Once there was a nymph; Es war einmal eine Nymphe.) Ill.: Artemis Nikolaidu.
Athenai: Chryse Penna.

Tarsule, Georgia: **Dyo ellenopula sta chronia tu Neronos.** (Two Greek children in *Nero's* time; Zwei Griechenkinder zu *Neros* Zeiten.) Ill.: Gerasimos Gregores.
Athenai: Estia 1968.

1969 Sarante, Galateia: **Charazei e leutheria.** Oi mparutomyloi tes Demetsanas. (The dawn of freedom. The gunpowder factories of Demetsana; Es dämmert die Freiheit. Die Pulvermühlen von Demetsana.) Ill.: Marios Angelopulos.
Athenai: Estia.

Surele, Galateia: **O spurgites me to kokkino gileko.** (The sparrow with the red waistcoat; Der Spatz mit der roten Weste.) Ill.: Petros Zampeles.
Athenai: Papyros 1971.

1970 Chatzigiannu, Chrysula: **Phterugismata.** (Fluttering; Flattern.) Ill.
Athenai: To elleniko biblio.

Maximu, Penelope: **26 charumenes istories.** (26 pleasant stories; 26 frohe Geschichten.) Ill.
Athenai: Astir 1973.

Palaiologu, Galateia: **Me to trechanteri.** (With the sailboat; Mit dem Segelboot.) Ill.: Chara Bienna.
Athenai: Karabias 1970.

Sakkas, Giorgos: **Milun ta buna mas.** (Our mountains speak; Unsere Berge sprechen.) Ill.: Tasos Chatzes.
Athenai: Typos Phytrake.

Tzortzoglu, Nitsa: **Tom Tommy kai sia.** (*Tom Tommy* and company; *Tom Tommy* und die Bande.)
Athenai: Ekdoseis epta.

Chatzinikolau, Ntina: **Chamogela.** (Smiles; Lächeln.) Ill.
Athenai:

1971 Gumenopulu, Maria: **Pes mu kati manula.** (Tell me something, mother; Erzähl mir etwas Mutter.) Ill.: Litsa Patrikiu.
Athenai: Elaphos.

Nikolopulu, Ankelike: **Eleutheria e thanatos.** (Freedom or death; Freiheit oder Tod.) Ill.: Nikos Kastrinakes.
Athenai: Ankyra.

Papamoschu, Ero: **Megales diakopes.** (Long vacations; Lange Ferien.) Ill.
Athenai:

Stathatu, Phranse: **Phos apo to Arkadi.** (Light from Arcady; Licht aus Arkadien.) Ill.: Paul Balasakes.
Athenai: Estia.

1972 Chatzigiannu, Chrysula: **Elie mu . . . elie mu.** (My sun . . . my sun; Meine Sonne . . . meine Sonne.) Ill.: K. Kolybe.
Athenai: Chrysula Chatzigiannu.

Karthaiu, Rena: **Chartaetoi ston urano.** (Kites in the sky; Papierdrachen am Himmel.) Ill.
Athenai: Rena Karthaiu.

Krokos, Giorges: **Aetopholies.** (Eagle eyries; Adlerhorste.) Ill.: Demos Anagnostopulos/A. Artinian/Rita Bergu-Charulare/Phaidon Kalogeru/Thanases Netas/Athena Tsukala.
Athenai: Giorgos Krokos 1972.

Pheruses, Demetres: **O ekatontarchos.** (The centurion; Der Zenturio.) Ill.
Athenai: Apostolike diankonia.

Tzamales, Kostas: **Sten Athena tu Perikle.** (In *Pericles' Athens;* Im Athen von *Perikles*,) Ill.: Nike Tzamale.
Athenai: Estia.

Zarambouka, Sofia: **O Phlit taxideuei.** (*Phlit* journeys; *Phlit* geht auf Reise.) Ill.: Sofia Zarambouka.
Athenai: Sofia Zarambouka 1972.

1973 Gulime, Alke: **Ta paramythia tes manulas.** (Mother's fairy tales; Mütterchens Märchen.) Ill.: Paulos Balasakes.
Athenai: Eleutherudakes.

Chatzinikolau, Ntina: **Kyklamina.** (Cyclamen; Alpenveilchen.) Ill.: Ntina Chatzinikolau.
Athenai: Nea skepsi.

1975 Gumenopulu, Maria: **O Michalakes kai to dikio tu.** (*Michalakes* and his rights; *Michalakes* und sein Recht.)
Athenai:

Petrobits-Andrutsopulu, Lote: **O mikros adelphos.** (The younger brother; Der jüngere Bruder.) Ill.: Paulos Balasakes.
Athenai: Ekdoseis ton philon 1976.

Sakellariu, Chare: **Poiemata.** (Poems; Gedichte.)
(Unpublished; Unveröffentlicht.)

1976 Balabane, Elene: **Taxidi st'Anapli.** (Journey to Anapli; Reise nach Anapli.) Ill.: Agenoras Asterides.
Athenai: Dodone 1977.

Barella, Angelike: **E politeia tu anemu.** (The city of the wind; Die Stadt des Windes.)
(Unpublished; Unveröffentlicht.)

Surele, Galateia: **Emena me noiazei.** (It's my concern; Es geht mich an.) Ill.
Athenai: Estia 1976.

1977 Philntisi, S.: **Thalasina diegemata.** (Tales of the sea; Erzählungen des Meeres.)
(Unpublished; Unveröffentlicht.)

Tzortzoglu, Nitza: **Nesia kai kymata.** (Islands and waves; Inseln und Wellen.)
(Unpublished; Unveröffentlicht.)

(Information was not given concerning the year the following titles were awarded the prize; consequently, they have been listed by author, in alphabetical order/ Bei den folgenden Titeln fehlen die Jahresangaben, so daß sie alphabetisch nach Autoren geordnet sind.)

Arbanies, Nikos: **O antreomenos.** (The brave one; Der Tapfere.) Ill.
Athenai: Paidikoi Orizontes, Seira ekdoseon apostolikes Diakonias.

Balabane, Elene: **Morphes tu neu Ellenismu.** (Figures of the new hellenism; Gestalten des neuen Hellenismus.) Ill.: Spyros Basileiu.
Athenai: Estia 1965.

Balabane, Elene: **Ta paputsia ki' ego.** (The shoes and I; Die Schuhe und ich.) Ill.
Athenai: Diphros.

Brachnas, Giannes: **Ekei pu pholiazun oi aetoi.** (Where the eagles nest; Dort wo die Adler horsten.) Ill.
Athenai: Basileiu.

Krinaios, Paulos: **Te tetradia ton angelon.** (The note-books of the angels; Die Hefte der Engel.) Ill.
Athenai: To elleniko spiti.

Krokos, Giorges: **Paidiko theatro — ephebiko theatro.** (Theatre for children — theatre for juveniles; Theater für Kinder — Theater für Jugendliche.) Ill.: Demos Anagnostopulos/A. Artinian/Rita Bergu-Chartulake/Giorgos Durbuphes.
Athenai: Giorges Krokos 1977.

Lappas, Takes: **Doxasmene exodus.** (Glorious exodus; Glorreicher Auszug.) Ill.: Nikos Zographu.
Athenai: Atlantis.

Maximu, Penelope: **Alethino paramythi.** (A true fairy tale; Ein wahres Märchen.) Ill.: St. Mpozinake.
Athenai: Basileiu.

Melissanthe: **O mikros adelphos.** (The younger brother; Der kleine Bruder.) Ill.
Athenai:

Mpumpe-Papa, Rita: E magike phlogera. (The enchanted flute; Die verzauberte Flöte.) Ill.
Athenai:

Mpurune, Demetra: **To galazio leibadi.** (The sky blue meadow; Die himmelblaue Wiese.) Ill.
Athenai: Diphros.

Phalare, Ntora: **Tik . . . tak to roloi.** (Tick . . . tock, the clock; Tik . . . tak die Uhr.) Ill.: Nephgele Raphtopulu.
Athenai: Ekdose "Mana Kore".

Sakellariu, Chare: **O pohilos mu o Tarzan.** (*Tarzan,* my friend; *Tarzan,* mein Freund.) Ill.
Athenai: Ekdose K. Loberdu "Prometheutikes."

Tsimikale, Pipina: **O chartaetos.** (the paper kite; Der Papierdrachen.) Ill.
Athenai: Basileiu.

Tsiomikale, Pipina: **E kokkine omprela.** (The red umbrella; Der rote Schirm.) Ill.: Panos Balasakes.
Athenai: Pipina Tsimikale.

Tsimikale, Pipina: **O Panagos.** (*Panagos.*) Ill.
Athenai: Kibotos.

Hungary/Ungarn

Jószef-Attila-dij

This prize was named in honour of the poet, Attila Jószef (1905—1937), who published his first expressionistic poems of social criticism at the age of seventeen in Hungary's famous literary magazine, "Nyugat" (West). Initially, the prize was awarded in three categories to individual titles, as well as the complete works of authors; but in 1971 the rules were changed and the prize was awarded only for the complete works of authors, still in three categories. From 1977 onwards, the prize has only been awarded to a single author for his complete works.

Dieser Preis wurde zu Ehren des Dichters Attila Jószef (1905—1937) gestiftet, der seine ersten expressionistischen sozialkritischen Gedichte im Alter von 17 Jahren in der bekannten ungarischen Literaturzeitschrift "Nyugat" (Der Westen) veröffentlichte. Ursprünglich wurde der Preis in drei Kategorien verliehen und zwar sowohl für einzelne Werke als auch für das Gesamtwerk eines Autors; 1971 wurden die Statuten geändert und der Preis wurde nur noch für Gesamtwerke vergeben, aber noch immer in drei Kategorien. Seit 1977 wird der Preis nur noch an einen Autor für dessen Gesamtwerk verliehen.

1950 Fehér, Klára: **Abecület.** (The honour; Die Ehre.)
Budapest: Ifjúsági kiadó 1950.
(1st category/1. Kategorie)

1951 Hegedűs, Géza: **Az erdöntúli veszedelem.** (The danger beyond the forest; Die Gefahr jenseits des Waldes.) Ill.: Miklós Győry.
Budapest: Ifjúsági kiadó 1951.
(2nd category/2. Kategorie)

Hegedűs, Géza: **A zálogbatett város.** (The pawned city; Die verpfändete Stadt.) Ill.: Miklós Győry.
Budapest: Śzépirodlmi kiadó 1951.
(2nd category/2. Kategorie)

Szüdi, György: **A forradalom katonája.** (The soldier of the revolution; „Der Soldat der Revolution.") Ill.: Miklós Győry.
Budapest: Ifjúsági kiadó 1951.
(2nd category/2. Kategorie)

Gáli, Jószef: **Erős, János. Mesejáték.** (Fairy tale theatre pieces to perform; Märchenspiele zum Aufführen.) Ill.: István Köpeczi Bócz.
Budapest: Ifjúsági kiadó 1951.
(3rd category/3. Kategorie)

Ill. 20 Lászlo Réber in E. Lázár: A hétfejú tündér

1952 Gergely, Márta: **Üttörébarátság.** (Pioneer friendship; Pionierfreundschaft.)
Budapest: Ifjúsági kiadó 1951.
(3rd category/3. Kategorie)

1953 The prize was not given; Der Preis wurde nicht vergeben.

1954 Thury, Zsuzsa: **A francia kislány.** (The little French girl; Das kleine französische Mädchen.) Ill.: Ágnes Kepes.
Budapest: Ifjúsági kiadó 1953.
(2nd category/2. Kategorie)

1955 Vészi, Endre: **A küldetés.** (The mission; Die Mission.) Ill.: Károly Raszler.
Budapest: Ifjúsági kiadó 1954.
(2nd category/2. Kategorie)

Kormes, István: **A tréfás mackók.** (The humorous bears; Die lustigen Bären.) Ill.: Piroska Szántó.
Budapest: Ifjúsági kiadó 1954.
(3rd category/3. Kategorie) and for his other works in the area of youth literature; und für seine anderen Werke auf dem Gebiet der Jugendliteratur.

1956 The prize was not given; Der Preis wurde nicht vergeben.

1957 Thury, Zsuzsa for: **Collected works in the area of children's literature;** Gesamtschaffen auf dem Gebiet der Kinderliteratur.
(2nd category/2. Kategorie)

1958 The prize was not given; Der Preis wurde nicht vergeben.

1959 Mesterházi, Lajes: **Pár lépés a határ. Regény.** (A few steps to the frontier; Ein paar Schritte bis zur Grenze.) Ill.: Gyula Szőnyi.
Budapest: Móra kiadó 1958.
(1st category/1. Kategorie)

Szántó, György for: **his historical novels for youth;** für seine geschichtlichen Jugendromane.
(1st category/1. Kategorie)

Gergely, Márta: **A mi lányunk.** (Our girl; Unser Mädchen.)
Ill.: Gyula Szőnyi.
Budapest: Móra kiadó 1959.
(3rd category/3. Kategorie)

Gergerly, Márta: **Szöszi. Regény.** (*Szöszi.* A novel; *Szöszi.* Roman.)
Ill.: Gyula Szőny.
Budapest: Móra kiadó 1959.
(3rd category/3. Kategorie)

1960 Fekete, István for: **his collected works in the area of youth novels;** sein Gesamtschaffen auf dem Gebiet des Jugendromans.
(2nd category/2. Kategorie)

1961 Tatay Sándor: **Puskák és galambok.** (Guns and pigeons; Flinten und Tauben.) Ill.: Ernő Zórád.
Budapest: Móra kiadó 1960.
(1st category/1. Kategorie)

Dékány, András for: **popular science youth novels;** seine populärwissenschaftlichen Jugendromane.
(2nd category/2. Kategorie)

1962 Földes, Péter for: **his collected work in the area of children's literature;** für sein Gesamtschaffen auf dem Gebiet der Jugendliteratur.
(3rd category/3. Kategorie)

1963 The prize was not given; Der Preis wurde nicht vergeben.

1967 Palotai, Boris for: **collected belletristic work, including numerous books for children and youth;** für ihr belletristisches Gesamtschaffen, zu dem zahlreiche Kinder- und Jugendbücher gehören.

1968 The prize was not given; Der Preis wurde nicht vergeben.

1969 Mándy, Iván for: **collected belletristic work;** für sein belletristisches Gesamtschaffen.

Nemes Nagy, Ágnes for: **collected lyrical works;** für ihr lyrisches Gesamtschaffen.

1970 The prize was not given; Der Preis wurde nicht vergeben.

1971 Gerő, Janós for: **works in the field of children's literature;** für seine schriftstellerische Tätigkeit auf dem Gebiet der Kinder- und Jugendliteratur.
(2nd category/2. Kategorie)

1972 The prize was not given; Der Preis wurde nicht vergeben.

1973 Varga, Domokos for: **works in the area of children's and youth literature;** für seine schriftstellerische Tätigkeit auf dem Gebiet der Kinder- und Jugendliteratur.
(2nd category/2. Kategorie)

1974 Lázár, Ervin for: **works in the area of children's and youth literature;** für seine schriftstellerische Tätigkeit auf dem Gebiet der Kinder- und Jugendliteratur.

Tóth, Eszter for: **works in the area of children's and youth literature;** für ihre schriftstellerische Tätigkeit auf dem Gebiet der Kinder- und Jugendliteratur.

Török, Sándor for: **his works in the area of children's and youth literature;** für seine schriftstellerische Tätigkeit auf dem Gebiet der Kinder- und Jugendliteratur.

1975 Bálint, Agnes for: **works in the area of children's and youth literature;** für ihre schriftstellerische Tätigkeit auf dem Gebiet der Kinder- und Jugendliteratur.

1976 Varga, Katakin for: **her works in the area of children's and youth literature;** für ihre schriftstellerische Tätigkeit auf dem Gebiet der Kinder- und Jugendliteratur.

1977 Janikovszky, Éva for: **her works in the area of children's and youth literature;** für ihre schriftstellerische Tätigkeit auf dem Gebiet der Kinder- und Jugendliteratur.

Csukás, István for: **his works in the area of children's and youth literature;** für seine schriftstellerische Tätigkeit auf dem Gebiet der Kinder- und Jugendliteratur.

1978 Gazdag, Erzsébet for: **her works in the area of children's and youth literature;** für ihre schriftstellerische Tätigkeit auf dem Gebiet der Kinder- und Jugendliteratur.

1979 Kántor, Zsuzsa for: **her works in the area of children's and youth literature;** für ihre schriftstellerische Tätigkeit auf dem Gebiet der Kinder- und Jugendliteratur.

Tatay, Sándor for: **his works in the area of children's and youth literature;** für seine schriftstellerische Tätigkeit auf dem Gebiet der Kinder- und Jugendliteratur.

1980 Szepesi, Attila for: **his children's poetry;** für seine Kindergedichte.

1981 Lengyel, Balázs for: **his youth books;** für seine Jugendbücher.

Simai, Mihály for: **his children's books;** für seine Kinderbücher.

Iceland/Island

Barnabókaverdlaun á Íslandi

Initiated in 1973, this prize is awarded annually to the best children's and youth books published in Iceland during the previous year. Award-winners, selected by a committee chosen by the educational council of Reykjavík, may be either authors or translators.

Der Preis wird seit 1973 vergeben und zwar jährlich für die besten Kinder- und Jugendbücher, die im vorangegangenen Jahr in Island veröffentlicht wurden. Die Preisträger, die vom Unterrichtsministerium in Reykjavik ausgewählt werden, können sowohl Autoren als auch Übersetzer sein.

Ill. 21 Halldór Pétursson in N. Njardvik: Helgi skodar heiminn

1973 *Original title/Originaltitel*
Stefánsson, Jenna/Steffánsson, Hreidar: **for their contribution to children's literature;**für ihren Beitrag zur Kinderliteratur.

Translation/Übersetzung
Briem, Steinunn for: Jannsson, Tove: **Eyjan hans múnínpabba.** (Father and the sea; Vater und das Meer; Swed.orig.title: Papp och havet.)
Reykjavík: Örn og Örlygur 1972.

1974 *Original title/Originaltitel*
Jónasson, Jónas: **Polli ég og allir hinir.** (*Polli,* I and all the others; *Polli,* ich und all die anderen.)
Reykjavík: Setberg 1973.

Tryggvason, Kári: **Úlla horfir á heiminn.** (*Ulla* looks at the world; *Ulla* betrachtet die Welt.)
Reykjavík: Isafold 1973.

Translation/Übersetzung
Valdimarsdóttir, Anna for: Gripe, Maria: **Jósefína.** (*Josephine*; *Josefine*; Swed.orig.title: *Josefin*.)
Reykjavík: Idunn 1973.

1975 *Original title/Originaltitel*
Helgadóttir, Guđrún: **Jón Oddur og Jón Bjarni.** (*John Oddur* and *John Bjarni; Johann Oddur* und *Johann Bjarni.*)
Reykjavík: Iđunn 1974.

Translation/Übersetzung
Thorarensen, Solveig for: Wilde, Oscar: **Prinsinn hamingjusami.** (Orig.Eng.title: The happy prince; Der glückliche Prinz.)
Reykjavík: Fjölvi 1974.

1976 *Original title/Originaltitel*
The prize was not awarded/Der Preis wurde nicht vergeben.

Translation/Übersetzung
Dagbjartsdóttir, Vilborg for: Gripe, Maria: **Húgó.** (*Hugo;* Orig.Swed.title: *Hugo.*)
Reykjavík: Iđunn 1975.

1977 *Original title/Originaltitel*
Samundsson, Thorvaldur: **Bjartir dagar.** (Bright days; Helle Tage.)
Reykjavík: Thorvaldur Samundsson 1976.

Translation/Übersetzung
Hauksson, Thorleifur for: Lindgren, Astrid: **Bróđir minn ljónsjarta.** (The brothers, *Lionheart*; Die Brüder Löwenherz; Orig.Swed.title: Bröderna *Lejonhjärta.*)
Reykjavík: Mál og menning 1976.

India/Indien

Children's Book Trust Award

The Children's Book Trust organises a yearly competition for writers of children's books. the competition was started in 1978. Manuscripts are accepted for three categories: fiction, non-fiction and picture books. Two cash awards are offered in each category. The competition is open to all.

Der Children's Book Trust veranstaltet jährlich einen Wettbewerb für Kinderbuchautoren; 1978 zum erstenmal. Die Manuskripte werden in drei Kategorien eingeteilt: Erzählende Literatur, Sachbücher, Bilderbücher. Für jede Kategorie werden zwei Geldpreise ausgesetzt. Jedermann kann sich am Wettbewerb beteiligen.

1978 *Fiction/Erzählende Literatur*
1st prize/1. Preis
Datta, Arup Kumar: **(The Kaziranga Trail;** (Der *Kaziranga Pfad.*)
Ill.: Jagdish Joshi.
New Delhi: Children's Book Trust 1979.

Ill. 22 Jagdish Joshi in A. Datta: The Kaziranga Trail

2nd prize/2. Preis
Allfrey, Katherine: **Dipak's quest.** (*Dipaks* Suche.)
3rd prize/3. Preis
Maitra, Rita: **Chiku sees the world.** (*Chiku* sieht die Welt.)

1979 *Fiction/Erzählende Literatur*
1st prize/1. Preis
Sinha, Nilima: **the Chandipur jewels.** (Die *Chandipur* Juwelen.) Ill.: Jagdish Joshi.
New Delhi: Children's Book Trust 1981.
2nd prize/2. Preis
Sengupta, Abhijit: **The story of Panchami.** (Die Geschichte von *Panchami.*)
Non-fiction/Sachbücher
1st prize/1. Preis
Rajagopalan, R.: **About computers.** (Über Computer.)
2nd prize/2. Preis
Bhagat, O.P.: **The king of fruits.** (Der König der Früchte.)
3rd prize/3. Preis
The prize was not given; Der Preis wurde nicht vergeben.

1980 *Fiction/Erzählende Literatur*
1st prize/1. Preis
The prize was not given; Der Preis wurde nicht vergeben.
2nd prize/2. Preis
Datta, Arup Kumar: **Trouble at Kolongijan.** (Schwierigkeiten in *Kolongijan.*)
Bulsara, C.N.: **Robin and the eagle.** (*Robin* und der Adler.)
3rd prize/3. Preis
Krishna Pillai, G. Radha: **The lion of Kerala.** (Der Löwe von Kerala.)
Sinha, Sarojini: **The treasure box.** (Die Schatzkiste.)
Non-fiction/Sachbücher
1st prize/1. Preis
The prize was not given; Der Preis wurde nicht vergeben.
2nd prize/2. Preis
Melwani, Mona: **Tipu Sultan.** (*Tipu Sultan.*)
3rd prize/3. Preis
The prize was not given; Der Preis wurde nicht vergeben.
Picture book/Bilderbuch
1st prize/1. Preis
Shankar, Alaka: **My Muffy.** (Mein *Muffy.*)

2nd prize/2. Preis
Swami, Minnie: **My wall.** (Meine Wand.)
3rd prize/3. Preis
Nath, Pratibha: **Barber-in-Chief.** (Der Chef-Friseur.)
Sinha, Shaiontani: **The elephant that ran away.** (Der Elefant, der davonlief.)

Shankar's Award

This award is named after the founder and executive trustee of the Children's Book Trust, Mr. K. Shankar Pillai, and is given to outstanding books published for children. This gold medal was awarded for the first time in 1979 to mark the International Year of the Child.

Der Preis hat seinen Namen nach dem Gründer und dem Treuhänder des Children's Book Trust, K. Shankar Pillai. Er wird für ein außergewöhnliches Kinderbuch verliehen. Die Goldmedaille wurde 1979 zum Internationalen Jahr des Kindes zum erstenmal vergeben.

1979 Datta, Arup Kumar: **The Kaziranga Trail.** (Der *Kaziranga Pfad.*) Ill.: Jagdish Joshi.
New Delhi: Children's Book Trust 1979.

1980 The prize was not given; Der Preis wurde nicht vergeben.

1981 The prize was not given; Der Preis wurde nicht vergeben.

Indian National Government Children's Literature Prizes

From the year 1955, the National Government of India started a programme for awarding prizes to the best books published for children (text books excluded). A committe of experts examines the books and manuscriptes received from authors and publishers, selecting the best books from all languages officially recognized by the Indian constitution (14 in number).

After the 14th competition it was noticed that the number of entries decreased; because of this, the government decided to discontinue the prize. After one year, however, the scheme was revived and the 15th competition was held in 1970.

The prize winning books along with the names of the authors are given below, by year.

(Note: Complete bibliographical data is lacking in these prize listings due to difficulties in obtaining the necessary information by the time this publication went to press. It is hoped that this problem will be rectified in the next edition.)

Lit.: Dey, Provash Ronjan: Children's literature of India. Calcutta: Academy for Documention and Research on Children's Literature 1977. 56 p.

Im Jahre 1955 begann die indische Regierung, die besten Kinderbücher — ausgenommen sind Schulbücher — zu prämieren. Eine Jury begutachtet alle Bücher und Manuskripte, die von Autoren und Verlegern eingereicht werden, und berücksichtigt dabei alle in der indischen Verfassung anerkannten Sprachen (insgesamt 14).

Nach dem 14. Wettbewerb stellte man fest, daß die Zahl der eingereichten Werke sank und daher beschloß die indische Regierung den Preis nicht mehr zu vergeben. Aber nach einem Jahr wurde der Wettbewerb erneut ins Leben gerufen und 1970 zum 15. mal veranstaltet.

Die Titel der prämierten Bücher und die Namen der Autoren werden nachfolgend chronologisch aufgeführt.

(Vollständige bibliographische Angaben zu diesem Preis fehlen leider, da bis zum Redaktionsschluß die nötigen Informationen nicht vorlagen. Wir hoffen, diese Angaben in der nächsten Auflage nachtragen zu können.)

Lit.: Dey, Provash Ronjan: Children's literature of India. Calcutta: Academy for Documentation and Research on Children's Literature 1977. 56p.

Assamese language/Assamesische Sprache

1955 Baxbarua, N.B.: **Junuka.**

1956 The prize was not given; Der Preis wurde nicht vergeben.

1957 Bakthakur, Dulal Ch.: **Ghumati jaiore.**
Barua, Naba Kanta: **Akharar jakhala.**

1958 Das, Hargovinda: **Sonar putalee.**
Sarma, H.N.: (*Ashoka.*)

1959 Bordoloi, Smt. Nirmal.: **Chil chil chial begi.**
Goswami, P.C.: **Phular sadhu.**

1960 Das, D.N.: **Adim zugar adi khata.**
Goswami, P.C.: **Jantur sadhu.**

1961 Sakia, Jogindra Nath: **Potanger katha.**
Shastri, Biswanarayan: **Nair sadhu.**

1962 Das, Bhuban Mohan: **Amar dore sinhote manab.**
Shastri, biswanarayan: **Sagorika.**

1963 Barua. Birinchi Kumar: **Jataka mala.**
1964 Mahanta, Smt. Punya Probha: **Daktar kaka.**
1965 Kalita, Haren: **Akasar katha.**
1966 Sharma, Harendra Nath: **Samay balir khojbor.**
1967 Tamuli, Santanu: **Mani bani aru akan phulani.**
1968 Chowdhury, Amikwapada: **Kalida.**
1969 The prize was not given; Der Preis wurde nicht vergeben.
1970 Kalitha, Harendra Nath: **Prithivir sadhu.**
1971 The prize was not given; Der Preis wurde nicht vergeben.
1972 Saikis, Nanda: **Desh videshor akoni.**
1973 Tamuli, Santanu: **Sarisrip.**
1974 Medhi, B.K.: **Ekhan desh alakh manush.**
1975 The prize was not given; Der Preis wurde nicht vergeben.
1976 Chowdhury, Mohan: **Bhuglar chirijan bikhyati.**

Bengali language/Bengalische Sprache

1955 Rao, Smt. Sukhalata: **Galpa aro galpa.**
Roy, Sukumar: **Pagla dasu.**
1956 Tagore, Abanindranath: **Sakuntala.**
Tagore, Rabindranath: **Chitra bichitra.**
1957 Mitra, Premendranath: **Ghanadar galpa.**
Rao, Smt. Sukhalata: **Nije parha.**
1958 Ghosh, Bimal: **Nakal nengti ghenga benga.**
Chakraborty, Saila: **Gari ghorar galpa.**
1959 Mazumder, Smt. Lila: **Halday pakhir palak.**
Chakraborta, Saila: **Manush elo kotha hotey.**
Acharya, Syama Prasad: **Tel non kadi.**
1960 Ghosh, Mohit: **Tapur tupur.**
Chakraborty, Purna: **Chobitey Mahabharat.**
Banerjee, Saradindu: **Sadasiver tin kanda.**
1961 Gupta, Amulya Bhusan: **Choto holayo chote nai.**
Chakraborty, Mon Mohan: **Chabite prithibi.**
Chakraborta, Saila: **Chotoder craft.**
1962 Chattopadhya, Dinesh: **Bhayankarer jiban katha.**
Gautam, Nirmalendu: **Khalagharer rajya.**
Mitra, Siva Sankar: **Sundarban.**

1963 Chakraborty, Amiya: **Chalo jai.**
1964 Dasgupta, Sashi Bhusan: **Chotader vyashadev rachita Mahabharat.**
Rao, Smt. Sukhalata: **Nanan desher Rupkatha.**
1965 Roy, Amar Nath: **Jhan bijnaner galpa.**
1966 Roy, Satyajit: **Professor Shanku.** (Professor *Shanku.*)
1967 Ghosh, Sailen: **Mitul.**
1968 Chakraborty, Nani Gopal: **Amader pratibesi keet patnaga.**
1969 The prize was not given; Der Preis wurde nicht vergeben.
1970 Guha, Mritunjoy: **Cholo jai chander deshey.**
1971 The prize was not given; Der Preis wurde nicht vergeben.
1972 Roy, sunirmal: **Jivoner bishmay.**
1973 Roy, Robidas Saha: **Amader bharat ratna Indira.**
1974 Roy, Robidas Saha: **Lenin.** (*Lenin*).
1975 The prize was not given; Der Preis wurde nicht vergeben.
1976 Mitra, Khagendra Nath: **Soumanta.**

Gujarati language/Gujaratische Sprache

1956 Jodhani, Manubhai: **Angana parkhi.**
Soni, Ramanlal: **Huen Tsang.**
1957 Jodhani, Manubhai: **Padarna pankhi.**
Soni, Ramanlal: **Pashu-no-kakko.**
1958 Patel, Somabhai: **Pimpi.**
1959 Sariya, Annie Chandrakant: **Tareliya.**
Dave, Balmukand: **Son champson.**
1960 Desai, Jaibhiku B.V.: **Dilna diwa.**
Shridharani, K.L.: **Hathrasno halthi.**
1961 Desai, Jaibhuku B.V.: **Sidhraj Jaya Singh.**
Kalarathi, Mukulbhai: **Ba ape Bapu.**
1962 Charya, Jitendra: **Geet gurjari.**
Desai, Jaibhiku B.V.: **Pali parwala.**
1963 Soni, Ramanlal: **Khavandavina khavum.**
1964 Desai, Jitendra: **Gandhi Bapu.** (*Gandhi Bapu.*)
Mangaldas, Leena: **Ek-ajab-gajab-nu-bulbul.**
1965 Gandhi, Manuben: **Virat sarshan.**
1966 Desai, Balabhai Virchand: **Hirani Khan.**

1967 Pavri, Soli/Shah, Rasik: **Sacharachar-ne-dhara khanchati.**
1968 Shah, Rasik: **Shakteepunja parmanu.**
1969 The prize was not given; Der Preis wurde nicht vergeben.
1970 Desai, Kumarpal: **Kedi katari khabhe dhal.**
1971 The prize was not given; Der Preis wurde nicht vergeben.
1972 Raval, Panditrao: **Sri Aravindayan.** (Sri *Aravindayan.*)
1973 Jadav, J.D.: **Apna kasabio.**
1974 Desai, Kumarpal: **Mot ne hath tali.**
1975 The prize was not given; Der Preis wurde nicht vergeben.
1976 The prize was not given; Der Preis wurde nicht vergeben.

Hindi language/Hindi Sprache

1955 Leaf, Munro: **Sachi nagrikta.**
Benipuri, Ram Briksha: **Bete hon to aise.**
Dinkar, Ramdhari Singa: **Mirch ka maza.**
Pandey, Ramniranjan: **Gaon ki kahaniyan.**
Nautiyal, Santosh Narayan: **Chandan mama ka dosh.**
Jain, Sri Chand: **Vindhya bhoomi ki lok khathayan.**
Sharma, Shree Ram: **Balakan ki kahaniyan.**
Majil, Valleru: **Nanhay langoor ki kahani.**
1956 Kaushal, Ganga Prasad: **Veer balak.**
Saran, Govinda: **Gharaunda.**
Narayan: **Hanshi khushi.**
Bhushan, Satyan/Shobharani: **Vigyan darshan chitrawali.**
Singh, Suresh: **Jivon ki duniya.**
Shankar, Uma: **Science ke kahaniyan.**
1957 Gupta, Brahma Nand: **Prakash ki baten.**
Chowdhari, Braj Rai: **Chitra-me-ek-do-tin-char.**
Dutta, Rudra: **Hamare pakshi.**
Misra, Smt. Sharoda: **Neelan-aur-mashari-ki-devi.**
Dwiveda, Schanlal: **Doodh batasha.**
1958 Razak, Abdul: **Hawa ki zabani.**
Jain, Nandlal: **Jar jagat ki kahaniyan.**
Tewari, Ramchandra: **Aao kren sawari.**
Mishra, Rudra Dutta: **Phool khilai hain dali dali.**

Vatsa, Shivmurti Singh: **Nat khat chun cnun.**

Mukhi, Smt. Suraj: **Dharti mata.**

1959 Shastri, Dharampal: **Ankur ka sapna.**

Garg, Kishore: **Sansar ke chirya Ghar. Main.**

Varma, R.C.: **Ghari kaise bani.**

Mishra, Smt. Sharda: **Carom board ki pariyan.**

1960 Sagar, Keshav: **Aag ki kahani.**

Sinha, Rajeshwar Prasad: **Hamare pakshi.**

Tyagi, Ram Avtar: **Main dilli hoon.**

1961 Shastri, Dharampal: **Duniya ke Acharya.**

Sagar, Keshav: **Awaz.**

Sing, Rajeshwar Narain: **Hamare venya pashu.**

Tiwari, Ramchad: **Apna desh.**

1962 Bandhu, Gupta: **Hawai ghora.**

Sagar, Keshav: **Pani.**

Awasthi, Rajendra: **Chota bari lahar.**

Vyas, Shavam Sundar: **Muthavaron ke mela.**

Bhai, Tarun: **Jal char.**

1963 Duraswami, H.: **Nani ki kahani.**

Verma, Smt. Savitri Devi: **Yeh ran bankure.**

1964 Bandhu, Gupta: **Kudarati cemara.**

Sheel, Ratna Prakash: **Vigyan ki kahaniyan.**

Hriday, Vyathit: **Main hawa hoon.**

Lalle, Yogendra: **Sare jahan se achha.**

1965 Singh, Ramji: **Bachon-ke-liye chumbuk.**

Kumar, Jitendra: **Dunia-ke-sat mahan asacharyon ki kahani.**

1966 Aggarwal, Sneh: **Aisey the cha cha Nehru.**

Singh, Ramji: **Bachon ke liye dhwani.**

1967 Jain, Shaken: **Tik tik tun tun.**

Mitra, Ved: **durbeen ki kahani.**

1968 Bharti, Jai Prakash: **Chalo chand par chalen.**

Mitra, Ved: **Vigyan ke jharokhe se tumhari duniya.**

1969 The prize was not given; Der Preis wurde nicht vergeben.

1970 Prakasan, Shakuu: **Sunoo ram ki katha.**

Joshi, Hem Chander: **Suraj aur uska pariwar.**

1971 The prize was not awarded; Der Preis wurde nicht vergeben.
1972 Krishan, Sri: **Desh videsh ke anokhe thevar.**
Verma, Manchar: Janwaren ke interview.
1973 Saxena, Dayal Sarveshwar Dayal: **Batuta ka juta.**
Nagar, Amrit Lal: **Bajrangi smuggleron ke phande me.**
1974 Baigar, A.: **Bharat mera desh.**
Bagga, K.: **Maharaja Ranjit Singh.** (Maharaja *Ranjit Singh.*)
1975 The prize was not given; Der Preis wurde nicht vergeben.
1976 Prasad, Sri: **Mera sasthi ghora.**
Rahi, Bal Swarrop: **Dadi amma mujhe batao.**

Kannada language/Kannadische Sprache

1956 Rao, Raja: **Makala sachitra ganita.**
Murthy, G.A. Narasimha: **Sachitra balaramayan.**
1957 Baliga, Damodar: **Namma bumi.**
1958 Alankar, Ashalata: **Munni maduve.**
1959 Vankataram, N.S.: **Sanka chithragalu.**
1960 The prize was not given; Der Preis wurde nicht vergeben.
1961 Kamalapur, J.N: **Nanu nari.**
Iyengar, H.L. Narasimha: **Vidu yava mara.**
1962 Hirematha, Gurpada Swami: **Halina gindi.**
Kamalapur, J.N.: **Harada mathu haruua paranigalu.**
1963 Sangamosh, Shishu: **Nanna mane.**
1964 Vittelsenoi, K.: **Vinoda.**
Kumara, Sashi: **Navu geleyaru.**
1965 Puranik, Siddayya: **Thuppa rotti ge ge ge.**
1966 Kumara, Sashi: **Chandranna mela ilidaru.**
1967 Kamalapur, J.N.: **Abba E.E. Puttaprmigalu.**
1968 Sangamesh, Sisu: **Nanna gelia japanado tara.**
1969 The prize was not given; Der Preis wurde nicht vergeben.
1970 Pukkamma, B.S.: **Papu ammanige halida kathegalu.**
1971 The prize was not given; Der Preis wurde nicht vergeben.
1972 Kumara, Sashi: **Minuguthare.**
1973 Mitra, Madav: **Nana hejjegalu.**
1974 Mitra, Madav: **Samrat ashok.**

1975 The prize was not given; Der Preis wurde nicht vergeben.
1976 Belagali, D.N.: **Badukuva bayake.**

Kashmiri language/Kashmiri Sprache

1959 Bhat, Shambhu: **Bala yar.**
1960 Kaul, Sankar Nath: **March pipin ta chanchipoot.**
1967 Sadhu, S.L.: **Don Quixote.** (Den *Quixote;* Don *Quichote.*)

Malayalam language/Malayalam Sprache

1955 Kurup, Sankara: **Elam chaundukal.**
1956 Ikkarama, A.: **Bala katha kal.**
1957 John, T.V.: **Onappakky.**
1958 Sethunath, K.G.: **Talappoli.**
John, T.V.: **Painkilli.**
1959 Sethunath, K.G.: **Nallalokam.**
1960 Pillai, K.N.: **Anakkaran.**
1961 Parameshwara, Evoor: **Pookalam.**
Narayanan, R.K.: **Rajavum katupopthum.**
1962 Basil, K.P. Alex: **Sindha avaludae katha pareyunnu.**
1963 Kesvan, Niranam M.P.: **Oru Karahaka balante atmakatha.**
1964 John, T.V.: **Idiyum minnalum.**
John, T.V.: **Kuttikalude indraprastham.**
1965 Namburdippad, O.P.: **Vimanam.**
1966 Narendranath, P.: **Kunhikoonan.**
1967 Balakrishnan, Tajamma: **Aadarshya jeevikalute.**
1968 Shah, Rasik: **Manushyan karangil ninno pisara.**
1969 The prize was not given; Der Preis wurde nicht vergeben.
1970 Devedas, Kumarapuram: **Poompattakal.**
1971 The prize was not given; Der Preis wurde nicht vergeben.
1972 John, T.V.: **Poochakku manikettiyathru.**
1973 Elias, P.: **Arun.**
1974 Karanawar, G.: **Namukku chuttarnulla.**
1975 The prize was not given; Der Preis wurde nicht vergeben.
1976 Marath, E.K.R.P.: **Kathamaduri.**
Prabhu, S.B.: **Satav wadiche lahanya.**

Marathi language/Marathi Sprache

1956 Bhagwat, B.R.: **Chandrawar sawari.**
Bhagwat, Lilavati: **Ghoda chalayala tap tap tap.**
1957 Dandikar, G.N.: **Bhilla vir kaliyngha.**
Paigaonkar, Smt. Sumati: **Badutaicha kak kak.**
1958 Paigaonkar, Smt. Sumati: **Minichi bahuli.**
Deshpande, P.L.: **Nava Gokul.**
1959 Rangnekar, Smt. Kumudani: **Bhartiya san va vtsav vaisakh.**
Shukla, N.G.: **Dulu dulu.**
1960 Patil, G.H.: **Pankharanchi shala.**
Hagaole, Leeladhar: **Pachuchen bet.**
Paigaonkar, Smt. Sumati: **Rangaonchi asagagadi.**
1961 Paranjpye, Sai: **Shepticha shap.**
Gavankar, V.S.: **Kokilecha dad.**
1962 Karandikar, Vinda: **Ekada kaya zale.**
Paranjpye, Sai: **Zali kasy gammat.**
Kakkar, M.G.: **Atpat nagarat.**
1963 Karandikar, G.V.: **Sashache kan.**
Mangalvedekar, Raja: **Bahurupi.**
1964 Champhekar, S.G.: **Bharatache paramavir.**
Bhagwat, Smt. Duraga: **Ranzara.**
1965 Mudgalkar, C.D.: **De tali ga gha tali.**
1966 Karandikar, G.V.: **Pari ga pari.**
1967 Dharap, Narayan Gopal: **Gogramacha chutar.**
1968 Begul, Devidas: **Pisara.**
1969 The prize was not given; Der Preis wurde nicht vergeben.
1970 Prabhu, Sudhakar: **Prani swatantra sale.**
1971 The prize was not given; Der Preis wurde nicht vergeben.
1972 Shirolkan, Smt. Shymala: **Ja udani pakhara.**
1973 Magalwedhekar, Raja: **Mukya.**
1974 Shirolkan, Smt. Shymala: **Chmbalechi mule.**

Oriya language/Oriya Sprache

1955 Tripathy, Pandit Upendra: **Ghanti ghangudi.**
1956 Devi, Bidyut Prava: **Jahakiv jiye.**
Mahapatra, Chakradhar: **Baghammamura chatasali.**

1957 Sarongi, Vidyanath: **Kutu kutu.**

1958 Senapati, A.M: **Duradeshara pilanka katha.**
Mahapatra, Godabarish: **Mo khela sathi.**

1959 Patnaik, Durga Prasad: **Tuao tuninka ghara.**
Mohanty, Jaykrishna: **Botia jatra.**

1960 Patnaik, Durga Prasad: **Tanka nua chara.**
Devi, Smt. Punnya Prava: **Kalia balada gala gala.**

1961 Patnaik, Durga Prasad: **Tapnera sapna.**
Acharya, Shantanu: **Kokatagbada katta kane.**

1962 Patnaik, Durga Prasad: **Langula banka gotina thina pila.**
Mohanty, Jagannath: **Jete salekhile kukur.**

1963 Archarya, Shantanu: **Akadaka satati pahacha.**

1964 Tripathi, Upendra: **Pilanke pasu pakhi purana.**

1965 Patnaik, Durga Prasad: **Nai bahila.**

1966 Bohura, Basanta Kumar: **Odisara benga.**

1967 Patnaik, Ananta: **Chhabitiki gabatie.**

1968 Patnaik, Anand: **Saltukutuku surajatia kiashe.**

1969 The prize was not given; Der Preis wurde nicht vergeben.

1970 Patnaik, Durga Prasad: **Bhoca teya.**

1971 The prize was not given; Der Preis wurde nicht vergeben.

1972 Behura, B.K.: **Dinosaur.**

1973 Mohanty, Mahaswar: **Chabbi kahuchi katha.**

Punjabi language/Punjabi Sprache

1956 Kaur, Bhagwat: **Chiri te gulela.**
Singh, Sohan: **Raj kumar sumer.**

1957 Ahluwalia, R.S.: **Vichari Everest.**

1958 Singh, Gurbachan: **Aag di kahani.**

1959 Gyani, Lal Singh: **Sunahri kukar.**

1960 Deepak, Avtar Singh: **Tasweeran boldian.**
Giani, Bal Singh: **Gulab kurani.**

1961 Singh, Gurbachan: **Moti-di-kahani.**
Ahluwalia, R.S.: **Kathputla.**

1962 Kaur, Smt. Anwant: **Sahid di makhi.**
Kapur, Krishan: **Bharat de mahan kavi.**

1963 Depak, Avtar Singh/Singh, Harinder: **Ghar ghar bole radio.**

1964 Singh, Gurbachan: **Chanan di kahani.**
Amole, S.S.: **Jal parian.**
1965 Amole, S.S.: **Annmulli dat.**
1966 Bali, Baljit Singh: **Morr sa da qaumi panchchi.**
1967 Singh, Harbinder: **Pullar yug ate rocket.**
1968 Sithal, Dhanwant Singh: **Dharti ke shingar.**
1969 The prize was not given; Der Preis wurde nicht vergeben.
1970 Sithal, Dhanwant Singh: **Dharti da parwar.**

Sindhi language/Sindhi Sprache

1957 Mahboobani, Govardhan: **Latiyoon.**
1958 Hiranand, Parasram: **Baugh bhar.**
1959 The prize was not given; Der Preis wurde nicht vergeben.
1960 Gogia, J.K.: **Dadi joon akhaniyoon.**
1961 Vaswani, Fatehchand: **Bharat darshan.**
1962 Mahboobani, Govardhan: **Naeen basti.**
1963 The prize was not given; Der Preis wurde nicht vergeben.
1964 Kauromal, Manohar Das: **Chanchita.**
Hans, Lekhraj: **Dadia ji dat.**
1965 Bhatia, Lachman: **Hikro hyo raja.**
1966 Deepchandra: **Jawahar darshan.**
1967 Bhambard, Lachman: **Murkandar makhayoon.**
1968 Bramachari, Prabhudas: **Bapu darshan.**
1969 The prize was not given; Der Preis wurde nicht vergeben.
1970 The prize was not given; Der Preis wurde nicht vergeben.
1971 The prize was not given; Der Preis wurde nicht vergeben.
1972 Asha, Dayal: **Dada darshan.**
1973 Prakash, Moti: **Gulran ja geet.**
1974 Bedi, A.: **Jhirmir.**
1975 The prize was not awarded; Der Preis wurde nicht vergeben.
1976 Parumal: **Vigvan jyoti.**

Tamil language/Tamil Sprache

1955 Nagarajan, N.K.: **Ramuvum nauum.**
1956 Vallippa, A.L.: **Malarum ullam.**
1957 Nagarajan, N.K.: **Kashthuriyin.**

1958 Gopalakrishan, Kalvi: **Parakkum pappa.**
1959 Srinavasan, Thambi: **Thanga kuzhandaigal.**
Rae, S. Krishna: **Pakshi patalu.**
1960 Thilakavathi A.: **Tagorin vacznile.**
Sivakithu, M.: **Muthu padalgal.**
Vajeswari, R.: **Goutimma Buddhar.** (*Gautama Buddha*; *Gautama Buddha*.)
1961 Mudalai, S.V. Duraiswamy: **Azhagana.**
Gopalkrishan, V.D.: **Kaverien anbu.**
1962 Gopalakrishan, Kalvi: **Manth avathiyin magan.**
Vanamamalai, N.: **Rubborin kathai.**
1963 Muthukrishan, P.A.: **Kuzhanthalp paakkal.**
1964 Gopalakrishan, Kalvi: **Pandaya ulgil parakkum pappa.**
1965 Muthu, Puvannan Chathiram: **Pulavar magan.**
Paramthaman, A.K.: **Engal thottam.**
1966 Subramanian, Vai: **Nehruvin kathai.**
1967 Kaliyaperumal, T.S.: **Nadu katha mnallavargal.**
1968 Aiyaswami, R.: **Balaramayanam.**
1969 The prize was not awarded; Der Preis wurde nicht vergeben.
1970 Valliappa, A.L.: **Patile Gandhi kathai.**
1971 The prize was not awarded; Der Preis wurde nicht vergeben.
1972 T.J.R.: **Kokarakko.**
1973 Subramaniam, S.: **Helicopter in kathai.**
1974 Soundarasajan, S.: **Nalla kaigal.**

Telugu language/Telugu Sprache

1955 Dikshatalu, Chinta: **Lekka pidthalu.**
Rao, Kavi: **Boomarillu.**
Bapineedu, M.: **Pillala bonmala bharatan.**
1956 Venkata, Gadyau: **Balanandam.**
Raghavarao, Nayapathi: **Badi ganta.**
1957 Krishna, Natraj Rama: **Narantana bala.**
1958 Rao, B.V. Narasimha: **Palabadi patalu.**
Suramanayam, Varanasi: **Janthuprapanchamu.**
1959 Rao, A. Lakshma: **Chilukamma chuttalu.**

1960 Rao, S.L. Narasimha: **Janthu purham.**
Rao, Vedula Kameswara: **Bommala Goutam Buddhu.**
Rao, Vissa Appa: **Akasam.**
1961 Rao, A.V.S. Rama: **Paramanu.**
Narasimhachari, K.: **Biddala caotipanal.**
1962 Rao, A.V.S. Rama: **Antarikshavijayam.**
Ramkrishna, Natraja: **Nartanaseema.**
1963 Rao, A.V.S. Rama: **Viswa Rahasyam.**
1964 Kumari, Smt. D. Kanya: **Pagalu rathri.**
1965 Moorthy, B. Satyanarayana: **Balala bommalu Nehruji.**
1966 Sadananda, K.: **Bengaru nandichina baats.**
1967 Ramakrishna, Mataraj: **Narthana katha.**
1968 Lakshmipatirao, V.: **Swatantra bharti.**
1969 The prize was not given; Der Preis wurde nicht vergeben.
1970 Rao, M. Ramkrishna: **Rangu rangula ratana deepalu.**
1971 The prize was not given; Der Preis wurde nicht vergeben.
1972 Rao, A.V.S. Rama: **Chandralok yatra.**
1973 Raghviah, Reddy: **Galele prayanam.**
1974 Rao, A.V.S. Rama: **Akasani choodam.**
1975 The prize was not given; Der Preis wurde nicht vergeben.
1976 Rao, A.V.S. Rama: **Bal migyan kadhanidhi.**

Urdu language/Urdu Sprache

1955 Begum, Smt. Qudesia: **Gandhi baba ki kahani.**
1956 Saiyidain, Saheeda: **Aao dost benaye.**
1957 Naqvi, Safdar Abbas: **Hazaron baras men.**
Fayzee, Sultana Asaf: **Samandar ke kinare.**
1958 Bedi, Freda M.: **Ranga ke aur rang.**
1959 Mudholi, Abdul Ghaffar: **Camp pire ki naklen.**
Hussain, Smt. Saliha Abid: **Sonehre balonk bachchon ka desh.**
1960 Siddigi, Mohamad Ishq: **Chand ki kahani.**
Naqvi, Safdar Abbas: **Ojhal parda.**
1961 Parveez, Athar: **Khala ka safar.**
Hasan, Fasahat: **Hamri abad duniya.**
1962 Mudholi, Abdul Ghaffar: **Madrasa-i-ibtedai-ki-kahani.**
Ansari, Masood: **Hamare tagore.**

1963 Parveez, Athar: **Tawanai ka raaz.**
1964 Mudholi, Abdul Ghaffar: **Talibilm ki kahani.**
Zaidi, Smt. Kishwar: **Zameen se chand tak.**
1965 Mahrum, Tilck Chand: **Bachchon ki duniya.**
1966 Parveez, Athar: **Anmol ratan.**
1967 Parveez, Athat: **Hamara Hindusthan.**
1968 Siddiqui, Saeed Ahmed: **Lo ek kahani suno.**
1969 The prize was not given; Der Preis wurde nicht vergeben.
1970 Lall, Inder Jit: **Babbar sher ki kahani.**
1971 The prize was not given; Der Preis wurde nicht vergeben.
1972 Bharti, S.H.: **Doctor Zakir Hussain.** (Doctor *Zakir Hussain..*)
1973 Khaver, Mahmood: **Netaji subhash Chandra Bose.**
1974 The prize was not given; Der Preis wurde nicht vergeben.
1975 The prize was not given; Der Preis wurde nicht vergeben.
1976 Pravea, Athar: **Paucous aur janwaron ki duniya.**

Iran

Prize of the Iranian Children's Book Council

The Iranian Children's Book Council established this prize for children's and youth books in 1963. The prize, with a plaque bearing the title, "The Book of the Year", is awarded annually to authors, translators and illustrators.

The jury consists of twenty-five members selected from the following professional groups: teachers, editors, translators, specialists for children's books, librarians and authors. The jury works under the supervision of the officers of the Children's Book Council. The number of prizes awarded each year varies according to the number of books published meeting the standards of excellence set forth by the Council.

Das iranische "Kuratorium der Kinderbücher" stiftete 1963 einen Preis für Kinder- und Jugendbücher. Der Preis wird jährlich im Mai, samt einer Plakette mit der Aufschrift "Das Buch des Jahres" an Autoren, Übersetzer und Illustratoren verliehen.

Der Preis wird von einer Jury gewählt, die aus 25 Personen folgender Berufsgruppen besteht: Lehrern, Lektoren, Übersetzern, Bibliothekaren und Autoren. Die Jury arbeitet unter der Aufsicht eines der Präsidiumsmitglieder des Kuratoriums.

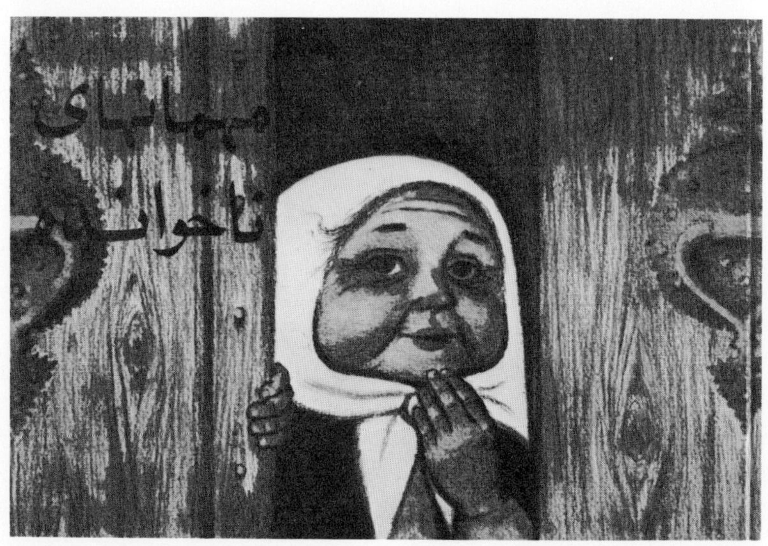

Ill. 23 Gudi Farmanfarmayian in F. Farǵam: Mihmanhay-i nahandah

Die Zahl der verliehenen Preis wechselt und hängt von dem qualitativen Angebot der Bücher ab.

1963 Fatḥ-Ā ǎzam, Hūšmand: **Qiṣṣah, Qiṣṣah.** (Tale, tale; Märchen, Märchen.) Ill.: Murtiḍā Mumaiyz.
Teheran: Bungāh-i tarǧumah wa našr-i kitab 1963.

Mirhadi, Fahimah: **Guftigūy-i dirahtān.** (Conversation of trees; Gespräch der Bäume.)
Teheran: Intišarāt-i murwārid 1963.

Translation/Übersetzung

Kiānūš, Pari for:
Thorn, Alice: **Madame Curie.** (Madame *Curie.*)
Teheran: Hānāh-i kitāb 1963.

Nikpur, Ardšir. for:
Valery, Giselle: **Dāstānhāy-i čini.** (Chinese tales; Chinesische Märchen.)
Teheran: Bungāh-i tarǧumah wa našr-i kitāb 1963.

Rušangar, Maǧid for:
Parker, Bertha Morris: **Abr wa bārān wa barf.** (Amer.orig.title: The cloud, the rain and the snow; Die Wolke, der Regen und der Schnee.)
Teheran: Ibn-i sinā 1963.

1964 Yazdi, Mihdi Ādar: **Qiṣṣah-hāy-i ḥūb.** (Nice tales; Schöne Märchen.)
Teheran: Amir Kabir 1964.

Translation/Übersetzung

eĀameri, Muhammed eĀli for:
Parker, Bertha Morris: **Kārhānah-i kaǧaḏsāzi.** (Plant factories; Pflanzenfabriken.)
Teheran: Ibn-i sina 1964.

eĀameri, Muhammed eĀli for:
Parker, Bertha Morris: Hurafāh ya eilm. (Superstition or science; Aberglaube oder Wissenschaft.)
Teheran: Ibn-i sinā 1964.

Arbāb, Rūhi for:
Bistroy, I.S.: **Dāstānhāy-i milal-i mašriqzamin.** (Tales of Oriental peoples; Märchen von orientalischen Völkern.)
Teheran: Bungāh-i tarǧumah wa našr-i kitab 1964.

1965 Šarif, eĀbbās Yamini: **Firi bah āsmān mirawad.** (**Firi** goes to the sky; *Firi* geht in den Himmel.)
Teheran: Amir Kabir 1965.

Translation/Übersetzung
Bahman for:
Prokofiev, Sergeji: **Peter wa gurg.** (*Peter* and the wolf; *Peter* und der Wolf; Russ.orig.title: *Petja* i volk.)
Teheran: Intišarāt-i padidah 1965.

Iman, Ruia for:
Anglund, Joan Walsh: **Kitab-i dusti wa muḥabbat.** (Eng.orig.title: A friend is someone who likes you; Ein Freund ist jemand der dich mag.)
Teheran: Ibn-i sinā 1965.

Nikpūr, Ardšir for:
Selter-Four, Helen: **Afsānah-hāy-i surhpustān.** (Tales of Indians; Märchen der Indianer.)
Teheran: Amir Kabir 1965.

1966 Farǧam, Faridah: **Mihmānhāy-i naḫāndah.** (The uninvited guests; Die ungeladenen Gäste.) Ill.: Gǧdi Farmānfarmayiān.
Teheran: Institute for the Intellectual Development of Children and Young Adults 1966.

Leon, Ruth: **Man čah hastam.** (What am I? Was bin ich?)
Teheran: Franklin 1966.

Yazdi, Mihdi Āḏar: **Bačah-i ădam.** (The man-child; Der Menschensohn.)
Teheran: Inišārāt-i ašrafi 1966.

Yazdi, Mihdi Āḏar: **Qiṣṣah-hāy-i qurān.** (The tales of the *Koran*; Die Märchen des *Koran*.)
Teheran: Āmir Kabir 1966.

Translation/Übersetzung
Marandi, Hasan for:
Ravielli, Anthony: **Šiguftihay-i tan-i adami.** (Eng.orig.title: Wonders of the human body; Die Wunder des menschlichen Körpers.)
Teheran: Amir Kabir 1966.

1967 Bahār, Mihrdād: **Ǧamšid šah.** (King *Gamsid*; König *Gamsid*.)
Ill.: Faršid Mitqali.
Teheran: Institute for the Intellectual Development of Children and Young Adults 1967.

Kasrāiy, Siāwuš: **Baed az zimistān dar ābādy-i mā.** (After winter in our village; Nach dem Winter in unserem Dorf.) Ill.: Hušang Maliknia.
Teheran: Institute for the Intellectual Development of Children and Young Adults 1967.

Translation/Übersetzung
Lālihzāri, Isḥaq for:
Drosher, Vitus: **Hawās asrārāmiz-i hiwānāt.** (Wonderful senses of animals; Wundersame Sinne der Tiere.)
Teheran: Intišārāt-i ašrafi 1967.

1968 Azad, Mušrif maḥmud (i.e. Maḥmud Mušrif Tihrāni): **Ṭouqi.** (Robin; Rotkehlchen.) Ill.: Nāhid Haqiqat.
Teheran: Institute for the Intellectual Development of children and Young Adults 1968.

Ibrāhimi, Nādir: **Dūr az ḫānah.** (Far from home; Weit vom Haus.) Ill.: Lili Nahāwandi.
Teheran: Institute for the Intellectual Development of Children and Young Adults 1968.

Bihrangi, Samad: **Māhy-i siāh-i kūčūlū.** (The little black fish; Der kleine schwarze Fisch.) Ill.: Faršid Miṯqali.
Teheran: Institute for the Intellectual Development of Children and Young Adults 1968.

Translation/Übersetzung
Irāni, Aḥmad for:
Sutherland, Lucile: **Safar bah faḍā.** (The journey in space; Die Reise ins All.)
Teheran: Intišārāt-i ḫārazmi 1968.

1969 Dulātābadi, Mahduht **Ǧumǧumak barg-i ḫazūn.** (The trembling autumn leaves; Die zitternden Herbstblätter.) Ill.: Parwiz Kalāntari.
Teheran: Intišārāt-i ǧibi 1969.

Hānlari, Zahrā: **Afsšnah-i símurġ.** (The legend of *Simurg*; Die Legende von *Simurg*.) Ill.: Nurudin Zarrinkilk.
Teheran: Intišārāt-i ǧibi 1969.

Kiānuš, Mahmud: **Ādam ya rūbah.** (The human of the fox; Der Mensch oder der Fuchs.)
Teheran: Intišārāt-i nil 1969.

Malāyari, Muhammad Haidari: **Šināḫt-i nūr.** (Knowledge about light; Kenntnisse über das Licht.)
Teheran: Bungāh-i tarǧumah wa našr-i kitāb 1969.

Nistāni, Manučihr: **Gul umad bahār umad.** (The coming of spring and flowers; Die Blumen und der Frühling kommen.) Ill.: Parwitz Kalāntari.
Teheran: Institute for the Intellectual Development of Children and Young Adults 1969.

Translation/Übersetzung
Dawāči, Parwin for:
McGregor, R.J.: **Karāghān-i ǧawān.** (Eng.orig.title: Young detectives; Junǧe Detektive.)
Teheran: Bunǧāh-i tarǧumah wa našr-i kitāb 1969.
Dulatābādi, Mahduht for:
Selam, May Sai̇̌nt: **Yik ǧāy-i Pa, du ǧāy-i Pā.** (One footprint, two footprints; Eine Fußspur, zwei Fußspuren.)
Teheran: Intišārāt-i bank-i sādirāt 1969.

1970 Āšūri, Dariūš: **Pul wa iqtisad.** (Money and economy; Geld und Wirtschaft.) Ill.: Nafisah Riāḫi.
Teheran: Institute for the Intellectual Development of Children and Young Adults 1970.
Baǧčah-bān, Ǧabbār: **Baba barfi.** (Daddy *Snowman; Schneevater.*) Ill.: Alan Biāš.
Teheran: Institute for the Intellectual Development of Children and Young Adults 1970.

Translation/Übersetzung
Dulatābādi, Mahduḫt for:
Clymer, Eleanor: **Ďar ǧustiǧūy-i fusil-i zindah.** (Eng.orig.title: Search for a living fossil; Auf der Suche nach lebenden Fossilien.)
Teheran: Ibn-i sinā 1970.
Garawi, Hamide for:
Wyler, Rose: **Dāstān-i ǎṣr-i yahbandan.** (The story of the ice age; Die Geschichte von der Eiszeit; Amer.orig.title: The ice age.)
Teheran: Ibn-i sinä 1970.
Hirḫah, eĀbbās for:
Highland, Esther Harris/Highland, Harold Joseph: **Šiguftihāy-i riādiāt.** (The wonder of mathematics; Die Wunder der Mathematik; Eng.orig.title: Mathematics.)
Teheran: Amir Kabir 1970.
Rūḫi, Hūma for:
Sperry, Armstrong: **In rā miguyand šuǧā eāt.** (Amer.orig.title: Call it courage; Nenn es Mut.)
Teheran: Amir Kabir 1970.
Ṣulhǧū, Ǎli for:
Mason, Miriam E.: **Ḥāhar-i wasaṭi.** (Eng.orig.title: The middle sister; Die mittlere Schwester.)
Teheran: Ibn-i sina 1970.

1971 Kišāwarz, Karim: **Yāddāšthāy-i ḥasanak yazdi.** (News from *Hasanak Yazdi*; Neuigkeiten von *Hasanak Yazdi.*)
Teheran: Institute for the Intellectual Development of Children and Young Adults 1971.

Translation/Übersetzung
Amiršāhi, Mahšid for:
White, Elwyn Brooks: **Kartunak šarlut.** (Amer.orig.title: *Charlotte's* web; Schweinchen *Wilbur* und seine Freunde.)
Teheran: Intišārāt-i ǧibi 1971.

Atašī, Manučihr for:
O'Dell, Scott: **Ǧazirah-i dilfinhāy-i ābirang.** (Amer.orig.title: Island of the blue delphins; Insel der blauen Delphine.)
Teheran: Intišārāt-i ǧibi 1971.

Imāmi, Guli for:
Lindgren, Astrid: **Pippe ǧurāb buland.** (*Pippi Longstocking; Pippi Langstrumpf;* Swed.orig.title: *Pippi Langstrump.*)
Teheran: Intišārāt-i ǧibi 1971.

Qahramān, D. for:
Fonvilliers, George: **Kudak, sarbāz wa daryā.** (The child, the soldier and the sea; Das Kind, der Soldat und das Meer; Fr.orig.title: L'enfant, le soldat et la mer.)
Teheran: Institute for the Intellectual Development of Children and Young Adults 1971.

Taraqi, Guli for:
Carlson, Natalie Savage: **Ḫaniwādah zir-i pul.** (Amer.orig.title: The family under the bridge; Die Familie unter der Brücke.)
Teheran: Intišārāt-i ǧibi 1971.

1972 Baiḍāiy, Bahram: **Haqiqat wa mard-i dānā.** (The truth and the wise man; Die Wahrheit und der Weise.) Ill.: Murtiḍā Mumaiyz.
Teheran: Institute for the Intellectual Development of Children and Young Adults 1972.

Qāḍinūr, Qudsi: **Du parandah.** (Two birds; Zwei Vögel.) Ill.: Qudsi Qāḍinūr.
Teheran: Sāzimān-i hamgam 1972.

Translation/Übersetzung
Ibrāhimi, Farzanah for:
Part, Judy: **Čira ǧāniwarān nabāyad libās bispušand.** (Why shouldn't animals wear clothes? Warum sollen Tiere keine Kleider tragen?)
Teheran: Sāzimān-i hamgam 1972.

Ibrāhimi, Nādir for:
Hughes, Ted: **Ādam-i āhani.** (Eng.orig.title: The iron man; Der Eisenmann.)
Teheran: Sāzimān-i hamgam 1972.

Haqiqi, Ibrāhim for:
Lebuda: **Hamahči bā qiči.** (All things with the scissors; Alles mit der Schere.)
Teheran: Intišārāt-i ǧibi 1972.

1973 Qāḍinur, Qudsi: **Ārizū.** (The wish; Der Wunsch.)
Teheran: Intišārāt-i gulšāiy 1973.

Translation/Übersetzung
Tusi, Ahmad for:
Day, Beth/Liley, H. Margaret: **Duniāy-i pinhān-i kudak.** (The secret world of the baby; Die geheime Welt des Kleinkindes.)
Teheran: Institute for the Intellectual Development of Children and Young Adults 1973.

1974 Baǧčik-ban, Tamin: **Nurūzhā wa bādbādakhā.** (*Nuruzha* and the kites; *Nuruzha* und die Drachen.) Ill.: Nurriddin Zarrinkilk.
Teheran: Institute for the Intellectual Development of Children and Young Adults 1974.

Zarrinkilk, Nurridin: **Waqti kah man bačih būdam.** (When I was a child; Als ich ein Kind war.) Ill.: Farhang Zarrinkilk.
Teheran: Institute for the Intellectual Development of Children and Young Adults 1974.

Israel

Lamdan Prize

This award was founded in 1954 by the municipality of Ramat-Gan and named in honour of the famous poet and editor, Yitzhak Lamdan (1899—1954). The prize is awarded annually to a deserving children's book, selected by a jury composed of representatives of the Israeli Writers' Association and the municipality of Ramat-Gan.

Der Preis wurde 1954 zu Ehren des berühmten Dichters und Herausgebers Yitzhak Lamdan (1899—1954) von der Stadt Ramat-Gan gestiftet. Eine Jury die sich aus Mitgliedern der Schriftstellervereinigung Israel und der Stadtverwaltung Ramat-Gan zusammensetzt, vergibt jährlich den Preis an ein hervorragendes Kinderbuch.

1954 Stavi, Moshe: **Ba-derekh le'ereẓ ha-ośer.** (On the way to the land of happiness; Unterwegs ins Land des Glückes.) Ill.: Bina Gvirtz. Tel Aviv: Sreberk 1953.

1955 Axelrad, Gurit: **Sin, Sung veani.** (China, *Sung* and I; China, *Sung* und ich.) Ill.: Gurit Axelrad. Ramat-Gan: Massada 1954.

Ill. 24 Nahum Guttman in M. Meir: Ani oher le-zayer

Naḥmani, Ḥayim Simḥa: **Harpatkot Sasson veGiora.** (The adventures of *Sasson* and *Giora*; Die Abenteuer von *Sasson* und *Giora.*) Ill.: Lidia Wolpert.
Tel Aviv: Chachik 1955.

1956 Ḥurgin, Yaakov: **Yahalem hapla'im.** (The wonderful diamond; Der wundervolle Diamant.) Ill.: Isah Hershkovitz.
Tel Aviv: Amichai 1955.

Talmi, Menaḥem: **Be'oz ruḥam.** (With their courage; Mit ihrem Mut.) Ill.: Arie Moskovitz.
Tel Aviv: Amichai 1956.

1957 Dagon, Barukh: **Kanaf el kanaf.** (Wing to wing; Flügel zu Flügel.) Photos.
Tel Aviv: Am Oved 1956.

Guttman, Naḥum: **Ha-hofeš hagadol.** (The great summer holiday; Die großen Sommerferien.) Ill.: Naḥum Guttman.
Tel Aviv: Am Oved 1957.

1958 Zawiri, Ẓevi: **Harpatkot Yuval.** (The adventures of *Yuval*; Die Abenteuer von *Yuval.*) Ill.: Naḥum Guttman.
Tel Aviv: Hakibbutz Hameuchad 1957.

Weinberg, Avraham: **Me'atim mul Rabim.** (Few against many; Einige gegen viele.) Ill.: Z. Gera.
Tel Aviv: Ma'arakhot 1958.

1959 Smilanski, Yizhar: **Beraglain Yeḥefot.** (Barefoot; Barfuß.) Ill.: Naomi Woolman.
Jerusalem: Tarshish 1959.

1960 Yonatan, Natan: **Bein aviv le'anan.** (Between spring and cloud; Zwischen Frühling und Wolke.) Ill.: Moshe Gat.
Tel Aviv: Sifriat Po'alim 1960.

1961 The prize was not given; Der Preis wurde nicht vergeben.

1962 Meltzer, Samson: **Alef.** (*Alpha.*) Ill.: Naftali Bezem.
Tel Aviv: Dvir 1961.

1963 Orland, Yaakov: **Beit ha-ẓa ẓu'im.** (House of toys; Ein Haus voller Spielzeug.) Ill.: Ẓevi Meirovitz.
Haifa: Megillot 1962.

1964 Galai, Benjamin: **Atalefei Akko.** (Bats of *Acre*; Fledermäuse von *Acre.*) Ill.: Beẓalel Shatz.
Tel Aviv: Machbarot Lesifrut 1963.

1965 Ofek, Uriel: **MeRobinson ad Lobengulu.** (From *Robinson* to *Lobengulu*; Von *Robinson* zu *Lobengulu.*) Ill.
Ramat-Gan: Massada 1965.

1966 Ben-Shaul, Moshe: **Halonet la-šamayim.** (Windows to the sky; Fenster zum Himmel.) Ill.: Moshe Ben-Shaul.
Tel Aviv: Newman 1964.

1967 Bieber, Yoash: **Gagot adumin.** (Red roofs; Rote Dächer.) Ill.: Ora Ethan.
Ramat-Gan: Massada 1965.

1968 Omer, Deborah: **Sara giborat Nili.** (*Sara,* the heroine of *Nili*; *Sara,* die Heldin von *Nili.*) Ill.: Tirẓa Tannai.
Tel Aviv: Sreberk 1967.

1969 Hanani, Yosef: **Šeloša ḥavserim ve-ḥaver.** (Three friends and a pal; Drei Freunde und ein Kumpan.) Ill.: Hanna Adolphi.
Tel Aviv: Yavne 1968.

1970 Beẓer, Oded: **Ha-ẓanḥanit selo sava.** (The girl paratrooper who did not come back; Das Fallschirmmädchen, das nicht zurückkam.) Ill.: Amaẓia Kaẓ.
Tel Aviv: Sreberk 1969.

1971 Gluzman, Sara: **Ben hamozeg.** (The tavernkeeper's son; Der Sohn des Wirts.)
Tel Aviv: Sreberk 1970.

1972 Zer, Pnina: **Hayadid halohem.** (The fighting friend; Der kämpfende Freund.) Ill.: Milo Shor.
Tel Aviv: Am Oved 1971.

1973 Cohen, Adir: **Alon ba-sa'ar.** (An oak in the storm; Eine Eiche im Sturm.) Ill.: Saul Baskin.
Tel Aviv: Milo 1972.

1974 Keren, Rivka: **Kati: Yomanah šel na'ara.** (*Kati:* a young girl's diary; *Kati:* Tagebuch eines jungen Mädchen.)
Tel Aviv: Am Oved 1973.

1975 The prize was not given; Der Preis wurde nicht vergeben.

1976 Kipnis, Levin: **Mo'adei Israel.** (Israeli holidays; Festtage in Israel.) Ill.: Yaakov Guttman.
Tel Aviv: Simson 1975.

1977 Liebmann, Irena: **Piki ze ani.** (I am *Piki*; Ich bin *Piki.*)
Tel Aviv: Amichai 1976.

1978 Bar, Amos: **Poretz hamahsomin.** (The block breakers; Die Steinbrecher.) Ill.: Yaakov Guterman.
Tel Aviv: Sreberk 1977.

Yatziv Prize

The Yatziv Prize was founded in 1954 by the editorial board of the children's weekly, Davar Liladim, and named after the first editor of this magazine, Yitzhak Yatziv (1890—1947). The prize is awarded annually to a deserving contributor to this publication. In the following list, only those works are mentioned which have appeared in book form.

Der Preis wurde 1954 von den Herausgebern der Kinderzeitschrift Davar Liladim (wöchentliche Erscheinungsweise) vergeben. der Preis erhielt seinen Namen vom ersten Herausgeber dieser Zeitschrift: Yitzhak Yatziv (1890—1947). Er wird jährlich an einen hervorragenden Beitrag dieser Zeitschrift verliehen. In der folgenden Liste sind nur die Titel verzeichnet, die in Buchform erschienen sind.

1958 Saporta, Raphael: **Gan gurim.** (A garden of cubs; Ein Garten mit Tierkindern.) Ill.: Isah Hershkovitz.
Tel Aviv: Beẓalel 1957.

1959 Omer, Deborah: **Dapei Tamar.** (*Tamar's* a diary; *Tamars* Tagebuch.) Ill.: Hava Natan.
Tel Aviv: Amichai 1959.

1960 Agmon, David: **Gešem rišon.** (First rain; Der erste Regen.) Ill.: Ẓilla Binder.
Tel Aviv: Dvir 1959.

1961 Kashti, Mat'ama: **Hašemeš orit.** (Bright sun; Helle Sonne.) Ill.: Ora Czernov.
Tel Aviv: Yavne 1960.

1963 Ḥaviv, Yifraḥ: **Ma 'ase betarnegolei hodu.** (A tale about turkeys; Eine Geschichte über Truthähne.) Ill.: Yoram Kleiner.
Ramat-Gan: Massada 1963.

1965 Bieber, Yoash: **Hakrav hagadol.** (The great fight; Der große Kampf.) Ill.: Ora Ethan.
Tel Aviv: Yavne 1968.

1967 Ben-Shalom, Ẓevia: **Hu baraḥ min habayit.** (He ran away from home; Er rannte von zu Hause weg.) Ill.: Yehezkel Kimḥi.
Tel Aviv: sifriat Po' alim 1970.

1968 Gamzu, Yosi: **Lo roẓim lišon, roẓim lehištagea.** (We don't want to sleep, we want to have fun; Wir wollen nicht schlafen, wir wollen fröhlich sein.) Ill.: Micha Ullman.
Tel Aviv: Tsherikover 1969.

1969 Druker, Yigal: **Ha'agam baḥolot.** (The lake in the sand; Der See im Sand.) Ill.: Shraga Heller.
Tel Aviv: Massada 1970.

1970 Levin, Amos: **Be'ikvot hasusa halevana.** (In the footsteps of the white mare; Auf den Spuren des Schimmels.) Ill.: Ilana Machlia.
Tel Aviv: Massada 1971.

1971 Druker, Yigal: **Haḥan al hagiv'a.** (The barrack on the hill; Die Baracke auf dem Hügel.) Ill.: Tirẓa Tanni.
Tel Aviv: Milo 1972.

1972 Vishnitzer, Naomi: **Ḥaruz kachel šel Mazal.** (A blue bead of luck; Eine blaue Perle des Glücks.) Ill.: Tirẓa Tanni.
Tel Aviv: Sifriat po'alim 1973.

1973 Shaham, Nurit: **Yomano hasodi šel Uzi Tapuzi.** (The secret diary of *Uzi Tapuzi*; Das geheime Tagebuch von *Uzi Tapuzi.*) Ill.: Nurit Shaham.
Tel Aviv: Davar 1973.

1974 Haviv, Ma'oz: **Hakašarim haẓe'irim.** (The young signallers; Die jungen Signalwärter.) Ill.: Nurit Yuval.
Tel Aviv: Mizrachi 1974.

1975 Putshu (i.e. Israel Wisler): **Havurat Metušelaḥ.** (*Methuselah's* gang; *Methuselahs* Bande.) Ill.: Yafa Talarek.
Tel Aviv: Sreberk 1977.

1976 Ben-Shaul, Moshe: **Rodfim aḥarekha, Yonatan.** (They are after you, *Jonathan;* Sie sind hinter dir, *Jonathan.*) Ill.: Moshe Ben-Shaul.
Tel Aviv: Hakibbutz Hameuchad 1976.

1977 Ruzanzky, Arie: **Melekh ha-Tsev'im.** (King of the hyenas; König der Hyänen.)
Tel Aviv: Yavne 1977.

1978 Zarḥi, Nurit: **Yaldat hutz.** (The exterior girl; Das Mädchen, das abseits steht.) Ill.: Ora Ethan.
Tel Aviv: Zmora, Bitan, Modan 1978.

1979 Golan, Zvia: **Sod givat hagamal.** (The secret of *Camel Hill*; Das Geheimnis des *Kamel-Berges.*) Ill.: Yaffa Talarek.
Tel Aviv: Davar Liladim 1979.

Ben Yitzhak Award

This, prize first awarded in 1978, was established by the Ben Yitzhak Memorial Fund in cooperation with the Youth Wing of the Israel Museum. The award, in the form of a medal, is given biennially to the illustrator of the best children's book published in Israel.

Three qualified judges are responsible for the selection of one book with distinguished illustrations worthy of the Ben Yitzhak Medal. They are also allowed to select additional books of merit for honourable mention. In the event no book is found to meet the standard of excellence of the prize, the judges have the right to decide not to give the award.

Dieser Preis wird seit 1978 verliehen. Er wurde von der Ben Yitzhak Gedächtnis-Stiftung und der Kinderabteilung des Israel Museums ins Leben gerufen. Der Preis, eine Medaille, wird alle zwei Jahre einem Illustrator mit seinen in Buchform veröffentlichten Illustrationen verliehen.

Eine Jury, die sich aus drei Juroren zusammensetzt, ist dafür verantwortlich. Darüberhinaus können sie noch andere Bücher erwähnen, die auf der Ehrenliste erscheinen. Ist kein preiswürdiges Buch vorhanden, wird der Preis nicht verliehen.

1978 Eitan, Ora in:
Regev, Menahen (ed.): **Hagiga shel shirim.** (An anthology of children's poetry; eine Anthologie Kinderdichtung.)
Tel Aviv: Am Oved 1977.

Honourable mention/Ehrenliste
Abulafia, Yosef in:
Sidon, Ephraim: **Alilot Ferdinand pedatzur bekitzur.** (The adventures of King *Ferdinand*; Die Abenteuer des Königs *Ferdinand.*)
Jerusalem: Keter-Li 1977.

Ayal, Ora in: Ayal, Ora: **Ugbo.** (*Ugbo.*)
Tel Aviv: Sifriat Po'alim 1977.

Frankel, Alona in:
Hillel, O.: **Mizevuv as pil.** (From a fly to an elephant; Von der Fliege zum Elefanten.)
Jerusalem: Keter-Li 1977.

Kerman, Danny in:
Atlas, Yehudah: **Vehayeled haze hu ani.** (And this child is me; Und das Kind bin ich.)
Jerusalem: Keter-Li 1977.

Zarfati, Ruth in:
Shavit, Yaakov. **Yotam vehahippoptam.** (*Yotam* and the hippopotamus; *Yotam* und das Nilpferd.)
Tel Aviv: Yariv Hadar 1977.

1980 Ullman, Gad in:
Friedman Sara/Sofer, Esther: **Telepele.** (TV wonders; Fernseh-Wunder.)
Ramat-Gan: Massada 1979.

Honourable mention/Ehrenliste
Bar-Adon, Ra'aya in:
Ya'ari, Mira Mintzer: **Mi shenish'ar im atzmo hu kevar lo Levad.** (He who stays with himself is no longer alone; Derjenige, der mit sich allein sein kann, ist nicht länger allein.)
Tel Aviv: Hakkibbutz Hameuchad 1978.

Ga'ash, Elisheva in:
Harel, Nira: **Sefat hasimanim shel Noa.** (*Noa's* sign language; *Noas* Zeichensprache.)
Jerusalem: Keter-Li 1979.

Gerstein, David in:
Orlev, Uri: **Siamina.** (*Siamina.*)
Tel Aviv: Am Oved 1979.

Katz, Avner in:
Katz, Avner: **Ve'az hatzav bana lo bayit.** (And then the turtle built himself a house; Und dann baute sich die Schildkröte ein Haus.)
Jerusalem: Keter-Li 1979.

Ze'ev Preis

This award was founded in 1970 by the Children's Book Department of the Ministry of Education and named in honour of the prominent children's poet, Ze'ev Aharen (1900—1968). (The prize (I£ 5000), awarded annually for the best books of the year, is selected by a jury composed of representatives from the Israeli Writers' Association, the Ministry of Education and the Ze'ev Perpetuation Board.

Der Preis wurde 1970 von der Kinderbuchabteilung des Kultusministeriums in Israel zu Ehren des berühmten Kinderbuchautors Ze'ev Aharon (1900—1968) gestiftet. Der Preis (I£ 5000) wird jährlich den besten Büchern verliehen. Eine Jury, die sich aus Mitgliedern der Schriftstellervereinigung Israel, dem Kultusministerium und dem Vorstand der Ze'ev Gesellschaft zusammensetzt, wählt die Preise aus.

1971 Tammuz, Benjamin: **Ḥayey hakelev Rizi.** (The life of *Rizi* the dog; Das Leben des Hundes *Rizi.*) Ill.: Ruth Ẓarfati.
Tel Aviv: Dvir 1971.

Amir, Aliza: **Hageśem Dom veYahalom.** (The stopping rain and a diamond; Der Regen hört auf und ein Diamant.) Ill.: Yeḥezkel Kimḥi.
Tel Aviv: Sifriat Po'alim 1971.

Zarḥi, Nurit: **Ani ohev liśrok ba-Reḥov.** (I love to whistle on the road; Unterwegs pfeife ich gerne.) Ill.: Samuel Katz.
Ramat-Gan: Massada 1971.

1972 Atar, Tirẓa: **Ya'el metayelet.** (*Ya'el* goes walking; *Ya'el* geht spazieren.) Ill.: Ẓilah Binder.
Tel Aviv: Hakibbutz Hameuchad 1971.

Yonatan, Natan: **Od sippurim bein Aviv le-Anan.** (More stories between spring and clouds; Noch mehr Geschichten zwischen Frühling und Wolken.) Ill.: Ruth Ẓarfati.
Tel Aviv: Sifriat Po'alim 1972.

1973 Tenne, Benjamin: **Be-Ẓel etz ha-Armon.** (Under the chestnut tree; Unter dem Kastanienbaum.) Ill.: Tirẓa Tannai.
Tel Aviv: Sifriat Po'alim 1972.

Meir, Mira: **Ani ohev le-ẓayer.** (I love drawing; Ich zeichne gerne.) Ill.: Naḥum Guttman.
Tel Aviv: Sifriat Po'alim 1973.

1974 Huppert, Samuel: **Arayot bi-Yruśalaim.** (Lions in Jerusalem; Löwen in Jerusalem.) Ill.: Joseph Stern.
Ramat-Gan: Massada 1974.

1975 Ofek, Uriel: **Ein Sodot ba-śekhuna.** (No secrets in the neighborhood; Keine Geheimnisse in der Nachbarschaft.) Ill.: Erela Horowitz.
Tel Aviv: Sifriat Po'alim 1975.

1976 Michael, Sammy: **Sufah bein Dekalim.** (Palm trees in the storm; Palmen im Sturm.) Ill.: Yaakov Kimche.
Tel Aviv: Am Oved 1976.

Vishnitzer, Naomi: **Yaldah shegadlah.** (A girl who grew up; Das Mädchen, das größer wird.)
Tel Aviv: Hakibbutz Hameuchad 1976.

1977 Atlas, Yehuda: **Vehayeled haze hu ani.** (And this child is me; Und das Kind bin ich.) Ill.: Danny Kerman.
Jerusalem: Keter-Li 1977.

1978 Betzer, Oded: **Ha-massa ha-mufla el lokhamei Bar-Kokhba.** (The incredible journey to the warriors of *Bar-Kokhba;* Die unmögliche Reise zu den Kriegern von *Bar-Kokhba.*) Ill.: Abba Fenichel.
Tel Aviv: Millo 1978.

Oz, Omes: **Sumchi.** (*Sumchi.*) Ill.: Ora Ethan.
Tel Aviv: Am Oved 1978.

1979 Atlas, Yehuda: **Ve'haYeled hazeh hoo Ani.** (And this boy is me; Und der Junge bin ich.) Ill.: Danny Kerman.
Jerusalem: Keter-Li 1977.

Oz, Omos: **Sumchi.** (*Sumchi.*) Orath Eitan.
Tel Aviv: Am Oved 1978.

Betzer, Oded: **Ha-massa ha-mufla el lokhamei Bar-Kokhba.** (The incredible journey to the warriors of *Bar-Kokhba;* Die unglaubliche Reise zu den Kriegern von *Bar-Kokhba.*) Ill.: Abba Fenichel.
Tel Aviv: Millo 1978.

1980 Naor, Leah: **Makhela Aliza.** (A gay choir; Ein lustiger Chor.) Ill.: Ayah Shmueli.
Tel Aviv: Yavneh 1979.

Kaniuk, Yoram: **HaBait shebo metim haJukim miSeiva tova.** (The house where the cockroaches die at a ripe old age; Das Haus, in dem die Küchenschaben in fortgeschrittenem Alter sterben.) Ill.: Ayah Kaniuk.
Tel Aviv: Sifriat Po'alim 1979.

Italy/Italien

Premio Giana Anguissola

This prize was founded in 1967 as a memorial to the well known Italian authoress, Giana Anguissola (1906—1966). The award was given annually by the publishing house, Ugo Mursia, Milan, in conjunction with the children's magazine, Corriere dei Piccoli, for an unpublished manuscript to meet the reading needs of 8 to 14 year olds. The text was to have been highly original an concerned with the problems of contemporary youth. The prize was cancelled in 1974.

Zum Andenken an die bekannte italienische Schriftstellerin Giana Anguissola (1906—1966) verleiht im jährlichen Turnus seit 1967 das Verlagshaus Ugo Mursia, zusammen mit dem Corriere der Piccoli einen Jugendliteraturpreis für Mädchen und Jungen zwischen 8 und 14 Jahren für ein noch nicht verlegtes Buch der erzählenden, italienischen Literatur, das besondere künstlerische Originalitäten aufweist und das für die Probleme und Notwendigkeiten der kindlichen Welt und der heutigen Jugend aufgeschlossen ist. Seit 1974 wird er nicht mehr vergeben.

1967 Dematté, Enzo: **Il regno sul fiume.** (The kingdom on the river; Das Reich am Fluß.) Ill.: Carlo Alberto Michelini. Milano: Mursia 1968.

1968 The prize was not given; Der Preis wurde nicht vergeben,

1969 Grazzani, Roberta: **Giovanna, il coraggio e la paura.** (*Giovanna*, courage and fear; *Giovanna*, Mut und Angst.)
Ill.: Aldo La Duca.
Brescia: La Scuola 1972.
Perrini, Antonio: **Viva i butteri.** (Long live the mounted herdsmen; Die berittenen Hirten, sie leben hoch!)
Milano: Mursia 1971.

1970 Rofinella Borzone, Gianna: **Quando si spengono le stelle**. (When the stars go out; Wenn die Sterne erlöschen.)
Milano: Mursia 1971.

1971/1973 The prize was not given; Der Preis wurde nicht vergeben.

1974 The prize was cancelled; Der Preis wurde nicht mehr vergeben.

Ill. 25 *Giancarlo Cereda and Giuseppe Lagana in G. Padoan: Robinson dello spazio*

Premio Bancarelino

The prize „Il Bancarelino" (which means a small sales-stand), is given to youth books which are both outstanding for their literary quality and for their high sales capacity. Book shop owners nominate three titles, from which a final selection is made by a jury of teen-agers.

Der Preis „Il Bancarelino" (so nennt man einen kleinen Verkaufsstand) wird für ein Jugendbuch verliehen, das sich sowohl durch Qualität als auch durch Verkaufserfolg auszeichnet. Von drei Büchern, die von Buchhändlern benannt werden, sucht eine Jury von Jugendlichen den besten Titel aus.

1958 Berretta, Dino Salvatore/Costa, Roberto: **La nave e l'uomo. L'uomo questo navigatore.** (The ship and man. Man as seafarer; Das Schiff und der Mensch. Der Mensch als Seefahrer.) Ill.
Milano: La Sorgente 1957.

1959 Dei, Cesare: **Il libro di Madur.** (The book of Madur; Das Buch von *Madur.*) Ill.: Fiorenzo Faorzi.
Firenze: Bemporad-Marzocco 1958.

1960 Oursler-Armstrong, April: **La bibbia racconta** (Stories from the Bible; Die Bibel erzählt.) Ill. A. Frigeria and Serio Romano Rizzato.
Milano: Garzanti 1959.

1961 Arpino, Giovanni: **Le mille e una Italia.** (Thousand an one Italy; Tausend und ein Italien.) Ill.: Bruno Caruso.
Torino: Einaudi 1960.

1962 Libenzi, Ermanno: **Il piccolo codice della strada. Divagazioni, norme, consigli di educazione stradale per i ragazzi.** (Traffic rules. Regulations and advice about traffic signs; Kleine Straßenverkehrsordnung. Hinweise, Regeln, Ratschläge zur Verkehrserziehung.) Ill.: Michelangelo Oppio.
Milano: Mursia 1961.

1963 Rigoni Stern, Mario: **Il sergente nella neve.** (The sergeant in the snow; Der Sergeant im Schnee.) Photos.
Torino: Einaudi 1962.

1964 Anguissola Giana: **Violetta la timida.** (Timid Violet; Violet die Schüchterne.) Ill.: Maria Luigia Falcioni Gioia.
Milano: Mursia 1963.

1965 Libenzi, Ermanno: **Ragazzi della resistenza.** (Children of the resistance; Kinder des Widerstands.) Ill.: Giuseppe Motte.
Milano: Mursia 1964.

1966 Triberti, Carlo: **La pattuglia**. (The patrol; Die Patrouille.) Ill.: Mario Uggeri.
Milano: Mursia 1965.

1967 Venturi, Marcello: **L'ultimo veliero**. (The last sailor; Der letzte Segler.) Ill.: Enrico Paolucci.
Torino: Einaudi 1966.

1968 Lofting, Hugh: **Il favoloso dottor Dolittle**. (The fabulous Doctor *Dolittle*; Der fabelhafte Doktor *Dolittle*; Engl. orig. title: The story of Doctor Dolittle.) Ill.: Giovanni Benvenuti.
Milano: Garzanti 1967.

1969 Rogier, Alberto: **L'ombra del gigante**. (The shadow of the giant; Der Schatten des Giganten.) Ill.: Roger Barcilon.
Milano: Mursia 1968.

1970 Padoan, Gianni: **Robinson dello spazio**. (*Robinson* in space; *Robinson* im Weltall.) Ill.: Giancarlo Cereda and Giuseppe Laganá.
Milano: AMZ 1969.

1971 Milani, Mino: **La grande avventura dell'uomo**. (The great adventure of mankind; Das große Abenteuer des Menschen.) Ill.: Cesare Colombi.
Milano: AMZ 1970.

1972 Kopciowski, Clara Costa: **Io spia, tu spia**. (I spy, you spy; Ich spioniere, du spionierst.) Ill. Antonio Lupatelli.
Milano: AMZ 1971.

Milani, Mino: **Aka-Hor.** (*Aka-Hor.*) Ill.: Gino D'Achille.
Milano: Mursia 1971.

1973 Battaglia, Romano: **Lettere dal domani**. (Lettres from tomorrow; Briefe von morgen.) Photos: Mariapia Vecchi.
Torino: SEI 1973.

1974 Pieroni, Piero/Gatteschi, Riccardo: **Indiani, maledetti indiani.** (Indians, damned Indians; Indianer, verdammte Indianer.) Ill.: Luciano Raimondi.
Milano: Fabbri 1973.

1975 Jarunková, Klará: **Il vento sull'erba nuova**. (The wind over the new grass; Der Wind über dem neuen Gras; Slovak. orig. title: Brat mlćanlivého Vlka.) Ill. Yean Ives Malbos.
Firenze: Salani 1975.

1976 Perrault, Gilles: **Il grande giorno**. (The great day; Der große Tag; Fr. orig. title: Le grand jour.) Ill.: Jean Olivier Héron.
Milano: Rizzoli 1975.

1977 Bertino, Serge: **Il conquistatori della terra**. (The conquerors of the earth; Die Eroberer der Erde.) Ill.: René Follet.
Milano: Mursia 1976.

Rutgers van der Loeff-Basenau, An: **I giorni delle valanghe**. (The day of the avalanche; Der Tag an dem die Lawine kam; Dutch. orgig.title: Lawines razen.) Ill.: Sanmarco.
Firenze: Salani 1976.

1978 Lindgren, Astrid: **I fratelli Cuordileone.** (The brothers, *Lionheart;* Die Brüder *Löwenherz; Swed.orig.title: Brödderna Lejonhjärta.*) Ill. Ilon Wikland.
Firenze: Vallecchi 1977.

1979 Padoan, Gianni for:
Free adaption of the film by/ Freie Bearbeitung nach dem gleichlautenden Film von Walter Santesso: **La carica delle patate**. (The load of potato hand grenades; Die Ladung Kartoffel-Hand-Granaten.) Film photos: Walter Santesso.
Milano: AMZ 1978.

1980 Rubbi, Clara: **Glaciazione anno 2079**. (Glacial year 2079; Eisjahr 2079.)
Torino: SEI 1979.

1981 Troiepolski, Gavril: **Bim bianco dall'orecchio nero.** (White Bim with black ears; Weißer Bim mit schwarzen Ohren.)
Firenze: Giunti Marzocco 1980.

Premio Castello

The community of Sanguinetto near Verona founded this prize in 1953 for high-quality children's books written by Italian authors. The first award presentation was given posthumously to Giuseppe Ernesto Nuccio (1874—1933) for his book, "La luce del mondo". The prize money was donated to poor children in a Palermo elemantary school. Nuccio had worked as an educator in Sicily.

Der Castello-Preis wird seit 1953 regelmäßig von der Gemeinde Sanguinetto bei Verona für Bücher italienischer Autoren verliehen. 1953 prämiierte man das nachgelassene Werk von Giuseppe Ernesto Nuccio (1874—1933) "La luce del mondo". Die Prämie wurde für arme Schüler einer Elementarschule in Palermo bestimmt — Nuccio wirkte als Pädagoge in Sizilien.

1953 Nuccio, Giuseppe Ernesto: **La luce del mondo**. (The light of the world; Das Licht der Welt.) Ill.: Vittorio Lucchi.
Milano: Garzanti 1952.

Anguissola, Giana: **Seguendo una lira.** (Following a lira; Einer Lira folgend.) Ill.: Gustavino (i.e. Gustavo Rosso).
Milano: Garzanti 1953.

Petrini, Enzo: **Il corsaro di Dio. San Francesco Saverio.** (The corsair of God. Saint *Francis Xavier*; Der Korsar Gottes. Heiliger *Franz Xaver.*)
Breschia: La Scuola 1953.

Uguccioni, Ruffillo: **Il cervo bianco.** Avventure di Cappa e Spada del secolo XVII. (The white deer. Adventures of *Cappa* and *Spada* in the 17th century; Der weiße Hirsch. Abenteuer von *Cappa* und *Spada* des 17. Jahrhunderts.) Ill.: Luigi Melandri.
Torino, Milano, Genova: S.E.I. 1953.

Lattes, Laura: **Lo specchio magico.** (The magic mirror; Der Zauberspiegel.) Ill. Ugo Fontana.
Firenze: Marzocco 1952.

1954 Gotta, Salvator: **Una bimba alla ventura.** (A small girl's adventure; Abenteuer eines kleinen Mädchens.) Ill. Pietro Nardini.
Milano: A.P.E. 1955.

Ugolini, Luigi: **Voci del mare e della terra.** *Novelle per tutti.* (Voices of the sea and earth. A story for all; Stimmen des Meeres und der Erde. Erzählungen für alle.) Ill.: Cafiero Filippelli, Roberto Lemmi, Renato Natali.
Torino, Milano, Genova: S.E.I. 1953.

1955 Anguissola, Giana: **Il diario di Giulietta. Romanzo.** (*Julia's* diary. Novel; *Julias* Tagebuch. Roman.)
Milano: La Sorgente 1954.

Cupisti, Mario: **Giona sulla balena.** (*Jonah* and the whale; *Jonas* und der Walfisch.) Ill.: Anna Ferrari.
Bologna: Cappelli 1954.

Drago, Ignazio: **Racconti e leggende.** (Stories and legends; Erzählungen und Legenden.) Ill.: Piero Bernardini.
Firenze: Marzocco 1954.

Paltrinieri, Bruno: **Mattutino Verdiano. Infanzia e giovinezza di Giuseppe Verdi.** (Dawning *Verdi*. Childhood and youth of *Giuseppe Verdi*; *Verdi*s Anfang. Kindheit und Jugend von *Giuseppe Verdi.*)
Torino, Genova, Milano: S.E.I. 1955.

1956 Fiori, Pacifico: **I rebelli della prateria.** (The rebellion of the prairie; Die Rebellen der Prärie.)
Torino, Genova, Milano: S.E.I. 1955.

1957 Ugolini, Luigi: **Pa delle caverne**. Romanzo. (*Pa* of the caves. Novel; *Pa* von den Höhlen. Roman.) Ill.: Pinardi.
Torino, Genova, Milano: S.E.I. 1956.

Ricci, Adriana Cumano: **Lo scoglio del diavolo**. (The devil's cliff; Die Klippe des Teufels.)
(Unpublished; Unveröffentlicht.)

Pascucci, Maria: **Sulla vetta**. Romanzo per ragazzi. (At the top. Novel for children; Auf dem Gipfel. Kinderroman.) Ill. Guido Bertello.
Torino, Genova, Milano: S.E.I. 1956.

1958 Paltrinieri, Bruno: **Il segreto di Sbadiglio**. (The secret of *Sbadiglio*; Das Geheimnis des *Sbadiglio*.) Ill.: Adolfi Busi.
Milano: Piccoli 1957.

1959 Berretta, Dino Salvatore/Costa, Roberto: **L'America in francobolli**. (*America* in postage stamps; *Amerika in Briefmarken*.) Ill.
Milano: La sorgente 1958.

1960 Gigli, Silvio: **Quattro ragazzi conquistano gli astri**. (Four children conquer the stars; Vier Kinder erobern die Sterne.) Ill.: Silvio Gigli.
Milano: Fabbri 1959.

1961 Zucconi, Giuglielmo: **Scaramacai**. (*Scaramacai*.) Ill.: Manlio Amodeo.
Milano: Mondadori 1960.

1962 Ugolini, Luigi: **Gli skua d'isola bianca**. Romanzo polare. (The skua of the white island. A polar story; Die Skua der weißen Insel. Eine Polargeschichte.) Ill.
Torino, Genova, Milano: S.E.I. 1961.

1963 Rodari, Gianni: **Gip nel televisore. Favola in orbita**. (*Gip* in the television. Tales in orbit; *Gip* im Fernsehen. Märchen im Weltraum.) Ill.: Giancarlo Carloni.
Milano: Mursia 1962.

1964 Ripani, Mina: **La conquista dello spazio**. (The conquest of space; Die Eroberung des Weltraums.) Ill.: Beniamino Bodini.
Milano: Signorelli 1963. (Ex aequo).

Sven, Anna: **Storia di un cavallo bizzarro.** (Story of a stubborn horse; Geschichte eines störrischen Pferdes.) Ill.
Milano: Ceschina 1961. (Ex aequo)

1965 *1st prize / 1. Preis*
Milani, Mino: **Tommy River e lo scozzese.** (*Tommy River* and the Scotsman; *Tommy River* und der Schotte.) Ill.: Mario Uggeri.
Milano: Mursia 1964.

2nd prize/2. Preis
Boldrini, Giuliana: **Il segreto etrusco. Infanzia e viaggi di Vel.** (The Etruscan secret, Childhood and travels of *Vel;* Das etruskische Geheimnis. Kindheit und Reisen von *Vel.*) Ill.: Ulla Kampmann.
Firenze: Valecchi 1965.

1966 Melegari, Vezio: **Missilino Fiordimarte**. Romanzino umoristico interplanetario per fanciulli promettenti. (The little Mars flower-rocket. A humorous interplanetary novelette for clever children; Kleinrakete Marsblume. Kleiner humoristischer interplanetarischer Roman für kluge Kinder.)
Milano: Rizzoli 1965.

1967 Trojani, Felice: **L'ultimo volo**. La drammatica avventura dell' Italia al Polo Nord. (The last flight. Italy's dramatic adventure at the North Pole; Der letzte Flug. Das dramatische Abenteuer Italiens am Nordpol.) Ill.: Marcello Cassinari Vettor.
Milano: Mursia 1967.

1968 Boldrini, Giuliana: **Il leone di Micene**. (The lion of Mycenae; Der Löwe von Mykene.) Ill.: Giovanni Caselli.
Firenze: Vallecchi 1967.

1969 Monchieri, Lino: **Il campione**. (The champion; Der Meister.) Ill.: Piero Mancini.
Milano: Massimo 1968.

1970 Padoan, Gianni: **Robinson dello spazio.** (*Robinson* in space; Robinson im Weltall.) Ill.: Giancarlo Cereda and Giuseppe Laganà.
Milano: AMZ 1969.

1971 Kopciowski, Clara Costa: **Shalom**. (Shalom.) Ill. Bruno Fraganello.
Milano: Mursia 1970.

1972 Cassini, Marino: **Torpedini umane**. (Human torpedoes; Menschliche Torpedos.) Ill.: Antonio de Rosa.
Milano: Mursia 1971.

1973 Minestrini, Walter: **Ogni uomo è mio fratello**. (Every man is my brother; Jeder Mensch ist mein Bruder.) Photos.
Milano: Mursia 1973.

1974 Geron, Gastone: **La banda della grava**. (The hard gang; Die schwere Bande.) Ill.: Guido Bertello.
Milano: Bietti 1974.

1975 Pratesi, Fulco: **Il salvanatura**. (Conservation of nature; Rettung der Natur.) Ill.: Fulco Pratesi and Roberto Diso. Photos: Renato Bazzoni, Giovanni Diana, Salvatore Felici et al.
Milano: Federico Motta 1974.

1976 Bufalari, Giuseppe: **La nave dei guerrieri**. (The ship of fighters; Das Schiff der Krieger.) Ill. Photos.
Milano: Fratelli Fabbri 1976.

1977 Caratelli, Gianni: **Vivranno, dottor Cleveland!** (You will live, Dr. Cleveland! Sie werden leben, Dr. Cleveland!)
Bologna: Capitol 1976.

1978 Pucci, Mario V.: **Guerra a primavera**. (War in spring; Krieg im Frühling.)
Milano: Ed. Scolastiche Bruno Mondadori 1977.

1979 Rho, Franco: **Il grande occhio del mondo**. (The great eye of the world; Das große Auge der Welt.) Photos.
Bergamo: Minerva Italica 1979.

1980 Bamonte, Gerardo/Marzotto, Lidia: **La guardiana delle acque.** (The guardian of the waters; Der Hüter der Gewässer.) Ill.: Giusi Corteggi.
Milano: Rizzoli 1980 (ex aequo)

Paolini, Alcide: **Il paese abbandonato**. (The abandoned village; Das verlassene Dorf.) Ill.: Flavio Faganello.
Firenze: Salani 1980. (ex aequo)

Premio letterario nazionale per la fiaba Hans Christian Andersen Baia delle favole Sesti Levante

This prize was founded in 1966 by the Sestri Levante Polytechnic together with the local tourist board. It is awarded annually to an unpublished fairy tale manuscript. It is an open competition to promote the writing of fairy tales of literary merit which will help counteract the materialistic trends of contemporary society. Since 1970 the prize has been under the sponsorship of the children's magazine, "Corriere dei Pccoli", with the help of AMZ publishers of Milan.

Der Premio „Hans Christian Andersen" Baia delle favole, wurde 1966 von der Volksuniversität Sestri Levante in Zusammenarbeit mit dem örtlichen Fremdenverkehrsamt für ein noch unverlegtes Märchenmanuskript im jährlichen Turnus ins Lebens gerufen. Der Preis ist ein nationaler, literarischer Märchenwettbewerb dessen Bestrebungen dahin gehen, das Märchen im Rahmen der Kinder- und Jugendliteratur in einer Zeit, in der der Mensch sich vom materiellen Alltag lösen sollte, aufzuwerten. Der Preis wurde ab 1970 zum ersten Mal auch unter Mitarbeit des Verlagshauses AMZ in Mailand und unter dem Patronat des "Corriere dei Piccoli" vergeben.

1967 Grazzani, Roberta Maria Rosa: **Il pagliaccio Fiordaliso.** (*Corn Blossom*, the clown; Der Clown *Kornblume*.)

Randazzo Tonon, Lidia: **Le tre monete d'oro**. (The three golden coins; Die drei goldenen Münzen.)

Lacava, Cora: **Principessa diamantina**. (The diamond princess; Die Diamantenprinzessin.)

1968 Remiddi, Maria: **Il testamento del re**. (The testament of the king; Das Testament des Königs.)

Martinelli, Elisabetta: **I funghi d'oro**. (The golden mushrooms; Die goldenen Pilze.)

Madia, Bianca: **I prodigi di re inverno**. (The miracle of the winter king; Die Wunder des Winterkönigs.)

1969 Richeri, Gabriella: **L'uomo dei desideri**. (The man who wishes; Der Mann der Wünsche.)

Eusebietti, Dora: *Il brutto re ossia. Celestina e la veritá.* (The ugly king. *Celestina* and the truth; Der häßliche König. *Celestina* und die Wahrheit.)

Melloni, Piero: **Le tre anfore**. (The three urns; Die drei Henkelkrüge.)

(From 1970 until 1977, the prize was divided into two categories: category A — for professional authors and journalists; category B — for new authors. Three prizes are awarded in category B.

Ab 1970 bis 1977 wurde der Preis in zwei Kategorien aufgeteilt: Kategorie A wird an professionelle Autoren und Journalisten vergeben und besteht aus einem einzigen Preis. Kategorie B wird an Autodidakten vergeben und besteht aus 3 Preisen.)

1970 *Category A/Kategorie A*

Mosca, Giovanni: **Fumo**. (Smoke; Rauch.)

Category B/Kategorie B

Roli, Costanza: **L'albero**. (The tree; Der Baum.)

Magnani, Bianca: **Il bricco miracoloso**. (The miraculous can; Die wundertätige Kanne.)

Guernieri, Dino: **La nuvoletta di Maestro Bastian**. (The little cloud of Master *Bastian*; Die kleine Wolke von Meister *Bastian*.)

1971 *Category A/Katergorie A*

Arpino, Giovanni: **Zio Computer**. (Uncle *Computer*; Onkel *Computer*.)

Category B/Kategorie B

Terrile, Gino: **Il calore del buon senso**. (The warmth of good courage; Die Wärme des guten Mutes.)

Gabanizza, Clara: **Il violino fedele**. (The faithful violin; Die treue Geige.)

Richeri, Gabriella: **Casimiro e Beniamino**. (*Casimir* and *Benjamin*; *Kasimir* und *Benjamin*.)

1972 Category A/Kategorie A

Zuconi, Giuglielmo: **Sole pazzo**. (The crazy sun; Die verrückte Sonne.)

Category B/Kategorie B

Grazzani, Roberta: **Il tram color fragola**. (The strawberry colored tram; Die erdbeerfarbene Straßenbahn.)

Cavalli Gazzo, Leonilda: **Senza bacchetta magica**. (Without magic wand; Ohne Zauberstab.)

Cassini, Marino: **Carusiello e la libertà**. (*Carusiello* and liberty; *Carusiello* und die Freiheit.)

1973 Category A/Kategorie A

Zavoli, Sergio: **Una favola per Valentina**. (A fable for *Valentina*; Eine Fabel für *Valentina*.)

Category B/Kategorie B

Di Caprio, Umberto: **Il pescastelle**. (The star fisher; Der Sternenfischer.)

Mallucci Converso-Chiavari, Anna Maria: **Le pillole Big**. (The pill, *Big*; Die Pillen *Big*.)

Paltro, Piera: **Salvezza alla S. SP-38**. (The salvage of *S. SP-38*; Die Rettung auf den *S. SP-38*.)

1974 Category A/Kategorie A

Filippo, Peppino de: **Pedrolino**. (Little *Pedro*; Der kleine *Pedro*.)

Category B/Kategorie B

Pezzata, Silvano: **Il trombettiere del re**. (The king's trumpeter; Der Trompeter des Königs.)

Borfecchia de Rocca, Noris: **Casimiro Perteghetta**. (Casimiro Perteghetta.)

Fornari, Oreste de: **La formica hippy**. (The ant hippy; Die Ameise Hippy.)

1975 Category A/Kategorie A

Chiosso, Leo: **Bel colpo, Fratelli Castori!**. (Well done, *Brother Beaver*; Gut gemacht, *Gebrüder Biber*!)

Category B/ Kategorie B

Frasconi, Giovanni: **Il falco d'acciaia**. (The steel falcon; Der Falke aus Stahl.)

Lemarque, Vivian: **Elisabetta**. (*Elizabeth*; *Elisabeth*.)

Melloni, Piero: **Esaù e il delfino**. (*Esau* and the dolphin; *Esau* und der Delphin.)

1976 Category A/Kategorie A

Moravia, Alberto: **Mustafà, la volpe del Sahara**. (*Mustafa, the fox of the Sahara; Mustafa*, der Fuchs der Sahara.)

Category B/Kategorie B

Crotti, Silvana: **Accadde davvero**. (It really happened; Es passierte wirklich.)

Zelli, Aldo: **Oscar al Luna Park**. (*Oscar* in *Luna Park*; *Oskar* im *Luna Park*.)

Fontani, Carlo: **Il chicco d'Etiopia**. (The corn of Ethiopia; Das Korn von Äthiopien.)

(Since 1977, the prize has reverted back to only one category;

Ab 1977 besteht der Preis nur aus einer Kategorie.)

1977 Calvino, Italo: **I disegni arrabbiati.** *(The angry drawings; Die verärgerten Zeichnungen.)*

Prono, Alfredo: **Le due cartelle**. (The two school bags; Die zwei Schultaschen.)

Valsecchi, Franca: **Un draghetto fuori tempo**. (A little dragon outside of time; Ein kleiner Drache außerhalb der Zeit.)

1978 The prize was not given; Der Preis wurde nicht vergeben.

1979 The prize was not given; Der Preis wurde nicht vergeben.

(In 1980 the rules ware changed to include both adults and elementary school children in the jury, and 6 prizes were given;

Im Gegensatz zu den vergangenen Jahren besteht die Jury seit 1980 aus einer Kommission von Erwachsenen und Kindern einer Grundschule und es werden 6 Preise vergeben.)

1980 1st prize/1. Preis

Allinovi, Valeria: **Come fu che la tigre maltese divenne regina.** (How the Maltese tiger became a queen; Wie war es möglich, daß der maltesische Tiger Königin wurde.)

2nd prize/2. Preis

Scaravelli, Enrico: **L'amuleto di Aniuk.** (The amulet of *Aniuk*; Das Amulett von *Aniuk*.)

3rd prize/3. Preis

Agnini, Amalia: **Il pesce nero.** (The black fish; Der schwarze Fisch.)

4th prize/4. Preis

Moretti Pacchielli, Viklinda: **Il sogno dello spaventapasseri.** (The scarecrow's dream; Der Traum der Vogelscheuche.)

5th prize/5. Preis

Converso, Anna Maria: **Il nido delle ghiandaie.** (The nest of the jays; Das Nest der Häher.)

6th prize/6. Preis

Gasparri Manfredini, Carla: **Un gatto blu a Bazibebel.** (A blue cat in *Bazibebel*; Eine blaue Katze in *Bazibebel*.)

Premio Monza

This annual prize, sponsored by the library "Regina Margherita", has as its purpose the selection of good books suitable for adaptation to other media and for transcription into braille for blind children. The final selections are made from a list of six titles by a group of sixteen children representing reading groups in different Italian cities. Since 1980, the competition has been open to translations.

Das Ziel dieses Preises, der jährlich von der "Regina Margherita"-Bibliothek verliehen wird, ist die Auswahl guter Bücher, die zur Adaption für andere Medien und für die Transkription in Brailleschrift für blinde Kinder geeignet sind. Die endgültige Auswahl wird aus einer Liste von sechs Titeln von einer Gruppe von 16 Kindern getroffen, die Lesegruppen aus verschiedenen Städten in Italien repräsentieren. Seit 1980 werden auch übersetzte Titel berücksichtigt.

1972 Argilli, Marcello: **Ciao Andrea.** (So long, *Andrea*; Auf Wiedersehen, *Andrea*.)
Milano: Mondadori 1971.

1973 Guarnieri, Rossana: **Gente d'Irlanda.** (People in Ireland; Menschen in Irland.) Ill.: Florenzio Corona.
Milano: Mursia 1972.

1974 Calanchi, Giuseppe: **Operazione Orne**. (Operation *Orne*; Unternehmen *Orne*.)
Torino: Paravia 1973.

1975 Sabbieti, Mario: **Una stagione per crescere**. (A season to grow up; Eine Jahreszeit um erwachsen zu werden.) Photos: Giovanni Renna.
Milano: Fabbri 1974.

1976 Mauri, Carlo: **Quando il rischio è vita**. (When life is risked; Wenn Risiko Leben ist.) Photos: Carlo Mauri.
Milano: La Sorgente 1975.

1977 *Fiction/Erzählende Literatur*

Petruccelli, Alessandro: **Un giovane di campagna**. (A youth from the country; Ein Junge vom Land.)
Roma: Riunti 1976.

Non-fiction/Sachbuch

Lanzillo, Luigi: **Continente di ghiaccio**. (Continents in the ice; Kontinente im Eis.) Photos.
Firenze: Giunti-Nardini 1976.

1978 *Fiction/Erzählende Literatur*

Argilli, Marcello: **Vacanze col padre**. (Vacation with father; Ferien mit Vater.)
Milano: Mondadori 1977.

Non-fiction/Sachbuch

Baberio Corsetti, Livia: **Il fondo del pozzo**. (The source of the fountain; Der Grund des Brunnens.)
Torino: Paoline 1977.

1979 *Fiction/Erzählende Literatur*

Guarnieri, Rossana: **Il corragio di viverve.** (Courage to live; Mut zu leben.)
Milano: Mursia 1978.

Non-fiction/Sachbuch

Turri, Eugenio: **Nomadi, gli uomini dei grandi spazi**. (Nomads, people of the wide open spaces; Nomaden, Menschen der großen Weiten.) Ill.: Maurizio Bajetti. Photos.
Milano: Fabbri 1978.

1980 *Fiction/Erzählende Literatur*

Sabietti, Marioi: **La città era un fiume.** (The town was a river; Die Stadt war ein Fluß.)
Roma: Riuniti 1979.

Non-fiction/Sachbuch
Cancrini, M.G./Harrison, L.: **Due + non fa quattro.** (Two + two don't make four; Zwei und zwei macht nicht vier.)
Roma: Riuniti 1979.

1981 *Fiction/Erzählende Literatur*
Paolini, Alcide: **Il paese abbandonato.** (The abandoned village; Das verlassene Dorf.) Ill.: Flavio Faganello.
Firenze: Salani 1980.

Non-fiction/Sachbuch
Bongiorno, Teresa: **Il romanzo di Marco Polo.** (A novel about Marco Polo; Roman über Marco Polo.) Ill.
Milano: Rusconi 1980.

Premio L'ancora d'oro

The authorities of the International Fair, Genoa, and the National Society for Shipbuilding and Allied Trades are the main sponsors of this award. Additional sponsors for this prize, founded in 1965, are the Study Centre for Youth Literature and the International Seafarers' Society. The Italian Library Association is responsible for the selection of the prize winning stories. Originally the prize was awarded only to published manuscripts on the theme of seafaring. The story could be historical, geographical, fiction, non-fiction or fairytale, provided it was intended for the young reader. First prize is called the Golden Anchor; second prize, the Silver Anchor; third and fourth place are given honorable mention. In 1972, publishers were allowed to participate with titles published on the theme of seafaring. This prize was cancelled in 1975.

Die Internationale Messegesellschaft, Genua, sowie die Nationale Vereinigung der Werften, Schiffahrtsindustrie und branchenähnliche Unternehmen, schreibt im Zusammenhang mit den Rahmenveranstaltungen der Internationalen Schiffsvereinigung, mit dem Studienzentrum für Jugendliteratur ein 1965 gegründetes, von der Direktion der Bibliotheken abhängiges Unternehmen, einen Wettbewerb für Jugendliteratur aus. Zugelassen sind nicht veröffentlichte Erzählungen aus dem Bereich der Seefahrt. Der Inhalt kann geschichtlicher oder geographischer Art sein, Abenteuergeschichten oder Märchen können ebenso teilnehmen, wie Erzählungen mit sportlichem oder wissenschaftlichem Hintergrund, wenn sie den Interessen der jugendlichen Leser Rechnung tragen. Der erste Preis nennt sich „Der goldene Anker", der zweite Preis „Der silberne Anker". Die Titel an dritter und vierter Stelle werden erwähnt. Seit 1972 können sich auch Verlage beteiligen, die in den letzten 3 Jahren Bücher für Jugendliche aus dem Bereich der Seefahrt verlegt haben. Der Preis wird seit 1975 nicht mehr verliehen.

1965 *Golden anchor/Goldene Anker*

Melegari, Vezio: **L'alpino che navigò**. (The alpinist who went to sea; Der Alpinist, der zur See fuhr.)

Silver anchor/Silberne Anker

Terrile, Gino: **Storia di Doghi, Pesce cucciolo**. (The story about *Doghi* the fish child; Geschichte von *Doghi*, dem Fischkind.)

Honorable mention/Ehrenliste

Cavalli Gazzo, Leonilda: **Tre giorni di sole**. (Three days of sun; Drei Tage Sonne.)

Dolcino, Michelangelo: **Agostino e il Real Ferdinando**. (*Augustine* and King *Ferdinand*; *Augustin* und der königliche *Ferdinand*.)

1966 The prize was not given; Der Preis wurde nicht vergeben.

1967 *Golden anchor/Goldene Anker*

Cassini, Marino: **Il Bernardo eremita e l'anemone di mare**. (*Bernard* the hermit and the sea anemone; *Bernhard* und die Seeanemone.)

Silver anchor/Silberne Anker

Caratelli, Gianni: **La gara del Lee**. (*Lee*'s contest; Der Wettkampf von *Lee*.)

Honorable mention/Ehrenliste

The prize was not given; Der Preis wurde nicht vergeben.

1968 *Golden anchor/Goldene Anker*

Belski Lagazzi, Ines: **Un giorno accadrà**, (One day it will happen; Es wird eines Tages passieren.)

Silver anchor/Silberne Anker

Jelpo, Vincenzo: **Barbara**. (*Barbara*.)

Honorable mention/Ehrenliste

Zanelli, Anna Maria: **Una notte con Columbo**. (A night with *Columbus*; Eine Nacht mit *Kolumbus*.)

Valle, Guglielo: **I pettirossi**. (The robin; Das Rotkehlchen.)

1969 *Golden anchor/Goldene Anker*

Cassini, Marino: **Il vecchio e il pescecane**. (The old man and the shark; Der Alte und der Haifisch.)

Silver anchor/Silberne Anker

Zanelli, Anna Maria: **Occhiali, corsaro all'italiana**. (*Occhiali*, the Italian pirate; *Occhiali* Seeräuber aus Italien.)

Honorable mention/Ehrenliste

Pedroni, Maria Luisa: **Maglione rosso**. (Red sweater; Roter Pullover.)

1970 *Golden anchor/Goldene Anker*

Bandini, Marina: **Il pagaro e i mostri**. (The pagaro [=fish] and the monsters; Der Pagaro [=Fisch] und die Ungeheuer.)

Silver anchor/Silberne Anker

Cassini, Marino: **Ritorno all'origine**. (Return to the beginning; Rückkehr zum Ursprung.)

Honorable mention/Ehrenliste

Cassini, Marino: **GESCAPP. Gestione case per pesci**. (*GESCAPP.* Fish management; *GESCAPP.* Fischereiverwaltung.)

Terrile Gino: **Lo straordinario caso dei pirati e del mago Sgiribi**. (The extraordinary case of the pirate and *Sgiribi*, the magician; Der außergewöhnliche Fall der Piraten und des Zauberers *Sgiribi*.)

1971 The prize was not given; Der Preis wurde nicht vergeben.

1972 *Golden anchor/Goldene Anker*

Bellugi, Ubaldo: **La città delle navi**. (The city of the ships; Die Stadt der Schiffe.)

Silver anchor/Silberne Anker

Richeri, Gabriella: **La barca meravigliosa**. (The marvelous boat; Die wunderbare Barke.)

Honorable mention/Ehrenliste

Zuccoli, Tina: **La conquista dei poli**. (The conquest of the poles; Die Eroberung der Pole.) Photos. Ill.
Firenze: Vallecchi 1969.

1973 *Golden anchor/Goldene Anker*

Guernieri, Dino: **Un ragazzo chiamato Jack London**. (A boy called *Jack London*; Ein Junge genannt *Jack London*.)

Silver anchor/Silberne Anker

Pogioli, Franco: **Il mito del Matteo Padre**. (The myth of Father *Matthew*; Die Doge von Vater *Matthäus*.)

The prize was not given; Der Preis wurde nicht vergeben.

1974 *Golden anchor/Goldene Anker*

Vangelista, Chiara: **La favola del mare quando arrivò a Torino**. (The fable of the sea when it arrives at Turin; Die Fabel vom Meer, das Turin erreichte.)

Silver anchor/Silberne Anker

Gnoli, Ines: **Albatros.** (Albatross; Albatros.)

Gold medal/Goldmedaille

Petrucci, Antonio: **Le meditazioni del granchio.** (A view of cancer; Die Überlegungen des Krebses.) (ex aequo)

Martinelli, Elisabetta: **Il veliero nella bottiglia.** (The sailing ship in the bottle; Das Segelschiff in der Flasche.) (ex aequo)

1975 The prize was cancelled; Der Preis wird nicht mehr verliehen.

Premio Laura Orvieto

This prize was named after Laura Orvieto Cantoni (1876—1953). Before 1960, it was awarded both to works of fiction and poetry, and in cases of works possessing equal literary quality, it was divided among them. Since 1960, however, the prize (offered every second year) is alternately given to a work of fiction and a work of poetry. In 1974, the prize was discontinued.

Vor 1960 wurde dieser, nach Laura Orvieto Cantoni (1876—1953) benannte Preis für ein Prosawerk und im selben Jahr auch für ein Werk aus dem Bereiche der Dichtkunst verliehen. Dabei konnte der Preis auch geteilt werden. Seit 1960 aber wird der Preis, für den ein zweijähriger Turnus üblich ist, das eine Mal für ein Werk der Poesie, das andere Mal nur für ein Werk in Prosa vergeben. Seit 1974 wird er nicht mehr verliehen.

1954 *Prose/Prosa*

Draghi, Laura: **Storia dell'angelo custode.** (Story of the guardian angel; Geschichte des Schutzengels.) Ill.: Ugo Fontana.
Firenze: Valecchi 1956. (Ex aequo)

Prose/Prosa

Momo, Natalia: **Borgo fra le risaia.** (Hamlet in the rice field; Der Weiler im Reisfeld.) Ill.: Maria Carla Prette.
Torino, Milano, Padova: Paravia 1955.

Prose/Prosa

Rinaldi, Luigi: **Un'avventura al Matto Grosso,** (An adventure in the *Matto Grosso*; Ein Abenteuer am *Matto Grosso*.) Ill. Roberto Lemmi.
Firenze: Bemporad-Marzocco 1955. (Ex aequo)

1956 *Poetry/Poesie*

Castoldi, Maggiorina: **Armonia delle stagioni.** Poesie. (Harmony of the seasons. Poetry; Harmonie der Jahreszeiten. Poesie.) Ill.: Fanny Giuntoli.
Torino, Genova, Milano: S.E.I. 1957. (Ex aequo)

Poetry/Poesie

Rompato, Romano: **Girotondo fiorito**. (Flowering ring; Blühender Reigen.) Ill.: Sara Ragazzini Fossati.
Firenze: Bemporad-Marzocco 1956. (Ex aequo)

1958 *Prose/Prosa*

Bellandi Taddei, Ada: **Il meraviglioso mare**. (The marvelous sea; Das wunderbare Meer.) Ill.: Roberto Lemmi.
Bologna: Cappelli 1961.

Poetry/Poesie

Dell'Era, Idilio: (i.e. Martin Giosé Ceccuzzi): **Il canzoniere del fanciullo**. (Children's song book; Kinderliederbuch.) Ill.
Firenze: Specchio del Libro per Ragazzi 1962.

1960 *Prose/Prosa*

Tumiati, Lucia: **Saltafrontiera**. (Border-jumper; Grenzüberspringer.) Ill.: Luca Checchi.
Firenze: Bemporad-Marzocco 1961.

1962 The prize was not given; Der Preis wurde nicht vergeben.

1964 *Prose/Prosa*

Reggiani, Renée: **Domani, dopodomani**. (Tomorrow, day after tomorrow; Morgen, übermorgen.)
Firenze: Valecchi 1964.

1966 *Poetry/Poesie*

Parri, Teresa: **Navigaluna**. (Moon traveler; Mondfahrer.)
Firenze: Valecchi 1971.

1968 The prize was not given; Der Preis wurde nicht vergeben.

1970 *Prose/Prosa*

Martini, Luciana: **Marco in Sicilia**. (*Marco* in Sicily; *Marco* in Sizilien.)
Firenze: Valecchi 1972.

1972 The prize was not given; Der Preis wurde nicht vergeben,

1964 The prize was cancelled; Der Preis wird nicht mehr verliehen.

Premio Biennale di letteratura per ragazzi „Olga Visentini"

The city government of Cerea, Italy established this prize in 1968 and it is awarded every two years for an unpublished manuscript. The prize is dedicated to the memory of Olga Visentini, who was one of the most famous writers and educators for youth. Her works contain strong elements of Christian morality and educational intent. Even today the best publishers print her books and children and young people read them with interest and enthusiasm.

Die Kommunalverwaltung von "Cerea" veranstaltet seit 1968 alle zwei Jahre einen Wettbewerb für noch nicht verlegte Werke der Jugendliteratur, der dem Andenken der Autorin Olga Visentini gewidmet ist. Olga Visentini, deren sterbliche Überreste in Cerea ruhen, war eine der berühmtesten Schriftstellerinnen und Erzieherin der Jugend. Ihre Bücher werden noch heute von den besten Verlagshäusern herausgegeben und von den Kindern und Jugendlichen mit Begeisterung gelesen. Wie ihre Lehrtätigkeit an einem Mailänder Bildungsinstitut, so sind auch ihre Werke von einer christlichen und erzieherischen Moral durchdrungen.

1968 Belski Lagazzi, Ines: **La storia di Lam Tahn**. (The story of *Lam Tahn*; Die Geschichte von *Lam Tahn.) Ill.: Roberto Molino.*
Milano: Le Stelle 1969.

1970 Pezzetta, Silvano: **Ragazzo indio**. (Indian boy; *Maipiki.) Ill.: Gianni Renna.*
Milano: Fabbri 1972.

1972 Guarnieri, Rossana Valeri: **Gente d'Irlanda**. (People of Ireland; Menschen in Irland.) Ill.: Florenzio Corona.
Milano: Mursia 1972.

1974 Pettoello Morrone, Carmen: **Scappa Bouc, scappa!**. (Run *Bouc*, run! Lauf *Bouc*, lauf!) Ill.: Maraja.
Milano: Rizzoli 1975.

1976 Enna di Sassari, Francesco: **Un anno a Punta Coìle**. (One year at *Punta Coìle*; Ein Jahr in *Punta Coìle*.) (Manuscript/Manuskript)

1978 Paltro, Piera: **Europa chiama Europa**: (Europe calling Europe; Europa genannt Europa.) (Manuscript/Manuskript)

Japan

Akai Tori Bungakushō

This prize, founded in 1971, was named after the magazine, "Akai Tori" (The red bird), which played an important role in the development of Japanese children's literature during the years 1918 to 1935. The prize was founded by the writer. Joji Tsubota, who was a member of Akai Tori. The award is given annually to the best children's book written in the previous year.

Akai Tori Bungakusho wurde 1971 zur Erinnerung an die Zeitschrift "Akai Tori" (Der rote Vogel), die 1918—1935 in der japanischen Jugendliteratur eine große Rolle spielte, gestiftet. Der Begründer ist Schriftsteller Joji Tsubota, der einer der Vereinsmitglieder der Zeitschrift war. Der Preis wird den besten für Kinder bestimmten literarischen Werken des jeweils vergangenen Jahres verliehen.

1971 Muku, Hatojū: **Maya no Issyō.** (*Maya's* life; *Mayas* Leben.) Ill.: Tadashi Yoshii.
Tokyo: Dainihon-Tosho 1970.

Muku, Hatojū: **Momo-chan to Akane.** (Little *Momo* and *Akane*; Die kleine *Momo* und *Akane.*) Ill.: Otsu Iwozumi.
Tokyo: Popurasha 1970.

1972 Shonō, Junzō: **Akio to Ryōji.** (*Akio* and *Ryoji.*) Ill.: Keimei Anzai.
Tokyo: Iwanami-Shoten 1971.

Seki, Hideo: **Chiisai Kokoro no Tabi.** (Travels of a small heart; Die Reise eines kleinen Herzens.) Ill.: Motoichiro Takebe.
Tokyo: Kaiseisha 1971.

Seki, Hideo: **Shiroi Chō no Ki.** (The life of a white butterfly; Das Leben eines weißen Schmetterlings.) Ill.
Tokyo: Shin'nihon-Shuppansha 1971.

1973 Andō, Mikio: **Dendenmushi no Keiba.** (The snail race; Das Wettrennen der Schnecken.) Ill.: Shōsuke Fukuda.
Tokyo: Kaiseisha 1972.

1974 Funazaki, Yoshihiko: **Poppen-sensei to Kaerazu no Numa.** (Dr. *Poppen* and the lost swamp; Dr. *Poppen* und der verlorengegangene Sumpf.) Ill.: Yoshihiko Funazaki.
Tokyo: Chikuma-Shobo 1973.

1975 Matsutani, Miyoko: **Momo-chan to Akane-chan.** (Little *Momo* and her sister, little *Akane*; Die kleine *Momo* und ihre kleine Schwester, *Akane.*) Ill.: Sadao Kikuchi.
Tokyo: Kodansha 1974.

1976 Nonagase, Masao: **Chiisana Boku no Ie.** (My little house; Mein kleines Haus.) Ill.: Motoichiro Takebe.
Tokyo: Kodansha 1975.

Ill. 26 Suekichi Akaba in H. Muku: Homan-Ike no Kappa

Kōzaki, Mieko: **Chapu-chappun no Hanashi.** (Tales of *Chapu-chappun*; Die Geschichten von *Chapu-chappun*.) Ill.: Yōsuke Inoue.
Tokyo: Obunsha 1975.

Kōzaki, Mieko: **Mahō no Benchi.** (The magic bench; Die Zauberbank.) Ill.: Yūichi Watanabe.
Tokyo: Popurasha 1975.

1977 Shono, Eiji: **Arufabetto Guntō.** (The island alphabet; Die Inselgruppe Alphabet.) Ill.: Eiji Shono.
Tokyo: Kaiseisha 1977.

Kogure, Masao: **Matashichi-Gitsune Jitensha ni noru.** (*Matashichi* the fox rides a bike; Der Fuchs *Matashichi* fährt Rad.) Ill.: Yūichi Watanabe.
Tokyo: Komine Shoten 1977.

1978 Miyagawa, Hiro: **Yoru no Kagebōshi.** (The night shadows; Der Nachtschatten.) Ill.: Genjirō Mita.
Tokyo: Kodansha 1977.

1979 Kobayashi, Junichi: **Shōnenshishū Mosaku-jīsan.** (Poetry collection for youth, "Old *Mosaku*"; Gedichtsammlung für Jugendliche "Der alte *Mosaku*".) Ill.: Masao Kubo.
Tokyo: Kyoiku Shuppan Sentā 1979.

Hama, Mitsuo: **Haru yo koi.** (Come, spring; Komm, Frühling!) Ill.: Motoichiro Takebe.
Tokyo: Kaiseisha 1979.

1980 Miyaguchi, Shize: **Miyaguchi-Shizue Dōwa Zenshū, Zen 8-kan.** (Collected stories of *Shizune Miyaguchi* in eight volumes; Gesammelte Erzählungen von *Shizue Miyaguchi* in 8 Bänden.) Ill.: Setsu Asakura.
Tokyo: Chikuma Shobo 1979.

1981 Iwamoto, Toshi: **Karasu ga kākā naite iru.** (The crows crow; Es schreien die Krähen.) Ill.: Sadami Azuma.
Tokyo: Kaiseisha 1980.

Nihon-Jidōbungakusha-Kyōkai-Kyōkaishō

This prize was founded in 1951 by the Nihon-Jidobungakusha-Kyokai (The Society of Japanese Children's Book Writers and Researchers) to promote democratic values in youth literature. The prize is awarded annually to the best youth book or theoretical work on youth literature published during the previous year.

Der Preis wurde 1951 von der Nihon-Jidobungakusha-Kyokai (Gesellschaft der japanischen Kinderbuchschriftsteller- und -forscher) gestiftet, um die demokratische Jugendliteratur zu fördern. Der Preis wird den besten Werken der Jugendliteratur und -forschung, die in der Regel im vergangenen Jahr erschienen sind, verliehen.

1951 Tsuboi, Sakae: **Kaki-no-Ki no aru Ie:** (The house with persimmon trees; Das Haus mit Dattelpflaumen-Bäumen.) Ill.: Toshiko Akamatsu.
Tokyo: Yamanoki-Shoten 1949.

Okamoto, Yoshio: **Itsumo shizukani.** (Always be calm; Sei immer ruhig.)
Tokyo: Nihon-Jidobungaku 1947.

Okamoto, Yoshio: **Rakudai-Yokchō.** (Failure street; Die Straße der Sitzenbleiber.)
Tokyo: Ginga 1947.

Okamoto, Yoshio: **Asu mo okashiika.** (Will tomorrow be amusing, also? Wird es morgen auch lustig sein?)
Tokyo: Ginga 1941.

1952 The prize was not given; Der Preis wurde nicht vergeben.

1953 The prize was not given; Der Preis wurde nicht vergeben.

1954 The prize was not given; Der Preis wurde nicht vergeben.

1955 Kokubun, Ichitarō: **Tetsu no Machi no Shōnen.** (Boys in the iron town; Die Jungen in der Eisenstadt.) Ill.: Sadao Ichikawa.
Tokyo: Shinchosa 1954.

1956 *Theory/Theorie*
Kan, Tadamichi: **Nihon no Jidōbungaku.** (Japanese juvenile literatur; Die japanische Jugendliteratur.)
Tokyo: Ōtsuki-Shoten 1956.

1957 The prize was not given; Der Preis wurde nicht vergeben.

1958 The prize was not given; Der Preis wurde nicht vergeben.

1959 The prize was not given; Der Preis wurde nicht vergeben.

1960 The prize was not given; Der Preis wurde nicht vergeben.

1961 Suzuki, Minoru et al: **Yama ga naiteru.** (The mountains cry; Die heulenden Berge.) Ill.: Kōichi Kume.
Tokyo: Rironsha 1960.

1962 Hayafune, Chiyo: **Hyūpora no aru Machi.** (The town with foundries; Die Stadt mit Giessereien.) Photos: Koichi Matsumoto.
Tokyo: Yayoi-Shobō 1961.

1963 Kōyama, Yoshiko: **Ariko no Ki.** (*Ariko's* report; *Arikos* Bericht.) Ill.: Toshiko Maruki.
Tokyo: Rironsha 1962.

1964 Shōno, Eiji: **Hoshi no Makiba.** (The starlit pasture; Die Wiese unter den Sternen.) Ill.: Shinta Chō.
Tokyo: Rironsha 1963.

Theory/Theorie

Jingu, Teruo: **Sekai-Jidobungaku-An'nai.** (The guide to children's literature of the world; Ein Führer zur Kinderliteratur der ganzen Welt.)
Tokyo: Rironsha 1964.

1965 Takashi, Yoichi: **Uzumoreta Nihon.** (Japan buried; Das begrabene Japan.) Ill.: Yoshi Kobayashi.
Tokyo: Maki-Shoten 1964.

Inagaki, Masako: **Ma-Obasan wa Neko ga suki.** (Aunt *Ma* likes cats; Tante *Ma* liebt Katzen.) Ill.: Shōsuke Fukuda.
Tokyo: Rironsha 1964.

1966 Imanishi, Sukeyuki: **Higo no Ishiku.** (The stonemason from *Higo*; Der Maurer aus *Higo*.) Ill.: Bunshū Iguchi.
Tokyo: Jitsugyō-no-Nihonsha 1965.

Nasuda, Minoru: **Shirakaba to Shōji.** (White birches and a girl; Die Birken und ein Mädchen.) Ill.: Yoshiharu Suzuki.
Tokyo: Jitsugyō-no-Nihonsha 1965.

1967 Furuta, Taruhi: **Shukudai-Hikiuke-Kabushikigaisha.** (The company that undertakes housework; Die Aktiengesellschaft, die Hausaufgaben übernimmt.) Ill.: Kōichi Kume.
Tokyo: Rironsha 1966.

1968 Nagasaki, Gen'nosuke: **Hyokotan no Yagi.** (*Hyokotan's* goat; *Hyokotans* Ziege.) Ill.: Shōsuke Fukuda.
Tokyo: Rironsha 1967.

1969 Kurusu, Yoshio: **Kurosuke.** (*Kurosuke.*) Ill.: Genjirō Mita.
Tokyo: Iwasaki-Shoten 1968.

1970 Maekawa, Yasuo: **Majin no Umi.** (The demon's sea; Das Meer des Dämons.) Ill.: Nuguri Toko.
Tokyo: Kōdansha 1969.

1971 Sunada, Hiroshi: **Saraba Haiuei.** (Goodbye, highway; Leb wohl, Autobahn.) Ill.: Toshi Onoda.
Tokyo: Rironsha 1970.

1972 Seki, Hideo: **Chiisai Kokoro no Tabi.** (Travels of a small heart; Die Reise eines kleinen Herzens.) Ill.: Motoichirō Takebe.
Tokyo: Kaiseisha 1971.

Theory/Theorie

Fujita, Tamao: **Nihon Dōyōshi.** (The history of Japanese children's songs; Die Geschichte der japanischen Kinderlieder.)
Tokyo: Akane-Shobō 1971.

1973 Kubo, Takashi: **Akai Ho no Fune.** (The ship with red sails; Das Schiff mit roten Segeln.) Ill.: Makoto Sakurai.
Tokyo: Kaiseisha 1972.

Andō, Mikio: **Dendenmushi no Keiba.** (The snail race; Wettrennen der Schnecken.) Ill.: Shōsuke Fukuda.
Tokyo: Kaiseisha 1972.

1974 Imae, Yoshitomo: **Bonbon.** (My little boy; Mein kleiner Junge.) Ill.: Shinta Chō.
Tokyo: Rironsha 1973.

Iwasaki, Kyōko: **Hanasaka.** (The flower gardener; Der Blumengärtner.) Ill.: Hiroyuki Saitō.
Tokyo: Kaiseisha 1973.

1975 Kō, Sa-Myon: **Ikiru Koto no Imi.** (The meaning of life; Der Sinn des Lebens.) Ill.: Jirō Mizuno.
Tokyo: Chikuma-Shobō 1974.

1976 Mado, Michio: **Shokubutsu no Uta.** (Plant poems; Pflanzengedichte.) Photos: Ken Kuramochi.
Tokyo: Gingasha 1975.

Theory/Theorie

Torigoe, Shin: **Nihon Jidobungakushi Nenpyō.** (The chronological history of Japanese juvenile literature; Die chronologische Tabelle der japanischen Jugendliteratur.)

1977 Goto, Ryuji: **Shiro-Aka-Dasuki Ko O no Hata.** (The red and white ribbon and the flag with the little circle; Das rot-weisse Band und die Fahne mit dem kleinen Kreis.)
Tokyo: Kodansha 1976.

Takezaki, Yuhi: **Ishikiriyama no Hitobito.** (The mountain of the stonemasons; Der Berg der Steinmetzen.)
Tokyo: Kaiseisha 1976.

Tomita, Hiroyuki: **Nihon Jidōengekishi.** (The story of Japanese children's theatre; Die Geschichte des japanischen Kindertheaters.)
Tokyo: Kaiseisha 1977.

1978 Nagasaki, Gennosuke: **Tonneru-yama no Kodomo-tachi.** (The children in the mountain tunnel; Die Kinder im Bergtunnel.)
Tokyo: Kaiseisha 1977.

Saito, Ryūsuke: **Ten no Akauma.** (The red horse in the sky; Das rote Pferd am Himmel.)
Tokyo: Iwasaki-Shoten 1977.

1979 Kanzawa, Toshiko: **Inai-inai-Bāya.** (My wet-nurse; Meine Amme.)
Ill.: Eizo Hirayama.
Tokyo: Iwanami Shoten 1978.

1980 Matsutani, Miyoko: **Watashi no Anne Frank.** (My *Anne Frank;* Meine *Anne Frank.*) Ill.: Osamu Tsukasa.
Tokyo: Kaiseisha 1979.

1981 Katsuo, Kinya: **Nanatsubanshi Hyakumangoku.** (Seven stories from a princedom; Sieben Geschichten eines Fürstentums.) Ill.: Sanzen Tashiro.
Tokyo: Kaiseisha 1980.

Kawamura, Takashi: **Hiru to Yoru no aida.** (Between day and night; Zwischen Tag und Nacht.)
Ill.: Yoshi Kobayashi.
Tokyo: Kaiseisha 1980.

Noma Jidōbungei-shō

The Noma Hokokai Foundation was established by Seiji Noma, founder and first president of Kodansha Publishing House. The Noma literature prize forms one part of the foundation's numerous activities. The special Noma Prize for juvenile literature was created in 1963 and is completely independent from the adult literature prize. Selections are made from the best juvenile books which appeared during the previus year. The ten members of the jury are permitted to choose from fiction, non-fiction, short stories, theatre pieces, poems and songs. The winning author receives both a medal and a cash award.

Noma Hokokai ist eine Stiftung von Seiji Noma, dem Gründer und ersten Präsidenten des Verlagshauses Kodansha. Zu den zahlreichen Tätigkeiten dieser Stiftung gehört der Noma-Literatur-Preis. Er wird für das beste für Kinder bestimmte literarische Werk des jeweils vergangenen Jahres verliehen; der zehnköpfigen Jury steht es frei, unter Romanen, Erzählungen, Theaterstücken, Sachbüchern, Gedichten, Liedern usw. auszuwählen. Die Auszeichnung erfolgt in Form einer Medaille und einer Geldprämie.

1963 Ishimori, Nobuo: **Ban no Miyage-banashi.** (*Ban's story of his travels; Bans* Geschichte von seinen Reisen.) Ill.: Senzaburo Ikeda. Tokyo: Tōto Shobō 1962.

1964 Shōno, Eiji: **Hoshi no Makiba.** (The starlit pasture; Die Wiese unter den Sternen.) Ill.: Shinta Chō. Tokyo: Rironsha 1963.

Matsutani, Miyoko: **Chiisai Momo-chen** (Little *Momo*; Die kleine *Momo*.) Ill.: Sadao Kikuchi. Tokyo: Kōdansha 1963.

1965 Inui, Tomiko: **Umineko no Sora.** (The sky is for albatrosses; Der Himmel für Sturmvögel.) Tokyo: Rironsha 1965.

1966 Fukuda, Kiyoto: **Aki no Medama.** (The eye of autumn; Das Auge des Herbstes.) Ill.: Ryūichi Terashima. Tokyo: Kodansha 1966.

1967 Kagawa, Shigeru: **Setoro no Umi.** (*Setoro's* sea; Das Meer von *Setoro*.) Ill.: Yoshiharu Suzuki. Tokyo: Tōto Shobō 1967.

Sato, Satoru: **Obāsan no Hikoki.** (*Grandma's* airplane; Omas Flugzeug.) Ill.: Tsutomu Murakami. Tokyo: Komine Shoten 1966.

1968 Michio, Mado: **Tempura Piripiri.** (*Tempura Piripiri.*) Ill.: Yutaka Sugita. Tokyo: Dainihon Tosho 1968.

1969 Imanishi, Sukeyuki: **Uragami no Tabibito-tachi.** (The travelers from *Uragami*; Die Reisenden aus *Uragami*.) Ill.: Daihachi Ohta. Tokyo: Jitsugyo-no-Nihonsha 1969.

Miyawaki, Toshio: **Yama no Ongoku-Monogatori.** (The story of a faraway mountain land; Die Geschichte vom fernen Bergland.) Tokyo: Kōdansha 1969.

1970 Iwasaki, Kyoko: **Koi no iru Mura.** (The village that cultivates carp; Das Dorf, in dem es Karpfen gibt.) Ill.: Chihiro Iwasaki et al. Tokyo: Shin-Nihon-Shuppansha 1969.

1971 Tsuchiya, Yukio: **Tokyokko Monogatari.** (The story of a Tokyo boy; Die Geschichte von einem Jungen aus Tokio.) Ill.: Shōsuke Fukuda. Tokyo: Tōto-Shobō 1971.

1972 Kitabatake, Yaho: **Oni o kau Goro.** (*Goro,* the demon raiser; *Goro,* der Dämonenzüchter.) Ill.: Selichi Katō. Tokyo: Jitsugyo-no-Nihonsha 1971.

1973 Yoda, Jun'ichi: **No-yuki Yama-yuki.** (Over the fields, over the mountains; Über Wiesen und Berge.) Ill.: Akio Ohkuni.
Tokyo: Dainihon-Tosho 1973.

Andō, Mikio: **Dendenmushi no Keiba.** (The snail race; Wettrennen der Schnecken.) Ill.: Shōsuke Fukuda.
Tokyo: Kaiseisha 1973.

1974 Tsubota, Jōji: **Nezumi no Ibiki.** (The snoring mouse; Die schnarchende Maus.) Ill.: Hisako Komatsu.
Tokyo: Kōdansha 1973.

1975 Koide, Shōgo: **Zinta no Ota.** (The sound of the band; Die Töne der Blaskapelle.) Ill.: Yoshiharu Suzuki.
Tokyo: Kaiseisha 1974.

1976 Nonagase, Masao: **Shishu "Chiisana boku no Ie".** (Poetry collection, "Our little house"; Gedichtsammlung "Unser kleines Haus".) Ill.: Motochiro Takebe.
Tokyo: Kōdansha 1976.

1977 Shōgenji, Haruko: **Yukkibokko Monogatari.** (The story of a snow boy; Die Geschichte eines Schneejungen.) Ill.: Sadao Ichikawa.
Tokyo: Doshinsha 1977.

Imae, Yoshitomo: **Aniki.** (My older brother; Mein älterer Bruder.) Ill.: Shinta Cho.
Tokyo: Rironsha 1976.

1978 Kawamura, Takashi: **Yama e iku Ushi.** (Today the cow climbs up the mountain; Heute steigt die Kuh auf den Berg.) Ill.: Hiroyuki Saito.
Tokyo: Kaiseisha 1977.

1979 Kanzawa, Toshiko: **Inai-inai-Bāya.** (My wet nurse; Meine Amme.) Ill.: Eizo Hirayama.
Tokyo: Iwanami Shoten 1978.

1980 Nagasaki, Gennosuke: **Wasurerareta Shima e.** (On a forgotten island; Auf einer vergessenen Insel.) Ill.: Miyoshi Akasaka.
Tokyo: Kaiseisha 1980.

Sakata, Hiroo: **Tora-jīchan no Bōken.** (The adventure of old *Tora*; Abenteuer des alten *Tora*.) Ill.: Fuyuji Yamanaka.
Tokyo: Kōdansha 1980.

Shōgakukan Bungakushō/Kaigashō

In 1952, the book and magazine publishing house, Shogakukan, established two prizes which are given annually: one for literature and the other for illustration. Books and magazine or newspaper articles, original texts or adaptations, poems and plays are eligible for the prize. There is no differentiation as to age groupings. Selections are made from the previous year's production (April — March). The literary jury, which has ten members, is made up of authors and critics. The fine arts jury, composed of artists, has six members. The final selection is made in October, with the public presentation taking place in November. The prize-winners receive a cash-award and a bronze statuette. (For the illustration prize, the authors are only indicated when the title is in book form.)

Der Buch- und Zeitschriftenverlag Shogakukan begründete 1952 sowohl einen literarischen als auch einen grafischen Preis für Veröffentlichungen in Buchform oder in Form von Zeitschriften- und Zeitungsbeiträgen. Der Literaturpreis kann Originaltexten, aber auch Nacherzählungen, Gedichten und Theaterstücken verliehen werden. Es gibt keine Altersdifferenzierungen, eingereicht werden Veröffentlichungen des jeweils vergangenen Produktionsjahres (April bis März), die Jurys bestehen aus zehn Schriftstellern und Kritikern bzw. aus sechs Künstlern. Nachdem im Oktober die endgültige Wahl getroffen wird, findet Anfang November die öffentliche Preisverteilung statt, bei der eine von Takashi Shimzu geschaffene Bronzstatuette und eine Geldprämie verliehen werden. (Die Autoren werden beim Illustrationspreis nur erwähnt, wenn die Titel in Buchform erschienen sind.)

1952 *Literature prize/Literaturpreis*

Namachi, Saburo: **Maigo no Dōnatsu.** (Doughnuts astray; Verirrte Krapfen.)
Tokyo: Yonen Kurabu 1951 (April).

Sumii, Sue: **Mikan.** (Orange.)
Tokyo: Shogaku 5-nensei 1952 (February).

Tsuchiya, Yukio: **Sambiki no Koneko.** (Three kittens; Drei Kätzchen.)
Tokyo: Yonen Kurabu 1951 (January); 1952 (December).

Illustration prize/Illustrationspreis

Yasu, Tai: **Illustration series; Illustrationsreihe.**

Iguchi, Bunshun: **Illustration series;** Illustrationsreihe.

Watanabe, Ikuko: **Illustration series;** Illustrationsreihe.

1953 *Literature prize/Literaturpreis*

Ito, Einosuke: **Gorō-gitsune.** (*Goro* the fox; *Goro* der Fuchs.)
Tokyo: Shōgaku 5-nensei 1953 (January).

Nagai, Rintaro: **Otsukisama wo tabeta Yakkodako.** (The kite that ate the moon; Der Drachen, der den Mond fraß.)
Tokyo: 1-nen no Gakushu 1953 (March).

Nitanosa, Nakaba: **Koushi no Nakama.** (The friendly calves; Freundliche Kälber.)
Tokyo: Shōgaku 5-nensei 5-nensei 1953 (February).

Illustration prize/Illustrationspreis
Kurakane, Shōsuke: **Illustration series;** Illustrationsreihe.

Miyoshi, Teikichi: **Illustration series;** Illustrationsreihe.

Suzuki, Toshio: **Illustration series;** Illustrationsreihe.

1954 *Literature prize/Literaturpreis*
Ochiai, Sōzaburo: **Tanjōbi no Okurimono.** (Birthday gifts; Geschenke zum Geburtstag.)
Tokyo: Sakurai Shoten 1953.

Illustration prize/Illustrationspreis
Motai, Takeshi for: **Illustrations in children's books;** Illustrationen in Kinderbüchern.

1955 *Literature prize/Literaturpreis*
Tsuruta, Tomoya: **Hattara wa waga Furusato.** (*Hattara* is my home; *Hattara* ist meine Heimat.)
Tokyo: Shōgaku 6-nensei 1954 (April) — 1955 (March).

Illustration prize/Illustrationspreis
Nakao, Akira: **Nakayoshi Yōchien.** (The friendly kindergarten; Der freundliche Kindergarten.)
Tokyo: Child Book 1954 (September)

Nakao, Akira: **Nikoniko Taro-chan.** (Little smiling *Taro*; Der lächelnde kleine *Taro*.)
Tokyo: Child Book 1955 (January).

Nakao, Akira: **Hituji-san to Oshikura.** (Pushing contest with sheep; Stoß-Spiel mit dem Schaf.)
Tokyo: Child Book 1955 (February).

1956 *Literature prize/Literaturpreis*
Koyama, Katsukiyo: **Yamainu-Shōnen.** (The coyote boy; Der Kojotenjunge.)
Tokyo: Chugakusei no Tomo 1955 (April).

Illustration prize/Illustrationspreis
Iwasaki, Chihiro: **Yūhi.** (The setting sun; Die untergehende Sonne.)
Tokyo: Hikari no Kuni 10—7.

1957 *Literature prize/Literaturpreis*
Uchiki, Muraji: **Yume no ma no koto.** (Dreams; Träume.)
Tokyo: Shōgaku 6-nensei 1956 (December).

Illustration prize/Illustrationspreis
Watanabe, Saburo: **Kumo-san.** (Clouds; Wolken.)
Tokyo: Child Book 1955 (September).

1958 *Literature prize/Literaturpreis*
Nishiyama, Toshio: **Yokohama Monogatari.** (The tale of *Yokohama*; Die Geschichte von *Yokohama.*)
Tokyo: Asa no Fue 1957 (June); 1958 (March).

Illustration prize/Illustrationspreis
Ohta, Daihachi: **Itazura-Usagi.** (Mischievous rabbits; Die unartigen Hasen.)
Tokyo: Kodomo no Tomo 1957 (September).

1959 *Literature prize/Literaturpreis*
Saeki, Chiaki: **Moeyo ki no Hana.** (The yellow flowers flame up; Die gelben Blumen leuchten.)
Tokyo: Jogakusei no Tomo 1958 (September).

Illustration prize/Illustrationspreis
Kakimoto, Kōzō: **Minato.** (The harbour; Der Hafen.)
Tokyo: 1-nen no Gakushu 1958 (July).

Kakimoto, Kōzō: **Kodamago.** (*Kodama Express; Kodama Express.)*
Tokyo: 1-nen no Gakushu 1958 (March).

1960 *Literature prize/Literaturpreis*
Shinkawa, Kazue: **Kisetu no Hana Shishu.** (Collection of poems on seasonal flowers; Gedichtsammlung von Blumen in den verschiedenen Jahreszeiten.)
Tokyo: Chugaku 1-nen Kosu 1959 (April); 1960 (March).

Illustration prize/Illustrationspreis
Fukazawa, Kuniro: **Nakayoshi Buranko.** (The friendly swing; Die freundliche Schaukel.)
Tokyo: Hikari no Kuni 1959 (April).

Fukazawa, Kuniro: **Zō no Hana wa naze nagai.** (Why the elephant has such a long nose; Warum hat der Elefant einen so langen Rüssel?)
Tokyo: Yochien 1959.

1961 *Literature prize/Literaturpreis*
The prize was not given; Der Preis wurde nicht vergeben.

Illustration prize/Illustrationspreis
Endo, Teruyo: **Natsukashi no Tomo.** (Dear friends; Liebe Freunde.)
Tokyo: Chugakusei no Tomo 2-nen 1960 (October).

Endo, Teruyo: **Uranai.** (Fortune teller; Der Wahrsager.)
Tokyo: 5-nen no Gakushu 1961 (January).

Endo, Teruyo: **Shimbun-Haitatsu.** (A newsboy; Ein Zeitungsjunge.)
Tokyo: 3-nen no Gakushu 1960 (April).

1962 *Literature prize/Literaturpreis*
Hanaoka, Daigaku: **Yūyake-Gakkō.** (The twilight school; Die Schule in der Abenddämmerung.) Ill.: Kōichi Kume.
Tokyo: Rironsha 1961.

Illustration prize/Illustrationspreis
The prize was not given; Der Preis wurde nicht vergeben.

1963 *Literature prize/Literaturpreis*
Manzoku, Takashi: **Oyadanuki to Kodanuki no Uta.** (The song of the badger family; Der Gesang der Dachsfamilie.)
Tokyo: Asahi Shuppansha 1963.

Oishi, Makoto: **Mienaku natta Kuro.** (*Kuro* is lost; *Kuro* ist verschwunden.)
Tokyo: Tanoshii 6-nensei 1963 (January).

Illustration prize/Illustrationspreis
Shimizu, Masaru in:
Furukawa, Haruo/Yajima, Minoru: **Konchū to Shokubutsu Kagaku-Zusetsu Siriziu.** (Insects and plants; Insekten und Pflanzen.)
Tokyo: Shogakukan 1962.

1964 *Literature prize/Literaturpreis*
Yamamoto, Kazuo: **Moeru Mizuumi.** (The burning lake; Der brennende See.) Ill.: Kōichi Kume.
Tokyo: Rironsha 1964.

Illustration prize/Illustrationspreis
Ie, Haruyo in:
Kaeru no Kero. (*Kero* the frog; *Kero* der Frosch.)
Tokyo: Hikari no Kuni 1963 (April).

1965 *Literature prize/Literaturpreis*
Kubo, Takashi: **Biru no Yamaneko.** (Wildcat in the building; Die Wildkatze im Hochhaus.) Ill.: Yoshiharu Suzuki.
Tokyo: Shinsei Shobo 1964.

Illustration prize/Illustrationspreis
Nakatani, Chiyoko in:
Kishida, Eriko: **Kabakun no Fune.** (*Hippo's* boat; *Hippos* Boot.)
Tokyo: Kodomo no Tomo 1964 (May).

Nakatani, Chiyoko in:
Nakatani, chiyoko: **Maigo no Chiro.** (*Chiro* loses himself; *Chiro* hat sich verirrt.)
Tokyo: Kodomo no Tomo 1965 (March).

Nakatani, Chiyoko in:
Nakatani, Chiyoko: **Ōkina Kuma-san.** (Big bear; Der große Bär.)
Tokyo: Hikari no Kuni 1964 (September).

1966 *Literature prize/Literaturpreis*
Nishizawa, Shōtaro: **Aoi Sukuramu.** (Blue team; Die blaue Mannschaft.) Ill.: Sadao Ichikawa.
Tokyo: Tōtō Shobō 1965.

Illustration prize/Illustrationspreis
Fukuda, Shōsuke in:
Hanaoka, Daigaku: **100-wa no Tsuru.** (One hundred cranes; Hundert Kraniche.)
Tokyo: Jitsugyo no Nihonsha 1965.

Fukuda, Shōsuke in:
Go Shō On: **Songoku.** (*Songoku.*)
Tokyo: Seikosha 1965.

1967 *Literature prize/Literaturpreis*
Yoshida, Toshi: **Jibun no Hoshi.** (My stars; Meine Sterne.)
Tokyo: Shōgaku 4-nensei 1965 (January); 5-nensei 1966 (December).

Illustration prize/Illustrationspreis
Murakami, Tsutomu in:
Sato, Satoru: **Uchū kara kita Mitsubachi.** (The bees from outer space; Die Biene aus dem Weltraum.)
Tokyo: Seikosha 1966.

Murakami, Tsutomu in:
Sato, Satoru: **Obāsan no Hikōki.** (Grandma's airplane; Omas Flugzeug.)
Tokyo: Komine Shoten 1967.

1968 *Literature prize/Literaturpreis*
Saito, Ryūsuke: **Berodashi Chomma.** (*Chomma* the doll; Die Puppe *Chomma.*) Ill.: Jirō Takidaira.
Tokyo: Rironsha 1967.

Illustration prize/Illustrationspreis
Segawa, Yasuo in:
Matsutani, Miyoko: **Yamamba no Nishiki.** (The brocade of the mountain witch; Der Brokat der Berghexe.)
Tokyo: Popurasha 1967.

1969 *Literature prize/Literaturpreis*
Yamashita, Yumiko: **2-nen 2-kumi wa Hiyoko no Kurasu.** (The class of the chicken teacher; Die Klasse der Küken-Lehrerin.) Ill.: Shinta Chō.
Tokyo: Rironsha 1968.

Illustration prize/Illustrationspreis
Suzuki, Yoshiharu in:
Nakamura, Misako: **Machi no Sentaku.** (The town laundry; Die Wäscherei der Stadt.)
Tokyo: Hikari no Kuni 1968 (August).

1970 *Literature prize/Literaturpreis*
Takegawa, Mizue: **Kūchū Atorie.** (An atelier in the air; Das Atelier in der Luft.) Ill.: Sumiko Ishizaki.
Tokyo: Jitsugyo-no-Hihonsha 1970.

Illustration prize/Illustrationspreis
Onoki, Gaku in:
Andō, Mikio: **Ondori to nimai no Kinka.** (The cock and two gold coins; Der Hahn und zwei Goldmünzen.)
Tokyo: Popurasha 1969.

1971 *Literature prize/Literaturpreis*
Ōe, Hide: **8-gatsu ga kuru tabini.** (When August comes; Wenn August kommt.)
Tokyo: Rironsha 1971.

Illustration prize/Illustrationspreis
Tanaka, Hiroaki in:
Ségur, Sophie Comptesse de: **Chitchana Shukujo-tachi.** (Little ladies; Die kleinen Damen.)
Tokyo: Shogakukan 1970.

1972 *Literature prize/Literaturpreis*
Sugi, Mikiko: **Chiisana Yuki no Machi no Monogatari.** (The story of the little city; Die Geschichte einer schneebedeckten kleinen Stadt.) Ill.: Chūryō Sato.
Tokyo: Doshinsha 1972.

Illustration prize/Illustrationspreis
Kosaka, Shigeru in:
Mitsukoshi, Sachio: **Orihime to Kengyū.** (*Vega* and *Altair.*)
Tokyo: Child Book 1971 (July).

Saito, Hiroyuki in:
Takashi, Yoichi: **Gawappa.** (*Gawappa.*)
Tokyo: Iwasaki Shoten 1971.

1973 *Literature prize/Literaturpreis*
Awa, Naoko: **Kaze to Ki no Uta.** (A song of the wind and the tree; Das Lied vom Wind und Baum.) Ill.: Osamu Tsukasa.
Tokyo: Jitsugyo-no-Nihonsha 1972.

Illustration prize/Illustrationspreis
Akasaka, Miyoshi in:
Tani, Shinsuke: **Kapura no Mori.** (*Kapura's* forest; *Kapuras* Wald.)
Tokyo: Kaiseisha 1972.

Akasaka, Miyoshi in:
Tani, Shinsuke: **Juni-sama.** (The god of the forest; Der Gott des Waldes.)
Tokyo: Kokudosha 1973.

Akasaka, Miyoshi in:
Tani, Shinsuke: **Kamakura.** (*Kamakura.*)
Tokyo: Kodansha 1972.

1974 *Literature prize/Literaturpreis*
Kobayashi, Seinosuke: **Yachō no Shiki.** (Four seasons of wild birds; Vier Jahresszeiten der wilden Vögel.) Ill.: Maki Ando.
Tokyo: Komine Shoten 1974.

Illustration prize/Illustrationspreis
Kajiyama, Toshio: **Ahoroku no Kawa-Daiko.** (*Ahoroku's* leather drum; *Ahorokus* Ledertrommel.)
Tokyo: Popurasha 1974.

1975 *Literature prize/Literaturpreis*
Yamashita, Haruo: **Hambun chōdai.** (Please give me half! Gib mir, bitte, die Hälfte!) Ill.: Ken'ichi Matsunaga.
Tokyo: Shogakukan 1975.

Illustration prize/Illustrationspreis
Akaba, Suekichi in:
Muku, Hatoju: **Homan-Ike no Kappa.** (*Kappa,* the nixie in *Homan Pond*; *Kappa,* die Nixe im *Homan-Teich.*)
Tokyo: Gingasha 1975.

1976 *Literature prize/Literaturpreis*
Yoshida, Hisako: **Makiko wa naita.** (*Makiko* cried; *Makiko* hat geweint.) Ill.: Setsu Asakura.
Tokyo: Rironsha 1975.

Illustration prize/Illustrationspreis
Kume, Kōichi in:
Sudo, Katsuzo: **Yamamba.** (*Yamamba.*)
Tokyo: Iwasaki Shoten 1976.

Kume, Kōichi in:
Kubo Takashi: **Kuroshio Saburo.** (*Saburo,* the boy of the black sea wave; *Saburo,* der Junge der schwarzen Meeresströmung.)
Tokyo: Kin-no-Hoshisha 1976.

1977 *Literature prize/Literaturpreis*
Takezake, Yūhi: **Ishikiriyama no Hitobito.** (The mountain of the stone masons; Der Berg der Steinmetzen.) Ill.: Shimpei Kitajima.
Tokyo: Kaiseisha 1976.

Illustration prize/Illustrationspreis
Anno, Mitsumasa in:
Anno, Mitsumasa: **No no Hana to Kobito-tachi.** (The flowers of the meadow and the elves; Die Blumen auf der Wiese und die Elfen.)
Tokyo: Iwasaki Shoten 1976.

1978 *Literature prize/Literaturpreis*
Haitani, Kenjiro: **Hitoribotchi no Dōbutsuen.** (Alone in the animal garden; Allein im Tiergarten.) Ill.: Shinta Chō.
Tokyo: Akane Shobo 1977.

Illustration prize/Illustrationspreis
Tsukasa, Osamu in:
Kawamura, Takashi: **Hana no Yubiwa.** (The ring of flowers; Der Ring aus Blumen.)
Tokyo: Bunken Shuppan 1977.

1979 *Literature prize/Literaturpreis*
Kishi, Takeo: **Hanabusa-Tōge.** (The flowering mountain pass; Der blühende Bergpaß.) Ill.: Shunsaku Umeda.
Tokyo: Kodansha 1979.

Saneto, Akira: **Jambokokko no Denki.** (Biography of *Jambokokko*; Biographie von *Jambokokko*.) Ill.: Tomoko Hasegawa.
Tokyo: Shogakukan 1979.

Illustration prize/Illustrationspreis
Sugiura, Norishige in:
Tsurumi, Massao: **Furuya no Mori.** (Holes in the old house; Löcher im alten Haus.)
Tokyo: Froebel-kan 1979.

1980 *Literature prize/Literaturpreis*
Imanishi, Sukeyuki: **Hikari to Kaze to Kumo to Ki to.** (The light and the wind, the clouds and the trees; Das Licht und der Wind, die Wolken und die Bäume.) Ill.: Sadao Ichikawa.
Tokyo: Shogakukan 1980.

Kagawa, Shigeru: **Kōkū 10.000 mētoru no kanata de.** (Over 10.000 meters high; Über 10.000 m Höhe.) Ill.: Nobuyoshi Arai.
Tokyo: Alice-kan Maki Shinsha 1980.

Illustration prize/Illustrationspreis
Harada, Yasuji in:
Harada, Yasuji: **Watashi no Shinshū. Kusabue no Uta.** (My country and Poems from the grass pipe; Mein Heimatland und Gedichte von der Graspfeife.)
Tokyo: Kodansha 1979.

The Netherlands/Niederlande

Het Kinderboek van het Jaar

In The Netherlands, the „Commissie voor de Collectieve Propaganda van het Nederlands Boek" (CPNB) — Committee for the General Promotion of the Dutch Book — annually presents a prize for the best children's book published in the previous year. The first such prize was presented in 1955. The ceremony of the award presentation is part of Children's Book Week, which takes place in autumn.

Since 1966, two prizes have been given: one for a book for children up to ten years of age, and another for a youth book for those ten and above. Since 1971, the titles of these two awards have officially been named, the „Gouden Griffel" (Golden Plaque) and the „Zilveren Griffel" (Silver Plaque).

In den Niederlanden vergibt die „Commissie voor de Collectieve Propaganda van het Nederlandse Boek (CPNB) seit 1955 jährlich anläßlich der Kinderbuchwoche im Herbst einen Preis für das beste Jugendbuch des vergangenen Jahres. Seit 1966 werden zwei Preise vergeben; für ein Kinderbuch bis zu 10 Jahren und für ein Jugendbuch ab 10 Jahren. Seit 1971 wird den preisgekrönten Büchern der „Gouden Griffel" (Goldene Griffel) und der „Zilveren Griffel" (Silberne Griffel) verliehen.

Ill. 27 *Wim Hofman in: Koning Wikkepokluk de merkwaardige zoekt een Rijk....*

1955 Rutgers van der Loeff-Basenau, An: **Lawines razen.** (Roaring avalanches; Die Lawinen toben.) Ill.: Alie Evers.
Amsterdam: Ploegsma 1954.

1956 Bruijn, Cor: **Lasse Länta.** (*Lasse Länta*) Ill.: Ger Sligte.
Amsterdam: Ploegsma 1955.

1957 Diekmann, Miep: **De boten van Brakkeput.** (The boat from Brakkeput; Die Boote von Brakkeput.) Ill.: Jenny Dalenoord.
'S-Gravenhage: Leopold 1956.

1958 Schmidt, Annie Maria Geertruida: **Wiplala.** (*Wiplala.*) Ill.: Jenny Dalenoord.
Amsterdam: De Arbeiderspers 1957.

1959 Laurey, Harriet: **Sinterklaas ende struikrovers.** (*Santa Claus* and the highwaymen; Der *Nikolaus* und die Strauchdiebe.) Ill.: Babs van Wely.
Amsterdam: U.M. Holland 1958.

1960 Pothast-Gimberg, Christina Elizabeth: **Corso, het ezeltje.** (*Corso*, the donkey; *Corso*, das Eselchen.) Ill.: Elly van Beek.
'S-Gravenhage: Van Goor 1959.

1961 Blokker, Jan Andries: **Op zoek naar een oom.** (In search of an uncle; Auf der Suche nach einem Onkel.) Ill.: Laura Gerding.
Amsterdam: De Bezige Bij 1960.

1962 Dulieu, Jean (i.e. Jan van Oort): **Paulus de Hulpsinterklaas.** (*Paul, Santa Claus's* helper; *Paulus* Der Hilfs-*Nikolaus.*) Ill.: Jean Dulieu.
Amsterdam: van der Peet 1961.

1963 Dragt, Tonke: **De brief voor de koning.** (The letter for the king; Der Brief für den König.) Ill.: Tonke Dragt.
'S-Gravenhage: Leopold 1962.

1964 Visser, Willem F.H.: **Niku de koerier.** (*Niku* the courier; *Niku* der Kurier.) Ill.: Jenny Dalenoord.
'S-Gravenhage: Van Goor 1963.

1965 Biegel, Paul: **Het sleutelkruid.** (The key herb; Das Schlüsselkraut.) Ill.: Babs van Wely.
Haarlem: U.M. Holland 1965.

1966 *Children's Book/Kinderbuch*
Bouhuys, Mies: **Kinderverhalten.** (Children's stories; Kindergeschichten.) Ill.: Babs van Wely.
Haarlem: U.M. Holland 1964.

Youth book/Jugendbuch
Blom, Toos: **Loeloedji, kleine rode bloem.** (*Loeloedji*, little red flower; *Loeloedji*, kleine rote Blume.) Ill.: Elly van Beek.
Amsterdam: De Arbeiderspers 1965.

1967 The prize was not given; Der Preis wurde nicht vergeben.

1968 *Children's book/Kinderbuch*
Werner, Hans: **Mattijs Mooimuziek.** (*Mattijs Mooimuziek.*) Ill.: Niek Hiemstra.
Hoorn: West-Friesland 1967.

Youth book/Jugendbuch
Iterson, Siny Rose van: **De adjudant van de vrachtwagen.** (The driver's mate on the truck; Der Beifahrer des Lastwagens.) Ill.: Dick Stolwijk.
's-Gravenhage: Leopold 1967.

1969 *Children's book/Kinderbuch*
Andreus, Hans: **Meester Pompelmoes en de Mompelpoes.** (Mr. *Grapefruit* and the pussy cat; Meister *Pampelmuse* und die Miezekatze.) Ill.: Babs van Wely.
Haarlem: Holland 1968.

Youth book/Jugendbuch
Kerkwijk, Henk van: **Komplott op volle zee.** (Conspiracy on the high sea; Verschwörung auf hoher See.) Ill.: R.P.E. Oxenaar.
Amsterdam: Ploegsma 1968.

1970 *Children's book/Kinderbuch*
Laurey, Haariet: **Verhalen van de spinnende kater.** (The story of the purring cat; Die Geschichte des schnurrenden Katers.) Ill.: Reintje Venema.
Haarlem: Holland 1969.

Youth book/Jugendbuch
Herzen, Frank: **De zoon van de woordbouwer.** (The son of the word builders; Der Sohn des Wortbauers.) Ill.: Frank Herzen.
Leiden: Sijthoff 1969.

1971 *Gouden Griffel*
Kooiker, Leonie: **Het malle ding van bobbistiek.** (*Bobbistiek's* humourous thing; Das lustige Ding von *Bobbistiek*.) Ill.: Carl Hollander.
Amsterdam: Ploegsma 1970.

Schouten, Alet: **De mare van de witte toren.** (The news from the white towers; Die Nachricht von den weißen Türmen.) Ill.: Alet Schouten.
Bussum: Van Holkema & Warendorf 1970.

Zilveren Griffel

Andreus, Hans: **De rommeltuin.** (The bewitched garden; Der verwunschene Garten.)
Haarlem: Holland 1970.

Beckman, Thea: **Met Korilu de griemel rond.** (Around the world with *Korilu*; Mit *Korilu* rund um die Welt.)
Rotterdam: Lemniscaat 1970.

Burger, Sacha: **Heraois en de beker.** (*Heraois* and the cup; *Heraois* und der Becher.)
Den Haag: Leopold 1970.

Iterson, Siny R. van: **Het gouden suikerriet.** (The golden sugar cane; Das goldene Zuckerrohr.)
Den Haag: Leopold 1970.

Kerkwijk, Henk van: **Schakelfout.** (Switch defect; Schaltfehler.)
Amsterdam: Ploegsma 1970.

Lobel, Arnold: **Valentijn.** (*Valentin.*)
Amsterdam: Ploegsma 1970.

Rodman, Maia: **Net als je vader, Manolo;** (Not as your father, *Manolo*; Nicht als dein Vater, *Manolo*.)
Den Haag: Leopold 1970.

Schmidt, Annie M.G.: **Minoes.** (*Minoes.*)
Amsterdam: De Arbeiderspers 1970.

Sutcliff, Rosemary: **De roemruchte daden van Robin Hood.** (The well known facts about *Robin Hood*; Die berühmten Taten von *Robin Hood*.)
Den Haag: Leopold 1970.

Zimnik, Reiner: **De kleine brultijger.** (The little roaring tiger; Der kleine Brülltiger.)
Amsterdam: Ploegsma 1970.

1972 *Gouden Griffel*

Biegel, Paul: **De kleine kapitein.** (The little captain; Der kleine Kapitän.) Ill.: Carl Hollander.
Haarlem: Holland 1971.

Terlouw, Jan: **Koning van Katoren.** (King from Katoren; König von Katoren.) Ill.: A. Bouwman.
Rotterdam: Lemniscaat 1971.

Zilveren Griffel

Biegel, Paul: **De twaalf rovers.** (The twelve robbers; Die zwölf Räuber.)
Haarlem: Holland 1971.

Cesco, Frederique de: **De prins van Mexico.** (The prince of Mexico; Der Prinz von Mexiko.)
Den Haag: Leopold 1971.

Dahl, Roald: **De fantastische meneer Vos.** (The fantastic Mr. *Vos*; Der phantastische Herr *Vos*.)
De Bilt: De Fontein 1971.

Hunt, Irene: **Het huis tussen de bomen.** (The house between the trees; Das Haus zwischen den Bäumen.)
Amsterdam: Deltos Elsevier 1971.

Jagt, Bouke: **De pozzebokken.** (The lazy billy goat; Der faule Ziegenbock.)
Bussum: Van Holkema & Warendorf 1971.

Preussler, Otfried: **De avonturen van sterke Wanja.** (The adventures of strong *Wanja*; Die Abenteuer des starken *Wanja*.)
Rotterdam: Lemniscaat 1971.

1973 *Gouden Griffel*

Barnard, Henk: **De Marokkaan en de kat van tante Da.** (The Moroccan and aunt *Da*'s cat; Der Marokkaner und die Katze von Tante *Da*.) Ill.: Reintje Venema.
Bussum: Van Holkema & Warendorf 1972.

Terlouw, Jan: **Oorlogswinter.** (Winter of war; Kriegswinter.)
Rotterdam: Lemniscaat 1972.

Zilveren Griffel

Ainsworth, Ruth: **Voor jou van vrouwtje Appelwang.** (For you from Mrs. *Apple-cheek*; Für Euch von Frau *Apfelwange*.)
Amsterdam: Ploegsma 1972.

Bödker, Cecil: **De luipaard.** (The leopard; Der Leopard; Dan. orig. title: Leoparden.)
Den Haag: Leopold 1972.

Garfield, Leon: **De avonturen van Jack Holborn.** (The adventures of *Jack Holborn*; Die Abenteuer des *Jack Holborn*.)
Den Haag: Leopold 1972.

Hunter, Kristin: **De Soul Brothers en Sister Lou.** (The soul brothers and sister *Lou*; Die Seelenbrüder und Schwester *Lou*.)
Den Haag: Leopold 1972.

Jong, Meindert de: **Candy, kom terug.** (*Candy*, come back; *Candy* komm zurück.)
Hoorn: West-Friesland 1972.

Lindgren, Astrid: **Lotta uit de Kabaalstraat.** (*Lotta* from Kabaal Street; *Lotta* aus der Kabaalstraße.)
Amsterdam: Ploegsma 1972.

Preussler, Otfried: **Meester van de zwarte molen.** (The satanic mill.; Germ.orig.title: *Krabat.*)
Rotterdam: Lemniscaat 1972.

Viorst, Judith: **Dat is heel wat voor een kat, vind je niet?** (This is something for the cat, don't you agree? Das ist etwas für eine Katze, findest du nicht?)
Amsterdam: Kosmos 1972.

1974 *Gouden Griffel*

Beckman, Thea: **Kruistocht in spijkerbroek.** (Crusade in jeans; Kreuzzug in Jeans.)
Rotterdam, Lemniscaat 1973.

Haar, Jaap ter: **Het wereldje van Beer Ligthart.** (*Beer Ligthart*'s little world; *Beer Ligtharts* kleine Welt.) Ill.: Rien Poortvliet.
Bussum: Van Holkema & Warendorf 1973.

Zilveren Griffel

Biegel, Paul: **Het Olifantenfeest.** (The elephant's party; Das Elefantenfest.)
Haarlem: Holland 1973.

Evenhuis, Gertie: **Stefan en Stefan.** (*Stefan* and *Stefan.*)
Amsterdam: Deltos Elsvier 1973.

Garfield, Leon: **Tussen galg en gekkenhuis.** (Between gallows and lunatic asylum; Zwischen Galgen und Irrenanstalt.)
Den Haag: Leopold 1973.

Haugaard, Erik Christian: **Dag van de koningsakker.** (The King's acre; Der Tag des Königsackers.)
Den Haag: Leopold 1973.

Kellogg, Steven: **Mag ik hem houden.** (Can I keep him? *Martin* wünscht sich einen Freund.)
Amsterdam: Fehmers 1973.

Manushkin, Fran: **Kindje.** (Child; Kindchen.)
Amsterdam: Kosmos 1973.

Procházka, Jan: **Lenka.** (*Lenka.*)
Den Haag: Leopold 1973.

Sachs, Marilyn: **Wie had gelijk Mary Rose?** (The truth about *Mary Rose*; Die Wahrheit über *Mary Rose.*)
Amsterdam: Querido 1973.

1975 *Gouden Griffel*

Schell, Simone: **De nacht van de heksenketelkandij.** (The night *van de heksenketelkandij* = witch's sugar candy cauldron; Die Nacht *van de heksenketelkandij* = Hexenkessel-Kandiszucker.) Ill.: Jes Preekmeester.
Amsterdam: Deltos Elsevier 1974.

Schouten, Alet: **Iolo komt niet spelen.** (*Iolo* won't come to play; *Iolo* kommt nicht zum Spielen.) Ill.: Paul Hulshof.
Bussum: Van Holkema & Warendorf 1974.

Zilveren Griffel

Eykman, Karel: **De vreselijk verlegen vogelverschrikker.** (The horribly embarrassed scarecrow; Die schrecklich verlegene Vogelscheuche.)
Amsterdam: De Harmonie 1974.

Fleischman, Sid: Djingo Django. (*Djingo Django.*)
Amsterdam: Kosmos 1974.

George, Jean Craighead: **Miyax, de wolven en de jager.** (Orig.Can.title: *Julie* of the wolves; *Julie* von den Wölfen.)
Amsterdam: Kosmos 1974.

Lee, Virigina: **Vlinder voor Marianne.** (Butterflies for *Marianne*; Schmetterling für *Marianne*.)
Rotterdam: Lemniscaat 1974.

Lindgren, Astrid: **De gebroeders Leeuwenhart.** (The brothers, *Lionheart*; Die Brüder *Löwenherz*.)
Amsterdam: Ploegsma 1974.

Maccauley, David: **De kathedraal.** (The cathedral; Die Kathedrale.)
Amsterdam: Ploegsma 1974.

Ungerer, Tomi: **Zeralda's reus.** (*Zeralda*'s giant; *Zeraldas* Riese.)
Utrecht: Bruna 1974.

Buchholz, Tony Vos-Dahmen von: **Arenden vliegenalleen.** (Eagles fly alone; Adler fliegen allein.)
Hoorn: West-Friesland 1974.

1976 *Gouden Griffel*

Kuijer, Guus: **Met de poppen gooien.** (Throwing with the puppets; Mit Puppen werfen.) Ill.: Mance Post.
Amsterdam: Querido 1975.

Zilveren Griffel

Buisman, Jantien: **Kees en Keetje.** (*Kees* and *Keetje*.)
Amsterdam: De Harmonie 1975.

Bolliger, Max: **De kleine reus.** (The little giant; Der kleine Riese.)
Rotterdam: Lemniscaat 1975.

Eilert, B.: **De kroondieven.** (The crown thieves; Die Krondiebe.)
Amsterdam: Ploegsma 1975.

Fox, Paula: **Duvelstoejager op een slavenschip.** (Orig.Amer.title: The slave dancer; Das Faktotum auf einem Sklavenschiff.)
Haarlem: Holland 1975.

Hall, Lynn: **Maak me niet kapot.** (Don't ruin me; Mach mich nicht kaputt.)
Rotterdam: Lemniscaat 1975.

Hoban, Russel: **Hoe Tom won van kapitein Najork en zijn gehuurde sportlingen.** (How *Tom* beat captain *Najork* and his hired sportsmen; Wie *Tom* Kapitän *Najork* und seine gemieteten Sportsmänner schlug.)
Amsterdam: Boelen 1975.

Klein, Eduard: **Severino.** (*Severino.*)
Bussum: Van Holkema & Warendorf 1975.

Lebacs, Diana: **Nancho van Bonaire.** (*Nancho* From Bonaire; *Nancho* von Bonaire.)
Den Haag: Leopold 1975.

Vries, Anke de: **Het geheim van Mories Besjoer.** (The mystery of *Mories Besjoer*; Das Geheimnis von *Mories Besjoer.*)
Rotterdam: Lemniscaat 1975.

1977 *Gouden Griffel*

Barnard, Henk: **Kom hesi baka/Kom gauw terug.** (Come, go back; Komm, geh zurück.)
Bussum: Van Holkema & Warendorf 1976.

Zilveren Griffel

Cressey, James: **De rattenvanger.** (The rat catcher; Der Rattenfänger.)
Rotterdam: Lemniscaat 1976.

Dahl, Roald: **Daantje de wereldkampioen.** (*Daantje.* The champion of the world; *Daantje*, der Weltmeister.)
De Bilt: De Fontein 1976.

Gernhardt, Robert: **Wie dit leest is het vierde beest.** (Who reads this is the fourth beast; Wer dies liest, ist das vierte Biest.)
Utrecht: Bruna 1976.

Hofman, Wim: **Wim.** (*Wim.*)
Bussum: Van Holkema & Warendorf 1976.

Kuijer, Guus: **Grote mensen daar kan je beter soep van koken.** (Don't trust grown-ups; Traue keinem Erwachsenen.)
Amsterdam: Querido 1976.

Procházka, Jan: **Milena.** (*Milena.*)
Den Haag: Leopold 1976.

Sachs, Marilyn: **Het boek van Dorrie.** (*Dorrie*'s book; Das Buch von *Dorrie.*)
Amsterdam: Querido 1976.

Smith, Doris Buchanan: **We gingen bramen plukken.** (We went off to pick berries; Wir gingen Beeren suchen.)
Amsterdam: Querido 1976.

Wernström, Sven: **De vergeten hacienda.** (The forgotten hacienda; Die vergessene Hacienda.)
Haarlem: Holland 1976.

1978 *Gouden Griffel*

Diekmann, Miep: **Wiele wiele stap.** (Turn, turn, step; Drehen, drehen, Schritt.) Ill.: Tjong Khing.
Amsterdam: Querido 1977.

Pelgrom, Els: **De kinderen van het Achtste Woud.** (Children of the Eighth Wood; Die Kinder vom Achten Wald.)
Amsterdam: Kosmos 1978.

Zilveren Griffel

Mahy, Margaret: **Ze lopen gewoon met me mee.** (They come with me usually; Sie laufen gewöhnlich mit mir mit.)
Rotterdam: Lemniscaat 1977.

Wagner, Jenny: **Borre en de nachtzwarte kat.** (*Borre* and the night-black cat; *Borre* und die nachtschwarze Katze; Orig.Amer.title: *John Brown*, *Rose* and the midnight cat.)
Rotterdam: Lemniscaat 1977.

Annett, Cora: **Hoe de heks ezeltje Alf te pakken kreeg.** (How the witch caught *Alf*, the donkey; Wie die Hexe Eselchen *Alf* zu fassen bekam.)
Antwerpen: Lotus 1977.

Byars, Betsy: **De dag van de Geitenman.** (Goat-man's day; Der Tag des Ziegenmannes.)
Amsterdam: Kosmos 1977.

Godden, Rumer: **De Diddakoi.** (The *Diddakoi*; Der *Diddakoi.*)
Baarn: Hollandia 1977.

Cesco, Federica de: **De gouden daken van Lhasa.** (The golden rooftops of Lhasa; Die goldenen Dächer von Lhasa.)
Den Haag: Leopold 1977.

Griffiths, Helen: **Het heksenkind.** (The witch-child; Das Hexenkind.)
Hoorn: Westfriesland 1977.

Hunter, Mollie: **Een toren tegen de romeinen.** (A tower against the Romans; Ein Turm gegen die Römer; Eng.orig.title: The stronghold.)
Haarlem: Holland 1977.

1979 *Gouden Griffel*

Kuijer, Guus: **Krassen in het tafelblad.** (Scratches in the tabletop; Risse in der Tischplatte.)
Amsterdam: Querido 1978.

Zilveren Griffel

Brands, Gerard: **Padden verhuizen niet graag.** (Toads don't like to move around; Kröten ziehen nicht gerne um.)
Amsterdam: Querido 1978.

Briggs, Raymond: **De sneeuwman.** (The snowman; Der Schneemann.) Ill.: Raymond Briggs.
Bussum: Van Holkema & Warendorf 1978.

Dahl, Roald: **Het wonderlijk verhaal van Hendrik Meier.** (The humourous story of *Hendrik Meier*; Die komische Geschichte von *Hendrik Meier*.)
Utrecht: Fontein 1978.

Hinton, Nigel: **Vluchten kan niet meer.** (Flight is no longer possible; Flucht ist nicht mehr möglich; Eng.orig.title: Collision course.)
Rotterdam: Lemniscaat 1978.

Lavalle, Sheila: **Allemaal appeltaart.** (Too many apple tarts; Zu viel Apfelkuchen.) Ill.: John Lawrence.
Nieuwkoop: Heuff 1978.

Schouten, Alet: **Het huis van Roos en Lap.** (The house of *Roos* and *Lap*; Das Haus von *Roos* und *Lap*.)
Bussum: Van Holkema & Warendorf 1978.

Steig, William: **Abels eiland.** (Amer.orig.title: *Abel*'s island; *Abel*'s Insel.) Ill.: William Steig.
Amsterdam: Querido 1978.

Verroen, Dolf: **De kat in de gordijen.** (The cat in the curtains; Die Katze hinter dem Vorhang.) Ill.: Tjong Khing.
Den Haag: Leopold 1978.

Vriens, Jacques: **Zondagmorgen.** (Sundy morning; Sonntagmorgen.)
Bussum: Van Holkema & Warendorf 1978.

1980 *Gouden Griffel*
Schell, Simone: **Zeesicht.** (Sea view; Seeblick.) Ill.: Annelies Schoth.
Amsterdam: Van Goor 1979.

Zilveren Griffels
Hughes, Shirley: **Knuffel.** (*Knuffel.*)
Nieuwkoop: Heuff 1979.

Lund, Doris H.: **Je zou Herberts huis eens moeten.** (*Herbert*'s house; *Herberts* Haus.) Ill.: Steven Kellogg.
Antwerpen: Lotus 1979.

Dubelaar, Thea: **Sjanetje.** (*Sjanetje.*) Ill.: Mance Post.
Amsterdam: Ploegsma 1979.

Leeuwen, Joke van: **Een huis met zeven kamers.** (A house with seven rooms; Ein Haus mit sieben Zimmern.) Ill.: Joke van Leeuwen.
Den Haag: Omniboek 1979.

Donnelly, Elfie: **De rommelkist van grootvader.** (Grandfather's old trunk; Die Rumpelkiste von Großvater.) Ill.: Bab Siljée.
Amsterdam: Ploegsma 1979.

Beckman, Thea: **Stad in de storm.** (Storm over the city; Sturm über der Stadt.)
Rotterdam: Lemniscaat 1979.

Coué, Jean: **...En de zon werd koud.** (The straw sun; Eine Sonne aus Stroh.)
Rotterdam: Lemniscaat 1979.

Müller, Jörg/Steiner, Jörg: **De beer, die een beer wou blijven.** (The bear that wanted to remain a bear; Der Bär, der ein Bär bleiben wollte.) Ill.: Jörg Steiner.
Leuven: Davidsfonds 1979.

Gouden Penseel

This prize, a continuation of the Kinderkijkboekenprijs, is awarded annually by the „Commissie vor Collectieve Propaganda van het Nederlandse Boek" (Commission for the Promotion of the Dutch Book) in conjunction with the Grafische Vormgevers Nederland" (Professional Graphic Artists' Association), and was originally intended to encourage unknown illustrators; but since 1977, the has been open to established illustrators, also.

Dieser Preis, eine Fortführung des Kinderkijkboekenprijs, wird jährlich vom „Commissie vor Collectieve Propaganda van het Nederlandse Boek" (Aus-

schuß für gemeinsame Werbung des Niederländischen Buches) in Zusammenarbeit mit dem „Beroepsvereiniging Grafische Vormgevers" (Berufsvereinigung graphischer Gestalter) als Ermutigungspreis für einen unbekannten Illustrator vergeben. Seit 1977 können sich alle Illustratoren an der Ausschreibung beteiligen.

1973 Heynmans, Margriet in:
Heymans, Margriet: **Hollidee de circuspony.** (Holiday of the circus ponies; Ferien des Zirkusponies.)
Rotterdam: Lemniscaat 1972.

1974 Hofman, Wim in:
Hofman, Wim: **Koning Wikkepokluk de merkwaardige zoet een Rijk.** (King *Wikkepokluk the Remarkable* searches for a kingdom; König *Wikkepokluk* der Merkwürdige sucht ein Reich.)
Bussum: Van Holkema & Warendorf 1973.

1975 Hulshof, Paul in:
Hulshof, Paul: **Iolo komt niet spelen.** (*Iolo* won't come to **play;** *Iolo* kommt nicht zum Spielen.)
Bussum: Van Holkema & Warendorf 1974.

1976 Postma, Lidia in:
Andersen, Hans Christian: **Sprookjes en vertellingen van Hans Christian Andersen.** (Fairy tales and stories from *Hans Christian Andersen;* Märchen und Erzählungen von *Hans Christian Andersen.*)
Bussum: Van Holkema & Warendorf 1975.

1977 Velthuijs, Max in:
Velthuijs, Max: **Het goedige monster en de rovers.** (The goodhearted monster and the robbers; Das gutherzige Ungeheuer und die Räuber.)
Den Haag: Junk 1976.

1978 Khing, Tjong in:
Diekmann, Miep: **Wiele wiele stap.** (Turn, turn, step; Drehen, drehen, Schritt.)
Amsterdam: Querido 1977.

Verburg, jan Marinus in:
Schmidt, Annie M.B.: **Tom Tippelaar.** *(Tom Tippelaar.)*
Amsterdam: Querido 1977.

1979 Eyzenbach, Tom in:
Dahl, Roald: **Het wonderlijk verhall van Hendrik Meier.** (The humourous story of *Hendrik Meier;* Die komische Geschichte von *Hendrik Meier.*)
Utrecht: Fontein 1978.

1980 Leeuwen, Joke van in:
Leeuwen, Joke van: **Een huis met zeven kamers.** (A house with seven rooms; Ein Haus mit sieben Zimmern.)
Den Haag: Omniboek 1979.

Nienke van Hichtumprijs

Since 1964, the Jan Campert Foundation has awarded this prize to Dutch authors of youth books. Nienke van Hichtum (1860-1939), for whom this prize was named, was a well known author and pioneer in the field of youth literature. Her pseudonym was Troelstra Bokma de Boer.

Seit 1964 wird dieser Preis an niederländische Autoren vergeben, die Jugendbücher schreiben. Er wird vom Vorstand der Jan Campert Stiftung vergeben. Nienke van Hichtum war ein bekannter Autor und ein Pionier auf dem Gebiet der Jugendliteratur (1860—1939). Das Pseudonym von Nienke van Hichtum lautet Troelstra Bokma de Boer.

1964 Evenhuis, Gertie: **Wij waren er ook bij.** (We were also there; Wir waren auch dabei.) Ill.: Otto Dicke.
s'Gravenhage: Van Goor 1964.

1965/
1970 The prize was not given; Der Preis wurde nicht vergeben.

1971 Dragt, Tonke: **Torenhoog en mijlen breed.** (Tower-high and milewide; Turmhoch und meilenweit.) Ill.: Tonke Dragt.
Den Haag: Leopold 1969.

1972 Haar, Jaap ter: **Geschiedenis van de lage landen.** (Stories from the low land; Geschichten vom Tiefland.)
Bussum: Fibula-Van Dishoeck 1972.

1973 Biegel, Paul: **De twaalf rovers.** (The twelve robbers; Die zwölf Räuber.) Ill.: Tineke Schinkel.
Haarlem: Holland 1973.

1974 The prize was not given; Der Preis wurde nicht vergeben.

1975 Diekmann, Miep: **Dan ben je nergens meer.** (Then, no longer will I go anywhere; Dann gehe ich nirgendwohin.)
Amsterdam: Querido 1975.

1976 The prize was not given; Der Preis wurde nicht vergeben.

1977 Hofman, Wim: **Wim.** (*Wim.*)
Bussum: Van Holkema & Warendorf 1977.

1978 The prize was not given; Der Preis wurde nicht vergeben.

1979 Barnard, Henk: **Laatste nacht in Jeque.** (Last night in *Jeque*; Letze Nacht in *Jeque*.) Ill.: Reintje Venema.
Bussum: Van Holkema & Warendorf 1979.

Kinderkijkboekenprijs

This prize was established by the "Commissie voor Collectieve Propaganda van het Nederlandse Book" (Committee for the Promotion of the Dutch Book) in conjunction with the "Beroepsvereniging Grafische Vormgevers" (Professional Graphic Artists Association) for the illustrator of the best picture book published in the last two years. The prize was discontinued after the first presentation and was renamed the "Gouden Penseel" (Golden Brush).

Der Preis wird von "Commissie voor Collectieve Propaganda von het Nederlandse Boek" (Ausschuß für gemeinsame Werbung des Niederländischen Buches) in Zusammenarbeit mit dem "Beroepsvereniging Grafische Vormgevers" (Berufsvereinigung graphischer Gestalter) in den letzten zwei Jahren erschienenen besten Bilderbuchs vergeben. Der Preis wurde einmal vergeben, die folgenden Jahre bekam er einen neuen Namen "Goldener Pinsel".

1970 Hoogendoorn, Ton In:
Hoogendoorn, Ton: **Stoep af stoep op.** (Step on, step up; Treppauf treppab.)
Groningen: Wolters-Nordhoff 1970.

Staatsprijs voor kinder- en jeugdliteratuur

This prize was established in 1964 by the Ministry of Education, Art and Science and is presented every three years by the Ministry of Culture, Recreation and Social Work.

Der Preis wurde vom Ministerium für Unterricht, Kunst und Wissenschaften 1964 eingeführt, und wird alle drei Jahre vom Ministerium für Kultur, Freizeit und Sozialarbeit vergeben.

1964 Annie M.G. Schmidt
1967 An Rutgers van der Loeff-Basenau
1970 Miep Diekmann
1973 Paul Biegel
1976 Tonke Dragt
1979 Guus Kuijer

New Zealand/Neuseeland

Esther Glen Award

This award was initiated in 1945 in honour of Esther Glen, a Christchurch journalist and authoress of children's books. Each year, books written for children by New Zealand authors are considered by a panel of three judges. Both fiction and non-fiction are eligible for the award and either an author or an illustrator may receive it. The award, consisting of a medal and small cash prize, is given only in those years in which a prize-worthy book is published.

Der Esther Glen Preis wurde 1945 ins Leben gerufen, und zwar zu Ehren von Esther Glen einer Journalistin und Kinderbuchautorin von Christchurch. Jährlich werden Kinderbücher, die von Neuseeländern geschrieben sind, von einer Jury, die aus drei Personen besteht, ausgewählt. Sowohl Sachbücher als auch schöne Literatur wird berücksichtigt; Autoren oder Illustratoren können den Preis gewinnen. Die Überreichung einer Medaille und eine kleine Summe Geldes wird nur stattfinden, wenn preiswürdige Bücher vorhanden sind.

Ill. 28 Jenny Williams in M. Mahy: A lion in the meadow

1945 Morice, Stella: **Book of *Wiremu*.** (Buch des Wiremu.) Ill.: Nancy Parker.
Hamilton: Paul's Book Arcade 1944.

1947 Ree, Alexander Wyclif: **Myths and legends of Maoriland.** (Mythen und Sagen aus dem Maoriland.) Ill.: George Woods and W. Dittmer.
Wellington: A.H. & A.W. Reed 1947.

1950 Smith, Joan: **Nimble, Rumble and Tumble.** (*Nimble, Rumble* und *Tumble.*) Ill.: Joan Smith.
Hamilton: Paul's Book Arcade 1949.

1960 Duggan, Maurice: **Falter Tom and the water boy.** (*Falter Tom* und der Seejunge.) Ill.: Kenneth Rowell.
London: Faber & Faber 1958.

1964 Powell, Lesley Cameron: **Turi. The story of a little boy.** (*Turi.* Die Geschichte von einem kleinen Jungen.) Photos: Pius Blank.
Hamilton: Paul's Book Arcade 1963.

1970 Mahy, Margaret May: **A lion in the meadow.** (Ein Löwe auf der Wiese.) Ill.: Jenny Williams.
London: Dent 1969.

1972 Mahy, Margaret May: **The first Margaret Mahy story book.** (Das erste *Margaret-Mahy*-Geschichtenbuch.) Ill.: Shirley Hughes.
London: Dent 1972.

1975 Sutton, Eve: **My cat likes to hide in boxes.** (Meine Katze versteckt sich gern in Schachteln.) Ill.: Lynley Dood.
London: Hamish Hamilton 1973.

1977 Armitage, Ronda: **The lighthouse keeper's lunch.** (Das Mittagessen des Leuchtturmwärters.) Ill.: David Armitage.
London: Andre Deutsch 1977.

1978 De Hamel, Joan: **Take the long path;** (Nimm den langen Weg.) Ill.: Gareth Floyd.
London: Lutterworth 1978.

1979 The award was not given; Der Preis wurde nicht vergeben.

Russel Clark Award

This prize was established in 1975 although it was not until 1978 that the first award presentation was made. In founding this award the New Zealand Library Association formally acknowledged the importance of recognising outstanding illustrators of New Zealand children's books just as, thirty years before, it had acknowledged in the Esther Glen Award the importance of recognising distinguished constributors to New Zealand's children's literature. The Russell Clark Award may be awarded annually to the New Zealander who has produced the most outstanding illustrations for a children's book. The award is named after Russell Clard (1905—1966) a notable New Zealand illustrator and artist best known, perhaps, for his work in the New Zealand „Listener" and the „School Journal" during the 1940s and 1950s. His figure drawing is particularly accomplished; in his drawings of the everyday activities of ordinary people he has left a lively record of a past era and of places that have changed almost beyond recognition.

Der Russell Clark Preis wurde 1975 gestiftet, obwohl bis 1978 kein Preis vergeben wurde. Die Bibliotheksvereinigung von Neuseeland unterstrich mit diesem Preis die Wichtigkeit hervorragender Illustrationen neuseeländischer Kinderbüchern. 30 Jahre vorher hatte die Bibliotheksvereinigung mit dem Esther Glen Preis die Bedeutung ausgezeichneter Mitarbeiter in der neuseeländischen Kinderliteratur anerkannt. Der Russell Clark Preis wird jährlich einem neuseeländischen Illustrator verliehen, der die besten Illustrationen für ein Kinderbuch gemacht hat. Der Preis hat seinen Namen nach Russell Clark einem bemerkenswerten neuseeländischen Illustrator berühmt vor allem für seine Arbeit in den Zeitschriften "Listener" und "School Journal" während der vierziger und fünfziger Jahre. Sein Personenzeichnen ist besonders gelungen, in seinen Zeichnungen alltäglicher Arbeiten der einfachen Leute hat er einen lebendigen Bericht einer vergangenen Zeit und von Plätzen gegeben, die heute fast verschwunden sind.

1978 Jahnke, Robert F. in:
Bacon, Ronald L.: **The house of the people.** (Das Haus der Leute.)
Auckland: Collins 1977.

1979 Treloar, Bruce in:
Treloar, Bruce: **King.** (*Kim.*)
Auckland: Collins 1978.

1980 The prize was not given; Der Preis wurde nicht vergeben.

Norway/Norwegen

Kirke- og undervisningsdepartements premier for bøker skikket for skolebiblioteker

This prize established by the Norwegian Ministry for Church and Education was first presented in 1949. The jury, consisting of ten members, includes delegates of the abovementioned ministry and representatives appointed by the Norwegian Teachers' Association, the Association of Youth Book Authors, the Association of Children's Librarians, the Association of Norwegian Psychologists and the Association of Pictorial Artists. The books must be written by Norwegian authors and suitable for school libraries. Only books published within a twelve-month period prior to the prize presentations are considered. Since 1958, illustrations are also eligible. A special prize for the best picture book was founded in 1962 and an award for the best translation was established in 1972. In 1974, a prize for comic strips was initiated.

Der Preis des norwegischen Ministeriums für Kirche und Erziehung wird seit 1949 vergeben. Die Jury setzt sich aus 10 Mitgliedern zusammen, aus Abgeordneten des oben angegebenen Ministeriums, Vertreter der norwegischen Lehrervereinigung, der Vereinigung von Jugendbuchautoren, der Vereinigung der Jugendbibliothekare, der norwegischen Vereinigung von Psychologen und der bildenden Künstler. Die Bücher müssen von norwegischen Autoren geschrieben und für Schulbibliotheken geeignet sein. Der Preis wird nur an Bücher vergeben, die nicht älter als 12 Monate nach der Wettbewerbsausschreibung sind. Seit 1958 können auch Illustrationen preisgekrönt werden. Seit 1962 gibt es einen Sonderpreis für das beste Bilderbuch, seit 1972 einen Preis für die beste Übersetzung, seit 1974 einen Preis für Comics.

1949 *1st prize/1. Preis*
By, Sverre: **Raudmerra.** (*Raudmerra.*)
Oslo: Noregs boklag 1948.

2nd prize/2. Preis
Holt, Kåre: **Cleng Peerson og Nils med luggen.** (*Cleng Peerson* and *Nils* with the tresses of hair; *Cleng Peerson* und *Nils* mit dem Schopf.)
Oslo: Gyldendal Norsk Forlag 1948.

Saelen, Frithjof: **En motig maur.** (A courageous ant; Eine mutige Ameise.) Ill.: Frithjof Saelen.
Bergen: Eide 1948.
(bokmal)

Saelen, Frithjof: **Ein modig maur.** (A courageous ant; Eine mutige Ameise.) Ill.: Frithjof Saelen.
Bergen: Eide 1948.
(Nynorsk)

Ill. 29 Kari Bøge in E. Økland: Slik er det

3rd prize/3. Preis
Brochmann, Odd: **Fortelligen om Marianne på sykehus.** (The story of *Marianne* in the hospital; Die Geschichte von *Marianne* im Krankenhaus.)
Oslo: Aschehoug 1948.

Gjengedal, Knut: **Kronekongen og andre soger.** (The crown king and other tales; Der Kronenkönig und andere Geschichten.)
Oslo: Noregs boklag 1948.

1950 *1st prize/1. Preis*
Vesaas, Halldis Moren: **Tidleg på våren.** (Early in spring; Zeitig im Frühjahr.)
Oslo: Aschehoug 1949.

2nd prize/2. Preis
Coucheron, Olaf: **Espen fra Svarttjernet.** (*Espen* from *Svarttjernet; Espen* von *Svarttjernet.*)
Oslo: Tiden Norsk Forlag 1949.

Lie, Haakon: **Villmark og villdyr.** (Wilderness and wild animals; Wildnis und wilde Tiere.) Ill.: Omar Andreen.
Oslo: Tiden Norsk Forlag 1949.

3rd prize/3. Preis
Bang-Hansen, Odd: **Mette og Tom og bokstavene.** (*Mette* and *Tom* and the alphabet; *Mette* und *Tom* und die Buchstaben.)
Oslo: Tiden Norsk Forlag 1949.

Tenfjord, Jo: **Venner verden over.** (Friends all over the world; Freunde in der ganzen Welt.) Ill.: Edvarda Lie.
Oslo: Aschehoug 1949.

1951 *1st prize/1. Preis*
Bjorgås, Nils: **Siste sommaren.** (The last summer; Der letzte Sommer.)
Oslo: Achehoug 1950.

2nd prize/2. Preis
Floden, Halvor: **Vi er vener.** 3. soga om Kari Trestakk.
(We are friends. The 3rd story about *Kari Trestakk*; Wir sind Freunde. 3. Geschichte von *Kari Trestakk.*)
Oslo: Norli 1950.

Sommerfelt, Aimée: **Miriam.** (*Miriam.*)
Oslo: Gyldendal Norsk Forlag 1950.

3rd prize/3. Preis
Borch, Anka (i.e. Anna Colban Berg: **Voksen kar fem år.** (A grown up chap, five years old; Ein erwachsener Mann, 5 Jahre alt.) Ill.: Vigdis Rojahn.
Oslo: Damm 1950.

Moen, Erling: **Kjell og andre ungar.** (*Kjell* and other children; *Kjell* und andere Kinder.) Ill.: Borghild Rud.
Oslo: Gyldendal Norsk Forlag 1950.

1952 *1st prize/1. Preis*
By, Sverre: **Turid og dei andre.** (*Turid* and the others; *Turid* und die anderen.)
Oslo: Noregs boklag 1951.

2nd prize/2. Preis
Gjengedal, Knut: **Bortanfor Blåbreen.** (Behind *Blabreen*; Hinter *Blabreen.*)
Oslo: Norsk barneblad 1951.

Hegge, Mary: **Beritungen.** (Little *Berit*; Die kleine *Berit.*)
Oslo: Fonna 1951.

3rd prize/3. Preis
Borch, Anka (i.e. Anna Colban Berg): **Jomfru Birgit.** (Maid *Birgit*; Jungfer *Birgit.*)
Oslo: Damm 1951.

Waage, Per: **Anders i Vesterisen.** (*Anders* in the western ice; *Anders* im Westeis.)
Oslo: Aschehoug 1951.

1953 *1st prize/1. Preis*
Havrevold, Finn: **Sommereventyret.** (Summer adventure; Sommerabenteuer.)
Oslo: Damm 1952.

Ørbech, Kari: **Hun som fikk navnet Loretta.** (The one called *Loretta*; Die den Namen *Loretta* erhielt.) Ill.: Finn Havrevold.
Oslo: Damm 1952.
(bo̊kmal)

Ørbech, Kari: **Ho som Namnet Loretta.** (The one called *Loretta;* Die den Namen *Loretta* erhielt.) Ill.: Finn Havrevold.
Oslo: Damm 1952.
(nynorsk)

2nd prize/2. Preis
Sommerfelt, Aimée: **Bare en jentunge?** (Only a little girl? Nur ein kleines Mädchen?)
Oslo: Tiden Norsk Forlag 1952.

3rd prize/3. Preis
Floden, Halvor: **Trond og venene hans.** (*Trond* and his friends; *Trond* und seine Freunde.)
Oslo: Norli 1952.

Rojahn, Vigdis: **Marit.** (*Marit.*) Ill.: Vigdis Rojahn.
Oslo: Damm 1952.

1954 *1st prize/1. Preis*
Egner, Thorbjørn: **Klatremus og de andre dyrene i Hakkebakkeskogen.** (*Klatremus* and the other animals in *Hakkebakke* Forest; *Klatremus* und die anderen Tiere im *Hakkebakke*-Wald.) Ill.: Thorbjørn Egner.
Oslo: Grøndahl 1953.

Rongen, Bjørn: **Bergtyeken i Risehola.** (Captured in the troll's mountain; Gefangen in der Trollhöhle des Berges.)
Oslo: Damm 1953.

2nd prize/2. Preis
Herje, Emil: **Farlig kar.** (A dangerous fellow; Ein gefährlicher Kerl.)
Oslo: Gyldendal Norsk Forlag 1953.

3rd prize/3. Preis
Østby, Jan: **Hvalkongen. Eventyret om Svend Foyn.** (The adventure of *Svend Foyn*; Das Abenteuer von *Svend Foyn*.)
Oslo: Gyldendal Norsk Forlag 1953.

Rojahn, Vigdis: **Prinsen som gråt.** (The prince who wept; Der weinende Prinz.) Ill.: Vigdis Rojahn.
Oslo: Damm 1953.

1955 *1st prize/1. Preis*
The prize was not given; Der Preis wurde nicht vergeben.

2nd prize/2. Preis
Colbjørnsen, Roar: **Annes hemmelighet.** (*Anne's* secret; *Annes* Geheimnis.)
Oslo: Damm 1954.

Tenfjord, Jo/Oxaal, Gunnar: **Jens krysser himmelrommet.** (*Jens* cruises through space; *Jens* durchkreuzt den Himmelsraum.)
Oslo: Aschehoug 1954.

3rd prize/3. Preis
Mykle, Jane/Mykle, Agnar: **Dukketeater.** (Puppet theatre; Puppentheater.) Ill.: Johan Holm.
Oslo: Gyldendal Norsk Forlag 1954.

Rynning-Tønnesen, Olaf: **Sjøspeidernes hytte.** (The sea scout's hut; Die Hütte der Seespäher.)
Oslo: Damm 1954.

1956 *1st prize/1. Preis*

Egner, Thorbjørn: **Folk og røvere i Kardemomme by.** (People and robbers in *Kardemomme;* Die Räuber von *Kardemomme.*) Ill.: Thorbjørn Egner.
Oslo: Cappelen 1955.

Rynning-Tønnesen, Olaf: **Løp, Jan, løp!** (Run, *Jan,* run! Lauf, *Jan,* lauf!)
Oslo: Damm 1955.

2nd prize/2. Preis

Havrevold, Finn: **Den ensomme kriger.** (The lonesome warrior; Der einsame Krieger.) Ill.: Ulf Aas.
Oslo: Damm 1955.

Svinsaas, Ingvald: **Tom i villmarka.** (*Tom* in the wilderness; *Tom* in der Wildnis.) Ill.: Ridley Borchgrevink.
Oslo: Damm 1955.

3rd prize/3. Preis

Vaage, Ragnvald: **Den gode sumaren.** (The good summer; Der gute Sommer.)
Oslo: Norli 1955.

Vestly, Anne-Catharina: **Ole Aleksander får skjorte.** (*Ole Aleksander* gets a shirt; *Ole Aleksander* erhält ein Hemd.) Ill.: Johan Vestly.
Oslo: Tiden Norsk Forlag 1955.

1957 *1st prize/1. Preis*

The prize was not given; Der Preis wurde nicht vergeben.

2nd prize/2. Preis

Bruheim, Jan-Magnus: **Skrythøna og andre barnerim.** (The boasting hen and other children's rhymes; Das prahlende Huhn und andere Kinderreime.) Ill.: Reidar Johan Berle.
Bergen: Eide 1956.

Rongen, Bjørn: **Anne Villdyrjente.** (*Anne,* the wild animal girl; *Anne,* das Wildtier-Mädchen.)
Oslo: Gyldendal Norsk Forlag 1956.

3rd prize/3. Preis

Holm Hannebo (i.e. Jo Tenfjord): **Skønnhetsdronning.** (Beauty queen; Schönheitskönigin.)
Oslo: Damm 1956.

1958 *1st prize/1. Preis*

Hamre, Leif: **Otter tre to kaller.** (8—3—2 calling; 8—3—2 ruft.) Ill.: Arne Johnson.
Oslo: Aschehoug 1957.

Havrevold, Finn: **Marens lille ugle.** (*Maren's* little owl; Marens kleine Eule.) Ill.: Finn Havrevold.
Oslo: Damm 1957.

2nd prize/2. Preis
Hamsun, Marie: **Bygdebarn. Folk og fe på langerud. (Country children. People and cattle in** *Langerud;* Landkinder. Leute und Vieh auf *Langerud.*)
Oslo: Aschehoug 1957.

Vestly, Anne-Catherina: **Åtte små, to store og en lastebil.** (Eight small, two big and one van; Acht Kleine, zwei Große und ein Lastwagen.) Ill.: Johan Vestly.
Oslo: Tiden Norsk Forlag 1957.

3rd prize/3. Preis
Herje, Emil: **Kamerater.** (Comrades/Kameraden.)
Oslo: Gyldendal Norsk Forlag 1957.

Olafsson, Albert: **Ørn frå Island.** (*Orn* from Iceland; *Orn* aus Island.)
Oslo: Noregs boklag 1957.

Prøysen, Alf: **Kjerringa som ble så lita som ei teskje.** (The old woman who became as small as a teaspoon; Die Alte, die so klein wie ein Teelöffel wurde.) Ill.: Borghild Rud.
Oslo: Tiden Norsk Forlag 1957.

Illustration — 1st prize/1. Preis
Førde, Runa in:
Berset, Inger/Bøe, Ingebjørg: **Jeg fant! Jeg fant! Barnas verden.** (I found! I found! Children's world; Ich fand! Ich fand! Die Welt der Kinder.)
Oslo: Mittet 1956.

Illustration — 2nd prize/2. Preis
Andreen, Omar in:
Svinsaas, Ingvald: **Gaupe i fjellet.** (Lynx in the mountains; Luchs in den Bergen.)
Oslo: Tiden Norsk Forlag 1957.

Johnson, Arne in: Hamre, Leif: **Otter tre to kaller.** (8—3—2 calling; 8—3—2 ruft.)
Oslo: Aschhoug 1957.

1959 *1st prize/1. Preis*
Hamre, Leif: **Blå to-hopp ut.** (Blue 2 — jump! Blau 2 — spring ab!)
Ill.: Arne Johnson.
Oslo: Aschehoug 1958.

2nd prize/2. Preis
Bruheim, Jan-Magnus: **Hornsmeden og andre barnerim.** (The hornsmith and other children's rhymes; Der Hornschmied und andere Kinderreime.) Ill.: Reidar Johan Berle.
Bergen: Eide 1958.

Vestly, Anne-Catharina: **Mormor og de åtte ungene i skogen.** (Grandmother and the eight children in the forest; Großmutter und die acht Kinder im Wald.) Ill.: Johan Vestly.
Oslo: Tiden Norsk Forlag 1958.

3rd prize/3. Preis
Jørgensen, Ingeborg Storm: **Parthenia seiler i natt.** (The *Parthenia* sails tonight; *Parthenia segelt heute Nacht.)*
Oslo: Aschehoug 1958.

Semb, Klara: **Danse-danse-dokka mi.** Songdansar, turdansar, ringleikar, turleikar. For barn og ungdom. (Dance, dance my doll. Singing dances, round dances, circle games. For children and youth; Tanz, tanz, Püppchen mein. Tänze, Reigentänze, Kreisspiele. Für Kinder und Jugend.) Ill.: Ole Ekornes.
Oslo: Noregs boklag 1958.

Illustration — 1st prize/1. Preis.
Egner, Thorbjørn in:
Wells, Herbert George: **Tommy og elefanten.** (*Tommy* and the elephant; *Tommy* und der Elefant.)
Oslo: Cappelen 1958.

Illustration — 2nd prize/2. Preis
Berle, Reidar Johan in:
Bruheim, Jan-Magnus: **Hornsmeden og andre barnerim.** (The hornsmith and other children's rhymes; Der Hornschmied und andere Kinderreime.)
Bergen: Eide 1958.

Rud, Borghild in:
Langbo, Kirsten: **Berte frå barnetimen.** (*Berte* from the children's hour; *Berte* aus der Kinderstunde.)
Oslo: Aschehoug 1958.

1960 *1st prize/1. Preis*
Hamre, Leif: **Klart fly.** (The airplane takes off; Flugzeug startklar.) Ill.: Arne Johnson.
Oslo: Aschehoug 1959.

Sommerfelt, Aimée: **Veien til Agra.** (The way to *Agra*; Der Weg nach *Agra*.) Ill.: Ulf Aas.
Oslo: Damm 1959.

2nd prize/2. Preis
Friis-Baastad, Babbis: **Aeresord.** (Word of honour; Ehrenwort.) Ill.: Ulf Aas.
Oslo: Damm 1959.

Senje, Sigurd (i.e. Sigurd Rasmussen): **Sleiven finner kursen.** (*Sleiven* finds the course; *Sleiven* findet den Kurs.) Ill.: Pedro (i.e. Salo Grenning).
Oslo: Aschehoug 1959.

3rd prize/3. Preis
Henriksen, Hild: **Vestover til Østen.** (Westward to the East; Westwärts nach Osten.) Ill.: Bibi Plahte.
Oslo: Aschehoug 1959.

Illustration — 1st prize/1. Preis
Johnson, Arne in:
Løland, Rasmus: **Kvitebjørnen.** (The polar bear; Der Eisbär.) Adapt.: Halldis Moren Vesaas.
Oslo: Det norske samlaget 1959.

Illustration — 2nd prize/2. Preis
Rojahn, Vigdis in:
Rojahn, Vigdis: **Sirkusloppen.** (The circus flea; Der Zirkus-Floh.)
Oslo: Green 1959.

Strøm, Tonje in:
Lind, Ebba: **Per-Pål-Espen på Sommerøya.** (*Per-Pal-Espen* on the summer island; *Per-Pal-Espen* auf der Sommerinsel.)
Oslo: Tiden Norsk Forlag 1959.

1961 *1st prize/1. Preis*
Havrevold, Finn: **Grunnbrott.** (Shipwreck; Schiffbruch.)
Oslo: Damm 1060.

2nd prize/2. Preis
Lie, Haakon: **Vegen til eventyret.** (The way to adventure; Der Weg zum Abenteuer.) Ill.: Unni-Lise Jonsmoen.
Oslo: Noregs boklag 1960.

Thesen, Kirsten: **En og to følge slo.** (One and two join each other; Eins und zwei schließen sich zusammen.)
Oslo: Damm 1960.

3rd prize/3. Preis
Haslund, Ebba: **Barskinger på Brånåsen.** (The *Barskinger* children of *Bran Hill*; Die *Barskinger* Kinder vom Hügel *Bran*.)
Oslo: Aschehoug 1960.

Lind, Ebba: **Per-Pål-Espen i Agategate** (Per-Pal-Espen in Agate Street; Per-Pal-Espen in der Agate-Straße.) Ill.: Tonje Strøm.
Oslo: Tiden Norsk Forlag 1960.

Illustration
Johnson, Arne in:
Rynning-Tønnesen, Olaf: **Hemmelig sender.** (Secret transmitter; Geheimsender.)
Oslo: Aschehoug 1960.

Jonsmoen, Unni-Lise in:
Davik, Ingebrigt: **Det hendte i Taremareby.** Forteljing og viser frå barnetimen. (It happened in *Taremareby.* Stories and songs from the children's hour; Es geschah in *Taremareby.* Erzählungen und Lieder aus der Kinderstunde.)
Oslo: Noregs boklag 1960.

Rud, Borghild in:
Prøysen, Alf: **Teskjekjerringa pa nye eventyr.** (The teaspoon woman's new adventures; Die Teelöffel-Alte erlebt neue Abenteuer.)
Oslo: Tiden Norsk Forlag 1960.

Strøm, Tonje in:
Linde, Ebba: **Per-Pål-Espen i Agategate.** (*Per-Pal-Espen* in Agate Street; *Per-Pal-Espen* in der Agate-Straße.)
Oslo: Tiden Norsk Forlag 1960.

1962 *1st prize/1. Preis*
Bruheim, Jan-Magnus: **Røyskatten og andre barnerin.** (The weasel and other children's rhymes; Das Hermelin und andere Kinderreime.) Ill.: Reidar Johan Berle.
Oslo: Noregs boklag 1961.

Hagerup, Inger: **Lille Persille. Barnevers.** (*Little Parsley.* Children's verse; *Kleine Petersilie.* Kinderverse.) Ill.: Paul René Gauguin.
Oslo: Aschehoug 1961.

2nd prize/2. Preis
Borch, Anka (i.e. Colban Berg): **Torarin.** (*Torarin.*)
Oslo: Gyldendal Norsk Forlag 1961.

Lie, Haakon: **I villdyrskog.** (In the forests of wild living animals; Im Wald der wild lebenden Tiere.)
Oslo: Noregs boklag 1961.

3rd prize/3. Preis
Rojahn, Vigdis: **Stribust** (*Stribust* [= rude and obstinate]; *Stribust* [= widerborstig].) Ill.: Vigdis Rojahn.
Oslo: Green 1961.

Rongen, Bjørn: **Slalåm for livet.** (Slalom for your life; Slalom um das Leben.)
Oslo: Damm 1961.

Picture book/Bilderbuch
Gauguin, Paul René in:
Hagerup, Inger: **Lille Persille. Barnevers.** (*Little Parsley.* Children's verse; *Kleine Petersilie.* Kinderverse.)
Oslo: Aschehoug 1961.

Illustration — 1st prize/1. Preis
Berle, Reidar Johan in:
Bruheim, Jan-Magnus: **Røyskatten og andre barnerim.** (The weasel and other children's rhymes; Das Hermelin und andere Kinderreime.)
Oslo: Noregs boklag 1961.

Berle, Reidar Johan in:
Buck, Pearl Sydenstricker: **Dragefisken.** (The dragon fish; Der Drachenfisch.)
Oslo: Aschehoug 1961.

Illustration — 2nd prize/2. Preis
Jonsmoen, Unni-Lise in:
Jonsmoen, Ola: **Singeling for rare ting.** (*singeling* [=onomatopoeia] for lovable things; *Singeling* [= Lautmalerei] um liebenswerte Dinge.)
Oslo: Noregs boklag 1961.

1963 *1st prize/1. Preis*
The prize was not given; Der Preis wurde nicht vergeben.

2nd prize/2. Preis
Heggland, Johannes: **Folket i dei kvite båtane.** (The people in the white boats; Die Leute in den weißen Booten.)
Oslo: Det norske samlaget 1962.

Sommerfelt, Aimée: **Den hvite bungalowen.** (The white bungalow; Der weiße Bungalow.) Ill.: Ulf Aas.
Oslo: Damm 1962.

3rd prize/3. Preis
Friis-Baastad, Babbis: **Kjersti.** (*Kjersti.*)
Oslo: Damm 1962.

Thesen, Kirsten: **Bare du og jeg.** (Only you and I; Nur du und ich.)
Oslo: Damm 1962.

Picture book/Bilderbuch
Aas, Tonje Strøm in:
Bilder, rim og regler. Barnas verden. 5. (Pictures, rhymes and funny tales. The children's world. 5; Bilder, Reime und lustige Geschichten. Die Welt der Kinder. 5.)
Oslo: Aschehoug 1962.

Illustration
Berle, Reidar Johan in:
Vi leser eventyr. (We read fairy tales; Wir lesen Märchen.)
Oslo: Aschehoug 1962.

Ranheimsaeter, Ørnulf in:
Vestly, Anne-Catharina: **Barnas store sangbok.** (The big songbook for children; Das große Liederbuch für Kinder.) Music/Noten: Johnny Nilsen.
Oslo: Cappelen 1962.

1964 *1st prize/1. Preis*
Prøysen, Alf: **Sirkus Mikkelikski.** (*Mikkelikski* circus Zirkus *Mikkelikski.*) Ill.: Hans Normann Dahl.
Oslo: Tiden Norsk Forlag 1963.

2nd prize/2. Preis
Heggland, Johannes: **Bronsesverdet.** (The bronze sword; Das Bronzeschwert.)
Oslo: Det norske samlaget 1963.

Olsen, Johanna Bugge: **Løsgjengeren.** (The vagabond; Der Vagabund.)
Oslo: Tiden Norsk Forlag 1963.

3rd prize/3. Preis
Nordang, Marit: **Tik-tal-taj.** (*Tik-tal-taj.*) Ill.: Unni-Lise Jonsmoen.
Oslo: Det norske samlaget 1963.

Picture book/Bilderbuch
Berle, Reidar Johan in:
Bruheim, Jan-Magnus: **Reinsbukken Kauto frå Kautokeino.** (*Kauto* the reindeer from *Kautokeino*; Der Renbock *Kauto* von *Kautokeino.*)
Oslo: Noregs boklag 1963.

Illustration
Dahl, Hans Normann in:
Prøysen, Alf: **Sirkus Mikkelikski.** (*Mikkelikski* circus; Zirkus *Mikkelikski.*)
Oslo: Tiden Norsk Forlag 1963.

Special prize for Lappish translation/Sonderpreis für die Übertragung ins Samische
Østmo, Isak in:
Bruheim, Jan-Magnus: **Guov'dagaeino Gab'ba.** (*Gab'ba,* the reindeer; Der Renbock *Gab'ba.*) Ill.: Reidar Johan Berle.
Oslo: Noregs boklag 1963.

1965 *1st prize/1. Preis*
Christensen, Christian Arthur Richardt: **Norge under okkupasjonen.** (Norway during the occupation; Norwegen während der Besatzung.)
Oslo: Damm 1964.

Friis-Baastad, Babbis: **Ikke ta Bamse.** (Donot take *Bamse*; Nimm *Bamse* nicht.)
Oslo: Damm 1964.

2nd prize/2. Preis
Prøysen, Alf: **Den grønne votten.** (The green mitten; Der grüne Fausthandschuh.)
Oslo: Tiden Norsk Forlag 1964.

Sommerfelt, Aimée: **Pablo og de andre.** (*Pablo* and the others; *Pablo* und die anderen.) Ill.: Hans Normann Dahl.
Oslo: Damm 1964.

3rd prize/3. Preis
Heggland, Johannes: **Skutelsveinen.** (The young guardsman; Der junge Bursche von der Leibwache.)
Oslo: Noregs boklag 1964.

Picture book/Bilderbuch
Berle, Reidar Johan in:
Øiestad, Per Christian: **Min første bibelbok.** (My first Bible; Meine erste Bibel.)
Bergen: Lunde 1964.
(Bokmål)

Berle, Reidar Johan in:
Øiestad, Per Christian: **Mi første bibelbok.** (My first Bible; Meine erste Bibel.)
Bergen: Lunde 1964.
(nynorsk)

Illustration — 1st prize/1. Preis
Rud, Borghild in:
Prøysen, Alf: **Den grønne votten.** (The green mitten; Der grüne Fausthandschuh.)
Oslo: Tiden Norsk Forlag 1964.

2nd prize/2. Preis
Dahl, Hans Normann in:
Sommerfelt, Aimée: **Pablo og de andre.** (*Pablo* and the others; *Pablo* und die anderen.)
Oslo: Damm 1964.

3rd prize/3. Preis
Vestly, Johan in:
Vestly, Anne-Catharina: **Knerten gifter seg.** (*Knerten* gets married; *Knerten* heiratet.)
Oslo: Tiden Norsk Forlag 1964.

1966 *1st prize/1. Preis*
Hamre, Leif: **Brutt kontakt.** (Interrupted contact; Abgerissene Verbindung.) Ill.: Stein Davidsen.
Oslo: Aschehoug 1965.

2nd prize/2. Preis
Waage, Jan Fr.: **Oppbrudd i savolaks.** (Departure from *Savolaks*; Aufbruch in *Savolaks.*) Ill.: Andreas Hauge.
Oslo: Damm 1965.

Illustration
Aas, Tonje Strøm in:
Hagerup, Anders: **Katten som kunne telle til seksti.** (The cat who could count up to sixty; Die Katze, die bis 60 zählen konnte.)
Oslo: Aschehoug 1965.

Aas, Ulf in:
Svendsen, Kari B.: **Eventyr for de minste.** (Fairy tailes for the smallest ones; Märchen für die Allerkleinsten.)
Oslo: Tiden Norsk Forlag 1965.

Jonsmoen, Unni-Lise in:
Nordang, Marit: **Bimbam i jungelen.** (*Bimbam* in the jungle; *Bimbam* im Dschungel.)
Oslo: Det Norske Samlaget 1965.

Løwe, Trygve Eivind in:
Ørback, Hans Børre: **Zakarias og sjørøver Røverø.** (*Zakarias* and the pirate, *Røverø; Zakarias* und der Seeräuber *Røverø.*)
Oslo: Fabritius 1965.

1967 *1st prize/1. Preis*
The prize was not given; Der Preis wurde nicht vergeben.

2nd prize/2. Preis.
Brunheim, Jan-Magnus: **Grashoppa og andre barnerim.** Grasshop-

per and other children's rhymes; Heuschreck und andere Kinderreime.) Ill.: Reider Johan Berle.
Oslo: Noregs boklag 1966.

Heggland, Johannes: **Syskenlaget.** Barne- og ungdomsroman frå midten av førre hundreåret. (Brothers and sisters. Children's and youth novel from the middle of the nineteenth century; Geschwister, Kinder- und Jugendroman aus der Mitte des vorigen Jahrhunderts.)
Oslo: Det Norske Samlaget 1966.

Thesen, Kirsten: **Samma det, bare tida går.** (It doesn't matter, anything to pass the time; Es ist gleich, wenn nur die Zeit vergeht.)
Oslo: Damm 1966.

3rd prize/3. Preis

Kvasbø, Alf: **En flaske i snøen.** Ungdomsroman. (A bottle in the snow. Youth novel; Eine Flasche im Schnee. Jugendroman.)
Oslo: Gyldendal Norsk Forlag 1966.

Rojahn, Vigdis:**Rabletusten.** The scribbled note; Der Kritzelwisch.)
Ill.: Vigdis Rojahn.
Oslo: Green 1966.

Picture book/Bilderbuch

Jonsmoen, Unni-Lise in:
Floden, Halvor: **Tommeliten på ikornrygg.** (*Little Thumbling* on the squirrel's back; Der Däumling auf dem Eichhornrücken.)
Oslo: Noregs boklag 1966.

Illustration

Berger, Grethe in:
Knagenhjelm, Ragnhild: **Plukke, plukke barnevers.** (Pluck, pluck children's verses; Pluck, pluck Kinderverse.)
Oslo: Dreyer 1966.

Berle, Reidar Johan in:
Bruheim, Jan-Magnus: **Grashoppa og andre barnerim.** (Grasshopper and other children's rhymes; Heuschreck und andere Kinderreime.)
Oslo: Noregs boklag 1966.

Pedersen, Tore Bernitz in:
Prøysen, Alf: **Frå Hompetitten til Bakvendtland.** 37 barneviser. (From *Hompetitten* to *Upside-down-Land.* 37 Children's songs; Von *Hompetitten* zum *Umgekehrt-Land.* 37 Kinderlieder.)
Music/Noten: Johnny Nilsen.
Oslo: Tiden Norsk Forlag 1966.

1968 *1st prize/1. Preis*
Døcker, Rolf: **Marius.** (*Marius.*) Ill.: Tonje Strøm Ass.
Oslo: Aschehoug 1967.

2nd prize/2. Preis
Brodtkorb, Reidar: **Rokkesteinen.** (The rocking stone; Der wippende Stein.) Ill.: Kjersti Scheen.
Oslo: Damm 1967.

Friis-Baastad, Babbis: **Du må våkne, Tor!** (You must wake up, *Tor*! Du mußt aufwachen, *Tor*!)
Ill.: Hans Norman Dahl.
Oslo: Damm 1967.

Prøysen, Alf.: **Teskjekjerringa på camping.** (The teaspoon woman goes camping; Die Teelöffel-Alte beim Camping.) Ill.: Borghild Rud.
Oslo: Tiden Norsk Forlag 1967.

Picture book/Bilderbuch
Berle, Reidar Johan in: Hagerup, Inger: **Trekkfuglene og skjaera.** (The birds of passage and the magpie; Die Zugvögel und die Elster.)
Oslo: Aschehoug 1967.

Toming, Hans Jørgen in:
Lybeck, Sebastian: **Da elefanten tok leketanten.** (When the elephant took the kindergarten teacher; Als der Elefant die Kindergärtnerin nahm.)
Oslo: Aschehoug 1967.

Illustration - 1st prize/1. Preis
Johnson, Kaare Espolin in:
Normann, Regine: **Ringelihorn og andre eventyr.** (*Ringelihorn* [= Curly Horn] and other fairy tales; Ringelihorn [=Geringeltes Horn] und andere Märchen.
Oslo: Aschehoug 1967.

2nd prize/2. Preis
Dahl, Hans Normann in:
Friis-Baastad, Babbis: **Du må våkne, Tor!** (You must wake up, *tor*! Du mußt aufwachen, *Tor*!)
Oslo: Damm 1967.

Rud, Borghild in:
Prøysen, Alf.: **Teskjerringa på camping.** (The teaspoon woman goes camping; Die Teelöffel-Alte beim Camping.)
Oslo: Tiden Norsk Forlag 1967.

1969 *1st prize/1. Preis*
The prize was not given; Der Preis wurde nicht vergeben.

2nd prize/2. Preis
Kvasbø, Alf: **Dueller.** (Duels; Duelle.) Ill.: Johann Kippenbroock.
Oslo: Gyldendal 1968.

Ljone, Oddmund: **På villstra.** (Gone astray; Verirrt.)
Oslo: Gyldendal 1968.

3rd prize/3. Preis
Brodtkorb, Reidar: **Tisledevollen.** (*Tislede* meadow; Die *Tislede*-Wiese.) Ill.: Kjersti Scheen Grep.
Oslo: Damm 1968.

Sem, Gunnar: **Veien til Vestmar.** (The way to *Vestmar*; Der Weg nach *Vestmar*.)
Oslo: Aschehoug 1968.

Picture book/Bilderbuch - 1st prize/1. Preis
Berle, Reidar Johan in:
Øiestad, Per Christian: **Den første julaften.** (The first Christmas Eve; Der erste Weihnachtsabend.)
Oslo: Gyldendal 1968.

2nd prize/2. Preis
Kapsberger, Sigrun Saebø in:
Langemyr, Ingvald: **Eit hus i stova.** (A house in the chamber; Ein Haus in der Stube.)
Bergen: Barnebladet Magne 1968.

Illustration - 1st prize/1. Preis
Dahl, Hans Normann in:
Friis-Baastad, Babbis: **Hest på ønskelisten.** (Horse on the wishing list; Pferd auf der Wunschliste.)
Oslo: Damm 1968.

Johnson, Arne in:
Dahl, Synnøve Gill: **Hånschen.** (*Hanschen*; *Hänschen*.)
Oslo: Gyldendal 1968.

2nd prize/2. Preis
Bjøgrum, Olav in:
Hagen, Ingeborg Refling: **Eventyr og historier frå Mostua.** (Fairy tales and stories from *Mostua*; Märchen und Geschichten aus *Mostua*.)
Oslo: Utgitt av Suttung 1968.

1970 *1st prize/1. Preis*
Bruheim, Jan-Magnus: **Romferda og andre barnerim.** (The space trip and other children's poems; Die Raumfahrt und andere Kindergedichte.) Ill.: Reidar Johan Berle.
Oslo: Noregs boklag 1969.

Hopp, Zinken (i.e. Signe Marie): **Arven frå Adamson.** (*Adamson's* inheritance; *Adamsons* Erbteil.) Ill.: Odd Brochmann.
Oslo: Aschehoug 1969.

2nd prize/2. Preis
Brodtkorb, Reidar: **Haiene gikk opp med tidevannet.** (The sharks arrived with the flood tide; Die Haifische tauchten mit den Gezeiten auf.) Ill.: Egil Torin Naesheim.
Oslo: Barnebladet Magne 1969.

Havrevold, Finn: **Lommekniven.** (The pocket knife; Das Taschenmesser.)
Oslo: Aschehoug 1969.

3rd prize/3. Preis
Kvasbø, Alf: **Kaldt vann i blodet.** (Cold water in the blood; Kaltes Wasser im Blut.)
Oslo: Gyldendal 1969.

Picture book/Bilderbuch - 1st prize/1. Preis
Bjørklid, Haakon in:
Bjørklid, Haakon: **Den store blå bukken.** (The big blue buck; Der große blaue Bock.)
Oslo: Gyldendal 1969.

2nd prize/2. Preis
Kapsberger, Sigrun Saebø in:
Langemyr, Ingvald: **Hos oss.** (With us; Bei uns).
Oslo: Barnebladet Magne 1969.

Illustration - 1st prize/1. Preis
Johnson, Arne in:
Normann, Regine: **Den grå katt og den sorte.** (The grey cat and the black cat; Die graue Katze und die schwarze Katze.)
Oslo: Aschehoug 1969.

2nd prize/2. Preis
Berle, Reidar Johan in:
Bruheim, Jan-Magnus: **Romferda og andre barnerim.** (The space trip and other children's poems; Die Raumfahrt und andere Kindergedichte.)
Oslo: Noregs boklag 1969.

Naesheim, Egil Torin in:
Brodtkorb, Reidar: **Haiene gikk opp med tidevannet.** (The sharks arrived with the flood tide; Die Haifische tauchten mit den Gezeiten auf.)
Oslo: Barnebladet Magne 1969.

1971 *1st prize/1. Preis*
Prøysen, Alf: The prize was awarded posthumously for his contribution to children's literature; Der Preis wurde ihm nach seinem Tod für seinen Beitrag zur Kinderliteratur verliehen.

2nd prize/2. Preis
Brodtkorb, Reidar: **Gutten som fant kirkesølvet.** (The boy who found the church silver; Der Junge, der das Kirchensilber fand.)
Ill.: Kjersti Scheen Grepp.
Oslo: Damm 1970.

Heggland, Johannes: **Den forfølgde.** (The pursued; Der Verfolgte.)
Larvik: Norsk barneblad 1970.

3rd prize/ 3. Preis
Breen, Else: **Mias kråke.** (*Mia's* crow; *Mias* Krähe.)
Oslo: Aschehoug 1970.

Erichsen, Eli: **Signe og Signora.** (*Signe* and *Signora* .)
Oslo: Aschehoug 1970.

Kvasbø, Alf: **En sjel av kork.** (A soul of cork; Eine Seele aus Kork.)
Ill.: Jan O. Henriksen.
Oslo: Gyldendal 1970.

Picture book/Bilderbuch
Berle, Reidar Johan in:
Berle, Reidar Johan: **Om natten skinner solen.** (The sun shines during the night; Während der Nacht scheint die Sonne.)
Oslo: Gyldendal 1970.

Kapsberger, Sigrun Saebø in:
Rud, Nils Johan: **Barna som gikk for å hente våren.** (The children who went searching for spring; Die Kinder, die auszogen, um den Frühling zu suchen.)
Oslo: Barnebladet Magne 1970.

Illustration
Bjørgum, Olaf in:
Hagen, Ingeborg Refling: **Eventyr og historier frå Mostua.** (Fairy tales and stories from *Mostua*; Märchen und Geschichten aus *Mostua* .)
Oslo: Suttung 1970.

Grepp, Kjersti Scheen in:
Brodtkorb, Reidar: **Gutten som fant kirkesølvet.** (The boy who found the church silver; Der Junge, der das Kirchensilber fand.)
Oslo: Damm 1970.

Rojahn, Vigdis in:
Rojan Vigdis: **Vesle-Laie's eventyr.** (Little *Laie's* fairy tales; Klein-*Laies* Märchen.)
Oslo: Green 1970.

Storsveen, Eva in:
Bruheim, Jan-Magnus: **På langferd med Mjo Monsemann.** (On a long journey with *Mjo Monsemann*; Auf großer Reise mit *Mjo Monsemann*.)
Oslo: Noregs boklag 1970.

1972 *1st prize/1. Preis*
Brodtkorb, Reidar: **Fuglen som fløy over land og hav.** (The bird flew over land and sea; Der Vogel, der über Land und See flog.) Ill.: Egil Torin Naesheim.
Oslo: Barnebladet Magne 1971.

2nd prize/2. Preis
Hanre, Leif: **Operasjon Arktis.** (*Operation Arctic*; *Operation Arktis.*)
Oslo: Aschehoug 1971.

3rd prize/3. Preis
Sommerfelt, Aimée: **Den farlige natten.** (The dangerous night; Die gefährliche Nacht.) Ill.: Borghild Rud.
Oslo: Damm 1971.

Picture book/Bilderbuch
Dahl, Hans Normann in:
Prøysen, Alf: **Snekker Andersen og julenissen.** (*Andersen* the carpenter and the Christmas brownie; Tischler *Andersen* und der Weihnachts-Wichtel.)
Oslo: Tiden Norsk Forlag 1971.

Illustration — 1st prize/1. Preis
Rud, Borghild in:
Sommerfelt, Aimée: **Den farlige natten.** (The dangerous night; Die gefährliche Nacht.)
Oslo: Damm 1971.

2nd prize/2. Preis
Berle, Reidar Johan in:
Tenfjord, Johanne Marie: **Ønsketreet. Eventyr fra fem verdensdeler.** (Fairy tales from five continents; Märchen aus den fünf Erdteilen.)
Bergen: Eide 1971.

3rd prize/3. Preis
Johnson, Arne in:
Falkberget, Johan: **Eventyrfjell.** (Fairy tale mountain; Märchen-Gebirge.)
Oslo: Aschehoug 1971.

1973 Bruheim, Jan-Magnus: **Syskenringen of andre barnedikt.** (The ring of brothers and sisters and other children's poetry; Der Ring der Geschwister und andere Kindergedichte.) Ill.: Reidar Johan Berle.
Bergen: Noregs koblag 1972.

Heggland, Johannes: **Selja frå Salmeli.** (*Selja* from *Salmeli*; *Selja* von *Salmeli.*)
Larvik: Norsk barneblad 1972.

Vinje, Karl: **Den vesle jenta og den store tyven.** (The little girl and the big thief; Das kleine Mädchen und der große Dieb.)
Stavnager: Nomi Forlag 1972.

Picture book/Bilderbuch
Berle, Reidar Johan in:
Tenfjord, Johanne Marie: **Regnbuebroen og andre fortellinger om da verden ble til.** (The rainbow bridge and other stories; Die Regenbogenbrücke und andere Erzählungen.)
Bergen: Eide 1972.

Rud, Borghild in:
Prøysen, Alf: **Teskjekjerringa og Kvitebjorn Kong Valemon.** (The teaspoon woman and the polar bear king, *Valemon*; Die Teelöffel-Alte und der Eisbär König *Valemon.*)
Oslo: Tiden Norsk Forlag 1972.

Illustration
Johnson, Arne in:
Armstrong, William H.: **Klang, den store hunden.** (*Klang*, the big dog; *Klang*, der große Hund; Am.orig.title: *Sounder.*)
Oslo: Gyldendal 1972.

Naesheim, Egil Torin in:
Olafsson, Albert: **Islandske eventyr.** (Icelandic fairy tales; Isländische Märchen.)
Oslo: Det Norske Samlaget 1972.

Translation/Übersetzen
Coucheron, Olaf für:
Thorvall, Kerstin: **Istedenfor en far.** (Instead of a father; Anstelle eines Vaters; Swed.orig.title: I stället for en pappa.)
Oslo: Damm 1972.

Stang, Jørgen für:
Rasmussen, Halfdan: **Trippe-trapp-treppestein.** (Trip, trap stepping-stone; Trippe-trapp-Treppenstein; Dan.orig.title: Børnerim. Tegninger.) Ill.: Ib Spang Olsen.
Oslo: Noregs boklag 1972.

1974 *1st prize/1. Preis*
Kvasbø, Alf: **Storm.** (Storm; Sturm.)
Oslo: Gyldendal 1973.

2nd prize/2. Preis
Brodtkorb, Reidar: **Minus 30 grader.** (Minus 30 degrees centigrade; Minus 30 Grad Celsius.)
Oslo: Damm 1973.

Ørbech, Kari: **Alt kan hende, Peder.** (Anything can happen, *Peder*; Es kann alles geschehen, *Peder*.)
Oslo: Tiden Norsk Forlag 1973.

Solås, Ragne: **Om Jonna og Emil.** (About *Jonna* and *Emil*; Über *Jonna* und *Emil*.) Ill.: Borghild Rud.
Oslo: Gyldendal 1973.

Picture book/Bilderbuch. Ist prize/1. Preis
Bjørklid, Haakon in:
Bjørklid, Haakon: **Mons Matglad.** (Gluttonous; Nimmersatt.)
Oslo: Gyldendal 1974.

2nd prize/2. Preis
Berle, Reidar Johan in:
Tenfjord, Johanne Marie: **Jørgen frå Helgeland.** (*Jorgen* from Helgoland; *Jørgen* von Helgoland.)
Bergen: Eide 1973.

Storsveen, Eva in:
Bruheim, Jan-Magnus: **Då dyra samlast til dyreting.** (When the animals gathered for a conference; Als sich die Tiere zum Rat versammelten.)
Oslo: Noregs boklag 1973.

Illustration
Dahl, Hans Normann in:
Preussler, Otfried: **Den vesle heksa.** (The little witch; Germ.orig.title: Die kleine Hexe.)
Oslo: Bokklubben 1973.

Kapsberger, Sigrun Saebø in:
Svinsass, Ingvald: **Laksen Glad.** (*Glad*, the salmon, der Lachs *Glad*.)
Oslo: Tiden Norsk Forlag 1973.

Kippenbroeck, Johan H.F. in:
Moe, Jørgen: **I brønnen og i tjernet.** (In the well and in the pond; Im Brunnen und im Teich.)
Oslo: Bokklubben 1973.

Translation/Übersetzen

Farestveit, Johannes for:
Haugaard, Erik Christian: **Bak krigens kjerre.** (Behind the war cart; Hinter dem Kriegskarren; Dan.orig.title: Bag krigens kaerre.)
Larvik: Norsk barneblad 1973.

Hagerup, Inger for:
Olsen, Ib Spang: **Regnet.** (Rain; Der Regen; Dan.orig.title; Regnet.)
Oslo: Gyldendal 1973.

1975 *1st prize/1. Preis*
Kvasbø, Alf: **Naerkamp.** (Close combat; Nahkampf.)
Oslo: Gyldendal 1974.

2nd prize/2. Preis
Brodtkorb, Reidar: "S.S. Vannrotta". ("S.S. Vannrotta" [= water rat]; "S.S. Vannrotta"; [= Wasserratte].)
Oslo: Damm 1974.

Orbech, Kari: **Stormdagon.** (Storm day; Sturmtag.)
Oslo: Tiden Norsk Forlag 1974.

Sommerfelt, Aimée: **Reisen til ingensteder.** (The voyage to nowhere; Die Reise nirgendwohin.)
Ill.: Egil Torin Naesheim.
Oslo: Damm 1974.

Picture book/Bilderbuch

Dahl, Hans Normann in:
Hansson, Per: **Herr Gummistrikk og vesle Henriette.** (Mr. *Gummistrikk [= elastic band] and little Henriette*; Herr *Gummistrikk* [= Gummiband] und die kleine *Henriette*.)
Oslo: Gyldendal 1974.

Rud, Borghild/Rud, Nils Johan in: **Ole Soppnisse.** (*Ole Soppnisse* [= mushroom brownie]; *Ole Soppnisse [= Pilzwichtel].)*
Oslo: Gyldendal 1974.

Illustration

Balke, Turid in:
Balke, Turid: **Det begynte en fredag i Finvik.** (It began on Friday in *Finvik*; Es begann an einem Freitag in *Finvik*.)
Oslo: Tiden Norsk Forlag 1974.

Bøge, Kari in:
Økland, Einar: **Det blir alvor.** (It's becoming serious; Es wird ernst.)
Oslo: Det Norske Samlaget 1974.

Olsen, Vivian Zahl in:
Rønningen, Bjorn: **Fru Pigalopp.** (Mrs. *Pigalopp;* Frau *Pigalopp.*)
Oslo: Gyldendal 1974.

Translation/Übersetzen
Tenfjord, Jo Giaever for:
Lindgren, Astrid: **Brødrene Løvehjerte.** (The brothers, *Lion Heart*; Die Brüder *Löwenherz*; Swed.orig.title: Bröderna *Lejonhjärta.)*
Oslo: Damm 1974.

Best comic strip award/Preis für die beste Comic-Serie
Newth, Mette: **Benjamin Fisker.** (*Benjamin Fisker.*)
Barnas Avis 1974.

1976 Bing, Jon: **Azur-kapteinens planet.** (The planet of the *Azur* captains; Der Planet des *Azur*-Kapitäns.) Ill.: Thore Hansen.
Oslo: Damm 1975.

Hanssen, Arvid: Den vonde vinteren. (The bad winter; Der schlimme Winter.)
Larvik: Norsk barneblad 1975.

Haugen, Tormod: **Nattfuglene.** (The night birds; Die Nachtvögel.)
Oslo: Gyldendal 1975.

Kvasbø, Alf: **Mørketid.** (Dark time; Dunkle Zeit.)
Oslo: Gyldendal 1975.

Picture book/Bilderbuch
Newth, Mette in:
Newth, Mette: **Lille Skrekk.** (Little *Terror;* Kleiner *Schreck.*)
Oslo: Aschehoug 1975.

Berle, Reidar Johan in:
Borseth, Helge: **Ello melle deg fortelle.** (Elle melle [= onomatopoeia] telling you; Elle melle [= Lautmalerei] erzählen dir.)
Bergen: Eide 1975.

Illustration
Bøge, Kari in:
Økland, Einar: **Slik er det.** (It's like that; So ist das.)
Oslo: Det Norsk Samlaget 1975.

Graff, Finn in:
McCuaig, Ronald: Fresi Fantastika. (*Fresi Fantastika.*)
Oslo: Bokklubben 1975.

Hansen, Thore in:
Bing, Jon: **Azur-kapteinens planet.** (The planet of the *Azur* captains; Der Planet des *Azur*-Kapitäns.)
Oslo: Damm 1975.

Naesheim, Egil Torion in:
Dybwad, Øyvind: **Katta på Grip som ikkje ville flytte til Kristiansund.** (*Katta* from *Grip,* who did not want to move to *Kristiansund*; *Katta* von *Grip*, die nicht nach *Kristiansund* umziehen wollte.)
Oslo: Noregs boklag 1975.

Translation/Übersetzen
Hopp, Zinken (i.e. Signe Marie for):
Nöstlinger, Christine: **Ned med agurk-kongen.** (Down with the cucumber king; Nieder mit dem Gurken-König; Aust.orig.title: Wir pfeifen auf den Gurkenkönig.) Ill.: Werner Maurer.
Oslo: Gyldendal 1975.

Ørjasaeter, Jo for:
Skote, Inger: **Dei teier meg ihjel.** (One ignores me as if I were dead; Man schweigt mich tot; Swed.orig.title: Dom tiger ihäl mej!)
Oslo: Det Norsk Samlaget 1975.

Best comic strip award/Preis für die beste Comic-Serie.
Bøge, Kari: **Sotus som.**
Oslo: Bokklubben 1975.

1977 Haugen, Tormod: **Zeppelin.** (*Zeppelin.*)
Oslo: Gyldendal 1976.

Lorentzen, Karin: **Stine Stankelben.** (*Stine* Stankelben [= skinny longlegs]; *Stine* stankelben [= Weberknecht].)
Oslo: Gyldendal 1976.

Tenfjord, Johanne Marie: **Tre trylleord.** (Three magic words; Drei Zauberworte.)
Bergen: Eide 1976.

Vinje, Kari: **Kamillas venn.** (*Kamilla's* friend; *Kamillas* Freund.)
Oslo: Luther Forlag 1976.

Picture book/Bilderbuch
Egner, Thørbjorn in:
Egner, Thørbjorn: **I Billedbokland. Series.** (In *Picture Book Land.* Series; Im *Bilderbuchland.* Serien.)
Oslo: Cappelen 1976.

Scheen, Kjersti in:
Scheen, Kjersti: **Fie og mørkret.** (*Fie* and the dark; *Fie* und das Dunkel.)
Oslo: Gyldendal 1976.

Illustration
Øyen, Wenche in:
Okkenhaug, Sigrun: **Helga.** (*Helga.*)
Oslo: Det Norsk Samlaget 1976.

Vestly, Johan in:
Vestly, Anne-Catharina: **Gro og nøkkerosene.** (*Gro* and the water lilies; *Gro* und die Wasserlilien.)
Oslo: Tiden Norsk Forlag 1976.

Translation/Übersetzen
Bull, Ella Holm for:
Clevin, Jørgen: **Jaahke jih Joakime.** (*Jacob* and *Joachim*; *Jakob* und *Joachim*; Dan.orig.title: *Jakob* og *Joakim*.)
Oslo: Aschehoug 1976.

Dalflyen, Gudny for:
Sandberg, Inger: Perry og usynlege Wrolf. (*Perry* and *Wrolf, the invisible; Perry* und *Wrolf,* der Unsichtbare; Swed.orig.title: *Perry* och osynlige *Wrolf.*) Ill.: Lasse Sandberg.
Oslo: Samlaget 1976.

Smedstad, Tove Gravem for:
Andersen, Leif Esperød: **Heksefeber.** (Witch fever; Hexenfieber; Dan.orig.title: Heksefeber.)
Oslo: Aschehoug 1976.

Best comic strip award/Preis für die beste Comic-Serie.
Newth, Mette/Newth, Philipp: **Bruse.** (*Bruse.*)
Oslo: Bokklubben 1976.

Kari-Plaketten

The Norwegian Committee for Juvenile Literature (Norsk kuratorium for barne- og ungdomsbøker), which is the Norwegian section of the International Board on Books for Young People, awarded the first Kari medal for an outstanding children's book in 1957. The intention of this award was to promote the art of illustration and picture book making. The last medal was presented in 1961, the year the prize of the Norwegian Ministry of Church and Cultural Affairs was extended to take in the field of illustration.

Das norwegische Kuratorium für Kinder- und Jugendbücher (Norsk kuratorium for barne- og ungdomsbøker), die norwegische Sektion des Internationalen Kuratoriums für das Jugendbuch, vergab 1957 zum erstenmal die Kari-Plakette für das schönste norwegische Kinder- und Jugendbuch, um die Bilderbuch- und Illustrationskunst zu fördern. Da inzwischen der Preis des

Kirchen- und Erziehungsministeriums auch auf dieses Gebiet ausgedehnt wurde, sah das norwegische Kuratorium seine Initiative aufgenommen und stellte die Vergabe der Plakette mit dem Jahre 1961 wieder ein.

1958 Berle, Reidar Johan in:
Slettemark, Nils: **Rull, rull, kjerre. Barnerim.** (Roll, roll, cart. Children's rhymes; Rolle, rolle, Karren. Kinderreime.) Music: Vera Slettemark.
Bergen: Eide 1957.

1959 Berle, Reidar Johan in:
Bruheim, Jan-Magnus: **Hornsmeden og andre barnerim.** (The hornsmith and other children's rhymes; Der Hornschmied und andere Kinderreime.)
Bergen: Eide 1958.

1960 Gauguin, Paul René in:
Hagerup, Inger: **Så rart. Barnevers.** (How curious. Children's rhymes. Wie wunderlich. Kinderreime.)
Oslo: Aschehoug 1959.

1961 Jonsmoen, Unni-Lise in:
Davik, Ingebrigt: **Det hendte i Taremareby.** Forteljing og viser fra barnetimen. (It happened in *Taremareby.* Stories and songs from the children's hour; Es geschah in *Taremareby.* Erzählungen und Lieder aus der Kinderstunde.)
Oslo: Noregs boklag 1960.

Peru

Premio Nacional de Literatura Infantil José María Eguren

The Institute of National Culture established this prize in 1968. The prize was descontinued in 1972.

Dieser Preis wurde 1968 vom nationalen Kulturinstitut gestiftet. 1972 wurde er nicht mehr verliehen.

1968 Alegria, Ciro: **Panky y el guerrero.** (*Panky* and the warrior; *Panky* und der Krieger.) Ill.: Paco Cisneros.
Lima: Ed. Industrial Gráfica S.A.

1969 Corcueta, Arturo: **Fábulas para Rosamar.** (Fables for *Rosamar*; Fabeln für *Rosamar*.) Ill.: Tilsa Tsuchiya.
Lima: Ed Omar Ames.

1970 Carvallo de Nuñez, Carlotta: **Cuentos de Navidad.** (Stories of Christmas; Weihnachtsgeschichten.) Ill.: Charo Núñez de Patrucco.
Lima: Peisa.

1971 Ibanez, Mercedes: **Las estrellas se pueden tocar.** (You can touch the stars; Du kannst die Sterne berühren.)
(Unpublished; Unveröffentlicht.)

Premio Juan Volatin

This prize was established by the Peruvian section of IBBY (International Board on Books for Young People), and was funded by the city of San Isidro. In 1973 the prize was discontinued.

Dieser Preis wurde 1964 von der peruanischen Sektion der IBBY gestiftet und von San Isidro unterhalten. Seit 1973 wird der Preis nicht mehr verliehen.

1964 Nieri de Dammert, Graciela: **Cuentos del Perú.** (Stories of Peru; Geschichten über Peru.) Ill.: R. Villanueva.
Lima: Sección Peruana de la Organización Internacional del Libro Juvenil 1964.

1965 Cerna Guardia, Rosa: **Los días de carbón.** (The days of coal; Die Tage der Kohlen.) Ill.: Francisco Izquierdo López.
Lima: Sección Peruana de la Organización Internacional del Libro Juvenil 1966.

1968 Hidalgo, José: **Muñeca de trapo.** (Rag doll; Flicken-Puppe.) Ill.: Charo Núñez de Patrucco.
Lima: Ed. San Isidro 1969.

Eguren, Mercedes: **El múñeco de aserrin.** (The saw-dust puppet; Die Drahtpuppe aus Sägespänen.) Ill.: Charo Núñez de Patrucco.
Lima: Ed. San Isidro 1969.

1972 Cerna Guardia, Rosa: **El hombre de paja.** (The straw man; Der Strohmann.) Ill.: Alicia Ferrarone.
Lima: Ed. Universo.

Ill. 30 *Charo Núñez de Patrucco in C. Carvallo de Nuñez: Cuentos de Navidad*

Poland/Polen

Hacerska Nagroda Literacka

The "Hacerska Nagroda Literacka" (Boy Scout's Literature Prize) was established at the 4th Congress of Polish Boy Scouts. Since 1970 the prize has been awarded annually. The prize-winning books must be of high literary worth, written by Polish authors, and possess artistic and educational qualities in alignment with the Boy Scout education programme. Further rules of the prize require that the books must have been published during

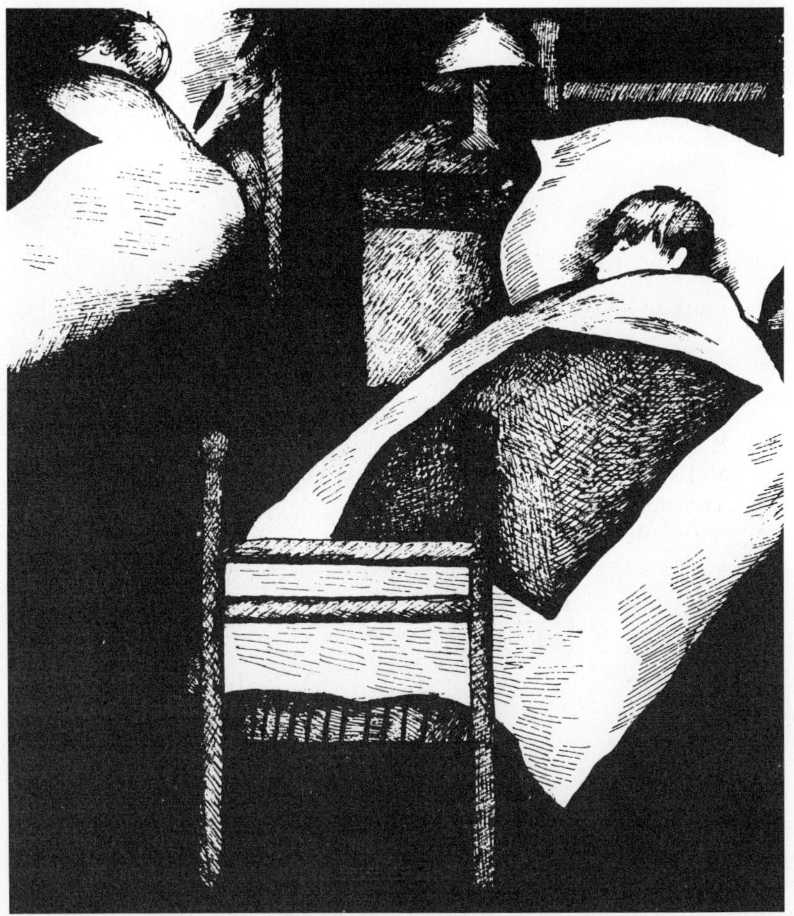

Ill. 31 Malgorzata Rózańska in H. Lothamer: Do zobaczenia, mamo

the previous year, should not have already received a prize elsewhere, and that they are geared for the age group, twelve to fifteen years. Proposals of titles for the prize are submitted by, publishers, children's book experts, cultural organizations, and by members of the Boy Scout's Cultural Council.

Der Pfadfinder-Literaturpreis wurde auf dem IV. Kongress des Polnischen Pfadfinderbundes gestiftet. Seit 1970 wird der Preis jährlich verliehen. Ausgezeichnet werden Bücher polnischer Autoren. Die vorgeschlagenen Werke müssen von hohem literarischen Wert sein, erzieherische und künstlerische Qualität aufweisen, mit dem Erziehungsprogramm des Pfadfinderbundes übereinstimmen und aktuelle Themen behandeln. Weitere Bedingungen sind, daß die Bücher im Vorjahr erschienen sind, bisher noch keinen Preis bekommen haben und für Jugendliche von 12—15 Jahren geeignet sind. Vorschläge werden von Verlagen, wissenschaftlichen und kulturellen Institutionen, Organisationen, die sich mit Erforschung und Verbreitung der Kinder- und Jugendliteratur befassen, sowie von Mitgliedern des Pfadfinderkulturrates eingereicht.

1970 Jurgielewiczowa, Irena: **Wszystko inaczej.** (Everything is different; Alles ist anders.) Ill.: Bożena Truchanowska.
Warszawa: Nasza Księgarnia 1968.

Bratkowski, Stefan: **Księga wróżb prawdziwych.** (The book of true prophecy; Das Buch der wahren Prophezeihungen.) Ill.: Mirosław Pokora.
Warszawa: Wydawnictwo Harcerskie "Horyzonty" 1968.

1971 Platówna, Stanisława: **Chłopiec na polnej drodze.** (The boy on the path in the field; Der Junge auf dem Feldweg.) Ill.: Mieczysław Majewski.
Warszawa: Nasza Księgarnia 1970.

1972 Minkowski, Aleksander: **Szaleństwo Majki Skowron.** (The madness of *Majka Skowron*; Die Verrücktheiten der *Majka Skowron*.)
Warszawa: Wydawnictwo Harcerskie "Horyzonty" 1972.

1973 Szczygieł, Jerzy: **Nigdy cię nie opuszczę.** (I will never leave you; Ich werde dich nie verlassen.) Ill.: Kazimierz Hałajkiewicz.
Warszawa: Nasza Księgarnia 1972.

1974 Dańkowsky, Maria: **Romans naszej mamy.** (The romance of our mother; Die Romanze unserer Mutter.) Ill.: Jolanta Kalita.
Warszawa: Wydawnictwo Harcerskie "Horyzonty" 1973.

1975 Bieńkowska, Danuta: **Chwila prawdy.** (The hour of truth; Die Stunde der Wahrheit.) Ill.: Elżbieta Murawska.
Warszawa: Nasza Księgarnia 1975.

1976 Kuczyński, Maciej: **Zwycięzca.** (The winner; Der Sieger.) Ill.: Waldemar Andrzejewski.
Warszawa: Nasza Księgarnia 1976.

1977 Wieczerska, Janina: **Lekcja dzielenia.** (The division lesson; Lektion des Dividierens.) Ill.: Leonia Janecka.
Warszawa: Wydawnictwo Harcerskie "Horyzonty" 1977.

1978 Sołonowicz-Olbrychska, Klementyna: **Majówka.** (The May excursion; Der Maiausflug.)
Warszawa: Ludowa Spółdzielnia Wydawnicza 1977.

Lothamer, Henryk: **Do zobaczenia, mamo!** (Good bye, mama! Auf Wiedersehen, Mama!) Ill.: Małgorazata Różańsky.
Warszawa: Krajowa Agencja Wydawnicza 1977.

1979 Kucharski, Jan E.: **Warszawiacy.** (The people of Warsaw; Die Warschauer.) Ill.: Stanisław Rozwadowski.
Warszawa: Nasza Księgarnia 1978.

Ostrowska, Ewa: **Długa lekcja.** (A long school lesson; Eine lange Schulstunde.)
Warszawa: Młodzieżowa Agencja Wydawnicza 1979.

1980 Nienacki, Zbigniew: **Pan Samochodzik i złota rękawica.** (Mr. Automobile and the golden glove; Herr Auto und der goldene Handschuh.) Ill.: Tomasz Borowski.
Warszawa: Nasza Księgarnia 1979.

Nagroda literacka Centralnej Rady Związków Zawodowych za twórczość dla młodych czytelników

This prize is awarded to authors whose books aim to inspire the future leaders of Polish Labor organizations. Founded by the Central Council of Labor Unions, this prize is given for books that will help to build character of young people. Since 1972, the award has been discontinued.

Der Preis wird an Jugendbuchautoren verliehen, die ihre Werke künftig führenden Mitgliedern der Arbeiterorganisation gewidmet haben. Es wurden Bücher ausgezeichnet, die die Persönlichkeit des jungen Menschen formen helfen. Nach 1972 wurde der Preis nicht mehr verliehen.

1969 Górkiewiczowa, Janina Barbara: **A jednak radość.** (And still a joy; Und dennoch eine Freude.) Ill.: Władysław Paweł Jabłoński.
Warszawa: Nasza Księgarnia 1967.

Domaglik, Janusz: **Koniec wakacji.** (The end of the holiday; Das Ende der Ferien.) Ill.: Juliusz Makowski.
Warszawa: Nasza Księgarnia 1966.

1970 Ziółkowska, Maria: **Szukaj wiatru w polu.** (Look for the wind in the field; Suche den Wind im Feld.) Ill.: Albin Dobiesz. Warszawa: Nasza Księgarnia 1969.

Twardecki, Alojzy: **Szkoła janczarów.** (The school of the *Janissary*; Die Schule der Janitscharen.) Warszawa: Iskry 1969.

1971 Bratkowski, Stefan: **Świat w którym żyjemy.** (The world in which we live; Die Welt in der wir leben.) Warszawa: Horyzonty 1970.

Dańkowska, Maria: **W cztery oczy.** (Face to face; Unter vier Augen.) Ill.: Tadeusz Pietrzyk. Warszawa: Horyzonty 1970.

1972 Chądzyńska, Żofia: **Życie za życie.** (Life for life; Leben für Leben.) Warszawa: Nasza Księgarnia 1971.

Warneńska, Monika: **Ścieżki przez dżunglę.** (Ways through the jungle; Wege durch den Dschungel.) Warszawa: Horyzonty 1971.

Nagroda Prezesa Rady Ministrów za twórczość literacką dla dzieci i młodziezy

After Julian Tuwim received the State Prize for Literature in 1951, the Prime Minister of Poland has since 1952 conferred annually a prize for the collected works of a children's book author.

Nachdem 1951 Julian Tuwim den höchsten Staatspreis für Literatur erhielt, verleiht der polnische Ministerpräsident seit 1952 jährlich einen Preis für das Gesamtschaffen eines Kinder- oder Jugendbuchautors.

1952 Krzemieniecka, Lucyna for: Collected works; Gesamtwerk.

1953 Porazińska, Janina for: Collected works; Gesamtwerk.

Szelburg-Zarembina, Ewa for: Collected works; Gesamtwerk.

1954 Januszewska, Hanna for: Collected works; Gesamtwerk.

1955 Centkiewicz, Alina for: Collected works; Gesamtwerk.

Centkiewicz, Czesław for: Collected works; Gesamtwerk.

Niziurski, Edmund for: Collected works; Gesamtwerk.

1956 Brzechwa, Jan for: Collected works; Gesamtwerk.

Kownacka, Maria for: Collected works; Gesamtwerk.

1957 Kann, Maria for: Collected works; Gesamtwerk.

1958 Jurgielewicz, Irena for: Collected works; Gesamtwerk.

1959 Ożogowska, Hanna for: Collected works; Gesamtwerk.

1960 Janczarski, Czesław for: Collected works; Gesamtwerk.

1961 Dziarnowska, Janina: Gdy inni dziećmi są. (When the others are still children; Wenn andere noch Kinder sind.) Ill.
Warszawa: Nasza Księgarnia.

Morcinek, Gustaw for: Collected works; Gesamtwerk.

1962/1972 The prize was not given; Der Preis wurde nicht vergeben.

1973 Broniewska, Janina for: Books dealing with problems concerning society and patriotism; Werke zur Gesellschaft und zum Patriotismus.

Siesicka, Krystyna for: Works dealing with children and their problems in the contemporary family structure; Werke, die sich durch Darstellung des Kindes und seiner Probleme in der zeitgenössischen Familie auszeichnen.

Szklarski, Alfred for: Collected works; Gesamtwerk.

Świrczyńska, Anna for: Collected works; Gesamtwerk.

1974 Bahdaj, Adam for: Collected works; Gesamtwerk.

Broszkiewicz, Jerzy for: Collected works; Gesamtwerk.

Fiedler, Arkady for: Collected works; Gesamtwerk.

Jaworczakowa, Mira for: Collected works; Gesamtwerk.

1975 Bechlerowa, Helena for: Works for small children; Werke für die Kleinsten.

Domagalik, Janusz for: Works dealing with youth problems; Werke, die der Jugend nahestehende Probleme behandeln.

Goździkiewicz, Teodor for: Works dealing with the love and protection of nature; Bücher, die die Liebe zur Natur fördern.

Paukszta, Eugeniuszs for: Works concerning problems of the Baltic und Oder regions; Werke, die die Problematik der Gebiete an Oder und Ostsee behandeln.

Anderska, Halina for: Radio plays; Hörspiele.

1976 Chotomska, Wanda for: Collected works, especially works for radio and television; Gesamtwerk mit besonderer Berücksichtigung der Werke für Rundfunk und Fernsehen.

Kern, Ludwik Jerzy for: Collected works; Gesamtwerk.

Kownacka, Maria for: Collected works; Gesamtwerk.

Kuliczkowska, Krystyna for: Collected works and the indroduction of Polish children's and youth literature in foreign countries; Gesamtwerk und Verbreitung polnischer Kinder- und Jugendliteratur im Ausland.

Sikirychi, Igor for: Collected works; Gesamtwerk.

Szczygieł, Jerzy for: Collected works; Gesamtwerk.

Nagroda Prezesa Rady Ministrów za twórczość dla dzieci i młodzieży w dziale plastyki

Since 1951 the Polish government has offered a prize for outstanding achievement in the field of illustration for children's books. The prize is awarded for the collected works of an illustrator.

Für herausragende Leistungen auf dem Gebiet der Kinder- und Jugendbuchillustration wird in der polnischen Volksrepublik seit 1951 das grafische Gesamtwerk eines Kinderbuchillustrators ausgezeichnet.

1951 Siemaszko, Olga for: Collected illustrations/Gesamtschaffen als Kinderbuchillustratorin.

1952 Szancer, Jan Marcin for: Collected illustrations/Gesamtschaffen als Kinderbuchillustrator.

1953 Marczyński, Adam for: Collected illustrations/Gesamtschaffen als Kinderbuchillustrator.

1954 Fijałkowska, Zofia for: Collected illustrations/Gesamtschaffen als Kinderbuchillustratorin.

Rychlicki, Zbigniew for: Collected illustrations/Gesamtschaffen als Kinderbuchillustrator.

1955 Czerwiński, Józef for: Collected illustrations/Gesamtschaffen als Kinderbuchillustrator.

Piotrowski, Mieczysław for: Collected illustrations/ Gesamtschaffen als Kinderbuchillustrator.

1956 Janecka, Leonia for: Collected illustrations/Gesamtschaffen als Kinderbuchillustratorin.

1957 Bylina, Michał for: Collected illustrations/Gesamtschaffen als Kinderbuchillustrator.

1958 Grabiański, Janusz for: Collected illustrations/Gesamtschaffen als Kinderbuchillustrator.

1959 Rożanska, Eugenia for: Collected illustrations/Gesamtschaffen als Kinderbuchillustratorin.

1960 Uniechowski, Antoni for: Collected illustrations/Gesamtschaffen als Kinderbuchillustrator

1961 Zieleniec, Bogdan for: Collected illustrations/Gesamtschaffen als Kinderbuchillustrator.

1962 The prize was not given; Der Preis wurde nicht vergeben.

1973 Rychlicki, Zbigniew for: Collected illustrations/Gesamtschaffen als Kinderbuchillustrator.

Kilian, Adam for: Collected illustrations/Gesamtschaffen als Kinderbuchillustrator.

1974 Butenko, Bogdan for: Collected word in the area of book graphic art and posters/Gesamtschaffen auf dem Gebiet der Buchgrafik und Plakate.

Stanny, Janusz for: Collected illustrations/Gesamtschaffen als Kinderbuchillustrator.

Wilkoń, Józef for: Collected illustrations/Gesamtschaffen als Kinderbuchillustrator.

1975 Truchanowska-Majchrzakowa, Bożena for: Collected illustrations/Gesamtschaffen als Kinderbuchillustrator.

Majchrzak, Wiesław for: Collected illustrations/Gesamtschaffen als Kinderbuchillustrator.

1976 Boratyński, Antoni for: Collected illustrations/Gesamtschaffen als Kinderbuchillustrator.

Nagroda literacka miasta Warszawy za twórczość dla dzieci i młodzieży

The city of Warsaw offers a prize for the collected works of a children's or youth book author.

Die Stadt Warschau vergibt einen Preis für das beste Gesamtwerk eines Kinder- oder Jugendbuchautors.

1948 Szelburg-Zarembina, Ewa for: Collected works/Gesamtwerk.

1949 The prize was not given; Der Preis wurde nicht vergeben.

1950 Krzemieniecka, Lucyna for: Collected works/Gesamtwerk.

1951 Kownacka, Maria for: Collected works/Gesamtwerk.

1952 The prize was not given; Der Preis wurde nicht vergeben.

1953 The prize was not given; Der Preis wurde nicht vergeben.

1954 The prize was not given; Der Preis wurde nicht vergeben.

1955 Brzechwa, Jan for: Collected works/Gesamtwerk.

1956 Januszewska, Hanna for: Collected works/Gesamtwerk.

1957 Porazińska, Janina for: Collected works/Gesamtwerk.

1958 Janczarski, Czesław for: Collected works/Gesamtwerk.

1959 Jurgielewicz, Irena for: Collected works/Gesamtwerk.

1960 Żabiński, Jan for: Collected works/Gesamtwerk.

1961/1964 The prize was not given; Der Preis wurde nicht vergeben.

1965 Przyrowski, Zbigniew for: Collected works/Gesamtwerk.

1966 The prize was not given; Der Preis wurde nicht vergeben.

1967 Żółkiewska, Wanda for: Collected works/Gesamtwerk.

1968/1970 The prize was not given; Der Preis wurde nicht vergeben.

1971 Auderska, Halina for: Collected works/Gesamtwerk.

1972/1975 The prize was not given; Der Preis wurde nicht vergeben.

1976 Żubrowski, Wojciech for: Collected works/Gesamtwerk.

Nagrody i wyróżnienia Polskiego Towarzystwa Wydawców Książek w konkursie "Najlepsze Książki Roku" przyznane "Naszej Księgarni"

The Polish Association of Publishers offers these prizes and honor awards for the best book of the year to Nasza Księgarnia Publishing House, Warsaw.

Preise und Anerkennungen des polnischen Verlegerverbandes, die innerhalb des Wettbewerbes – "Das schönste Buch des Jahres" – dem Verlag "Nasza Księgarnia" zuerkannt wurden.

1971 *Honourable mention/Anerkennung*
Perrault, Charles: **Bajki.** (Fairy tales; Märchen; Fr.orig.title: Histoires ou Contes du temps passé avec des moralitez.) Adapt.: Hanna Januszewska. Ill.: Janusz Grabiański.
Warszawa: Nasza Księgarnia 1971.

1972 *Honourable mention/Anerkennung*
Jarzyna, Zdzisław: **Wśród drzew.** (In the midst of trees; Inmitten von Bäumen.) Ill.: Józef Wilkoń.
Warszawa: Nasza Księgarnia 1972.

Kern, Ludwig Jerzy: **Mądra poduszka. Wiersze dla dzieci.** (The wise pillow. Verse for children; Das kluge Kopfkissen. Verse für Kinder.) Ill.: Zbigniew Rychlicki.
Warszawa: Nasza Księgarnia 1972.

Papuzińska, Joanna: **A gdzie ja się biedniuteńki podzieję?** (And where shall a poor boy like me find shelter? Und wo soll ich armer Kleiner hin?) Ill.: Teresa Wilbik.
Warszawa: Nasza Księgarnia 1972.

1973 *1st prize/1. Preis*
Baum, Lyman Frank: **W krainie czarnoksiężnika Oza.** (Amer. orig.title: The marvellous land of *Oz;* Das wunderbare Land von *Oz.*) Ill.
Warszawa: Nasza Księgarnia 1972.

Honourable mention/Anerkennung
Kubiak, Tadeusz: **List do Warsawy.** (A letter to Warsaw; Ein Brief nach Warschau.) Ill.: Józef Wilkoń.
Warszawa: Nasza Księgarnia 1973.

Topelius, Zakarias: **Perła Adalminy.** (*Adalmina's* pearl; *Adalminas* Perle.) Ill.: Olga Siemaszko.
Warszawa: Nasza Księgarnia 1973.

1974 *Honourable mention/Anerkennung*
Szafer, Tadeusz: **Odkrycie Afryki.** (The discovery of Africa; Die Entdeckung Afrikas.) Ill.
Warszawa: Nasza Księgarnia 1974.

1975 *Honourable mention/Anerkennung*
Badalska, Wiera: **Ballady.** (Ballads; Balladen.) Ill.: Krystyna Michałowska.
Warszawa: Nasza Księgarnia 1975.

Duché, Jean: **Całe życie Marianny czyli historia Francji.** (The life of *Marianna* or, the history of France; Das ganze Leben *Mariannes,* oder die Geschichte Frankreichs; Orig.Fr.title: L'histoire de France racontée a *Françis* et Caroline.) Ill.: Bohdan Butenko.
Warszawa: Nasza Księgarnia 1975.

Nagrody i wyróżnienia Polskiego Towarzystwa Wydawców Ksiezek w konkursie "Najpiekniejsze Książki Roku" przyznana Krajowej Agencji Wydawniczej

The Polish Association of Publishers awards this prize and honour awards for the best book of the year published by Krajowa Agencja Wydawnicza publishing house (formerly, Ruch).

Preise und Auszeichnungen des polnischen Verlegerverbandes, die innerhalb des Wettbewerbs — "Das schönste Buch des Jahres" — dem Verlag Krajowa Agencja Wydawnicza (früher "Ruch") zuerkannt wurden.

1964 *Honourable mention/Anerkennung*
Gałczyńska, Natalia: **Iv i Finetta.** (*Iv* and *Finetta.*) Ill.: Józef Wilkoń.
Warszawa: Krajowa Agencja Wydawnicza 1962.

1965/1966 The prize was not given; Der Preis wurde nicht vergeben.

1967 *Honourable mention/Anerkennung*
Iłłakowiczówna, Kazimiera: **Wierszyki nałęczowskie.** (Children's poems from *Naleczów;* Kindergedichte aus *Naleczów.*) Ill.: Janusz Stanny.
Warszawa: Krajowa Agencja Wydawnicza 1967.

1968 *Honourable mention/Anerkennung*
Hlebowicz, Bohdan: **O jarząbku i jarzębinie.** (About the hazel-hen and mountain-ash berry; Vom Haselhuhn und der Vogelbeere.) Ill.: Bożena Truchanowska.
Warszawa: Krajowa Agencja Wydawnicza 1967.

Górski, Ludwik: **Krople na start.** (Drops for the start; Tropfen für den Start.) Ill.: Bohdan Butenko.
Warszawa: Krajowa Agencja Wydawnicza 1967.

Janczarski, Cresław: **Strzelba zajączka.** (The rabbit's rifle; Die Flinte des Hasen.) Ill.: Janusz Stanny.
Warszawa: Krajowa Agencja Wydawnicza 1967.

Stanny, Janusz: **Koń i kot.** (Horse and cat; Pferd und Katze.) Ill.: Janusz Stanny.
Warszawa: Krajowa Agencja Wydawnicza 1967.

1969 *1st prize/1. Preis*
Ficowski, Jerzy: **Maciupinka.** (The tiny little one; Die winzig Kleine.) Ill.: Józef Wilkoń.
Warszawa: Krajowa Agencja Wydawnicza 1968.

Honourable mention/Anerkennung
Buczkówna, Mieczysława: **Mój słoń.** (My elephant; Mein Elefant.) Ill.: Mieczysław Piotrowski.
Warszawa: Krajowa Agencja Wydawnicza 1968.

Kamieńska, Anna: **Dębowa kołyska.** (The oaken cradle; Die eichene Wiege.) Ill.: Adam Kilian.
Warszawa: Krajowa Agencja Wydawnicza 1967.

Terlikowska, Maria: **Malowana awantura.** (The painted adventure; Das gemalte Abenteuer.) Ill.: Bohdan Wróblewski.
Warszawa: Krajowa Agencja Wydawnicza 1968.

Illustration prize/Illustrationspreis
Stanny, Janusz in:
Witkowski, Jan: **Awantura w kopcie.** (Adventure in the earth hill; Abenteuer im Erdhügel.)
Warszawa: Krajowa Agencja Wydawnicza 1968.

1970 *1st prize/1. Preis*
Woroszylski, Wiktor: **Czterdzieści szczygłów.** (Forty goldfinches; Vierzig Stieglitze.) Ill.: Bohdan Butenko.
Warszawa: Krajowa Agencja Wydawnicza 1968.

Honourable mention/Anerkennung
Bielicki, Marian: **Chłopiec z glinianą Tabliczką.** (The boy with the clay tablet; Der Junge mit der Tontafel.) Ill.: Antoni Boratyński.
Warszawa: Krajowa Agencja Wydawnicza 1969.

1971 *1st prize/1. Preis*
Januszewska, Hanna: **Grajmy.** (Let's play; Laß' uns spielen.) Ill.: Józef Wilkoń.
Warszawa: Krajowa Agencja Wydawnicza 1970.

Honourable mention/Anerkennung
Kulmowa, Joanna: **Wiersze dla Kaji.** (Poems for *Kaja*; Gedichte für *Kaja*.) Ill.: Janusz Grabiański.
Warszawa: Krajowa Agencja Wydawnicza 1970.

1972 *1st prize/1. Preis*
Kulmowa, Joanna: **Deszczowa muzyka.** (Rain music; Die Regenmusik.) Ill.: Janusz Stanny.
Warszawa: Krajowa Agencja Wydawnicza 1971.

Honourable mention/Anerkennung
Stanny, Janusz: **Baśń o królu Dardanelu.** (The fable about King *Dardanell;* Die Fabel vom König *Dardanell.*) Ill.: Janusz Stanny.
Warszawa: Krajowa Agencja Wydawnicza 1971.

Leja, Magda: **Kot pięciokrotny.** (The quintuple cat; Die fünffache Katze.) Ill.: Mieczysław Piotrowski.
Warszawa: Krajowa Agencja Wydawnicza 1971.

Chotomska, Wanda: **Koziołki pana zegarmistrza.** (The little goats of Mr. *Watchmaker;* Die Zicklein des Herrn *Uhrmacher.*) Ill.: Jerzy Srokowksi.
Warszawa: Krajowa Agencja Wydawnicza 1971.

1973 *Honourable mention/Anerkennung*
Pollakówna, Joanna: **Kólko graniaste.** (The edged circle; Der eckige Kreis.) Ill.: Jerzy Jaworowski.
Warszawa: Krajowa Agencja Wydawnicza 1972.

1974 *Honourable mention/Anerkennung*
Woroszylski, Wiktor: **Żółw, żaba, żbik.** (Turtle, frog, wild cat; Schildkröte, Frosch, Wildkatze.) Ill.: Danuta Żukowska.
Warszawa: Krajowa Agencja Wydawnicza 1973.

Zonn, Włodzimierz/Milewska, Elwira: **Niebo i kalendarz.** (The sky and the calendar; Der Himmel und der Kalender.) Ill.: Bohdan Butenko.
Warszawa: Krajowa Agencja Wydawnicza 1973.

1975 *1st prize/1. Preis*
Kierst, Jerzy: **Od gór do morza.** (From the mountains to the sea; Von den Bergen bis zum Meer.) Ill.: Józef Wilkoń.
Warszawa: Krajowa Agencja Wydawnicza 1974.

Honourable mention/Anerkennung
Januszewska, Hanna: **Lwy.** (The lions; Die Löwen.) Ill.: Janusz Stanny.
Warszawa: Krajowa Agencja Wydawnicza 1974.

Kamieńska, Anna: **Złote litery.** (Golden letters; Goldene Buchstaben.) Ill.: Janusz Stanny.
Warszawa: Krajowa Agencja Wydawnicza 1974.

1976 *1st prize/1. Preis*
Michalowska, Mira: **Ania i Ewa i Marian io Rusak i inni . . .** (*Anya* and *Eva* and *Marian* and *Rusak* and others; *Anja* und *Eva* und *Marian* und *Rusak* und andere . . .) Ill.: Janusz Stanny.
Warszawa: Krajowa Agencja Wydawnicza 1975.

Honourable mention/Anerkennung
Butenko, Bohdan: **Pierwszy, drugi, trzeci.** (First, second, third; Erster, zweiter, dritter.) Ill.: Bohdan Butenko.
Warszawa: Krajowa Agencja Wydawnicza 1975.

Lewandowska, Barbara: **Trzy po trzy z minusem.** (Three times three minus; Drei mal drei minus.) Ill.: Jan Bokiewicz.
Warszawa: Krajowa Agencja Wydawnicza 1975.

Portugal

Prémio "O Ambiente na Literatura Infantil"

This prize was established by the Comissão Nacional do Ambiente (National Environmental Commission) in 1976 to promote the writing of books for children and young people dealing with environmental problems and the protection of nature. The award is in the form of a cash-prize (20,000 escudos) and is given annually. Competition for the prize is open to all authors, native-born and foreign, who write in the Portuguese language. The award presentation takes place at a public ceremony on April 2nd each year.

Dieser Preis wurde 1976 von der Comissao Nacional do Ambiente (Nationalen Umwelt-Kommission) gestiftet, um Bücher für Kinder und Jugendliche, die Umwelt- und Umweltschutzprobleme behandeln, zu fördern. Der Preis ist mit einer Geldsumme (20.000 escudos) verbunden und wird jährlich verliehen. Er kann an jeden Autor gegeben werden, der in portugiesischer Sprache schreibt. Die Preis-Verleihung findet jedes Jahr am 2. April statt.

1976 Muralha, Sidónio: **Valéria e a vida.** (*Valeria* and life; *Valeria* und das Leben.) Ill.: Soares Rocha.
Lisboa: Livros Horizonte 1976.

1977 Baptista, Eurico: **O julgamento do cuco.** (The judgement of the cuckoo; Das Urteil des Kuckucks.) Ill.: José de Moura, Zé Manuel Mendes.
Lisboa: Scrire 1977.

Montarroyos, Silvia: **Histórias do bichinho qualquer.** (Stories about insects; Insektengeschichten.) Ill.: Gonçalo Cabral.
Porto: Afrontamento 1977.

1978 The prize was not given; Der Preis wurde nicht vergeben.

Prémio Maria Amàlia Vaz de Carvalho

This award was presented by the National Secretariat for Information of Portugal up until 1961. The prize which consisted of a cash-award, has since been discontinued. It was named after the Portuguese writer, Maria Amàlia Vaz de Carvalho, whose books were held in high esteem around the turn of the century. Some of Mrs. Carvalho's books dealt with questions concerning the education of the young. Together with her husband, the writer Gonçalves Crespo, she also translated Grimm and Andersen. She was a member of the Portuguese Academy of Science.

Das Informationssekretariat Portugals, eine staatliche Organisation, vergab den Maria-Amàlia-Vaz-de-Carvalho Preis in Form einer Geldprämie. Seit

1961 wird der Preis nicht mehr ausgeschrieben. Er war nach der um die Jahrhundertwende sehr geschätzten Schriftstellerin benannt, die sich unter anderem auch mit Fragen der Jugenderziehung beschäftigte. Zusammen mit ihrem Mann, dem Schriftsteller Gonçalves Crespo, übersetzte sie Grimm und Andersen; sie war Mitglied der Akademie der Wissenschaften.

Ill. 32 Gonçalo Cabral in S. Montarroyos: Historias do bichinho qualquer

1937 Müller, Adolfo Simões: **Caixinha de brinquedos.** (The little toy box; Die kleine Spielzeugkiste.) Ill.: Rudy (i.e. Manuel Joaquim Baptista).
Lisboa: Ed. Império 1937.

1938 Archer, Maria: **Viagem à roda de Africa.** Romance de aventuras infantis. (Travels in Africa. Adventure stories for children; Reisen in Afrika. Abenteuergeschichten für Kinder.)
Lisboa: Ed. O. Século 1938.

1939 Leal, Olavo d'Eça: **História extraordinária de Iratan e Iracema, os meninos mais malcriados do mundo.** (The extraordinary story of *Iratan* and *Iracema*, the naughtiest children in the world; Die außergewöhnliche Geschichte von *Iratan* und *Iracema*, den ungezogensten Kindern der Welt.) Ill.: Paulo (i.e. Paulo Guilherma d'Eça Leal.)
Lisboa: O Jornal do Comércio e das Colónias 1939.

1940 The prize was not given; Der Preis wurde nicht vergeben.

1941 The prize was not given; Der Preis wurde nicht vergeben.

1942 Müller, Adolfo Simões: **O feiticeiro da cabana azul.** (The sorcerer from the blue house; Der Zauberer vom blauen Haus.) Ill.: Manuel Lapa.
Lisboa: Agência Geral das Colónias 1942.

1943 Leal, Olavo d'Eça: **História de Portugal para meninos preguiçosos.** (The story of Portugal for lazy children; Die Geschichte Portugals für faule Kinder.) Ill.: Manuel Lapa.
Porto: Tavares Martins 1943.

1944 Lemos, José Neves de: **O sábio que sabia tudo e outras histórias.** (The man who knew everything and other stories; Der weise Mann, der alles wußte und andere Geschichten.) Ill.: José Neves de Lemos.
Lisboa: Ed. Gama 1944.

1945 Almeida, Salomé de: **Falam os animais.** (The animals speak; Die Tiere sprechen.) Ill.: Alfredo de Morais.
Lisboa: Empresa Literária Universal 1945.

1946 Santos, Isaura Correia: **O senhor sabe tudo, conta . . .** (The man who knows everything, tells . . .; Der Mann der alles weiß, erzählt . . .)
Porto: Figueirinhas 1946.

1947 Lemos, José Neves de: **Histórias e bonecos.** (Stories and dolls; Geschichten und Puppen.) Ill.: José Neves de Lemos.
Lisboa: Ed. Atica 1947.

1948 Constança, Aurora: **Aventuras do coelho Káluzu.** (The adventures of *Kaluzu* the rabbit; Die Abenteuer des Kaninchen, *Kaluzu.*) Ill.: Fernando Bento.
Lisboa: Published by the author; Selbstverlag 1948.

1949 The prize was not given; Der Preis wurde nicht vergeben.

1950 The prize was not given; Der Preis wurde nicht vergeben.

1951 The prize was not given; Der Preis wurde nicht vergeben.

1952 Constança, Aurora: **Estrelinhas de oiro, grinaldas de prata.** (Golden stars and a silver garland; Goldene Sterne und eine Girlande aus Silber.) Ill.: Fernando Bento.
Lisboa: Published by the author; Selbstverlag 1952.

1953 Correia, Maria Cecilia: **Histórias da minha rua.** (Stories of my state; Geschichten aus meinem Land.) Ill.: Maria Keil do Amaral.
Lisboa: Portugalia Ed. 1953.

1954 Oliveira, Maria Elisa Nery de: **A quinta das amendoeiras.** (The almond farmer; Der Mandelbauer.) Ill.: E. Loureiro.
Lisboa: Bertrad 1954.

1955 The prize was not given; Der Preis wurde nicht vergeben.

1956 The prize was not given; Der Preis wurde nicht vergeben.

1957 Queiroz, Mauricio de: **A história linda de Portugal.** (A beautiful story about Portugal; Eine schöne Geschichte über Portugal.) Ill.: Carlos Carneiro.
Porto: Figueirinhas 1957.

1958 The prize was not given; Der Preis wurde nicht vergeben.

1959 Alberty, Ricardo: **A galinha verde.** (The green hen; Die grüne Henne.) Ill.: Júlio Gil.
Lisboa: Atica 1959.

1960 The prize was not given; Der Preis wurde nicht vergeben.

1961 Bió (i.e. Isabel Maria Vaz Raposo): **O menino gordo.** (The fat boy; Der fette Junge.) Ill.: Bió.
Lisboa: Ed. Verbo 1961.

Bió (i.e. Isabel Maria Vaz Raposo): **A formiga.** (The ant; Die Ameise.) Ill.: Bió.
Lisboa: Ed. Verbo 1961.

Bió (i.e. Isabel Maria Vaz Raposo): **O sábio e a borboleta.** (The wise man and the butterfly; Der weise Mann und der Schmetterling.) Ill.: Bió.
Lisboa: Ed. Verbo 1961.

Rumania/Rumänien

Premiul Asociaţiei Scriitorilor

The Writer's Association of Bucharest, since 1972, has awarded an annual prize for children's and youth literature. The Writer's Association applies the same criteria in making its selection of the prize-winning titles as does the Writer's Union. The jury is elected through balloting by the members of the Association. The various literary forms eligible for the competition are prose, poetry, drama or literary essay, suitable for children and young people up to the age of 15 years. The prize consists of a diploma and cash-award of 10.000 Lei. The award presentation takes place before an audience which includes members of the press media.

Ill. 33 György Mihail in M. Cozmin: Croitorul de poveşti

Seit 1972, werden neben den Preisen des Schriftstellerverbandes der Sozialistischen Republik Rumänien, jährlich eine Reihe von Preisen der Schriftstellervereine der Hauptstadt oder der bedeutendsten Städte des Landes verliehen. Allerdings ist im Rahmen der Schriftstellervereine der von Bukarest der einzige, der einen oder höchstens zwei Preise für die besten Werke der Kinder- und Jugendliteratur verleiht. Der Preis für die Kinder- und Jugendliteratur wird aufgrund derselben Kriterien bestimmt wie jener des Schriftstellerverbandes. Die Kommission, die die Preisverleihung vornimmt, wird von den Mitgliedern des Schriftstellervereins aus Bukarest in geheimer Abstimmung gewählt. Eine Arbeit in Versform, Prosa, Bühnenstück oder literarischer Essay, für Kinder oder Jugendliche bis zu 15 Jahren wird mit einem Diplom und mit einem Geldbetrag in Höhe von 10.000 Lei prämiert. Die Preisverleihung veranstaltet man in einem festlichen Rahmen, in Gegenwart der Presse.

1972 Ion, Dumitru M.: **Povestea minunatelor călătorii.** (The story of wonderful journeys; Die Erzählung wunderbarer Reisen.)
București: Editura Ion Creangă 1972.

1973 Zotta, Ovidiu: **O şansă pentru fiecare.** (A chance for all; Eine Gruppe für jedermann.)
Bucureşti: Editura Ion Creangă 1973.

Sintimbreanu, Mircea: **Recreaţia mare.** (The long pause; Die große Pause.) Ill.: Iurie Darie.
Bucureşti: Editura Ion Creangă 1973.

1974 Tulbure, Victor: **Basme pentru toată săptămîna.** (Fairy tales for the whole week; Märchen für die ganze Woche.) Ill.: Nicu Russu.
Bucureşti: Editura Ion Creangă 1974.

1975 Ioachim, Alexandra: **O idee isteaţă nu se vinde la piaţă.** (A clever idea is not sold in the marketplace; Eine kluge Idee verkauft man nicht auf dem Markt.)
Bucureşti: Editura Ion Creangă 1975.

1976 Băran, Vasile: **Ambarcaţiunea eroică.** (The heroic boat trip; Heldenhafte Bootsfahrt.)
Bucureşti: Editura Ion Creangă 1976.

Anton, Costache: **Dimineţile lungi.** (The long mornings; Die langen Morgen.)
Bucureşti: Editura Cartea Romanească 1976.

1977 The prize was not given; Der Preis wurde nicht vergeben.

1978 Iuteş, Gică: **Mar roşu ca focul.** (The apple as red as fire; Der Apfel ist so rot wie Feuer.)
Bucureşti: Editura Ion Creangă 1978.

Bulyčev, Kirill: **Fetiţa de pe Terra.** (The girl from planet earth; Das Mädchen vom Planeten Erde; Russ.orig.title: Devočka s zemli.)
Bucureşti: Editura Ion Creangă 1978.

1979 Neagu, Nicolae: **Ninsoarea care ne trebuie.** (The snowfall we need; Der Schneefall den wir brauchen.) Ill.: György Mihail.
Bucureşti: Editura Ion Creangă 1979.

Sălăjan, Doina: **Samlţuri.** (Glazes; Glasuren.)
Bucureşti: Editura Ion Creangă 1979.

Nicutá, Tanase: **Telfonul e la ora 19.** (The telephone call at 9 o'clock. Der Anruf um 19 Uhr.)
Bucureşti: Editura Ion Creangă 1979.

1980 Crohmălniceanu, Ovid S.: **Istorii insolite.** (Unusual history; Ungewöhnliche Geschichte.)
Bucureşti: Ed. Cartea Românească 1980.

Gruia, Călin: **Moara lui Elisei.** (*Elisei's* mill; *Eliseis* Mühle.)
Iaşi: Ed. Junimea 1979.

Stefănescu, Alexandru Ion: **Aventură la Braşov.** (Adventures in *Braşov*; Abenteuer in *Braşov.*)
Bucureşti: Ed. Albatros 1980.

Premiul Uniunii Scriitorilor

Since 1958, the Writer's Union of the Socialist Republic of Rumania has awarded annually a series of prizes to authors of literary works of high quality. The prizes honour the best works of poetry, prose, drama, translation, literary criticism and history. One or two works, at most, are awarded the prize for children's and youth literature. These books must appeal to children and young people up to the age of fifteen years of age. The prize-winning titles are selected by a board of specialists (elected by ballot vote) on the suggestions made by the Council of the Writer's Union. The prize consists of a certificate and a cash-award of 10.000 Lei. The award-winning books are given wide publicity in the press.

Seit 1958 verleiht der Schriftstellerverband der Sozialistischen Republik Rumänien, für eine literarische Schöpfung des vergangenen Jahres eine Reihe von Preisen. Die Preise honorieren die besten Werke in Versform, Prosa, Dramaturgie, Übersetzungen, Kritik und Literaturgeschichte.
Ein oder zwei Werke der Kinder- und Jugendliteratur werden mit dem Preis des Schriftstellerverbandes ausgezeichnet. Die Auslese der Werke nimmt eine aus Spezialisten bestehende Kommission vor, die aufgrund der Vorschläge des Konsiliums des Schriftstellerverbandes, von der Vollversammlung in geheimer Wahl bestimmt wird. Die Bücher wenden sich an Kinder und Jugendliche bis

zu 15 Jahren. Der Preis besteht aus einem Diplom und einem Geldbetrag in Höhe von 10.000 Lei. Die preisgekrönten Bücher werden von der Presse vorgestellt.

1963 Iuteş, Gică: **Faima detaşamentului.** (The good name of the group; Der gute Ruf der Gruppe.) Ill.: Tia Peltz.
Bucureşti: Editura tineretului 1963.

1964 Naum, Gellu: **A doua carte cu Apolodor.** (The second book of *Apolodor;* Das zweite Buch von *Apolodor.*) Ill.: Gellu Naum.
Bucureşti: Editura tineretului 1964.

Popescu, Dumitru Radu: **Vara oltenilor.** (The *Oltenian* summer; Der Sommer der *Oltenier.*)
Bucureşti: Editura tineretului 1964.

1965 Alexandru, Ion: **Viaţa deocamdata.** (Life for the present; Das heutige Leben.)
Bucureşti: Editura tineretului 1965.

Chiriţă, Constantin: **Cireşarii.** (The people of Cherryham; Die Kirschwinkler.) Ill.: Alexandru Alexe.
Bucureşti: Editura tineretului 1965.

Stoian, Mihai: **Reporter în anchetă.** (A reporter investigates; Ein Reporter forscht.)
Bucureşti: Editura tineretului 1965.

1966 Fodor, Sándor: **Csipike, a gonosz törpe.** (*Csipike,* the bad-tempered dwarf; *Csipike,* der böse Zwerg.) Ill.: Livia Rusz.
Bucureşti: Ifjúsági Könyvkiadó 1966.

Fulga, Laurenţiu: **Alexandra şi infernul.** (*Alexandra* and hell; *Alexandra* und die Hölle.)
Bucureşti: Editura tineretului 1966.

1967 The prize was not given; Der Preis wurde nicht vergeben.

1968 Doinaş, Stefan Augustin: **Ipostaze.** (Hypostases; Hypostasen.)
Bucureşti: Editura tineretului 1968.

Mitru, Alexandru: **Săgeata căpitanului Ion.** (Captain *Ion's* arrow; Der Pfeil des Hauptmanns *Ion.*) Ill.: Ion Deak.
Bucureşti: Editura tineretului 1967.

Pillat, Monica: **Cei 13 şi misterul.** (The 13 and the secret; Die 13 und das Geheimnis.) Ill.: Lena Constante.
Bucureşti: Editura tineretului 1968.

1969 The prize was not given; Der Preis wurde nicht vergeben.

1970 Chimet, Iordan: **Inchide ochií şi vei vedea oraşul.** (Close your eyes and you will see the town; Schließe die Augen und du siehst die Stadt.)
București: Editura Ion Creangă 1970.

Pancu-Iaşi, Octav: **Nu fugi, ziua mea frumoasă!** (Don't run away, beautiful day! Geh nicht weg, schöner Tag!) Ill.: Puiu Manu.
Bucureşti: Editura Ion Creangă 1970.

1971 Porumbacu, Veronica: **Ferestre deschise.** (Open windows; Offene Fenster.) Ill.: Maria Constantin.

1972 Anton, Costache: **Ochii aurii ai Roxanei.** (*Roxana's* golden eyes; *Roxanas* goldene Augen.)
Bucureşti: Editura Albatros 1972.

Buzinschi, Corneliu: **Hotii de vise.** (The dream thieves; Die Traumdiebe.) Ill.: Mihai Sînzianu.
Bucereşti: Editura Ion Creangă 1972.

1973 The prize was not given; Der Preis wurde nicht vergeben.

1974 Balan, Ion Dodu: **Copilăria unui Icar.** (The childhood of an *Icarus*; Kindheit eines *Ikarus*.) Ill.: Damian Petrescu.
Bucureşti: Editura Ion Creangă 1974.

1975 Neamţu, Leonida: **Comoara locotenentului Balica.** (Lieutenant *Balica's* treasure; Der Schatz des Leutnants *Balica*.)
Bucureşti: Editura Ion Creangă 1975.

1976 Larian, Sonia: **Biblioteca fantastică.** (Fantastic library; Phantastische Bibliothek.)
Bucureşti: Editura Cartea Romanească 1976.

1977 Hauser, Hedi: **Eine Tanne ist kein Hornissennest.** (A pine tree is not a hornet's nest.)
Bucureşti: Editura Ion Creangă 1977.

1978 Băran, Vasile: **Diamantul viu.** (The living diamond; Der lebendige Diamant.)
Bucureşti: Editura Cartea Romanească 1978.

Desliu, Dan: **Un haiduc pe bicicletă sau contratimp şi spaţiu cu Marin Niculescu.** (A partisan on bicycle or, counter-time and space for *Marin Niculescu*; Ein Freischärler auf dem Fahrrad oder Unzeit und Raum für *Marin Niculescu*.)
Iaşi: Editura Junimea 1978.

Foartă, Serban: **Simpleroze.** (*Simpleroze.*)
Timişoara: Editura Facla 1978.

1979 Hobana, Ion: **Douăzeci de mii pagini în căutarea lui Jules Verne.** (Twenty thousand pages in search of *Jules Verne*; Zwanzigtausend Seiten auf der Suche nach *Jules Verne*.)
Bucureşti: Editura Univers 1979.

Beniuc, Mihai: **Ajun de răscoală.** (On the eve of insurrection; Am Vorabend des Aufstandes.)
Bucureşti: Editura Albatros 1979.

Zinca, Haralambie: **Eu, H.Z., aventurierul.** (I, H.Z., adventurer; Ich, H.Z., der Abenteurer.)
Bucureşti: Editura Cartea Romanească 1979.

1980 Blandiana, Ana: **Intîmplări din grădina mea.** (Events in my garden; Ereignisse in meinem Garten.) Ill.: Doina Botez.
Bucureşti: Editura Ion Creangă 1980.

Cozmin, Marta: **Croitorul de poveşti.** (The fairy tale tailor; Der Märchenschneider.) Ill.: György Mihail.
Bucureşti: Ed. Ion Creangă 1980.

Sintimbreanu, Mircea: **Mama mamuţilor mahmuri.** (The mother of the bad-tempered mammoths; Die Mutter mißgestimmter Mammute.) Ill.: Gheorghe Marinescu.
Bucureşti: Ed. Ion Creangă 1980.

Republic of South Africa/ Südafrikanische Republik

Tienie Hollowaymedalje

Since 1970, the South African Academy for Science and Art has awarded the Tienie Holloway Medal for books in Afrikaans suitable for children under the age eight years. The prize was named after Tienie Holloway who was noted for her verse for young children in the early part of this century. The medal is not awarded regularly. It is only given when a title or author merits recognition.

Seit 1970 verleiht die Südafrikanische Akademie der Wissenschaften und Künste die Tienie Holloway Medaille für afrikanische Bücher für Kinder unter acht Jahren. Der Preis ist nach Tienie Holloway benannt, die durch Gedichte für Kinder bekannt wurde. Die Medaille wird sporadisch verliehen, nur wenn Titel oder Schriftsteller diese Anerkennung verdient haben.

1970 Mer (i.e. M.E. Rothmann): **Karlien en Kandas.** (*Karlien* and *Kandas.*) Ill.: Anna Rothmann.
Kaapstad: Tafelberg 1969.

1971 Grobbelaar, Pieter Willem: **Complete works;** Gesamtschaffen.

1973 Linde, Freda: **Jos en die bok.** (*Jos* and the goat; *Jos* und die Ziege.) Ill.: Marjorie Wallace.
Kaapstad: Malherbe 1972.

1976 Heese, Hester: **Complete works;** Gesamtschaffen.

1977 The prize was not given; Der Preis wurde nicht vergeben.

1978 The prize was not given; Der Preis wurde nicht vergeben.

1979 Holloway, Tienie: **Complete works;** Gesamtschaffen.

1980 The prize was not given; Der Preis wurde nicht vergeben.

C.P. Hoogenhoutmedalje

To promote the developoment of Afrikaans children's books, the South African Librarians Association founded a prize for the best children's book for readers up to the age of twelve. The book must meet certain literary standards. Author and illustrator of the prize winning work are honoured by a gold medal; the publisher receives a certificate. The first presentation took place in 1960. The prize is named after the first author of a children's book in Afrikaans, C.P. Hoogenhout. Hoogenhout was a Dutch teacher who published his book, "De geschiedenis von Josef voor Kinders en huisouwens geschrijve door en vrind", in 1873 under the pseudonym, Klaas

Waarzegger. The Association, in addition to the prize book, publishes an honour list of twelve titles and a list of outstanding translations.

Um die Entwicklung des afrikaansen Kinderbuches voranzutreiben, stiftete der Südafrikanische Bibliotheksverein einen Preis für das beste Kinderbuch, das für Kinder bis zu zwölf Jahren geeignet ist und bestimmte literarische Kriterien

Ill. 34 Marjorie Wallace in F. Linde: Jos en Klos

erfüllt. Der Autor und Illustrator des Preisbuches werden durch eine Goldmedaille geehrt, der Verleger erhält eine Urkunde. 1960 wurde der Preis zum ersten Mal vergeben. Er ist nach dem Mann benannt, der das erste Kinderbuch in Afrikaans schrieb: C.P. Hoogenhout, holländischer Lehrer, veröffentlichte 1873 unter dem Pseudonym Klaas Waarzegger das Buch "De geschiedenis van Josef voor Kinders en huisouwens geschrijve door een vrind". Neben dem Preis stellt der Bibliotheksverein jedes Jahr eine Auswahlliste von höchstens zwölf Titeln auf, sowie eine Liste der besten Übersetzungen.

1960 Kühne, Wilhelm Otto: **Huppel verjaar.** (*Huppel's* birthday; *Huppels* Geburtstag.) Ill.: Dorothy Hill Kühne.
Kaapstad: Tafelberg 1960.

1961 Bouwer, Alba: **Katrientjie van Keerweder.** (*Katrientjie* from Keerweder; *Katrientjie* von Keerweder.) Ill.: Katrine Harries.
Kaapstad: Tafelberg 1961.

1962 The prize was not given; Der Preis wurde nicht vergeben.

1963 Du Plessis, Flooi J.: **Rympieboek vir kinders.** (Rhyme book for children; Reimbuch für Kinder. Ill.: Katrine Harries.
Kaapstad: Tafelberg 1963.

1964 Linde, Freda: **Snoet-Alleen.** (*Snoet* alone; *Snoet* allein.) Ill.: Peter Clarke.
Kaapstad: Malherbe 1964.

1965 The prize was not given; Der Preis wurde nicht vergeben.

1966 Komnick, Günther in: Linde, Freda: **Botter-aas.** (Butter-bait; Butterköder.)
Kaapstad: Malherbe 1966.

1967 Komnick, Günther in: Linde, Freda: **Die stadsmusikante.** (The town muscians; Die Stadtmusikanten.)
Kaapstad: Malherbe 1967.

1968 Grobbelaar, Pieter Willem: **Die mooiste Afrikaanse sprokies.** (The most beautiful Afrikaans folk tales; Die schönsten Afrikanischen Märchen.) Ill.: Katrine Harries.
Kaapstad: Numan & Rousseau 1968.

1969 The prize was not given; Der Preis wurde nicht vergeben.

1970 The prize was not given; Der Preis wurde nicht vergeben.

1971 Bouwer, Alba: **'n Hennetjie met kuikens.** (A little hen with chicks; Eine kleine Henne mit Küken.) Ill.: Katrine Harries.
Kaapstad: Tafelberg 1971.

1972 The prize was not given; Der Preis wurde nicht vergeben.

1973 Linde, Freda: **Jos en Klos.** (*Jos* and *Klos*.) Ill.: Marjorie Wallace. Kaapstad: Malherbe 1973.

1974 Linde, Freda: **By die oog van die fontein; twee-en-sestig spreukryme.** (By the fountain; sixty-two proverb rhymes; An der Quelle; 62 Sprichwörter.) Ill.: Fred Mouton. Kaapstad: Human & Rousseau 1974.

1975 The prize was not given; Der Preis wurde nicht vergeben.

1976 Rupert, Rona: **Wat maak jy, Hektor?** (What are you doing, *Hector?* Was machst du, *Hektor?*) Ill.: Alida von der Merwe. Kaapstad: Tafelberg 1976.

1977 Linde, Freda: **Die kokkewiet en sy vrou.** (The kokkewiet [= a bird] and his wife; Der Kokkewiet [= ein Vogel] und seine Frau.) Ill.: Ann Walton. Kaapstad: Malherbe 1977.

1978 The prize was not given; Der Preis wurde nicht vergeben.

1979 Heese, Hester: **Sera Madera.** (*Sera Madera*.) Ill.: Ann Walton. Kaapstad: Tafelberg 1979.

Soviet Union/Sowjetunion

Vsesojuznyj konkurs

This prize is presented annually during the All-Unions Competition. The prize winning books receive a certificate for first or second prize. The prize is mainly awarded to books with good illustrations or outstanding polygraphic design.

Because we have not been able to obtain information about the early years of the prize presentations, the books have been listed chronologically. From 1966 awards, the year of the prize presentations is given.

Der Preis wird jährlich auf einem Allunionswettbewerb verliehen. Prämierte Bücher bekommen ein Diplom 1. oder 2. Grades. Den Preis bekommen vor allem diejenigen Bücher, die sich durch gute Illustrationen oder gute polygrafische Bearbeitung auszeichnen.

Da für die ersten Auszeichnungen das Jahr der Preisverleihung nicht bekannt ist, sind die Bücher in chronologischer Reihenfolge geordnet. Ab 1966 ist das entsprechende Jahr angegeben.

Ill. 35 Maj Miturič in A. Barto: U nas pod krylom

Ill. 36 Kaljo Põllu in A. Põldmäe: Mitmekesi maateral

1st prize/1. Preis

Končalovskaja, Natal'ja Petrovna: **Naša drevnja ja stolica.** (Our old capitol city; Unsere alte Hauptstadt.) Ill.: Vladimir Andreevic Favorskij.
Moskva: Detgiz 1962.

Puškin, Aleksandr Sergeevič: **Skazka o care Saltane.** (The fairy tale about czar *Saltan*; Das Märchen vom Zaren *Salten*.) Ill.: Tatjana Alekseevna Mavrina (i.e. Tatjana Alekseevna Lebedeva.)
Moskva: Detgiz 1962.

Twain, Mark (i.e. Samuel Langhorne Clemens): **Priljučenija Gekl'berri Finna.** (Amer.orig.title: The adventures of *Huckleberry Finn*; Abenteuer des *Huckleberry Finn*.) Ill.: Vitalij Nikolaevič Gorjaev.
Moskva: Detgiz 1962.

Koroleva-Lebed.: Litovskie narodnye skazki. (Swan queen. Lithuanian folk tales; Schwankönigin. Litauische Volksmärchen.) Ill.: Albina Iono Makunaite.
Vilnius: Valstybine grozines literaturos Leidykla 1963.

Makrusenko, Pavlo (i.e. Pavel Il'ic Makrusenko): **Elka v Gorkach.** (*Elka* in Gorka.) Ill.: Vladimir Aleksandrovic Vasil'ev.
Sverdlovsk: Sverdlovskoe knižnoe izdatal'stvo 1963.

Maršak, Samuil Jakovlerič: **Plyvet, plyvet korablik.** (The little ship floats; Es schwimmt ein Schifflein.) Ill.: Vladimir Michajlovič Konašević.
Moskva: Detskaja literatura 1963.

Puškin, Aleksandr Sergeevič: **Skazka o zolotom petuške.** (The fairy tale about the little golden cock; Das Märchen vom goldenen Hähnchen.) Ill.: Vladimir Michajlovič Konaševič.

Puškin, Aleksandr Sergeevič: **Skazka o mertvoj carevne.** (The fairy tale about the czar's dead daughter; Das Märchen von der toten Zarentochter.) Ill.: Vladimir Michajlovič Konaševič.
Moskva: Detskaja literatura 1963.

Russkie skazki. (Russian fairy tales; Russische Märchen.) Ill.: Tatjana Alekseevna Mavrina (i.e. Tatjana Alekseevna Lebedeva.)
Moskva: Chudožestvennaja literatura 1963.

Shakespeare, William: **Romeo i Džul'etta.** (*Romeo* and *Juliet*.) Ill.: Dementij Alekseevič Smarinov.
Moskva: Detskaja literatura 1963.

Puškin, Aleksandr Sergeevič: **Ruslan i Ljudmila.** (*Rusland* and *Ludmila.*) Ill.: Tatjana Alekseevna Mavrina (i.e. Tatjana Alekseevna Lebedeva).
Moskva: Detskaja literatura 1964.

Sakse, Anna Ottovna: **Kaspar – syn kuzneca.** (*Kaspar,* the smith's son; *Kaspar,* Sohn des Schmiedes.) Ill.: Rozkali.
Riga: Liesma 1964.

Laduški. Russkie narodnye skazki, pesenki, poteski. (*Laduški.* Russian folk tales, songs; *Laduški.* Russische Volksmärchen, Lieder.) Ill.: Jurij Alekseevič Vasnecov.
Moskva: Detskaja literatura 1964.

Puškin, Aleksandr Sergeevič: **Boris Godunov.** (*Boris Godunov.*) Ill.: Boris Aleksandrovič Dechterev.
Moskva: Detskaja literatura 1965.

Puškin, Aleksandr Sergeevič: **Skazki.** (Fairy tales; Märchen.) Ill.: Vladimir Michajlovič Konaševič.
Moskva: Detskaja literatura 1965.

Shaekspeare, William: **Gamlet.** (*Hamlet.*) Ill.: Boris Aleksandrovič Dechterev.
Moskva: Detskaja literatura 1965.

2nd prize/2. Preis

Kubilinskas, Kostas: **Ljaguška-koroleva.** (Frog queen; Froschkönigin.) Ill.: Algirdas Steponavičius.
Vilnius: Valstybine grozines literaturos leidykla 1962.

Afrikanskie skazki. (African fairy tales; Afrikanische Märchen.) Ill.: I. Nekrasov.
Minsk: Belorus' 1963.

Andersen, Hans Christian: **Princessa na gorošine.** (The princess and the pea; Prinzessin auf der Erbse; Dan.orig.title: Prinsessin på aerten.) Ill.: Valerij Sergeevič Alfeevskij.
Moskva: Detskaja literatura 1963.

Baruzdin, Sergej Alekseevič: **Strana, gde my živem.** (The land where we live; Das Land, in dem wir leben.) Ill.: Fedor Viktorovič Lemkul'.
Moskva: Detskaja literatura 1963.

Čarušin, Evgenij Ivanovič: **Tjupy, Tomka i soroka.** (*Tjupy* the cat, *Tomka* the dog and the magpie. Die Katze *Tjupy,* der Hund *Tomka* und die Elster.) Ill.: Evgenij Ivanovič Čarušin.
Moskva: Detskaja literatura 1963.

Čukovskij, Kornej Ivanovič: **Mojdodyr.** (*Mojdodyr.*) Ill.: Adminadav Mojseevič Kanevskij.
Moskva: Detskaja literatura 1963.

Dva žadnych medvežonka. (Two greedy little bears; Zwei gierige Bären.) Ill.: Evgenij Michajlovič Račev.
Moskva: Detskaja literatura 1963.

Fedin, Konstantin Aleksandrovič: **Sazany.** (Carp; Karpfen.) Ill.: Andria Michajlovič Ermolaev.
Moskva: Detskaja literatura 1963.

Gusi-lebedi. (Swan-geese; Gänse-Schwäne.) Ill.: Viktor Michajlovič Vasnecov.
Moskva: Detskaja literatura 1963.

Ljubimov, Lev: **Velikaja živopis' Niderlandov.** (The great art of the Netherlanders; Die große Kunst der Niederländer.) Ill.: Iraida Ivanovna Fomian.
Moskva: Detskaja literatura 1963.

Mar, Evgenij Petrovič (i.e. Evgenij Petrovič Vysockij): **Glina i ruki.** (The clay and the hands; Der Lehm und die Hände.) Ill.: Il'ja Josifović Kabakov.
Moskva: Detskaja literatura 1963.

Oskokin, Vasilij I.: **Rasskazy o russkom pejzaže.** (Stories about Russian landscape painting; Erzählungen vom russischen Landschaftsbild.) Ill.: Iraida Ivanovna Fomina.
Moskva: Detskaja literatura 1963.

Ovsjannikov, J.: **Pero Žar-pticy.** (The feather of the firebird; Die Feder des Feuervogels.) Ill.: Solomon Benediktovič Telingater.
Moskva: Sovetskaja Rossija 1963.

Paustovskij, Konstantin Georgievič: **Stal'noe kolečko.** (A little steel ring; Ein Ringlein aus Stahl.) Ill.: Tatjana Aleseevna Eremina.
Moskva: Detskaja literatura 1963.

Krošečka-Chavrošečka. Russkaja narodnaja skazka. (Tiny little piggy. Russian folk tales; Winzig kleines Schweinchen. Russisches Volksmärchen.)
Ill.: Nadežda Iosifovna Lopuchova.
Kiev: Veselka 1964.

Sutockij, S.: **Bednijaga dvadcat'vos'moj.** (The 28th poor fellow; Der 28. arme Tropf.) Ill.: Vitalij Nikolaevič Gorjaev.
Moskva: Detskaja literatura 1964.

Dva moroza. Belorusskaja narodnaja skazka. (Two frosts. White Russian folk tales; Zwei Fröste. Weißrussisches Volksmärchen.) Ill.: I. Nekrasov.
Minsk: Belorus' 1965.

Kudaševa, Raisa Adamovna: **Petušok.** (The little cockerel; Der kleine Hahn.) Ill.: Maj Petrovič Miturič.
Moskva: Malyš 1965.

Palčinkaite, Violeta: **Gorochovyj stručok.** (The pea shell; Die Erbsenhülse.) Ill.: Sigute Valiuviene.
Vilnius: VAGA 1965.

Sergeev, M. (i.e. Mark Davidovič Gantvarger): **Kapel'ka po kapel'ke.** (Drop by drop; Tröpfchen auf Tröpfchen.) Ill.: V. Losin, Evgenij Grigor'evič Monin and V. Percev.
Moskva: Malyš 1965.

Zlatovlaska. Češskaja narodnaja skazka. (The golden-haired girl. Czech folk tales; Die Goldhaarige. Tschechisches Volksmärchen.) Ill.: Fedor Viktorovič Lemkul'.
Moskva: Detskaja literatura 1965.

1966 Gogol', Nikolaj Vasilevič: **Peterburgskie povesti.** (Petersburg stories; Petersburger Erzählungen.) Ill.: V.N. Vorjaev.
Moskva: Detskaja literatura 1965.

Maršak, Samuil Jakovlevič: **Detjam.** (For children; Für Kinder.) Ill.: Vladimir V. Lebedev.
Moskva: Detskaja literatura 1965.

Maršak, Samuil Jakovlevič: **Stichi dlja detej.** (Poems for children; Gedichte für Kinder.) Ill.: Maj Miturič.
Moskva: Sovetskaja Rossija 1966.

Pryhora, Marija A.: **Kozak Holota.** (*Kozak Holota.*)
Kyiv: Veselka 1966.

1967 **Bolšoj dom čelovečestva.** (The large house of mankind; Das große Haus der Menschheit.) Ill.: B. Kišimov.
Moskva: Detskaja literatura 1966.

Čukovskij, Kornej Ivanovič: **Dže pokoritel' velikanov.** (*Jack*, the giant killer; *Jack*, der Bezwinger der Riesen.) Ill.: Fedor Viktorovič Lemkul'.
Moskva: Detskaja literatura 1966.

Panova, Vera Fedorovna: **Sereža.** (*Sereža.*) Ill.: L. Podljasska.
Leningrad: Detskaja literatura 1966.

1968 Nekrasov, Nikolaj Alekseevič: **Komu na Rusi žit' chorośo.** (Who lives good in Russia; Wer in Russland gut lebt.) Ill.: S. Gerasimov. Moskva: Chudožestvennaja literatura 1968.

Oj konyky syvaši. Ukrains'ki narodni dytjači pisen'ky. (Hey, little grey horses. Ukrainian folk songs for children; Hei, kleine graue Pferde. Ukrainische Kinder-Volkslieder.) Ill.: Marija Prymaćenko. Kyiv: Veselka 1968.

Počemu l'va net na Kavkaze? (Why are there not lions in the Caucasus? Warum gibt es im Kaukasus keinen Löwen?) Ill.
Nalčik: Degestanskoe učebnoe pedagogićeskoe izdatel'stvo 1968.

1969 Andersen, Hans Christian: **Skazki.** (Fairy tales; Märchen; Dan.orig.title: Eventyr og historier.) Ill.: G.A.V. Traugot.
Leningrad: Detskaja literatura 1969.

Cyferov, Gennadij Michailovič: **Skazki.** (Fairy tales; Märchen.) Ill.: V. Cižikov.
Moskva: Detskaja literatura 1969.

Čukovskij, Kornej Ivanovič: **Doktor Ajbolit.** (Dr. *Ajbolit;* Doktor *Ajbolit.*) Ill.: V. Duvidov.
Moskva: Detskaja literatura 1969.

Kogda žili velikany. (As the giant lived; Als die Riesen lebten.) Ill.: Kalinaskas.
Vilnius: VAGA 1969.

Kuročka rjaba. (The little speckled hen; Das scheckige Hühnchen.) Ill.: L. Majorova.
Moskva: Malyš 1969.

Oleša, Jurij Karlovič: **Tri tolstjaka.** (The three fat men; Die drei dicken Männer.) Ill.: Vitalij Nikolaevič Gorjaev.
Moskva: Detskaja literatura 1969.

Raduga-duga. (Rainbow bow; Regenbogen-Bogen.) Ill.: Jurij Alekseevič Vasnecov.
Moskva: Detskaja literatura 1969.

Skazočnaja azbuka. (The fairy tale ABC; Das Märchen-ABC.) Ill.: Tat'jana Alekseevna Mavrina.
Moskva: Gosznak 1969.

Vovčok, Marko: **Vedmid.** (The bear; Der Bär.) Ill.: N. Danylova.
Kyiv: Veselka 1969.

1970/1971 Priležaeva, Marija Pavlovna: **Zizn' Lenina.** (*Lenin's* life; *Lenins* Leben.) Ill.: Orest G. Verejskij.
Moskva: Detskaja literatura 1970.

Raud, Eno: **Ogon' v zatemnennom gorode.** (Fire in a darkened town; Feuer in einer verdunkelten Stadt; Orig.Estn.title: Tuli primendatud linnas.) Ill.
Tallinn: Eesti Raamt 1970.

Vasil'ev, Boris L'vovič: **A zori zdes' tichie . . .** (Here, the dawn is quiet . . .; Das Morgenrot ist hier still . . .) Ill.: P. Pinkisevič.
Moskva: Detskaja literatura 1971.

1971/ Andersen, Hans Christian: **Novoe plat'e korola.** (The emperor's
1972 new clothes; Des Kaisers neue Kleider; Dan.orig.title: Kejserens nye klaeder.) Ill.: G.A.V. Traugot.
Kišineu: Lumina 1971.

Andersen, Hans Christian: **Olej-Lukoje.** (*Ole Lukøje;* Dan.orig.title: Ole-Lukøje.) Ill.: G.A.V. Traugot.
Moskva: Malyś 1971.

Maršak, Samuil Jakovlevič: **Stichi dlja detej.** (Poems for children; Gedichte für Kinder.) Ill.: Maj Miturić.
Moskva: Sovetskaja Rossija 1971.

Neris, Salomeja: **Mama! Kur tu?** (Mama! Where are you? Mutti! Wo bist du?) Ill.: Kystytis Juodikaitis.
Vilnius: Vaga 1971.

Sirotka Elenite i Jonikas barašek. (*Elenite,* the orphan and *Jonikas,* the little lamb. Das Waisenkind *Elenite* und das Lämmchen *Jonikas.*) Ill.: P. Riapšis.
Vilnius: Vaga 1971.

1973/ Alekseev, Michail Nikolaevič: **Miškino detstvo.** (*Miška's* childhood;
1974 *Miškas* Kindheit.) Ill.: G. Pavišin.
Charabovsk: Knižnoe izdatel'stvo 1973.

Alekseev, Michail Nikolaevič: **Miškino detstvo.** (*Miska's* childhood; *Miskas* Kindheit.) Ill.: M. Petrov.
Moskva: Malyš 1973.

Andersen, Hans Christian: **Skazki.** (Fairy tales; Märchen.) Dan.orig.title: Eventyr og historier.) Ill.: A. Kokorin.
Moskva: Malyš 1973.

Blaginina, Elena Aleksandrovna: **Žusravuška.** (*Žuravuška.*) Ill.: Jurij Molokanov.
Moskva: Detskaja literatura 1973.

Čego na svete ne byvaet. Skazki. (Nearly everything in the world is possible. Fairy tales; Was es nicht alles gibt auf der Welt. Märchen.) Ill.: E. Monin.
Moskva: Malyš 1974.

Čerešečka. Russkaja narodnaja skazka. (*Čerešečka.* Russian folk tales; *Čerešečka.* Russisches Volksmärchen.) Ill.: Jurij Kokorin.
Moskva: Detskaja literatura 1973.

Creangă, Ion: **Za čerešnjami.** (Picking cherries; Kirschen holen.) Ill.: E. Cildescu.
Kišineu: Lumina 1973.

Dmitriev, Jurij Dmitrievič: **Čelovek i ževotnye. kn.2.** (Humans and animals. vol 2.; Der Mensch und die Tiere. Bd.2.) Ill.
Moskva: Detskaja literatura 1974.

Pestra planeta. (The coloured planet; Der bunte Planet.)
Charkiv: Prapor 1974.

Prišvin, Michail Michajlovič: **Lisičkin chleb.** (The fox bread; Das Fuchsbrot.) Ill.: N. Ustinov.
Moskva: Detskaja literatura 1973.

Shakespeare, William: **Romeo i Džulietta.** (*Romeo* and *Juliet*; *Romeo* und *Julia.*) Ill.: Dementij Smarinov.
Moskva: Detskaja literatura 1973.

Sisoev, V.: **Udivitel'nye zveri.** (Remarkable animals; Merkwürdige Tiere.) Ill.: G. Pavlišin.
Charabovsk: Knźnoe izdatel'stvo 1974.

Sladkov, Nikolaj Ivanović: **Podvodnaja gazeta.** (Underwater newspaper; Unterwasser-Zeitung.) Ill.: E. Bianki.
Moskva: Detskaja literatura 1973.

Zukova, A.: **V.I. Lenin v risunkach chudoźnika.** (*V.I. Lenin in the drawings of an artist; V.I. Lenin* in den Zeichnungen eines Künstlers.) Ill.: Jurij Kopejko.
Moskva: Malyś 1973

1975 Collodi, Carlo: **Prikljućenija Pinokkio.** (The adventures of *Pinocchio; Pinocchios* Abenteuer; Ital.orig.title: Le avventure di Pinocchio.)
Moskva: Progress 1974.

Dmitriev, Jurij Dmitriević: **Bol'śaja kniga lesa.** (The big book of forests; Das große Buch des Waldes.) Ill.: V. Osver/N. Mićenko.
Moskva: Detskaja literatura 1974.

Kubilinskas, Kostas: **Stovi Pasaku namelis.** (A little fairy tale house; Es steht ein Märchenhäuschen.) Ill.: Virute Zilytė.
Vilnius: Vaga 1974.

Leskov, Nikolaj Semenovič: **Levša.** (Left-hander: Linkshänder.) Ill.: Kukryniksy (i.e. N.V. Kuprijanov/P.N. Krylov/ N.A. Sokolov).
Moskva: Detskaja literatura 1974.

Maršak, Samuil Jakovlevič: **Gde obedal vorobej. Soroka-beloboka.** (Where the sparrow ate lunch. The magpie with white-feathered sides; Wo der Spatz zu Mittag aß. Die Elster mit den weißen Wangen.) Ill.: L. Majorova.
Moskva: Malyš 1974.

Nachodčivyj soldat, Skazka. (The clever soldier. Fairy tale; Der findige Soldat. Märchen.) Ill.: V. Petrov.
Moskva: Malyš 1974.

Ostrovskij, Aleksandr Nikolaevič: **Groza.** (Tempest; Das Gewitter.) Ill.: S. Gerasimov.
Moskva: Detskaja literatura 1974.

Puškin, Aleksandr Sergeevič: **Skazki.** (Fairy tales; Märchen.) Ill.: Tatjana Mavrina.
Moskva: Detskaja literatura 1974.

Puškin, Aleksandr Sergeevič: **Kapitanskaja dočka.** (The captain's daughter; Die Kapitänstochter.) Ill.: A. Itkin.
Moskva: Sovetskaja Rossija 1974.

Russkie skazki. (Russian fairy tales; Russische Märchen.) Ill.: Jurij A. Vasnecov.
Leningrad: Detskaja literatura 1974.

Seton, Ernest Thompson: **Krēg-kutenejskij baran.** (Amer.orig.title: *Krag,* the Kootenay ram; *Krag* der Widder von Kootenay.) Ill.: G. Nikolskij.
Moskva: Malyš 1974.

Voronkova, Ljubov F.: **Solnečnyj denek.** (A sunny day; Ein sonniger Tag.) Ill.: N. Ustinov.
Moskva: Detskaja literatura 1974.

Zolotaja jablonka. Belorusskaja narodnaja skazka. (The golden apple tree. White Russian folk tales; Der goldene Apfelbaum. Weißrussisches Volksmärchen.) Ill.: J. Kastitis.
Vilnius: Vaga 1975.

1976 Andersen, Hans Christian: **Skazki.** (Fairy tales; Märchen; Dan.orig.title: Eventyr og historier.) Ill.: V. Pivovarov.
Moskva: Detskaja literatura 1975.

Anglijskie skazki. (English fairy tales; Englische Märchen.) Ill.: Fedor V. Lemkul'.
Moskva: Progress 1975.

Antonov, Sergej Petrovič: **Alenka.** (*Alenka.*) Ill.: M.Z. Rudakov.
Moskva: Sovetskaja Rossija 1975.

Astaf'ev, Viktor Petrovič: **Pereval.** (Mountain pass; Gebirgspaß.) Ill.: M.Z. Rudakov.
Moskva: Sovetskaja Rossija 1975.

Averbuch, J.: **Upokorennja velykaniv.** (The taming of the giants; Zähmung der Riesen.) Ill.: V. Hončarenko.
Kyiv: Veselka 1975.

Bianki, Vitalij Valentinovič: **Lesnye domiški.** (Forest cottages; Waldhütten.) Ill.: Nikita Čarušin.
Moskva: Detskaja literatura 1975.

Dickens, Charles: **Priključenija Olivera Tvista.** (*Oliver Twist's* adventure; *Oliver Twists* Abenteuer; Eng.orig.title: *Oliver Twist.*) Ill.: A. Konstantinovskij.
Moskva: Detskaja literatura 1975.

Dmitriev, Jurij Dmitrieivič: **Čelovek i životnye. Kniga 2.** (Humans and animals. Book 2.; Der Mensch und die Tiere. Buch 2.) Ill.: Kičinov.
Moskva: Detskaja literatura 1975.

Donelaitis, K.: **My prostye buri.** (We commonplace storm winds; Wir einfachen Sturmwinde.) Ill.: Albina Makūnătė.
Vilnius: Vaga 1975.

Dva pivnyky. Ukrains'ka narodna pisen'ka-kazka. (Two cockerels. Ukrainian folk song; Zwei Hähne. Ukrainisches Volkslied.) Ill.: Valerij Holozubiv.
Kyiv: Veselka 1975.

Emin, G.: **Tanec sasuncev.** (The dance of the *Sasunians*; Der Tanz der *Sasuner.*) Ill.: G. Chandžjan.
Erevan: Ajastan 1975.

Eršov, Petr Pavlovič: **Konek Gorbunok.** (*Gorbunok,* the little horse; Das Pferdchen *Gorbunok.*) Ill. V.A. Milaševskij.
Moskva: Detskaja literatura 1975.

Grimm, Jakob/Grimm, Wilhelm: **Skazki.** (Fairy tales; Märchen; Germ.orig.title: Kinder- und Hausmärchen.) Ill.: N. Cejtlin.
Moskva: Detskaja literatura 1975.

Ključ ščastja. Skazki narodov Sibirii. (The lucky key. Siberian fairy tales; Der Glücksschlüssel. Märchen der Völker Sibiriens.) Ill.: L. Serkov.
Novosibirsk: Zapadno-sibirskoe knižnoe izdatelstvo 1975.

Michalkov, Sergej Vladimirovič: **Basni.** (Fables; Fabeln.) Ill.: Evgenij Račev.
Moskva: Detskaja literatura 1975.

Nagiškin, Dmitrij Dmitrievič: **Amurskie skazki.** (Fairy tales from Amur; Märchen vom Amur.) Ill.: Gennadij Pavlišin.
Charabovsk: Charabovsk'oe knižoe izd. 1975.

Petkavičius, Vytautas: **Aršin syn Verška.** (*Aršin,* son of the summit; *Aršin,* Sohn des Gipfels; Lit.orig.title: Sieksnis, Sprindzio vaikas.) Ill.: J. Kastitis.
Vilnius: Vaga 1975.

Puškin, Aleksandr Sergeevič: **Mednyj vsadnik.** (The bronze rider; Der bronzene Reiter.) Ill.: Fedor Konstantinov.
Moskva: Detskaja literatura 1975.

Sacharnov, Svjatoslav Vladimirovič: **Po morjam vokrug zemli.** (On the oceans around the world; Auf den Meeren um die Welt.)
Ill.: E. Benjaminson/B. Kyštymov.
Moskva: Detskaja literatura 1976.

Šolochov, Michail Aleksandrovič: **Nachalenok.** (The impudent fellow; Der Frechdachs.) Ill.: V. Judin.
Moskva: Malyš 1975.

Šolochov, Michail Aleksandrovič: **Sud'ba čeloveka.** (A human destiny; Ein Menschenschicksal.) Ill.: Orest Verejskij.
Moskva: Detskaja literatura 1975.

Tolstoj, Lev Nikolaevič: **Tri kalača i odna baranka.** (Three round white loaves of bread and a ringshaped roll; Drei runde Weißbrote und ein Kringel.) Ill.: A.F. Pachomov.
Leningrad: Detskaja literatura 1975.

1977 Andersen, Hans Christian: **Skazki.** (Fairy tales; Märchen; Dan.orig.title; Eventyr og historier.) Ill.: A. Kokorin.
Moskva: Moskovskij rabočij 1976.

Avyžius, Jonas: **Soročie chitrosti.** (The cunning magpie; List der Elster; Lit.orig.title: Sarkos grudryba.) Ill.: Bronius Leonabičius.
Vilnius: Vaga 1976.

Barto, Agnija L'vovna: **U nas pod krylom.** (Under our protection; Unter unserem Schutz.) Ill.: Maj Miturič.
Moskva: Sovetskaja Rossija 1976.

Čukovskij, Kornej Ivanovič: **Doktor Ajbolit.** (Dr. *Ajbolit*; Doktor *Ajbolit.*) Ill.: V. Duvidov.
Moskva: Detskaja literatura 1976.

Damian, A.: **Pinja.** (Bread; Brot.) Ill.: I. Kirmu.
Kišineu: Lumina 1976.

Defoe, Daniel: **Robinson Kruso.** (*Robinson Crusoe*; Eng.orig.title: The life and strange surprising adventures of *Robinson Crusoe.*) Ill.: N. Kozlov.
Minsk: Mastackaja literatura 1977.

Franko, Ivan Ja: **Koly šče zviri hovoryly.** (When animals could speak; Als die Tiere sprechen konnten.) Ill.: Artjušenko.
Kyiv: Veselka 1976.

Harris, Joel Chandler: **Skazki deduški Rimusa.** (Uncle *Remus'* fairy tales; Onkel *Remus* Märchen; Amer.orig.title: Uncle *Remus.*) Ill.: G. Kalinovskij.
Moskva: Detskaja literatura 1976.

Kipling, Rudyard: **Maugli.** (*Maugli;* Eng.orig.title: The jungle book.) Ill.: Maj Miturič.
Moskva: Malyš 1976.

Lebedev, Aleksandr Aleksandrovič: **Desjat knižek dlja detej.** (Ten books for children; Zehn Bücher für Kinder.) Ill.
Leningrad: Chudožnik RSFSR 1976.

Mora, Ferenc: **Volšebmaja šubejka.** (The magic jacket; Die Zauberjacke.) Ill.: B. Diodorov.
Moskva: Detskaja literatura 1976.

Perrault, Charles: **Skazki Matuški gusyni.** (*Mother Goose* fairy tales; Märchen des *Mütterchens Gans*; Fr.orig.title: Histoires ou contes du temps passé avec des moralitez.) Ill.: G.A.V. Traugot.
Leningrad: Chudoŭestvennaja literatura 1976.

Prišvin, Michail Michajlovič: **Kladovaja solnca.** (Storeroom of the sun; Vorratskammer der Sonne.) Ill.: I. Bruni.
Moskva: Sovetskaja Rossija 1976.

Puškin, Aleksandr Sergeevič: **Kapitanskaja dočka.** (The captain's daughter; Die Kapitänstochter.) Ill.: V. Smarinov.
Moskva: Detskaja literatura 1976.

Skučaite, R.: **Kolokol'čiki.** (The little bells; Die Glöckchen.) Ill.: A. Skiliutauskaite.
Vilnius: Vaga 1976.

Suslov, Volt Nikolaevič: **Mir, v kotorom ty živeš.** (The world in which you live; Die Welt, in der du lebst.) Ill.: B. Kyštymov.
Moskva: Detskaja literatura 1976.

Tolstoj, Aleksej Nikolaevič: **Zolotoj ključik ili priključenija Buratino.** (The little golden key, or *Buratino's* adventures; Das goldene Schlüsselchen oder *Buratinos* Abenteuer.) Ill.: M. Skobelev.
Moskva: Malyš 1976.

Važdaev, Viktor: **Volšebnye spicy.** (The enchanted needles; Die Zaubernadeln.) Ill.: M. Majofis.
Moskva: Malyš 1976.

Juhan Smuuli nimelised kirjanduslikud aastapreemiad

This prize was established by the Council of Ministers of the Estonian SSR in 1970 at the suggestion of the Writer's Union and the Publishing Committee. It is awarded to authors of outstanding literary works, including children's and juvenile books, critical reviews and translations. It is also awarded to translations published in other republics of the Soviet Union. The prize consists of a certificate, a medal and a cash-award. In 1971 this annual award was named after Juhan Smuul (1922—1971), People's Writer of the Estonian SSR, and for many years chairman of the Writer's Union.

Der Preis wurde 1970 vom Ministerrat der estnischen Volksrepublik auf Vorschlag der Schriftstellergewerkschaft sowie dem Verlegerkomitee der estnischen SSR gegründet. Der Preis wird an Autoren für hervorragende literarische Arbeiten verliehen, einschließlich Kinder- und Jugendbüchern, Kritiken und Übersetzungen. Der Preis kann auch an Übersetzungen vergeben werden die in anderen Sowjetrepubliken erscheinen. Der Preis setzt sich aus einem Diplom, einer Medaille und einer Geldsumme zusammen. Im Jahre 1971 wurde der jährlich verliehene Preis nach Juhan Smuul (1922—1971) benannt, einem estnischen Volksschriftsteller der jahrelang Vorsitzender der Schriftstellergewerkschaft der estnischen SSR war.

1970 Raud, Eno: **Uudishimulik filmkaamera.** (The curious film camera; Die neugierige Filmkamera.)
Tallinn: Eesti Raamat 1969.

Raud, Eno: **Lugu lendavate taldrikutega.** (The story about flying saucers; Die Geschichte von den fliegenden Untertassen.) Ill.: Edgar Valter.
Tallinn: Eesti Raamat 1969.

1971 Niit, Ellen: **Lahtiste uste päev.** (Day of open doors; Tag der offenen Türen.) Ill.: Heldur Laretei.
Tallinn: Eesti Raamat 1970.

1972 Rannap, Jaan: **Jefreitor Jõmm,** (Private *Jomm*; Gefreiter *Jomm.*) Ill.: Edgar Valter.
Tallinn: Eesti Raamat 1971.

1973 Beekman, Vladimir: **Raua-Roobert.** (Iron *Robert*; Der eiserne Robert.) Ill.: Iivi Sampu-Raudsepp.
Tallinn: Eesti Raamat 1972.

1974 Maran, Iko: **Londiste, oige Vant.** (*Londiste,* otherwise called Vant; *Londiste,* oder auch *Vant* genannt.) Ill.: Heldur Laretei.
Tallinn: Eesti Raamat 1972.

1975 Pukk, Holger: **Mida te teate Oskarist?** (What do you know about *Oscar?* Was wissen Sie über *Oskar?*) Ill.: Asta Vender.
Tallinn: Eesti Raamat 1974.

1976 Pervik, Aino: **Kunksmoor ja kapten Trumm.** (*Kunks* the witch and captain *Trumm*; Die Hexe *Kunks* und Kapitän *Trumm.*) Ill.: Edgar Valter.
Tallinn: Eesti Raamat 1975.

1977 Luik, Viivi: **Leopold aitab linnameest.** (*Leopold* helps the citizens; *Leopold* hilft den Einwohnern.) Ill.: Asta Vender.
Tallinn: Eesti Raamat 1977.

1978 Niit, Ellen: **Triinu ja Taavi uued ja vanad lood.** (New and old stories about *Triinu* and *Taavi*; Neue und alte Geschichten über *Triinu* und *Taavi.*)
Tallinn: Eesti Raamat 1977.

1979 Põldmäe, Asta: **Mitmekesi maateral.** (Together on the earth; Zusammen auf der Erde.) Ill.: Kaljo Põllu.
Tallinn: Eesti Raamat 1978.

1980 Karusoo, Merle: **Olen kolmeteistkümne aastane.** (I am thirteen; Ich bin dreizehn.)
(Unpublished; Unveröffentlicht.)

Eestimaa Leninliku Kommunistliku Noorsooühingu kirjanduse ja kunsti preemiad

The Literature and Art Prizes of the Young Communist League of Estonia were established in 1968 and are presented every two years for outstanding achievements in the field of literature, journalism, art music, theatre, cinema, television and interpretation. There are five prizes altogether and they are never repeatedly given to the same person. The following children's book authors were awarded the prize.

Der Preis wurde 1968 ins Leben gerufen und wird alle zwei Jahre für außergewöhnliche Leistungen auf dem Gebiet der Literatur, des Journalismus, der Kunst, der Musik des Theaters, des Kinos, des Fernsehens, der Interpretation vergeben. Er besteht aus insgesamt fünf Preisen und darf nur einmal an ein und dieselbe Person verliehen werden. Die folgenden Kinderbuchautoren wurden ausgezeichnet.:

1968 Rannap, Jaan: **Salu Juhan je ta sõbrad.** (*Salu Juhan* and his friends; *Salu Juhan* und seine Freunde.) Ill.: Asta Vender.
Tallinn: Eesti Raamat 1964.

1970 Pukk, Holger: **Öine lahing.** (The battle at night; Kampf in der Nacht.) Ill.: Edgar Valter.
Tallinn: Eesti Raamat 1970.

1972/ There was no children's book prize given; wurde kein Kinderbuch-
1980 preis vergeben.

Spain/Spanien

"Barco de Vapor" Concurso de Libro Infantil de la Fundación Santa Maria

This prize for manuscripts was established by the Santa Maria Foundation in Madrid to promote children's and youth literature. The selected manuscripts must be of high literary quality and capable of inspiring humanitarian sentiments in youthful readers. The jury, appointed by the Santa Maria Foundation, is composed of specialists working in the field of children's literature. The first award presentation took place in 1978.

Dieser Preis für Manuskripte wird von der Santa Maria Stiftung in Madrid verliehen, um die Kinder- und Jugendliteratur zu fördern. Die preiswürdigen Manuskripte müssen hohen literarischen Ansprüchen genügen und müssen fähig sein im jugendlichen Leser menschenfreundliche Gefühle zu erwecken. Die Jury, die von der Santa Maria Stiftung benannt wird, setzt sich aus Spezialisten auf dem Gebiet der Kinderliteratur zusammen. Die erste Preisverleihung fand 1978 statt.

1978 *1st prize/1. Preis*

Armijo, Consuelo: **El Paminoplas.** (The *Pampinoplas*; Der *Pampinoplas.*) Ill.: Ill.: Antonio Tello.
Madrid: Ed. S.M. 1979.

2nd prize/2. Preis

Pilar Molina, María del: **El mensaje de Maese Zamaor.** (The message of Master *Zamaor;* Botschaft von Meister *Zamaor.*) Ill.: Francisco Solé.
Madrid: Ed. S.M. 1981.

3rd prize/3. Preis

The prize was not given; Der Preis wurde nicht vergeben.

1979 *1st prize/1. Preis*

Muñoz Martín, Juan: **Fray Perico y su borrico.** (Brother *Perico* and his donkey; Bruder *Perico* und sein Esel.) Ill.: Antonio Tello.
Madrid: Ed. S.M. 1980.

2nd prize/2. Preis

Jimenez Frontin, José Luis: **Aventuras y desventuras de Nessi, la pelota de golf.** (The adventures and misadventures of *Nessi* the golf ball; Geschicke und Mißgeschicke des Golfballs *Nessi.*)
(Unpublished; Unveröffentlicht.)

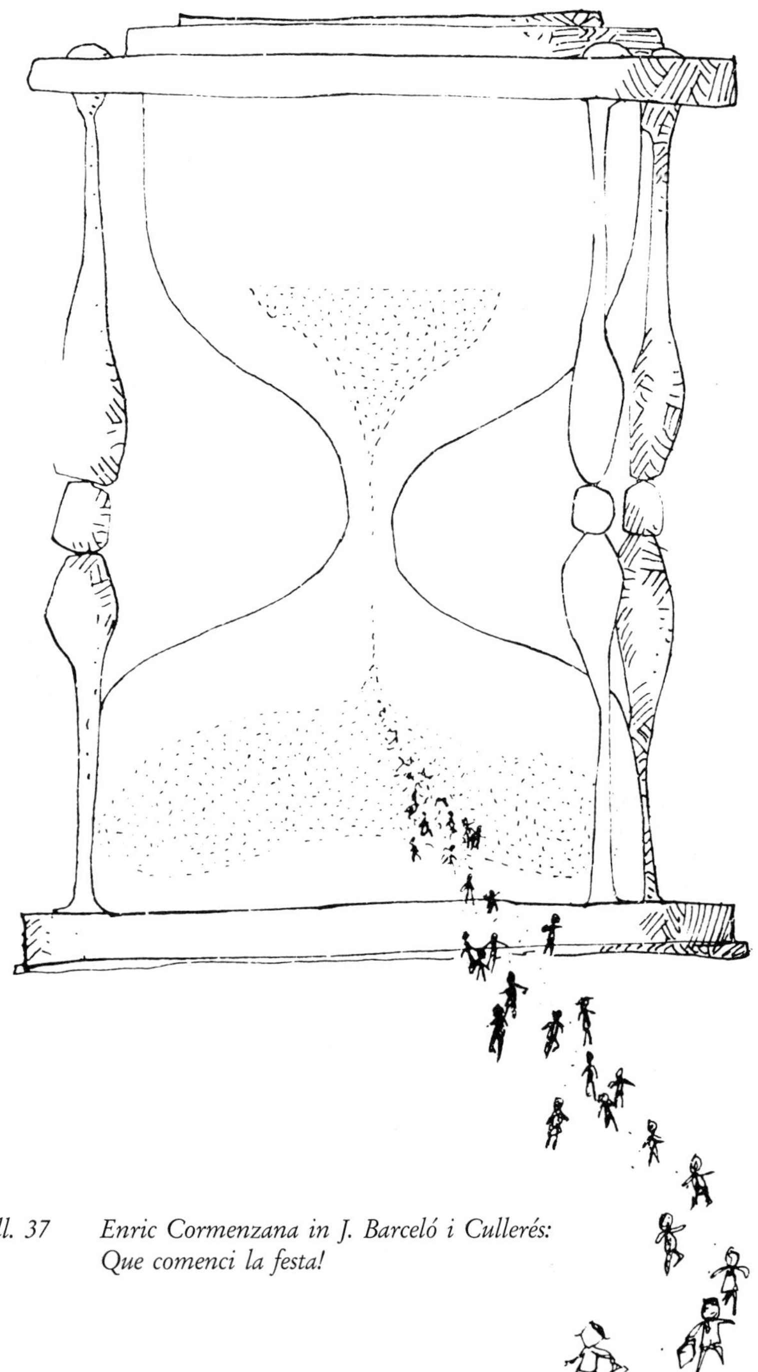

Ill. 37 *Enric Cormenzana in J. Barceló i Cullerés: Que comenci la festa!*

3rd prize/3. Preis
García Dominguez, Ramón: **Carta bolitelepática sobre un grillo del año dos mil y pico.** (Telepathic-pen letter about a cricket from the year 2000 or so; Ein telepathischer Kugelschreiberbrief über eine Grille etwa aus dem Jahr 2000.)
(Unpublished; Unveröffentlicht.)

Ill. 38 Ulises Wensell in: Maria Puncel: Operación Pata de Oso

1980 *1st prize/1. Preis*
The prize was not given; Der Preis wurde nicht vergeben.

2nd prize/2. Preis
Baquedano Azcona, Lucia: **La muñeca que tenía 24 pecas.** (The doll with 24 pimples; Die Puppe mit 24 Pickeln.)
(Unpublished; Unveröffentlicht.)

Mateos Martín, Pilar: **Historias de ninguno.** (Stories about nobody; Geschichten über niemanden.) Ill.: Juan Antonio Rojo.
Madrid: Ed. S.M. 1981.

3rd prize/3. Preis
Borrego, Juan José: **La aventura de Martín.** (*Martin's* adventure; *Martins* Abenteuer.)
(Unpublished; Unveröffentlicht.)

Ill. 39 Galician children in: Bernadino Graña: O Leon e o paxaro rebelde

Premio C.C.E.I.

The prize of the Spanish Catholic Children's Commission (Spanish section of B.I.C.E.) was established in 1962. The purpose of this award is to influence publishers to bring out books of high quality for children and young people.

Der Preis der Katholischen Kinderkommission Spaniens (spanische Sektion B.I.C.E.) wurde 1962 gegründet. Der Preis soll die Verleger ermuntern, Kinder- und Jugendliteratur von hoher Qualität zu veröffentlichen.

1962 Aguirre Bellver, Joaquín: **El bordón y la estrella.** (The staff and the star; Der Stock und der Stern.) Ill.: Antonio Valdivieso.
Madrid: Doncel 1962.

1963 Sánchez Coquillat, María Marcela: **Un castillo en el campo.** (A castle in the countryside; Das Schloß auf dem Lande.) Ill.: Elvira Elías.
Barcelona: Juventud 1962.

1964 Kurtz, Carmen: **Oscar, espía atómico.** (*Oscar,* atomic spy; *Oskar,* der Atomspion.) Ill.: Carlos María Alvarez.
Barcelona: Juventud 1963.

1965 Ruiz Acosta, Juan: **Tienes que vivir.** (You must live; Du mußt leben.)
Madrid: Santillana 1964.

1966 Molina, María Isabel: **Las ruinas de Numancia.** (The ruins of *Numancia*; Die Ruinen von *Numancia.*) Ill.: Julián Nadel.
Madrid: Doncel 1965.

1967 Kurtz, Carmen: **Oscar, espeleólogo.** (*Oscar,* the cave explorer; *Oskar,* der Höhlenforscher.) Ill.: Odile Madrid.
Madrid: Cid 1966.

1968 Sánchez-Silva, José María: **Ladis, un gran pequeño.** (*Ladis,* the big little one; *Ladis,* der große Kleine.) Ill.: José Luis macías.
Alcoy: Marfil 1971.

1969 Espinás, José María: **Todos tenemos hermanos pequeños.** (Everyone has little brothers; Jeder hat kleine Brüder.) Ill.: Eulalia Sariola.
Barcelona: La Galera 1968.

1970 Vallverdù, José: **Polvorón.** (*Polvorón.*) Ill.: Narmas (i.e. Narcis Masferrer).
Barcelona: La Galera 1969.

1971 Amo, Montserrat del: **Chitina y su gato.** (*Chitina* and her cat; *Chitina* und ihre Katze.) Ill.: María Rius.
Barcelona: Juventud 1970.

1972 Muelas, Federico: **Angeles albriciadores.** (Guardian angels; Schutzengel.) Ill.: Pepi Sánchez.
Madrid: Doncel 1971.

1973 Sorribas i Roig, Sebastià: **Los astronautas del "Mochuelo".** (The astronauts of the "*Owl*"; Die Astronauten der "*Eule*".) Ill.: Pilarín Bayés.
Barcelona: La Galera 1972.

1974 Molina Llorente, Pilar: **El terrible Florentino.** (The terrible Florentine; Der schreckliche Florentiner.)
Madrid: Doncel 1973.

1975 Puncel Reparaz, María: **Operación "Pata de Oso";** (Operation "*Bear Paw*", Operation "*Bärenpfote*".) Ill.: Ulises Wensell.
Madrid: Doncel 1971.

1976 Armijo, Consuelo: **Los batautos.** (The batautos; Die Batautos.) Ill.: Jordi Ciuró.
Barcelona: Juventud 1975.

1977 Blázquez, Feliciano: **Caminos abiertos por Juan XXIII.** (Paths opened by *John XXIII;* Offene Wege durch *Johannes XXIII.*) Photos.
Madrid: Hernando 1976.

1978 Llimona, Mercedes: **Juegos y canciones para niños.** (Games and songs for children; Kinderlieder und Spiele.) Ill.: Mercedes Llimona.
Barcelona: Hymsa 1977.

1979 Vallverdù, Josep: **Mir, el ardilla.** (*Mir,* the squirrel; *Mir,* das Eichhörnchen; Cat.orig.title: En *Mir,* l'esquirol.) Ill.: Joan Andreu Vallvé.
Barcelona: La Galera 1979.

1980 Lanuza i Hurtado, Empar: **El sabio rey loco.** (The crazy wise king; Der irre weise König; Cat.orig.title: El savi rei boig i alltre contes.) Ill.: Montserrat Ginesta.
Barcelona: La Galera 1979.

Gisbert, Joan Manuel: **Escenarios fantásticos.** (Fantastic scenes; Fantastische Schauplätze.) Ill.: Miguel Calatayud.
Barcelona: Labor 1979.

Premi Josep Maria Folch i Torres

The Josep Maria Folch i Torres Prize was founded in 1963 by Spes publishing house in order to encourage the production of children's books in Catalan language. It is awarded annually and the works submitted must be in manuscript form (unpublished). The publishing house, La Galera (Barcelona), publishes the prize-winning manuscript, as well as those of the runners-up. A simultaneous edition in Castilian language is also published. The prize is awarded each year in the month of December.

Im Jahre 1963 stiftete der Verlag Spes den Josep-Maria-Folch-i-Torros-Preis, mit dem Kinder- und Jugendbuch-Manuskripte in katalanischer Sprache ausgezeichnet werden. Das preisgekrönte Manuskript, sowie in die engere Wahl gezogene unveröffentlichte Werke, bringt der Verlag La Galera (Barcelona) in katalanischer und kastilischer Sprache heraus. Die Preisverleihung findet jährlich im Dezember statt.

1964 Mussons, Montserrat: **Piu piu.** (Peep. peep; Piep, Piep.) Ill.: Roser Rius.
Barcelona: La Galera 1967.

1965 Sorribas, Sebastià: **El zoo d'en Pitus.** (*Pitus'* zoo; Der Zoo von *Pitus.*) Ill.: Pilarin Bayés.
Barcelona: La Galera 1966.

1966 Novell, Maria: **Les presoneres de Tabriz.** (The prisoners of Tabriz; Die Gefangenen von Tabriz.) Ill.: Llucià Navarro.
Barcelona: La Galera 1967.

1967 The prize was not given; Der Preis wurde nicht vergeben.

1968 Vallverdú, Josep: **Rovelló.** (*Rovelló.*) Ill.: Narmas (i.e. Narcís Masferrer).
Barcelona: La Galera 1969.

1969 Carbó, Joaquim: **I tu, què hi fas aquí?** (And you, what are you doing here? Und du, was machst du hier?) Ill.: Enric Cormenzana.
Barcelona: La Galera 1970.

1970 Vallverdú, Josep: **En Roc drapaire.** (*Roc,* the rag merchant; *Roc,* der Lumpensammler.) Ill.: Joan Corbera.
Barcelona: La Galera 1971.

1971 The prize was not given; Der Preis wurde nicht vergeben.

1972 Solà, Maria Lluïsa: **Anna** (*Anna.*) Ill.: Isidre Monés.
Barcelona: La Galera 1973.

1973 Murià, Anna: **El Meravellós viatge de Nico Huehuetl a travès de Mèxic.** (The wonderful journey of *Nico Huehuetl* through Mexico; Die wunderbare Reise des Nico *Huehuetl* durch Mexiko.) Ill.: Christa Gottschewsky.
Barcelona: La Galera 1974.

1974 The prize was not given; Der Preis wurde nicht vergeben.

1975 Janer i Manila, Gabriel: **El rei Gaspar.** (*Casper* the king; Der König *Kasper.*) Ill.: Montserrat Torres.
Barcelona: La Galera 1976.

1976 Canela Garayoa, Mercè: **L'escarabat verd.** (The green beetle; Der grüne Käfer.) Ill.: Andreu Vallvé.
Barcelona: La Galera 1977.

1977 Vergés, Oriol: **La ciutat sense muralles.** (The city without walls; Die Stadt ohne Mauern.) Ill.: Isidre Monés.
Barcelona: La Galera 1978.

1978 Lanuza i Hurtado, Empar de: **El savi rei boig.** (The wise crazy king; Der weise verrückte König.) Ill.: Montserrat Ginesta.
Barcelona: La Galera 1979.

1979 Lanuza i Hurtado, Empar: **El savi rei boig i altres contes.** (The crazy wise king and other stories; Der irre weise König und andere Geschichten.) Ill.: Montserrat Ginesta.
Barcelona: La Galera 1979.

1980 Barceló i Cullerés, Joan: **Que comenci la festa.** (The feast begins; Das Fest soll beginnen.) Ill.: Enric Cormenzana.
Barcelona: La Galera 1980.

"Gran Angular" Concurso de Libro Juvenil de la Fundación Santa Maria

This prize for manuscripts was established by the Santa Maria Foundation in Madrid to promote children's and youth literature. The selected manuscripts must be of high literary quality and capable of inspiring humanitarian sentiments in youthful readers. The jury, appointed by the Santa Maria Foundation, is composed of specialists working in the field of children's literature. The first award presentation took place in 1978.

Dieser Preis für Manuskripte wird von der Santa Maria Stiftung in Madrid verliehen, um die Kinder- und Jugendliteratur zu fördern. Die preiswürdigen Manuskripte müssen hohen literarischen Ansprüchen genügen und müssen fähig sein im jugendlichen Leser menschenfreundliche Gefühle zu erwecken. Die Jury, die von der Santa Maria Stiftung benannt wird, setzt sich aus Spezialisten auf dem Gebiet der Kinderliteratur zusammen. Die erste Preisverleihung fand 1978 statt.

1978 The prize was not given; Der Preis wurde nicht vergeben.

1979 *1st prize/1. Preis*
The prize was not given; Der Preis wurde nicht vergeben.
2nd prize/2. Preis
Maritín Vigil, José Luis: **El misterio del Almak.** (The mystery of *Almak*; Das Geheimnis von *Almak*.)
(Unpublished; Unveröffentlicht.)

Riaño Martín, José: **La promesa.** (The promise; Das Versprechen.) (Unpublished/Unveröffentlicht)

3rd prize/3. Preis

Baquedano Azcona, Lucia: **Cinco panes de cebada.** (Five loaves of barley bread; Fünf Gerstenbrote.)
Madrid: Ed. S.M. 1981.

1980 *1st prize/1. Preis*

Sierra i Fabra, Jordi: **El cazador.** (The hunter; Der Jäger.)
Madrid: Ed. S.M. 1981.

2nd prize/2. Preis

Martiín Vigíl, José Luis: **Doce indeseables.** (Twelve undesirables; Zwölf Unerwünschte.)
(Unpublished; Unveröffentlicht.)

3rd prize/3. Preis

Herrera García, Juan Ignacio: **Regreso a la naturaleza.** Return to nature; Rückkehr zur Natur.)
(Unpublished; Unveröffentlicht.)

Premio Lazarillo

Spain has a number of private prizes for children's and school books. The Lazarillo Prize was founded in 1958 under the patronage of the Ministry of Information and Tourism and the Ministry of Education and Science. Each year, the commission for juvenile literature of the National Institute for the Spanish Book (Instituto Nacional del Libro Español) appoints a jury.

The prize has three categories: 1) a cash-award for the author of the best children's and youth book. (It is now custromary to alternate: one year the best children's book receives the prize and the next year, the best youth book). The book may be in manuscript form or published the previous year. 2) A cash-award for the best illustration (both published and unpublished illustrations can be submitted). 3) An honorary citation, without cash-award to the publishing house (discontinued since 1971).

The prizes are usually presented on National Book Day. The first two categories apply to Spanish and Hispano-American candidates; the publishers do not necessarily have to be Spanish citizens, but they must have residence in Spain and appear in the lists of the Instituto Nacional del Libro Español. All three categories can go to the producers of one book. It is important to note that since 1968 no distinction is made between the four official Spanish Languages. Therefore, the prizes can be awarded to Castillian, Catalonian, Basque and Galician books, provided the books published in the regional language are submitted together with a translation in Castillian.

Neben einer Anzahl privater Preise für Kinder- und Schulbücher besteht seit 1958 in Spanien unter dem Patronat des Ministeriums für Erziehung und Wissenschaft und des Ministeriums für Information und Fremdenverkehr der Lazarillo-Preis. Jedes Jahr stellt die Kommission für Kinder- und Jugendliteratur des Nationalinstituts für das spanische Buch (Instituto Nacional del Libro Español) eine Jury auf.

Der Preis setzt sich aus drei Kategorien zusammen: 1. eine Geldprämie für den Verfasser des besten Kinder- oder Jugendbuches (neuerdings wechselt man ab: in einem Jahr wird das beste Kinderbuch ausgewählt, im folgenden das beste Jugendbuch) — wobei es keinen Unterschied macht, ob das Buch im vergangenen Jahr bereits veröffentlicht wurde oder lediglich im Manuskript vorlag, 2. eine Geldprämie für die beste Illustration (es können sowohl bereits veröffentlichte als auch noch nicht gedruckte Illustrationen eingereicht werden, 3. eine ehrenvolle Auszeichnung eines Verlages ohne Geldprämie. (dieser Ehrenpreis wird seit 1971 nicht mehr verliehen).

Die Preise werden gewöhnlich im Juni anläßlich des Nationalen Tages des Buches vergeben. Die beiden ersten Preise können an spanische und hispanoamerikanische Bewerber verliehen werden; bei den Verlegern genügt es, daß sie sich in Spanien niedergelassen und im Instituto Nacional del Libro Español eingeschrieben haben. Die drei Preise können gleichzeitig an die Urheber ein und desselben Buches fallen. Wichtig ist, daß seit 1968 kein Unterschied mehr zwischen den vier spanischen Sprachen gemacht wird. Es können also Preise sowohl an kastilische und katalanische als auch an baskische und galegische Bücher verliehen werden — Bedingung ist lediglich, daß zu Publikationen in einer spanischen Regionalsprache die kastilische Übersetzung vorgelegt wird.

1958 Iniesta, Corredor, Alfonso: **Dicen las florecillas . . . Estampas franciscanas.** (The little flowers say . . . Franciscan pictures; Die kleinen Blumen sprechen . . . Franziskanische Bilder.) Ill.: Narmas (i.e. Narcís Masferrer.).
Gerona: Charles Dalmau, Pla 1957.

Illustration

Aguirre, José Francisco in:
Herrera, José Luis: **El libro del desierto.** (The book of the desert; Das Buch der Wüste.)
Madrid: Aguilar 1958.

Publisher/Verleger

Editorial Mateu, Barcelona for:
Castro Montaner, Ramón: **Enciclopedia del muchacho español.** (The Spanish boy's encyclopedia; Die Enzyklopädie des spanischen Jungen.)
Barcelona: Mateu 1958.

1959 Buñuel, Miguel: **El niño, la golondrina y el gato.** (The boy, the swallow and the cat; Der Junge, die Schwalbe und die Katze.) Ill.: Lorenzo Goñi.
Madrid: Doncel 1959.

Illustration
Munoa, Rafael in:
Espina, Antonio: **Exploradores de Africa.** (Explorer of Africa; Erforscher Afrikas.)
Madrid: Aguilar 1958.

Publisher/Verleger
Dalmau y Jover, Barcelona for:
Muedra, Vicente: **La Naturaleza.** (Nature; Die Natur.) Ill.: José Maria Thomas.
Barcelona: Dalmau y Jover 1958.

1960 Del Amo y Gili, Montserrat: **Rastro de Dios.** (God's trail; Spur Gottes.) Ill.: Dora Roda.
Madrid: Cid 1960.

Illustration
Jiménez Arnalot, Manuel in:
Fabra, Luis R.: **Yo soy el gato.** (I am the cat; Ich bin die Katze.)
Barcelona: Gamma 1960.

Publisher/Verleger
Gamma, Barcelona for:
Fabra, Luis R.: **Yo soy el gato.** (I am the cat; Ich bin die Katze.) Ill.: Manuel Jiménez Arnalot.
Barcelona: Gamma 1960.

1961 Aguirre Bellver, Joaquín: **El juglar del Cid.** (The *Cid's* juggler; Der Gaukler des *Cid.*) Ill.: Julián Nadel.
Madrid: Doncel 1960.

Illustration
Narro, José in:
Defoe, Daniel: **Robinsón Crusoe.** (*Robinson Crusoe; Engl.orig.title:* The life and adventures of *Robinson Crusoe.*)
Barcelona: Juventud 1960.

Publisher/Verleger
Doncel, Madrid for:
Aguirre Bellver, Joaquín: **El juglar del Cid.** (The *Cid's* juggler; Der Gaukler des *Cid.*) Ill.: Julián Nadal.
Madrid: Doncel 1960.

1962 Fernández Luna, Concepción: **Fiesta en Marilandia.** (Festival in *Sealand*; Das Fest in *Seeland*.) Ill.: Daniel Zarza.
Salamanca: Anaya 1963.
Illustration
Picó, José in:
Picó, José: **Fantasía.** (Fantasy; Fantasie.)
(Unpublished; Unveröffentlicht.)
Publisher/Verleger
Ediciones Gaisa, S.L., Valencia, for the series/Mit der Reihe: **Vidas y aventuras de animales salvajes.** (Lives and adventures of wild animals; Leben und Abenteuer der wilden Tiere.)
Valencia: Gaisa.

1963 Ionescu, Angela C.: **De un país lejano.** (From a far country; Aus einem fernen Land.) Ill.: Máximo San Juan.
Madrid: Doncel 1962.
Illustration
Perellón, Celedonio in:
Draghi, Laura: **Cuentos del Angel Custodio.** (Tales of the guardian angel; Erzählungen vom Schutzengel.)
Madrid: Doncel 1961.
Publisher/Verleger
The prize was not given; Der Preis wurde nicht vergeben.

1964 Kurtz, Carmen: **Color de fuego.** (Color of fire; Feuerfarbe.)
Ill.: Pablo Ramírez.
Madrid: Cid 1964.
Illustration
Zarza, Daniel in:
Fernández Luna, Concepción: **Fiesta en Marilandia** (Festival in *Sealand*; Das Fest in *Seeland*.)
Salamanca: Anaya 1963.
Publisher/Verleger
Ediciones Anaya, Salamanca for:
Fernández Luna, Concepción: **Fiesta en Marilandia.** (Festival in *Sealand*; Das Fest in *Seeland*.)
Ill.: Daniel Zarza.
Salamanca: Anaya 1963.

1965 Mature, Ana Maria: **El polizón del "Ulises".** (The stowaway on the *Ulysses*; Der blinde Passagier der *Ulysses*.) Ill.: Cesca Jaume (i.e. Francesca Jaume).
Barcelona: Lumen 1965.

Illustration

Balzola, Asunción in:
Gil, Bonifacio: **Cancionero infantil universal.** (Universal children's songbook; Kinderlieder aus aller Welt.)
Madrid: Aguilar 1964.

Publisher/Verleger

Santillana S.A. de Ediciones, Madrid for:
Colección aficiones. (Hobby series; Hobby-Serie.)
Madrid: Santillana 1962—1965.

1966 Osorio, Marta: **El caballito que quería volar.** (The little horse who wanted to fly; Das kleine Pferd, das fliegen wollte.) Ill.: Maria Luísa Jover.
Barcelona: La Galera 1968.
(Manuscript orig.title: El caballito.)

Illustration

Horna, Luis de in:
Martín Barrigós, José: **Gino, Comino y el camello, Moja-Jamón.** (*Gino, Comino* and the camel, *Moja-Jamón; Gino, Comino* und das Kamel *Moja-Jamón.*)
Alcoy: Marfil 1970.

Publisher/Verleger

Ediciones La Galera, Barcelona for:
Quality of combined production; Verlagsschaffen im allgemeinen.

1967 Tiraboschi de Grim, Lita: **Historia del gato que vino con Solís.** (The story of the cat that came with *Solís;* Die Geschichte der Katze, die mit *Solís* kam.) Ill.: Ricardo Zamorano.
Madrid: Aguilar 1970.

Illustration

Riera Rojas, Roque in:
Cervantes Saavedra, Miguel de: **Don Quijote de la Mancha. Vols, 1.2.** (Don *Quixote* from *La Mancha;* Don *Quichotte* von *La Mancha.*)
Adapt.: Fernando Gutiérrez.
Barcelona: Cresda 1966.

Publisher/Verleger

The prize was not given; Der Preis wurde nicht vergeben.

1968 Ferrán, Jaime: **Ángel en Colombia.** (*Angel* in Colombia; *Engel* in Kolumbien.) Ill.: María Antonio Dans.
Madrid: Doncel 1967.

Illustration
Rius, María in:
Benet, Amèlia: **Per què canten els ocells.** (Why the birds sing; Warum die Vögel singen.)
Barcelona: Teide 1968.

Rius, María in: Benet, Amèlia: **Per què són útils els ocells.** (Why the birds are useful; Warum die Vögel nützlich sind.)
Barcelona: Teide 1968.

Publisher/Verleger
Editorial Cantábrica S.A., Bilbao.

1969 Aleixandre, José Javier: **Froilán, el amigo de los pájaros.** (*Froilan*, the friend of the birds; *Froilan*, der Freund der Vögel.) Ill.: Ramón Castañer.
Alcoy: Marfil 1968.

Illustration
Sáez González, Fernando in:
El Lazarillo de Tormes. (*Lazarillo* de Tormes; *Lazarillo* von Tormes.)
Madrid: Susaeta 1969.

Publisher/Verleger
Luís Verón Climent (Editor), Barcelona for:
Five classic works; Fünf klassische Werke: Cervantes Saavedra, Miguel de: **Don Quijote de la Mancha.** (Don *Quixote* from *La Mancha*; Don *Quichotte* von *La Mancha*.)
Homeros: **Ilíada.** (Iliad; Iliade.)
Homeros: **La Odisea.** (Odyssey; Odyssee.)
Milton, John: **El Paraíso perdido.** (Paradise lost; Das verlorene Paradies.)
Vergilius Maro, Publius: **La Eneida.** (Aeneid; Aeneis.)
Barcelona: Ediciones Verón.

1970 Sadot, Fernando: **Cuentos del zodíaco.** (Tales of the zodiac; Die Märchen von den Tierkreiszeichen.) Ill.: Begoña (i.e. Begoña Fernández.)
Madrid: Doncel 1971.

Illustration
Montero Suárez, Felicidad in:
Los músiocos de Bremen. (The musicians of Bremen; Die Bremer Stadtmusikanten.)
(Unpublished; Unveröffentlicht.)

Publisher/Verleger
Editorial Teide, Barcelona.

1971 Puncel Reparaz, María: **Operación Pata de Oso.** (*Operation Bear Paw; Operation Bärenpfote.)* Ill.: Ulises Wensell.
Madrid: Doncel 1971.

Illustration
Sáez González, Fernando in:
Losada, Basilio: **Goya.** (*Goya.*)
Barcelona: Verón 1972.

Publisher/Verleger
The prize was not given; Der Preis wurde nicht vergeben.

1972 Cupit, Aarón: **Cuentos del año 2100.** (Tales of the year 2100; Geschichten auf dem Jahr 2100.) Ill.: Miguel Calatayud.
Madrid: Doncel 1973.

Illustration
Boix Álvarez, Manuel in:
Ionescu, Ángela C.: **El país de las cosas perdidas.** (The land of lost things; Das Land der verlorenen Sachen.)
Madrid: Doncel 1971.

1973 Váquez Vigo, Carmen: **Caramelos de menta.** (Mint candy; Pfefferminzbonbons.) Ill.: Viví Escrivá.
Madrid: Doncel 1973.

Illustration
Pacheco, Miguel Ángel in:
Maestros de la fantasia. (Masters of fantasy; Meister der Fantasie.) Vol. 14.
Madrid: Santillana 1972.

1974 Armijo Navarro Reverter, Consuelo: **Los batautos.** (The batautos; Die Batautos.) Ill.: Jordi Ciuró.
Barcelona: Juventud 1975.

Illustration
Calatayud, Miguel in:
Cupit, Aarón: **Cuentos del año 2100.** (Tales of the year 2100; Geschichten aus dem Jahr 2100.)
Madrid: Doncel 1973.

1975 Perera de Díaz, Hilda: **Cuentos para chicos y grandes.** (Tales for children and adults; Erzählungen für Kinder und Erwachsene.) Ill.: Ana Bermejo.
Valladolid: Miñon 1976.

Illustration
Vázquez de Parga, Margarita for:
Once ilustraciones inéditas. (Eleven unpublished Illustrations; Elf unveröffentlichte Illustrationen.)

1976 The prize was not given; Der Preis wurde nicht vergeben.

1977 Alonso, Fernando: **El hombrecito vestido de gris y otros cuentos,** (The little man dressed in grey and other stories; Der kleine grau gekleidete Mann und andere Geschichten.) Ill.: Ulises Wensell.
Madrid: Alfaguara 1978.

Illustration
The prize was not given; Der Preis wurde nicht vergeben.

1978 Perera, Hilda: **Podria ser una vez . . .** (Once, it could have been that. . .; Es könnte einmal gewesen sein daß . . .)
(Unpublished; Unveröffentlicht.)

Illustration
Sánchez, José Ramón in:
Garcia Sánchcz, Josć Luis: **Los libros dcl aprcndiz dc brujo.** (The books of the sorcerer's apprentice; Die Bücher vom Zauberlehrling.)
Valladolid: Miñon 1977.

1979 The prize was not given; Der Preis wurde nicht vergeben.

Illustration
Wensell, Ulises in:
Puncel, Maria: Cuando sea mayor seré marino. (When I get big, I will be a sailor; Wenn ich groß bin, werde ich Seemann.)
Madrid: Altea 1979.

Wensell, Ulises in:
Puncel, Ulises: **Cuando sea mayor seré enfermera.** (When I get big, I will be a nurse; Wenn ich groß bin, werde ich Krankenschwester.)
Madrid: Altea 1979.

1980 Gisbert, Joan: **El misterio de la isla de Tokland.** (The mystery of *Tokland Island*; Das Geheimnis der *Toklandinsel.*)
(Unpublished; Unveröffentlicht.)

Illustration
Escrivá, Vivi (i.e. Maria Victoria Escrivá) in:
Puncel, Maria: **Dos cuentos de princesas.** (Two stories about princesses; Zwei Geschichten über Prinzessinnen.)
Madrid: Altea 1980.

Libros de Interés Infantil y Juvenil

This prize was founded on September 29, 1975 by the Ministry of Culture. The Jury evaluates the creative contents of the books, the educational and literary elements, as well as the illustration and typography. The president of the jury is the general director of Books and Libraries. Originally the rules of the prize stipulated that the titles must be first editions; later, this was changed to include second editions, also. The works submitted must be written in Castilian or one of the other official languages of Spain. In 1978, the prize was expanded to include didactic literature and encyclopedias. It was also decided, in the same year, to limit the prize to children's books only.

Das Kultusministerium rief diesen Wettbewerb am 29.9.1975 ins Leben. Die Jury, deren Vorsitzender der Generaldirektor der Bibliotheken ist, bewertet sowohl den Gehalt des Buches, die literarische Qualität, als auch die Illustrationen und die Typografie. Die Bücher, die für diesen Wettbewerb angemeldet werden, müssen Erstveröffentlichungen in kastilischer Sprache sein oder in einer anderen in Spanien offiziellen Sprache. 1978 wurde der Wettbewerb erweitert, so daß nun auch Lehrbücher, Enzyklopädien und Neuauflagen, berücksichtigt werden können. Außerdem entschloß sich die Jury den Wettbewerb auf Kinderbücher zu beschränken.

1975 *Children's books/Kinderbücher*

Bruna, Dick: **Canelo.** (Canelo.) Ill.: Dick Bruna.
Madrid: Aguilar 1975.

García Sanchez, José Luís: **El último lobo y caperudita.** (The last wolf and little *Red Cap*; Der letzte Wolf und das kleine *Rotkäppchen*.) Ill.: Miguel Angel Pacheco.
Barcelona: Labor 1975.

Torre, Bautista de la: **Gasparitu¡ Pum! y otros cuentos.** (*Gasparitu.* Bang! and other stories; *Gasparitu.* Päng! und andere Geschichten.)
Madrid: Almena 1975.

Grée, Alain: *Tom, Irene* y animales domésticos. (*Tom, Irene* and the domestic animals; *Tom, Irene* und ihre Haustiere.) Ill.: Gérard Grée.
Barcelona: Juventud 1975.

Gasset, Angeles: **Títeres con cabeza.** (Puppets with heads; Puppen mit Köpfen.) Ill.: F. Goico Aguirre.
Madrid: Aguilar 1967.

Cervantes y Saavedra, Miguel de: **Don Quijote de la Mancha.** (Don *Quixote* from La Mancha; Don *Quichotte* von La Mancha.) Adapt./Photos: Antonio Albarrán, A. Perera.
Madrid: Sedmay 1975.

Youth Books/Jugendbücher

Kipling, Rudyard: **Cuatro cuentos del "Libro de la Selva".** (Four stories from the "Jungle Book"; Vier Geschichten aus dem "Dschungelbuch".)
Barcelona: Timun Más 1975.

Kurtz, Carmen: **Oscar en Africa.** (*Oscar* in Africa; *Oskar* in Afrika.) Ill.: Odile Kurz.
Barcelona: Juventud 1974.

Enciclopedia Juvenil Pala. Vol. 1—7. (*Pala* youth encyclopedia; *Palas* Jugendenzyklopädie.)
San Sebastián: Pala 1974.

Steinacker, Conrado: **Gentes y países. Vol. 1.2.** (People and countries; Leute und Länder.)
Bilbao: Fher 1974.
Dickens, Charles: **Una canción de Navidad.** (Eng.orig.title: A Christmas carol; Weihnachtserzählungen.) Ill.: Chiqui de la Fuente.
Madrid: Sedmay 1974.

Ionescu, Angela C.: **Donde duerme el agua.** (Where the water sleeps; Wo das Wasser schläft.) Ill.: Nestor Salas.
Barcelona: Labor 1975.

1976 *Children's books/Kinderbücher*
Lemos, Montserrat: **Pepo.** (*Pepo.*)
Barcelona: Hymsa.

Janer Manila, Gabriel: **El rey Gaspar.** (*Casper,* the king; *Kasper,* der König.) Ill.: Montserrat Torres.
Barcelona: La Galera 1976.

Tomlinson, Jill: **El buho que tenía miedo a la oscuridad.** (Amer.orig.title: The owl who was afraid of the dark; Die Eule, die vor der Dunkelheit Angst hatte.) Ill.: Ana Bermejo.
Valladolid: Miñon 1976.

Tison, Anette/Taylor, Talus: **Barbapapá.** (*Barbapapa; Fr. orig.title: Barbapapa.*) Ill.: Anette Tison.
Barcelona: Juventud 1973.

Ionescu, Angela C.: **De un país lejano.** (From a far country; Aus einem fernen Land.)
Ill.: Máximo San Juan.
Madrid: Doncel 1969.

Primer diccionario en color. (First dictionary in color; Das erste bunte Lexikon.)
León: Everest.

Youth books/Jugendbücher
Matute, Ana María: **Paulina.** (*Paulina.*) Ill.: Francesca Jaume.
Barcelona: Lumen 1969.

Golowanjuk, Jascha: **La ruta de las caravanas.** (The caravan route; Der Weg der Karawanen.)
Barcelona: Juventud 1976.

Lavolle, Louise Nöelle: **Las llaves del desierto.** (The keys of the desert; Die Schlüssel der Wüste; Fr.orig.title: Les clés du désert.)
La Coruña: Adara.

Maravillas del saber. Vol.1—10. (Marvels of knowledge; Wunder des Wissens.)
Barcelona: Oredas.

Qué sabes de . . . (Who knows about . . .; Wer kennt . . .) Vol.1—10.
Barcelona: Nauta 1975—1976.

Verne, Jules: **20.000 leguas de viaje submarino.** (20,000 leagues under the sea; 20.000 Meilen unter dem Meer; Fr.orig.title: Vingt mille lieues sous les mers.)
Madrid: Altea 1976.

1977 *Children's books/Kinderbücher*

Enciclopedia de la enseñanza general básica. Vol. 1—10. (General encyclopedia for basic teaching; Allgemeine Enzyklopädie des gründlichen Unterrichts.)
Barcelona: Plaza y Janés 1977.

Preussler, Otfried: **El geniecillo del agua.** (The little water sprite; Germ.orig.title: Der kleine Wassermann.) Ill.: Winnie Gayler.
Barcelona: Noguer 1977.

Capdevila Font, Juan: **Teo en tren.** (*Theo* in the train; *Theo* im Zug.) Ill.: Violeta Denou.
Barcelona: Timun Más 1977.

Ionescu, Angela C.: **Detrás de las nubes.** (Behind the clouds; Hinter den Wolken.) Ill.: Jesús Casaus.
Madrid: Doncel 1977.

Philippart de Foy, Guy: **Waki, el pequeño pigmeo de la selva.** (*Waki,* the little pygmy and the jungle animals; *Waki,* der kleine Pygmäe und die Tiere des Waldes.)
Bilbao: Fher 1977.

Brunhoff, Jean de: **Historia de Babar, el elefantito.** (The story of *Babar,* the little elephant; Die Geschichte von *Babar,* dem kleinen Elefanten; Fr.orig.title: Histoire de *Babar,* le petit éléphant.) Ill.: Jean de Brunhoff.
Madrid: Alfaguara 1972.

Youth books/Jugendbücher

Jiménez, Juan Ramón: **Platero y yo.** (*Platero* and I; *Platero* und ich.) Ill.: Rafael Munoa.
Madrid: Aguilar 1972.

Molina, Natacha: **Caminos abiertos. Madame Curie.** (Open roads. Madame *Curie*; Offene Wege. Madame *Curie*.)
Madrid: Hernando 1977.

Manzi, Alberto: **Orzowei.** (*Orzowei.*) Ill.: Maria Matons de Malagrida.
Barcelona: Noguer 1966.

Molina, María Isabel: **Las ruinas de Numancia.** (The ruins of *Numancia;* Die Ruinen von *Numancia.* Ill.: Julián Nadal.
Madrid: Doncel 1969.

Vallverdú, Josep: **Chacales en la ciudad.** (Jackals in the city; Hyänen in der Stadt.) Ill.: Jordi Bulbena.
Barcelona: La Galera 1977.

Jiménez Landi, Antonio: **Leyendas de España.** (Legends of Spain; Legenden aus Spanien.) Ill.: Ricardo Zamorano.
Madrid: Aguilar 1971.

1978 Kurtz, Carmen: **Oscar en las islas.** (*Oscar* in the islands; *Oskar* auf den Inseln.) Ill.: Odile Kurz.
Barcelona: Juventud 1977.

Verges, Oriol: **La ciutat sense muralles.** (The city without walls; Die Stadt ohne Mauern.) Ill.: Isidre Monés.
Barcelona: La Galera 1978.

Garcia Sanchez, José Luís: **La niña sin nombre.** (The girl without name; Das Mädchen ohne Namen.) Ill.: Asunción Balzola.
Madrid: Altea 1978.

Alonso, Fernando: **El hombrecito vestido de gris y otros cuentos.** (The little man dressed in grey and other stories; Der kleine grau gekleidete Mann und andere Geschichten.) Ill.: Ulises Wensell.
Madrid: Alfaguara 1978.

Senell, Joles: **La guia fantàstica.** (The fantastic guide; Der fantastische Führer.) Ill.: Montserrat Brucart.
Barcelona: Abadia de Monserrat 1977.

Marzot, Janet/Marzot, Livio: **Las liebres blancas.** (The white books; Die weißen Bücher.)
Barcelona: Juventud 1978.

1979 Adams, Richard: **El viaje de los tigres.** (The voyage of the tigers; Die Reise der Tiger; Eng.orig.title: Tyger voyage.) Ill.: Nicola Bayley.
Barcelona: Lumen 1979.

Alonso, Fernando: **El hombrecillo de papel.** (The paper man; Das Männchen aus Papier.) Ill.: Fernando Alonso.
Valladolid: Miñon 1978.

Ceserani, Gian Paolo: **El viaje de Marco Polo.** (*Marco Polo's* voyage; *Marco Polos* Reise; Ital.orig.title: Il viaggio di *Marco Polo.*) Ill.: Piero Ventura.
Madrid: Magisterio Español 1979.

García Sanchez, José Luís/Pacheco, Miguel Angel: **Las 100 y una actividades, juegos, inventos y aventuras de Camembert en el mar.** (The 101 activities, games, inventions and adventures of *Camembert* in the sea; Die 101 Unternehmungen, Spiele, Erfindungen und Abenteuer von *Camembert* im Meer.) Ill.: José Ramón Sanchez.
Madrid: Altea 1979.

Kurtz, Carmen: **Oscar, Kina y el laser.** (*Oscar, Kina* and the laser; *Oskar, Kina* und der Laser.) Ill.
Barcelona: Juventud 1979.

Vallverdú i Aixala, Josep: **Mir, el ardilla.** (*Mir,* the squirrel; *Mir,* das Eichhörnchen; Cat.orig.title: En *Mir* l'esquirol.) Ill.: Joan Andreu Vallvé.
Barcelona: La Galera 1979.

1980 Ceserani, Gian Paolo: **El viajes de Magallanes.** (*Magellan's* voyage; *Magellans* Reise; Ital.orig.title: Il viaggio di *Magellano.) Ill.: Piero Ventura.*
Madrid: Magisterio Español 1980.

Galeano, Eduardo: **La piedra arde.** (The stone burns; Der Stein brennt.) Ill.: Luís de Horna.
Salamanca: Lóguez 1980.

MacAmlay, David: **Castillo medieval.** (Medieval castle; Mittelalterliches Schloß.) Ill.: David MacAmlay.
Barcelona: Timun Mas 1980.

Obiols, Miguel: **El misteri de Buster Keaton.** (The mystery of *Buster Keaton;* Das Geheimnis von *Buster Keaton.*) Ill.: Marta Balaguer.
Barcelona: Abadia de Montserrat 1980.

Preussler, Otfried: **Las aventuras de Vania el forzudo.** (The adventures of strong *Vania*; Germ.orig.title: Die Abenteuer des starken *Wanja.*) Ill.: Antonio Tello.
Madrid: Ed. S.M. 1980.

Vazquez Vigo, Carmen: **Animales charlatanes.** (Chattering animals; Geschwätzige Tiere.) Ill.: Sánchez Muñoz.
Barcelona: Noguer 1980.

Premios Nacionales de Literatura Infantil

This prize was founded in 1978 by the Ministry of Culture as a project motivated by the "International Year of the Child". This national award, which is to be given annually, is designed to promote all areas of children's book production.

Dieser Preis wurde 1978 vom Kultusminister zum "Internationalen Jahre des Kindes" gestiftet. Dieser Nationalpreis, der jährlich verliehen wird, soll alle Gebiete der Kinderbuchproduktion fördern.

1978 *Best editorial work/Beste Verlagsarbeit*
La Galera, Barcelona

Best lay-out and printing/Beste grafische Gestaltung und bester Druck
Novograph S.A., Madrid.

Illustration
Ulises Wensell
(1st prize/1. Preis.)

Asunción Balzola
(2nd prize/2. Preis)

Translation/Übersetzung
Balseiro, Maria Luisa for:
Gardner, John: **Dragón, dragón.** (Dragon, dragon; Drache, Drache; Amer.orig.title: Dragon, dragon and other timeless tales.)

Bookshop/Buchladen
Talentum, Madrid
(1st prize/1. Preis)

Garbancito, Madrid
(2nd prize/2. Preis)

1979 *Best book/Das beste Buch*
Martinez Gil, Fernando: **El rio de los castores.** (The river of the beavers; Der Fluß der Biber.)
Barcelona: Noguer 1981.
(1st prize/1. Preis)

Chozas Pedrero, Mercedes: **Palabras de cuento.** (Words of stories; Worte aus Erzählungen.)
Valladolid: Miñon 1981.
(2nd prize/2. Preis)

Illustration
Solé, Carme in:
Pierini, Fabio: **El niño que queria volar.** (The boy who wanted to fly; Das Kind, das fliegen wollte.)
Valladolid: Miñon 1979.
(1st prize/1. Preis)

Sole΄, Carme in:
Levert, Claude: **Pedro y su roble.** (*Pedro* and his oak tree; *Pedro* und seine Eiche.)
Valladolid: Miñon 1979.
(1st prize/1. Preis)

Solé, Carme in:
Leclercq, Jean Paul: **Peluso y la cometa.** (*Peluso* and the comet; *Peluso* und der Komet.)
Valladolid: Miñon 1979.
(1st prize/1. Preis)

Horna, Luis de in:
Alberti, Rafael:¡ **Aire, que me lleva el aire!** (The air takes me into the air; Die Luft trägt mich in die Luft.)
Barcelona: Labor 1979.
(2nd prize/2. Preis)

Translation/Übersetzung
Hombria, Concha in:
Jarrell, Randall: **La familia animal.** (Amer.orig.title: Animal family; Die Tierfamilie.) Ill.: Maurice Sendak.
Madrid: Alfaguara 1979.

Best editorial work/Beste Verlagsarbeit
Editorial Miñon, Valladolid

Best lay-out and printing/Beste grafische Gestaltung und bester Druck
The prize was not given; Der Preis wurde nicht vergeben.

Best bookshop/Der beste Buchladen
Libreria Amics, Valencia.
(1st prize/1. Preis)

Libreria Garbancito, Madrid

1980 *Best book/Das beste Buch*
Díaz-Noriega, Juan Farias: **Algunos niños, tres perros y más cosas.** (Some boys, three dogs and more things; Einige Kinder, drei Hunde und andere Sachen.)
(1st prize/1. Preis)
(Unpublished; Unveröffentlicht.)

Vergés i Mundo, Oriol: **Les trifulques dels herois.** (The sufferings of the heros; Die Leiden der Helden.)
(2nd prize/2. Preis)
(Unpublished; Unveröffentlicht.)

Illustration
Miguel Angel Fernández Pacheco
(1st prize/1. Preis)

Mercedes Llimona
(2nd prize/2. Preis)

Translation/Übersetzung
Ambrosy, Manuel in:
Pelot, Pierre: **La jangada.** (The raft; Das Floß; Fr.orig.title: La drave.)
Madrid: Ed. S.M. 1980.

Best publisher/Der beste Verlag
Editorial Altea, Madrid

Premio "O Facho"

This prize for children's stories was founded in 1968 by the O Facho Cultural Association in order to encourage children's book production in the Galician language. It is sponsored by the savings bank, Caja de Ahorros-Monte de Piedad, of La Coruña and Lugo. It is awarded each year on May 17th, the "Day of Galician Children's Literature".

Die Kultur-Organisation "O Facho" stiftete den gleichnamigen Preis im Jahre 1968, um Kinderbücher in galicischer Sprache hervorzuheben. Geldgeber sind die Sparkassen Caja de Ahorros-Monte de Piedad aud La Coruña und Lugo. Der Preis wird jährlich am 17. Mai, dem "Tag der galicischen Kinderliteratur" verliehen.

1968 Casares, Carlos: **A galiña azul.** (The blue hen; Das blaue Huhn.) Ill.: Galician children; galicische Kinder.
Vigo: Galaxia 1969.

1969 Graña, Bernadino: **O león e o paxaro rebelde.** (The lion and the rebellious bird; Der Löwe und der aufrührerische Vogel.) Ill.: Galician children; galicische Kinder.)
Vigo: Galaxia 1969.

1970 Paradela, Alvaro: **Dous contos.** (Two stories; Zwei Erzählungen.)
La Coruña: Alvaro Paradela 1971.

1971 Agrelo Hermo, Xosé: **O espanta-paxaros.** (The scarecrow; Die Vogelscheuche.) Ill.: Galician children; galicische Kinder.
Vigo: Galaxia 1972.

1972 López-Casanova, Arcadio: **O bosque de Ouriol.** (*Ouriol's* forest; *Ouriols* Wald.) Ill.: Galician children; Galicische Kinder.
(Unpublished; Unveröffentlicht.)

1973 Martín, Paco: **Sabeliña e os ratos.** (*Sabeliña* and the mice; *Sabeliña* und die Mäuse.)
(Unpublished; Unveröffentlicht.)

1974 Barbarro González, Xoán: **Zoca zoqueira.** (*Zoca zoqueira* = play on words; *Zoca zoqueira = Wortspiel.)*
(Unpublished; Unveröffentlicht.)

1975 Moreno Márquez, María Victoria: **O cataventos.** (The weather vane; Der Wetterhahn.)
(Unpublished; Unveröffentlicht.)

1976 Vázquez, Dora: **Cascabel, o cabaliño do circo.** (**Cascabel** the little circus pony; *Cascabel,* das kleine Zirkuspferd.)
(Unpublished; Unveröffentlicht.)

1977 Fernández Martínez, Ana María: **Os amigos do cabaleiro.** (The gentleman's friends; Die Freunde des Herren.)
(Unpublished; Unveröffentlicht.)

1978 Guisán Seixas, Xoán: **Pallaso parado.** (The stopped clown; Der verhinderte Clown.)
(Unpublished; Unveröffentlicht.)

Premio Joaquim Ruyra

This prize for youth literature was created in homage to the Catalan author, Joaquim Ruyra (1858—1939), and is awarded annually to an unpublished manuscript. Between 1970 and 1975, the jury did not convene to award the prize; but in 1976 the prize was reactivated once again due to the support of the Congress of Catalan Culture.

Dieser Preis für Jugendliteratur wurde zu Ehren des katalanischen Autors Joaquim Ruyra (1858—1939) gestiftet und wird jährlich für ein unveröffentlichtes Manuskript verliehen. 1970—1975 trat die Jury nicht zusammen, aber 1976 wurde der Preis mit Unterstützung des Kongresses der katalanischen Kultur wieder vergeben.

1963 Vallverdù, Josep: **Trampa sota les aigües.** (Trap under the water; Falle unter dem Wasser.)
Barcelona: Estela 1965.

1964 Macia, Carles: **Un paracaigudes sobre Vall-Ferrera.** (A parachute over *Vall-Ferrera;* Ein Fallschirmjäger über *Vall-Ferrera.)*
Barcelona: Estela 1965.

1965 The prize was not given; Der Preis wurde nicht vergeben.

1966 *Saladrigas Riera, Robert:* **Entre Juliol i Setembre.** (Between July and September; Zwischen Juli und September.)
Barcelona: Estela 1967.

1967 Teixidor, Emili: **Les rates malaltes.** (The sick mice; Die kranken Mäuse.)
Barcelona: Estela 1968.

1968 The prize was not given; Der Preis wurde nicht vergeben.

1969 The prize was not given; Der Preis wurde nicht vergeben.

1970/1975 The jury did not convene; Die Jury trat nicht zusammen.

1976 Albanell, Pep: **El Barcelonauta.** (The Barcelonian; Der Barcelonese.)
Barcelona: Laia 1977.

1977 Cabré, Jaume: **Galcerán, l'heroi de la guerra negra.** (*Galcerán,* the hero of the black war; *Galcerán,* der Held des schwarzen Krieges.)
Barcelona: Laia 1978.

1978 Vergés, Oriol: **El superfenomen.** (The superphenomenon; Das Superphänomen.)
(Unpublished; Unveröffentlicht.)

1979 The prize was not given; Der Preis wurde nicht vergeben.

1980 Vilatoro, Vicens: **Papers robats que cremen.** (Stolen papers that burn; Gestohlene Papiere, die brennen.
(Unpublished; Unveröffentlicht.)

Sweden/Schweden

Elsa Beskow-Plaketten

The Elsa Beskow Award, named after the Swedish illustrator of picture books, Elsa Beskow, neé Maartman (1874—1953), was established in 1958 by the Swedish Library Association. Presentations take place during the annual convention of the Association. The illustrator of the best Swedish picture book published during the previous year receives the award. Also eligible are the collected works of an illustrator or a photographer. The committee that selects the Nils Holgersson prize also selects the recipient of the Elsa Beskow Award.

Die Elsa Beskow Plakette, ist nach der schwedischen Bilderbuchillustratorin Elsa Beskow, geb. Maartman (1874—1953) benannt. Er wurde 1958 vom schwedischen Bibliotheksverband gestiftet und wird jährlich auf seiner Jahrestagung verliehen. Die Auszeichnung erhält der Illustrator des besten, im Vorjahr erschienenen schwedischen Bilderbuches. Es kann auch das Gesamtwerk eines Illustrators oder Photographen prämiert werden. Das Komitee, das die Nils Holgersson Plakette vergibt, verleiht auch diesen Preis.

Ill. 40 Harald Wiberg in H. Peterson: Den stora snöstormen

1958 Jansson, Tove in:
Jansson, Tove: **Trollvinter.** (Troll winter; Trollwinter.)
Stockholm: Geber 1957.

1959 Lamm, Martin in:
Tetzner, Lisa: **All världens vackra sagor.** Bd 4. (The most beautiful fairy tales of the world. Vol.4.; Die schönsten Märchen der Welt. Bd 4.)
Stockholm: Bonnier 1958.

1960 Löfgren, Ulf in:
Krantz, Leif: **Barnen i djungeln.** (The children in the jungle; Die Kinder im Dschungel.)
Stockholm: Rabén & Sjögren 1959.

1961 Billow, Eva in:
Billow, Eva: **Filippa Hallondoft och andra pysslingar och smysslingar och älvor och knytt, som bor litet varstans i skog och mark.** (*Filippa Hallondoft* and other elves and brownies that live in the woods; *Filippa Hallondoft* und andere Elfen und Kobolde, die in den Wäldern leben.)
Stockholm: Nordisk Rotogravyr 1960.

1962 The prize was not given; Der Preis wurde nicht vergeben.

1963 Riwkin-Brick, Anna: **Samlad produktion som barnboks illustratör.** (Collected works as childrens book illustrator; Gesamtschaffen als Kinderbuchillustratorin.)

1964 Hald, Fibben (i.e. Niels Christian Hald) in:
Hellsing, Lennart: **Katten blaste i silverhorn.** (The cat blew the silver horn; Die Katze blies in das Silberhorn.)
Stockholm: Rabén & Sjögren 1963.

1965 Södersten, Stig: **Samlad produktion som barnboks illustratör.** (Collected works as children's book illustrator; Gesamtschaffen als Kinderbuchillustrator.)

1966 Sandberg, Lasse in:
Sandberg, Inger: **Lilla spöket Laban.** (*Laban*, the little ghost; *Laban*, der kleine Geist.)
Stockholm: Almqvist & Wiksell, Geber 1965.

1967 Ströyer, Poul: **Samlad produktion som barnboks illustratör.** (Collected works as children's book illustrator; Gesamtschaffen als Kinderbuchillustrator.)

1968 Palmquist, Eric: **Samlad produktion som barnboks illustratör.** (Collected works as children's book illustrator; Gesamtschaffen als Kinderbuchillustrator.)

1969 Wikland, Ilon: **Samlad produktion som barnboks illustratör.** (Collected works as children's book illustrator; Gesamtschaffen als Kinderbuchillustratorin.)

1970 Borg, Inga: **Samlad produktion som barnboks illustratör.** (Collected works as children's book illustrator; Gesamtschaffen als Kinderbuchillustratorin.)

1971 Berg, Björn: **Samlad produktion som barnboks illustratör.** (Collected works as children's book illustrator; Gesamtschaffen als Kinderbuchillustrator.)

1972 Gripe, Harald: **För hans illustrationer i Maria Gripes böcker.** (For his illustrations in Maria Gripe's books; Für seine Illustrationen in Maria Gripes Büchern.)

1973 Beckman, Kaj: **Samlade verk.** (Collected works; Gesamtschaffen.)

1974 Hemmel, Sven: **Samlade verk.** (Collected works; Gesamtschaffen.)

1975 Andersson, Mats: **Samlade verk.** (Collected works; Gesamtschaffen.)

1976 Wiberg, Harald in:
Peterson, Hans: **Den stora snöstormen.** (The big snowstorm; Der große Schneesturm.)
Stockholm: Rabén & Sjögren 1975.

1977 Lööf, Jan in:
Lööf, Jan: **Skrot-Nisse.** (*Skrot-Nisse.*)
Stockholm: Carlsen if 1976.

1978 The Information was not obtained; Wir erhielten keine Informationen.

1979 The information was not obtained; Wir erhielten keine Informationen.

1980 Nygren, Tord: **complete works;** Gesamtschaffen.

1981 Eriksson, Eva in:
Lindgren, Barbro: **Mama och den vilda bebin.** (Mama and the wild baby; Mama und das wilde Baby.)
Stockholm: Rabén & Sjögren 1980.

Expressens Heffaklump

Expressens Heffaklump was established in 1966 by the Stockholm evening newspaper, Expressen, and is named after the Heffalump in Alan Alexander Milne's "Winnie-the-Pooh". The award, a sculpture by the Swedish artist, K.G. Bejemark, is given annually to the author of the best Swedish children's book. On the jury are representatives from the newspaper itself, a children's librarian and an author.

Expressens Heffaklump wurde 1966 von der Stockholmer Abendzeitung "Expressen" gestiftet und ist nach dem Heffaklump in Alan Alexander Milnes "Winnie the Pooh" (Pooh der Bär) benannt. Der Preis, eine Skulptur des schwedischen Künstlers K.G. Bejemark, wird alljährlich an den Autor des besten schwedischen Kinderbuches verliehen. Die Jury besteht aus einem Vertreter der Zeitung, einem Jugendbibliothekar und einem Autor.

1966 *Gripe, Maria:* **Hugo.** (*Hugo.*) Ill.: Harald Gripe.
Stockholm: Bonnier 1966.

1967 Lundgren, Max: **Pojken med guldbyxorna.** (The boy with the golden trousers; Der Junge mit den Goldhosen.)
Stockholm: Bonnier 1967.

1968 Kullman, Harry: **De rödas uppror.** (The Red's revolt; Aufruhr in Stockholm.)
Stockholm: Bonnier 1968.

1969 Sandberg, Inger/Sandberg, Lasse: **Pappa kom ut!** (Come out, daddy; Vati komm doch.)
Stockholm: Rabén & Sjögren 1969.

1970 Jansson, Tove: **Sent i november.** (Moominvalley in November; Spät im November.) Ill.: Tove Jansson.
Stockholm: Geber 1970.

Lindgren, Astrid: **Än lever Emil i Lönneberga.** (Emil and his clever pig; Michel bringt die Welt in Ordnung.) Ill.: Björn Berg.
Stockholm: Rabén & Sjögren 1970.

1971 Lindgren, Barbro: **Jättehemligt.** (Top secret; Streng geheim.) Ill.: Olof Landström.
Stockholm: Rabén & Sjögren 1971.

1972 Reuterswärd, Maud: **Han-där.** (He — there; Er — dort!)
Stockholm: Bonnier 1972.

1973 The prize was not given; Der Preis wurde nicht vergeben.

1974 Lööf, Jan: **Sagan om det röda äpplet.** (The story of the red apple; Die Geschichte von dem roten Apfel.) Ill.: Jan Lööf.
Stockholm: Carlsen if 1974.

1975 Mattson, Olle: **Talejten väntar i väst.** (*Talejten* waits in the west; *Talejten* wartet im Westen.)
Stockholm: Bonnier 1975.

1976 Holmqvist, Stig/Talle, Aud: **Barn i Belfast.** (Children in *Belfast*; Kinder in *Belfast*.)
Stockholm: Liber Förlag 1976.

1977 Gelotte, Ann-Madeleine: **Ida Maria från Arfliden.** (*Ida Maria* of *Arfliden*; *Ida Maria* von *Arfliden.*) Ill.: Ann-Madeleine Gelotte.
Stockholm: Tiden 1977.

Nils Holgersson-Plaketten

The Nils Holgersson Plaque was established by the Swedish Library Association and has been offered since 1950. Presentations take place during the annual convention of the Association. The author of the best Swedish children's book published during the previous year receives the award. The collected works of an author are also eligible for the competition. The prize is announced by a committee, appointed for three years by the representative assembly of the Swedish Library Association. It is made up of two delegates each from the division of public library service and school library service, and one delegate from the division of library service for children and young adults. The latter acts as chairman. The plaque is named in honour of Selma Lagerlöf's famous character in "The wonderful adventures of Nils", first published in 1907.

Die Nils Holgersson-Plakette wurde 1950 vom Schwedischen Bibliotheksverband gestiftet; die Verleihung erfolgt jährlich auf der Jahrestagung des Verbandes. Die Plakette wird dem Autor des besten im Vorjahr erschienenen schwedischen Kinderbuches verliehen. Es kann auch das Gesamtwerk eines Autors prämiert werden. Der Preis wird von einem Komitee vergeben, das für jeweils drei Jahre von der Delegiertenversammlung des schwedischen Bibliotheksverbandes gewählt wird. Das Komitee besteht aus jeweils zwei Vertretern des Öffentlichen Bibliothekswesens und des Schulbibliothekswesen und einem Delegierten der Abteilung Bibliotheksdienst für Kinder und junge Erwachsene, der gleichzeitig als Vorsitzender fungiert. Die Plakette wurde nach der berühmten Hauptperson von Selma Lagerlöfs Roman "Wunderbare Reise des kleinen Nils Holgersson mit den Wildgänsen" (erschienen 1907) benannt.

1950 Lindgren, Astgrid: **Nils Karlsson-Pyssling.** (*Nils Karlsson-Pyssling.*) Ill.: Eva Billow.
Stockholm: Rabén & Sjögren 1949.

1951 Hellsing, Lennart: **Summa summarum. Ramsor.** (Summa summarum. Rhymes; Summa summarum. Reime.) Music: Knut Brodin. Ill.: Poul Strøyer.
Stockholm: Rabén & Sjögren 1950.

1952 Bergman, Sten: **Vildar och paradisfåglar.** Ungdomsupplaga. (Wild animals and birds of paradise. Youth edition; Wilde- und Paradiesvögel. Jugendausgabe.)
Stockholm: Bonnier 1951.

Beskow, Elsa: **Samlade verk.** (Collected works; Gesamtschaffen.)

1953 Jannson, Tove: **Hur gick det sen? Boken om Mymlan, Mumintrollet och lilla My.** (What happened then? *Mymlan, Mumintrollet* and litte *My*; Und was passierte dann? Das Buch über *Mymlan, Mumintrollet* und *Klein-My*.)
Stockholm: Geber 1952.

1954 The prize was not given; Der Preis wurde nicht vergeben.

1955 Kullman, Harry: **Hemlig resa.** (The secret journey; Heimliche Reise.) Ill.: Claes Bäckström.
Stockholm: Rabén & Sjögren 1953.

1956 Mattson, Olle: **Briggen Tre Lijor.** (The brig, "*Three Lilies*"; *Die Brigg "Drei Lilien"*.)
Stockholm: Bonnier 1955.

1957 Unnerstad, Edith: **Farmorsresan.** (The journey to father's mother; Die Reise zu Vaters Mutter.) Ill.: Iben Clante.
Stockholm: Rabén & Sjögren 1956.

1958 Peterson, Hans: **Magnus, Mattias och Mari.** (*Magnus, Matthew* and *Mari; Magnus, Matthias* und *Mari*.) Ill.: Ilon Wikland.
Stockholm: Rabén & Sjögren 1957.

1959 Oterdahl, Jeanna: **Samlade verk.** (Collected works; Gesamtschaffen.)

Claque (i.e. Anna Lisa Wärnlöf): **Pellas bok.** (*Pella's* book; *Pellas* Buch.)
Stockholm: Svensk Läraretidnings förlag 1958.

1960 Söderhjelm, Kai: **Mikko i kungens tjänst. En berättelse från det tjugofemåriga krigets tid, 1570—1595.** (*Mikko* in the king's service. A story from the time of the 25 year's War 1570—1595; *Mikko* im Dienst des Königs. Eine Erzählung aus der Zeit des 25-jährigen Krieges, 1570—1595.)
Stockholm: Rabén & Sjögren 1959.

1961 Holmberg, Åke: **Ture Sventon, privatdetektiv.** (*Ture Sventon*, private detective; *Ture Sventon*, Privatdetektiv.) Ill.: Sven Hemmel.
Stockholm: Rabén & Sjögren 1960.

1962 Hallqvist, Britt Gerda: **Festen i Hulabo.** (The party in *Hulabo*; Das Fest in *Hulabo*.) Ill.: Helga Henschen.
Lund: Gleerup 1961.

1963 Gripe, Maria: **Hugo och Josefin.** (*Hugo* and *Josephine*.) Ill.: Harald Gripe.
Stockholm: Bonnier 1962.

1964 Anckarsvärd, Karin: **Doktorns pojk'.** (Doctor's son; Der Sohn des Doktors.)
Stockholm: Bonnier 1963.

1965 Linde, Gunnel: **Den vita stenen.** (The white stone; Der weiße Stein.) Ill.: Eric Palmquist.
Stockholm: Bonnier 1964.

1966 The prize was not given; Der Preis wurde nicht vergeben.

1967 Brattström, Inger: **Samlad produktion som ungdomsboks författare.** (Collected output of youth books; Gesamtschaffen als Jugendbuchverfasserin.)

1968 Lundgren, Max: **Pojken med guldbyxorna.** (The boy with the golden trousers; Der Junge mit den Goldhosen.)
Stockholm: Bonnier 1976.

1969 Carpelan, Bo: **Bågen.** (Bow Island; Bogeninsel.)
Stockholm: Bonnier 1968.

1970 Ericson, Stig: **Akta er för rödskinn.** (Look out for red-skins; Achtung Rothäute.) Ill.: Nils Stödberg.
Stockholm: Bonnier 1969.

Ericson, Stig: **Dan Henrys flykt.** (*Dan Henry's* flight; *Dan Henrys* Flucht.)
Stockholm: Bonnier 1969.

1971 Hellberg, Hans-Eric: **Samlade verk.** (Collected works; Gesamtschaffen.)

1972 Sandman-Lilius, Irmelin: **Gullkrona gränd.** (Gullkrona Street; Gullkrona Straße.) Ill.: Irmelin Sandman-Lilius.
Stockholm: Bonnier 1969.

Sandman-Lilius, Irmelin: **Gripanderska gården.** (*Gripander's* manor; *Gripanders* Gutshof.) Ill.: Irmelin Sandman-Lilius.
Stockholm: Bonnier 1970.

Sandman-Lilius, Irmelin: **Gångande Grå.** (*Going Gray*; *Gehendes Grau.*) Irmelin Sandman-Lilius.
Stockholm: Bonnier 1971.

1973 Sandberg, Inger: **Samlade verk.** (Collected works; Gesamtschaffen.)

1974 Wernström, Sven: **Trälarna.** (*Trälarna.*)
Stockholm: Gidlund 1973.

1975 Beckman, Gunnel: Samlade verk. (Collected works; Gesamtschaffen.)

1976 Reuterswärd, Maud: **För hennes samlade verk för barn.** (Collected works for children; Gesamtschaffen für Kinder.)

1977 Lindgren, Barbro: **Lilla Sparvel.** (Little *Sparvel*; Kleine *Sparvel.*) Ill.: Andreas Lindgren and Mathias Lindgren. Stockholm: Rabén & Sjögren 1976.

1978 Widerberg, Siv: **Samlade verk.** (Collected works; Gesamtschaffen.)

1979 The information was not obtained; Wir erhielten keine Informationen.

1980 Lagercrantz, Rose: **Samlade verk.** (collected works; Gesamtschaffen.

1981 Linderholm, Helmer: **for his books about "Amisko"**; für seine Bücher über "Amisko".

Astrid Lindgren-Priset

To honour Astrid Lindgren on her 60th birthday in 1967, her Swedish publisher, Rabén & Sjögren, established an annual prize to be awarded to a Swedish author for a substantial and lasting contribution to literature for children. The prize (at present 12,500 SwCr) is announced by a committee made up of Astrid Lindgren, a representative from Rabén & Sjögren, a children's librarian and a critic of children's books.

Zu Ehren von Astrid Lindgren stiftete ihr schwedischer Verleger Rabén & Sjögren anläßlich ihres 60. Geburtstages einen Preis, der jährlich an einen schwedischen Autor verliehen wird, der einen wesentlichen und dauerhaften Beitrag zur Kinderliteratur geleistet hat. Der Preis, zur Zeit 12.500 Schwedenkronen, wird von einer Jury vergeben, die aus Astrid Lindgren, einem Vertreter des Verlages Rabén & Sjögren, einem Jugendbibliothekar und einem Kritiker der Jugendliteratur besteht.

1967 Åke Homberg

1968 Ann Mari Falk

1969 Harry Kullman

1970 Lennart Hellsing

1971 Hans Peterson

1972 Maria Gripe

1973 Barbro Lindgren

1974 Inger Sandberg and Lasse Sandberg

1975 Hans-Eric Hellberg

1976 Irmelin Sandman-Lilius

1977 Kerstin Thorvall

Switzerland/Schweiz

Jugendbuchpreis des Schweizerischen Lehrervereins und des Schweizerischen Lehrerinnenvereins

Upon the suggestion of Hans Cornioley (1896—1977), member and later president of the Swiss Committee on Children's Books, the Board of the Swiss Teacher's Association was invited on June 20, 1942 to establish a prize for children's books in order to promote Swiss juvenile literature. The suggestion was officially recognized by the delegates' convention. Since then, the two Swiss teachers' associations (Schweizerischer Lehrer- und Schweizerischer Lehrerinnenverein) jointly offer the sum of 1000 Swiss france each year for the prize. Either one particular book or the collected works of an author in the field of juvenile literature are selected. Author and publisher of the prize-winning book must be Swiss. Following this ruling, the Association has since the inception of the award recognized single titles or called attention to the collected works of a children's book author.

Auf Antrag ihres Mitgliedes und späteren Präsidenten Hans Cornioley (1896—1977) lud die Schweizerische Jugendschriftenkommission am 20.6.1942 den Zentralvorstand des Schweizerischen Lehrervereins ein, einen Preis für Jugendschriften auszusetzen, mit der einheimische Jugendliteratur gefördert werden sollte. Die Delegiertenversammlung erhob den Antrag zum Beschluss. Der Schweizerische Lehrerverein und der Schweizerische Lehrerinnenverein stellen seitdem alljährlich gemeinsam eine Summe von 1000 Franken zur Verfügung. Durch diesen Preis wird ein Jugendbuch ausgezeichnet. Die für den Jugendbuchpreis in Betracht kommenden Bücher müssen nach Verfasser und Verlag schweizerisch sein. Nach diesem Reglement wird jedes Jahr ein Buch besonders ausgezeichnet oder auf das Werk eines Jugendschriftstellers hingewiesen.

1943 Büchli, Arnold: **Sagen aus Graubünden.** Bd. 1—2. (Fables from Graubünden. Vol. 1—2) Ill.: August Meinrad Bächtiger.
Aarau: Sauerländer 1933; 1934.

1944 Reinhart, Josef: **Complete works,** especially for; Gesamtwerk, insbesondere: **Brot der Heimat,** (Bread of the homeland.)
Aarau: Sauerländer 1940.

1945 Meyer, Olga: **Complete works,** especially; Gesamtwerk, insbesondere: **Anneli.** (*Anneli.*) Ill.: Hans Witzig.
Zürich: Rascher 1919.

1946 Müller, Elisabeth: **Complete works**; Gesamtschaffen.
Bern: Francke; Zollikon: Evangelischer Verlag.

1947 Haller, Adolf: **Complete works**; Gesamtschaffen.
Aarau: Sauerländer (et al; u.a.).

Ill. 41 Klaus Brunner in Hans Reutimann: Das Drachenfest

1948 Carigiet, Alois in:
Chönz, Selina; **Schellenursli.** (*Bell Ursli.*)
Zürich: Schweizer Spiegel Verlag 1945.

1949 Vogel, Traugott: **Complete works**; Gesamtschaffen.
Aarau: Sauerländer (et al; u.a.)

1950 *Special honour to youth magazine editors/Ehrengabe an Jugendzeitschriften-Redakteure*

Aebli, Fritz for: **Schweizer Kamerad.** (Swiss comrade.)
Zürich: Pro Juventute.

Frei-Uhler, Reinhold for: **Illustrierte Schweizerische Schülerzeitung.** (Illustrated Swiss school magazine.)
Wabern bei Bern: Büchler.

Reinhart, Josef for: **Jugendborn.** (Youth fountain.)
Aarau: Sauerländer.

1951 *Award for pamphlet series/Prämiierung der Heftreihe*
Schweizerisches Jugendschriftenwerk (SJW). (Swiss youth writings.)
Zürich.

1952 The prize was not given; Der Preis wurde nicht vergeben.

1953 Voegli, Max: **Die wunderbare Lampe.** (The wonderful lamp.)
Ill.: Felix Hoffmann.
Aarau: Sauerländer 1952.

1954 Häusermann, Gertrud: **Heimat am Fluß.** (At home on the river.)
Aarau: Sauerländer 1953.

1955 Kreidolf, Ernst: **Complete works**; Gesamtschaffen.
Zürich: Rotapfel Verlag.

1956 Meyer, Olga: **Heimliche Sehnsucht.** (Secret longing.) Ill.: Maja von Arx.
Aarau: Sauerländer 1955.

1957 Hoffmann, Felix: **Complete works**; Gesamtschaffen.
Aarau: Sauerländer.

1958 Keller, Anna: **Complete works**; Gesamtschaffen.
Aarau: Sauerländer.

1959 Brunner, Fritz: **Complete works**; Gesamtschaffen.
Aarau: Sauerländer.

1960 Halter, Toni: **Culan.** (*Culan.*) Ill.: Alois Carigiet.
Disentis: Desertina Verlag 1959.

1961 Schmitter, Hans: **Benz.** (*Benz.*) Ill.: Heiner Bauer.
Bern: Francke 1960.

1962 Cornioley, Hans: **Complete works**; Gesamtschaffen.
Aarau: Sauerländer.

1963 Gardi, René: **Complete works**; Gesamtschaffen.
Aarau: Sauerländer.

1964 Lauber, Cécile: **Land deiner Mutter.** Bd 1—4. (Land of your mother. Vol. 1—4.)
Zürich: Atlantis Verlag 1946—1957.

1965 Wartenweiler, Fritz: **Complete works**; Gesamtschaffen.
Zürich: Rotapfel Verlag (et al; u.a.).

1966 Carigiet, Alois: **Zottel, Zick und Zwerg**. (*Zottel, Zick* and *Zwerg*.)
Zürich: Schweizer Spiegel Verlag 1965.

1967 Haller, Adolf: **Der Mann unseres Jahrhunderts.** Das Leben Winston Churchills. (The man of our century. The life of *Winston Churchill*.)
Aarau: Sauerländer 1966.

1968 Kappeler, Ernst: **Complete works**; Gesamtschaffen.
Solothurn: Schweizer Jugend Verlag (et al; u.a.).

1969 Witzig, Hans: **Complete works**; Gesamtschaffen.
Erlenbach, Zürich: Rentsch (et al; u.a.).

1970 Keller, Therese: **Complete works for the puppet theatre**; Für ihr Gesamtwerk für das Puppentheater.

1971 The prize was not given; Der Preis wurde nicht vergeben.

1972 Keller, Agathe: **Happy End mit Skarabäus**. (Happy end with *Skarabäus*.)
Aarau: Sauerländer 1971.

Reutimann, Hans: **Das Drachenfest**. (The dragon's feast.) Ill.: Klaus Brunner.
Dietikon-Zürich: Stocker-Schmid 1970.

1973 Bolliger, Max: **Complete works**; Gesamtschaffen.
Zürich: Artemis (et al; u.a.).

1974 Nussbaumer, Paul: **Children's book illustrations**; für seine Kinderbuch-Illustrationen.
Zürich: Atlantis (et al; u.a.).

Schaad, Hans-Peter: **Children's book illustrations**; Für seine Kinderbuch-Illustrationen.
Zürich: Diogenes (et al; u.a.).

1975 Heizmann, Gertrud: **Complete works**; Gesamtschaffen.
Bern: Francke Verlage (et al; u.a.).

1976 The prize was not given; Der Preis wurde nicht vergeben.

1977 Müller, Jörg: **Children's book illustriations**; für seine Kinderbuch-Illustrationen.
Aarau: Sauerländer Verlag (et al; u.a.).

1978 Hasler, Eveline: **Complete works**; Gesamtschaffen.

1979 Kätterer, Lisbeth: **Complete works**; Gesamtschaffen.

1980 Steiger, Otto: **Complete works**; Gesamtschaffen.

1981 Wyss, Hedi: **Welt hinter Glas**. (World behind glass.)
Zürich, Köln: Benzinger 1979.

Zürcher Kinderbuchpreis

This prize was initiated in 1977 by the Kinderbuchladen (Children's Book Shop) of Zürich. It is given to a children's book one year and to a youth book the next. The jury consists of eleven members. The award is limited to a book by a German-speaking author that has been published in the autumn of the preceding year or spring of the current year. In addition to the prize-winning book, a list of six runners-up titles is published.

The prize consists of a wooden statue executed by Antonio Vitali, showing a Swiss cow, „La vache qui lit" (the cow that reads) and a cash-award of SF 2000, which is provided by the Zürich newspaper, „Tages-Anzeiger".

Dieser Preis wurde 1977 vom Kinderbuchladen Zürich angeregt. Er wird - jährlich wechselnd zwischen Kinder- und Jugendbuch - von einer elfköpfigen Jury nach einem Punktsystem vergeben. Ausgezeichnet werden können Bücher deutschsprachiger Autoren aus der Frühjahrsproduktion des laufenden und der Herbstproduktion des vergangenen Jahres. Zusätzlich zum Preisträger wird eine 6 Titel umfassende Auswahlliste ermittelt.

Der Preis besteht aus einer von Antonio Vitali geschnitzten Schweizer Kuh - „La vache qui lit" (Wanderpreis) und einer vom Tages-Anzeiger gestifteten Geldprämie von 2000.- SF.

1977 Kirsch, Hans-Christian: **Lorcan zieht in den Krieg**. (*Lorcan* goes to war.)
Baden-Baden: Signal Verlag 1977.

1978 Brechbühl, Beat: **Schnüff, Herr Knopf und andere Freunde**. (*Schnüff*, Mr. *Knopf* and other friends.)
Zürich, Köln: Benziger 1977.

1979 Korschunow, Irina: **Er heißt Jan**. (He's called *Jan*.)
Zürich, Köln: Benziger 1979.

1980 Härtling, Peter: **Ben liebt Anna**. (*Ben* loves *Anna*.)
Weinheim: Beltz & Gelberg 1979.

Härtling, Peter: **Sofie macht Geschichten**. (*Sofie* makes stories.)
Weinheim: Beltz & Gelberg 1980.

United States of America/ Vereinigte Staaten von Amerika

Jane Addams Book Award

This award, initiated in 1953, is given by the Women's International League for Peace and Freedom and the Jane Addams Peace Association. A certificate is offered annually to the childrens book of the year that best combines literary merit and themes of brotherhood.

Dieser Preis, der 1953 ins Leben gerufen wurde, wird von der Internationalen Frauenliga für Frieden und Freiheit (Women's International League for Peace and Freedom) und der Jane Addams Friedensorganisation (Jane Addams Peace Association) vergeben. Jährlich wird dem besten Buch eine Urkunde verliehen,

Ill. 42 Paul Goble in: The girl who loved wild horses

daß das Thema der zwischenmenschlichen Verständigung literarisch beispielhaft schildert.

1953 Evans, Eva Knox: **People are important**. (Menschen sind wichtig.) Ill.: Vana Earle.
Irvington-on-Hudson, New York: Capitol 1951.

1954 Ketchum, Jean: **Stick-in-the-mud**. A tale of a village, a custom and a little boy. (Der Faulenzer. Eine Geschichte eines Dorfes, ein Brauch und ein kleiner Junge.) Ill.: Fred Ketchum.
Glenview, Illinois: Scott 1953.

1955 Yates, Elizabeth: **Rainbow round the world.** A story of UNICEF. (Der Regenbogen rund um die Welt. Eine Geschichte von UNICEF.) Ill.: Betty Alden.
Indianapolis: Bobbs-Merrill 1954.

1956 Bontemps, Arna Wendell: **Story of the Negro**. (Die Geschichte der Neger.) Ill.: Raymond Lufkin.
New York: Knopf 1955.

1957 Benary-Isbert, Margot: **Blue mystery**. (Blaues Geheimnis.) Ill.: Enrico Arno.
New York: Harcourt Brace 1958.

1958 Steele, William Owen: **The perilous road**. (Die gefährliche Straße.) Ill.: Paul Galdone.
New York: Harcourt, Brace 1958.

1959 The prize was not given; Der Preis wurde nicht vergeben.

1960 Meyer, Edith Patterson: **Champions of peace. Winners of the Nobel Peace Prize**. (Menschen des Friedens. Die Preisträger des Nobelpreises.) Ill.: Eric von Schmidt.
Boston: Little, Brown 1959.

1961 Arora, Shirley Lease: **What then, Raman**? (Was dann, *Raman*?) Ill.: Hans Guggengeim.
Chicago: Follett 1960.

1962 Sommerfelt, Aimée: **The road to Agra**. (Der Weg nach *Agra*.) Ill.: Ulf Aas.
New York: Criterion 1961.

1963 Johnson, Walter Ryerson: **The monkey and the wild, wild wind.** (Der Affe und der wilde, wilde Wind.) Ill.: Lois Lignell.
London, New York: Abelard-Schuman 1961.

1964 Kennedy, John Fitzgerald: **Profiles in courage**. (Mutige Männer.) Ill.: Emil Weiss.
New York: Harper & Row 1964.

1965 Bradley, Duane: **Meeting with a stranger**. (Die Zusammenkunft mit einem Fremden.) Ill.: E. Harper Johnson.
Philadelphia: Lippencott 1964.

1966 Neville, Emily Cheney: **Berries Goodman**. (*Berries Goodman*.)
New York: Harper & Row 1965.

1967 Burch, Robert: **Queenie Peavy**. (*Queenie Peavy*.) Ill.: Jerry Lazare.
New York: Viking Press 1966.

1968 Haugaard, Eric Christian: **The little fishes**. (Die kleinen Fische.) Ill.: Milton Johnson.
Boston: Houghton mifflin 1967.

1969 Hautzig, Esther: **The endless steppe. Growing up in Siberia**. (Die endlose Steppe. Eine Kindheit in Sibirien.)
New York: Crowell 1968.

1970 Taylor, Theodore: **The cay**. (Die Sandbank.)
New York: Doubleday 1969.

1971 Meigs, Cornelia Lynde: **Jane Addams. Pioneer for social justice. A biography**. (*Jane Addams*. Vorläufer für die soziale Gerechtigkeit. Eine Biographie.)
Boston: Little, Brown, 1970.

1972 Underwood, Betty: **The tamarack tree**. (Die Lärche.) Ill.: Bea Holmes.
Boston: Houghton Mifflin 1971.

1973 Hirsch, S. Carl: **The riddle of racism**. (Das Rätsel des Rassismus.)
New York: Viking Press 1972.

1974 Mohr, Nicholasa: **Nilda**. (*Nilda*.) Ill.: Nicholasa Mohr.
New York: Harper & Row 1973.

1975 Pomerantz, Charlotte: **The princess and the admiral**. (Die Prinzessin und der Admiral.)
Reading, Massachusetts: Addison-Wesley 1974.

1976 Greenfield, Eloise: **Paul Robeson**. (*Paul Robeson*.) Ill.: George Ford.
New York: Crowell 1975.

1977 Meltzer, Milton: **Never to forget. The Jews of the holocaust**. (Sie dürfen nie vergessen werden. Die Juden als Opfer der Massentötung.)
New York: Harper & Row 1976.

1978 Yep, Laurence: **Child of the owl**. (Das Kind der Eule.)
New York: Harper & Row 1977.

1979 Highwater, Jamake: **Many smokes, many moons**. (Viel Rauch, viele Monde.)
New York: Lippincott 1978.

1980 Kherdian, David: **The road from home. The story of an Armenian girl.** (Die Straße nach Hause. Die Geschichte eines armenischen Mädchens.)
New York: Greenwillow 1979.

The Aurianne Award

The Aurianne Award — a modest cash-prize and a certificate designed by Valenti Angelo — had been presented annually since 1958 to the author of the best book about animals (for children eight to fourteen years of age). Both fiction and non-fiction were eligible for the prize. The winning book had to help instill in children a humane attitude toward animals. The prize was made possible through the bequest of Augustine Aurianne, a school librarian in New Orleans who died in 1947. The legacy was to honor the memory of her father, Pierre and that of her sister, Adelle. It was administered by the American Library Association. The jury was made up of school librarians who were members of the ALA. In 1966, funds for the prize were depleted and consequently, it was cancelled.

Der Aurianne-Preis, der aus einer kleinen Geldprämie und einem von Valenti Angelo entworfenen Diplom bestand, wurde seit 1958 jährlich dem Autor des besten Tierbuches für Kinder zugesprochen (von 8—14 Jahren, gleich ob Erzählung oder Sachbuch), das eine humane Haltung zu entwickeln verstand. Der Preis war durch Stiftung von Augustine Aurianne ermöglicht worden, einer Schulbibliothekarin in New Orleans, die 1947 starb und mit ihrer Stiftung das Andenken ihres Vater, Pierre Aurianne, und ihrer Schwester, Adele Aurianne, ehren wollte. Die Stiftung wurde von der Amerikanischen Bibliotheksvereinigung (American Library Association) verwaltet, die Jury setzte sich aus Kinderbibliothekaren der American Library Association zusammen. 1966 war die Stiftung erschöpft und der Preis konnte nicht mehr verliehen werden.

1958 George, Jean Craighead/George, John Lothar: **Dipper of Copper Creek.** (Wasserschöpfer am *Copper Creek.*) Ill.: Jean Craighead George.
New York: Dutton 1956.

1959 The prize was not given; Der Preis wurde nicht vergeben.

1960 De Jong, Meindert: **Along came a dog.** (Ein Hund kam vorbei.) Ill.: Maurice Sendak.
New York: Harper 1958.

1961 Smith, Agnes: **An edge of the forest.** (Am Rande des Waldes.) Ill.: Roberta Moynihan.
New York: Viking Press 1969.

1962 Schaefer, Jack: **Old Ramon.** (Alter *Ramon.*) Ill.: Harold West. Boston: Houghton Mifflin 1960.

1963 Burnford, Sheila: **The incredible journey**. (Die unglaubliche Reise.) Ill.: Carl Burger.
Boston, Toronto: Little, Brown 1961.

1964 Liers, Emil Ernest: **A black bear's story**. (Die Geschichte vom schwarzen Bären.) Ill.: Ray Sherin.
New York: Viking Press 1962.

1965 North, Sterling: **Rascal. A memoir of a better era**. (*Rascal*. Erinnerung an eine bessere Zeit.) Ill.: John Schoenherr.
New York: Dutton 1963.

1966 Gage, Wilson: **Big blue island**. (Große blaue Insel.) Ill.: Glen Rounds.
Cleveland: World 1964.

The Mildred L. Batchelder Award

Since 1968, the Mildred L. Batchelder Award is annually presented in honor of Miss Batchelder and her outstanding achievements. She had encouraged and promoted the translation of the world's best children's books. The prize is given to the publisher who presented the English translation of an outstanding foreign children's book twelve months prior to the prize selection. The jury, annually appointed by the president of the American Library Association's Children's Services Division, selects the titles which are considered for the final balloting. This final choice is made by members of the Children's Services Division.

Seit 1968 wird der Mildred L. Batchelder-Preis jährlich zu Ehren jener Frau verliehen, die sich im Sinne internationaler Verständigung für die Übersetzung der besten Kinderbücher aus aller Welt einsetzte. Den Preis erhält derjenige Verleger, der das bedeutendste, ursprünglich in einer fremden Sprache im Ausland erschienenen Kinderbuch in den Vereinigten Staaten in englischer Übersetzung verlegt. Die Übersetzung muß im Jahr vor der Preisverleihung in den USA erschienen sein. Das Preiskomitee, jährlich vom Präsidenten der Kinderbüchereisektion der amerikanischen Bibliotheksvereinigung ernannt (Children's Services Division der American Library Association), schlägt drei bis fünf herausragende Titel zur engeren Wahl vor. Der endgültige Preisbeschluß wird dann von Mitgliedern der Kinderbüchereisektion gefaßt.

1968 Alfred A. Knopf, New York for:
Kästner, Erich: **The little man**. (Germ.orig.title: Der Kleine Mann.) Ill.: Rick Schreiter. Transl.: James Kirkup.
New York: Knopf 1966.

1969 Charles Scribner's Sons, New York, for:
Friis-Baastad, Babbis: **Don't take Teddy**. (Nimm *Teddy* nicht weg; Norw.orig.title: Ikke ta *Bamse*.) Transl.: Lise Søme McKinnon.
New York: Scribner 1967.

1970 Holt, Rinehart & Winston, New York, for:
Zei, Aliki: **Wildcat under glass**. (Wildkatze unter Glas; Gr.orig.title: To kaplani tis vitrinas.) Transl.: Edward Fenton.
New York: Holt, Rinehart & Winston 1968.

1971 Pantheon Books, New York, for:
Baumann, Hans: **In the land of Ur. The discovery of ancient Mesopotamia**. (Germ.orig.title: Im Lande *Ur*. Die Entdeckung Altmesopotamiens.) Transl.: Stella Humphries.
New York: Pantheon 1969.

1972 Holt, Rinehart & Winston, New York, for:
Richter, Hans Peter: **Friedrich**. (Germ.orig.title: Damals war es Friedrich.) Transl: Edite Kroll.
New York: Holt, Rinehart & Winston 1970.

1973 William Morrow & Co., New York, for:
Iterson, Siny Rose van: **Pulga**. (Der Adjutant des Lastwagens; Dutch orig.title: De adjutant van de vrachtwagen.) Transl.: Alexander Gode and Alison Gode.
New York: William Morrow 1971.

1974 E.P. Dutton, New York, for:
Zei, Aliki: **Petro's war**. (*Petros* Krieg; Gr.orig. title: O megalos peripatos tou *Petrou*.) Transl.: Edward Fenton.
New York: E.P. Dutton 1972.

1975 Crown Publishers, New York, for:
Linevskii, Aleksandr Mikhailovitch: **An old tale carved out of stone.** (Ein altes Märchen aus Stein gemeißelt; Russ.orig.title: Listy kammenoj knigi.) Transl: Maria Polushkin.
New York: Crown 1973.

1976 Henry Z. Walck, New York, for:
Hürlimann, Ruth: **The cat and mouse who shared a house**. (Germ.orig.title: Katze und Maus in Gesellschaft.) Transl.: Anthea Bell.
New York: Walck 1974.

1977 Atheneum Publishers, New York, for:
Bødker, Cecil: **The leopard**. (Geisterleopard; Dan.orig.title: Leoparden.) Transl.: Gunnar Poulsen.
New York: Atheneum 1975.

1978 The prize was not given; Der Preis wurde nicht vergeben.

1979 Franklin Watts, New York, for:
Konrad. (Germ.orig.title: *Konrad*.) Transl.: Anthea Bell.
New York: Franklin Watts 1977.

Harcourt Brace Jovanovich, New York, for:
Steiner, Jörg: **Rabbit Island**. (Germ.orig.title: Kanincheninsel.)
Ill.: Jörg Müller. Transl.: Ann Conrad Lammers.
New York: Harcourt Brace Jovanovich 1978.

1980 E.P.Dutton, New York, for:
Zei, Alki: **The sound of the dragon's feet**. (Der Klang der Füße des Drachens; Gr.orig.title: Konda stis Raghes.) Transl.: Edward Fenton.
New York: E.P. Dutton 1979.

1981 Pelgrom, Els: **The winter when time was frozen**. (Der Winter, als die Zeit eingefroren war.)
New York: Morrow 1980.

The Randolph Caldecott Medal

The Randolph Caldecott Medal was established in 1937 upon the suggestion of Frederic G. Melcher; it is named after the children's book illustrator Randolph Caldecott (1846—1886), who started a new era in picturebook making, together with Walter Crane and Kate Greenaway. The medal is designed by René Chambellan and is offered to the best illustrator of a children's book, published the previous year. The book is selected according to rules and regulations of the Newbery Medal. The Caldecott Medal was first presented in 1938.

Der Randolph-Caldecott-Preis wurde 1937 auf Vorschlag von Frederic G. Melcher ins Leben gerufen und nach dem englischen Kinderbuchillustrator Randolph Caldecott (1846—1886) benannt, der zusammen mit Walter Crane und Kate Greenaway eine neue Ära des Bilderbuches schuf. Die Medaille, von René Chambellan entworfen, wird dem besten Illustrator eines Kinderbuches verliehen, das jeweils im Laufe des vergangenen Jahres in den Vereinigten Staaten erschienen ist. Das Buch wird von demselben Komitee und nach denselben Regeln prämiiert wie die mit der Newbery Medaille ausgezeichneten Bücher. Die Caldecott-Medaille wurde erstmalig im Juni 1938 verliehen.

1938 Lathrop, Dorothy Pulis in:
Fish, Helen Dean: **Animals of the Bible. A picture book**. (Tiere der *Bibel*. Ein Bilderbuch.)
New York: Stokes 1937 (now: Philadelphia: Lippincott).

1939 Handforth, Thomas in:
Handforth, Thomas: **Mei Li.** (*Mei Li.*)
New York: Doubleday 1938.

1940 D'Aulaire, Ingri Parin and D'Aulaire, Edgar Parin in:
D'Aulaire, Ingri Parin/D'Aulaire, Edgar Parin: **Abraham Lincoln.** (*Abraham Lincoln.*)
New York: Doubleday 1939.

1941 Lawson, Robert in:
Lawson, Robert: **They were strong and good.** (Sie waren stark und gut.)
New York: Viking Press 1940.

1942 McCloskey, Robert in:
McCloskey, Robert: **Make way for ducklings.** (Straße frei für Enten.)
New York: Viking Press 1941.

1943 Burton, Virginia Lee in:
Burton, Virginia Lee: **The little house.** (Das kleine Haus.)
Boston: Houghton Mifflin 1942.

1944 Slobodkin, Louis in:
Thurber, James: **Many moons.** (Viele Monde.)
New York: Harcourt 1943.

1945 Jones, Elizabeth Orton in:
Field, Rachel: **Prayer for a child.** (Ein Gebet für ein Kind.)
New York: Macmillan 1944.

1946 Petersham, Maud and Petersham, Miska in:
Petersham, Maud/Petersham, Miska: **The rooster crows. A book of American rhymes and jingles.** (Der Erpel schreit. Ein Buch amerikanischer Reime und Melodien.)
New York: Macmillan 1945.

1947 Weisgard, Leonard in:
Macdonald, Golden (i.e. Margaret Wise Brown): **The little island.** (Die kleine Insel.)
New York: Doubleday 1946.

1948 Duvoisin, Roger in:
Tresselt, Alvin: **White snow, bright snow.** (Weißer Schnee, heller Schnee.)
New York: Lothrop, Lee & Shepard 1947.

1949 Hader, Berta and Hader, Elmer in:
Hader, Berta/Hader, Elmer: **The big snow.** (Der große Schnee.)
New York: Macmillan 1948.

1950 Politi, Leo in:
Politi, Leo: **Song of the swallows**. (Lied der Schwalben.)
New York: Scribner 1949.

1951 Milhous, Katherine in:
Milhouse, Katherine: **The egg tree**. (Der Eierbaum.)
New York: Scribner 1950.

1952 Nicolas (i.e. Nicolas Mordvinoff) in:
Will (i.e. William Lipkind): **Finders keepers**. (Der Finder behält es.)
New York: Harcourt, Brace 1951.

1953 Ward, Lynd in:
Ward, Lynd: **The biggest bear**. (Der größte Bär.)
Boston: Houghton Mifflin 1952.

1954 Bemelmans, Ludwig in:
Bemelmans, Ludwig: **Madeline's rescue**. (*Magdalenens* Rettung.)
New York: Viking Press 1953.

1955 Brown, Marcia in:
Perrault, Charles: **Cinderella or The glass slipper**. (*Cinderella* oder der kleine gläserne Schuh.)
New York: Scribner 1954.

1956 Rojankovsky, Feodor in:
Langstaff, John: **Frog went a-courtin'**. (Der Froschwerber.)
New York: Harcourt, Brace 1955.

1957 Simont, Marc in:
Udry, Janice May: **A tree is nice**. (Der Baum ist schön.)
New York: Harper & Row 1956.

1958 McCloskey, Robert in:
McCloskey, Robert: **Time of wonder**. (Zeit der Wunder.)
New York: Viking Press 1957.

1959 Cooney, Barbara in:
Chaucer, Geoffrey: **Chanticleer and the fox**. (*Chanticleer* und der Fuchs.)
New York: Crowell 1958.

1960 Ets, Marie Hall in:
Ets, Marie Hall/Labastida, Aurora: **Nine days to Christmas**. (Neun Tage bis *Weihnachten*.)
New York: Viking Press 1959.

1961 Sidjakov, Nicolas in:
Robbins, Ruth: **Baboushka and the three kings**. (*Baboushka* und die drei Könige.)
Berkeley: Parnassus Press 1960.

1962 Brown, Marcia Joan in:
Brown, Marica Joan: **Once a mouse...** (Es war einmal eine Maus...)
New York: Scribner 1961.

1963 Keats, Ezra Jack in:
Keats, Ezra Jack: **The snowy day**. (Der Schneetag.)
New York: Viking Press 1962.

1964 Sendak, Maurice in:
Sendak, Maurice: **Where the wild things are**. (Wo die wilden Kerle wohnen.)
New York: Harper & Row 1963.

1965 Montresor, Beni in:
Schenk de Regniers, Beatrice: **May I bring a friend?** (Darf ich einen Freund nach Haus bringen?)
New York: Atheneum 1964.

1966 Hogrogian, Nonny in:
Leodhas, Sorche Nic (i.e. G. Alger Leclaire): **Always room for one more**. (Immer Platz für einen mehr.)
New York, Chicago, San Francisco: Holt, Rinehart & Winston 1965.

1967 Ness, Evaline in:
Ness, Evaline: **Sam, Bangs and moonshine**. (*Sam*, *Bangs* und Mondschein.)
New York, Chicago, San Francisco: Holt, Rinehart & Winston 1966.

1968 Emberley, Ed in:
Emberley, Barbara: **Drummer Hoff**. (Trommler *Hoff*.)
Englewood Cliffs, N.J.: Prentice-Hall 1967.

1969 Shulevitz, Uri in:
Ransome, Arthur: **The fool of the world and the flying ship. A Russian tale**. (Der Narr der Welt und das fliegende Schiff. Eine Russische Erzählung.)
New York: Farrar, Straus & Giroux 1968.

1970 Steig, William in:
Steig, William: **Sylvester and the magic pebble**. (Sylvester und der Zauber Kieselstein.)
New York: Windmill Books 1969.

1971 Haley, Gail E. in:
Haley, Gail E.: **A story, a story. An African tale**. (Eine Geschichte, eine Geschichte. Eine afrikanische Erzählung.)
New York: Atheneum 1970.

1972 Hogrogian, Nonny in:
Hogrogian, Nonny: **One fine day.** (Ein schöner Tag.)
New York: Macmillan 1971.

1973 Lent, Blair in:
Mosel, Arlene: **The funny little woman.** (Die komische kleine Frau.)
New York: Dutton 1972.

1974 Zemach, Margot in:
Zemach, Harve: **Duffy and the devil. A Cornish tales.** (*Duffy* und der Teufel. Eine Geschichte aus Cornwall.)
New York: Farrar, Straus & Giroux 1973.

1975 McDermott, Gerald in:
McDermott, Gerald: **Arrow to the sun. A Pueblo Indian tale.** (Pfeil zur Sonne. Eine Pueblo Indianergeschichte.)
New York: Viking Press 1974.

1976 Dillon, Leo/Dillon, Diane in:
Aardema, Verna: **Why mosquitoes buzz in people's ears. A west African tale.** (Warum stechen Moskitos die Ohren der Menschen. Eine westafrikanische Geschichte.)
New York: Dial Press 1975.

1977 Dillon, Leo/Dillon, Diane in:
Musgrove, Margaret: **Ashanti to Zulu. African traditions.** (Von den *Ashantis* zu den *Zulus*. Afrikanische Tradition.)
New York: Dial Press 1976.

1978 Spier, Peter in:
Spier, Peter: **Noah's ark.** (Die Arche *Noah*.)
New York: Doubleday 1977.

1979 Goble, Paul in:
Goble, Paul: **The girl who loved wild horses.** (Das Mädchen, das Wildpferde liebte.)
Scarsdale, New York: Bradbury Press 1978.

1980 Cooney, Barbara in:
Hall, Donald: **Ox-cart man.** (Der Ochsenkarrenmann.)
New York: Viking Press 1979.

1981 Lobel, Arnold in:
Lobel, Arnold: **Fables.** (Fabeln.)
New York: Harper & Row 1980.

1982 Allsburg, Chris van: in:
Allsburg, Chris van: **Jumanji.** (*Jumanji*.)
Boston: Houghton Mifflin 1981.

Golden Kite Award

This award, which was established in 1973 by the Society of Children's Book Writers, is presented annually to a member of the Society whose book „best exhibits excellence in writing and genuinely appeals to the interests and concerns of children." A pewter statuette is given to the award-winning author.

Dieser Preis wurde von der Vereinigung der Kinderbuchschriftsteller im Jahr 1973 gegründet. Er wird jährlich an ein Mitglied der Vereinigung vergeben. Der Inhalt des Buches muß mit den Interessen der Kinder und Jugendlichen übereinstimmen. Der Preisträger erhält einen Pokal.

1973 Greene, Bette: **Summer of my German soldier**. (Der Sommer meines deutschen Soldaten.)
New York: Dial Press 1973.

1974 Yolen, Jane: **The girl who cried flowers**. (Das Mädchen, das Blumen weinte.) Ill.: David Palladini.
New York: Crowell 1974.

1975 Farley, Carol J.: **The garden is doing fine**. (Der Garten blüht.) Ill.: Lynn Sweat.
New York: Atheneum 1975.

1976 Bunting, Eve: **One more flight**. (Noch ein Flug.) Ill.: Diane De Groat.
New York: Frederick Warne 1975.

1977 *Fiction/Roman*
Rabe, Bernice: **The girl who had no name**. (Das Mädchen ohne Namen.)
New York: E.P. Dutton 1977.

Non-fiction/Sachbuch
McClung, Robert: **Peeper, first voice of spring**. (*Peeper*, Erste Stimme des Frühlings.) Ill.: Carol Lerner.
New York: William Morrow 1977.

1978 *Fiction/Roman*
Pevsner, Stella: **And you give me a pain, Elaine**. (Und du verletzt mich, *Elaine*.)
New York: Seabury Press 1978.

Non-fiction/Sachbuch
Naylor, Phyllis Reynolds: **How I came to be a writer**. (Wie ich Schriftsteller wurde.)
New York: Atheneum 1978.

1979 *Fiction/Roman*
Adler, Carole S.: **The magic of the Glits.** (Der Zauber der *Glits.*) Ill.: Ati Forberg.
New York: Macmillan 1979.
Non-fiction/Sachbuch
Madison, Arnold: **Runaway teens: An American tragedy.** (Teenager, die wegrennen. Eine amerikanische Tragödie.)
New York: Elsevier, Nelson 1979.

1980 *Fiction/Roman*
MacLachlan, Patricia: **Arthur, for the very first time.** (*Arthur*, zum allererstenmal.) Ill.: Lloyd Bloom.
New York: Harper & Row 1980.
Non-fiction
Patent, Dorothy Hinshaw: **The lives of spiders.** (Das Leben der Spinnen.)
New York: Holiday 1980.

National Book Awards (Children's Book Category)

In 1969, the National Book Awards included for the first time a prize in the category of children's books. The award, contributed by the Children's Book Council, is administered by the American Publishers Association and its General Publishing Division. It is presented annually to the most distinguished children's book published in the United States during the preceding year. The award consists of a citation and a $1, 000 cash prize.

1969 wurde zum erstenmal vom Nationalen Buchpreis (National Book Award) ein Preis für Kinderbücher vergeben. Der Preis, der vom Children's Book Council gestiftet ist, wird von der amerikanischen Verlegervereinigung verliehen. Der Preis wird jährlich dem besten im laufenden Jahr in USA erschienenem Titel verliehen. Er besteht aus einem Diplom und $ 1,000.

1969 De Jong, Meindert: **Journey from Peppermint Street.** (Die Reise aus der *Pfefferminzstraße.*) Ill.: Emily Arnold McCully.
New York: Harper & Row 1968.

1970 Singer, Isaac Bashevis: **A day of pleasure. Stories of a boy growing up in Warsaw.** (Ein Tag der Freude. Geschichten einer Kindheit in *Warschau.*) Photos: Roman Vishniac.
New York: Farrar, Straus & Giroux 1969.

1971 Alexander, Lloyd: **The marvellous misadventures of Sebastian.** (Das Missgeschick des *Sebastian.*)
New York: E.P. Dutton 1970.

1972 Barthelme, Donald: **The slightly irregular fire engine**. (Die kleinste unregelmäßige Feuerspritze.) Ill.: Donald Barthelme.
New York: Farrar, Straus & Giroux 1971.

1973 LeGuin, Ursula Kroeber: **The farthest shore**. (Das fernste Ufer.) Ill.: Gail Garraty.
New York: Atheneum 1972.

1974 Cameron, Eleanor: **The court of the stone children.** (Der Hof der steinernen Kinder.)
New York: E.P. Dutton 1973.

1975 Hamilton, Virginia: **M.C. Higgins, the great**. (Der große *M.C. Higgins.*)
New York: Macmillan 1974.

1976 Edmonds, Walter Dumaux: **Bert Breen's barn**. (*Bert Breens* Scheune.)
Boston: Little, Brown 1975.

1977 Paterson, Katherine: **The master puppeteer**. (Der Meister der Puppenspieler.) Ill.: Haru Wells.
New York: Crowell 1975.

1978 Kohl, Judith/Kohl, Herbert: **A view from the oak**. (Aussicht von der Eiche.) Ill.: Roger Bayless.
New York: Scribners 1977.

1979 Paterson, Katherine: **The great Gilly Hopkins**. (Die große *Gilly Hopkins.*)
New York: Crowell 1978.

The John Newbery Medal

Since 1922, the John Newbery Medal has been annually presented by the American Library Association to the best American children's and juvenile book. The world's oldest prize for juvenile literature is named after John Newbery (1713—1767), publisher in London and initiator of the English children's book. The selections are based upon suggestions of librarians in the juvenile field; the final choice is made by a special committee. The creation of the first prize for children's literature was the idea of Frederic Gershom Melcher, friend and patron of literature for young people and late president of the publishing firm, Bowker & Co. The bronze medal was designed by René Paul Chambellan and bears the name of the prize-winning author. The presentation of the prize is part of the Annual Convention of the American Library Association.

Seit 1922 wird die John-Newbery-Medaille jährlich von der amerikanischen Bibliotheksvereinigung (American Library Association) an das beste amerikanische Kinder- und Jugendbuch verliehen. Der älteste Kinderbuchpreis der Welt ist nach John Newbery, dem im 18. Jahrhundert in London lebenden Herausgeber und eigentlichen Begründer des englischen Kinderbuches benannt (1713—1767). Die Bücher werden nach den Vorschlägen von Jugendbibliothekaren ausgewählt; die engere Auswahl liegt bei einem besonderen Komitee. Die Idee zu dieser Medaille ist Frederic Gershom Melcher zu danken, dem früheren Direktor des Verlages Bowker & Co. Frederic G. Melcher war ein besonderer Freund und Förderer der Jugendliteratur. Die von René Paul Chambellan entworfene Medaille ist in Bronze gegossen und zeigt den Namen des Preisträgers. Die Überreichung des Preises findet jeweils anläßlich der Jahrestagung der American Library Association statt.

1922 Van Loon, Hendrik Willem: **The story of mankind**. (Die Geschichte der Menschheit.) Ill.: Hendrik Willem van Loon.
New York: Liveright 1921.

1923 Lofting, Hugh: **The voyages of Doctor Dolittle**. (Die Reisen des *Doktor Dolittle*.) Ill.: Hugh Lofting.
New York: Stokes 1922 (now: Philadelphia: Lippincott).

1924 Hawes, Charles Boardman: **The dark frigate**. (Das dunkle Boot.) Ill.: Anton Otto Fischer.
Boston: Little, Brown 1923.

1925 Finger, Charles Joseph: **Tales from Silver Lands**. (Geschichten aus dem Silberland.) Ill.: Paul Honoré.
New York: Doubleday 1924.

1926 Chrisman, Arthur Bowie: **Shen of the sea. A book for children**. (*Shen* vom Meer. Ein Buch für Kinder.) Ill.: Else Hasselriis.
New York: Dutton 1925.

1927 James, Will: **Smoky, the cowhorse**. (*Smoky*, das Kuhpferd.) Ill.: Will James.
New York: Scribner 1926.

1928 Merkji, Dhan Gopal: **Gay-Neck, the story of a pigeon**. (*Gay-Neck*, die Geschichte einer Taube.) Ill.: Boris Artzybasheff.
New York: Dutton 1927.

1929 Kelly, Eric Philbrook: **The trumpeter of Krakow. A tale of the fifteenth century**. (Der Trompeter von *Krakou*. Eine Geschichte aus dem 15. Jahrhundert.) Ill.: Angela Pruszynska.
New York: Macmillan 1928.

1930 Field, Rachel Lyman: **Hitty, her first hundred years.** (*Hitty*, ihre ersten hundert Jahre.) Ill.: Dorothy Pulis Lathrop.
New York: Macmillan 1929.

1931 Coatsworth, Elizabeth Jane: **The cat who went to heaven.** (Die Katze, die in den Himmel ging.) Ill.: Lynd Ward.
New York: Macmillan 1930.

1932 Armer, Laura Adams: **Waterless mountain.** (Trockener Berg.) Ill.: Sidney Armer and Laura Adams Armer.
New York: Longmans, Green 1931.

1933 Lewis, Elizabeth Foreman: **Young Fu of the Upper Yangtze.** (*Young Fu* vom oberen *Yangtze.*) Ill.: Kurt Wiese.
Philadelphia: Winston 1932.

1934 Meigs, Cornelia: **Invincible Louisa.** (Unverwundbare *Luisa.*) Photos.
Boston: Little, Brown 1933.

1935 Shannon, Monica: **Dobry.** (*Dobry.*) Ill.: Atanas Katchamakoff.
New York: Viking Press 1934.

1936 Brink, Carol Ryrie: **Caddie Woodlawn.** (*Caddie Woodlawn.*) Ill.: Kate Seredy.
New York: Macmillan 1935.

1937 Sawyer, Ruth: **Roller skates.** (Rollschuhe.) Ill.: Valenti Angelo.
New York: Viking Press 1936.

1938 Seredy, Kate: **The white stag.** (Der weiße Hirsch.) Ill.: Kate Seredy.
New York: Viking Press 1937.

1939 Enright, Elizabeth: **Thimble summer.** (Fingerhutsommer.) Ill.: Elizabeth Enright.
New York: Farrar & Rinehart 1938.

1940 Daugherty, James Henry: **Daniel Boone.** (*Daniel Boone.*) Ill.: James Henry Daugherty.
New York: Viking Press 1939.

1941 Sperry, Armstrong: **Call it courage.** (Nenn es Mut.) Ill.: Armstrong Sperry.
New York: Macmillan 1940.

1942 Edmonds, Walter Dumaux: **The matchlock gun.** (Das Luntengewehr.) Ill.: Paul Lantz.
New York: Dodd, Mead 1941.

1943 Gray, Elizabeth Janet: **Adam of the road.** (*Adam*, von der Straße.) Ill.: Robert Lawson.
New York: Viking Press 1942.

1944 Forbes, Esther: **Johnny Tremain. A novel for young and old.** (*Johnny Tremain*. Eine Erzählung für jung und alt.) Ill.: Lynd Ward. Boston: Houghton Mifflin 1943.

1945 Lawson, Robert: **Rabbit Hill**. (Kaninchenhügel.) Ill.: Robert Lawson.
New York: Viking Press 1944.

1946 Lenski, Lois: **Strawberry girl**. (Das Erdbeermädchen.) Ill.: Lois Lenski.
Philadelphia: Lippincott 1945.

1947 Bailey, Carolyn Sherwin: **Miss Hickory**. (*Miss Hickory*.) Ill.: Ruth Gannett.
New York: Viking Press 1946.

1948 Du Bois, William Pène: **The twenty-one balloons**. (Die einundzwanzig Ballons.) Ill.: William Pène Du Bois.
New York: Viking Press 1947.

1949 Henry, Marguerite: **King of the wind**. (Der König der Winde.) Ill.: Wesley Dennis.
Chicago: Rand McNally 1948.

1950 De Angeli, Marguerite: **The door in the wall**. (Die Tür in der Wand.) Ill.: Marguerite De Angeli.
New York: Doubleday 1949.

1951 Yates, Elizabeth: **Amos Fortune, free man**. (*Amos Fortune*, ein freier Mensch.) Ill.: Nora Spicer Unwin.
New York: Aladdin 1950.

1952 Estes, Eleanor Ruth: **Ginger Pye**. (*Ginger Pye*.) Ill.: Eleanor Ruth Estes.
New York: Harcourt, Brace 1951.

1953 Clark, Ann Nolan: **Secret of the Andes**. (Das Geheimnis der *Anden*.) Ill.: Jean Charlot.
New York: Viking Press 1952.

1954 Krumgold, Joseph: **...and now Miguel**. (... und nun Michael.) Ill.: Jean Charlot.
New York: Crowell 1953.

1955 De Jong, Meindert: **The wheel on the school**. (Das Rad auf der Schule.) Ill.: Maurice Sendak.
New York: Harper 1954.

1956 Latham, Jean Lee: **Carry on, Mr. Bowditch**. (Machen Sie weiter, *Mr. Bowditch*.) Ill.: John O'Hara Cosgrave.
Boston: Houghton Mifflin 1955.

1957 Sorensen, Virginia: **Miracles on Maple Hill**. (Wunder in *Maple Hill*.) Ill.: Beth Krush and Joe Krush.
New York: Harcourt, Brace 1956.

1958 Keith, Harold: **Rifles for Watie**. (Gewehre für *Watie*.)
New York: Crowell 1957.

1959 Speare, Elizabeth George: **The witch of Blackbird Pond**. (Die Hexe vom Amselteich.) Ill.: Witold T. Mars.
Boston: Houghton Mifflin 1958.

1960 Krumgold, Joseph: **Onion John**. (Zwiebel *John*.) Ill.: Symeon Shimin.
New York: Crowell 1959.

1961 O'Dell, Scott: **Island of the blue dolphins**. (Die Insel der blauen Delphine.)
Boston: Houghton Mifflin 1960.

1962 Speare, Elizabeth George: **The bronze bow**. (Der bronzene Bogen.)
Boston: Houghton Mifflin 1961.

1963 L'Engle, Madeleine: **A wrinkle in time**. (Eine Falte zur rechten Zeit.)
New York: Farrar Straus 1962.

1964 Neville, Emily Cheney: **It's like this, cat**. (Es ist so, wie es ist, Katze.) Ill.: Emil Weiss.
New York, Evanston, London: Harper & Row 1963.

1965 Wojciechowska, Maia: **Shadow of a bull**. (Der Schatten eines Bullen.) Ill.: Alvin Smith.
New York: Atheneum 1964.

1966 Borton de Treviño, Elizabeth: **I, Juan de Pareja**. (Ich, *Juan de Pareja*.)
New York: Farrar, Straus & Giroux 1965.

1967 Hunt, Irene: **Up a road slowly**. (Langsam, die Straße hinauf.)
Chicago, New York: Follett 1966.

1968 Konigsburg, Elaine L.: **From the mixed-up files of Mrs. Basil E. Frankweiler**. (Von den vertauschten Ordnern der Frau *Basil E. Frankweiler*.) Ill.: Elaine L. Konigsburg.
New York: Atheneum 1967.

1969 Alexander, Lloyd: **The high king**. (Der hohe König.)
New York: Holt, Rinehart & Winston 1968.

1970 Armstrong, William Howard: **Sounder**. (*Sounder*.) Ill.: James Barkley.
New York: Harper & Row 1969.

1971 Byars, Betsy: **The summer of the swans.** (Als die Schwäne kamen.) Ill.: Ted CoConis.
New York: Viking Press 1970.

1972 O'Brien, Robert C.: **Mrs. Frisby and the rats of Nimh.** (Frau *Frisby* und die Ratten von *Nimh.*) Ill.: Zena Bernstein.
New York: Atheneum 1971.

1973 George, Jean Craighead: **Julie of the wolves.** (*Julie* von den Wölfen.) Ill.: John Schoenherr.
New York: Harper & Row 1972.

1974 Fox, Paula: **The slave dancer.** (Der Sklaven Tänzer.) Ill.: Eros Keith.
Scarsdale, New York: Bradbury 1973.

1975 Hamilton, Virginia: **M.C. Higgins, the great.** (*M.C. Higgins* der Große.)
New York: Macmillan 1974.

1976 Cooper, Susan: **The grey king.** (Der graue König.) Ill.: Michael Helsop.
New York: Atheneum 1975.

1977 Taylor, Mildred D.: **Roll of thunder, hear my cry.** (Donnerrollen, hör' mein Schreien.)
New York: Dial 1976.

1978 Paterson, Katherine: **Bridge to Terabithia.** (Brücke nach *Terabithia.*) Ill.: Donna Diamond.
New York: Crowell 1977.

1979 Raskin, Ellen: **The Westing game.** (Das Spiel des Herren *Westing.*)
New York: E.P. Dutton 1978.

1980 Blos, Joan W.: **A gathering of days.** (Eine Sammlung von Tagen.)
New York: Scribners 1979.

1981 Paterson, Katherine: **Jacob have I loved.** (Ich liebte *Jacob.*)
New York: Crowell 1980.

1982 Willard, Nancy: **A visit to william Blake's inn.** Poems for innocent and experienced travelers. (Ein Besuch bei *William Blakes* Wirtshaus. Gedichte für unschuldige und erfahrene Reisende.)
Ill.: Alice Provensen and Martin Provensen.
New York: Harcourt Brace Jovanovich 1981.

New York Academy of Sciences Children's Science Book Award

This award was instituted in 1972 by the New York Academy of Sciences to encourage the writing and publishing of more books of high quality in the field of science for children. In 1973, the award was divided into two categories: one for children's books, the other for youth books. The jury that selects the winning titles is composed of scientists and children's literature specialists.

Dieser Preis wurde 1972 von der New Yorker Akademie der Wissenschaften mit der Absicht gestiftet, die Veröffentlichung von anspruchsvollen Sachbüchern für Kinder zu fördern. 1973 wurde der Preis geteilt – einer für Kinderbücher und einer für Jugendbücher. Die Jury, die die Preisträger ermittelt, besteht aus Wissenschaftlern und Kinderbuchspezialisten.

1972 Richardson, Robert S.: **The stars and Serendipity**. (Die Sterne und *Serendipity*.) Ill.: Robert S. Richardson.
New York: Pantheon 1971.

1973 *Children's book/Kinderbuch*
Gallob, Edward: **City leaves, city trees**. (Blätter in der Stadt, Bäume in der Stadt.) Photos: Edward Gallob.
New York: Scribner 1972.

Juvenile book/Jugendbuch
Cottrell, Leonard: **Reading the past**. (Lektüre der Vergangenheit.)
New York: Macmillan 1971.

1974 *Children's book/Kinderbuch*
Freschet, Berniece: **The web in the grass**. (Das Spinnwebnetz im Gras.) Ill.: Roger Duvoisin.
New York: Scribner 1973.

Juvenile book/Jugendbuch
MacClintock, Dorcas: **A natural history of giraffes**. (Die Naturgeschichte der Giraffen.) Ill.: Ugo Mochi.
New York: Scribner 1973.

1975 *Children' book/Kinderbuch*
Duvoisin, Roger: **See what I am**. (Schau was ich bin.) Ill.: Roger Duvoisin.
New York: Lothrop 1974.

Juvenile book/Jugendbuch
Kirk, Ruth/Daugherty, Richard D.: **Hunters of the whale**. (Walfischjäger.) Ill.: Ruth Kitk and Louis Kirk.
New York: William Morrow 1974.

1976 *Children's book/Kinderbuch*
Deguine, Jean-Claude: **Emperor penguin**. (Der Kaiser der Pinguine.) Ill.
Brattleboro, Vermont: Stephen Greene 1974.
Juvenile book/Jugendbuch
Buchenholz, Bruce: **Doctor in the zoo**. (Doktor im Zoo.) Photos: Bruce Buchenholz.
New York: Viking Press 1974.

1977 *Children's book/Kinderbuch*
Aliki (i.e. Aliki Brandenberg): **Corn is maize**. (Mais.) Ill.: Aliki (i.e. Aliki Brandenberg.)
New York: Crowell 1976.
Juvenile book/Jugendbuch
Kevles, Bettyann Holtzmann: **Watching the wild apes**. (Beobachtung der wilden Affen.) Photos.
New York: E.P. Dutton 1976.

1978 *Children's book/Kinderbuch*
Brady, Irene: **Wild mouse**. (Feldmaus.) Ill.: Irene Brady.
New York: Scribner 1976.
Juvenile book/Jugendbuch
Brown, Elizabeth Burton: **Grains**. (Körner.) Ill.: Elizabeth Burton Brown.
Englewood Cliffs: Prentice-Hall 1976.

1979 *Children's book/Kinderbuch*
Anderson, Lucia: **The smallest life around us**. (Das kleinste Leben um uns.) Ill.: Leigh Grant.
New York: Crown 1978.
Juvenile book/Jugendbuch
Schneider, Herman: **Laser light**. (Laserlicht.) Ill.: Radu Vero.
New York: McGraw Hill 1979.

1980 *Children's book/Kinderbuch*
Kuskin, Karla: **A space story**. (Eine Raumfahrtgeschichte.) Ill.: Marc Simont.
New York: Harper & Row 1980.
Juvenile book/Jugendbuch
Salvadori, Mario: **Building. The fight against gravity**. (Bau. Der Kampf gegen die Anziehungskraft der Erde.) Ill.: Saralinda Hooker and Christopher Ragus.
New York: Atheneum 1980.

1981 *Children's book/Kinderbuch*
Cobb, Vicki/Darling, Kathy: **Bet you can't!** (Ich wette Du kannst es nicht!) Ill.: Martha Weston.
New York: Lothrop 1980
Juvenile book/Jugendbuch
Adkins, Jan: **Moving heavy things**. (Das Bewegen schwerer Gegenstände.)
Boston: Houghton, Mifflin 1980.

The Regina Medal

The Regina Medal was first presented in 1959. It is a distinction given away by the Catholic Library Association for outstanding work in the field of juvenil literature, regardless of creed and nationality of author and reader. The prize was given to authors, publishers, illustrators, editors. The silver medal is presented every year during the Convention of the Catholic Library Association.

Die Regina-Medaille wurde erstmalig 1959 von der katholischen Bibliotheksvereinigung der USA (Catholic Library Association), ohne Berücksichtigung des religiösen Bekenntnisses oder der Nationalität, für das Lebenswerk einer Persönlichkeit verliehen, die sich in besonderer Weise um die Jugendliteratur verdient gemacht hat. Unter den Preisträgern befinden sich sowohl Autoren als auch Verleger, Herausgeber oder Illustratoren. Die Silbermedaille wird jedes Jahr während der Konferenz der Catholic Library Association vergeben.

1959 Eleanor Farjeon
1960 Anne Carroll Moore
1961 Padraic Colum
1962 Frederic Gershom Melcher
1963 Ann Nolan Clark
1964 May Hill Arbuthnot
1965 Ruth Sawyer
1966 Leo Politi
1967 Bertha Mahony Miller
1968 Marguerite de Angeli
1969 Lois Lenski
1970 Ingri und Edgar Parin d'Aulaire
1971 Tasha Tudor

1972 Meindert DeJong
1973 Frances Clarke Sayers
1974 Robert McCloskey
1975 Lynd Ward and May McNeer Ward
1976 Virginia Haviland
1977 Marcia Brown
1978 Scott O'Dell
1979 Morton Schindel
1980 Beverly Cleary

The Laura Ingalls Wilder Award

The Laura Ingalls Wilder Award medal is presented every fifth Year to an author or illustrator, whose books have proven, over many years, to be outstanding achievements in the field of juvenile literature. The books must have been published in the United States. The suggestions for the prize are made by the Children's Services Division of the American Library Association. The medal is presented during the Annual Convention of the American Library Association in commemoration of Laura Ingalls Wilder (1867—1957) and her tales about the era of the American pioneers.

Die Laura-Ingalls-Wilder-Medaille wird alle fünf Jahre an einen Autor oder einen Illustrator verliehen, dessen Bücher über lange Jahre hinweg einen bedeutenden Beitrag auf dem Gebiete der Kinderliteratur geleistet haben. Die Bücher müssen in den Vereinigten Staaten erschienen sein. Die Preisträger werden von Mitgliedern der Kinderbüchereisektion der Amerikanischen Bibliotheksvereinigung (Children's Services Division der American Library Association) vorgeschlagen und ausgewählt. Die Medaille wird auf der Jahreskonferenz der American Library Association im Gedenken an Laura Ingalls Wilder (1867—1957) und ihre Bücher über die amerikanische Pionierzeit verliehen.

1954 Laura Ingalls Wilder
1960 Clara Ingram Judson
1965 Ruth Sawyer
1970 Elwyn Brooks White
1975 Beverly Cleary
1980 Theodor Geisel

Yugoslavia/Jugoslawien

Nagrada Ivana Brlić-Mažuranić

The publishing house Školska knjiga of Zagreb founded, on the occasion of its 20th anniversary, an annual prize for children's literature and children's book illustrations. The prize was named after the Croatian children's book author, Ivana Brlić-Mažuranić (1874—1939). Each year, the prize is awarded to the best author and the best illustrator of a children's book. The winning titles are selected by two juries composed of five members each, which are chosen by the worker's committee of Školska knjiga publishing house. The prize-winners receive a citation, a statuette of Hlapić, the shoemaker's apprentice (hero of one of Ivana Brlić-Mažuranić's novels) and a cash prize.

Der Verlag Školska knjiga in Zagreb stiftete zum Jubiläum seines zwanzigjährigen Bestehens einen jährlichen Preis für Kinderliteratur und Kinderbuchillustration. Er erhielt den Namen der klassischen kroatischen Kinderbuchautorin

Ill. 43 Ivan Antolčič in Hrvoje Hitrec: Petrica Kerempuh

Ivana Brlić-Mažuranić (1874—1939). Er wird jährlich dem Autor des erfolgreichsten literarischen Werkes für Kinder und dem erfolgreichsten Illustrator eines Kinderbuches verliehen. Über die Preisverleihung entscheiden zwei Kommissionen aus je 5 Mitgliedern, die vom Arbeiterrat des Verlages Školska knjiga bestimmt werden. Die Preisträger erhalten ein besonderes Diplom, eine Statuette des Schuhmacherlehrlings Hlapić und eine Summe Geldes.

Ill. 44 Marjanca Jemec-Božič in Branka Jurca: Ko Nina spi

1971 Kanižaj, Pajo: **Bila jednom jedna plava.** (Once upon a time there was a blue; Es war einmal eine Blaue.) Ill.: Vilko Selan Gliha.
Zagreb: Školska knjiga 1970.
Illustration
Binički, Stevo in:
Iveljić, Nada: **Kiki-mala polarna lisica.** (*Kiki,* the little polar fox; *Kiki,* die kleine Polarfüchsin.)
Zagreb: Školska knjiga 1971.

1972 Kuśan, Ivan: **Koko i duhovi.** (*Koko* and the ghosts; *Koko* und die Gespenster.) Ill.: Đuro Seder.
Zagreb: Mladost 1972.
Illustration
Stranić, Bojan in:
Horvatić, Dubravko: **Hej, vatrogasci, požurite.** (Forward, firemen, hurry; Los, Feuerwehrleute, beeilt euch.)
Zagreb: Školska knjiga 1972.

1973 Paljetak, Luko: **Miševi i mačke naglavačke.** (Mice and cats go topsy-turvy; Mäuse und Katzen machen Kopfstand.) Ill.: Diana Kosec-Bourek.
Zagreb: Mladost 1973.
Illustration
Kinert, Albert in:
Hribar, Branko: **Ekčapoan i druge smiješne žalosti.** (*Ekčapoan* and other funny troubles; *Ekčapoan und anderer komischer Verdruß.*
Zagreb: Školska knjiga 1973.

1974 Matošec, Milivoj: **Okuka na Zlatnoj rijeci.** (The bend in the golden river; Die Biegung im goldenen Fluß.) Ill.: Stero Binički.
Zagreb: Školska knjiga 1973.
Illustration
Bourek, Zlatko in:
Vitez, Grigor: **Antuntun.** (*Antuntun.*)
Zagreb: Školska knjiga 1974.

1975 Balog, Zvonimir: **Pjesme sa šlagom ili šumar ima šumu na dlanu.** (Poems with cream or the forester has the forest in his hand; Gedichte mit Sahne oder der Förster hat den Wald in der Hand.) Ill.: Ivica Antolčić.
Zagreb: Školska knjiga 1975.
Illustration
Antolčić, Ivica in:
Balog, Zvonimir: **Pjesme sa šlagom ili šumar ima šumu na dlanu.**

(Poems with cream or the forester has the forest in his hand; Gedichte mit Sahne oder der Förster hat den Wald in der Hand.)
Zagreb: Školska knjiga 1975.

1976 Mihalić, Slavko: **Petrica Kerempuh u starim i novim pričama**. (*Petrica Kerempuh* in old and new tales; *Petrica Kerempuh* in alten und neuen Geschichten.) Ill.: Zlatko Bourek.
Zagreb: Školska knjiga 1975.

Illustration
Bourek, Zlatko in:
Mihalić, Slavko: **Petrica Kerempuh un starim i novim pričama**. (*Petrica Kerempuh* in old and new tales; *Petrica Kerempuh* in alten und neuen Geschichten.)
Zagreb: Školska knjiga 1975.

1977 Martić, Andelka: **Djed pričalo i čarobni vrutak**. (Grandfather the storyteller and the magic fountain; Großvater der Geschichtenerzähler und der Zauberquell.) Ill.: Branko Vujanović.
Zagreb: Mladost 1977.

Illustration
Bifel, Josip in:
Balog, Zvonimir: **Zeleni mravi**. (Green ants; Grüne Ameisen.)
Zagreb: Naša djeca 1977.

1978 The prize was not given; Der Preis wurde nicht vergeben.

1979 The prize was not given; Der Preis wurde nicht vergeben.

1980 Hitrec, Hrvoje: **Eko-Eko**. (*Eko-Eko*.) Ill.: Joško Marušić.
Zagreb: Mladost 1980.

Krilić, Zlatko: **Čudnovata istina**. (Amazing truth; Wundersame Wahrheit.) Ill.: Nedeljko Dragić.
Zagreb: Mladost 1980.

Illustration
Haramija, Živko in:
Mažuranić, Ivan: **Smrt Smail-age Čengića**. (The death of the *Smail-Aga Čengić*; Der Tod des *Smail-Aga Čengić*.)
Zagreb: Školska knjiga 1980.

1981 Škrinjarić, Sunčana: **Ulica predaka**. (The street of the ancestors; Die Straße der Vorfahren.)
Zagreb: Mladost 1980.

Illustration
Kavurić-Kurtović, Nives in:
Balog, Zvonimir: **Tko je čega sit**. (Who has enough of that; Wer was satt hat.)
Zagreb: Mladost 1980.

Levstikova Nagrada

The Slovenian publishing house, Mladinska knjiga, Ljubljana, has awarded this prize each year, beginning in 1950. It is named after the classic writer of Slovenian literature, Fran Levstik (1831—1887). Levstik was the author of numerous children's books. This award is given annually for the best fiction, collections of children's poems and songs, non-fiction and illustrations. The prize, although intended for annual presentation, is given only in those years in which prizeworthy books are published.

Der slowenische Verlag Mladinska knjiga, Ljubljana, verleiht seit 1949 den Levstik-Preis, der seinen Namen nach dem Klassiker der slowenischen Literatur, auch der Kinderliteratur trägt. Jedes Jahr werden Preise für die besten belletristischen Werke, die besten Sammlungen von Kindergedichten, die besten Sachbücher und die besten Illustrationen vergeben. Im Wettbewerb steht immer die Kinder- und Jugendliteratur des vorangegangenen Jahres. Wenn es keine preiswürdigen Bücher gibt, wird der Preis nicht vergeben.

1950 *Fiction/Belletristik*

Bevk, France: **Tonček**. (*Tonček*.) Ill.: Riko Debenjak.
Ljubljana: Mladinska knjiga 1948.

Prežihov, Voranc (i.e. Lovro Kuhar): **Solzice.** (Lilies of the valley; Die Maiglöckchen.) Ill.: France Miheliž.
Ljubljana: Mladinska knjiga 1949.

Ribičič, Josip: **Tinče in Binče**. (*Tinče* and *Binče*.) Ill.: Evgen Sajovic.
Ljubljana: Mladinska knjiga 1949.

Seliškar, Tone: **Mule**. (Mule; Maulesel.) Ill.: Evgen Sajovic.
Ljubljana: Mladinska knjiga 1948.

Špur, Katja for her editorial creativity, especially; für ihr publizistisches Schaffen, insbesondere:
Špur, Katja: **Plugi orjejo**. (The plows, plow; Die Pflüge pflügen.)
Ljubljana: Mladinska knjiga 1949.

Špur, Katja: **Po novih poteh**. (Along new ways; Auf neuen Wegen.)
Ljubljana: Mladinska knjiga 1947.

Illustration

Gaspari, Maksim in:
Čukovskij, Kornej Ivanovič: **Šuri-Muri velikan**. (*Šuri-Muri* the giant; *Šuri-Muri* der Riese.)
Ljubljana: Mladinska knjiga 1946.

Mihelič, France in:
Prežihov, Vorance (i.e. Lovro Kuhar): **Solzice**. (Lilies of the valley; Maiglöckchen.)
Ljubljana: Mladinska knjiga 1949.

Podrekar, France in:
Milčinski, Fran: **Butalci**. (The citizens of *Butale*; Die Schildbürger von *Butale*.)
Ljubljana: Mladinska knjiga 1949.

Pregelj, Marij in:
Bevk, France: **Otroška leta**. (Years of childhood; Die Kinderjahre.)
Ljubljana: Mladinska knjiga 1949.

Šubic, Ive in:
Hudales, Zoran: **Nejček**. (*Nejček*.)
Ljubljana: Mladinska knjiga 1949.

1951 *Fiction/Belletristik*
Golia, Pavel: **Sneguljčica**. (*Snow-White*; *Schneewittchen*.) Ill.:Tone Kralj.
Ljubljana: Mladinska knjiga 1950.

Non-fiction/Sachbuch
Polenec, Anton: **Iz Življenja Žuželk**. (The life of insects; Aus dem Leben der Insekten.) Ill.: Ljubo Ravnikar.
Ljubljana: Mladinska knjiga 1950.

Illustration
Kralj, Tone in:
Šilih, Igor: **Pravlejica o carjeviču Jeruslanu**. (A tale of the tsarevich, *Jeruslan*; Ein Märchen über Zarevitsch *Jeruslan*.)
Ljubljana: Mladinska knjiga 1950.

Omersa, Nikolaj in:
Sega, Milan: **Zgodbe o zivalih**. (Stories about animals; Erzählungen über Tiere.)
Ljubljana: Mladinska knjiga 1950.

Stupica, Marlenka in:
Gruden, Igo: **Na Krasu**. (On stony ground; Aus dem Karst.)
Ljubljana: Mladinska knjiga 1949.

Vidic, Janez in:
Premagane zverine. Slovenska ljudska pesem. (The defeated carnivores. Slovenian folk poems; Besiegte Raubtiere. Slowenische Volksgedichte.) Adapt.: Mile Klopčič.
Ljubljana: Mladinska knjiga 1950.

1952 *Fiction/Belletristik*

Bevk, France: **Mali upornik**. (The little rebel; Der kleine Rebell.) Ill.: Nikolaj Omersa.
Ljubljana: Mladinska knjiga 1951.

Non-fiction/Sachbuch

Križanič, France: **Kratkočasna matematika**. (Fun with mathematics; Unterhaltende Mathematik.) Ill.: Milos Požar.
Ljubljana: Mladinska knjiga 1951.

Matanović, Drago: **Pogled v elektrotehniko**. (A glance at electricity; Ein Blick in die Elektrotechnik.) Ill.
Ljubljana: Mladinska knjiga 1951.

Naglič, Vladimir: **Kratke zanimivosti iz pomorstva**. (Remarkable facts about navigation; Bemerkenswerte Tatsachen von der Schiffahrt.) Ill.: Rudi Gorjup.
Ljubljana: Mladinska knjiga 1951.

Pahor, Jože: **Hodil po zemlji sem naši...Potopis po Jugoslaviji**. (A walk in our country...A travel guide through Yugoslavia; Ich ging in unserem Land herum...Reisebericht von Jugoslawien.)
Ljubljana: Mladinska knjiga 1951.

Illustration

Birolla, Gvido in:
Širok, Karel: **Trije bratje in trije razbojniki**. (Three brothers and three robbers; Drei Brüder und drei Räuber.)
Ljubljana: Mladinska knjiga 1951.

Mihelič, France in:
Levstik, Fran: **Najdihojca**. (*Najdihojca.*) Adapt.: Marja Boršnik.
Ljubljana: Mladinska knjiga 1951.

Pengov, Slavko in:
Finžgar, Fran Saleški: **Pod svobodnim soncem**. (Under the free sun; Unter der freien Sonne.)
Ljubljana: Mladinska knjiga 1951.

Petrič, Dusan in:
Prunk-Utva, Ljudmila: **Kaj je videl Mižek Figa.** (What *Mišek Figa* saw; Was *Mižek Figa* gesehen hat.)
Ljubljana: Mladinska knjiga 1951.

Šubic, Ive in:
Kralj Matjaž resi svojo nevesto. Slovenska narodna pesem. (King *Matjaž* saves his bride. Slovenian folksong; König *Matjaž* rettet seine Braut. Slowenisches Volkslied.) Adapt.: Mile Klopčič.
Ljubljana: Mladinska knjiga 1951.

Vidic, Janez in:
Valjavec, Matija: **Živalske pripovedke**. (Animal tales; Tiererzählungen.) Adapt.: Viktor Smolej.
Ljubljana: Mladinska knjiga 1951.

1953 *Non-fiction/Sachbuch*

Adlešič, Miroslav: **Od mehanike do elektronike**. (From mechanics to electronics; Von der Mechanik bis zur Elektronik.) Ill.
Ljubljana: Mladinska knjiga 1952.

Polenec, Anton: **Iz življenja pajkov**. (From the world of the spider; Aus der Welt der Spinnen.) Ill.: Ljubo Ravnikar.
Ljubljana: Mladinska knjiga 1952.

Zei, Miroslav: **Iz ribjega sveta**. (From the world of fish; Aus der Welt der Fische.) Ill.: Viktor Cotic.
Ljubljana: Mladinska knjiga 1952.

Illustration

Kobe, Boris in:
Tavčar, Ivan: Visoška kronika. (The chronicles of *Visoko*. Chronik von *Visoko*.)
Ljubljana: Mladinska knjiga 1953.

Krošelj, Rado in:
Barčica. (The little ship; Das Schiffchen.)
Ljubljana: Mladinska knjiga 1952.

Mihelič, France in:
Bevk, France: **Pesterna**. (The nurse; Das Kindermädchen.)
Ljubljana: Mladinska knjiga 1952.

Stupica, Marlenka in:
Župančic, Oton: **Mehurčki**. (Little soap bubbles; Seifenbläschen.) Adapt.: Alenka Glazer.
Ljubljana: Mladinska knjiga 1952.

Vidic, Janez in:
Vidic, Janez: **Letni casi**. (The seasons; Jahreszeiten.)
Ljubljana: Mladinska knjiga 1952.

1954 *Fiction/Belletristik*

Finžgar, Fran Saleški: **Iz mladih dni**. (From the time of my youth; Aus der Zeit meiner Jugend.) Ill.: Ive Šubic.
Ljubljana: Mladinska knjiga 1953.

Kranjec, Miško: **Imel sem jih rad**. (I was fond of them; Ich habe sie gerne gehabt.) Ill.: Lajci Pandur.
Ljubljana: Mladinska knjiga 1953.

Non-fiction/Sachbuch

Cermelj, Lavo: **Nikola Tesla in Razvoj elektrotechnike**. (*Nicola Tesla* and the development of electronics; *Nikola Tesla* und die Entwicklung der Elektrotechnik.)
Ljubljana: Mladinska knjiga 1953.

Illustration

Sajovic, Evgenin:
Andersen, Hans-Christian: **Snežna kraljica in druge pravljice**. (The snow queen and other fairy tales; Die Schneekönigin und andere Märchen.)
Ljubljana: Mladinska knjiga 1953.

Sedej, Maksim in:
Tisoč in ena noč. (Thousand and one nights; Tausend und eine Nacht.)
Ljubljana: Mladinska knjiga 1953.

1955 *Fiction/Belletristik*

Bratko, Ivan: **Teleskop**. (The telescope; Das Teleskop.) Ill.: Niko Pirnat.
Ljubljana: Mladinska knjiga 1954.

Non-fiction/Sachbuch

Petek, Božo: **Letalsko modelarstvo**. (Model airplane building; Flugzeugbasteln.) Ill.
Ljubljana: Mladinska knjiga 1953.

Illustration

Ciuha, Jože in:
Jovanovič Zmaj, Jovan: **Cekin**. (The ducat; Der Dukate.)
Ljubljana: Mladinska knjiga 1954.

Piščanec, Roža in:
Spyri, Johanna: **Heidi**. (*Heidi*.)
Ljubljana: Mladinska knjiga 1954.

Sedej, Maksim in:
Magajna, Bogomir: **Racko in Lija**. (*Racko* and *Lija*.)
Ljubljana: Mladinska knjiga 1954.

Stupica, Marlenka in:
Grimm, Jakob/Grimm, Wilhelm: **Trnuljcica**. (*Sleeping Beauty*; *Dornröschen*.)
Ljubljana: Mladinska knjiga 1954.

1956 *Fiction/Belletristik*

Peroci, Ela: **Moj dežnik je lahko balon.** (My umbrella can fly like a balloon; Mein Schirm kann fliegen wie ein Ballon.) Ill.: Leo Koporc.
Ljubljana: Mladinska knjiga 1955.

Ribičič, Josip: **Rdeča pest.** (The red fist; Die rote Faust.) Ill.: Janez Vidic.
Ljubljana: Mladinska knjiga 1955.

Seliškar, Tone: **Posadka brez ladje.** (The crew without a ship; Die Besatzung ohne Schiff.) Ill.: Ive Seljak-Čopič.
Ljubljana: Mladinska knjiga 1955.

Non-fiction/Sachbuch

Rudolf, Branko: **Maske in časi.** Kratka kulturna zgodvina za gledalisca. (Masks and time. Short cultural history of the theatre; Masken und Zeiten. Kurze Kulturgeschichte des Theaters.) Ill.
Ljubljana: Mladinska knjiga 1955.

Škerlj, Božo: **Nevšečno sorodstvo.** (The unloved relatives; Die mißliebigen Verwandten.) Ill.: Viktor Cotič.
Ljubljana: Mladinska knjiga 1955.

Škerlj, Božo: **Neznana Amerika.** (Unknown America; Unbekanntes Amerika.) Ill.
Ljubljana: Mladinska knjiga 1955.

Illustration

Omersa, Nikolaj in:
Jajčkov zvonček. Madzarska ljudska pravljica. (The hare's little bell. Hungarian folktale; Das Glöcklein des Hasen. Ungarische Volkserzählung.) Adapt.: Viko Novak.
Ljubljana: Mladinska knjiga 1955.

Seljak-Čopič, Ive in:
Bevk, France: **Knjiga o Titu.** (The book about *Tito*; Das Buch über *Tito*.)
Ljubljana: Mladinska knjiga 1955.

Seljak-Čopič, Ive in:
Seliškar, Tone: **Posadka brez ladje.** (The crew without a ship; Die Besatzung ohne Schiff.)
Ljubljana: Mladinska knjiga 1955.

1957 *Fiction/Belletristik*

Kranjec, Miško: **Čarni nasmeh.** (An enchanting smile; Bezauberndes Lächeln.) Ill.: Lajči Pandur.
Ljubljana: Mladinska knjiga 1976.

Peroci, Ela: **Tisočkratlepa**. (Thousand-beauty; Tausendschön.) Ill.: Maksim Sedej.
Ljubljana: Mladinska knjiga 1956.

Non-fiction/Sachbuch

Matjašič, Janez: **Iz življenja najmlajših**. (From the smallest one's world; Aus der Welt der Kleinsten.) Ill.
Ljubljana: Mladinska knjiga 1956.

Illustration

Mihelič, France in:
Mihelič, Mira: **Štirje letni časi**. (Four seasons; Vier Jahreszeiten.)
Ljubljana: Mladinska knjiga 1956.

Sedej, Maksim in:
Langus (i.e. Vitomil Zupan): **Potovanje v tisocera mesta**. (A journey to one thousand cities; Eine Reise in die tausend Städte.)
Ljubljana: Mladinska knjiga 1956.

Sedej, Maksim in:
Pastircek. (The shepherd; Der Hirt.)
Ljubljana: Mladinska knjiga 1956.

1958 *Fiction/Belletristik*

Zupanc, Lojze: **Povodni mož v savinji**. (The aquarian in *Savinja*; Der Wassermann in *Savinja*.) Ill.: Jože Ciuha.
Ljubljana: Mladinska knjiga 1957.

Non-fiction/Sachbuch

Adlešič, Miroslav: **Svet svetlobe in barv**. (The world of light and colors; Die Welt des Lichtes und der Farben.) Ill.
Ljubljana: Mladinska knjiga 1957.

Zei, Miroslav: **Iz zivljenja sesalcev**. (From the world of animals; Aus der Welt der Tiere.) Ill.: Zlatko Zei.
Ljubljana: Mladinska knjiga 1957.

Illustration

Pregelj, Marij in:
London, Jack: **Beli očnjak**. (Amer.orig.title: *White Fang*; *Weißer Hauzahn.*)
Ljubljana: Mladinska knjiga 1957.

Vork, Melita in:
Šega, Milan: **Zgode in nezgode kraljevega dvora**. (Curious stories about the royal court; Seltsame Geschichten vom Königshof.)
Ljubljana: Mladinska knjiga 1957.

1959 *Fiction/Belletristik*

Ingolič, Anton: **Tajno društvo PGC.** (The secret organization, *PGC*; Der geheime Verein *PGC*.) Ill.: Stefan Planinc.
Ljubljana: Mladinska knjiga 1958.

Pavček, Tone: **Juri-Muri v Afriki.** (*Juri-Muri* in Africa; *Juri-Muri* in Afrika.) Ill.: Melita Vovk.
Ljubljana: Mladinska knjiga 1958.

Non-fiction/Sachbuch

Neubauer, Robert: **Ceylon.** (*Ceylon*.) Ill.
Ljubljana: Mladinska knjiga 1957.

Savnik, Dušan: **Svet nasprotij.** (The world of contradictions; Die Welt der Gegensätze.)
Ljubljana: Mladinska knjiga 1958.

Illustration

Bizovičar, Milan in:
Bizovičar, Milan: **Maghellanovo potovanje okoli sveta.** (*Magellan*'s voyage around the world; *Maghellans* Reise rund um die Welt.)
Ljubljana: Mladinska knjiga 1958.

Omersa, Nikolj in:
Bevk, France: **Pisani svet.** (Multicolored world; Bunte Welt.)
Ljubljana: Mladinska knjiga 1958.

Omersa, Nikolaj in:
Grey, Zane: **Skrivnostni jezdec.** (Amer.orig.title: The mysterious rider; Geheimnisvoller Reiter.)
Ljubljana: Mladinska knjiga 1958.

Omersa, Nikolaj in:
Kipling, Rudyard: **Pogumni kapitani.** (Eng.orig.title: Captains courageous; Tapfere Kapitäne.)
Ljubljana: Mladinska knjiga 1958.

Planinc, Štefan in:
Ingolič, Anton: **Tajno društvo PGC.** (The secret organization, *PGC*; Der geheime Verein *PGC*.)
Ljubljana: Mladinska knjiga 1958.

Stupica, Marlenka in:
Valjavec, Matija: **Pastir.** (The shepherd; Der Hirt.)
Ljubljana: Mladinska knjiga 1958.

1960 *Fiction/Belletristik*

Milčinski, Frane Ježek: **Zvezdica Zaspanka.** (The little star, *Lazybones*; Das Sternchen *Siebenschläfer*.) Ill.: Mara Kraljeva.
Ljubljana: Mladinska knjiga 1959.

Non-fiction/Sachbuch
Čermelj, Lavo: **Z raketo v vesolje**. (A rocket into space; Mit der Rakete ins Weltall.) Ill.
Ljubljana: Mladinska knjiga 1959.

Illustration
Planinc, Štefan in:
Montgomery, Rutherford: **Karkažu**. (Amer.orig.title: Carcajou; Carcajou.)
Ljubljana: Mladinska knjiga 1960.

Planinc, Štefan in:
Vrščaj, Zima: **Sinička nas je obiskala**. (A titmouse visited us; Ein Meischen hat uns besucht.)
Ljubljana: Mladinska knjiga 1959.

Planinc, Štefan in:
Wells, Herbert Georg: **Prvi ljudje na mesecu**. (Eng.orig.title: First men in the moon; Erste Menschen auf dem Mond.)
Ljubljana: Mladinska knjiga 1959.

Pregelj, Marij in:
Hemingway, Ernest: **Starec i morje**. (Amer.orig.title: The old man and the sea; Der alte Mann und das Meer.)
Ljubljana: Mladinska knjiga 1959.

1961 *Fiction/Belletristik*
Jurca, Branka: **Okoli in okoli**. (Round and round about; Rund und rund herum.) Ill.: Cita Potokar.
Ljubljana: Mladinska knjiga 1960.

Kajzer, Janez: **Mimo dnevega načrta. Humoreske**. (To put aside. Humoresques; Am Tagesplan vorbei. Humoresken.) Ill.: Jože Ciuha.
Ljubljana: Mladinska knjiga 1960.

Non-fiction/Sachbuch
Križanič, France: **Elektronski aritmetični računaltik**. (Electronic arithmetical computers; Elektronische arithmetische Rechenmaschine.)
Ljubljana: Mladinska knjiga 1960.

Križanič, France: **Križem po matematiki**. (Exploring mathematics; Kreuz und quer durch die Mathematik.) Ill.: Jože Vedral.
Ljubljana: Mladinska knjiga 1960.

Illustration
Gošnik-Godec, Ančka in:
Martić, Anđjelka: **Decek in gozd**. (The boy and the forest; Der Knabe und der Wald.)
Ljubljana: Mladinska knjiga 1959.

Gošnik-Godec, Ančka in:
Peroci, Ela: **Pticke so odletele**. (The birds have flown away; Die Vögel sind ausgeflogen.)
Ljubljana: Mladinska knjiga 1960.

Gošnik-Godec, Ančka in:
Perrault, Charles: **Vile**. (The fairies; Die Feen.)
Ljubljana: Mladinska knjiga 1960.

Stupica, Marlenka in:
Collodi, Carlo (i.e. Carlo Lorenzini): **Ostržek**. (*Pinoccio*; Ital.orig.title: Le avventure di *Pinocchio*.)
Ljubljana: Mladinska knjiga 1960.

1962 *Fiction/Belletristik*

Pavček, Tone: **Velesenzacija**. (A great sensation; Große Sensation.) Ill.: Zdenka Golob-Borčič.
Ljubljana: Mladinska knjiga 1961.

Pečjak, Vid: **Drejček in trije Marsovčki**. (*Drejček* and the three little martians; Drejček und die drei Marsjungen.) Ill.: Štefan Planinc.
Ljubljana: Mladinska knjiga 1961.

Non-fiction/Sachbuch

Ramovš, Anton: **Geološki izleti po ljubljanski okolici**. (Geological excursions around Ljubljana; Geologische Ausflüge in die Ljubljaner Umgebung.) Ill.
Ljubljana: Mladinska knjiga 1961.

Ramovš, Anton: **Zemlja skozi milijone let**. (The earth through millions of years; Die Erde in Jahrmillionen.)
Ljubljana: Mladinska knjiga 1960.

Illustration

Piščanec, Roža in:
Hrubin, František: **Medenjakova hišica**. (The gingerbread house; Das Lebkuchenhaus.)
Ljubljana: Mladinska knjiga 1961.

1963 *Fiction/Belletristik*

Krakar, Lojze: **Sonce v knjigi**. (The sun in the book; Die Sonne im Buch.) Ill.: Miklavz Omersa.
Ljubljana: Mladinska knjiga 1962.

Non-fiction/Sachbuch

Likar, Miha: **Bakterije**. (Bacteria; Bakterien.) Ill.
Ljubljana: Mladinska knjiga 1961.

Likar, Miha: **Glivice**. (Fungi; Pilze.) Ill.
Ljubljana: Mladinska knjiga 1962.

Illustration
Bizovičar, Milan in:
Kovačič, Lojze: **Zgodbe iz mesta Rič-Rač**. Tales from the town of *Rič-Rač*; Geschichten aus der Stadt *Rič-Rač*.)
Ljubljana: Mladinska knjiga 1962.

Potokar, Ciat in:
Jurca, Branka: **Lizike za vse**. (Sweets for everyone; Lutschbonbons für alle.)
Ljubljana: Mladinska knjiga 1962.

1964 *Fiction/Belletristik*
Kovič, Kajetan: **Franca izpod klanca**. (Little *Franz* behind the hill; *Fränzchen* hinter dem Hügel.) Ill.: Marjanca Jemec.
Ljubljana: Mladinska knjiga 1963.

Smolnikar, Breda: **Ptročki, življenje teče dalje**. (Life goes on, children; Kinder, das Leben geht weiter.) Ill.: Božo Kos.
Ljubljana: Mladinska knjiga 1963.

Non-fiction/Sachbuch
Cvetko, Ciril: **Opera in njeni mojstri**. (Masters of the opera; Die Oper und ihre Meister.) Ill.
Ljubljana: Mladinska knjiga 1963.

Illustration
Planinc, Štefan in:
Pesmi za otroke. (Children's rhymes; Kinderreime.) Adapt.: Janko Glazer.
Ljubljana: Mladinska knjiga 1963.

Seljak-Čopič, Ive in:
Andrić, Ivo: **Aska in volk**. (*Aska* and the wolf; *Aska* und der Wolf.)
Ljubljana: Mladinska knjiga 1963.

1965 *Fiction/Belletristik*
Avčin, France: **Kjer tišina šepeta**. (Where silence whispers; Wo die Stille flüstert.) Ill. Adapt.: Tine Orel.
Ljubljana: Mladinska knjiga 1964.

Non-fiction/Sachbuch
Adelsic, Miroslav: **Svet zvoka in glasbe**. (The world of sound and music; Die Welt des Tons und der Musik.) Ill.
Ljubljana: Mladinska knjiga 1964.

Illustration
Gošnik-Godec, Ančka in:
O treh grahih. Slovenska ljudska pravljica. (About three peas. A Slovenian folktale; Über drei Erbsen. Slowenische Volksmärchen.)
Ljubljana: Mladinska knjiga 1964.

Gošnik-Godec, Ančka in:
Peroci, Ela: **Za lahko noč**. (For a good night; Zur guten Nacht.)
Ljubljana: Mladinska knjiga 1964.

Gošnik-Godec, Ančka in:
Zlata ptica. (The golden bird; Goldvogel.)
Ljubljana: Mladinska knjiga 1964.

Osterc, Lidija in:
Peroci, Ela: **Hisica iz kock**. (The house made of little blocks; Das Haus aus Klötzchen.)
Ljubljana: Mladinska knjiga 1964.

Sovre, Savo in:
Muhvić, Zlatko: **Nemška vadnica za V. in VI. razred osnovne sole**. (A German reader for grades V and VI; Deutsches Lesebuch für V. und VI. Klasse der Volksschule.)
Ljubljana: Mladinska knjiga 1963.

·Žnidaršič, Tone in:
Pirc, Vera: **Nauk o človeku za VII. razred osnovih sol**. (Human sciences for grade VII; Menschenkunde für die VII. Klasse der Volksschule.)
Ljubljana: Mladinska knjiga 1964.

1966 *Fiction/Belletristik*
Suhodolčan, Leopold: **Velikan in pajac**. (The giant and the clown; Der Riese und der Bajazzo.) Ill.: Irina Rahovsky-Kralj.
Ljubljana: Mladinska knjiga 1965.

Illustration
Ciuha, Jože in:
Zupančič, Beno: **Deček Jarbol**. (The boy, *Jarbol*; Der Knabe *Jarbol*.)
Ljubljana: Mladinska knjiga 1965.

Ciuha, Jože in:
Šinkovec, Črtomir: **Pomlad ob soči**. (Spring on the *Soča River*; Der Frühling an der *Soča*.)
Ljubljana: Mladinska knjiga 1965.

Ciuha, Jože in:
Kraigher, Nada: **Nina na Ceylonu**. (*Nina* in Ceylon; *Nina* auf Ceylon.)
Ljubljana: Mladinska knjiga 1965.

Vovk-Štih, Melita in:
Krylov, Ivan Andreevič: **Petdeset Basni**. (Fifty fables; Fünfzig Fabeln.) Adapt.: Mile Klopčič.
Ljubljana: Mladinska knjiga 1965.

Vovk-Štih, Melita in:
Albreht, Vera: **Pustov god.** (A day during carnival; Ein Tag im Fasching.)
Ljubljana: Mladinska knjiga 1965.

Vovk-Štih, Melita in:
Mihelič, Mira: **Puhek v Denetkah.** (*Puhek* in Venice; *Puhek* in Venedig.)
Ljubljana: Mladinska knjiga 1965.

1967 *Fiction/Belletristik*

Ciuha, Jože: **Popotovanje v deseto deželo.** (The journey to the land of milk and honey; Die Reise ins Schlaraffenland.) Ill.: Jože Ciuha.
Ljubljana: Mladinska knjiga 1966.

Jurca, Branka: **Vohljači in prepovedane skrivnosti.** (Spies and the forbidden secrets; Die Spione und die verbotenen Geheimnisse.) Ill.: Božo Kos.
Ljubljana: Mladinska knjiga 1966.

Illustration

Ciuha, Jože in:
Golia, Pavel: **Gospod Baroda in Druge ljudske pesmi.** (Mr. *Baroda* and other popular songs; Herr *Baroda* und andere Volkslieder.)
Ljubljana: Mladinska knjiga 1966.

Mavec, Aco in:
Stevenson, Robert Louis: **Otok zakladov.** (Eng.orig.title: Treasure Island; Die Schatzinsel.)
Ljubljana: Mladinska knjiga 1966.

Osterc, Lidija in:
Milčinski, Fran: **Desetnica.** (The tenth daughter; Die zehnte Tochter.)
Ljubljana: Mladinska knjiga 1966.

Osterc, Lidija in:
Grimm, Jakob/Grimm, Wilhelm: **Lonček, kuhaj.** (The magic cooking pot; Töpfchen koch! Germ.orig.title: Der süße Brei.)
Ljubljana: Mladinska knjiga 1966.

Osterc, Lidija in:
Grimm, Jakob/Grimm, Wilhelm: **Sneguljčica in druge Grommove pravljice.** (*Snow White* and other Grimm fairy tales; Germ.orig.title: *Schneewittchen* und andere Grimm-Märchen.)
Ljubljana: Mladinska knjiga 1966.

1968 *Fiction/Belletristik*

Ingolič, Anton: **Gimnazijka**. (The high school girl; Die Gymnasiastin.) Ill.: Aco Mavec.
Ljubljana: Mladinska knjiga 1967.

Non-fiction/Sachbuch

Planina, France: **Jugoslavija**. (Yugoslavia; Jugoslawien.) Ill.: Ive Subic and Jože Ciuha.
Ljubljana: Mladinska knjiga 1968.

Illustration

Bizovičar, Milan in:
Prežihov, Voranc (i.e. Lovro Kuhar): **Solzice**. (Lilies of the valley; Maiglöckchen.)
Ljubljana: Mladinska knjiga 1967.

Bizovičar, Milan in:
Haggard, Henry Rider: **Salomonovi rudniki**. (Eng.orig.title: King *Salomon*'s mines; König *Salomons* Bergwerke.)
Ljubljana: Mladinska knjiga 1968.

Ciuha, Jože/Šubic, Ive in:
Planina, France: **Jugoslavija**. (Yugoslavia; Jugoslawien.)
Ljubljana: Mladinska knjiga 1968.

1969 *Fiction/Belletristik*

Rozmon, smiljan: **Reporter Tejč poroca**. (Reporter *Tejč* reports the news; Reporter *Tejč meldet.) Ill.: Božo Kos.*
Ljubljana: Mladinska knjiga 1968.

Non-fiction/Sachbuch

Stanič, Janez: **Onkraj Kremlja**. (Beyond the Kremlin; Jenseits des Kreml.)
Ljubljana: Mladinska knjiga 1968

Gerlovič, Alenka/Gregorač, Ignac: **Likovni pouk otrok**. (Drawing lessons for children; Zeichenlehre für Kinder.) Ill.: Ignac Greorač.
Ljubljana: Mladinska knjiga 1968.

Illustration

Kos, Božo in:
Suhodolčan, Leopold: **Veliki in mali kapitan**. (The big and the small captains; Der große und der kleine Kapitän.)
Ljubljana: Mladinska knjiga 1968.

Kos, Božo in:
Pionirski list: **Kavboj Pipec in Rdeča pesa**. (Cowboy *Pipec* and *Red Beet*; Cowboy *Pipec* und *Rote Rübe*.)
Ljubljana: Pionirski list (Children's magazine; Kinderzeitschrift). 1969.

Kos, Božo in:
Pionirski, list: **Vesela šola**. (Delightful school; Lustige Schule.)
Ljubljana: Pionirski list 1969.

1970 *Fiction/Belletristik*

Snoj, Jože: **Barabákos in kosi, ali kako si Pokovčev Igor po pravici prislužil in pošteno odslužil to ime**. (*Barabákos* and the thrushes, or how *Pokovčev Igor* justly deserved that name and how he honestly paid off by service; *Barabákos* und die Amseln, oder wie *Pokovčev Igor* sich gerechterweise diesen Namen verdient und wie er ihn sich ehrlich abgedient hat.) Ill.: Božo Kos.
Ljubljana: Mladinska knjiga 1969.

Zorman, Ivo: **V tem mesecu se osipa mak**. (In this month the leaves of the poppy fall; In diesem Monat fallen die Blätter des Mohns.)
Ljubljana: Mladinska knjiga 1969.

Non-fiction/Sachbuch

Kotnik, Stanko: **Po domovih nasih pisateljev**. (The houses where our writers were born; Die Geburtshäuser unserer Schriftsteller.)
Ljubljana: Mladinska knjiga 1969.

Illustration

Osterc, Lidija in:
Grottet, Robert: **Laponske pripovedke**. (Lappish stories; Lappländische Erzählungen.)
Ljubljana: Mladinska knjiga 1969.

Osterc, Lidija in:
Pavček, Tone: **Strašni lovec Bumbum**. (*Bumbum*, the terrible hunter; Der schreckliche Jäger *Bumbum*.)
Ljubljana: Mladinska knjiga 1969.

Osterc, Lidija in:
Peroci, Ela: **Očala tete Bajavaje**. (Aunt *Bajavaja*'s spectacles; Die Brille der Tante *Bajavaja*.)
Ljubljana: Mladinska knjiga 1969.

Šubic, Ive in:
Kuntner, Tone: **Lesnika**. (The crab apple; Der Holzapfel.)
Ljubljana: Mladinska knjiga 1969.

Šubic, Ive in:
Gopal, Dhan: **Mladost v džungli**. (Youth in the jungle; Jugend im Urwald.)
Ljubljana: Mladinska knjiga 1969.

1971 *Fiction/Belletristik*
Forsternič, France: **Srakač**. (Magpie boy; Elsterjunge.) Ill.: Janez Vidic.
Ljubljana: Mladinska knjiga 1970.

Non-Fiction/Sachbuch
Šmit, Jože: **Kako bomo umirali**. (How we will die; Wie wir sterben werden.)
Ljubljana: Mladinska knjiga 1970.

Hadži, Jovan: **Razvojna pota živalstva**. (The ways that animals develop; Die Entwicklung der Tiere.)
Ljubljana: Mladinska knjiga 1970.

Illustration
Stupica, Marlenka in:
Suhodolčan, Leopold: **Krojaček Hlaček**. (*Taylor Tim*; Schneiderlein *Hosenmatz*.)
Ljubljana: Mladinska knjiga 1970.

Stupica, Marlenka in:
Števile. (Numbers; Zahlen.)
Ljubljana: Mladinska knjiga 1970.

Stupica, Marlenka in:
Babica v cirkusu. (Grandmother in the circus; Die Großmutter im Zirkus.)
Ljubljana: Mladinska knjiga 1970.

Seljak-Čopič, Ive in:
Ciciban, Pionir and Pionirski list (Children's magazines; Kinderzeitschriften.)
Ljubljana

1972 *Ficition/Belletristik*
Zupanc, Lojze: **Zlato pod Blegošem**. (Gold under the *Blegoš*; Das Gold unter dem *Blegoš*.) Ill.: Ive Šubic.
Ljubljana: Mladinska knjiga 1971.

Bitenc, Janez: **Ciciban poje**. (*Ciciban* sings; *Ciciban* singt.)
Ljubljana: Mladinska knjiga 1971.

Non-fiction/Sachbuch
Menaše, Luc: **Evropski umetnostno zgodovinski leksikon**. (European art history lexicon; Europäisches kunsthistorisches Lexikon.)
Ljubljana: Mladinska knjiga 1971.

Illustration
Šubic, Ive in:
Godina, Ferdo: **Kos rženega kruha.** (A piece of rye bread; Ein Stück Roggenbrot.)
Ljubljana: Mladinska knjiga 1971.

1973 *Fiction/Belletristik*
Brenk, Kristina: **Deklica Delfina in lisica Zvitorepka.** (The girl *Delfina* and *Reinecke* the fox; Das Mädchen *Delfina* und *Reinecke* Fuchs.) Ill.: Marlenke Stupica.
Ljubljana: Mladinska knjiga 1972.

Non-fiction/Sachbuch
Kremenšek, Slavko: **slovensko študentsko gibanje 1919—1941.** (The Slovenian student movement 1919—1941; Slovenische Studentenbewegung von 1919—1941.)
Ljubljana: Mladinska knjiga 1972.

Illustration
Kos, Božo in:
Jurca, Branka: **Rodiš se samo enkrat.** (You are born only once; Du wirst nur einmal geboren.)
Ljubljana: Mladinska knjiga 1972.

1974 *Fiction/Belletristik*
Makarovič, Svetlana: **Miška spi.** (The little mouse sleeps; Das Mäuschen schläft.) Ill.: Milan Bizovičar.
Ljubljana: Mladinska knjiga 1972.

Non-fiction/Sachbuch
Matičetov, Milko: **Zverinice iz Rezije.** (Little wild animals from *Rezija*; Die Raubtierchen aus *Rezija*.) Ill.:Ančka Gosnik-Godec.
Ljubljana: Mladinska knjiga 1973.

Illustration
Stupica, Marlenka in:
Andersen, Hans-Christian: **Kraljična na zrnu fraha.** (The princess and the pea; Die Prinzessin auf der Erbse; Dan.orig.title: Prinsessen på aerten.)
Ljubljana: Mladinska knjiga 1973.

1975 *Fiction/Belletristik*
Godina, Ferdo: **Sezidala si bova hišico.** (We two will build a small house; Wir beide werden uns ein Häuschen bauen.) Ill.: Ive Šubic.
Ljubljana: Mladinska knjiga 1974.

Non-fiction/Sachbuch
Ogrin, Miran: **Od Kalifornije do Ognjene zemlje.** (From *California* to *Fireland*; Von *Kalifornien* bis *Feuerland*.)
Ljubljana: Mladinska knjiga 1974.

Illustration
Bizovičar, Milan in:
Kovačič, Lojze: **Možicek med dimniki**. (The little man between the chimnies; Das Männlein zwischen den Schornsteinen.)
Ljubljana: Mladinska knjiga 1974.

1976 *Fiction/Belletristik*
Makarovič, Svetlana: **Kam pa kam, kosovirja?** (*Glili* and *Glal*, where to now? *Glili* und *Glal*, wohin nun?) Ill.: Lidija Osterc.
Ljubljana: Mladinska knjiga 1975.

Makarovič, Svetlana: **Kosovirja na leteči žlici**. (*Glili* and *Glal* on the flying spoon; *Glili* und *Glal* auf dem fliegenden Löffel.) Ill.: Lidija Osterc.
Ljubljana: Mladinska knjiga 1974.

Makarović, Svetlana: **Pekarna Mišmaš**. (The *Mishmash Backerey*; Die *Bäckerei Mischmasch*.) Ill.: Marija Lucija Stupica.
Ljubljana: Mladinska knjiga 1974.

Non-fiction/Sachbuch
Tarman, Kazimir: **Zakaj zato v ekologiji**. (The why of ecology; Das warum und wofür in der Ökologie.) Ill.: Božo Kos.
Ljubljana: Mladinska knjiga 1975.

Illustration
Bizovičar, Milan in:
Zajc, Dane: **Abecedarija**. (Alphabet; ABC.)
Ljubljana: Mladinska knjiga 1975.

1977 *Fiction/Belletristik*
Snoj, Jože: **Avtomoto mravlje**. (The Antland auto; Das Auto-Ameisenland.) Ill.: Melita Vovk-Stih.
Ljubljana: Mladinska knjiga 1975.

Snoj, Jože: **Pesmi za punčke**. (Poems for girls; Gedichte für Mädchen.) Ill.: Lidija Osterc.
Ljubljana: Mladinska knjiga 1976.

Non-fiction/Sachbuch
Pavlovec, Rajko: **Kras**. (Stoney ground; Der Karst.) Ill.: Božo Kos/Leon Koporc.
Ljubljana: Mladinska knjiga 1976.

Illustration
Seljak-Čopič, Ive in:
Defoe, Daniel: **Robinson Crusoe**. (*Robinson Crusoe*.)
Ljubljana: Mladinska knjiga 1975.

Seljak-Čopič, Ive in:
Afriške pripovedke. (African tales; Afrikanische Erzählungen.)
Ljubljana: Mladinska knjiga 1976.

Seljak-Čopič, Ive in:
Bevk, France: **Knjiga o Titu.** (A book about *Tito*; Ein Buch über *Tito*.)
Ljubljana: Mladinska knjiga 1976.

1978 *Fiction/Belletristik*

Pregl, Slavko: **Geniji v kratkih hlačeh.** (A genius in short pants; Ein Genie in kurzen Hosen.)
Ljubljana: Mladinska knjiga 1978.

Non-fiction/Sachbuch

Jerin, Zoran: **Himalaja, rad te imam.** (*Himalaya*, I love you; *Himalaya*, ich habe dich gern.)
Ljubljana: Mladinska knjiga 1978.

Illustration

Amalietti, Marjan in:
Dostoevskij, Feodor Michajlovič: **Netočka Nezvanova.** (Netočka Nezvanova.)
Ljubljana: Mladinska knjiga 1978.

Amalietti, Marjan in:
Kolář, Jiři: **Ulenspiegel.** (Owlglass; Eulenspiegel.)
Ljubljana: Mladinska knjiga 1978.

1979 *Fiction/Belletristik*

Suhodolčan, Leopold: **Piko Dinozaver.** (Piko the dinosaur; Piko der Dinosaurier.) Ill.: Marjanca Jemec-Božič.
Ljubljana: Mladinska knjiga 1978.

Suhodolčan, Leopold: **Cepecepetavček.** (The little wiggle-waggle man; Das Zappelzappelmännchen.) Ill.: Jelka Reichman.
Ljubljana: Mladinska knjiga 1979.

Suhodolčan, Leopold: **Peter Nos je vsemu kos.** (*Peter Nose* manages everything; *Peter Nase* schafft alles.) Ill.: Marjan Manček.
Ljubljana: Mladinska knjiga 1979.

Suhodolčan, Leopold: **Levi in desni klovn.** (The left and the right clown; Der linke und der rechte Clown.) Ill.: Matjaž Schmidt.
Ljubljana: Mladinska knjiga 1979.

Suhodolčan, Leopold: **Norčije v gledališču.** (Nonsense in the mirror; Unsinn im Spiegel.)
Ljubljana: Mladinska knjiga 1979.

Vegri, Saša: **Mama pravi, da v očkovi glavi.** (Mama tells what's in father's head; Mama erzählt, was in Vaters Kopf ist.) Ill.: Marjan Manček.
Ljubljana: Mladinska knjiga 1978.

Non-fiction/Sachbuch
Makarovič, Marija: **Kmečka abeceda.** (The farmer's ABC; Das Bauern-ABC.) Ill.: Lidija Osterc.
Ljubljana: Mladinska knjiga 1979.

Makarovič, Marija: **Kmečko gospodarstvo na Slovenskem.** (Farming in Slovenia; Landwirtschaft in Slovenien.) Ill.: France Golob.
Ljubljana: Mladinska knjiga 1978.

Illustration
Reichman, Jelka in:
Suhodolčan, Leopold: Cepecepetavček. (The little wiggle-wiggle man; Das Zappelzappelmännchen.)
Ljubljana: Mladinska knjiga 1979.

1980 *Fiction/Belletristik*
Grafenauer, Niko: **Nebotičniki, sedite.** (Sky scrappers, sit down; Wolkenkratzer, setzt euch.) Ill.: Matjač Schmidt.
Ljubljana: Mladinska knjiga 1979.

Non-fiction/Sachbuch
Prosen, Marijan: **Utrinki iz astronomije.** (Shooting stars of astronomy; Sternschnuppen der Astronomie.) Ill.: Matjaž Schmidt.
Ljubljana: Mladinska knjiga 1979.

Illustration
Jemec-Bežič, Marjanca in:
Jurca, Branka: **Ko Nina spi.** (*When* Nina sleeps; Wenn *Nina* schläft.)
Ljubljana: Mladinska knjiga 1980.

Jemec-Božič, Marjanca in:
Kovač, Polonca: **Deževen dan je krasen dan.** (A rainy day is a nice day; Ein Regentag ist ein schöner Tag.)
Ljubljana: Mladinska knjiga 1979.

Jemec-Božič, Marjanca in:
Župančič, Oton: **Pomladna ladja.** (The spring ship; Das Frühlingsschiff.)
Ljubljana: Mladinska knjiga 1980.

Jemec-Božič, Marjanca in:
Cernej, Anica: **Metuljčki.** (Butterflies; Schmetterlinge.)
Ljubljana: Mladinska knjiga 1980.

Jemec-Božič in:
Glazer, Alenka: **Žigažaga**. (Zigzag; Zickzack.)
Ljubljana: Mladinska knjiga 1980.

Nagrada Mlado pokolenje

The Mlado pokolenje prize is awarded annually to the best children's book and also to the best illustrations for a children's book. Books submitted for the prize may be in any of the different Yugoslavian languages, and printed in either Latin or Cyrillic letters. The name of this prize means, „Young Generations".

Der Mlado-pokolenje-Preis wird jährlich sowohl für das beste Kinderbuch als auch für die beste Kinderbuchillustration verliehen, gleichgültig in welcher Sprache Jugoslawiens es verfaßt ist, ob es in kyrillischen oder lateinischen Lettern gedruckt ist. Der Name des Preises bedeutet: Junge Generation.

1956 Seliškar, Tone: **Complete works**; Gesamtschaffen.

Čopič, Branko: **Doživljaji mačka Toše**. (The adventures of Toša the tom-cat; Die Erlebnisse des Katers Toša.) Ill.: Miloš Bajoć.
Beograd: Dečja kniga 1954.

Illustration
Ciuha, Jože: **Complete works**; Gesamtschaffen.

1957 Lovrak, Mato: **Complete works**; Gesamtschaffen.

Prize for the best book was not given; Der Preis für den besten Text wurde nicht vergeben.

Illustration
Nikolić, Save: **Complete works**; Gesamtschaffen.

1958 Maksimović, Desanka: **Complete works**; Gesamtschaffen.

Peroci, Ela: **Majhno kot mezinec**. (Small as the little finger; Klein wie der kleine Finger.) Ill.: Ančka Gošnik-Godec.
Ljubljana: Mladinska knjiga 1957.

Illustration
Vogelnik, Marija in:
Legiša, Lino: **Pojte, pojte drohne ptice**. (Sing, sing little birds; Singt, singt kleine Vögel.)
Ljubljana: Mladinska knjiga 1955.

1959 Bevk, France: **Complete works**; Gesamtschaffen.

Oblak, Danko: **Modri prozori**. (Blue windows; Blaue Fenster.) Ill.: Albert Kinert.
Sarajevo: Veselin Masleša 1959.

Illustration
Sokič, Ljubica: **Complete works**; Gesamtschaffen.

1960 Tartalja, Gvido: **Complete works**; Gesamtschaffen.

Danojlić, Milovan: **Kako apvaju tramvaji**. (How the tram cars sleep; Wie die Straßenbahnen schlafen.) Ill.: Danica Rusjan.
Zagreb: Lykos 1959.

Illustration
Ciuha, Jože in:
Puškin, Aleksandr Serveevič: **Pravljice**. (Fairy tales; Märchen; Russ.orig.title: Poslovenila Oton Župančič in Mile Klopčič.)
Ljubljana: Mladinska knjiga 1960.

1961 Pavičič, Josip: **Complete works**; Gesamtschaffen.

Pavčič, Tone: **Velesenzacija**. (Great sensation; Große Sensation.) Ill.: Zdenka Golob-Boršič.
Ljubljana: Mladinska knjiga 1961.

Illustration
Gošnik-Godec, Ančka: **Complete works**; Gesamtschaffen.

1962 Radović, Dušan: **Smešne reči**. (Funny words; Lustige Worte.) Ill.: Đorđe Milanović.
Beograd: Prosveta 1961.

Essay on children's literature; Essay über Kinderliteratur
Tahmiššič, Hussein: **U lepom krugu. Studija o pesmama za decu jovana Jovanovića Zmaja**. (In the beautiful circle. A study of the poems for children by *Jovan Jovanović Zmaj*; Im schönen Kreis. Studie über die Gedichte von *Jovan Jovanović Zmaj*.)
Kruševac: Bagdala 1963.

Tahmiššič, Hussein: **Ponova osvojen grad**. (The reconquered city; Die wiedereroberte Stadt.)
Sarajevo: Svjetlost 1961.

Illustration
Milanović, Đorđe: **Complete works**; Gesamtschaffen.

Milanović, Đorđe in: **Smešne reči**. (Funny words; Lustige Worte.)
Beograd: Prosveta 1961.

1963 Vitez, Grigor: **Complete works**; Gesamtschaffen.

Crnčević, Branislav: **Bosonogi i nebo**. (The barefooted ones and the sky; Die Barfüssigen und der Himmel.) Ill.: Vladimir Stojiljković.
Beograd: Prosveta 1963.

Illustration
Seljak-Čopič, Ive in:
Andrić, Ivo: **Aska in volk**. (*Aska* and the wolf; *Aska* und der Wolf.)
Ljubljana: Mladinska knjiga 1963.

1964 Čopič, Branko: **Complete works**; Gesamtschaffen.
Ceković, Ivan: **Kad bi mjesec bio balon**. (If the moon were a balloon; Wenn der Mond ein Ballon wäre.) Ill.: Gordana Popović.
Beograd: Mlado pokolenje 1964.

Illustration
Šubic, Ive in:
Brenk, Kristina: **Dolgi pot**. (The long way; Der lange Weg.)
Ljubljana: Mladinska knjiga 1965.

1965 Mihelič, Mira: **Pridi, mili moj Ariel**. (Come, dear *Ariel*; Komm, mein lieber *Ariel*.) Ill.: Roza Piščanec.
Ljubljana: Mladinska knjiga 1965.

Illustration
Vovk, Melita in:
Krylov, Ivan Andreevič: **Petdeset basni**. (Fifteen fables; Fünfzehn Fabeln.)
Ljubljana: Mladinska knjiga 1964.

1966 Brenk, Kristina: **Complete works**; Gesamtschaffen.
Podgorec, Vidoje: **Beloto ciganče**. (The white gipsy child; Das weiße Zigeunerkind.)
Skopje: Nova Makedonija 1966.
Šćekić, Draško: **Planina**. (The mountains; Das Gebirge.)
Sarajevo: Svetlost 1966.

Illustration
Rusjan, Danica in:
Hromadžić, Ahmet: **Zlatorum**. (*Zlatorum*.)
Sarajevo: Svetlost 1966.

1967 Ivanji, Ivan: **Kengur, helikopter i drugi**. (The kangaroo, the helicopter and other things; Känguruh, Helikopter und anderes.) Ill.: Marjan Lehner.
Beograd: Prosveta 1967.

Illustration
Petlevski, Ordan in:
Vitez, Grigor: **Igra se nastavlja**. (The game continues; Das Spiel geht weiter.)
Zagreb: Mladost 1967.

1968 Mikić, Aleksa: for his long and fertile artistic creation for children and his many successes in the creation and development of periodicals for children; für sein langjähriges und fruchtbares künstlerisches Schaffen für Kinder und für seine Erfolge im Schaffen und Entwickeln einer Zeitschrift für Kinder.

Janevski, Slavko: **Crni i Žolti**. (Blacks and yellows; Schwarze und Gelbe.) Ill.: Dimitar Kondovski.
Skopje: Makedonska kniga 1967.

Erić, Dobrica: **Slavuj i sunce**. (The nightingale and the sun; Die Nachtigall und die Sonne.) Ill.: Saša Mišić.
Beograd: Mlado pokolenje 1968.

Matošec, Milivej: **Strah u ulici lipa**. (Fear in Linden Street; Die Angst in der Lindenstraße.) Ill.: Branko Vujanović.
Zagreb: Mladost 1968.

Illustration
Ćirić, Ida in:
Ko umije njemu dvije. (He who can, has two; Wers kann, hat zwei.)
Beograd: Vuk Kradžić 1968.

1969 Krlec, Gustav: **Complete works**; Gesamtschaffen.

Nikoleski, Vančo: **Complete works;** Gesamtschaffen.

Lukić, Dragan: **Hiljadu reči o tri reči**. (One thousand words about three words; 1000 Worte über drei Worte.) Ill.: Marko Krsmanović.
Beograd: Mlado pkolenje 1968.

Katalinić, Palma: **Pričanje cvrčka moreplovca**. (The tale of the seafaring cricket; Die Erzählung der Seefahrergrille.) Ill.: Diana Kosec-Bourek.
Zagreb: Mladost 1969.

Illustration
Bourek, Zlatko in:
Kolar, Boris: **Dječak i lopta**. (The boy and the ball; Der Junge und der Ball.)
Zagreb: Skolska knjiga 1969.

Kos, Božo in:
Snoj, Jože: **Barbakos in kosi**. (*Barabakos* and the thrushes; *Barabakos* und die Amseln.)
Ljubljana: Mladinska knjiga 1969.

1970 Vučo, Aleksandar: for his poetic works which opened a new period in children's literature; für das dichterische Werk, das eine neue Epoche in der Kinderliteratur einleitet.

Kunoski, Vasil: for his pioneer work in the development of Macedonian poetry for children; für seine Pionierarbeit in der Entwicklung einer makedonischen Poesie für Kinder.

Tešić, Momčilo: **Complete works**; Gesamtschaffen.

Rsumović, Ljubivoje: **Ma šta mi reče**. (What you don't say; Was du nicht sagst!) Ill.: Dušan Petričić.
Novi Sad: Zmajeve decje igre.-Kulturni centar 1970.

Balog, Zvonimir: **Nevidljiva Iva**. (Invisible *Iva*; Die unsichtbare *Iva*.) Ill.: Marija Putra-Žižić.
Zagreb: Mladost 1970.

Illustration
Seljak-Copic, Ive: for his illustration output of the previous year; für das reiche illustratorische Werk im vergangenen Jahr.

1971/ Jurca, Branka: **Complete works**; Gesamtschaffen

1972 Horkić, Dragutin: **Čadeve zgode.** (Sooty adventures; Rußige Abenteuer.) Ill.: Aleksandar Marks and Pavao Štalter.
Zagreb: Školska knjiga 1971.

Németh, István: **Sebestyén**. (*Sebestyén*.)
Novi Sad: Forum 1972.

Popovski, Gligor: **Bilana**. (*Biljana*.)
Skopje: Misla 1972.

1973 Janevski, Slavko: **Complete works**; Gesamtschaffen.

Antić, Miroslav: **Garavi sokak**. (The street of the black dog; Die Straße des schwarzen Hundes.)
Čortanovici: Umetnička kolonija „Plavi Dunav" 1973.

Kulidžan, Dragan: **Deco, dobar dan**. (Good day, children; Kinder, guten Tag.)
Titograd: Pionirksi kulturni centar 1973.

Matičetov, Milko: **Zverinice iz Rezije**. (The little forest animals from *Rezija*; Die kleinen Waldtiere aus *Rezija*.) Ill.: Ančka Gošnik-Godec.
Ljubljana: Mladinska knjiga 1973.

Illustration
Selan Gliha, Vilko: **Complete works**; Gesamtschaffen.

Lukić, Jovan in:
The books of Juraj Tušjak, Pavel Grnja and Dobrica Erić; In den Büchern von Juraj Tušjak, Pavel Grnja und Dobrica Erić.

1974 Tušjak, Juraj: for prolific literary creation over many years for children; für langjähriges, fruchtbares literarisches Schaffen für Kinder.

Illustration
Petričić, Dušan: for his illustrations in the children's magazine „Poletarac" during 1974; für seine Illustrationen in der Kinderzeitschrift „Poletarac" im Jahre 1974.

1975 Kulidžan, Dragan: for his long and prolific literary creations for children; für langjähriges, fruchtbares literarisches Schaffen für Kinder.

Pandžo, Šukrija: **Zeleni strah**. (The green horror; Der grüne Schreck.) Ill.: Omer Omerović.
Sarajevo: Veselin Masleša 1975.

Illustration
Dogan, Boris in:
Dragojević, Danijel: **Bajka o vratima**. (The fairy tale about the door; Das Märchen von der Tür.)
Zagreb: Naprijed 1975.

1976 Radičević, Branko: **Devetaci**. (The nine; Die Neun.) Ill.: Boslijka Kićevac-Popović.
Beograd: Vuk Karadžić 1976.

Milček, Zvonimir: **Zviždukh s Bukovca**. (The whistle from *Bukovac*; Der Pfiff von *Bukovac*.) Ill.: Oto Reisinger.
Zagreb: Mladost 1975.

Ratković, Milenko: **Dvoboj u gradu dečeka**. (A duel in the city of boys; Zweikampf in der Stadt der Jungen.)
Titograd: Pobjeda 1975.

Illustration
Dragić, Nedeljko in:
Šporer, Zlatko: **Uh, ta matematika**. (Ugh, this math; Uch, diese Mathematik.)
Zagreb: Školska knjiga 1975.

1977 Penjin, Dragiša: **Tajna breskvinog cveta**. (The secret of the peach blossom; Das Geheimnis der Pfirsichblüte.) Ill.: Dragana Atanasović.
Beograd: Beogradski izdavažko-grafižki zavod 1977.

Nikolova, Olivera: **Mojot zvuk**. (My sound; Mein Klang.) Ill.: Ordan Manevski.
Skopje: Detska radost 1977.

Illustration
Lipovac, Vasko in:
Jelić, Vojin: **Kapetan gola brka**. (The captain without a moustache; Der Kapitän ohne Schnauzbart.)
Zagreb: Školska knjiga 1977.

1978 Diklić, Arsen: **Jesen u Mrtvaji**. (Autumn in the stagnant water; Herbst im Altwasser.) Ill.: Children's drawing; Kinderzeichnungen. Beograd: Narodna knjiga 1978.

Škrinjarič, Sunčana: **Pisac i vrijeme**. (The writer and the time; Der Schriftsteller und die Zeit.) Ill.: Josip Bifel. Zagreb: Naša djeca 1978.

Jovanović, Zoran: **Sunce je cvet na reveru dana**. (The sun is a flower on the lapel of the day; Die Sonne ist eine Blume auf dem Revers des Tages.) Sarajevo: Svjetlost 1978.

Illustration
Krsmanović, Marko in:
Lukić, Dragan: **Kapetanov slanik**. (The captain's saltshaker; Das Salzfaß des Kapitäns.) Beograd: BIGZ, Nolit, Prosveta, Vuk Karadžić 1978.

1979 Stojiljković, Vlada: **Blok 39**. (Block 39.) Beograd: BIGZ 1979.

Olujić, Gvozdana: **Sedefna ruža i druge bajke**. (The mother-of-pearl rose and other fairy tales; Die Perlmuttrose und andere Märchen.) Ill.: biserka Baretić. Zagreb: Mladost 1979.

Illustration
Marušić, Joško in:
Kišević, Enes: **Mačak u trapericama**. (The cat in jeans; Der bejeanste Kater.) Zagreb: Školska knjiga 1979.

1980 Šehović, Feda: **Vidra**. (The otter; Der Otter.) Ill.: Ivo Grbić. Zagreb: Školska knjiga 1980.

Subotić, Radovan: **Put oko cvta**. (Journey around the flower; Reise um die Blume.) Ill.: Slobodan Kuzmanov Kuza. Novi Sad: Radivoj Ćirpanov 1980.

Illustration
Antoločič, Ivan in:
Hitric, Hrvoje: **Petrica Kerempuh**. *(Petrica Kerempuh.)* Zagreb: Školska knjiga 1980.

Nagrada Neven

Since 1955, the Neven prize has been awarded to the best children's book written in Serbo-Croatian and published in the Serbian Socialist Republic. Books submitted for the prize can be in either Latin or Cyrllic type. In some years, outstanding illustrations are also given an award. The prize was named after "Neven" (1852—1858), the magazine devoted to entertainment and education, which in turn was named after the collection of poems by the well known Serbian author, Zmaj Jovan Jovanovich. Founded after the abortive revolution of 1848, this magazine, edited by the Matice ilirske, played an important part in the formation of the inner resistance against the absolutist regime of that time.

Für das beste Kinderbuch in serbokroatischer Sprache, soweit es im Bereich der Serbischen Sozialistischen Republik erschienen ist, wird seit 1955 der Neven-Preis verliehen. Die Bücher können sowohl in kyrillischer wie in lateinischer Schrift eingereicht werden, auch zeichnet man gelegentlich beste Kinderbuchillustrationen aus. Benannt wurde der Preis nach dem serbischen Autor Zmaj Jovan Jovanović und seiner Gedichtsammlung "Neven" (Ringelblume). Zugleich ist dies auch der Name einer Zeitschrift zur Unterhaltung und Belehrung (1852—1858). Sie wurde kurz nach der fehlgeschlagenen Revolution von 1848 gegründet und von Matice ilirske herausgegeben. Sie spielte eine wichtige Rolle im Widerstand gegen das absolutistische Regime jener Zeit.

1955 *Copić, Branko:* **Dozivljaji mačka Toše.** (*Toša* the tomcat; Der Kater *Toša.*) Ill.: Miloš Bajić.
Beograd: Dečja knjiga 1954.

Kostić, Živko: **Izmedu igre i hemije.** (Between play and chemistry; Zwischen Spiel und Chemie.) Ill.: Živko Kostić.
Beograd: Tehnička knjiga 1954.

Milošević, Slavka: **Zanimljiva geografija.** (Exciting geography; Spannende Geografie.)
Beograd: Znanje 1954.

Radović, Dušan: **Poštovana dec!** (Honourable children! Sehr geehrte Kinder!) Ill.: Đorde Milanović.
Beograd: Dečja knjiga 1954.

Illustration
Antić, Danica in:
Vasić, Hrvoje: **Srcegrad.** (Heart town, Herzenstadt.)
Beograd: Dečja knjiga 1955.

Milanović, Đorde in:
Radović, Dušan: **Poštovana deco!** Honourable children! Sehr geehrte Kinder!)
Beograd: Dečja knjiga 1954.

1956 *Illustration*
Nikolić, Sava in:
Bajko iz 1001 noći. (Tales from 1001 nights; Märchen aus 1001 Nacht.) Adapt: Besim Korkut.
Beograd: Dečja knjiga 1956.

1957 Vučo, Aleksandar: **san i java hrabrog Koče.** (Dream and awakening of brave *Koča;* Traum und Wachen des tapferen *Koča.*) Ill.: Dragan Savić.
Beograd: Dečja knjiga 1957.

1958 The prize was not given; Der Preis wurde nicht vergeben.

1960 Raičković, Stevan: **Družina pod suncem.** (The comrades under the sun; Die Gefährten unter der Sonne.) Ill.: Boško Risimović.
Beograd: Prosveta 1960.

Vujačić, Mirko: **Tužni cirkusanti.** (Strange circus people; Fremde Zirkusleute.) Ill.: Sava Nikolić.
Beograd: Kosmos 1960.

1961 Lukić, Dragan: **Ovde stanuju pesme.** (Poems live here; Hier wohnen Gedichte.) Ill.: Sava Nikolić.
Beograd: Mlado pokolenje 1961.

Popović, Vojislav: **Čudotvorna iskra.** (The miraculous spark; Der wundervolle Funke.)
Beograd: Prosveta 1961.

1962 Stefanović, Mirjana: **Vlatko Pidžula.** (*Vlatko Pidźula.*)Ill.: Mihailo Pisanjuk.
Beograd: Prosveta 1962.

1963 Krišković, Josip: **Praznik lepih želja.** (Holiday of beautiful wishes; Feiertag der schönen Wünsche.)
Beograd: Mlado pokolenje 1963.

Illustration
Pisanjuk, Mihailo in:
Maksimović, Desanka: **Pisma iz šume.** (Letters from the forest; Briefe aus dem Wald.)
Beograd: Prosveta 1963.

1964 Petrović, Mirko: **Dečaci sa trouglastog trga.** (The children from the triangular square; Die Kinder vom dreieckigen Platz.) Ill.: Sava Nikolić.
Beograd: Mlado pokolenje 1964.

Illustration
Ćirić, Ida in:
Đavo i njegov šegrt. Devojka cara nadmudrila. (The devil and his apprentice. The girl that tricked the tsar; Der Teufel und sein Lehrling. Das Mädchen, das den Zaren überlistete.) Adapt.: Uglješa Krstić.
Beograd: Vuk Karadžić 1964.

1965 Antić,Miroslav: **Plavi čuperak.** (The blond tuft of hair; Der blonde Haarschopf.) Ill.: Milorad Mihailović.
Beograd: Mlado pokolenje 1965.

Illustration
Sokić, Ljibica in:
Hodža, Mehmedali: **Mali zastavnik.** (The little flag bearer; Der kleine Fahnenträger.) Adapt.: Uglješa Krstić.
Beograd: Vuk Karadžić 1965.

Sokić, Ljubica in:
Maksimović, Desanka: **Neću ovim vozom.** (I won't take this train; Ich nehme nicht diesen Zug.)
Beograd: Vuk Karadžić 1965

1966 Kukaj, Rifat: **Harmonika e Vogël.** (The little harmonica; Die kleine Harmonika.)
Priština: Pioniere 1966.

Matejić, Aleksandar: **Pioniri jugoslovenske nauke.** (Pioneers of Yugoslavian science; Pioniere der jugoslavischen Wissenschaft.) Ill.: Ljubodrag Janković.
Beograd: Mlado pokolenje 1966.

Illustration
Janković, Ljubodrag in:
Matejić, Aleksandar: **Pioniri jugoslovenske nauke.** (Pioneers of Yugoslavian science; Pioniere der jugoslavischen Wissenschaft.)
Beograd: Mlado pokolenje 1966.

1967 Ceković, Ivan: **Šetači laganije.** (The walking lie; Die spazierende Lüge.) Đorde Milanović.
Beograd: Mlado pokolenje 1967.

1968 Jorgačević, Jovanka: **Šestotina slova.** (600 letters; 600 Buchstaben.) Ill.: Bosiljka Kičevac.
Beograd: Mlado pokolenje 1968.

Kikaj, Vehbi: **Sarajet e bardha.** (White courts; Weisse Höfe.) Ill.: Veli Gervalla.
Priština: Rilindja 1968.

Babinka, Mihal: **Zvonce za dobro jutro.** (A little bell for a good morning; Ein Glöckchen zum Guten Morgen.)
Novi Sad: Mlad Obzor 1968.

Illustration
Krsmanović, Marke in:
Lukić, Dragan: **Hiljadu reči o tri reči.** (One thousand words about three words; 1000 Worte über drei Worte.)
Beograd: Mlado pokolenje 1968.

1969 Danojlić, Milovan: **Furunica jogunica.** The capricious stove; Der eigensinnige Ofen.) Ill.: Ankica Oprešnik.
Novi Sad: Kulturni centar 1969.

Deak, Ferenc: **Sova i čizma.** (Owl and boot; Eule und Stiefel.)
Novi Sad: Zmajeve dečje igre i Radnicki univerzitet "Radivcj Ćirpanov" 1969.

Tušjak, Juraj: **Jednostavne reči.** (Simple words; Einfache Worte.) Ill.: Budimir Vojnović.
Bratislava: Mladé letá; Bački Petrovac: Obzor 1969.

Budinski, Miron: **Vodenica na srebernom potoku.** (The mill on the silver brook; Die Mühle am Silberbach.)
Novi Sad: Ruske slovo 1969.

Hoxha, Rexhep: **Gecatarët.** (The children from *Geca*; Die Kinder von *Geca.*) Ill.: Veli Gërvalla.
Priština: Rilindja 1969.

1970 Ršumović, Ljubivoje: **Ma šta mi reče.** (What you didn't say; Was du nicht sagst.) Ill.: Dusan Petričić.
Novi Sad: Zmajeve dečje igre i Kulturni centar 1970.

Németh, István: **A vadalma.** (The wild apple; Der wilde Apfel.)
Novi Sad: Forum 1970.

Shehu, Maksut: **Agimi** (Dawn; Morgenröte.)
Priština: Rilindja 1970.

1971 Stanojević, Zoran: **Rođak Glo.** (The relative; *Glo*; Der Verwandte *Glo.*)
Novi Sad: Zmajeve dečje igre i Kulturni centar 1971.

Čakan, Štefan: **Basne.** (Favles; Fabeln.) Ill.: Melanija Mudri.
Novi Sad: Ruske slovo 1971.

Batalli, Qamil: **Tri dritare.** (Three windows; Drei Fenster.) Ill.: Nevruz Musa.
Priština: Rilindja 1971.

Bogdánfi, Sándor: **Óriások.** (Giants; Riesen.)
Novi Sad: Forum 1971.

Illustration
Kovačević, Živojin in:
Priče stare puške. (Tales of an old gun; Erzählungen einer alten Kanone.)
Beograd: Beogradski izdavačko grafički zavod, Prosveta 1971.

1972 Danojlić, Milovan: **Rodna godina.** (The year of birth; Das Geburtsjahr.) Ill.: Ivan Lacković.
Beograd: Beogradski izdavačko grafički zavod 1972.

Antić, Miroslav: **Šašava knjiga.** (Crazy book; Verrücktes Buch.) Ill.: Mića Mihailović.
Beograd: Beogradski izdavačko grafički zavod 1972.

Dedaj, Rrahman: **Zogu dhe kulla.** (The bird and the tower; Der Vogel und der Turm.) Ill.: Shyqri Nimani.
Prištana: Rilindja 1972.

Illustration
Kičevac, Bosiljka in:
Bio jednom. (Once upon a time; Es war einmal.)
Beograd: Vuk Karadžić 1972.

1973 Lazić, Laza: **Na drvetu čavka.** (In the tree there is a jackdaw; Auf dem Baum sitzt eine Dohle.) Ill.: Milena Ćorak.
Beograd: Beogradski izdavačko grafički zavod 1973.

Németh, István: **Ki látta azt a kisfiút?** (Who saw this boy? Wer hat jenen Jungen gesehen?) Ill.: Oszkar Stefan.
Novi Sad: Forum 1973.

Deva, Agim: **Gishti ngjyre vjollce.** (The violet finger; Der violette Finger.) Ill.: Nusret Salihamixhiq.
Priština: Rilindja 1973.

Brasnyó, István: **Kései csillag.** (The late star; Der späte Stern.)
Novi Sad: Forum 1973.

Illustration
Petričić, Dušan in:
Ršumović, Ljubivoje: **Još nam samo ale fale.** (We miss the dragons; Drachen haben uns grad noch gefehlt.)
Beograd: Beogradski izdavačko grafički zavod 1973.

1974 Popović, Aleksandar: **Lek protiv starenja.** (Medicine against aging; Medizin gegen Altwerden.) Ill.: Milica Andrije.
Beograd: Beogradski izdavačko grafički zavod 1974.

Krasniqi, Mark: **Lepuri analfabet.** (The illiterate rabbit; Der Hase Analfabet.) Ill.: Abdylkader Pagarusha.
Priština: Rilindja 1974.

Brasnyó, István: **Holdfény.** (Moonshine; Mondschein.) Ill.: Oszkár Stefan.
Novi Sad: Forum 1974.

Kočiš, Evgenij m.: **Čajka.** (The seagull; Die Möwe.) Ill.: Petar Mojak.
Novi Sad: Ruske slovo 1974.

Illustration
Zečević, Radoslav in:
Lukić, Dragan: **Šta tata kaže.** (What papa says; Was Papa sagt.)
Beograd: Beogradski izdavačko grafički zavod 1974.

1975 Kulenović, Skender: **Gromovo dule.** Thunder roses; Donnerrosen.) Ill.: Mihailo Ćoković-Tikalo.
Beograd: Beogradski izdavačko grafički zavod 1975.

Elshani, Ymer: **Avanturat mbi trotinetin e vjeter.** (Adventures of an old scooter; Abenteuer auf einem alten Roller.)
Priština: Rilindja 1975.

Pavlovič, Melanija: **Veselinka.** (*Veselinka.*) Ill.: Jovan Lukić.
Novi Sad: Ruske slovo 1975.

Jung, Károly: **Bájoló.** (The sorcerer; Der Zauberer.)
Novi Sad: Forum 1975.

Illustration
Gavela, Dušan in:
Čudić, Predrag: **Jesen u cirkusu.** (Autumn in the circus; Herbst im Zirkus.)
Beograd: Vuk Karadžić 1975.

1976 Borisavljević, Miodrag: **Šumskim stazama.** (On the trail in the forest; Auf den Spuren im Wald.)
Beograd: Vuk Karadžić 1976.

Kanjuh, Miron: **Dobridzenjka.** (The good day girl; Das Guten-Tag-Mädchen.) Ill.: Olja Kovač.
Novi Sad: Ruske slovo 1976.

Bunjaku, Abdyl: **Djaloshi pas plepit.** (The boy behind the poplars; Der Junge hinter den Pappeln.) Ill.: Smajo Musoviq.
Priština: Rilindja 1976.

Illustration
Student group from the faculty of fine arts in Beograd; Gruppe von Studenten der Fakultät für angewandte Künste in Beograd in:

Ršumović, Ljubivoje: **Vesti iz nevesti.** (News from unconsciousness; Nachrichten aus der Ohnmacht.)
Beograd: Beogradski izdavačko grafički zavod 1976.

1977 Borisavljević, Miodrag: **Šumskim stazama.** (On forest paths; Auf Waldwegen.) Ill.: Emilija Kićvac.
Beograd: Vuk Karadžić 1978.

Kanjuh, Miron: **Dobridzenska.** (The good day girl; Das Guten-Tag-Mädchen.) Ill.: Olja Kovač.
Novi Sad: Ruske slovo 1976.

Bunjaku, Abdyl: **Djaloshi pas plepit.** (The boy behind the poplar; Der Junge hinter der Pappel.) Ill.: Smajo Musoviq.
Priština: Rilindja 1976.

1978 Jovović, Milena: **Mravlje srce.** (Ant heart; Ameisenherz.) Ill.: Ida Čirić.
Beograd: BIGZ 1977.

Kovač, Mihailo: **Perši radosci.** (The first joys; Die ersten Freuden,) Ill.: Olja Kovač.
Novi Sad: Ruske slovo 1977.

Gion, Nandor: **A kárókatonak még nem jötteg visza.** (The cormorants did not yet return; Die Kormorane sind noch nicht zurückgekommen.)
Novi Sad: Forum 1977.

Mučaji, Pavel: **Červená šatka.** (The red scarf, Das rote Tuch.) Ill.: Pavel Pop.
Novi Sad: Obzor 1977.

1979 Diklić, Arsen: **Moriški snegovi.** (Snow on the *Moriš*; Schnee an der Moriš.) Ill.: Bole Miloradović.
Beograd: Narodna knjiga 1978.

Diklić, Arsen: **Jesen u mrtvaji.** (Stagnant water in autumn; Herbst im Altwasser.) Ill.: Bole Miloradović.
Beograd: Narodna knjiga 1978.

Rambaja, Rushit: **Gjergj Elez Alia.** (*Gjergj Elez Alia.*)
Priština: Rilindja 1978.

Molnar, Maria: **Szobálany voltam Londonban.** (I was a chambermaid in London; Ich war Zimmermädchen in London.)
Novi Sad: Forum 1978.

Demák, Miroslav: **O truch umelcoch.** (About the three artists; Von den drei Künstlern.) Ill.: Vladimir Kardelis.
Novi Sad: Obzor 1977.

Nagrada Grigor Vitez

Through the initiative of the Center for Adult Education in Zagreb, this prize, the first for the best Croatian children's book, was established in 1967. It was named after the Slavonic children's book author, Grigor Vitez (1911-1966). The prize is offered to authors and illustrators who live and work in the Croatian Socialist Republic and consists of a cash-award, a certificate and a bronze sculture of a bird in flight. The jury of seven members is made up of three authors, two illustrators, one educator and one librarian.

1967 wurde durch die Initiative des Zentrums für außerschulische Erziehung in Zagreb zum erstenmal ein kroatischer Kinderbuchpreis geschaffen. Er wurde nach dem aus Slawonien stammenden Kinderschriftsteller Grigor Vitez (1911—1966) benannt und kann sowohl Autoren wie auch Illustratoren verliehen werden - soweit sie im Gebiet der Sozialistischen Republik Kroatien leben und arbeiten. Der Preis besteht aus einer Summe Geldes, einem Diplom und einer Bronze, die einen Vogel im Flug darstellt. Die siebenköpfige Jury besteht aus drei Autoren, zwei Illustratoren und aus je einem Pädagogen und einem Bibliothekar.

1967 Krklec, Gustav: **Majmun i naočale.** (The monkey and the spectacles; Der Affe und die Brille.) Ill.: Nives Kavurić-Kurtović.
Zagreb: Mladost 1966.

Zvrko, Ratko: **Grga Čvarak.** (*Grga Čvarak.*) Ill.: Branko Vujanović.
Zagreb: Mladost 1967.

Illustration
Gliha, Vilko Selan in:
Andrić, Ivo: **Priče iz djetinjstva.** (Stories from childhood; Erzählungen aus der Kindheit.)
Zagreb: Naša djeca 1967.

Job, Cvijeta in:
Brlić-Mažuranić, Ivana: **Šuma Striborova.** (*Stribor*'s forest; *Stribors* Wald.)
Zagreb: Mladost 1967.

1968 Matošec, Milivoj: **Strah u ulici lipa.** (Fear in Linden Street; Die Angst in der Lindenstraße.) Ill.: Branko Vujanović.
Zagreb: Mladost 1968.

Parun, Vesna: **Mačak Džingiskan i Miki Tarsi.** (*Džingiskan* the tomcat and *Miki Tarsi*; Der Kater *Džingiskan* und *Miki Tarsi.*) Ill.: Biserka Baretić.
Zagreb: Spektar 1968.

Illustration
Kinert, Albert in:
Najljepši klasični mitovi. (The most beautiful classical myths; Die schönsten klassischen Mythen.)
Zagreb: Školska knjiga 1968.

Kovačević, Edo in:
Horkić, Dragutin: **Dragocjene sestrice.** (Precious little sisters; Teure Schwestern.)
Zagreb: Školska knjiga 1968.

Rusjan, Danica in:
Iveljić, Nada: **Konjić sa zlatnim sedlom.** (The little horse with the golden saddle; Das Pferdchen mit dem goldenen Sattel.)
Zagreb: Mladost 1968.

1969 Stahuljak, Višnja: **Začarani putovi.** (Bewitched paths; Verzauberte Wege.) Ill.: Nives Kavurić-Kurtović.
Zagreb: Mladost 1969.

Horvatić, Dubravko: **Stanari u slonu.** (Dwellers in an elephant; Bewohner eines Elefanten.) Ill.: Ferdo Kulmer.
Zagreb: Školska knjiga 1969.

Illustration
Bourek, Zlatko in:
Kolar, Boris: **Dječak i lopta.** (The boy and the ball; Der Junge und der Ball.)
Zagreb: Školska knjiga 1969.

1970 Balog, Zvonimir: **Nevidljiva Iva.** (Invisible *Iva*; Die Unsichtbare *Iva*.) Ill.: Marija Putra-Žižić.
Zagreb: Mladost 1970.

Ivanac, Ivica: **Najljepši posao na svijetu.** (The nicest job in the world; Die schönste Arbeit der Welt.) Ill.: Zlatko Bourek.
Zagreb: Školska knjiga 1970.

Škrinjarić, Sunčana: **Kaktus bajke.** (Cactus fairy tales; Kaktusmärchen.) Ill.: Biserka Baretić.
Zagreb: Mladost 1970.

Illustration
Gliha, Vilko Selan in:
Kanižaj, Pajo: **Bila jedna plava.** (Once upon a time there lived a blue; Es war einmal eine Blaue.)
Zagreb: Školska knjiga 1970.

1971 Horkić, Dragutin: **Čadeve zgode.** (Sooty adventures; Rußige Abenteuer.) Ill.: Aleksandar Marks and Pavao Štalter.
Zagreb: Školska knjiga 1971.

Publić, Nikola: **Posljednja igra.** (The last game; Das letzte Spiel.)
Zagreb: Mladost 1971.

Illustration
Marks, Aleksandar/Štalter, Pavao in:
Horkić, Dragutin: **Čadave zgode.** (Sooty adventures; Rußige Abenteuer.)
Zagreb: Školska knjiga 1971.

1972 Kušan, Ivan: **Koko u Parizu.** (*Koko* in Paris.) Ill.: Đuro Seder.
Zagreb: Mladost 1972.

Ugrešić, Dubravka: **Mali plamen.** (Little flame; Kleine Flamme.) Ill.: Zlata Živković-Žilić.
Zagreb: Mladost 1972.

Iveljić, Nada: **Šestinski kišobran.** (The umbrella from Šestina; Der Regenschirm von Šestina.)
Zagreb: Nada Iveljić 1972.

1973 Majer, Vjekoslav: **Grič u suncu, Grič u sjeni.** (*Grič* in the sun; *Grič* in the shade; *Grič* in der Sonne, *Grič* im Schatten.) Photos: Tošo Dabac and Josip Vranić.
Zagreb: Školska knjiga 1973.

Balog, Zvonimir: **Ja magarac.** (I am a donkey; Ich Esel.) Ill.: Nives Kavurić-Kurtović.
Zagreb: Mladost 1973.

Illustration
Veža, Mladen in:
Škrinjarić, Sunčana: **Ljeto u modrom kaputu.** (The summer in the blue coat; Der Sommer im blauen Mantel.)
Zagreb: Školska knjiga 1972.

1974 Prica, Čedo: **Crna kraljica.** (The black queen; Die schwarze Königin.) Ill.: Boris Dogan.
Zagreb: Školska knjiga 1974.

Illustration
Dogan, Boris in:
Prica, Čedo: **Crna kraljica.** (The black queen; Die schwarze Königin.)
Zagreb: Školska knjiga 1974.

1975 Šoljan, Antun: **Ovo i druga mora.** (This and other seas; Dieses und andere Meere.) Ill.: Vjekoslav Brešić.
Zagreb: Školska knjiga 1975.

Illustration
Antolčić, Ivica in:
Balog, Zvonimir: **Pjesme sa šlagom ili šumar ima šumu na dlanu.** (Poems with cream, or the forester has the forest in his hand; Gedichte mit Sahne oder der Förster hat den Wald in der Hand.)
Zagreb: Školska knjiga 1975.

1976 Hribar, Branko: **Adam Vučjak.** (*Adam Vučjak.*) Ill.: Zlatko Bourek.
Zagreb: Mladost 1976.

Milčec, Zvonimir: **Zvižduk od Bukovca.** (The whistle of *Bukovac*; Der Pfiff von *Bukovac.*) Ill.: Oto Reisinger.
Zagreb: Mladost 1975.

1977 Klarić, Kazimir: **Imam rep.** (I have a tail; Ich habe einen Schwanz.) Ill.: Ivan Antolčić.
Zagreb: Školska knjiga 1976.

Illustration
Lipovac, Vasko in:
Jelić, Vojin: **Kapetan gola brka.** (The captain without a beard; Der Kapitän ohne Bart.)
Zagreb: Školska knjiga 1977.

1978 Škrinjarić, Sunčana: **Pisac i vrijeme.** (The writer and the time; Der Schriftsteller und die Zeit.) Ill.: Josip Bifel.
Zagreb: Naša djeca 1978.

Bilopavlović, Tito: **Paunaš.** (The peacock man; Der Pfauenmann.)
Zagreb: Školska knjiga 1978.

1979 Bauer, Ljudevit: **Parnjača Colombina.** (The steamboat, *Columbina*; Der Dampfer *Columbina.*) Ill.: Antun Babić.
Zagreb: Školska knjiga 1979.

Illustration
Marušić, Joško in:
Kišević, Enes: **Mačak u trapericama.** (The cat in jeans; Der bejeanste Kater.)
Zagreb: Školska knjiga 1979.

1980 Šehović, Feđa: **Vidra.** (The otter; Der Otter.) Ill.: Ivo Grbić.
Zagreb: Školska knjiga 1980.

Illustration

Veža, Mladen in:
Puškin, Aleksandr Sergeevič: **Bajka o ribaru i ribici.** (The fairy tale about the fisherman and the little fish; Das Märchen vom Fischer und vom Fischchen.)
Zagreb: Naša djeca 1980.

Antolčić, Ivan in:
Hitrec, Hrvoje: **Petrica Kerempuh.** (Little *Peter Kerempuh*; *Peterchen Kerempuh.*)
Zagreb: Mladost 1980.

International Prizes/Internationale Preise

Hans Christian Andersen Prize

The International board on Books for Young People presents the „International Children's Book Award Hans Christian Andersen" to an author whose collected works are considered an outstanding achievement in the field of juvenile literature. The prize is awarded biennially. The winning author is awarded a medal; and for those who receive honourable mention, a certificate is given. (The latter are not included in the list below.) Since 1966, the Andersen Medal has also been awarded to illustrators. Candidates for the prize are chosen by the national sections. The award presentation ceremony is part of the Congress of the International Board on Books for Young People.

Das „Internationale Kuratorium für das Jugendbuch" verleiht alle zwei Jahre den „Internationalen Jugendbuchpreis Hans Christian Andersen" an einen lebenden Schriftsteller, der sich durch ein hervorragendes Gesamtwerk auf dem Gebiete der Jugendliteratur verdient gemacht hat. Der Preis wird in Form einer Medaille verliehen. Die Autoren der in die Ehrenliste aufgenommenen Bücher werden mit einer Urkunde ausgezeichnet. Seit 1966 können auch Illustratoren die Andersenmedaille erhalten. Vorschläge und Unterlagen für die Verleihung des Preises werden bei den Ländersektionen des Internationalen Kuratoriums für das Jugendbuch eingereicht. Die Überreichung der Medaillen

Ill. 45 Svend Otto S. in: Tim og Trine

und Urkunden findet im Rahmen der Kongresse des Internationalen Kuratoriums statt.

1956 Eleanor Farjeon

1958 Astrid Lindgren

1960 Erich Kästner

1962 Meindert DeJong

1964 René Guillot

1966 *Author/Autor*
Tove Jansson
Illustrator
Alois Carigiet

1968 *Author/Autor*
James Krüss
José Maria Sanchez-Silva
Illustrator
Jiři Trnka

1970 *Author/Autor*
Gianni Rodari
Illustrator
Maurice Sendak

1972 *Author/Autor*
Scott O'Dell
Illustrator
Ib Spang Olsen

1974 *Author/Autor*
Maria Gripe
Illustrator
Farshid Mesghali

1976 *Author/Autor*
Cecil Bødker
Illustrator
Tatjana Mawrina

1978 *Author/Autor*
Paula Fox
Illustrator
Svend Otto S.

1980 *Author/Autor*
Bohumil Řiha
Illustrator
Suekichi Akaba

Premio Critici in Erba

During the International Children's Book Fair, the Bologna Fair Association presents a prize in the form of a gold plaque for the most beautifully illustrated children's books. The plaque is given to the publisher of the prize-winning book, and the publisher of the book must be represented at the fair. The selections are made by a jury of children: nine boys and girls aged eight to fourteen years. These children, named by the school administration, are selected from fifty pupils of schools in Bologna. The president of the jury is a professor of pedagogy. In translation, this prize's title means „budding critic".

Die Messegesellschaft Bologna verleiht während der Internationalen Kinderbuchmesse für das bestillustrierte Kinder- oder Jugendbuch einen Preis in Form einer Goldplakette. Die Plakette ist für den Verlag des preisgekrönten Werkes bestimmt. Der Verlag muß Teilnehmer an der Messe in Bologna sein. Ausgewählt wird das Buch von einer Kinderjury, bestehend aus neun Jungen und Mädchen zwischen acht und vierzehn Jahren, die von den Schulbehörden dafür ausgesucht und aus 50 Schülern der Schulen in Bologna ausgelost werden. Präsident der Jury ist ein Dozent der Pädagogik, der Name des Preises bedeutet soviel wie: junge Kritiken.

Ill. 46 *Tatjana Hauptmann in:*
Ein Tag im Leben der Dorothea Wutz

1966 Saint-Justh, Xavier: **L'album de Bambi.** (The album of *Bambi*; Das Album von *Bambi*.) Ill.: Xavier Saint-Justh.
Paris: Bias 1965.

1967 Barberis, Franco: **Ich schenk Dir einen Papagei.** (I give you a parrot.) Ill.: Franco Barberis.
Zürich: Diogenes Verlag 1964.

1968 *1st prize/1. Preis*
Quilici, Folco: **Alla scoperta dell'Africa.** (The discovery of Africa; Die Entdeckung Afrikas.) Ill.
Firenze: Vallechi 1966.

2nd prize/2. Preis
Cocagnac, Augustin-Maurice: **La création du monde.** (The creation of the world; Die Schöpfung der Welt.) Ill.: Colette Portal.
Paris: Ed. du Cerf 1967.

3rd prize/3. Preis
Guareschi, Giovanni: **La calda estate di Gigino pestifero.** (The hot summer of naughty *Gigino*; Der heiße Sommer des bösen *Gigino*.) Ill.: Paul.
Bologna: Ed. Il Borgo 1967.

1969 *1st prize/1. Preis*
Wahl, Jan: **Pocahontas in London.** (*Pocahontas* in London.) Ill.: John Alcorn.
New York: Seymour Lawrence 1967.

2nd prize/2. Preis
Blake, Quentin: **Patrick.** (*Patrick*.) Ill.: Quentin Blake.
London: Jonathan Cape 1968.

3rd prize/3. Preis
Quilici, Brando: **Io in Africa.** (I in Africa; Ich in Afrika.) Photos: Folco Quilici.
Milano: Emme 1968.

1970 *1st prize/1. Preis*
La storia di Francesco e Chiara raccontata dai bambini di Croce. (The story of *Francis* and *Clara* as told by the children of *Croce*; Die Geschichte von *Franziskus* und *Klara*, erzählt von den Kindern von *Croce*.) Ill.
Padua: Stediv/Aquila 1968.

2nd prize/2. Preis
Wölfflin, Kurt: Wer fängt den Wollknäuel? (Who catches the ball of yarn.) Ill.: Dorothea Stiehl-Dimow.
Wien: Österreichischer Bundesverlag 1969.

3rd prize/3. Preis
Ast, Janine/Grée, Alain: **Serafin und seine Wundermaschine.** (*Serafin* and his wonder machine.) Ill.: Philippe Fix.
Zürich: Diogenes 1970.

1971 Guggenmos, Josef: **Alle meine Blätter...** (All my leaves...) Ill.: Irmgard Lucht.
Köln: Middelhauve 1970.

1972 Paterson, Andrew Barton: **Waltzing Matilda.** (Die walzertanzende *Mathilda.*) Ill.: Desmond Digby.
Sydney, London: Collins 1970.

1973 Grimm, Jakob/Grimm, Wilhelm: **Snow White and the seven dwarfs.** (Schneewittchen und die sieben Zwerge.) Ill.: Nancy Ekholm Burkert.
New York: Farrar, Strauss and Giroux 1972.

1974 Sokolov, J. Mikitov: **God v lesu.** (A year in the woods; Ein Jahr in den Wäldern.) Ill.: Georgij Nikol'sky.
Moskva: Detskaja literatura 1972.

1975 Wilde, Oscar (i.e. Fingall O'Flahertie Wills): **Il principe felice.** (The happy prince; Der glückliche Prinz.) Ill.: Piero Crida.
Torino, Roma: Paoline 1974.

1976 Janus Hertz, Grete: **Das gelbe Haus.** (The yellow house.) Ill.: Iben Clante.
Reinbek b. Hamburg: Carlsen 1976.

1977 Brunhoff, Jean de: **Die Geschichten von Babar, den kleinen Elefanten.** (The story of *Babar*, the little elephant.) Ill.: Jean de Brunhoff.
Zürich: Diogenes 1976.

1978 Way, Mark: **Nicholas and the moon eggs.** (*Nikolaus* und die Mondeier.) Ill.: Mark Way.
Sydney: Collins 1977.

1979 Hauptmann, Tatjana: **Ein Tag im Leben der Dorothea Wutz.** (A day in the life of *Dorothea Wutz.*) Ill.: Tatjana Hauptmann.
Zürich: Diogenes 1978.

1980 Bärwinkel, Birke/Mose, Wilfried: **Das Buch vom Dorf.** (The book of the village.) Ill.: Birke Bärwinkel and Wilfried Mose.
Bad Aibling: Fabula 1979.

1981 Partridge, Jenny: **Mr. Squint.** (Mr. *Squint.*) Ill.: Jenny Partridge.
Tadworth: World's Work 1980.

Premio grafico Fiera di Bologna

Since 1966, the Fair Association of Bologna has offered a prize for the best typographically designed children's and youth books. All publishers represented at the International Children's Book Fair are eligible to enter the competition. The publisher (not the author or illustrator) of the prize winning book receives a gold plaque. The selection is made by an international jury which is appointed by the management of the fair. The jury does not judge the quality of either text or illustration, but the general lay-out, relationship between illustration and printed text, the cover and quality of manufacture. An honorary list of titles is published simultaneously with the award presentations, but because of space considerations, is not included in the list below.

Die Messegesellschaft Bologna schreibt seit 1966 einen Typografiepreis für das bestgestaltete Kinderbuch und für das bestgestaltete Jugendbuch aus. Alle an der Internationalen Kinderbuchmesse teilnehmenden Verleger sind zu diesem

Ill. 47 Etienne Delessert in A. van der Essen: Yok Yok

Wettbewerb zugelassen. Dem Verleger des ausgezeichneten Buches (nicht dem Illustrator oder dem Autor wird eine Goldplakette verliehen. Die Auswahl trifft eine internationale Jury, die von der Messeleitung ernannt wird. Sie beurteilt nicht die Qualität der Texte oder der Illustrationen, sondern das Lay-out, das Verhältnis von Illustration und Drucktext, den Umschlag und die Qualität der Verarbeitung. Es wird gleichzeitig eine Ehrenliste veröffentlicht, die wegen Platzmangels hier nicht aufgenommen ist.

1966 Radius, Emilio: **Gesù oggi.** (*Jesus* today; *Jesus heute.) Ill.*
Milano: Rizzoli 1965.

1967 Heyduck, Hilde: **Drei Vögel.** (Three birds.) Ill.: Hilde Heyduck.
Ravensburg: O. Maier 1966.

1968 *Children's book/Kinderbuch*
Grimm, Jakob/Grimm, Wilhelm: **Die Wichtelmänner.** (The dwarves.) Ill.: Katrin Brandt.
Zürich, Freiburg i.Br.: Atlantis 1967.
Youth book/Jugendbuch
Hostomská, Anna: **Přiběhy, pověsti a pohádky paní Hudby.** (Stories, fables and fairy tales of Mrs. *Hudba*; Geschichten, Sagen und Märchen der Frau *Hudba*.) Ill.: Zdenek Seydl.
Praha: SNDK 1966.

1969 *Children's book/Kinderbuch*
Behrangi, Samad: **Mahi-siah koo-choo-loo.** (The little black fish; Der kleine schwarze Fisch.) Ill.: Farshid Mesghali.
Teheran: The Institute for the Intellectual Development of Children and Young Adults 1968.
Youth book/Jugendbuch
Ragon, Michel: **La cité de l'an 2000.** (The city of the year 2000; Die Stadt im Jahr 2000.) Ill.
Tournai, Paris: Casterman 1968.

1970 *Children's book/Kinderbuch*
Carle, Eric: **1, 2, 3 ein Zug zum Zoo.** (One, two, three a train to the zoo.) Ill.: Eric Carle.
Oldenburg: Stalling 1969.
Youth book/Jugendbuch
Sinnema, Jac. J./De Vries, C.M.: **Vertel het uw kinderen.** (Tell us children a story; Erzählt uns Kindern eine Geschichte.)
Amsterdam: Nederlandsche Zondagsschool Vereeniging; Den Haag: Van Goor 1969.

1971 *Children's book/Kinderbuch*
Charlip, Remy: **Arm in arm.** (Arm in Arm.) Ill.: Remy Charlip. New York: Parents' Magazine 1969.
Youth book/Jugendbuch
Alberti, O./Avi-Yonah, M.: **Tutto su Gerusalemme biblica.** (Everything about biblical Jerusalem; Alles über das biblische Jerusalem.) Ill.
Firenze: Bemporad-Marzocco 1970.

1972 *Children's book/Kinderbuch*
Hürlimann, Ruth: **Stadtmaus und Landmaus.** (City mouse and country mouse.) Ill.: Ruth Hürlimann.
Zürich, Freiburg i.Br.: Atlantis 1971.
Youth book/Jugendbuch
Stanovský, Vladislav/Sirovátka, Oldřich/Lužik, R.: **Slawische Märchen.** (Slavic fairy tales.) Ill.: Mária Želibská.
Praha: Artia 1971.

1973 *Children's book/Kinderbuch*
Rodari, Gianni: **Kopfblumen.** (Head flowers.) Ill.: Eberhard Binder-Strassfurt.
Berlin: Kinderbuchverlag 1972.
Youth book/Jugendbuch
Krügerová, Maria: **Hodina nachové růže.** (Hour of the crimson rose; Stunde der puterroten Rose.) Ill.: Jana Sigmundová.
Praha: Albatros 1972.

1974 *Children's book/Kinderbuch*
Grimm, Jakob/Grimm, Wilhelm: **Rotkäppchen.** (*Little Red Cap.*) Zürich: Diogenes 1974.
Youth book/Jugendbuch
Cooper, James Fenimore: **The last of the Mohicans.** (Der letzte der *Mohikaner.*) Ill.: Christopher Bradbury.
London: Studio Vista Books 1973.

1975 *Children's book/Kinderbuch*
Barokas, Bernhard: **Trois petits flocons.** (Three small flakes; Drei kleine Flocken.) Ill.: Joelle Boucher.
Paris: Grasset-Jeunesse 1974.
Youth book/Jugendbuch
Das Sprachbastelbuch. (The wordcraft book.) Ill.: Gerri Zotter.
Wien, München: Jugend und Volk 1975.

1976 *Children's book/Kinderbuch*
Okuda, Tsuguo: **Mahō oshiemasu.** (Magic for sale; Zauber zu verkaufen.) Ill.: Masakane Yonekura.
Tokyo: Kaiseisha 1975.

Youth book/Jugendbuch
Puškin, Aleksandr Sergeevič: **Mednyj vsadnik.** (The bronze horseman; Der bronzene Reiter.) Ill.: Födor Konstantinov.
Moskva: Detskaja Literatura 1975.

1977 *Children's book/Kinderbuch*
Heide, Florence: **Schorschi schrumpft.** (*Georgy* shrinks). Ill.: Edward Gorey.
Zürich: Diogenes 1976.

Youth book/Jugendbuch
Yonekura, Masakane: **Takeru.** (*Takeru.*) Ill.: Masakane Yonekura.
Tokyo: Kaiseisha 1976.

1978 *Children's book/Kinderbuch*
Grabiánski, Janusz: **Grabianskis Stadtmusikanten.** (*Grabianski*'s town musicians.) Ill.: Janusz Grabiánski.
Wien, Heidelberg: Ueberreuter 1977.

Youth book/Jugendbuch
Anno, Mitsumasa: **Anno Mitsumasa no Gashū.** (*Anno*'s unique world; *Anno*s einzigartige Welt.) Ill.: Mitsumasa Anno.
Tokyo: Kodansha 1977.

1979 *Children's book/Kinderbuch*
Twain, Mark (i.e. Samuel Langhorne Clemens): **Histoire du petit Stephen Girard.** (Poor little *Stephen Girard*; Armer kleiner *Stephen Girard.*) Ill.: Jean-Michel Nicollet.
Paris: Gallimard 1978.

Youth book/Jugendbuch
Turin, Adela: **Aurora.** (*Aurora.*) Ill.: Annie Goetzinger/Francesca Cantarelli.
Milano: Dalla parte delle bambine 1978.

1980 *Children's book/Kinderbuch*
Akutagawa, Yasushi (ed.): **Uta no Ehon II.** (Songbook II; Liederbuch II.) Ill.: Mitsumasa Anno.
Tokyo: Kodansha 1979.

Youth book/Jugendbuch
Mühlbauer, Rita/Rink, Hanno: **Himmelszelt und Schneckenhaus.** (Vault of heaven and snail house.) Ill.: Rita Mühlbauer and Hanno Rink.
Aarau: Frankfurt: Sauerländer 1979.

1981 *Children's book/Kinderbuch*
Essen, Anne van der: **Yok-Yok.** (*Yok-Yok.*) Ill.: Etienne Delessert. Paris: Gallimard 1979.

Youth book/Jugendbuch
Pérennou, Marie/Nuridsany, Claude/Very, Jacques/Les enfants du lycée de Sisteron: **Insecte.** (Insects; Insekten.) Ill.: Les enfants du lycée de Sisteron. Photos: Marie Pérennou, Claude Nuridsany and Jacques Very.
Paris: La Noria; Genève: Lid 1980.

Premio Europeo „Provincia di Trento"

This prize, formerly called Premio Europeo „Città di Caorle", is organized by the Cultural Activities Board of the city of Trento in cooperation with the Children's Literature Department of the University of Padua, which originally founded the award. An international jury makes the selections and a prize of one million lire is awarded to the author of the best published work. Since 1976, the jury has also awarded prizes in the follow-

Ill. 48 Eva Eriksson in B. Lindgren: Sagen om den lilla farbrorn

ing categories: picture book (small chilren); picture book (older children); poetry; didactic literature; unpublished manuscript; historical novel and translation.

Dieser Preis, früher „Città di Caorle“, wurde vom Kulturreferat der Stadt Trento zusammen mit der Sektion der Kinderliteratur der Universität Padua, gestiftet. Eine internationale Jury wählt die Bücher aus, ein Preis von 1.000.000 Liren wird dem Autor des bestgeschriebenen Buches verliehen. Seit 1976 unterscheidet die Jury des Premio Europeo die folgenden Kategorien: Bilderbücher (kleinere Kinder); Bilderbücher (ältere Kinder); Poesie; didaktische Literatur; unveröffentlichte Manuskripte; historische Romane und Übersetzungen.

1962 Père Castor (i.e. Paul Faucher) for the series; mit der Reihe: **Les enfants de la terre.** (The children of the earth; Die Kinder der Erde.)
Paris: Flammarion 1948—1962.

Alberti, Aldo: **Storie meravigliose degli animali in paradiso.** (Wonderful stories of animals in paradise; Wunderbare Geschichten von den Tieren im Paradies.) Ill.: Alfonso Artoli.
Roma: Tumminelli 1961.

1964 Opie, Iona/Opie, Peter: **The Puffin Book of nursery rhymes.** (Das Puffin-Buch der Wiegenlieder.) Ill.: Pauline Baynes.
Harmondsworth: Penguin 1964.

Ziliotto, Donatella: **Mister Master.** (Mr. *Master*; Herr *Master*.) Ill.: Leo Mattioli.
Firenze: Valecchi 1962.

1966 Bourliaguet, Léonce: **Les canons de Valmy.** (The cannons of *Valmy*; Die Kanonen von *Valmy*.) Ill.: René Péron.
Paris: Société Nouvelle des Ed. G.P. 1964.

1968 *1st prize/1. Preis* (Premio Europeo)
Reggiani, Renée: **Carla degli Scávi.** (*Carla* of the rocks; *Carla* aus den Felsen.)
Milano: Garzanti 1968.

2nd prize/2. Preis
Řiha, Bohumil: **Divoký koník Ryn.** (*Ryn*, the wild colt; Das wilde Pferdchen *Ryn*.) Ill.: Mirko Hanák.
Praha: SNDK 1966.

Stow, Randolph: **Midnight.** (*Mitternacht*.) Ill.: Ralph Steadman.
London: Macdonald 1967.

1973 Preussler, Otfried: **Krabat.** (*Krabat*.) Ill.: Herbert Holzing.
Würzburg: Arena 1972.

1976 *1st prize/1. Preis* (Premio Europeo).
Pelot, Pierre: **Le coeur sous la cendre.** (The heart under the ashes; Das Herz unter der Asche.)
Paris: Ed. de l'Amitié, Rageot 1974.

Picture book (small children)/Bilderbuch (kleinere Kinder)
Januszewska, Hanna: **Lwy.** (The lions; Die Löwen.) Ill.: Janusz Stanny.
Warszawa: Biuro Wydawniczo-Propagandowe 1974.

Picture book (older children)/Bilderbuch (ältere Kinder)
Déon, Michel: **Thomas et l'infini.** (*Thomas* and the infinite; *Thomas* und die Unendlichkeit.) Ill.: Etienne Delessert.
Paris: Gallimard 1975.

Poetry/Poesie
Pedagogie Freinet: **Poèmes d'adolescents.** (Poems of adolescents; Gedichte vom Erwachsenwerden.)
Tournai: Casterman 1974.

Didactic literature/Didaktische Literatur
Ori: **Joan Mirò L. Il diario del sole rosso.** (*Joan Mirò*. The diary of the red sun; *Joan Mirò*. Das Tagebuch der roten Sonne.) Ill.: Joan Mirò.
Milano: Vallardi 1974.

Historical novel/Historischer Roman
Beckman, Thea: **Kruistocht in spijkerbrock.** (Crusade in jeans; Kreuzzug in Jeans.)
Rotterdam: Lemniscaat 1973.

1978 *1st prize/1. Preis* (Premio Europeo)
Coué, Jean: **Pierre est vivant.** (*Pierre is alive; Pierre* lebt.)
Paris: Ed. de l'Amitié G.T. Rageot 1977.

Picture book (small children)/Bilderbuch (kleinere Kinder)
Cipelletti, Tiziana: **Il mare dei delfini.** (The sea of the delphins; Das Meer der Delphine). Ill.: Michele Sambin.
Conegliano: Quadragono Libri 1977.

Picture book (older children)/Bilderbuch (ältere Kinder)
Müller, Jörg: **Hier fällt ein Haus, dort steht ein Kran und ewig droht der Baggerzahn oder die Veränderung der Stadt.** (Here falls a house, there stand a crane and the bulldozer eternally threatens, or the transformation of the city.) Ill.: Jörg Müller.
Aarau, Frankfurt: Sauerländer 1976.

Poetry/Poesie
Ďuričková, Mária: **Zlatá Brána.** (The golden gate; Das goldene Tor.) Ill.: Miroslav Cipár.
Bratislava: Mladé letá 1977.

Wawiłow, Danuta: **Rupaki.** (*Rupaki.*) Ill.: Elźbieta Gaudasińska.
Warszawa: Nasza Księgarnia 1977.

Didactic literature/Didaktische Literatur
McNaughton, Colin: **C'era una volta.** (Once upon a time; Es war einmal.) Ill.: Luisa Bigiaretti and Sergio Vezzali.
Roma: Le nuove edizioni romane 1977.

Historical book/Historisches Buch
Langmann, Gerhard: **600 Jahre Römer in Österreich.** (600 years of the Romans in Austria.) Ill.
Innsbruck, Wien, München: Tyrolia 1977.

Manuscript (special prize for unpublished work)/Manuskript (Spezialpreis für unveröffentlichte Werke)
Vannini de Gerulewicz, Marisa: **La fogata.** (The camp fire; Das Freudenfeuer.)

Translation/Übersetzungen
Baumann, Hans in:
Netschajew, Wadim: **Die Insel am Rande der Welt.** (The island at the edge of the world; Russ.orig.title: Vižu zemlju.)
Stuttgart: Thienemann 1976.

1980 *1st prize/1. Preis (Premio Europeo)*
Ende, Michael: **Die unendliche Geschichte.** (The endless story.) Ill.: Roswitha Quadflieg.
Stuttgart: Thienemann 1979.
(ex aequo)

Manzi, Alberto: **El loco.** (The fool; Der Spinner.) Ill.: Alfredo Brasioli.
Firenze: Salani 1979
(ex aequo)

Picture book/Bilderbuch
Lindgren, Barbro: **Sagan om den lilla.** (Story about a little man; Die Erzählung von einem kleinen Mann.) Ill.: Eva Eriksson.
Stockholm: Raben & Sjögren 1979.

Special prize „Arge Alp"/Spezialpreis „Arge Alp"
Rho, Franco: **Il grande occhio del mondo.** (The big eye of the world; Das große Auge der Welt.) Photos.
Bergamo: Minerva Italica 1979.

Historical book/Historisches Buch
Volpi, Domenico: **La vita e i costumi nel Medioevo.** (Life and customs in the Middle Ages; Leben und Bräuche im Mittelalter.) Ill.
Milano: Mursia 1978.

Prize for topical book/Preis für Aktuelle Literatur
Hartman, A. Evert: **Oorlog zonder vrienden.** (There are no friends in war; Krieg ohne Freunde.)
Rotterdam: Lemniscaat 1979.

Manuscript (special prize for unpublished work)/Manuskript (Spezialpreis für unveröffentlichte Werke
Cassiers, Bruno: **Storia di Dustam.** (The story of *Dustam*; Geschichte von *Dustam.*)
(ex aequo)
Guggenmos, Josef: **Ballata dei 12 cassetti.** (Ballad of 12 drawers; 12 Schubladen-Balladen.)
(ex aequo)

Bienále Ilustrácií Bratislava

During the Biennale for Illustrative Arts, Bratislava 1967, two competitions were established: one for children‘s book illustrations which had won national or international awards (the winners of this competition received the „Golden Apple“), and an international competition for illustrations which up to the time of the Biennale had not yet received any prizes (these winners received plaques). an international jury, appointed by the International Committee (highest agency of the BIB), presented the awards. This jury also made selctions for the „Grand Prix“, the highest distinction of the Biennale, which is offered independently of the other two competitions. A comprehensive exhibition of the original illustrations is held at the Museum of Art on the day of the prize presentations.

Auf der Biennale der Illustrationen in Bratislava wurden zum ersten Male 1967 zwei Wettbewerbe nebeneinander veranstaltet: ein Wettbewerb der Kinderbuchillustrationen, die bereits mit nationalen oder internationalen Preisen ausgezeichnet wurden (die Preisträger erhielten einen „Goldenen Apfel“), sowie ein internationaler Wettbewerb von bisher noch nicht ausgezeichneten Illustrationen (die Preisträger erhielten Plaketten). Eine internationale Jury, die vom Internationalen Komitee, dem obersten Organ der BIB, gewählt wurde, verlieh die Preise. Unabhängig von den beiden Wettbewerben erkannte die Jury als höchste Auszeichnung einen Grand Prix zu. Mit der Preisverleihung war im Haus der Kunst eine umfassende Ausstellung der Originalillustrationen verbunden.

1967 *Grand Prix*
Segawa, Yasuo in:
Matsuno, Masako: **Fushigina takenoko.** (*Taro* and the bamboo shoot; *Taro* und der Bambussprößling.)
Tokyo: Fukuinkan Shoten 1963.

Golden Apple/Goldener Apfel
Bombová, Viera in:
Obrova stupaj. Maorijské rozprávky. (Giant footsteps. Maori fairy tales; Riesen Fußspur. Maorie Märchen.)
Bratislava: Mladé letá 1965.

Ill. 49 *Oleg Zotov in A. Puškin: Skazki*

Klemke, Werner in:
Leaf, Munroe: **Ferdinand der Stier.** (Amer.orig.title: The story of Ferdinand.)
Berlin: Holz 1965.

Lionni, Leo in:
Lionni, Leo: **Swimmy.** (*Swimmy.*)
New York: Pantheon 1963.

Murawska, Elźbieta/Murawski, Marian in:
Woroszylski, Wiktor: **Podmuch malowanego wiatru.** (A breath of painted wind; Ein Hauch gemalten Windes.)
Warszawa: Nasza Księgarnia 1965.

Stepanovičius, Algirdas in:
Kubilinskas, Kostas: **Varlé karaliené.** (Frog queen; Froschkönigin.)
Vilnius: Vaga 1967.

Plaques/Plaketten

Brunovský, Albin in:
Andersen, Hans Christian: **Malá morská panna.** (The little mermaid; Die kleine Seejungfrau; Dan.orig.title: Den lille havfrue.)
Bratislava: Mladé letá 1967.

Fromm, Lilo in:
Grimm, Jakob/Grimm, Wilhelm: **Der goldene Vogel.** (The golden bird.)
München: Ellermann 1966.

Gianini, Giulio in:
Luzzati, Emanuele: **La gazza ladra.** (The thieving magpie; Die diebische Elster.)
Milano: Mursia 1964.

Miturič, Maj Petrovič in:
Čukovskij, Kornej Ivanovič: **Kradenoe solnce.** (The stolen sun; Die gestohlene Sonne.)
Moskva: Malyš 1966.

Nussbaumer, Paul in:
Hürlimann, Bettina: **Der Knabe des Tell.** (The son of *Tell.*)
Zürich: Atlantis 1965.

Sandberg, Lasse in:
Sandberg, Inger: **Pojken med de hundra bilarna.** (The boy and one hundred autos; Ein Junge und hundert Autos.)
Stockholm: Rabén & Sjögren 1966.

Kass, János in:
Hajnal, Anna: **Halászik a róka.** (The fox goes fishing; Der Fuchs geht fischen.)
Budapest: Móra kiadó 1967.

Perellón, Celedonio in:
Gómez de la Serna, Gaspar: **Cartas a mi hijo.** (Letters to my son; Briefe an meinen Sohn.)
Madrid: Doncel 1966.

Witkowska, Krystyna in:
Ratajczak, Jósef: **Zamki na lodzie.** (Castles on the ice; Schlösser auf dem Eis.)
Warszawa: Nasza Księgarnia 1966.

1969 *Grand Prix*
Bednářová, Eva in:
Štavičková, Dana: **Chinesische Volksmärchen.** (Chinese folk tales.)
Praha: Artia 1969.

Golden Apple/Goldener Apfel
Bombová, Viera in:
Czambel, Samo: **Janko Gondášik a zlatá pani.** (*Janko Gondašik* and the golden lady; *Janko Gondašik* und die goldene Frau.)
Bratislava: Mladé letá 1969.

Henstra, Friso in:
Williams, Jay: **The practical princess.** (Die geschickte Prinzessin.)
New York: Parents' Magazine Press 1969.

Spohn, Jürgen in:
Spohn, Jürgen: **Das Riesenross.** (The giant steed.)
Gütersloh: Bertelsmann Jugendbuchverlag 1968.

Tashima, Seizo in:
Imae, Yoshitomo: **Chikaratarō.** (*Taro* the strong; *Taro* der Starke.)
Tokyo: Popura-Sha 1968.

Žilytė, Birutė in:
Rainis, Janis: **Aukso sietelis.** (The little golden sieve; Das goldene Sieblein.)
Vilnius: Vaga 1967.

Plaques/Plaketten
Akino, Isamu in:
Otsuka, Yuzo: **Punku Maincha.** (*Punku Maincha.*)
Tokyo: Fukuinkan Shoten 1968.

Beskow, Bo in:
Mall, Viktor: **Figge bygger snäckhuis.** (*Figge* builds a snackbar; *Figge* baut eine Snackbar.)
Stockholm: Albert Bonniers förlag 1967.

Bo, Lars, in:
Andersen, Hans Christian: **Snedronningen.** (The snow queen; Die Schneekönigin.)
København: Carlsen Illustrationsforlaget 1967.

Delhumeau, Annick in:
Claude-Lafontain, Pascal: **Bussy le hamster doré.** (*Bussy* the golden hamster; *Bussy der goldene Hamster.)*
Paris: Ed. Pierre Tisné 1968.

Jacques, Robin in:
Manning-Sanders, Ruth: **A book of ghosts and goblins.** (Ein Buch von Geistern und Kobolden.)
London: Methuen 1968.

Lent, Blair in:
Lent, Blair: **From King Boggen's hall to nothing-at-all.** (Von der Empfangshalle des König Boggen zu nichts mehr.)

Stupica, Marlenka in:
Stupica, Marlenka: **Kape.** (Caps; Mützen.)
Ljubljana: Mladinska knijga 1969.

Wilkoń, Jósef in:
Kamieńska, Ahha: **W Nieparyżu i gdzie indziej.** (In *Notparis* and somewhere else; In *Nichtparis* und woanders.)
Warszawa: Nasza Księgarnia 1967.

Zimka, Ondrej in:
Feldek, Lubomír: **Zelené jelene.** (The green deer; Die grünen Hirsche.)
Bratislava: Mladé letá 1968.

1971 *Grand Prix*
Strumiłło, Andrzej in:
Stiller, Robert: **Narzeczony z morza.** (The bridegroom from the sea; Der Bräutigam aus dem Meer.)
Warszawa: Nasza Księgarnia 1971.

Golden Apple/Goldener Apfel
Appelmann, Karl Heinz in:
Appelmann, Karl Heinz: **Kjambaki.** (*Kjambaki.*)
Berlin: Junge Welt 1970.

Golozubov, Vladimir in:
Dva pivnyky. (Two little chickens; Zwei kleine Hähne.)
Kiev: Veselka 1970.

Maruki, Iri/Maruki, Toshi in:
Nihon no Densetsu. (Japanese legends; Japanische Sagen.)
Tokyo: Fukuinkan Shoten 1970.

Schröder, Binette in:
Schröder, Binette: **Lupinchen.** (Little *Lupin.*)
Mönchaltorf: Nord-Süd Verlag 1969.

Zarrinkelk, Nooredin in:
Ebrahimi, Nader:**Kalagh-ha.** (The crows; Die Krähen.)
Teheran: Institute for the Intellectual Development of Children and Young Adults 1970.

Plaques/Plaketten

Aichinger, Helga in:
Guggenmos, Josef: **Ein Körnchen für den Pfau.** (A seed for the peacook.)
Lahr: Kaufmann 1970.

Hürlimann, Ruth in:
Hürlimann, Ruth: **Stadtmaus und Landmaus.** (City mouse and country mouse.)
Zürich: Atlantis Verlag 1971.

Kudlaček, Jan in:
Hejna, Olga: **Petruška.** (*Petruška.*)
Praha: Artia 1970.

Löfgren, Ulf in:
Löfgren, Ulf: **Det underbara trädet.** (The wonderful tree; Der wunderbare Baum.)
Stockholm: Almquist et Wiksell 1969.

Nuñez de Patrucco, Charo in:
Carvallo de Nuñez, Carlota: **Cuentos de Navidad.** (Christmas stories; Weihnachtsgeschichten.)
Lima: Peisa 1970.

Pacheco, Miguel Angel in:
Bravo Villasante, Carmen: **Antologia de la literatura infantil universal. Vols.1—2.** (Anthology of the world's children literature; Anthologie der Weltkinderliteratur. Bd 1—2.)
Madrid: Doncel 1971.

Stupica, Marlenka in:
Suhodolčan, Leopold: **Kroljaček Hlaček.** (Little taylor *Hosenmatz*; Schneiderlein *Hosenmatz*.)
Ljubljana: Mladinska knjiga 1970.

Velthuijs, Max in:
Velthuijs, Max: **Der Junge und der Fisch.** (The boy and the fish.)
Mönchaltorf: Nord-Süd Verlag 1969.

Würtz, Adám in:
Sebök, Eva: **Mimóza.** (Mimosa; Mimose.)
Budapest: Móra Ferenc Könyvkiadó 1970.

Zimka, Ondrej in:
Feldek, Lubomír: **Rozprávka na niti.** (Tales on a thread; Märchen auf einem Faden.)
Bratislava: Mladé letá 1970.

1973 *Grand Prix*
Schwarz, Liselotte in:
Schwarz, Liselotte: **Traummacher.** (Dream maker.)
München: Ellermann 1972.

Golden Apple/Goldener Apfel
Boix, Manuel in:
Cotovad, Olga: **El cangrejo de oro.** (The golden crab; Der goldene Krebs.)
Madrid: Doncel 1971.

Ensikat, Klaus in:
Könner, Alfred: **Die Hochzeit des Pfaus.** (The peacock's wedding.)
Berlin: Altberliner Verlag 1972.

Kajiyama, Toshio in:
Inui, Tomiko: **Kaze no Omatsuri.** (The wind festival; Das Windfestival.)
Tokyo: Fukuinkan Shoten 1972.

Kállay, Dušan in:
Horák, Jozef: **Leteli sokoli nad Javorinou.** (The falcons flew over *Javorina*; Die Falken flogen über *Javorina*.)
Bratislava: Mladé letá 1972.

Mesghalí, Farshid in:
Kasrai, Siavoosh: **Aresh kamangir.** (*Aresh* the bowman; *Aresh* der Bogenschütze.)
Teheran: Institute for the Intellectual Development of Children and Young adults 1970.

Plaques/Plaketten

Akasaka, Miyoshi in:
Saito, Ryusuke: **Kamakura.** (Snow cave; Schneehöhle.)
Tokyo: Kodansha 1972.

Cipár, Miroslav in:
Ďuríčová, Mária: **Biela kňažná.** (The white princess; Die weiße Fürstin.)
Bratislava: Mladé letá 1973.

Čarušin, Nikita in:
Suvorov, E.: **Putešestvie k pelikanam.** (Journey to the land of the pelicans; Die Reise zu den Pelikanen.)
Moskva: Detskaja literatura 1971.

Dadkah, Bahman in:
Ushij, Nima: **Tukāiy dar gafas.** (An ortolan in the cage; Ein Ortolan im Käfig.)
Teheran: Institute for the Intellectual Development of Children and Young Adults 1972.

Kaufmann, Angelika in:
Kaufmann, Angelika: **Ein Pferd erzählt.** (A horse tells a story.)
Bad Goisern: Neugebauer Press 1971.

Kass, János in:
Móra, Ferenc: **A didergő király.** (The freezing king; Der frierende König.)
Budapest: Móra Ferenc Könyvkiadó 1971.

Koren, Edward in:
Koren, Edward: **Behind the wheel.** (Hinter dem Steuer.)
New York: Holt Rinehart & Winston 1971.

Löfgren, Ulf in:
Löfgren, Ulf: **Der verzauberte Drache.** (The enchanted kite.)
Budapest: Móra Ferenc Könyvkiadó 1973.

Rychlicki, Zbigniew in:
Baum, Lyman Frank: **Czaroksiężnik szmaragdowego grodu.** (The wizard of Oz; Der Zauberer Oz.)
Warszawa: Nasza Księgarnia 1973.

Skorčev, Rumen in:
Korn, Ilse/Korn, Vilmos: **Majstor Chans Rekle i Mistr Ognenos.** (Master *Hans Roeckle* and *Mr. Firefoot*; Germ.orig.title: Meister *Hans Röckle* und Mister *Flammfuß*.)
Sofia: Narodna Mladež 1971.

1975 *Grand Prix*
Popov, Nikolaj in:
Defoe, Daniel: **Robinson Crusoe.** (*Robinson Crusoe.*)
Moskva: Chudožestvenaja literatura 1974.

Golden Apple/Goldener Apfel
Hausmann, René in:
Hausmann, René: **Le bestiare insolite.** (Unusual animal stories; Ungewöhnliche Tiererzählungen.)
Bruxelles: Dupuis 1972.

Jeffers, Susan in:
Jeffers, Susan [adapt.]: **Three jovial huntsmen.** (Drei lustige Jäger.)
New York: Bradbury Press 1973.

Kállay, Dušan in:
Cibula, Václav: **Rytier Roland.** (Knight *Roland; Ritter Roland.)*
Bratislava: Mladé letá 1975.

Keeping, Charles in:
Keeping, Charles: **Railway Passage.** (*Railway Passage.*)
London: Oxford University Press 1974.

Pavlišin, Genadij in:
Nagiškin, Dmitrij: **Amurskie skazki.** (Fairy tales from *Amur*; Märchen vom *Amur.*)
Chabarovsk: Chabarovskoe knižnoe izdatelstvo 1975.

Plaques/Plaketten
Akasaka, Miyoshi in:
Tani, Shinsuke: **Juni-sama.** (*Juni-sama.*)
Tokyo: Kodansha 1973.

Berková, Dagmar in:
Cirkl, Jiří: **Kytička pro štěstí.** (A little bouquette of happiness; Ein Sträusschen zum Glück.)
Praha: Albatros 1973.

Butzmann, Manfred in:
Gesse, N./Sadunaiskaja, S.: **Die Kranichfeder.** (The crane feather.)
Berlin: Kinderbuchverlag 1975.

Claveloux, Nicole in:
Carroll, Lewis: **Les aventures d'Alice au Pays de Merveilles.** (*Alice*'s adventures in wonderland; Die Abenteuer von *Alice* im Wunderland.)
Grasset, Jeunesse 1974.

Dúbravec, Robert in:
Križanová-Brindzová, Helena: **Bohatierske byliny.** (Epic poetry; Helden-Epos.)
Bratislava: Mladé letá 1974.

Hürlimann, Ruth in:
Grimm, Jakob/Grimm, Wilhelm: **Katze und Maus in Gesellschaft.** (Cat and mouse in society.)
Zürich: Atlantis Verlag 1973.

Kaslow, Gisela in:
Bröger, Achim: **Das wunderbare Bettmobil.** (The wonderful bedmobile.)
Stuttgart: Thienemanns Verlag 1975.

Longoni, Alberto in:
Soldati, Mario: **Il polipo e i pirati.** (the octopus and the pirates; Der Polyp und die Piraten.)
Milano: Emme Edizioni 1975.

Löfgren, Ulf in:
Löfgren, Ulf: **Tuffa gumman.** (The tough woman; Die energische Frau.)
Stockholm: Almquist & Wiksell Gebers, 1974.

Stanny, Janusz in:
Januszewska, Hanna: **Lwy.** (The lions; Die Löwen.)
Warszawa: Biuro Wydawniczo Propagandowe 1974.

1977 *Grand Prix*
Löfgren, Ulf in:
Löfgren, Ulf: **Harlekin.** (Harlequin; Harlekin.)
Stockholm: Almquist & Wiksell Gebers 1974.

Golden Apple/Goldener Apfel
Anno, Mitsumasa in:
Anno, Mitsumasa: **A.I.U.E.O no Hon.** (A.I.U.E.O. book; A.I.U.E.O. Buch.)
Tokyo: Fukuinkan Shoten 1977.

Brunovský, Albín in:
Bodenek, Ján: **Koza rohatá a jež.** (The goat with horns and hedgehog; Die Ziege mit Hörnern und der Igel.)
Bratislava: Mladé letá 1977.

Kalinovskij, Gennadij in:
Harris, Joel Chandler: **Skazki deduški Rimusa.** (Uncle *Remus* tales; Onkel *Remus* Märchen.)
Moskva: Detskaja literatura 1976.

Murawski, Marian in:
Barzewski, Aleksander: **Niewyczerpany dzban.** (The never emptying pitcher; Der unerschöpfliche Krug.)
Warszawa: Ludowa Spółdzielnia Wydawnicza 1976.

Tolli, Vive in:
Jaaksoo, Andres (ed): **Zaklinatel' zmej.** (The story of the man who knew magic words; Geschichte vom Mann, der Zauberworte wußte; Est.orgin.title: Jutt mehest kes teadis ussisõnu.)
Tallinn: Eesti Raamat 1977.

Plaques/Plaketten

Cipár, Miroslav in:
Ďuríčková, Mária: **dunajská kral' ovný.** (Queen of the Danube; Donaukönigin.)
Bratislava: Mladé letá 1977.

Patrucco, Rosario Nuñez de in:
Nuñez, Carlota Carvallo de: **El Amaru.** (The *Amaru*; Der *Amaru.*)
Lima: ENCA S.A. 1976.

Henstra, Friso in:
Williams, Jay: **Forgetful Fred.** (Der vergeßliche *Fred.*)
New York: Parents' Magazine Press 1974.

Holzing, Herbert in:
Preussler, Otfried: **Krabat.** (Krabat.)
Würzburg: Arena Verlag 1971.

Noel, Roni in:
Slavici, Joan: **Doi feţi cu stea in frunte.** (Two boys with a star on their foreheads; Zwei Knaben mit einem Stern auf der Stirn.)
Bucureşti: Ed. Ion Creangă 1976.

Pohl, Norbert in:
Ruika-Franz, Viktoria: **Der Recke im Tigerfell.** (The wild man in the tiger trap.)
Berlin: Kinderbuchverlag 1976.

Schmid, Eleonore in:
Schmid, Eleonore: **Das schwarze Schaf.** (The black sheep.)
Mönchaltorf: Nord-Süd Verlag 1976.

Stanny, Janusz in:
Stanny, Janusz: **Baśnie.** (Fables; Fabeln.)
Warszawa: Państwowy Instytut Wydawniczy 1976.

Tajima, Yukihiko in:
Tajima, Yukihiko: **Gion-Matsuri.** (*Gion-Matsuri.*)
Tokyo: Doshin-Sha 1977.

Stupica, Marlenka in:
Andersen, Hans Christian: **Palcica.** (Thumbelina; Däumelinchen; Dan.orig.title: Tommelise.)
Ljubljana: Mladinska knjiga 1976.

1979 *Grand Prix*

Ensikat, Klaus in:
Perrault, Charles: **Der kleine Däumling.** (*Tom thumb*; Fr.orig.title: Le petit poucet.) Adapt.: Moritz Hartmann.
Berlin: Kinderbuchverlag 1977.

Ensikat, Klaus in:
Melville, Herman: **Tapai.** (Amer.orig.title: Typee.)
Berlin: Verlag Neues Leben 1977.

Golden Apple/Goldener Apfel

Anno, Mitsumasa: **Tabi no Ehon.** (My journey; Meine Reise.)
Tokyo: Fukuinkan 1978.

Born, Adolf in:
Brzechwa, Jan: **Akadémia pána Machuľku.** (The academy of Mr. *Klecks*; Die Akademie des Herrn *Klecks*; Pol.orig.title: Akademia pana *Kleksa*.)
Bratislava: Mladé letá 1978.

Postma, Lidia in:
Postma, Lidia: **De heksentuin.** (The witch garden; Der Hexengarten.)
Rotterdam: Lemniscaat 1978.

Postma, Lidia in:
Postma, Lidia: **De gestolen spiegel.** (The stolen mirror; Der gestohlene Spiegel.)
Rotterdam: Lemniscaat 1976.

Taniuchi, Kōta in:
Kuratomi, Chizuko: **Norainu.** (*Pim* and the fish box; *Pim* und der Fischkasten.)
Tokyo: Shiko-sha 1979.

Wilbik, Teresa in:
Kulmowa, Joanna: **Moje próżnowanie.** (My laziness; Meine Faulenzerei.)
Warszawa: Krajowa agencja wydawnicza 1979.

Plaques/Plaketten

Stoev, Borislav in:
Brumabarovi palati. (The beetle palace; Der Käferpalast.)
Sofija: Narodna mladež 1978.

Stoev, Borislav in:
Jankov, Nikolaj (ed.): **Koj kakŭv e i za što takŭv e.** (How he is and why he is like that; Wie er ist und warum er so ist.)
Sofija: Bulgarski chudožnik 1978.

Otto S, Svend in:
Otto S, Svend: **A Christmas book.** (Ein Weihnachtsbuch.)
London: Pelham Books 1978.

Kaila, Kaarina in:
Mikkola, Marja-Leena: **Anni Manninen.** (*Anni Manninen.*)
Helsinki: Helsingissä Kustannusosakeyhtiö 1978.

Kovács, Tamás in:
Dornbach, Mária (ed.): **Butuk Miska.** (*Butuk Miska.*)
Budapest: Móra 1978.

Janosch (i.e. Horst Eckert) in:
Janosch (i.e. Horst Eckert): **Die Maus hat rote Strümpfe an.** (The mouse has red stockings on.)
Weinheim: Beltz 1979.

Nuñez de Patrucco, Rosario in:
Camino. (The road; Die Landstraße.)
Ed. Quipu 1978.

Munteanu, Val in:
Daudet, Alphonse: **Extraordinarele aventuri ale lui Tartarin din Tarascon.** (The extraordinary adventures of *Tartarin* from Tarascon; Die außergewöhnlichen Abenteuer des *Tartarin* von Tarascon; Fr.orig.title: Aventures prodigieuses de *Tartarin* de Tarascon.)
Bucureşti: Ed. Ion Creangá 1978.

Delessert, Etienne in:
Essen, Anne van der: **Die Maus und was ihr bleibt.** (The mouse and what he had remaining.)
Köln: Middelhauve 1977.

Delessert, Etienne in:
Lear, Edward: **Les sept familles du lac Pipple-Popple.** (The seven Families from lake *Pipple Popple*; Die sieben Familien vom *Pipple-Popple-See.*)
Paris: Gallimard 1978.

Eidrigevičius, Stasys in:
Žilinskaite, Vytaute: **Robotas ir peteliške.** (The robot and the doll; Der Roboter und die Puppe.)
Vilnius: Vaga 1978.

Konćekova-Vesela, L'uba in:
Ende, Michael: **Hodinový kvet.** (*Momo*; Germ.orig.title: *Momo.*)
Bratislava: Mladé letá 1979.

1981 *Grand Prix*
Als, Roald in:
Børner, Hanne: **Kristoffers Rejse.** (*Kristoffer*'s journey; *Kristoffers* Reise.)
København: Borgen 1980.

Golden Apple/Goldener Apfel
Brunovský, Albin in:
Aulnoy, Marie-Catherine d': **Páví král'.** (The peacock king; Der Pfauenkönig; Fr.orig.title: Le rameau d'or et autres contes.)
Bratislava: Mladé letá 1979.

Diodorov, Boris in:
Lagerlöf, Selma: **Čudesnoe putešestvie Nil'sa s dikimi gusjami.** (*Nils Holgersson*'s wonderful journey with the wild geese; Die wunderbare Reise des kleinen *Nils Holgersson* mit den Wildgänsen; Swed.orig.title: *Nils Holgerssons* underbara resa genom Sverige.)
Moskva: Detskaja literatura 1979.

Qyen, Wenche in:
Økland, Einar: **Ein god tag.** (A good day; Ein guter Tag.)
Oslo: Det Norske Samlaget 1981.

Taniuchi, Kōta in:
Naito, Hatsue: **Tsuki to asobō.** (Play with the moon; Spiel mit dem Mond.)
Tokyo: Shiko-sha 1980.

Zotov, Oleg in:
Puškin, Aleksandr Sergeevič: **Skazki.** (Fairy tales; Märchen.)
Moskva: Malyš 1980.

Plaques/Plaketten
Bohdal, Susanne in:
Bohdal, Susanne: **Selina, Pumpernickel und die Katze Flora.** (*Selina*, *Pumpelnickel* and *Flora* the cat.)
Mönchaltorf: Nord-Süd Verlag 1981.

Eriksson, Eva in:
Lindgren, Barbro: **Mamman och vilda Bebin.** (Mama and the wild baby; Mama und das wilde Baby.)
Stockholm: Rabén & Sjögren 1980.

Felix, Monique in:
Felix, Monique: **Histoire d'une petite souris qui enfermée dans un livre.** (The story of a little mouse imprisoned in a book; Die Geschichte einer kleinen Maus, die in einem Buch gefangen ist.)
Paris: Gallimard 1980.

Hogeweg, Martin in:
Moonen, Ries: **De groene kikker.** (The green frog; Der grüne Frosch.)
Utrecht: Bruna 1979.

Jágr, Miloslav in:
Čtvrtek, Václav: **Jak ševci zvedli vojnu pro červenou sukni.** (How the taylors waged war over a red shirt; Wie die Schneider Krieg führten wegen eines roten Hemdes.)
Praha: Albatros 1979.

Mirčin, Jutta in:
Nedo, Pawoł: **Sylny wotročk.** (The strong peasant; Der starke Knecht.)
Budyšin: Domowina 1981.

Novák, Vladimír in:
Skřivan, A.: **Moře, objevy, staletí.** (The sea, discoveries, centuries; Meer, Entdeckungen, Jahrhunderte.)
Praha: Mladá fronta 1980.

Popov, Nikolaj in:
Skazki i legendy Portugalii. (Fairy tales and legends from Portugal; Märchen und Legenden Portugals.)
Moskva: Chudožestvennaja literatura 1980.

Sienkiewicz, Lucia/Eidrigevičius, Stasys in:
Delarue, Paul: **Król kurków. Baśń gaskońska.** (The king of the crows. Fairy tales from Gascogne; Der König der Krähen. Märchen aus der Gascogne.)
Warszawa: Krajowa agencja wydawnicza 1980.

Zwerger, Lisbeth in:
Grimm, Jacob/Grimm, Wilhelm: **Die sieben Raben.** (The seven ravens.)
Salzburg: Neugebauer 1981.

Zwerger, Lisbeth in:
Andersen, Hans Christian: **Däumelieschen.** (Thumbelina; Dan.orig.title: Tommelise.)
Salzburg: Neugebauer 1980.

International Janusz Korczak Prize

This prize was founded in 1978 by the Polish section of IBBY to honour the 100th birthday of Janusz Korczak, and is awarded every two years. The first presentation was made in 1979.

All national sections of IBBY can propose titles which are judged by an international jury. In addition to the main prizes, the jury awards medals to runners-up titles and publishes an honour list.

Der Preis wurde 1978 aus Anlaß des 100. Geburtstages von Janusz Korczak von der polnischen IBBY-Sektion gestiftet und wird alle zwei Jahre vergeben. Die erste Preisvergabe fand im Jahre 1979 statt.

Die nationalen IBBY-Sektionen können Preisvorschläge einreichen, die Jury ist international besetzt. Neben den Preisen vergibt die Jury noch Korczak-Medaillen für weiter herausragende Titel, außerdem wird eine Ehrenliste besonders empfehlenswerter Titel veröffentlicht.

1979 *Lindgren, Astrid:* **Bröderna Lejonhjärta.** (The brothers *Lionheart*; Die Brüder *Löwenherz*.) Ill.: Ilon Wikland. Stockholm: Rabén & Sjögren 1973.

Ill. 50 Ilon Wikland in A. Lindgren: Bröderna Lejonhjärta

Říha, Bohumil: **Nový Gulliver.** (The new *Gulliver*; Der neue *Gulliver.*) Ill.: Jan Kudláček.
Praha: Albatros 1973.

1981 Ende, Michael: **Die unendliche Geschichte.** (The unending story.) Ill.: Roswitha Quadflieg.
Stuttgart, Thienemann 1979.
(ex aequo)

Navratil, Jan: **Lampáš malého plavčika.** (The cabin boy's lamp; Die Lampe des Schiffsjungen.) Ill.: Marián Minarovič.
Bratislava: Mladé letá 1980.
(ex aequo)

Index of Authors / Autorenregister

Index of Illustrators / Register der Illustratoren

Index of Translators / Register der Übersetzer

Was wissen Fernsehproduzenten von ihren jungen Zuschauern?

Empirische Untersuchungen in vier Ländern
Herausgegeben von der Stiftung Prix Jeunesse
Redaktionelle Bearbeitung: Erentraud Hömberg

1979. 170 Seiten. Br. DM 18,–
ISBN 3-598-10091-4

Seit gut einem Jahrzehnt führen Wissenschaftler im Auftrag der Stiftung Prix Jeunesse Untersuchungen in Kooperation von Forschungsinstituten und Rundfunkanstalten vieler Länder durch. Die Ergebnisse dieses internationalen Forschungsprojektes werden hiermit vorgestellt, um bekanntzumachen, welche Bedürfnisse und Interessen sich im Jugendfernsehen widerspiegeln. Eines der Hauptziele bestand im Sammeln von Informationen, die für Produzenten von Bedeutung sind. Ebenso sind die Vorstellungen der Programmacher untersucht worden, und so konnte verglichen werden, welches Image die Produzenten von ihrem Publikum haben und wie sich demgegenüber die Zuschauer selbst einschätzen.

Das Forschungsprojekt war außerdem so konzipiert, daß es den Produzenten ermöglichen sollte, aus den Ergebnissen praktischen Nutzen ziehen zu können.

Lernen durch Fernsehen in Schule und Ausbildung

Eine Bibliographie ausgewählter Forschungsliteratur der Jahre 1967 bis 1979

Bearbeitet von Manfred Meyer, Frieder von Krusenstjern, Ursula Nissen und Sylvia Huth
Hrsg.: Internationales Zentralinstitut für das Jugend- und Bildungsfernsehen (IZI), München

1980. 121 S. Br. DM 24,–
ISBN 3-598-20683-6
(Bibliographischer Dienst Nr. 3)

Vorliegender Forschungsbericht befaßt sich mit dem Wirkungen des Lehrfernsehens auf Lernprozesse in der Vorschulerziehung sowie in Schule und Ausbildung.

Bei den untersuchten Fernsehsendungen handelt es sich um Lehrprogramme, bei deren Konzeption Wissenserwerb, Wissenszuwachs beabsichtigt waren. Aufgenommen wurden vor allem jene Begleituntersuchungen zu Schulfernsehprogrammen, die nicht nur Einsatz und Nutzung dieser Programme ermitteln wollten, sondern darüber hinaus deren Lernwirkungen festzustellen hatten.

K·G·Saur München·New York·London·Paris

K·G·Saur Verlag KG · Postfach 711009 · 8000 München 71 · Tel. (089) 798901
K·G·Saur Publishing, Inc. · 1995 Broadway · New York, N.Y. 10023 · Tel. 212873-2100
K·G·Saur Ltd. · Shropshire House · 2-20 Capper Street · London WC1E 6JA · Tel. 01-637-1571
K·G·Saur, Editeur SARL. · 40, rue du Fer-à-Moulin · 75005 Paris · Téléphone 7074964